Derivatives and Portfolio Management

CFA® PROGRAM CURRICULUM · VOLUME 6

LEVEL II
2008

CFA INSTITUTE

PEARSON
Custom
Publishing

Printed in the United States of America

10 9 8 7 6 5 4 3 2

ISBN 0-536-34240-7

2006160834

AG/JS

Please visit our web site at *www.pearsoncustom.com*

PEARSON CUSTOM PUBLISHING
501 Boylston Street, Suite 900, Boston, MA 02116
A Pearson Education Company

CONTENTS

indicates an optional segment   www.cfainstitute.org/toolkit—Your online preparation resource

HOW TO USE THE CFA PROGRAM CURRICULUM

Congratulations on passing Level I of the Chartered Financial Analyst (CFA®) Program. This exciting and rewarding program of study reflects your desire to become a serious investment professional. You are participating in a program noted for its requirement of ethics and breadth of knowledge, skills, and abilities.

The credential you seek is respected around the world as a mark of accomplishment and dedication. Each level of the program represents a distinct achievement in professional development. Successful completion of the program is rewarded with membership in a prestigious global community of investment professionals. CFA charterholders are dedicated to life-long learning and maintaining currency with the ever-changing dynamics of a challenging profession.

The CFA examination measures your degree of mastery of the assigned CFA Program curriculum. Effective study and preparation based on that curriculum are keys to your success on the examination.

Curriculum Development

The CFA Program curriculum is grounded in the practice of the investment profession. CFA Institute regularly conducts a practice analysis survey of investment professionals around the world to determine the knowledge, skills, and abilities that are relevant to the profession. The survey results define the Candidate Body of Knowledge (CBOK™), an inventory of knowledge and responsibilities expected of the investment management professional at the level of a new CFA charterholder. The survey also determines how much emphasis each of the major topic areas receives on the CFA examinations.

A committee made up of practicing charterholders, in conjunction with CFA Institute staff, designs the CFA Program curriculum to deliver the CBOK to candidates. The examinations, also written by practicing charterholders, are designed to allow you to demonstrate your mastery of the CBOK as set forth in the CFA Program curriculum. As you structure your personal study program, you should emphasize mastery of the CBOK and the practical application of that knowledge. For more information on the practice analysis, CBOK, and development of the CFA Program curriculum, please visit www.cfainstitute.org/toolkit.

Organization

The Level II CFA Program curriculum is organized into 10 topic areas. Each topic area begins with a brief statement of the material and the depth of knowledge expected.

Each topic area is then divided into one or more study sessions. These study sessions—18 sessions in the Level II curriculum—should form the basic structure of your reading and preparation.

Each study session includes a statement of its structure and objective, and is further divided into specific reading assignments. The outline on the inside front cover of each volume illustrates the organization of these 18 study sessions.

The reading assignments are the basis for all examination questions, and are selected or developed specifically to teach the CBOK. These readings are drawn from textbook chapters, professional journal articles, research analyst reports, CFA Program-commissioned content, and cases. Many readings include problems and solutions as well as appendices to help you learn.

Reading-specific Learning Outcome Statements (LOS) are listed in the pages introducing each study session as well as at the beginning of each reading. These LOS indicate what you should be able to accomplish after studying the reading. We encourage you to review how to properly use LOS, and the descriptions of commonly used LOS "command words," at www.cfainstitute.org/toolkit. The command words signal the depth of learning you are expected to achieve from the reading. You should use the LOS to guide and focus your study, as each examination question is based on an assigned reading and one or more LOS. However, the readings provide context for the LOS and enable you to apply a principle or concept in a variety of scenarios. It is important to study the whole of a required reading.

Features of the Curriculum

▶ **Required vs. Optional Segments** - You should read all of the pages for an assigned reading. In some cases, however, we have reprinted an entire chapter or article and marked those parts of the reading that are not required as "optional." The CFA examination is based only on the required segments, and the optional segments are included only when they might help you to better understand the required segments (by seeing the required material in its full context). When an optional segment begins, you will see an icon and a solid vertical bar in the outside margin that will continue until the optional segment ends, accompanied by another icon. *Unless the material is specifically marked as optional, you should assume it is required.* Keep in mind that the optional material is provided strictly for your convenience and will not be tested. You should rely on the required segments and the reading-specific LOS in preparing for the examination.

▶ **Problems/Solutions** - *All questions and problems in the readings as well as their solutions (which are provided in an appendix at the end of each volume) are required material.* When appropriate, we have included problems after the readings to demonstrate practical application and reinforce your understanding of the concepts presented. The questions and problems are designed to help you learn these concepts. Many of the questions are in the same style and format as the actual CFA examination and will give you test-taking experience in that format. Examination questions that come from a past CFA examination are marked with the CFA logo in the margin.

2006 exam

▶ **Margins** - The wide margins in each volume provide space for your note-taking.

▶ **Two-color Format** - To enrich the visual appeal and clarity of the exhibits, tables, and text, the curriculum is printed in a two-color format.

▶ **Six-volume Structure** - For portability of the curriculum, the material is spread over six volumes.

▶ **Glossary and Index** - For your convenience, we have printed a comprehensive glossary and index in each volume. Throughout the curriculum, a **bolded blue** word in a reading denotes a term defined in the glossary.

Designing Your Personal Study Program

Create a Schedule - An orderly, systematic approach to examination preparation is critical. You should dedicate a consistent block of time every week to reading and studying. Complete all reading assignments and the associated problems and solutions in each study session. Review the LOS both before and after you study each reading to ensure that you have mastered the applicable content and can demonstrate the knowledge, skill, or ability described by the LOS and the assigned reading.

CFA Institute estimates that you will need to devote a minimum of 10–15 hours per week for 18 weeks to study the assigned readings. Allow a minimum of one week for each study session, and plan to complete them all at least 30–45 days prior to the examination. This schedule will allow you to spend the final four to six weeks before the examination reviewing the assigned material and taking multiple online sample examinations.

At CFA Institute, we believe that candidates need to commit to a *minimum* of 250 hours reading and reviewing the curriculum, and taking online sample examinations, to master the material. This recommendation, however, may substantially underestimate the hours needed for appropriate examination preparation depending on your individual circumstances, relevant experience, and academic background.

You will undoubtedly adjust your study time to conform to your own strengths and weaknesses, and your educational and professional background. You will probably spend more time on some study sessions than on others. You should allow ample time for both in-depth study of all topic areas and additional concentration on those topic areas for which you feel least prepared.

Candidate Preparation Toolkit - We have created the online toolkit to provide a single comprehensive location for resources and guidance for candidate preparation. In addition to in-depth information on study program planning, the CFA Program curriculum, and the online sample examinations, the toolkit also contains curriculum errata, printable study session outlines, sample examination questions, and more. Errata identified in the curriculum are corrected and listed periodically in the errata listing in the toolkit. We encourage you to use the toolkit as your central preparation resource during your tenure as a candidate. Visit the toolkit at www.cfainstitute.org/toolkit.

Online Sample Examinations - After completing your study of the assigned curriculum, use the CFA Institute online sample examinations to measure your knowledge of the topics and to improve your examination-taking skills. After each question, you will receive immediate feedback noting the correct response and indicating the assigned reading for further study. The sample examinations are designed by the same people who create the actual CFA examinations, and reflect the question formats, topics, and level of difficulty of the actual CFA examinations, in a timed environment. Aggregate data indicate that the CFA examination pass rate was higher among candidates who took one or more online sample examinations than among candidates who did not take the online sample examinations. For more information on the online sample examinations, please visit www.cfainstitute.org/toolkit.

Preparatory Providers - After you enroll in the CFA Program, you may receive numerous solicitations for preparatory courses and review materials. Although preparatory courses and notes may be helpful to some candidates, you should view these resources as *supplements* to the assigned CFA Program curriculum. The CFA examinations reference only the CFA Institute assigned curriculum—no preparatory course or review course materials are consulted or referenced.

Before you decide on a supplementary prep course, do some research. Determine the experience and expertise of the instructors, the accuracy and currency of their content, the delivery method for their materials, and the provider's claims of success. Most importantly, make sure the provider is in compliance with the CFA Institute Prep Provider Guidelines Program. Three years of prep course products can be a significant investment, so make sure you're getting a sufficient return. Just remember, there are no shortcuts to success on the CFA examinations. Prep products can enhance your learning experience, but the CFA curriculum is the key to success. For more information on the Prep Provider Guidelines Program, visit www.cfainstitute.org/cfaprog/resources/prepcourse.html.

SUMMARY

Every question on the CFA examination is based on specific pages in the required readings and on one or more LOS. Frequently, an examination question is also tied to a specific example highlighted within a reading or to a specific end-of-reading question/problem and its solution. To make effective use of the curriculum, please remember these key points:

1. All pages printed in the Custom Curriculum are required reading for the examination except for occasional sections marked as optional. You may read optional pages as background, but you will not be tested on them.

2. All questions/problems printed at the end of readings and their solutions in the appendix to each volume are required study material for the examination.

3. Make appropriate use of the CFA Candidate Toolkit, the online sample examinations, and preparatory courses and review materials.

4. Commit sufficient study time to cover the 18 study sessions, review the materials, and take sample examinations.

Feedback

At CFA Institute, we are committed to delivering a comprehensive and rigorous curriculum for the development of competent, ethically grounded investment professionals. We rely on candidate and member feedback as we work to incorporate content, design, and packaging improvements. You can be assured that we will continue to listen to your suggestions. Please send any comments or feedback to curriculum@cfainstitute.org. Ongoing improvements in the curriculum will help you prepare for success on the upcoming examinations, and for a lifetime of learning as a serious investment professional.

ANALYSIS OF DERIVATIVE INVESTMENTS

STUDY SESSIONS

Study Session 16 Forwards and Futures

Study Session 17 Options, Swaps, and Interest Rate and Credit Derivatives

TOPIC LEVEL LEARNING OUTCOME

The candidate should be able to value futures, forwards, options, and swaps, and demonstrate how they may be used in various strategies.

STUDY SESSION 16
DERIVATIVE INVESTMENTS:
Forwards and Futures

This study session looks at derivative investments and markets and focuses on the concepts of derivative pricing and valuation and credit risk evaluation. To assist in determining the relative cost/benefit of using derivative instruments or investments with embedded derivatives, it is essential to know and understand the factors that affect valuation. This study session addresses interest rate, equity, and currency forwards and futures.

READING ASSIGNMENTS

Reading 62 Forward Markets and Contracts
Reading 63 Futures Markets and Contracts

LEARNING OUTCOMES

Reading 62: Forward Markets and Contracts
The candidate should be able to:

a. explain how the value of a forward contract is determined at initiation, during the life of the contract, and at expiration;

b. calculate and interpret the price and the value of an equity forward contract, assuming dividends are paid either discretely or continuously;

c. calculate and interpret the price and the value of 1) a forward contract on a fixed income security, 2) a forward rate agreement (FRA), and 3) a forward contract on a currency;

d. evaluate credit risk in a forward contract, and explain how market value is a measure of the credit risk to a party in a forward contract.

Reading 63: Futures Markets and Contracts
The candidate should be able to:

a. explain why the futures price must converge to the spot price at expiration;

b. determine the value of a futures contract;

c. explain how forward and futures prices differ;

d. identify the different types of monetary and non-monetary benefits and costs associated with holding the underlying asset, and explain how they affect the futures price;

e. describe backwardation and contango;

f. discuss whether futures prices equal expected spot prices;

g. describe the difficulties in pricing Eurodollar futures and creating a pure arbitrage opportunity;

h. calculate and interpret the price of Treasury bond futures, stock index futures, and currency futures.

FORWARD MARKETS AND CONTRACTS
by Don M. Chance

LEARNING OUTCOMES

The candidate should be able to:

a. explain how the value of a forward contract is determined at initiation, during the life of the contract, and at expiration;

b. calculate and interpret the price and the value of an equity forward contract, assuming dividends are paid either discretely or continuously;

c. calculate and interpret the price and the value of 1) a forward contract on a fixed income security, 2) a forward rate agreement (FRA), and 3) a forward contract on a currency;

d. evaluate credit risk in a forward contract, and explain how market value is a measure of the credit risk to a party in a forward contract.

INTRODUCTION 1

Recall the definition of a forward contract: *A forward contract is an agreement between two parties in which one party, the buyer, agrees to buy from the other party, the seller, an underlying asset or other derivative, at a future date at a price established at the start of the contract.* Therefore, it is a commitment by two parties to engage in a transaction at a later date with the price set in advance. The buyer is often called the **long** and the seller is often called the **short**.[1] Although any two parties can agree on such a contract, in this book we are interested only in forward contracts that involve large corporations, financial institutions, nonprofit organizations, or governments.

---

[1]The derivatives industry often uses nouns, verbs, adjectives, and adverbs as parts of speech other than what they are. Hence, words like *long* and *short* are used not as adjectives but as nouns.

Analysis of Derivatives for the CFA® Program, by Don M. Chance. Copyright © 2003 by AIMR. Reprinted with permission.

5

As an example, a pension fund manager, anticipating the receipt of cash at a future date, might enter into a commitment to purchase a stock portfolio at a later date at a price agreed on today. By doing so, the manager's position is unaffected by any changes in the value of the stock portfolio between today and the date of the actual investment in the stock portfolio. In this sense, the manager is hedged against an increase in stock prices until the cash is received and invested. The disadvantage of such a transaction is that the manager is also hedged against any decreases in stock prices. If stock prices fall between the time the commitment is established and the time the cash is received, the manager will regret having entered into the forward contract because the stock could have been acquired at a lower price. But that is the nature of a forward contract hedge: It locks in a price.

An important feature of a forward contract is that neither party pays any money at the start. The parties might require some collateral to minimize the risk of default, but we shall ignore this point. So keep in mind this very important aspect of forward contracts: *No money changes hands at the start.*

1.1 Delivery and Settlement of a Forward Contract

When a forward contract expires, there are two possible arrangements that can be used to settle the obligations of the parties. A deliverable forward contract stipulates that the long will pay the agreed-upon price to the short, who in turn will deliver the underlying asset to the long, a process called **delivery**. An alternative procedure, called **cash settlement**, permits the long and short to pay the net cash value of the position on the delivery date. For example, suppose two parties agree to a forward contract to deliver a zero-coupon bond at a price of $98 per $100 par. At the contract's expiration, suppose the underlying zero-coupon bond is selling at a price of $98.25. The long is due to receive from the short an asset worth $98.25, for which a payment to the short of $98.00 is required. In a cash-settled forward contract, the short simply pays the long $0.25. If the zero-coupon bond were selling for $97.50, the long would pay the short $0.50. Delivery of a zero-coupon bond is not a difficult thing to do, however, and cash-settled contracts are more commonly used in situations where delivery is impractical.[2] For example, if the underlying is the Russell 3000 Index, the short would have to deliver to the long a portfolio containing each of the Russell 3000 stocks proportionate to its weighting in the index. Consequently, cash settlement is much more practical. Cash-settled forward contracts are sometimes called NDFs, for **nondeliverable forwards**, although this term is used predominately with respect to foreign exchange forwards.

1.2 Default Risk and Forward Contracts

An important characteristic of forward contracts is that they are subject to default. Regardless of whether the contract is for delivery or cash settlement, the potential exists for a party to default. In the zero-coupon bond example above,

---

[2] Be aware, however, that the choice of delivery or cash settlement is not an option available at expiration. It is negotiated between the parties at the start.

the long might be unable to pay the $98 or the short might be unable to buy the zero-coupon bond and make delivery of the bond to the long. Generally speaking, however, forward contracts are structured so that only the party owing the greater amount can default. In other words, if the short is obligated to deliver a zero-coupon bond selling for more than $98, then the long would not be obligated to make payment unless the short makes delivery. Likewise, in a cash settled contract, only one party—the one owing the greater amount—can default. We discuss the nature of this credit risk in the following section and in Section 5 after we have determined how to value forward contracts.

1.3 Termination of a Forward Contract

Let us note that a forward contract is nearly always constructed with the idea that the participants will hold on to their positions until the contract expires and either engage in delivery of the asset or settle the cash equivalent, as required in the specific contract. The possibility exists, however, that at least one of the participants might wish to terminate the position prior to expiration. For example, suppose a party goes long, meaning that she agrees to buy the asset at the expiration date at the price agreed on at the start, but she subsequently decides to terminate the contract before expiration. We shall assume that the contract calls for delivery rather than cash settlement at expiration.

To see the details of the contract termination, suppose it is part of the way through the life of the contract, and the long decides that she no longer wishes to buy the asset at expiration. She can then re-enter the market and create a new forward contract expiring at the same time as the original forward contract, taking the position of the seller instead. Because of price changes in the market during the period since the original contract was created, this new contract would likely have a different price at which she would have to commit to sell. She would then be long a contract to buy the asset at expiration at one price and short a contract to sell the asset at expiration at a different price. It should be apparent that she has no further exposure to the price of the asset.

For example, suppose she is long to buy at $40 and short to deliver at $42. Depending on the characteristics of the contract, one of several possibilities could occur at expiration. Everything could go as planned—the party holding the short position of the contract on which she is long at $40 delivers the asset to her, and she pays him $40. She then delivers the asset to the party who is long the contract on which she is short at $42. That party pays her $42. She nets $2. The transaction is over.

There is always a possibility that her counterparty on the long contract could default. She is still obligated to deliver the asset on the short contract, for which she will receive $42. But if her counterparty on the long contract defaults, she has to buy the asset in the market and could suffer a significant loss. There is also a possibility that the counterparty on her short contract could fail to pay her the $42. Of course, she would then not deliver the asset but would be exposed to the risk of changes in the asset's price. This type of problem illustrates the credit risk in a forward contract. We shall cover credit risk in more detail in Section 5 of this reading.

To avoid the credit risk, when she re-enters the market to go short the forward contract, she could contact the same counterparty with whom she engaged in the long forward contract. They could agree to cancel both contracts. Because she would be owed $2 at expiration, cancellation of the contract would result in the counterparty paying her the present value of $2. This termination or offset of the original forward position is clearly desirable for both counterparties because it eliminates the credit risk.[3] It is always possible, however, that she might receive a better price from another counterparty. If that price is sufficiently attractive and she does not perceive the credit risk to be too high, she may choose to deal with the other counterparty and leave the credit risk in the picture.

2   THE STRUCTURE OF GLOBAL FORWARD MARKETS

The global market for forward contracts is part of a vast network of financial institutions that make markets in these instruments as well as in other related derivatives, such as swaps and options. Some dealers specialize in certain markets and contracts, such as forward contracts on the euro or forward contracts on Japanese equity products. These dealers are mainly large global banking institutions, but many large non-banking institutions, such as Goldman Sachs and Merrill Lynch, are also big players in this market.

Dealers engage in transactions with two types of parties: end users and other dealers. An end user is typically a corporation, nonprofit organization, or government.[4] An end user is generally a party with a risk management problem that is searching for a dealer to provide it with a financial transaction to solve that problem. Although the problem could simply be that the party wants to take a position in anticipation of a market move, more commonly the end user has a risk it wants to reduce or eliminate.

As an example, Hoffman-LaRoche, the large Swiss pharmaceutical company, sells its products globally. Anticipating the receipt of a large amount of cash in U.S. dollars and worried about a decrease in the value of the dollar relative to the Swiss franc, it could buy a forward contract to sell the dollar and buy Swiss francs. It might seek out a dealer such as UBS Warburg, the investment firm affiliated with the large Swiss bank UBS, or it might approach any of the other large multinational banks with which it does business. Or it might end up dealing with a non-bank entity, like Merrill Lynch. Assume that Hoffman-LaRoche enters into this contract with UBS Warburg. Hoffman-LaRoche is the end user; UBS Warburg is the dealer.

Transactions in forward contracts typically are conducted over the phone. Each dealer has a quote desk, whose phone number is well known to the major participants in the market. If a party wishes to conduct a transaction, it simply phones the dealer for a quote. The dealer stands ready to take either side of the transaction, quoting a bid and an ask price or rate. The bid is the price at which the dealer is willing to pay for the future purchase of the asset, and the ask is the price at which the dealer is willing to sell. When a dealer engages in a forward transaction, it has then taken on risk from the other party. For example, in the aforementioned transaction of Hoffman-LaRoche and UBS Warburg, by entering into the contract, UBS Warburg takes on a risk that Hoffman-LaRoche has eliminated. Specifically, UBS Warburg has now committed to buying dollars and selling Swiss francs at a future date. Thus, UBS Warburg is effectively long the dollar and stands to gain from a strengthening dollar/weakening Swiss franc.

---

[3] This statement is made under the assumption that the parties do not want the credit risk. Credit risk, like other risks, however, can be a risk that some parties want because of the potential for earning attractive returns by using their expertise in measuring the actual credit risk relative to the credit risk as perceived by the market. In addition, credit risk offers diversification benefits.

[4] The U.S. government does not transact in forward contracts or other derivatives, but some foreign governments and central banks do. Within the United States, however, some state and local governments do engage in forward contracts and other derivatives.

Typically dealers do not want to hold this exposure. Rather, they find another party to offset the exposure with another derivative or spot transaction. Thus, UBS Warburg is a wholesaler of risk—buying it, selling it, and trying to earn a profit off the spread between its buying price and selling price.

One might reasonably wonder why Hoffman-LaRoche could not avoid the cost of dealing with UBS Warburg. In some cases, it might be able to. It might be aware of another party with the exact opposite needs, but such a situation is rare. The market for financial products such as forward contracts is made up of wholesalers of risk management products who use their technical expertise, their vast network of contacts, and their access to critical financial market information to provide a more efficient means for end users to engage in such risk management transactions.

Dealers such as UBS Warburg lay off the risk they do not wish to assume by transacting with other dealers and potentially other end users. If they do this carefully, quickly, and at accurate prices, they can earn a profit from this market-making activity. One should not get the impression, however, that market making is a highly profitable activity. The competition is fierce, which keeps bid–ask spreads very low and makes it difficult to earn much money on a given transaction. Indeed, many market makers do not make much money on individual transactions—they typically make a small amount of money on each transaction and do a large number of transactions. They may even lose money on some standard transactions, hoping to make up losses on more-complicated, nonstandard transactions, which occur less frequently but have higher bid–ask spreads.

Risk magazine conducts annual surveys to identify the top dealers in various derivative products. Exhibit 1 presents the results of those surveys for two of the forward products we cover here, currency and interest rate forwards. **Interest rate forwards** are called forward rate agreements (FRAs). In the next section, we shall study the different types of forward contracts and note that there are some others not covered in the *Risk* surveys.

One of these surveys was sent to banks and investment banks that are active dealers in over-the-counter derivatives. The other survey was sent to end users. The tabulations are based on respondents' simple rankings of who they think are the best dealers. Although the identities of the specific dealer firms are not critical, it is interesting and helpful to be aware of the major players in these types of contracts. Most of the world's leading global financial institutions are listed, but many other big names are not. It is also interesting to observe that the perceptions of the users of these dealer firms' services differ somewhat from the dealers' self-perceptions. Be aware, however, that the rankings change, sometimes drastically, each year.

TYPES OF FORWARD CONTRACTS   3

In this section, we examine the types of forward contracts that fall within the scope of this reading. By the word "types," we mean the underlying asset groups on which these forward contracts are created. Because the CFA Program focuses on the asset management industry, our primary interest is in equity, interest rate and fixed-income, and **currency forwards**.

3.1 Equity Forwards

An **equity forward** is a contract calling for the purchase of an individual stock, a stock portfolio, or a stock index at a later date. For the most part, the differences

| EXHIBIT 1 | *Risk* Magazine Surveys of Banks, Investment Banks, and Corporate End Users to Determine the Top Three Dealers in Currency and Interest Rate Forwards |

	Respondents	
Currencies	**Banks and Investment Banks**	**Corporate End Users**
Currency Forwards		
$/€	UBS Warburg	Citigroup
	Deutsche Bank	Royal Bank of Scotland
	JP Morgan Chase	JP Morgan Chase/Bank of America
$/¥	UBS Warburg	Citigroup
	Citigroup	Bank of America
	JP Morgan Chase	JP Morgan Chase/UBS Warburg
$/£	UBS Warburg	Royal Bank of Scotland
	Royal Bank of Scotland	Citigroup
	Hong Kong Shanghai Banking Corporation	UBS Warburg
$/SF	UBS Warburg	UBS Warburg
	Credit Suisse First Boston	Citigroup
	BNP Paribas	Credit Suisse First Boston
Interest Rate Forwards (FRAs)		
$	JP Morgan Chase	JP Morgan Chase
	Bank of America	Royal Bank of Scotland
	Deutsche Bank	Bank of America
€	Deutsche Bank	Royal Bank of Scotland
	Intesa BCI	JP Morgan Chase
	Royal Bank of Scotland	Deutsche Bank
¥	Mizuho Securities	Citigroup
	JP Morgan Chase	Merrill Lynch
	BNP Paribas	Hong Kong Shanghai Banking Corporation
£	Royal Bank of Scotland	Royal Bank of Scotland
	Commerzbank	Bank of America/ING Barings
	Deutsche Bank	
SF	Credit Suisse First Boston	UBS Warburg
	UBS Warburg	Credit Suisse First Boston
	Deutsche Bank	Citigroup/ING Barings

Note: $ = U.S. dollar, € = euro, ¥ = Japanese yen, £ = U.K. pound sterling, SF = Swiss franc.

Source: Risk, September 2002, pp. 30–67 for banks and investment banking dealer respondents, and June 2002, pp. 24–34 for end user respondents. The end user survey provides responses from corporations and asset managers. The above results are for corporate respondents only.

in types of equity forward contracts are only slight, depending on whether the contract is on an individual stock, a portfolio of stocks, or a stock index.

3.1.1 Forward Contracts on Individual Stocks

Consider an asset manager responsible for the portfolio of a high-net-worth individual. As is sometimes the case, such portfolios may be concentrated in a small number of stocks, sometimes stocks that have been in the family for years. In many cases, the individual may be part of the founding family of a particular company. Let us say that the stock is called Gregorian Industries, Inc., or GII, and the client is so heavily invested in this stock that her portfolio is not diversi-fied. The client notifies the portfolio manager of her need for $2 million in cash in six months. This cash can be raised by selling 16,000 shares at the current price of $125 per share. Thus, the risk exposure concerns the market value of $2 million of stock. For whatever reason, it is considered best not to sell the stock any earlier than necessary. The portfolio manager realizes that a forward contract to sell GII in six months will accomplish the client's desired objective. The manager contacts a forward contract dealer and obtains a quote of $128.13 as the price at which a forward contract to sell the stock in six months could be constructed.[5] In other words, the portfolio manager could enter into a contract to sell the stock to the dealer in six months at $128.13. We assume that this contract is deliverable, meaning that when the sale is actually made, the shares will be delivered to the dealer. Assuming that the client has some flexibility in the amount of money needed, let us say that the contract is signed for the sale of 15,600 shares at $128.13, which will raise $1,998,828. Of course when the contract expires, the stock could be selling for any price. The client can gain or lose on the transaction. If the stock rises to a price above $128.13 during the six-month period, the client will still have to deliver the stock for $128.13. But if the price falls, the client will still get $128.13 per share for the stock.

3.1.2 Forward Contracts on Stock Portfolios

Because **modern portfolio theory** and good common sense dictate that investors should hold diversified portfolios, it is reasonable to assume that forward contracts on specific stock portfolios would be useful. Suppose a pension fund manager knows that in three months he will need to sell about $20 million of stock to make payments to retirees. The manager has analyzed the portfolio and determined the precise identities of the stocks he wants to sell and the number of shares of each that he would like to sell. Thus the manager has designated a specific subportfolio to be sold. The problem is that the prices of these stocks in three months are uncertain. The manager can, however, lock in the sale prices by entering into a forward contract to sell the portfolio. This can be done one of two ways.

The manager can enter into a forward contract on each stock that he wants to sell. Alternatively, he can enter into a forward contract on the overall portfo-lio. The first way would be more costly, as each contract would incur administra-tive costs, whereas the second way would incur only one set of costs.[6] Assume that the manager chooses the second method. He provides a list of the stocks and

---

[5] In Section 4, we shall learn how to calculate forward prices such as this one.

[6] Ignoring those costs, there would be no difference in doing forward contracts on individual stocks or a single forward contract on a portfolio. Because of the non-linearity of their payoffs, this is not true for options. A portfolio of options is not the same as an option on a portfolio, but a portfolio of forward contracts is the same as a forward contract on a portfolio, ignoring the aforementioned costs.

number of shares of each he wishes to sell to the dealer and obtains a quote. The dealer gives him a quote of $20,200,000. So, in three months, the manager will sell the stock to the dealer and receive $20,200,000. The transaction can be structured to call for either actual delivery or cash settlement, but in either case, the client will effectively receive $20,200,000 for the stock.[7]

3.1.3 Forward Contracts on Stock Indices

Many equity forward contracts are based on a stock index. For example, consider a U.K. asset manager who wants to protect the value of her portfolio that is a Financial Times Stock Exchange 100 index fund, or who wants to eliminate a risk for which the FTSE 100 Index is a sufficiently accurate representation of the risk she wishes to eliminate. For example, the manager may be anticipating the sale of a number of U.K. blue chip shares at a future date. The manager could, as in our stock portfolio example, take a specific portfolio of stocks to a forward contract dealer and obtain a forward contract on that portfolio. She realizes, however, that a forward contract on a widely accepted benchmark would result in a better price quote, because the dealer can more easily hedge the risk with other transactions. Moreover, the manager is not even sure which stocks she will still be holding at the later date. She simply knows that she will sell a certain amount of stock at a later date and believes that the FTSE 100 is representative of the stock that she will sell. The manager is concerned with the systematic risk associated with the U.K. stock market, and accordingly, she decides that selling a forward contract on the FTSE 100 would be a good way to manage the risk.

Assume that the portfolio manager decides to protect £15,000,000 of stock. The dealer quotes a price of £6,000 on a forward contract covering £15,000,000. We assume that the contract will be cash settled because such index contracts are nearly always done that way. When the contract expiration date arrives, let us say that the index is at £5,925—a decrease of 1.25 percent from the forward price. Because the manager is short the contract and its price went down, the transaction makes money. But how much did it make on a notional principal of £15,000,000?

The index declined by 1.25 percent. Thus, the transaction should make $0.0125 \times £15,000,000 = £187,500$. In other words, the dealer would have to pay £187,500 in cash. If the portfolio were a FTSE 100 index fund, then it would be viewed as a portfolio initially worth £15,000,000 that declined by 1.25 percent, a loss of £187,500. The forward contract offsets this loss. Of course, in reality, the portfolio is not an index fund and such a hedge is not perfect, but as noted above, there are sometimes reasons for preferring that the forward contract be based on an index.

3.1.4 The Effect of Dividends

It is important to note the effect of dividends in equity forward contracts. Any equity portfolio nearly always has at least a few stocks that pay dividends, and it is inconceivable that any well-known equity index would not have some component

---

[7] If, for example, the stock is worth $20,500,000 and the transaction calls for delivery, the manager will transfer the stocks to the dealer and receive $20,200,000. The client effectively takes an opportunity loss of $300,000. If the transaction is structured as a cash settlement, the client will pay the dealer $300,000. The client would then sell the stock in the market, receiving $20,500,000 and netting $20,200,000 after settling the forward contract with the dealer. Similarly, if the stock is selling for less than the amount guaranteed by the forward contract, the client will deliver the stock and receive $20,200,000 or, if the transaction is cash settled, the client will sell the stock in the market and receive a cash payment from the dealer, making the effective sale price still $20,200,000.

stocks that pay dividends. Equity forward contracts typically have payoffs based only on the price of the equity, value of the portfolio, or level of the index. They do not ordinarily pay off any dividends paid by the component stocks. An exception, however, is that some equity forwards on stock indices are based on total return indices. For example, there are two versions of the well-known S&P 500 Index. One represents only the market value of the stocks. The other, called the S&P 500 Total Return Index, is structured so that daily dividends paid by the stocks are reinvested in additional units of the index, as though it were a portfolio. In this manner, the rate of return on the index, and the payoff of any forward contract based on it, reflects the payment and reinvestment of dividends into the underlying index. Although this feature might appear attractive, it is not necessarily of much importance in risk management problems. The variability of prices is so much greater than the variability of dividends that managing price risk is considered much more important than worrying about the uncertainty of dividends.

In summary, equity forwards can be based on individual stocks, specific stock portfolios, or stock indices. Moreover, these underlying equities often pay dividends, which can affect forward contracts on equities. Let us now look at bond and interest rate forward contracts.

3.2 Bond and Interest Rate Forward Contracts

Forward contracts on bonds are similar to forward contracts on interest rates, but the two are different instruments. Forward contracts on bonds, in fact, are no more difficult to understand than those on equities. Drawing on our experience of Section 3.1, we simply extend the notion of a forward contract on an individual stock, a specific stock portfolio, or a stock index to that of a forward contract on an individual bond, a specific bond portfolio, or a bond index.[8]

3.2.1 Forward Contracts on Individual Bonds and Bond Portfolios

Although a forward contract on a bond and one on a stock are similar, some basic differences nonetheless exist between the two. For example, the bond may pay a coupon, which corresponds somewhat to the dividend that a stock might pay. But unlike a stock, a bond matures, and a forward contract on a bond must expire prior to the bond's maturity date. In addition, bonds often have many special features such as calls and convertibility. Finally, we should note that unlike a stock, a bond carries the risk of default. A forward contract written on a bond must contain a provision to recognize how default is defined, what it means for the bond to default, and how default would affect the parties to the contract.

In addition to forward contracts on individual bonds, there are also forward contracts on portfolios of bonds as well as on bond indices. The technical distinctions between forward contracts on individual bonds and collections of bonds, however, are relatively minor.

The primary bonds for which we shall consider forward contracts are default-free zero-coupon bonds, typically called Treasury bills or T-bills in the United States, which serve as a proxy for the risk-free rate.[9] In a forward contract

---

[8] It may be useful to review Chapters 1 and 3 of *Fixed Income Analysis for the Chartered Financial Analyst Program* by Frank J. Fabozzi, New Hope, PA: Frank J. Fabozzi Associates (2000).

[9] A government-issued zero-coupon bond is typically used as a proxy for a **risk-free asset** because it is assumed to be free of default risk. It can be purchased and held to maturity, thereby eliminating any market value risk, and it has no reinvestment risk because it has no coupons. If the bond is liquidated before maturity, however, some market value risk exists in addition to the risk associated with reinvesting the market price.

on a T-bill, one party agrees to buy the T-bill at a later date, prior to the bill's maturity, at a price agreed on today. T-bills are typically sold at a discount from par value and the price is quoted in terms of the discount rate. Thus, if a 180-day T-bill is selling at a discount of 4 percent, its price per \$1 par will be \$1 − 0.04(180/360) = \$0.98. The use of 360 days is the convention in calculating the discount. So the bill will sell for \$0.98. If purchased and held to maturity, it will pay off \$1. This procedure means that the interest is deducted from the face value in advance, which is called **discount interest**.

The T-bill is usually traded by quoting the discount rate, not the price. It is understood that the discount rate can be easily converted to the price by the above procedure. A forward contract might be constructed that would call for delivery of a 90-day T-bill in 60 days. Such a contract might sell for \$0.9895, which would imply a discount rate of 4.2 percent because \$1 − 0.042(90/360) = \$0.9895. Later in this reading, we shall see how forward prices of T-bills are derived.

In addition to forward contracts on zero-coupon bonds/T-bills, we shall consider forward contracts on default-free coupon-bearing bonds, also called Treasury bonds in the United States. These instruments pay interest, typically in semiannual installments, and can sell for more (less) than par value if the yield is lower (higher) than the coupon rate. Prices are typically quoted without the interest that has accrued since the last coupon date, but with a few exceptions, we shall always work with the **full price**—that is, the price including accrued interest. Prices are often quoted by stating the yield. Forward contracts call for delivery of such a bond at a date prior to the bond's maturity, for which the long pays the short the agreed-upon price.

3.2.2 Forward Contracts on Interest Rates: Forward Rate Agreements

So far in Section 3.2 we have discussed forward contracts on actual fixed-income securities. Fixed-income security prices are driven by interest rates. A more common type of forward contract is the interest rate forward contract, more commonly called a **forward rate agreement** or **FRA**. Before we can begin to understand FRAs, however, we must examine the instruments on which they are based.

There is a large global market for time deposits in various currencies issued by large creditworthy banks. This market is primarily centered in London but also exists elsewhere, though not in the United States. The primary time deposit instrument is called the **Eurodollar**, which is a dollar deposited outside the Unites States. Banks borrow dollars from other banks by issuing Eurodollar **time deposits**, which are essentially short-term unsecured loans. In London, the rate on such dollar loans is called the London Interbank Rate. Although there are rates for both borrowing and lending, in the financial markets the lending rate, called the **London Interbank Offer Rate** or **LIBOR**, is more commonly used in derivative contracts. LIBOR is the rate at which London banks lend dollars to other London banks. Even though it represents a loan outside of the United States, LIBOR is considered to be the best representative rate on a dollar borrowed by a private, i.e., nongovernmental, high-quality borrower. It should be noted, however, that the London market includes many branches of banks from outside the United Kingdom, and these banks are also active participants in the **Eurodollar market**.

A Eurodollar time deposit is structured as follows. Let us say a London bank such as NatWest needs to borrow \$10 million for 30 days. It obtains a quote from the Royal Bank of Scotland for a rate of 5.25 percent. Thus, 30-day LIBOR is 5.25 percent. If NatWest takes the deal, it will owe \$10,000,000 × [1 + 0.0525 (30/360)] = \$10,043,750 in 30 days. Note that, like the Treasury bill market, the convention in the Eurodollar market is to prorate the quoted interest rate over 360 days. In contrast to the Treasury bill market, the interest is not deducted from the principal. Rather, it is added on to the face value, a procedure appropriately called **add-on interest**. The market for Eurodollar time deposits is quite large, and the rates on these instruments are assembled by a central organization and quoted in financial newspapers. The British Bankers Association publishes a semi-official Eurodollar rate, compiled from an average of the quotes of London banks.

The U.S. dollar is not the only instrument for which such time deposits exist. Eurosterling, for example, trades in Tokyo, and Euroyen trades in London. You may be wondering about Euroeuro. Actually, there is no such entity as Euroeuro, at least not by that name. The Eurodollar instrument described here has nothing to do with the European currency known as the euro. Eurodollars, Euroyen, Eurosterling, etc. have been around longer than the euro currency and, despite the confusion, have retained their nomenclature. An analogous instrument does exist, however—a euro-denominated loan in which one bank borrows euros from another. Trading in euros and euro deposits occurs in most major world cities, and two similar rates on such euro deposits are commonly quoted. One, called EuroLIBOR, is compiled in London by the British Bankers Association, and the other, called **Euribor**, is compiled in Frankfurt and published by the European Central Bank. Euribor is more widely used and is the rate we shall refer to in this book.

Now let us return to the world of FRAs. FRAs are contracts in which the underlying is neither a bond nor a Eurodollar or Euribor deposit but simply an interest payment made in dollars, Euribor, or any other currency at a rate appropriate for that currency. Our primary focus will be on dollar LIBOR and Euribor, so we shall henceforth adopt the terminology LIBOR to represent dollar LIBOR and Euribor to represent the euro deposit rate.

Because the mechanics of FRAs are the same for all currencies, for illustrative purposes we shall use LIBOR. Consider an FRA expiring in 90 days for which the underlying is 180-day LIBOR. Suppose the dealer quotes this instrument at a rate of 5.5 percent. Suppose the end user goes long and the dealer goes short. The end user is essentially long the rate and will benefit if rates increase. The dealer is essentially short the rate and will benefit if rates decrease. The contract covers a given notional principal, which we shall assume is $10 million.

The contract stipulates that at expiration, the parties identify the rate on new 180-day LIBOR time deposits. This rate is called 180-day LIBOR. It is, thus, the underlying rate on which the contract is based. Suppose that at expiration in 90 days, the rate on 180-day LIBOR is 6 percent. That 6 percent interest will be paid 180 days later. Therefore, the present value of a Eurodollar time deposit at that point in time would be

$$\frac{\$10,000,000}{1 + 0.06\left(\dfrac{180}{360}\right)}$$

At expiration, then, the end user, the party going long the FRA in our example, receives the following payment from the dealer, which is the party going short:

$$\$10,000,000\left[\frac{(0.06 - 0.055)\left(\dfrac{180}{360}\right)}{1 + 0.06\left(\dfrac{180}{360}\right)}\right] = \$24,272$$

If the underlying rate is less than 5.5 percent, the payment is calculated based on the difference between the 5.5 percent rate and the underlying rate and is paid by the long to the short. It is important to note that even though the contract

OPTIONAL SEGMENT

expires in 90 days, the rate is on a 180-day LIBOR instrument; therefore, the rate calculation adjusts by the factor 180/360. The fact that 90 days have elapsed at expiration is not relevant to the calculation of the payoff.

Before presenting the general formula, let us review the calculations in the numerator and denominator. In the numerator, we see that the contract is obviously paying the difference between the actual rate that exists in the market on the contract expiration date and the agreed-upon rate, adjusted for the fact that the rate applies to a 180-day instrument, multiplied by the notional principal. The divisor appears because when Eurodollar rates are quoted in the market, they are based on the assumption that the rate applies to an instrument that accrues interest at that rate with the interest paid a certain number of days (here 180) later. When participants determine this rate in the London Eurodollar market, it is understood to apply to a Eurodollar time deposit that begins now and matures 180 days later. So the interest on an actual Eurodollar deposit would not be paid until 180 days later. Thus, it is necessary to adjust the FRA payoff to reflect the fact that the rate implies a payment that would occur 180 days later on a standard **Eurodollar deposit**. This adjustment is easily done by simply discounting the payment at the current LIBOR, which here is 6 percent, prorated over 180 days. These conventions are also followed in the market for FRAs with other underlying rates.

In general, the FRA payoff formula (from the perspective of the party going long) is

$$
\text{Notional principal} \left[\frac{\left(\begin{array}{c} \text{Underlying rate at expiration} \\ - \text{ Forward contract rate} \end{array} \right) \left(\dfrac{\text{Days in underlying rate}}{360} \right)}{1 + \text{Underlying rate at expiration} \left(\dfrac{\text{Days in underlying rate}}{360} \right)} \right]
$$

where *forward contract rate* represents the rate the two parties agree will be paid and *days in underlying rate* refers to the number of days to maturity of the instrument on which the underlying rate is based.

One somewhat confusing feature of FRAs is the fact that they mature in a certain number of days and are based on a rate that applies to an instrument maturing in a certain number of days measured from the maturity of the FRA. Thus, there are two day figures associated with each contract. Our example was a 90-day contract on 180-day LIBOR. To avoid confusion, the FRA markets use a special type of terminology that converts the number of days to months. Specifically, our example FRA is referred to as a 3 × 9, reflecting the fact that the contract expires in three months and that six months later, or nine months from the contract initiation date, the interest is paid on the underlying Eurodollar time deposit on whose rate the contract is based.[10]

FRAs are available in the market for a variety of maturities that are considered somewhat standard. Exhibit 2 presents the most common maturities. Most dealers follow the convention that contracts should expire in a given number of exact months and should be on the most commonly traded Eurodollar rates such as 30-day LIBOR, 60-day LIBOR, 90-day LIBOR, 180-day LIBOR, and so on. If a party wants a contract expiring in 37 days on 122-day LIBOR, it would be considered an exception to the standard, but most dealers would be willing to make a market in such an instrument. Such nonstandard instruments are called *off the run*. Of course, FRAs are available in all of the leading currencies.

---

[10] The notation "3 × 9" is pronounced "three by nine."

EXHIBIT 2	FRA Descriptive Notation and Interpretation	
Notation	**Contract Expires In**	**Underlying Rate**
1 × 3	1 month	60-day LIBOR
1 × 4	1 month	90-day LIBOR
1 × 7	1 month	180-day LIBOR
3 × 6	3 months	90-day LIBOR
3 × 9	3 months	180-day LIBOR
6 × 12	6 months	180-day LIBOR
12 × 18	12 months	180-day LIBOR

Note: This list is not **exhaustive** and represents only the most commonly traded FRAs.

The FRA market is large, but not as large as the swaps market. It is important, however, to understand FRAs before trying to understand swaps. As we will show in Reading 65, a swap is a special combination of FRAs. But let us now turn to another large forward market, the market for currency forwards.

3.3 Currency Forward Contracts

Spurred by the relaxation of government controls over the exchange rates of most major currencies in the early 1970s, a currency forward market developed and grew extremely large. Currency forwards are widely used by banks and corporations to manage foreign exchange risk. For example, suppose Microsoft has a European subsidiary that expects to send it €12 million in three months. When Microsoft receives the euros, it will then convert them to dollars. Thus, Microsoft is essentially long euros because it will have to sell euros, or equivalently, it is short dollars because it will have to buy dollars. A currency forward contract is especially useful in this situation, because it enables Microsoft to lock in the rate at which it will sell euros and buy dollars in three months. It can do this by going short the forward contract, meaning that it goes short the euro and long the dollar. This arrangement serves to offset its otherwise long-euro, short-dollar position. In other words, it needs a forward contract to sell euros and buy dollars.

For example, say Microsoft goes to JP Morgan Chase and asks for a quote on a currency forward for €12 million in three months. JP Morgan Chase quotes a rate of $0.925, which would enable Microsoft to sell euros and buy dollars at a rate of $0.925 in three months. Under this contract, Microsoft would know it could convert its €12 million to 12,000,000 × $0.925 = $11,100,000. The contract would also stipulate whether it will settle in cash or will call for Microsoft to actually deliver the euros to the dealer and be paid $11,100,000. This simplified example is a currency forward hedge.

Now let us say that three months later, the spot rate for euros is $0.920. Microsoft is quite pleased that it locked in a rate of $0.925. It simply delivers the euros and receives $11,100,000 at an exchange rate of $0.925.[11] Had rates risen,

---

[11] Had the contract been structured to settle in cash, the dealer would have paid Microsoft 12,000,000 × ($0.925 − $0.920) = $60,000. Microsoft would have converted the euros to dollars at the current spot exchange rate of $0.920, receiving 12,000,000 × $0.920 = $11,040,000. Adding the $60,000 payment from the dealer, Microsoft would have received $11,100,000, an effective rate of $0.925.

however, Microsoft would still have had to deliver the euros and accept a rate of $0.925.

A few variations of currency forward contracts exist, but most of them are somewhat specialized and beyond the objectives of this reading. Let us now take a very brief look at a few other types of forward contracts.

3.4 Other Types of Forward Contracts

Although we focus primarily on the financial derivatives used by asset managers, we should mention here some of the other types. **Commodity forwards**— in which the underlying asset is oil, a precious metal, or some other commodity—are widely used. In addition, the derivatives industry has created forward contracts and other derivatives on various sources of energy (electricity, gas, etc.) and even weather, in which the underlying is a measure of the temperature or the amount of disaster damage from hurricanes, earthquakes, or tornados.

Many of these instruments are particularly difficult to understand, price, and trade. Nonetheless, through the use of derivatives and indirect investments, such as hedge funds, they can be useful for managing risk and investing in general. They are not, however, our focus.

In the examples and illustrations used above, we have made reference to certain prices. Determining appropriate prices and fair values of financial instruments is a central objective of much of the process of asset management. Accordingly, pricing and valuation occupies a major portion of the CFA Program. As such, we turn our attention to the pricing and valuation of forward contracts.

OPTIONAL SEGMENT ENDS

4   PRICING AND VALUATION OF FORWARD CONTRACTS

Before getting into the actual mechanics of pricing and valuation, the astute reader might wonder whether we are being a bit redundant. Are pricing and valuation not the same thing?

An equity analyst often finds that a stock is priced at more or less than its fair market value and uses this conclusion as the basis for a buy or sell recommendation.[12] In an efficient market, the price of a stock would always equal its value or the price would quickly converge to the value. Thus, for all practical purposes, pricing and valuation would be the same thing. In general, when we speak of the value and price of an *asset,* we are referring to what that asset is worth and what it sells for. With respect to certain *derivatives,* however, value and price take on slightly different meanings.

So let us begin by defining value: *Value is what you can sell something for or what you must pay to acquire something.* This applies to stocks, bonds, derivatives, and used cars.[13] Accordingly, *valuation is the process of determining the value of an asset or service.* Pricing is a related but different concept; let us explore what we mean by pricing a forward contract.

---

[12] From your study of equity analysis, you should recall that we often use the discounted cash flow model, sometimes combined with the capital asset pricing model, to determine the fair market value of a stock.

[13] Be careful. You may think the "value" of a certain used car is $5,000, but if no one will give you that price, it can hardly be called the value.

A forward **contract price** is the fixed price or rate at which the transaction scheduled to occur at expiration will take place. This price is agreed to on the contract initiation date and is commonly called the **forward price** or **forward rate**. Pricing means to determine the forward price or forward rate. Valuation, however, means to determine the amount of money that one would need to pay or would expect to receive to engage in the transaction. Alternatively, if one already held a position, valuation would mean to determine the amount of money one would either have to pay or expect to receive in order to get out of the position. Let us look at a generic example.

4.1 Generic Pricing and Valuation of a Forward Contract

Because derivative contracts have finite lives, it is important to carefully specify the time frame in which we are operating. We denote time in the following manner: Today is identified as time 0. The expiration date is time T. Time t is an arbitrary time between today and the expiration. Usually when we refer to "today," we are referring to the date on which the contract is created. Later we shall move forward to time t and time T, which will then be "today."

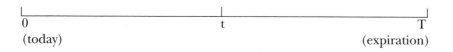

0	t	T
(today)		(expiration)

The price of the underlying asset in the spot market is denoted as S_0 at time 0, S_t at time t, and S_T at time T. The forward contract price, established when the contract is initiated at time 0, is $F(0,T)$. This notation indicates that $F(0,T)$ is the price of a forward contract initiated at time 0 and expiring at time T. The value of the forward contract is $V_0(0,T)$. This notation indicates that $V_0(0,T)$ is the value at time 0 of a forward contract initiated at time 0 and expiring at time T. In this reading, subscripts always indicate that we are at a specific point in time.

We have several objectives in this analysis. First, we want to determine the forward price $F(0,T)$. We also want to determine the forward contract value today, denoted $V_0(0,T)$, the value at a point during the life of the contract such as time t, denoted $V_t(0,T)$, and the value at expiration, denoted $V_T(0,T)$. Valuation is somewhat easier to grasp from the perspective of the party holding the long position, so we shall take that point of view in this example. Once that value is determined, the value to the short is obtained by simply changing the sign.

If we are at expiration, we would observe the **spot price** as S_T. The long holds a position to buy the asset at the already agreed-upon price of $F(0,T)$. Thus, the value of the forward contract at expiration should be obvious: $S_T - F(0,T)$. If the value at expiration does not equal this amount, then an arbitrage profit can be easily made. For example, suppose the forward price established at the initiation of the contract, $F(0,T)$, is $20. Now at expiration, the spot price, S_T, is $23. The contract value must be $3. If it were more than $3, then the long would be able to sell the contract to someone for more than $3—someone would be paying the long more than $3 to obtain the obligation of buying a $23 asset for $20. Obviously, no one would do that. If the value were less than $3, the long would have to be willing to sell for less than $3 the obligation of buying a $23 asset for $20. Obviously, the long would not do that. Thus, we state that the value at expiration of a forward contract established at time 0 is

$$V_T(0,T) = S_T - F(0,T)$$ **(62-1)**

Note that the value of a forward contract can also be interpreted as its profit, the difference between what the long pays for the underlying asset, $F(0,T)$, and what the long receives, the asset price S_T. Of course, we have still not explained how $F(0,T)$ is determined, but the above equation gives the value of the contract at expiration, at which time $F(0,T)$ would certainly be known because it was agreed on at the initiation date of the contract.

Now let us back up to the time when the contract was originated. Consider a contract that expires in one year. Suppose that the underlying asset is worth $100 and that the forward price is $108. We do not know if $108 is the correct forward price; we will simply try it and see.

Suppose we buy the asset for $100 and sell the forward contract for $108. We hold the position until expiration. We assume that there are no direct costs associated with buying or holding the asset, but we must recognize that we lose interest on the $100 tied up in the asset. Assume that the interest rate is 5 percent.

Recall that no money changes hands at the start with a forward contract. Consequently, the $100 invested in the asset is the full outlay. At the end of the year, the forward contract expires and we deliver the asset, receiving $108 for it—not bad at all. At a 5 percent interest rate, we lose only $5 in interest on the $100 tied up in the asset. We receive $108 for the asset regardless of its price at expiration. We can view $108 − $105 = $3 as a risk-free profit, which more than covered the cost. In fact, if we had also borrowed the $100 at 5 percent, we could have done this transaction without putting up any money of our own. We would have more than covered the interest on the borrowed funds and netted a $3 risk-free profit. This profit is essentially free money—there is no cost and no risk. Thus, it is an arbitrage profit. We would certainly want to execute any transaction that would generate an arbitrage profit.

In the market, the forces of arbitrage would then prevail. Other market participants would execute this transaction as well. Although it is possible that the spot price would bear some of the adjustment, in this reading we shall always let the derivative price make the full adjustment. Consequently, the derivative price would have to come down to $105.

If the forward price were below $105, we could also earn an arbitrage profit, although it would be a little more difficult because the asset would have to be sold short. Suppose the forward price is $103. If the asset were a financial asset, we could borrow it and sell it short. We would receive $100 for it and invest that $100 at the 5 percent rate. We would simultaneously buy a forward contract. At expiration, we would take delivery of the asset paying $103 and then deliver it to the party from whom we borrowed it. The short position is now covered, and we still have the $100 invested plus 5 percent interest on it. This transaction offers a clear arbitrage profit of $2. Again, the forces of arbitrage would cause other market participants to undertake the transaction, which would push the forward price up to $105.

If short selling is not permitted, too difficult, or too costly, a market participant who already owns the asset could sell it, invest the $100 at 5 percent, and buy a forward contract. At expiration, he would pay $103 and take delivery on the forward contract, which would return him to his original position of owning the asset. He would now, however, receive not only the stock but also 5 percent interest on $100. Again, the forces of arbitrage would make this transaction attractive to other parties who held the asset, provided they could afford to part with it for the necessary period of time.[14]

---

[14] In other words, a party holding the asset must be willing to part with it for the length of time it would take for the forces of arbitrage to bring the price back in line, thereby allowing the party to capture the risk-free profit and return the party to its original state of holding the asset. The period of time required for the price to adjust should be very short if the market is relatively efficient.

Going back to the situation in which the forward contract price was $103, an arbitrage profit could, however, be eliminated if the party going long the forward contract were required to pay some money up front. For example, suppose the party going long the forward contract paid the party going short $1.9048. Then the party going long would lose $1.9048 plus interest on this amount. Notice that $1.9048 compounded at 5 percent interest equals precisely $2, which not surprisingly is the amount of the arbitrage profit.

Thus, if the forward price were $103, the value of the contract would be $1.9048. With T = 1, this value equals

$$V_0(0,T) = V_0(0,1) = \$100 - \$103/1.05 = \$1.9048$$

Therefore, to enter into this contract at this forward price, one party must pay another. Because the value is positive, it must be paid by the party going long the forward contract to the party going short. Parties going long must pay positive values; parties going short pay negative values.[15]

If the forward price were $108, the value would be

$$V_0(0,T) = \$100 - \$108/1.05 = -\$2.8571$$

In this case, the value is negative and would have to be paid from the short to the long. Doing so would eliminate the arbitrage profit that the short would have otherwise been able to make, given the forward price of $108.

Arbitrage profits can be eliminated with an up-front payment from long to short or vice versa that is consistent with the forward price the parties select. The parties could simply negotiate a forward price, and any resulting market value could be paid from one party to the other. *It is customary, however, in the forward market for the initial value to be set to zero.* This convention eliminates the necessity of either party making a payment to the other and results in a direct and simple determination of the forward price. Specifically, setting $V_0(0,T) = 0$ and letting r represent the interest rate,

$$V_0(0,T) = S_0 - F(0,T)/(1 + r) = 0$$

which means that $F(0,T) = S_0(1 + r)$. In our example, $F(0,T) = \$100(1.05) = \$105$, which is the forward price that eliminates the arbitrage profit.

Our forward price formula can be interpreted as saying that the forward price is the spot price compounded at the risk-free interest rate. In our example, we had an annual interest rate of r and one year to expiration. With today being time 0 and expiration being time T, the time $T - 0 = T$ is the number of years to expiration of the forward contract. Then we more generally write the forward price as

$$F(0,T) = S_0(1 + r)^T \qquad \textbf{(62-2)}$$

Again, this result is consistent with the custom that no money changes hands at the start of a forward contract, meaning that the value of a forward contract at its start is zero.

Exhibit 3 summarizes the process of pricing a forward contract. At time 0, we buy the asset and sell a forward contract for a total outlay of the spot price of the asset.[16] Over the life of the contract, we hold the asset and forgo interest on the

---

[15] For example, when a stock is purchased, its value, which is always positive, is paid from the long to the short. This is true for any asset.

[16] Remember that in a forward contract, neither party pays anything for the forward contract at the start.

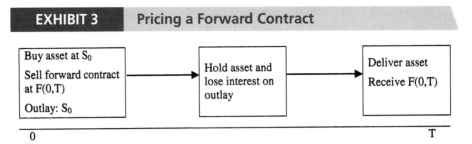

| EXHIBIT 3 | Pricing a Forward Contract |

The transaction is risk free and should be equivalent to investing S_0 dollars in a risk-free asset that pays $F(0,T)$ at time T. Thus, the amount received at T must be the future value of the initial outlay invested at the risk-free rate. For this equality to hold, the forward price must be given as

$$F(0,T) = S_0(1 + r)^T$$

Example: The spot price is \$72.50, the risk-free rate is 8.25 percent, and the contract is for five years. The forward price would be

$$F(0,T) = F(0,5) = 72.50(1.0825)^5 = 107.76$$

money. At expiration, we deliver the asset and receive the forward price for a payoff of $F(0,T)$. The overall transaction is risk free and equivalent to investing the spot price of the asset in a risk-free bond that pays $F(0,T)$ at time T. Therefore, the payoff at T must be the future value of the spot price invested at the risk-free rate. This equality can be true only if the forward price is the spot price compounded at the risk-free rate over the life of the asset.

A contract in which the initial value is intentionally set at a nonzero value is called an **off-market FRA**. In such a contract, the forward price is set arbitrarily in the process of negotiation between the two parties. Given the chosen forward price, the contract will have a nonzero value. As noted above, if the value is positive, the long pays that amount up front to the short. If it is negative, the short pays that amount up front to the long. Although off-market FRAs are not common, we shall use them in Reading 65 when studying swaps.

Now suppose we are at a time t, which is a point during the life of the contract. We may want to know the value of the forward contract for several reasons. For one, it makes good business sense to know the monetary value of an obligation to do something at a later date. Also, accounting rules require that a company mark its derivatives to their current market values and report the effects of those values in income statements and balance sheets. In addition, the market value can be used as a gauge of the credit exposure. Finally, the market value can be used to determine how much money one party can pay the other to terminate the contract.

Let us start by assuming that we established a long forward contract at time 0 at the price $F(0,T)$. Of course, its value at time 0 was zero. But now it is time t, and we want to know its new value, $V_t(0,T)$. Let us consider what it means to hold the position of being long at time t a forward contract established at time 0 at the price $F(0,T)$ and expiring at time T:

We will have to pay $F(0,T)$ dollars at T.
We will receive the underlying asset, which will be worth S_T, at T.

At least part of the value will clearly be the present value of a payment of $F(0,T)$, or in other words, $-F(0,T)/(1 + r)^{T - t}$. The other part of the contract value comes from the fact that we have a claim on the asset's value at T. We do not know what S_T (the asset value at T) will be, but we do know that the market tells us its present value is S_t, the current asset price. *By definition, an asset's value today is the present value of its future value.*[17] Thus we can easily value our forward contract at time t during the life of the contract:

$$V_t(0,T) = S_t - F(0,T)/(1 + r)^{(T-t)}$$

(62-3)

Consider our earlier example in which we entered into a one-year forward contract to buy the asset at $105. Now assume it is three months later and the price of the asset is $102. With $t = 0.25$ and $T = 1$, the value of the contract would be

$$V_t(0,T) = V_{0.25}(0,1) = \$102 - \$105/(1.05)^{0.75} = \$0.7728$$

Again, why is this the value? The contract provides the long with a claim on the asset at expiration. That claim is currently worth the current asset value of $102. That claim also obligates the long to pay $105 at expiration, which has a present value of $105/(1.05)^{0.75} = \$101.2272$. Thus, the long position has a value of $102 − $101.2272 = $0.7728.

As noted above, this market value may well affect the income statement and balance sheet. In addition, it gives an idea of the contract's credit exposure, a topic we have touched on and will cover in more detail in Section 5. Finally, we noted earlier that a party could re-enter the market and offset the contract by paying the counterparty or having the counterparty pay him a cash amount. This cash amount is the market value as calculated here.[18]

Exhibit 4 summarizes how we value a forward contract. If we went long a forward contract at time 0 and we are now at time t prior to expiration, we hold a claim on the asset at expiration and are obligated to pay the forward price at expiration. The claim on the asset is worth its current price; the obligation to pay the forward price at expiration is worth the negative of its present value. Thus, the value of the forward contract is the current spot price minus the forward price discounted from expiration back to the present.

Therefore, we have seen that the forward contract value is zero today: the asset price minus the present value of the forward price at a time prior to expiration, and the asset price minus the forward price at expiration. It may be helpful to note that in general, we can always say that *the forward contract value is the asset price minus the present value of the exercise price,* because given $V_t(0,T) = S_t - F(0,T)/(1 + r)^{(T - t)}$:

If $t = 0$, $V_t(0,T) = V_0(0,T) = S_0 - F(0,T)/(1 + r)^T = 0$
   because $F(0,T) = S_0(1 + r)^T$

If $t = T$, $V_t(0,T) = V_T(0,T) = S_T - F(0,T)/(1 + r)^0 = S_T - F(0,T)$

The formulas for pricing and valuation of a forward contract are summarized in Exhibit 5.

---

[17] This statement is true for any type of asset or financial instrument. It always holds by definition.

[18] If the market value is positive, the value of the asset exceeds the present value of what the long promises to pay. Thus, it makes sense that the short must pay the long. If the market value is negative, then the present value of what the long promises to pay exceeds the value of the asset. Then, it makes sense that the long must pay the short.

| EXHIBIT 4 | Valuing a Forward Contract |

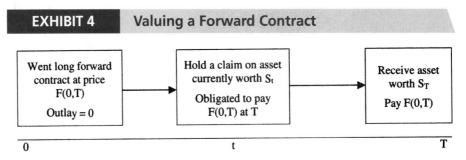

The value of the forward contract at t must be the value of what it will produce at T:

$$V_t(0,T) = S_t - F(0,T)/(1 + r)^{(T - t)}$$

Example: A two-year forward contract was established with a price of \$62.25. Now, a year and a half later (t = 1.5), the spot price is \$71.19 and the risk-free rate is 7 percent. The value of the forward contract is

$$V_t(0,T) = V_{1.5}(0,2) = 71.19 - 62.25/(1.07)^{0.5} = 11.01$$

| EXHIBIT 5 | Pricing and Valuation Formulas for a Forward Contract |

Today = time 0
Arbitrary point during the contract's life = time t
Expiration = time T

Value of a forward contract at any time t:

$$V_t(0,T) = S_t - F(0,T)/(1 + r)^{(T - t)}$$

Value of a forward contract at expiration (t = T):

$$V_T(0,T) = S_T - F(0,T)$$

Value of a forward contract at initiation (t = 0):

$$V_0(0,T) = S_0 - F(0,T)/(1 + r)^T$$

Customarily, no money changes hands at initiation so $V_0(0,T)$ is set equal to zero. Thus,

$$F(0,T) = S_0(1 + r)^T$$

EXAMPLE 1

An investor holds title to an asset worth €125.72. To raise money for an unrelated purpose, the investor plans to sell the asset in nine months. The investor is concerned about uncertainty in the price of the asset at that time. The investor learns about the advantages of using forward contracts to manage this risk and enters into such a contract to sell the asset in nine months. The risk-free interest rate is 5.625 percent.

A. Determine the appropriate price the investor could receive in nine months by means of the forward contract.

B. Suppose the counterparty to the forward contract is willing to engage in such a contract at a forward price of €140. Explain what type of transaction the investor could execute to take advantage of the situation. Calculate the rate of return (annualized), and explain why the transaction is attractive.

C. Suppose the forward contract is entered into at the price you computed in Part A. Two months later, the price of the asset is €118.875. The investor would like to evaluate her position with respect to any gain or loss accrued on the forward contract. Determine the market value of the forward contract at this point in time from the perspective of the investor in Part A.

D. Determine the value of the forward contract at expiration assuming the contract is entered into at the price you computed in Part A and the price of the underlying asset is €123.50 at expiration. Explain how the investor did on the overall position of both the asset and the forward contract in terms of the rate of return.

Solution to A:
$$T = 9/12 = 0.75$$
$$S_0 = 125.72$$
$$r = 0.05625$$

$$F(0,T) = 125.72(1.05625)^{0.75} = 130.99$$

Solution to B: As found in Part A, the forward contract should be selling at €130.99, but it is selling for €140. Consequently, it is overpriced—and an overpriced contract should be sold. Because the investor holds the asset, she will be hedged by selling the forward contract. Consequently, her asset, worth €125.72 when the forward contract is sold, will be delivered in nine months and she will receive €140 for it. The rate of return will be

$$\left(\frac{140}{125.72}\right) - 1 = 0.1136$$

This risk-free return of 11.36 percent for nine months is clearly in excess of the 5.625 percent annual rate. In fact, a rate of 11.36 percent for nine months annualizes to

$$(1.1136)^{12/9} - 1 = 0.1543$$

An annual risk-free rate of 15.43 percent is clearly preferred over the actual risk-free rate of 5.625 percent. The position is not only hedged but also earns an arbitrage profit.

Solution to C: $t = 2/12$

$$T - t = 9/12 - 2/12 = 7/12$$
$$S_t = 118.875$$
$$F(0,T) = 130.99$$

$$V_t(0,T) = V_{2/12}(0,9/12) = 118.875 - 130.99/(1.05625)^{7/12} = -8.0$$

The contract has a negative value. Note, however, that in this form, the answer applies to the holder of the long position. This investor is short. Thus, the value to the investor in this problem is positive 8.0.

Solution to D: $S_T = 123.50$

$$V_T(0,T) = V_{9/12}(0,9/12) = 123.50 - 130.99 = -7.49$$

This amount is the value to the long. This investor is short, so the value is a positive 7.49. The investor incurred a loss on the asset of $125.72 - 123.50 = 2.22$. Combined with the gain on the forward contract, the net gain is $7.49 - 2.22 = 5.27$. A gain of 5.27 on an asset worth 125.72 when the transaction was initiated represents a return of $5.27/125.72 = 4.19$ percent. When annualized, the rate of return equals

$$(1.0419)^{12/9} - 1 = 0.05625$$

It should come as no surprise that this number is the annual risk-free rate. The transaction was executed at the no-arbitrage forward price of €130.99. Thus, it would be impossible to earn a return higher or lower than the risk-free rate.

In our examples, there were no costs or cash flows associated with holding the underlying assets. In the specific examples below for equity derivatives, fixed-income and interest rate derivatives, and currency derivatives, we present cases in which cash flows on the underlying asset will slightly alter our results. We shall ignore any costs of holding assets. Such costs are primarily associated with commodities, an asset class we do not address in this reading.

4.2 Pricing and Valuation of Equity Forward Contracts

Equity forward contracts are priced and valued much like the generic contract described above, with one important additional feature. Many stocks pay dividends, and the effects of these dividends must be incorporated into the pricing and valuation process. Our concern is with the dividends that occur over the life of the forward contract, but not with those that may come after the contract ends. Following standard procedure, we assume that these dividends are known or are a constant percentage of the stock price.

We begin with the idea of a forward contract on either a single stock, a portfolio of stocks, or an index in which dividends are to be paid during the life of the contract. Using the time notation that today is time 0, expiration is time T, and there is an arbitrary time t during its life when we need to value the contract, assume that dividends can be paid at various times during the life of the contract between t and T.[19]

In the examples that follow, we shall calculate present and future values of this stream of dividends over the life of the forward contract. Given a series of these dividends of $D_1, D_2, \ldots D_n$, whose values are known, that occur at times $t_1, t_2, \ldots t_n$, the present value will be defined as PV(D,0,T) and computed as

$$PV(D,0,T) = \sum_{i=1}^{n} \frac{D_i}{(1 + r)^{t_i}}$$

The future value will be defined as FV(D,0,T) and computed as

$$FV(D,0,T) = \sum_{i=1}^{n} D_i(1 + r)^{T - t_i}$$

Recall that the forward price is established by eliminating any opportunity to arbitrage from establishing a forward contract without making any cash outlay today, as is customary with forward contracts. We found that the forward price is the spot price compounded at the risk-free interest rate. To include dividends, we adjust our formula slightly to

$$F(0,T) = [S_0 - PV(D,0,T)](1 + r)^T \tag{62-4}$$

In other words, we simply subtract the present value of the dividends from the stock price. Note that the dividends reduce the forward price, a reflection of the fact that holders of long positions in forward contracts do not benefit from dividends in comparison to holders of long positions in the underlying stock.

For example, consider a stock priced at $40, which pays a dividend of $3 in 50 days. The risk-free rate is 6 percent. A forward contract expiring in six months (T = 0.5) would have a price of

$$F(0,T) = F(0,0.5) = [\$40 - \$3/(1.06)^{50/365}](1.06)^{0.5} = \$38.12$$

If the stock had more than one dividend, we would simply subtract the present value of all dividends over the life of the contract from the stock price, as in the following example.

The risk-free rate is 4 percent. The forward contract expires in 300 days and is on a stock currently priced at $35, which pays quarterly dividends according to the following schedule:

Days to Ex-Dividend Date	Dividend
10	$0.45
102	$0.45
193	$0.45
283	$0.45

[19] Given the way dividends are typically paid, the right to the dividend leaves the stock on the ex-dividend date, which is prior to the payment date. To precisely incorporate this feature, either the dividend payment date should be the ex-dividend date or the dividend should be the present value at the ex-dividend date of the dividend to be paid at a later date. We shall ignore this point here and assume that it would be taken care of in practice.

The present value of the dividends is found as follows:

$$PV(D,0,T) = \$0.45/(1.04)^{10/365} + \$0.45/(1.04)^{102/365}$$
$$+ \$0.45/(1.04)^{193/365} + \$0.45/(1.04)^{283/365} = \$1.77$$

The time to expiration is $T = 300/365$. Therefore, the forward price equals

$$F(0,T) = F(0,300/365) = (\$35 - \$1.77)(1.04)^{300/365} = \$34.32$$

Another approach to incorporating the dividends is to use the future value of the dividends. With this forward contract expiring in 300 days, the first dividend is reinvested for 290 days, the second for 198 days, the third for 107 days, and the fourth for 17 days. Thus,

$$FV(D,0,T) = \$0.45(1.04)^{290/365} + \$0.45(1.04)^{198/365}$$
$$+ \$0.45(1.04)^{107/365} + \$0.45(1.04)^{17/365} = \$1.83$$

To obtain the forward price, we compound the stock value to expiration and subtract the future value of the dividends. Thus, the forward price would be

$$F(0,T) = S_0(1 + r)^T - FV(D,0,T) \tag{62-5}$$

This formula will give the same answer as the one using the present value of the dividends, as shown below:

$$F(0,300/365) = \$35(1.04)^{300/365} - \$1.83 = \$34.32$$

An alternative way to incorporate dividends is to express them as a fixed percentage of the stock price. The more common version of this formulation is to assume that the stock, portfolio, or index pays dividends continuously at a rate of δ^c. By specifying the dividends in this manner, we are allowing the dividends to be uncertain and completely determined by the stock price at the time the dividends are being paid. In this case, the stock is constantly paying a dividend at the rate δ^c. In Reading 63, we will again discuss how to incorporate dividends.

Because we pay dividends continuously, for consistency we must also compound the interest continuously. The continuously compounded equivalent of the discrete risk-free rate r will be denoted r^c and is found as $r^c = \ln(1 + r)$.[20] The future value of \$1 at time T is $\exp(r^cT)$. Then the forward price is given as

$$F(0,T) = (S_0 e^{-\delta^c T}) e^{r^c T} \tag{62-6}$$

The term in parentheses, the stock price discounted at the dividend yield rate, is equivalent to the stock price minus the present value of the dividends. This value

---

[20] The notation "ln" stands for natural logarithm. A logarithm is the power to which its base must be raised to equal a given number. The base of the natural logarithm system is e, approximately 2.71828. With an interest rate of $r = 0.06$, we would have $r^c = \ln(1.06) = 0.058$. Then $e^{0.058} = 1.06$ is called the exponential function and often written as $\exp(0.058) = 1.06$. The future value factor is thus $\exp(r^c)$. The present value factor is $1/\exp(r^c)$ or $\exp(-r^c)$. If the period is more or less than one year, we also multiply the rate by the number of years or fraction of a year—that is, $\exp(-r^cT)$ or $\exp(r^cT)$.

is then compounded at the risk-free rate over the life of the contract, just as we have done in the other versions.

Some people attach significance to whether the forward price is higher than the spot price. It is important to note that the forward price should not be interpreted as a forecast of the future price of the underlying. This misperception is common. If the forward price is higher than the spot price, it merely indicates that the effect of the risk-free rate is greater than the effect of the dividends. In fact, such is usually the case with equity forwards. Interest rates are usually greater than dividend yields.

As an example, consider a forward contract on France's CAC 40 Index. The index is at 5475, the continuously compounded dividend yield is 1.5 percent, and the continuously compounded risk-free interest rate is 4.625 percent. The contract life is two years. With $T = 2$, the contract price is, therefore,

$$F(0,T) = F(0,2) = (5475 \times e^{-0.015(2)})e^{0.04625(2)} = 5828.11$$

This specification involving a continuous dividend yield is commonly used when the underlying is a portfolio or stock index. If a single stock in the portfolio pays a dividend, then the portfolio or index can be viewed as paying a dividend. Given the diversity of dividend policies and ex-dividend dates, such an assumption is usually considered a reasonable approximation for stock portfolios or stock indices, but the assumption is not as appropriate for individual stocks. No general agreement exists on the most appropriate approach, and you must become comfortable with all of them. To obtain the appropriate forward price, the most important point to remember is that one way or another, the analysis must incorporate the dividend component of the stock price, portfolio value, or index level. If the contract is not trading at the correct price, then it is mispriced and arbitrage, as described in the generic forward contract pricing section, will force an alignment between the market forward price and the theoretical forward price.

Recall that the value of a forward contract is the asset price minus the forward price discounted back from the expiration date. Regardless of how the dividend is specified or even whether the underlying stock, portfolio, or index pays dividends, the valuation formulas for a forward contract on a stock differ only in that the stock price is adjusted by removing the present value of the remaining dividends:

$$V_t(0,T) = S_t - PV(D,t,T) - F(0,T)/(1 + r)^{(T-t)} \qquad \textbf{(62-7)}$$

where we now note that the dividends are only those paid after time t. If we are using continuous compounding,

$$V_t(0,T) = S_t e^{-\delta^c(T-t)} - F(0,T)e^{-r^c(T-t)} \qquad \textbf{(62-8)}$$

At the contract initiation date, $t = 0$ and $V_0(0,T)$ is set to zero because no cash changes hands. At expiration, $t = T$ and no dividends remain, so the valuation formula reduces to $S_T - F(0,T)$.

The formulas for pricing and valuation of equity forward contracts are summarized in Exhibit 6.

EXHIBIT 6	Pricing and Valuation Formulas for Equity Forward Contracts

Forward price = (Stock price − Present value of dividends over life of contract) $\times (1 + r)^T$

or (Stock price) $\times (1 + r)^T$ − Future value of dividends over life of contract

Discrete dividends over the life of the contract:

$$F(0,T) = [S_0 - PV(D,0,T)](1 + r)^T \text{ or } S_0(1 + r)^T - FV(D,0,T)$$

Continuous dividends at the rate δ^c:

$$F(0,T) = (S_0 e^{-\delta^c T}) e^{r^c T}$$

Value of forward contract:

$$V_t(0,T) = S_t - PV(D,t,T) - F(0,T)/(1 + r)^{(T - t)}$$

or

$$V_t(0,T) = S_t e^{-\delta^c(T - t)} - F(0,T) e^{-r^c(T - t)}$$

EXAMPLE 2

An asset manager anticipates the receipt of funds in 200 days, which he will use to purchase a particular stock. The stock he has in mind is currently selling for $62.50 and will pay a $0.75 dividend in 50 days and another $0.75 dividend in 140 days. The risk-free rate is 4.2 percent. The manager decides to commit to a future purchase of the stock by going long a forward contract on the stock.

A. At what price would the manager commit to purchase the stock in 200 days through a forward contract?

B. Suppose the manager enters into the contract at the price you found in Part A. Now, 75 days later, the stock price is $55.75. Determine the value of the forward contract at this point.

C. It is now the expiration day, and the stock price is $58.50. Determine the value of the forward contract at this time.

$$S_0 = \$62.50$$
$$T = 200/365$$
$$D_1 = \$0.75, t_1 = 50/365$$
$$D_2 = \$0.75, t_2 = 140/365$$
$$r = 0.042$$

Solution to A: First find the present value of the dividends:

$$\$0.75/(1.042)^{50/365} + \$0.75/(1.042)^{140/365} = \$1.48$$

Then find the forward price:

$$F(0,T) = F(0,200/365) = (\$62.50 - \$1.48)(1.042)^{200/365} = \$62.41$$

Solution to B: We must now find the present value of the dividends 75 days after the contract begins. The first dividend has already been paid, so it is not relevant. Because only one remains, the second dividend is now the "first" dividend. It will be paid in 65 days. Thus, $t_1 - t = 65/365$. The present value of this dividend is $\$0.75/(1.042)^{65/365} = \$0.74$. The other information is

$$t = 75/365$$
$$T - t = (200 - 75)/365 = 125/365$$
$$S_t = \$55.75$$

The value of the contract is, therefore,

$$V_t(0,T) = V_{75/365}(0,200/365) = (\$55.75 - \$0.74) - \$62.41/(1.042)^{125/365} = -\$6.53$$

Thus, the contract has a negative value.

Solution to C: $S_T = \$58.50$

The value of the contract is

$$V_{200/365}(0,200/365) = V_T(0,T) = \$58.50 - \$62.41 = -\$3.91$$

Thus, the contract expires with a value of negative $3.91.

4.3 Pricing and Valuation of Fixed-Income and Interest Rate Forward Contracts

Forward contracts on fixed-income securities are priced and valued in a virtually identical manner to their equity counterparts. We can use the above formulas if S_t represents the bond price at time t and D_i represents a coupon paid at time t_i. We denote B^c as a coupon bond and then use notation to draw attention to those coupons that must be included in the forward contract pricing calculations. We will let $B_t^c(T + Y)$ represent the bond price at time t, T is the expiration date of the forward contract, Y is the remaining maturity of the bond on the forward contract expiration, and $(T + Y)$ is the time to maturity of the bond at the time the forward contract is initiated. Consider a bond with n coupons to occur before its maturity date. Converting our formula for a forward contract on a stock into that for a forward contract on a bond and letting

CI be the coupon interest over a specified period of time, we have a forward price of

$$F(0,T) = \left[B_0^c(T + Y) - PV(CI,0,T)\right](1 + r)^T \qquad \textbf{(62-9)}$$

where PV(CI,0,T) is the present value of the coupon interest over the life of the forward contract. Alternatively, the forward price can be obtained as

$$F(0,T) = \left[B_0^c(T + Y)\right](1 + r)^T - FV(CI,0,T) \qquad \textbf{(62-10)}$$

where FV(CI,0,T) is the future value of the coupon interest over the life of the forward contract.

The value of the forward contract at time t would be

$$V_t(0,T) = B_t^c(T + Y) - PV(CI,t,T) - F(0,T)/(1 + r)^{(T-t)} \qquad \textbf{(62-11)}$$

at time t; note that the relevant coupons are only those remaining as of time t until expiration of the forward contract. As in the case for stock, this formula will reduce to the appropriate values at time 0 and at expiration. For example, at expiration, no coupons would remain, t = T, and $V_T(0,T) = B_T^c(T + Y) - F(0,T)$. At time t = 0, the contract is being initiated and has a zero value, which leads to the formula for F(0,T) above.

Consider a bond with semiannual coupons. The bond has a current maturity of 583 days and pays four coupons, each six months apart. The next coupon occurs in 37 days, followed by coupons in 219 days, 401 days, and 583 days, at which time the principal is repaid. Suppose that the bond price, which includes accrued interest, is \$984.45 for a \$1,000 par, 4 percent coupon bond. The coupon rate implies that each coupon is \$20. The risk-free interest rate is 5.75 percent. Assume that the forward contract expires in 310 days. Thus, T = 310, T + Y = 583, and Y = 273, meaning that the bond has 273 days remaining after the forward contract expires. Note that only the first two coupons occur during the life of the forward contract.

The present value of the coupons is

$$\$20/(1.0575)^{37/365} + \$20/(1.0575)^{219/365} = \$39.23$$

The forward price if the contract is initiated now is

$$F(0,T) = (\$984.45 - \$39.23)(1.0575)^{310/365} = \$991.18$$

Thus, we assume that we shall be able to enter into this contract to buy the bond in 310 days at the price of \$991.18.

Now assume it is 15 days later and the new bond price is \$973.14. Let the risk-free interest rate now be 6.75 percent. The present value of the remaining coupons is

$$\$20/(1.0675)^{22/365} + \$20/(1.0675)^{204/365} = \$39.20$$

The value of the forward contract is thus

$$\$973.14 - \$39.20 - \$991.19/(1.0675)^{295/365} = -\$6.28$$

The contract has gone from a zero value at the start to a negative value, primarily as a result of the decrease in the price of the underlying bond.

EXHIBIT 7	Pricing and Valuation Formulas for Fixed Income Forward Contracts

Forward price = (Bond price − Present value of coupons over life of contract) $(1 + r)^T$ or (Bond price)$(1 + r)^T$ − Future value of coupons over life of contract

Price of forward contract on bond with coupons CI:

$$F(0,T) = [B_0^c(T + Y) - PV(CI,0,T)](1 + r)^T$$
$$\text{or } [B_0^c(T + Y)](1 + r)^T - FV(CI,0,T)$$

Value of forward contract on bond with coupons CI:

$$V_t(0,T) = B_t^c(T + Y) - PV(CI,t,T) - F(0,T)/(1 + r)^{(T - t)}$$

If the bond is a zero-coupon bond/T-bill, we can perform the same analysis as above, but we simply let the coupons equal zero.

Exhibit 7 summarizes the formulas for the pricing and valuation of forward contracts on fixed-income securities.

EXAMPLE 3

An investor purchased a bond when it was originally issued with a maturity of five years. The bond pays semiannual coupons of $50. It is now 150 days into the life of the bond. The investor wants to sell the bond the day after its fourth coupon. The first coupon occurs 181 days after issue, the second 365 days, the third 547 days, and the fourth 730 days. At this point (150 days into the life of the bond), the price is $1,010.25. The bond prices quoted here include accrued interest.

A. At what price could the owner enter into a forward contract to sell the bond on the day after its fourth coupon? Note that the owner would receive that fourth coupon. The risk-free rate is currently 8 percent.

B. Now move forward 365 days. The new risk-free interest rate is 7 percent and the new price of the bond is $1,025.375. The counterparty to the forward contract believes that it has received a gain on the position. Determine the value of the forward contract and the gain or loss to the counterparty at this time. Note that we have now introduced a new risk-free rate, because interest rates can obviously change over the life of the bond and any calculations of the forward contract value must reflect this fact. The new risk-free rate is used instead of the old rate in the valuation formula.

Solution to A: First we must find the present value of the four coupons over the life of the forward contract. At the 150th day of the life of the bond, the coupons occur 31 days from now, 215 days from now, 397 days from now, and 580 days from now. Keep in mind that we need consider only the first four coupons because the owner will sell the bond on the day after the fourth coupon. The present value of the coupons is

$$\$50/(1.08)^{31/365} + \$50/(1.08)^{215/365} + \$50/(1.08)^{397/365}$$
$$+ \$50/(1.08)^{580/365} = \$187.69$$

Because we want the forward contract to expire one day after the fourth coupon, it expires in $731 - 150 = 581$ days. Thus, $T = 581/365$.

$$F(0,T) = F(0,581/365) = (\$1,010.25 - \$187.69)(1.08)^{581/365} = \$929.76$$

Solution to B: It is now 365 days later—the 515th day of the bond's life. There are two coupons to go, one occurring in $547 - 515 = 32$ days and the other in $730 - 515 = 215$ days. The present value of the coupons is now

$$\$50/(1.07)^{32/365} + \$50/(1.07)^{215/365} = \$97.75$$

To address the value of the forward contract and the gain or loss to the counterparty, note that $731 - 515 = 216$ days now remain until the contract's expiration. Because the bondholder would sell the forward contract to hedge the future sale price of the bond, the bondholder's counterparty to the forward contract would hold a long position. The value of the forward contract is the current spot price minus the present value of the coupons minus the present value of the forward price:

$$\$1,025.375 - \$97.75 - \$929.76/(1.07)^{216/365} = \$34.36$$

Because the contract was initiated with a zero value at the start and the counterparty is long the contract, the value of \$34.36 represents a gain to the counterparty.

Now let us look at the pricing and valuation of FRAs. Previously we used the notations t and T to represent the time to a given date. The expressions t or T were, respectively, the number of days to time point t or T, each divided by 365. In the FRA market, contracts are created with specific day counts. We will use the letter h to refer to the day on which the FRA expires and the letter g to refer to an arbitrary day prior to expiration. Consider the time line shown below. We shall initiate an FRA on day 0. The FRA expires on day h. The rate underlying the FRA is the rate on an m-day Eurodollar deposit. Thus, there are h days from today until the FRA expiration and $h + m$ days until the maturity date of the Eurodollar instrument on which the FRA rate is based. The date indicated by g will simply be a date during the life of the FRA at which we want to determine a value for the FRA.

0	g	h	h + m
(today)		(expiration)	

Now let us specify some notation. We let $L_i(j)$ represent the rate on a j-day LIBOR deposit on an arbitrary day i, which falls somewhere in the above period from 0 to h, inclusive. Remember that this instrument is a j-day loan from one bank to another. For example, the bank borrowing \$1 on day i for j days will pay back the amount

$$\$1\left[1 + L_i(j)\left(\frac{j}{360}\right)\right]$$

in j days.

The rate for m-day LIBOR on day h, $L_h(m)$, will determine the payoff of the FRA. We denote the fixed rate on the FRA as FRA(0,h,m), which stands for the rate on an FRA established on day 0, expiring on day h, and based on m-day LIBOR. We shall use a \$1 notional principal for the FRA, which means that at expiration its payoff is

$$\frac{[L_h(m) - FRA(0,h,m)]\left(\dfrac{m}{360}\right)}{1 + L_h(m)\left(\dfrac{m}{360}\right)} \qquad \textbf{(62-12)}$$

The numerator is the difference between the underlying LIBOR on the expiration day and the rate agreed on when the contract was initiated, multiplied by the adjustment factor m/360. Both of these rates are annual rates applied to a Eurodollar deposit of m days; hence, multiplying by m/360 is necessary. The denominator discounts the payoff by the m-day LIBOR in effect at the time of the payoff. As noted earlier, this adjustment is necessary because the rates in the numerator apply to Eurodollar deposits created on day h and paying off m days later. If the notional principal is anything other than \$1, we also must multiply the above payoff by the notional principal to determine the actual payoff.

To derive the formula for pricing an FRA, a specific arbitrage transaction involving Eurodollars and FRAs is required. We omit the details of this somewhat complex transaction, but the end result is that the FRA rate is given by the following formula:

$$FRA(0,h,m) = \left[\frac{1 + L_0(h + m)\left(\dfrac{h + m}{360}\right)}{1 + L_0(h)\left(\dfrac{h}{360}\right)} - 1\right]\left(\frac{360}{m}\right) \qquad \textbf{(62-13)}$$

This somewhat awkward-looking formula is actually just the formula for a LIBOR forward rate, given the interest payment conventions in the FRA market. The numerator is the future value of a Eurodollar deposit of h + m days. The denominator is the future value of a shorter-term Eurodollar deposit of h days. This ratio is 1 plus a rate; subtracting 1 and multiplying by 360/m annualizes the rate.[21]

Consider a 3 × 9 FRA. This instrument expires in 90 days and is based on 180-day LIBOR. Thus, the Eurodollar deposit on which the underlying rate is

---

[21] To compare with the traditional method of calculating a forward rate, consider a two-year rate of 10 percent and a one-year rate of 9 percent. The forward rate is $[(1.10)^2/(1.09)] - 1 = 0.1101$. The numerator is the future value of the longer-term bond, and the denominator is the future value of the shorter-term bond. The ratio is 1 plus the rate. We do not need to annualize in this example, because the forward rate is on a one-year bond.

based begins in 90 days and matures in 270 days. Because we are on day 0, h = 90, m = 180, and h + m = 270. Let the current rates be

$$L_0(h) = L_0(90) = 0.056$$
$$L_0(h + m) = L_0(270) = 0.06$$

In other words, the 90-day rate is 5.6 percent, and the 270-day rate is 6 percent.

With h = 90 and m = 180, using our formula for the FRA rate, we obtain

$$FRA(0,h,m) = FRA(0,90,180) = \left[\frac{1 + 0.06\left(\frac{270}{360}\right)}{1 + 0.056\left(\frac{90}{360}\right)} - 1\right]\left(\frac{360}{180}\right) = 0.0611$$

So to enter into an FRA on day 0, the rate would be 6.11 percent.[22]

As noted, the initial outlay for entering the forward contract is zero. Thus, the initial value is zero. Later during the life of the contract, its value will rise above or fall below zero. Now let us determine the value of an FRA during its life. Specifically, we use the notation $V_g(0,h,m)$ to represent the value of an FRA on day g, prior to expiration, which was established on day 0, expires on day h, and is based on m-day LIBOR. Omitting the derivation, the value of the FRA will be

$$V_g(0,h,m) = \frac{1}{1 + L_g(h - g)\left(\frac{h - g}{360}\right)} - \frac{1 + FRA(0,h,m)\left(\frac{m}{360}\right)}{1 + L_g(h + m - g)\left(\frac{h + m - g}{360}\right)} \quad \textbf{(62-14)}$$

This formula looks complicated, but the ideas behind it are actually quite simple. Recall that we are at day g. The first term on the right-hand side is the present value of $1 received at day h. The second term is the present value of 1 plus the FRA rate to be received on day h + m, the maturity date of the underlying Eurodollar time deposit.

Assume that we go long the FRA, and it is 25 days later. We need to assign a value to the FRA. First note that g = 25, h − g = 90 − 25 = 65, and h + m − g = 90 + 180 − 25 = 245. In other words, we are 25 days into the contract, 65 days remain until expiration, and 245 days remain until the maturity of the Eurodollar deposit on which the underlying LIBOR is based. First we need information about the new term structure. Let

$$L_g(h - g) = L_{25}(65) = 0.059$$
$$L_g(h + m - g) = L_{25}(245) = 0.065$$

We now use the formula for the value of the FRA to obtain

$$V_g(0,h,m) = V_{25}(0,90,180) = \frac{1}{1 + 0.059\left(\frac{65}{360}\right)} - \frac{1 + 0.0611\left(\frac{180}{360}\right)}{1 + 0.065\left(\frac{245}{360}\right)} = 0.0026$$

Thus, we went long this FRA on day 0. Then 25 days later, the term structure changes to the rates used here and the FRA has a value of $0.0026 per $1

---

[22] It is worthwhile to point out again that this rate is the forward rate in the LIBOR term structure.

EXHIBIT 8	**Pricing and Valuation Formulas for Interest Rate Forward Contracts (FRAs)**

Forward price (rate):

$$FRA(0,h,m) = \left[\frac{1 + L_0(h + m)\left(\dfrac{h + m}{360}\right)}{1 + L_0(h)\left(\dfrac{h}{360}\right)} - 1 \right]\left(\frac{360}{m}\right)$$

Value of FRA on day g:

$$V_g(0,h,m) = \frac{1}{1 + L_g(h - g)\left(\dfrac{h - g}{360}\right)} - \frac{1 + FRA(0,h,m)\left(\dfrac{m}{360}\right)}{1 + L_g(h + m - g)\left(\dfrac{h + m - g}{360}\right)}$$

notional principal. If the notional principal is any amount other than $1, we multiply the notional principal by $0.0026 to obtain the full market value of the FRA.

We summarize the FRA formulas in Exhibit 8. We have now looked at the pricing and valuation of equity, fixed-income, and interest rate forward contracts. One of the most widely used types of forward contracts is the currency forward. The pricing and valuation of currency forwards is remarkably similar to that of equity forwards.

EXAMPLE 4

A corporate treasurer needs to hedge the risk of the interest rate on a future transaction. The risk is associated with the rate on 180-day Euribor in 30 days. The relevant term structure of Euribor is given as follows:

30-day Euribor	5.75%
210-day Euribor	6.15%

A. State the terminology used to identify the FRA in which the manager is interested.

B. Determine the rate that the company would get on an FRA expiring in 30 days on 180-day Euribor.

C. Suppose the manager went long this FRA. Now, 20 days later, interest rates have moved significantly downward to the following:

10-day Euribor	5.45%
190-day Euribor	5.95%

The manager would like to know where the company stands on this FRA transaction. Determine the market value of the FRA for a €20 million notional principal.

D. On the expiration day, 180-day Euribor is 5.72 percent. Determine the payment made to or by the company to settle the FRA contract.

Solution to A: This transaction would be identified as a 1 × 7 FRA.

Solution to B: Here the notation would be h = 30, m = 180, h + m = 210. Then

$$
FRA(0,h,m) = FRA(0,30,180) = \left[\frac{1 + 0.0615\left(\frac{210}{360}\right)}{1 + 0.0575\left(\frac{30}{360}\right)} - 1 \right]\left(\frac{360}{180}\right) = 0.0619
$$

Solution to C: Here g = 20, h − g = 30 − 20 = 10, h + m − g = 30 + 180 − 20 = 190. The value of the FRA for a €1 notional principal would be

$$
V_g(0,h,m) = V_{20}(0,30,180) = \frac{1}{1 + 0.0545\left(\frac{10}{360}\right)} - \frac{1 + 0.0619\left(\frac{180}{360}\right)}{1 + 0.0595\left(\frac{190}{360}\right)} = -0.0011
$$

Thus, for a notional principal of €20 million, the value would be €20,000,000(−0.0011) = −€22,000.

Solution to D: At expiration, the payoff is

$$
\frac{[L_h(m) - FRA(0,h,m)]\left(\frac{m}{360}\right)}{1 + L_h(m)\left(\frac{m}{360}\right)} = \frac{(0.0572 - 0.0619)\left(\frac{180}{360}\right)}{1 + 0.0572\left(\frac{180}{360}\right)} = -0.0023
$$

For a notional principal of €20 million, the payoff would then be €20,000,000(−0.0023) = −€46,000. Thus, €46,000 would be paid by the company, because it is long and the final rate was lower than the FRA rate.

4.4 Pricing and Valuation of Currency Forward Contracts

Foreign currency derivative transactions as well as spot transactions must be handled with care. The exchange rate can be quoted in terms of units of the domestic currency per unit of foreign currency, or units of the foreign currency per unit of the domestic currency. In this reading, we shall always quote exchange rates in terms of units of the domestic currency per unit of the foreign currency, which is also called a direct quote. This approach is in keeping with the way in which other underlying assets are quoted. For example, from the perspective of a U.S. investor, a stock that sells for $50 is quoted in units of the domestic currency per unit (share) of stock. Likewise, if the euro exchange rate is quoted as $0.90, then the euro sells for $0.90 per unit, which is one euro. Alternatively, we could quote that $1 sells for 1/$0.90 = €1.1111—that is, €1.1111 per $1; in this case, units of foreign currency per one unit of domestic currency from the perspective of a U.S. investor. In fact, this type of quote is commonly used and is called an indirect quote. Taking that approach, however, we would quote the stock price as $1/\$50 = 0.02$ shares per $1, a very unusual and awkward way to quote a stock price.

By taking the approach of quoting prices in terms of units of the domestic currency per unit of foreign currency, we facilitate a comparison of currencies and their derivatives with equities and their derivatives—a topic we have already covered. For example, we have previously discussed the case of a stock selling for S_0, which represents units of the domestic currency per share of stock. Likewise, we shall treat the currency as having an exchange rate of S_0, meaning that it is selling for S_0. We also need the foreign interest rate, denoted as r^f, and the domestic interest rate, denoted as r.[23]

Consider the following transactions executed today (time 0), assuming a contract expiration date of T:

Take $S_0/(1 + r^f)^T$ units of the domestic currency and convert it to $1/(1 + r^f)^T$ units of the foreign currency.[24]

Sell a forward contract to deliver one unit of the foreign currency at the rate F(0,T) expiring at time T.

Hold the position until time T. The $1/(1 + r^f)^T$ units of foreign currency will accrue interest at the rate r^f and grow to one unit of the currency at T as follows:

$$\left(\frac{1}{1 + r^f}\right)^T (1 + r^f)^T = 1$$

Thus, at expiration we shall have one unit of the foreign currency, which is then delivered to the holder of the long forward contract, who pays the amount F(0,T). This amount was known at the start of the transaction. Because the risk has been hedged away, the exchange rate at expiration is irrelevant. Hence, this transaction is risk-free. Accordingly, the present value of F(0,T), found by discounting at the domestic risk-free interest rate, must equal the initial outlay of $S_0/(1 + r^f)^T$. Setting these amounts equal and solving for F(0,T) gives

$$F(0,T) = \left[\frac{S_0}{(1 + r^f)^T}\right](1 + r)^T \qquad \textbf{(62-15)}$$

The term in brackets is the spot exchange rate discounted by the foreign interest rate. This term is then compounded at the domestic interest rate to the expiration day.[25]

Recall that in pricing equity forwards, we always reduced the stock price by the present value of the dividends and then compounded the resulting value to the expiration date. We can view currencies in the same way. The stock makes

---

[23] We do not use a superscript "d" for the domestic rate, because in all previous examples we have used r to denote the interest rate in the home country of the investor.

[24] In other words, if one unit of the foreign currency costs S_0, then $S_0/(1 + r^f)^T$ units of the domestic currency would, therefore, buy $1/(1 + r^f)^T$ units of the foreign currency.

[25] It is also common to see the above Equation 62-15 written inversely, with the spot rate divided by the domestic interest factor and compounded by the foreign interest factor. This variation would be appropriate if the spot and forward rates were quoted in terms of units of the foreign currency per unit of domestic currency (indirect quotes). As we mentioned earlier, however, it is easier to think of a currency as just another asset, which naturally should have its price quoted in units of the domestic currency per unit of the asset or foreign currency.

cash payments that happen to be called dividends; the currency makes cash payments that happen to be called interest. Although the time pattern of how a stock pays dividends is quite different from the time pattern of how interest accrues, the general idea is the same. After reducing the spot price or rate by any cash flows over the life of the contract, the resulting value is then compounded at the risk-free rate to the expiration day.

The formula we have obtained here is simply a variation of the formula used for other types of forward contracts. In international financial markets, however, this formula has acquired its own name: **interest rate parity** (sometimes called covered interest rate parity). It expresses the equivalence, or parity, of spot and forward exchange rates, after adjusting for differences in the interest rates in the two countries. One implication of interest rate parity is that the forward rate will exceed (be less than) the spot rate if the domestic interest rate exceeds (is less than) the foreign interest rate. With a direct quote, if the forward rate exceeds (is less than) the spot rate, the foreign currency is said to be selling at a premium (discount). One should not, on the basis of this information, conclude that a currency selling at a premium is expected to increase or one selling at a discount is expected to decrease. A forward premium or discount is merely an implication of the relationship between interest rates in the two countries. More information would be required to make any assumptions about the outlook for the exchange rate.

If the forward rate in the market does not equal the forward rate given by interest rate parity, then an arbitrage transaction can be executed. Indeed, a similar relationship is true for any of the forward rates we have studied. In the foreign exchange markets, however, this arbitrage transaction has its own name: covered interest arbitrage. If the forward rate in the market is higher than the rate given by interest rate parity, then the forward rate is too high. When the price of an asset or derivative is too high, it should be sold. Thus, a trader would 1) sell the forward contract at the market rate, 2) buy $1/(1 + r^f)^T$ units of the foreign currency, 3) hold the position, earning interest on the currency, and 4) at maturity of the forward contract deliver the currency and be paid the forward rate. This arbitrage transaction would earn a return in excess of the domestic risk-free rate without any risk. If the forward rate is less than the rate given by the formula, the trader does the opposite, selling the foreign currency and buying a forward contract, in a similar manner. The combined actions of many traders undertaking this transaction will bring the forward price in the market in line with the forward price given by the model.

In Equation 62-15, both interest rates were annual rates with discrete compounding. In dealing with equities, we sometimes assume that the dividend payments are made continuously. Similarly, we could also assume that interest is compounded continuously. If that is the case, let r^{fc} be the continuously compounded foreign interest rate, defined as $r^{fc} = \ln(1 + r^f)$, and as before, let r^c be the continuously compounded domestic interest rate. Then the forward price is given by the same formula, with appropriately adjusted symbols, as we obtained when working with equity derivatives:

$$F(0,T) = (S_0 e^{-r^{fc}T}) e^{r^c T} \qquad \textbf{(62-16)}$$

Now consider how we might value a foreign currency forward contract at some point in time during its life. In fact, we already know how: We simply apply to foreign currency forward contracts what we know about the valuation of equity forwards during the contract's life. Recall that the value of an equity forward is the stock price minus the present value of the dividends over the remaining life of the contract minus the present value of the forward price over the remaining life of the contract. An analogous formula for a currency forward gives us

$$V_t(0,T) = \frac{S_t}{(1 + r^f)^{(T-t)}} - \frac{F(0,T)}{(1 + r)^{(T-t)}} \quad \textbf{(62-17)}$$

In other words, we take the current exchange rate at time t, S_t, discount it by the foreign interest rate over the remaining life of the contract, and subtract the forward price discounted by the domestic interest rate over the remaining life of the contract. Under the assumption that we are using continuous compounding and discounting, the formula would be

$$V_t(0,T) = (S_t e^{-r^{fc}(T-t)}) - F(0,T) e^{-r^c(T-t)} \quad \textbf{(62-18)}$$

For example, suppose the domestic currency is the U.S. dollar and the foreign currency is the Swiss franc. Let the spot exchange rate be \$0.5987, the U.S. interest rate be 5.5 percent, and the Swiss interest rate be 4.75 percent. We assume these interest rates are fixed and will not change over the life of the forward contract. We also assume that these rates are based on annual compounding and are not quoted as LIBOR-type rates. Thus, we compound using formulas like $(1 + r)^T$, where T is the number of years and r is the annual rate.[26]

Assuming the forward contract has a maturity of 180 days, we have T = 180/365. Using the above formula for the forward rate, we find that the forward price should be

$$F(0,T) = F(0,180/365) = \left[\frac{\$0.5987}{(1.0475)^{180/365}} \right] (1.055)^{180/365} = \$0.6008$$

Thus, if we entered into a forward contract, it would call for us to purchase (if long) or sell (if short) one Swiss franc in 180 days at a price of \$0.6008.

Suppose we go long this forward contract. It is now 40 days later, or 140 days until expiration. The spot rate is now \$0.65. As assumed above, the interest rates are fixed. With t = 40/365 and T − t = 140/365, the value of our long position is

$$V_t(0,T) = V_{40/365}(0,180/365) = \frac{\$0.6500}{(1.0475)^{140/365}} - \frac{\$0.6008}{(1.055)^{140/365}} = \$0.0499$$

So the contract value is \$0.0499 per Swiss franc. If the notional principal were more than one Swiss franc, we would simply multiply the notional principal by \$0.0499.

If we were working with continuously compounded rates, we would have $r^c = \ln(1.055) = 0.0535$ and $r^{fc} = \ln(1.0475) = 0.0464$. Then the forward price would be $F(0,T) = F(0,180/365) = (0.5987 e^{-0.0464(180/365)}) e^{0.0535(180/365)} = 0.6008$, and the value 40 days later would be $V_{40/365}(0,180/365) = 0.65 e^{-0.0464(140/365)} - 0.6008 e^{-0.0535(140/365)} = 0.0499$. These are the same results we obtained working with discrete rates.

Exhibit 9 summarizes the formulas for pricing and valuation of currency forward contracts.

---

[26] If these were LIBOR-style rates, the interest would be calculated using the factor 1 + [Rate(Days/360)].

EXHIBIT 9	Pricing and Valuation Formulas for Currency Forward Contracts

Forward price (rate) = (Spot price discounted by foreign interest rate) compounded at domestic interest rate:

$$\text{Discrete interest: } F(0,T) = \left[\frac{S_0}{(1 + r^f)^T} \right] (1 + r)^T$$

$$\text{Continuous interest: } F(0,T) = (S_0 e^{-r^{fc}T}) e^{r^c T}$$

Value of forward contract:

$$\text{Discrete interest: } V_t(0,T) = \left[\frac{S_t}{(1 + r^f)^{(T-t)}} \right] - \frac{F(0,T)}{(1 + r)^{(T-t)}}$$

$$\text{Continuous interest: } V_t(0,T) = [S_t e^{-r^{fc}(T-t)}] - F(0,T) e^{-r^c(T-t)}$$

Note: The exchange rate is quoted in units of domestic currency per unit of foreign currency.

EXAMPLE 5

The spot rate for British pounds is $1.76. The U.S. risk-free rate is 5.1 percent, and the U.K. risk-free rate is 6.2 percent; both are compounded annually. One-year forward contracts are currently quoted at a rate of $1.75.

A. Identify a strategy with which a trader can earn a profit at no risk by engaging in a forward contract, regardless of her view of the pound's likely movements. Carefully describe the transactions the trader would make. Show the rate of return that would be earned from this transaction. Assume the trader's domestic currency is U.S. dollars.

B. Suppose the trader simply shorts the forward contract. It is now one month later. Assume interest rates are the same, but the spot rate is now $1.72. What is the gain or loss to the counterparty on the trade?

C. At expiration, the pound is at $1.69. What is the value of the forward contract to the short at expiration?

Solution to A: The following information is given:

$$S_0 = \$1.76$$
$$r = 0.051$$
$$r^f = 0.062$$
$$T = 1.0$$

The forward price should be

$$F(0,T) = \left(\frac{\$1.76}{1.062} \right) (1.051) = \$1.7418$$

With the forward contract selling at $1.75, it is slightly overpriced. Thus, the trader should be able to buy the currency and sell a forward contract to earn a return in excess of the risk-free rate at no risk. The specific transactions are as follows:

▶ Take $1.76/(1.062) = $1.6573. Use it to buy 1/1.062 = £0.9416.

▶ Sell a forward contract to deliver £1.00 in one year at the price of $1.75.

▶ Hold the position for one year, collecting interest at the U.K. risk-free rate of 6.2 percent. The £0.9416 will grow to (0.9416)(1.062) = £1.00.

▶ At expiration, deliver the pound and receive $1.75. This is a return of

$$\frac{1.75}{1.6573} - 1 = 0.0559$$

A risk-free return of 5.59 percent is better than the U.S. risk-free rate of 5.1 percent, a result of the fact that the forward contract is overpriced.

Solution to B: We now need the value of the forward contract to the counterparty, who went long at $1.75. The inputs are

$$t = 1/12$$
$$S_t = \$1.72$$
$$T - t = 11/12$$
$$F(0,T) = \$1.75$$

The value of the forward contract to the long is

$$V_t(0,T) = \frac{1.72}{(1.062)^{11/12}} - \frac{1.75}{(1.051)^{11/12}} = -0.0443$$

which is a loss of $0.0443 to the long and a gain of $0.0443 to the short.

Solution to C: The pound is worth $1.69 at expiration. Thus, the value to the long is

$$V_T(0,T) = 1.69 - 1.75 = -0.06$$

and the value to the short is +$0.06. Note the minus sign in the equation $V_T(0,T) = -0.06$. The value to the long is always the spot value at expiration minus the original forward price. The short will be required to deliver the foreign currency and receive $1.75, which is $0.06 more than market value of the pound. The contract's value to the short is thus $0.06, which is the negative of its value to the long.

We have now seen how to determine the price and value of equity, fixed-income and interest rate, and currency forward contracts. We observed that the price is determined such that no arbitrage opportunities exist for either the long or the short. We have found that the value of a forward contract is the amount we would pay or receive to enter or exit the contract. Because no money changes hands up front, the value of a forward contract when initiated is zero. The value at expiration is determined by the difference between the spot price or rate at expiration and the forward contract price or rate. The value prior to expiration can also be determined and is the present value of the claim at expiration.

Determining the value of a forward contract is important for several reasons. One, however, is particularly important: Forward contracts contain the very real possibility that one of the parties might default. By knowing the market value, one can determine the amount of money at risk if a counterparty defaults. Let us now look at how credit risk enters into a forward contract.

5   CREDIT RISK AND FORWARD CONTRACTS

To illustrate how credit risk affects a forward contract, consider the currency forward contract example we just finished in the previous section. It concerns a contract that expires in 180 days in which the long will pay a forward rate of $0.6008 for each Swiss franc to be received at expiration. Assume that the contract covers 10 million Swiss francs. Let us look at the problem from the point of view of the holder of the long position and the credit risk faced by this party.

Assume it is the contract expiration day and the spot rate for Swiss francs is $0.62. The long is due to receive 10 million Swiss francs and pay $0.6008 per Swiss franc, or $6,008,000 in total. Now suppose that perhaps because of bankruptcy or insolvency, the short cannot come up with the $6,200,000 that it would take to purchase the Swiss francs on the open market at the prevailing spot rate.[27] In order to obtain the Swiss francs, the long would have to buy them in the open market. Doing so would incur an additional cost of $6,200,000 − $6,008,000 = $192,000, which can be viewed as the credit risk at the point of expiration when the spot rate is $0.62. Not surprisingly, this amount is also the market value of the contract at this point.

This risk is an immediate risk faced at expiration. Prior to expiration, the long faces a potential risk that the short will default. If the long wanted to gauge the potential exposure, he would calculate the current market value. In the example we used in which the long is now 40 days into the life of the contract, the market value to the long is $0.0499 per Swiss franc. Hence, the long's exposure would be 10,000,000($0.0499) = $499,000. Although no payments are due at this point, $499,000 is the market value of the claim on the payment at expiration. Using an estimate of the probability that the short would default, the long can gauge the expected credit loss from the transaction by multiplying that probability by $499,000.

The market value of a forward contract reflects the current value of the claim at expiration, given existing market conditions. If the Swiss franc rises significantly, the market value will increase along with it, thereby exposing the long to the potential for even greater losses. Many participants in derivatives markets estimate this potential loss by running simulations that attempt to reflect the potential market value of the contract along with the probability of the counterparty defaulting.

We have viewed credit risk from the viewpoint of the long, but what about the short's perspective? In the case in which we went to expiration and the short owed the long the greater amount, the short faces no credit risk. In the case prior to expiration in which the contract's market value was positive, the value of the future claim was greater to the long than to the short. Hence, the short still did not face any credit risk.

---

[27] Even if the short already holds the Swiss franc, she might be declaring bankruptcy or otherwise unable to pay debts such that the forward contract claim is combined with the claims of all of the short's other creditors.

The short would face credit risk, however, if circumstances were such that the value of the transaction were negative to the long, which would make the value to the short positive. In that case, the scenario discussed previously in this section would apply from the short's perspective.

There are various methods of managing the credit risk of various types of derivatives transactions. At this point, however, it will be helpful to specifically examine one particular method. Let us go back to the long currency forward contract that had a market value of $499,000. As it stands at this time, the holder of the long position has a claim on the holder of the short position that is worth $499,000. Suppose the two parties had agreed when they entered into the transaction that in 40 days, the party owing the greater amount to the other would pay the amount owed and the contract would be repriced at the new forward rate. Now on the 40th day, the short would pay the long $499,000. Recalling that the U.S. interest rate was 5.5 percent and the Swiss interest rate was 4.75 percent, the contract, which now has 140 days to go (T = 140/365), would then be repriced to the rate

$$F(0,T) = F(0,140/365) = \left[\frac{\$0.65}{(1.0475)^{140/365}} \right] (1.055)^{140/365} = \$0.6518$$

In other words, from this point, the contract has a new rate of $0.6518. The long now agrees to pay $0.6518 for the currency from the short in 140 days.

What the two parties have done is called **marking to market**. They have settled up the amount owed and marked the contract to its current market rate. If the parties agree in advance, a forward contract can be marked to market at whatever dates the parties feel are appropriate. Marking to market keeps one party from becoming too deeply indebted to the other without paying up. At the dates when the contract is marked to market, the parties restructure the contract so that it remains in force but with an updated price.

Forward contracts and swaps are sometimes marked to market to mitigate credit risk. In Reading 63, we shall examine futures contracts. A distinguishing characteristic of futures contracts is that they are marked to market every day. In essence, they are forward contracts that are marked to market and repriced daily to reduce the credit risk.

THE ROLE OF FORWARD MARKETS

6

In this reading we have discussed many aspects of forward contracts and forward markets. We will conclude the reading with a brief discussion of the role that these markets play in our financial system. Although forward, futures, options, and swap markets serve similar purposes in our society, each market is unique. Otherwise, these markets would consolidate.

Forward markets may well be the least understood of the various derivative markets. In contrast to their cousins, futures contracts, forward contracts are a far less visible segment of the financial markets. Both forwards and futures serve a similar purpose: They provide a means in which a party can commit to the future purchase or sale of an asset at an agreed-upon price, without the necessity of paying any cash until the asset is actually purchased or sold. In contrast to futures contracts, forward contracts are private transactions, permitting the ultimate in customization. As long as a counterparty can be found, a party can structure the contract completely to its liking. Futures contracts are standardized and may not have the exact terms required by the party. In addition, futures contracts, with their daily marking to market, produce interim cash flows that can lead to imperfections in a hedge transaction designed not to hedge interim events but to hedge a specific event at a target horizon date. Forward markets also provide secrecy and have only a light degree of regulation. In general, forward markets serve a specialized clientele, specifically large corporations and institutions with specific target dates, underlying assets, and risks that they wish to take or reduce by committing to a transaction without paying cash at the start.

As Reading 65 will make clear, however, forward contracts are just miniature versions of swaps. A swap can be viewed as a series of forward contracts. Swaps are much more widely used than forward contracts, suggesting that parties that have specific risk management needs typically require the equivalent of a series of forward contracts. A swap contract consolidates a series of forward contracts into a single instrument at lower cost.

Forward contracts are the building blocks for constructing and understanding both swaps and futures. Swaps and futures are more widely used and better known, but forward contracts play a valuable role in helping us understand swaps and futures. Moreover, as noted, for some parties, forward contracts serve specific needs not met by other derivatives.

In Reading 63 we shall look at futures contracts. We shall demonstrate how similar they are to forward contracts, but the differences are important, and some of their benefits to society are slightly different and less obvious than those of forwards.

SUMMARY

▶ The holder of a long forward contract (the "long") is obligated to take delivery of the underlying asset and pay the forward price at expiration. The holder of a short forward contract (the "short") is obligated to deliver the underlying asset and accept payment of the forward price at expiration.

▶ At expiration, a forward contract can be terminated by having the short make delivery of asset to the long or having the long and short exchange the equivalent cash value. If the asset is worth more (less) than the forward price, the short (long) pays the long (short) the cash difference between the market price or rate and the price or rate agreed on in the contract.

▶ A party can terminate a forward contract prior to expiration by entering into an opposite transaction with the same or a different counterparty. It is possible to leave both the original and new transactions in place, thereby leaving both transactions subject to credit risk, or to have the two transactions cancel each other. In the latter case, the party owing the greater amount pays the market value to the other party, resulting in the elimination of the remaining credit risk. This elimination can be achieved, however, only if the counterparty to the second transaction is the same counterparty as in the first.

▶ A dealer is a financial institution that makes a market in forward contracts and other derivatives. A dealer stands ready to take either side of a transaction. An end user is a party that comes to a dealer needing a transaction, usually for the purpose of managing a particular risk.

▶ Equity forward contracts can be written on individual stocks, specific stock portfolios, or stock indices. Equity forward contract prices and values must take into account the fact that the underlying stock, portfolio, or index could pay dividends.

▶ Forward contracts on bonds can be based on zero-coupon bonds or on coupon bonds, as well as portfolios or indices based on zero-coupon bonds or coupon bonds. Zero-coupon bonds pay their return by discounting the face value, often using a 360-day year assumption. Forward contracts on bonds must expire before the bond's maturity. In addition, a forward contract on a bond can be affected by special features of bonds, such as callability and convertibility.

▶ Eurodollar time deposits are dollar loans made by one bank to another. Although the term "Eurodollars" refers to dollar-denominated loans, similar loans exist in other currencies. Eurodollar deposits accrue interest by adding it on to the principal, using a 360-day year assumption. The primary Eurodollar rate is called LIBOR.

▶ LIBOR stands for London Interbank Offer Rate, the rate at which London banks are willing to lend to other London banks. Euribor is the rate on a euro time deposit, a loan made by banks to other banks in Frankfurt in which the currency is the euro.

▶ An FRA is a forward contract in which one party, the long, agrees to pay a fixed interest payment at a future date and receive an interest payment at a rate to be determined at expiration. FRAs are described by a special notation. For example, a 3×6 FRA expires in three months; the underlying is a Eurodollar deposit that begins in three months and ends three months later, or six months from now.

▶ The payment of an FRA at expiration is based on the net difference between the underlying rate and the agreed-upon rate, adjusted by the notional principal and the number of days in the instrument on which the underlying rate is based. The payoff is also discounted, however, to reflect the fact that the underlying rate on which the instrument is based assumes that payment will occur at a later date.

▶ A currency forward contract is a commitment for one party, the long, to buy a currency at a fixed price from the other party, the short, at a specific date. The contract can be settled by actual delivery, or the two parties can choose to settle in cash on the expiration day.

▶ A forward contract is priced by assuming that the underlying asset is purchased, a forward contract is sold, and the position is held to expiration. Because the sale price of the asset is locked in as the forward price, the transaction is risk free and should earn the risk-free rate. The forward price is then obtained as the price that guarantees a return of the risk-free rate. If the forward price is too high or too low, an arbitrage profit in the form of a return in excess of the risk-free rate can be earned. The combined effects of all investors executing arbitrage transactions will force the forward price to converge to its arbitrage-free level.

▶ The value of a forward contract is determined by the fact that a long forward contract is a claim on the underlying asset and a commitment to pay the forward price at expiration. The value of a forward contract is, therefore, the current price of the asset less the present value of the forward price at expiration. Because no money changes hands at the start, the value of the forward contract today is zero. The value of a forward contract at expiration is the price of the underlying asset minus the forward price.

▶ Valuation of a forward contract is important because 1) it makes good business sense to know the values of future commitments, 2) accounting rules require that forward contracts be accounted for in income statements and balance sheets, 3) the value gives a good measure of the credit exposure, and 4) the value can be used to determine the amount of money one party would have to pay another party to terminate a position.

▶ An off-market forward contract is established with a nonzero value at the start. The contract will, therefore, have a positive or negative value and require a cash payment at the start. A positive value is paid by the long to the short; a negative value is paid by the short to the long. In an off-market forward contract, the forward price will not equal the price of the underlying asset compounded at the risk-free rate but rather will be set in the process of negotiation between the two parties.

▶ An equity forward contract is priced by taking the stock price, subtracting the present value of the dividends over the life of the contract, and then compounding this amount at the risk-free rate to the expiration date of the contract. The present value of the dividends can be found by assuming the dividends are risk-free and calculating their present value using the risk-free rate of interest. Or one can assume that dividends are paid at a constant continuously compounded rate and then discount the stock price by the exponential function using the continuously compounded dividend rate. Alternatively, an equity forward can be priced by compounding the stock price to the expiration date and then subtracting the future value of the dividends at the expiration date. The value of an equity forward contract is the stock price minus the present value of the dividends minus the present value of the forward price that will be paid at expiration.

▶ To price a **fixed-income forward** contract, take the bond price, subtract the present value of the coupons over the life of the contract, and compound this amount at the risk-free rate to the expiration date of the contract. The value of a fixed-income forward contract is the bond price minus the present value of the coupons minus the present value of the forward price that will be paid at expiration.

▶ The price of an FRA, which is actually a rate, is simply the forward rate embedded in the term structure of the FRA's underlying rate. The value of an FRA based on a Eurodollar deposit is the present value of $1 to be received at expiration minus the present value of $1 plus the FRA rate to be received at the maturity date of the Eurodollar deposit on which the FRA is based, with appropriate (days/360) adjustments.

▶ The price, which is actually an exchange rate, of a forward contract on a currency is the spot rate discounted at the foreign interest rate over the life of the contract and then compounded at the domestic interest rate to the expiration date of the contract. The value of a currency forward contract is the spot rate discounted at the foreign interest rate over the life of the contract minus the present value of the forward rate at expiration.

▶ Credit risk in a forward contract arises when the counterparty that owes the greater amount is unable to pay at expiration or declares bankruptcy prior to expiration. The market value of a forward contract is a measure of the net amount one party owes the other. Only one party, the one owing the lesser amount, faces credit risk at any given time. Because the market value can change from positive to negative, however, the other party has the potential for facing credit risk at a later date. Counterparties occasionally mark forward contracts to market, with one party paying the other the current market value; they then reprice the contract to the current market price or rate.

▶ Forward markets play an important role in society, providing a means by which a select clientele of parties can engage in customized, private, unregulated transactions that commit them to buying or selling an asset at a later date at an agreed-upon price without paying any cash at the start. Forward contracts also are a simplified version of both futures and swaps and, therefore, form a basis for understanding these other derivatives.

PRACTICE PROBLEMS FOR READING 62

1. Consider a security that sells for $1,000 today. A forward contract on this security that expires in one year is currently priced at $1,100. The annual rate of interest is 6.75 percent. Assume that this is an off-market forward contract.

   A. Calculate the value of the forward contract today, $V_0(0,T)$.

   B. Indicate whether payment is made by the long to the short or vice versa.

2. Assume that you own a security currently worth $500. You plan to sell it in two months. To hedge against a possible decline in price during the next two months, you enter into a forward contract to sell the security in two months. The risk-free rate is 3.5 percent.

   A. Calculate the forward price on this contract.

   B. Suppose the dealer offers to enter into a forward contract at $498. Indicate how you could earn an arbitrage profit.

   C. After one month, the security sells for $490. Calculate the gain or loss to your position.

3. Consider an asset currently worth $100. An investor plans to sell it in one year and is concerned that the price may have fallen significantly by then. To hedge this risk, the investor enters into a forward contract to sell the asset in one year. Assume that the risk-free rate is 5 percent.

   A. Calculate the appropriate price at which this investor can contract to sell the asset in one year.

   B. Three months into the contract, the price of the asset is $90. Calculate the gain or loss that has accrued to the forward contract.

   C. Assume that five months into the contract, the price of the asset is $107. Calculate the gain or loss on the forward contract.

   D. Suppose that at expiration, the price of the asset is $98. Calculate the value of the forward contract at expiration. Also indicate the overall gain or loss to the investor on the whole transaction.

   E. Now calculate the value of the forward contract at expiration assuming that at expiration, the price of the asset is $110. Indicate the overall gain or loss to the investor on the whole transaction. Is this amount more or less than the overall gain or loss from Part D?

4. A security is currently worth $225. An investor plans to purchase this asset in one year and is concerned that the price may have risen by then. To hedge this risk, the investor enters into a forward contract to buy the asset in one year. Assume that the risk-free rate is 4.75 percent.

   A. Calculate the appropriate price at which this investor can contract to buy the asset in one year.

   B. Four months into the contract, the price of the asset is $250. Calculate the gain or loss that has accrued to the forward contract.

   C. Assume that eight months into the contract, the price of the asset is $200. Calculate the gain or loss on the forward contract.

   D. Suppose that at expiration, the price of the asset is $190. Calculate the value of the forward contract at expiration. Also indicate the overall gain or loss to the investor on the whole transaction.

   E. Now calculate the value of the forward contract at expiration assuming that at expiration, the price of the asset is $240. Indicate the overall gain or loss to the investor on the whole transaction. Is this amount more or less than the overall gain or loss from Part D?

5. Assume that a security is currently priced at $200. The risk-free rate is 5 percent.

    A. A dealer offers you a contract in which the forward price of the security with delivery in three months is $205. Explain the transactions you would undertake to take advantage of the situation.

    B. Suppose the dealer were to offer you a contract in which the forward price of the security with delivery in three months is $198. How would you take advantage of the situation?

6. Assume that you own a dividend-paying stock currently worth $150. You plan to sell the stock in 250 days. In order to hedge against a possible price decline, you wish to take a short position in a forward contract that expires in 250 days. The risk-free rate is 5.25 percent. Over the next 250 days, the stock will pay dividends according to the following schedule:

Days to Next Dividend	Dividends per Share
30	$1.25
120	$1.25
210	$1.25

    A. Calculate the forward price of a contract established today and expiring in 250 days.

    B. It is now 100 days since you entered the forward contract. The stock price is $115. Calculate the value of the forward contract at this point.

    C. At expiration, the price of the stock is $130. Calculate the value of the forward contract at expiration.

7. A portfolio manager expects to purchase a portfolio of stocks in 90 days. In order to hedge against a potential price increase over the next 90 days, she decides to take a long position on a 90-day forward contract on the S&P 500 stock index. The index is currently at 1145. The continuously compounded dividend yield is 1.75 percent. The discrete risk-free rate is 4.25 percent.

    A. Calculate the no-arbitrage forward price on this contract.

    B. It is now 28 days since the portfolio manager entered the forward contract. The index value is at 1225. Calculate the value of the forward contract 28 days into the contract.

    C. At expiration, the index value is 1235. Calculate the value of the forward contract.

8. An investor purchased a newly issued bond with a maturity of 10 years 200 days ago. The bond carries a coupon rate of 8 percent paid semiannually and has a face value of $1,000. The price of the bond with accrued interest is currently $1,146.92. The investor plans to sell the bond 365 days from now. The schedule of coupon payments over the first two years, from the date of purchase, is as follows:

Coupon	Days after Purchase	Amount
First	181	$40
Second	365	$40
Third	547	$40
Fourth	730	$40

A. Should the investor enter into a long or short forward contract to hedge his risk exposure? Calculate the no-arbitrage price at which the investor should enter the forward contract. Assume that the risk-free rate is 6 percent.

B. The forward contract is now 180 days old. Interest rates have fallen sharply, and the risk-free rate is 4 percent. The price of the bond with accrued interest is now $1,302.26. Determine the value of the forward contract now and indicate whether the investor has accrued a gain or loss on his position.

9. A corporate treasurer wishes to hedge against an increase in future borrowing costs due to a possible rise in short-term interest rates. She proposes to hedge against this risk by entering into a long 6 × 12 FRA. The current term structure for LIBOR is as follows:

Term	Interest Rate
30 day	5.10%
90 day	5.25%
180 day	5.70%
360 day	5.95%

A. Indicate when this 6 × 12 FRA expires and identify which term of the LIBOR this FRA is based on.

B. Calculate the rate the treasurer would receive on a 6 × 12 FRA.

Suppose the treasurer went long this FRA. Now, 45 days later, interest rates have risen and the LIBOR term structure is as follows:

Term	Interest Rate
135 day	5.90%
315 day	6.15%

C. Calculate the market value of this FRA based on a notional principal of $10,000,000.

D. At expiration, the 180-day LIBOR is 6.25 percent. Calculate the payoff on the FRA. Does the treasurer receive a payment or make a payment to the dealer?

10. A financial manager needs to hedge against a possible decrease in short term interest rates. He decides to hedge his risk exposure by going short on an FRA that expires in 90 days and is based on 90-day LIBOR. The current term structure for LIBOR is as follows:

Term	Interest Rate
30 day	5.83%
90 day	6.00%
180 day	6.14%
360 day	6.51%

    A. Identify the type of FRA used by the financial manager using the appropriate terminology.

    B. Calculate the rate the manager would receive on this FRA.

    It is now 30 days since the manager took a short position in the FRA. Interest rates have shifted down, and the new term structure for LIBOR is as follows:

Term	Interest Rate
60 day	5.50%
150 day	5.62%

    C. Calculate the market value of this FRA based on a notional principal of $15,000,000.

11. Consider a U.S.-based company that exports goods to Switzerland. The U.S. company expects to receive payment on a shipment of goods in three months. Because the payment will be in Swiss francs, the U.S. company wants to hedge against a decline in the value of the Swiss franc over the next three months. The U.S. risk-free rate is 2 percent, and the Swiss risk-free rate is 5 percent. Assume that interest rates are expected to remain fixed over the next six months. The current spot rate is $0.5974.

    A. Indicate whether the U.S. company should use a long or short forward contract to hedge currency risk.

    B. Calculate the no-arbitrage price at which the U.S. company could enter into a forward contract that expires in three months.

    C. It is now 30 days since the U.S. company entered into the forward contract. The spot rate is $0.55. Interest rates are the same as before. Calculate the value of the U.S. company's forward position.

12. The euro currently trades at $1.0231. The dollar risk-free rate is 4 percent, and the euro risk-free rate is 5 percent. Six-month forward contracts are quoted at a rate of $1.0225. Indicate how you might earn a risk-free profit by engaging in a forward contract. Clearly outline the steps you undertake to earn this risk-free profit.

13. Suppose that you are a U.S.-based importer of goods from the United Kingdom. You expect the value of the pound to increase against the U.S. dollar over the next 30 days. You will be making payment on a shipment of imported goods in 30 days and want to hedge your currency exposure. The U.S. risk-free rate is 5.5 percent, and the U.K. risk-free rate is 4.5 percent. These rates are expected to remain unchanged over the next month. The current spot rate is $1.50.

    A. Indicate whether you should use a long or short forward contract to hedge the currency risk.

    B. Calculate the no-arbitrage price at which you could enter into a forward contract that expires in 30 days.

    C. Move forward 10 days. The spot rate is $1.53. Interest rates are unchanged. Calculate the value of your forward position.

14. Consider the following: The U.S. risk-free rate is 6 percent, the Swiss risk-free rate is 4 percent, and the spot exchange rate between the United States and Switzerland is $0.6667.

   A. Calculate the continuously compounded U.S. and Swiss risk-free rates.

   B. Calculate the price at which you could enter into a forward contract that expires in 90 days.

   C. Calculate the value of the forward position 25 days into the contract. Assume that the spot rate is $0.65.

15. The Japanese yen currently trades at $0.00812. The U.S. risk-free rate is 4.5 percent, and the Japanese risk-free rate is 2.0 percent. Three-month forward contracts on the yen are quoted at $0.00813. Indicate how you might earn a risk-free profit by engaging in a forward contract. Outline your transactions.

FUTURES MARKETS AND CONTRACTS
by Don M. Chance

READING

63

LEARNING OUTCOMES

The candidate should be able to:

a. explain why the futures price must converge to the spot price at expiration;

b. determine the value of a futures contract;

c. explain how forward and futures prices differ;

d. identify the different types of monetary and non-monetary benefits and costs associated with holding the underlying asset, and explain how they affect the futures price;

e. describe backwardation and contango;

f. discuss whether futures prices equal expected spot prices;

g. describe the difficulties in pricing Eurodollar futures and creating a pure arbitrage opportunity;

h. calculate and interpret the price of Treasury bond futures, stock index futures, and currency futures.

INTRODUCTION · 1

In Reading 62, we focused on forward markets. Now we explore futures markets in a similar fashion. Although we shall see a clear similarity between forward and futures contracts, critical distinctions nonetheless exist between the two.

Like a forward contract, *a futures contract is an agreement between two parties in which one party, the buyer, agrees to buy from the other party, the seller, an underlying asset or other derivative, at a future date at a price agreed on today.* Unlike a forward contract, however, a futures contract is not a private and customized transaction but rather a public transaction that takes place on an organized futures exchange. In addition, a futures contract is standardized—the

Analysis of Derivatives for the CFA® Program, by Don M. Chance. Copyright © 2003 by AIMR. Reprinted with permission.

exchange, rather than the individual parties, sets the terms and conditions, with the exception of price. As a result, futures contracts have a secondary market, meaning that previously created contracts can be traded. Also, parties to futures contracts are guaranteed against credit losses resulting from the counterparty's inability to pay. A clearinghouse provides this guarantee via a procedure in which it converts gains and losses that accrue on a daily basis into actual cash gains and losses. Futures contracts are regulated at the federal government level; as we noted in Reading 62, forward contracts are essentially unregulated. Futures contracts are created on organized trading facilities referred to as **futures exchanges**, whereas forward contracts are not created in any specific location but rather initiated between any two parties who wish to enter into such a contract. Finally, each futures exchange has a division or subsidiary called a **clearinghouse** that performs the specific responsibilities of paying and collecting daily gains and losses as well as guaranteeing to each party the performance of the other.

In a futures transaction, one party, the long, is the buyer and the other party, the short, is the seller. The buyer agrees to buy the underlying at a later date, the expiration, at a price agreed on at the start of the contract. The seller agrees to sell the underlying to the buyer at the expiration, at the price agreed on at the start of the contract. Every day, the futures contract trades in the market and its price changes in response to new information. Buyers benefit from price increases, and sellers benefit from price decreases. On the expiration day, the contract terminates and no further trading takes place. Then, either the buyer takes delivery of the underlying from the seller, or the two parties make an equivalent cash settlement. We shall explore each of these characteristics of futures contracts in more detail. First, however, it is important to take a brief look at how futures markets came into being.

1.1 A Brief History of Futures Markets

Although vestiges of futures markets appear in the Japanese rice markets of the 18th century and perhaps even earlier, the mid-1800s marked the first clear origins of modern futures markets. For example, in the United States in the 1840s, Chicago was becoming a major transportation and distribution center for agricultural commodities. Its central location and access to the Great Lakes gave Chicago a competitive advantage over other U.S. cities. Farmers from the Midwest would harvest their grain and take it to Chicago for sale. Grain production, however, is seasonal. As a result, grain prices would rise sharply just prior to the harvest but then plunge when the grain was brought to the market. Too much grain at one time and too little at another resulted in severe problems. Grain storage facilities in Chicago were inadequate to accommodate the oversupply. Some farmers even dumped their grain in the Chicago River because prices were so low that they could not afford to take their grain to another city to sell.

To address this problem, in 1848 a group of businessmen formed an organization later named the Chicago Board of Trade (CBOT) and created an arrangement called a "to-arrive" contract. These contracts permitted farmers to sell their grain before delivering it. In other words, farmers could harvest the grain and enter into a contract to deliver it at a much later date at a price already agreed on. This transaction allowed the farmer to hold the grain in storage at some other location besides Chicago. On the other side of these contracts were the businessmen who had formed the Chicago Board of Trade.

It soon became apparent that trading in these to-arrive contracts was more important and useful than trading in the grain itself. Soon the contracts began trading in a type of secondary market, which allowed buyers and sellers to discharge their obligations by passing them on, for a price, to other parties. With the addition of the clearinghouse in the 1920s, which provided a guarantee against default, modern futures markets firmly established their place in the financial world. It was left to other exchanges, such as today's Chicago Mercantile Exchange, the New York Mercantile Exchange, Eurex, and the London International Financial Futures Exchange, to develop and become, along with the Chicago Board of Trade, the global leaders in futures markets.

We shall now explore the important features of futures contracts in more detail.

1.2 Public Standardized Transactions

A private transaction is not generally reported in the news or to any price-reporting service. Forward contracts are private contracts. Just as in most legal contracts, the parties do not publicly report that they have engaged in a contract. In contrast, a futures transaction is reported to the futures exchange, the clearinghouse, and at least one regulatory agency. The price is recorded and available from price reporting services and even on the Internet.[1]

We noted that a futures transaction is not customized. Recall from Reading 62 that in a forward contract, the two parties establish all of the terms of the contract, including the identity of the underlying, the expiration date, and the manner in which the contract is settled (cash or actual delivery) as well as the price. The terms are customized to meet the needs of both parties. In a futures contract, the price is the only term established by the two parties; the exchange establishes all other terms. Moreover, the terms that are established by the exchange are standardized, meaning that the exchange selects a number of choices for underlyings, expiration dates, and a variety of other contract-specific items. These standardized terms are well known to all parties. If a party wishes to trade a futures contract, it must accept these terms. The only alternative would be to create a similar but customized contract on the forward market.

With respect to the underlying, for example, a given asset has a variety of specifications and grades. Consider a futures contract on U.S. Treasury bonds. There are many different Treasury bonds with a variety of characteristics. The futures exchange must decide which Treasury bond or group of bonds the contract covers. One of the most actively traded commodity futures contracts is oil, but there are many different types of oil.[2] To which type of oil does the contract apply? The exchange decides at the time it designs the contract.

The parties to a forward contract set its expiration at whatever date they want. For a futures contract, the exchange establishes a set of expiration dates. The first specification of the expiration is the month. An exchange might establish that a given futures contract expires only in the months of March, June, September, and December. The second specification determines how far the expirations go out

---

[1] The information reported to the general public does not disclose the identity of the parties to transactions but only that a transaction took place at a particular price.

[2] Some of the main types are Saudi Arabian light crude, Brent crude, and West Texas intermediate crude.

into the future. For example, in January of a given year, there may be expirations of March, June, September, and December. Expirations might also be available for March, June, September, and December of the following year, and perhaps some months of the year after that. The exchange decides which expiration months are appropriate for trading, based on which expirations they believe would be actively traded. Treasury bond futures have expirations going out only about a year. Eurodollar futures, however, have expirations that go out about 10 years.[3] The third specification of the expiration is the specific day of expiration. Many, but not all, contracts expire some time during the third week of the expiration month.

The exchange determines a number of other contract characteristics, including the contract size. For example, one Eurodollar futures contract covers $1 million of a Eurodollar time deposit. One U.S. Treasury bond futures contract covers $100,000 face value of Treasury bonds. One futures contract on crude oil covers 1,000 barrels. The exchange also decides on the price quotation unit. For example, Treasury bond futures are quoted in points and 32nds of par of 100. Hence, you will see a price like 104 21/32, which means 104.65625. With a contract size of $100,000, the actual price is $104,656.25.

The exchange also determines what hours of the day trading takes place and at what physical location on the exchange the contract will be traded. Many futures exchanges have a trading floor, which contains octagonal-shaped pits. A contract is assigned to a certain pit. Traders enter the pits and express their willingness to buy and sell by calling out and/or indicating by hand signals their bids and offers. Some exchanges have electronic trading, which means that trading takes place on computer terminals, generally located in companies' offices. Some exchanges have both floor trading and electronic trading; some have only one or the other.

1.3 Homogenization and Liquidity

By creating contracts with generally accepted terms, the exchange standardizes the instrument. In contrast, forward contracts are quite heterogeneous because they are customized. Standardizing the instrument makes it more acceptable to a broader group of participants, with the advantage being that the instrument can then more easily trade in a type of secondary market. Indeed, the ability to sell a previously purchased contract or purchase a previously sold contract is one of the important features of futures contracts. A futures contract is therefore said to have liquidity in contrast to a forward contract, which does not generally trade after it has been created.[4] This ability to trade a previously opened contract allows participants in this market to offset the position before expiration, thereby obtaining exposure to price movements in the underlying without the actual requirement of holding the position to expiration. We shall discuss this characteristic further when we describe futures trading in Section 2.

1.4 The Clearinghouse, Daily Settlement, and Performance Guarantee

Another important distinction between futures and forwards is that the futures exchange guarantees to each party the performance of the other party, through a mechanism known as the clearinghouse. This guarantee means that if one

---

[3] You may be wondering why some Eurodollar futures contracts have such long expirations. Dealers in swaps and forward rate agreements use Eurodollar futures to hedge their positions. Many of those over-the-counter contracts have very long expirations.

[4] The notion of liquidity here is only that a market exists for futures contracts, but this does not imply a high degree of liquidity. There may be little trading in a given contract, and the bid–ask spread can be high. In contrast, some forward markets can be very liquid, allowing forward contracts to be offset, as described in Reading 62.

party makes money on the transaction, it does not have to worry about whether it will collect the money from the other party because the clearinghouse ensures it will be paid. In contrast, each party to a forward contract assumes the risk that the other party will default.

An important and distinguishing feature of futures contracts is that the gains and losses on each party's position are credited and charged on a daily basis. This procedure, called **daily settlement** or **marking to market**, essentially results in paper gains and losses being converted to cash gains and losses each day. It is also equivalent to terminating a contract at the end of each day and reopening it the next day at that **settlement price**. In some sense, a futures contract is like a strategy of opening up a forward contract, closing it one day later, opening up a new contract, closing it one day later, and continuing in that manner until expiration. The exact manner in which the daily settlement works will be covered in more detail later in Section 3.

1.5 Regulation

In most countries, futures contracts are regulated at the federal government level. State and regional laws may also apply. In the United States, the Commodity Futures Trading Commission regulates the futures market. In the United Kingdom, the Securities and Futures Authority regulates both the securities and futures markets.

Federal regulation of futures markets generally arises out of a concern to protect the general public and other futures market participants, as well as through a recognition that futures markets affect all financial markets and the economy. Regulations cover such matters as ensuring that prices are reported accurately and in a timely manner, that markets are not manipulated, that professionals who offer their services to the public are qualified and honest, and that disputes are resolved. In the United States, the government has delegated some of these responsibilities to an organization called the National Futures Association (NFA). An industry self-regulatory body, the NFA was created with the objective of having the industry regulate itself and reduce the federal government's burden.

FUTURES TRADING 2

In this section, we look more closely at how futures contracts are traded. As noted above, futures contracts trade on a futures exchange either in a pit or on a screen or electronic terminal.

We briefly mentioned pit trading, also known as floor-based trading, in Section 1.2. Pit trading is a very physical activity. Traders stand in the pit and shout out their orders in the form of prices they are willing to pay or accept. They also use hand signals to indicate their bids and offers.[5] They engage in transactions with other traders in the pits by simply agreeing on a price and number of contracts to trade. The activity is fast, furious, exciting, and stressful. The average pit trader is quite young, owing to the physical demands of the job and the toll it takes on body and mind. In recent years, more trading has come off of the exchange floor to electronic screens or terminals. In electronic or screen-based trading, exchange members enter their bids and offers into a computer system, which then displays this information and allows a trader to consummate a trade

---

[5] Hand signals facilitate trading with someone who is too far away in the pit for verbal communication.

electronically. In the United States, pit trading is dominant, owing to its long history and tradition. Exchange members who trade on the floor enjoy pit trading and have resisted heavily the advent of electronic trading. Nonetheless, the exchanges have had to respond to market demands to offer electronic trading. In the United States, both pit trading and electronic trading are used, but in other countries, electronic trading is beginning to drive pit trading out of business.[6]

A person who enters into a futures contract establishes either a long position or a short position. Similar to forward contracts, long positions are agreements to buy the underlying at the expiration at a price agreed on at the start. Short positions are agreements to sell the underlying at a future date at a price agreed on at the start. When the position is established, each party deposits a small amount of money, typically called the **margin**, with the clearinghouse. Then, as briefly described in Section 1.4, the contract is marked to market, whereby the gains are distributed to and the losses collected from each party. We cover this marking-to-market process in more detail in the next section. For now, however, we focus only on the opening and closing of the position.

A party that has opened a long position collects profits or incurs losses on a daily basis. At some point in the life of the contract prior to expiration, that party may wish to re-enter the market and close out the position. This process, called **off-setting**, is the same as selling a previously purchased stock or buying back a stock to close a short position. The holder of a long futures position simply goes back into the market and offers the identical contract for sale. The holder of a short position goes back into the market and offers to buy the identical contract. It should be noted that when a party offsets a position, it does not necessary do so with the same counterparty to the original contract. In fact, rarely would a contract be offset with the same counterparty. Because of the ability to offset, futures contracts are said to be fungible, which means that any futures contract with any counterparty can be offset by an equivalent futures contract with another counterparty. Fungibility is assured by the fact that the clearinghouse inserts itself in the middle of each contract and, therefore, becomes the counterparty to each party.

For example, suppose in early January a futures trader purchases an S&P 500 stock index futures contract expiring in March. Through 15 February, the trader has incurred some gains and losses from the daily settlement and decides that she wants to close the position out. She then goes back into the market and offers for sale the March S&P 500 futures. Once she finds a buyer to take the position, she has a long and short position in the same contract. The clearinghouse considers that she no longer has a position in that contract and has no remaining exposure, nor any obligation to make or take delivery at expiration. Had she initially gone short the March futures, she might re-enter the market in February offering to buy it. Once she finds a seller to take the opposite position, she becomes long and short the same contract and is considered to have offset the contract and therefore have no net position.

3 THE CLEARINGHOUSE, MARGINS, AND PRICE LIMITS

As briefly noted in the previous section, when a trader takes a long or short position in a futures, he must first deposit sufficient funds in a **margin account**. This amount of money is traditionally called the margin, a term derived from the

---

[6] For example, in France electronic trading was introduced while pit trading continued. Within two weeks, all of the volume had migrated to electronic trading and pit trading was terminated.

stock market practice in which an investor borrows a portion of the money required to purchase a certain amount of stock.

Margin in the stock market is quite different from margin in the futures market. In the stock market, "margin" means that a loan is made. The loan enables the investor to reduce the amount of his own money required to purchase the securities, thereby generating leverage or gearing, as it is sometimes known. If the stock goes up, the percentage gain to the investor is amplified. If the stock goes down, however, the percentage loss is also amplified. The borrowed money must eventually be repaid with interest. The margin percentage equals the market value of the stock minus the market value of the debt divided by the market value of the stock—in other words, the investor's own equity as a percentage of the value of the stock. For example, in the United States, regulations permit an investor to borrow up to 50 percent of the initial value of the stock. This percentage is called the initial margin requirement. On any day thereafter, the equity or percentage ownership in the account, measured as the market value of the securities minus the amount borrowed, can be less than 50 percent but must be at least a percentage known as the maintenance margin requirement. A typical **maintenance margin** requirement is 25 to 30 percent.

In the futures market, by contrast, the word **margin** is commonly used to describe the amount of money that must be put into an account by a party opening up a futures position, but the term is misleading. When a transaction is initiated, a futures trader puts up a certain amount of money to meet the **initial margin requirement**; however, the remaining money is not borrowed. The amount of money deposited is more like a down payment for the commitment to purchase the underlying at a later date. Alternatively, one can view this deposit as a form of good faith money, collateral, or a performance bond: The money helps ensure that the party fulfills his or her obligation.[7] Moreover, both the buyer and the seller of a futures contract must deposit margin.

In securities markets, margin requirements are normally set by federal regulators. In the United States, maintenance margin requirements are set by the securities exchanges and the NASD. In futures markets, margin requirements are set by the clearinghouses. In further contrast to margin practices in securities markets, futures margins are traditionally expressed in dollar terms and not as a percentage of the futures price. For ease of comparison, however, we often speak of the futures margin in terms of its relationship to the futures price. In futures markets, the initial margin requirement is typically much lower than the initial margin requirement in the stock market. In fact, futures margins are usually less than 10 percent of the futures price.[8] Futures clearinghouses set their margin requirements by studying historical price movements. They then establish minimum margin levels by taking into account normal price movements and the fact that accounts are marked to market daily. The clearinghouses thus collect and disburse margin money every day. Moreover, they are permitted to do so more often than daily, and on some occasions they have used that privilege. By carefully setting margin requirements and collecting margin money every day, clearinghouses are able to control the risk of default.

In spite of the differences in margin practices for futures and securities markets, the effect of leverage is similar for both. By putting up a small amount of money, the trader's gains and losses are magnified. Given the tremendously

---

[7] In fact, the Chicago Mercantile Exchange uses the term "performance bond" instead of "margin." Most other exchanges use the term "margin."

[8] For example, the margin requirement of the Eurodollar futures contract at the Chicago Mercantile Exchange has been less than one-tenth of one percent of the futures price. An exception to this requirement, however, is individual stock futures, which in the United States have margin requirements comparable to those of the stock market.

low margin requirements of futures markets, however, the magnitude of the leverage effect is much greater in futures markets. We shall see how this works as we examine the process of the daily settlement.

As previously noted, each day the clearinghouse conducts an activity known as the daily settlement, also called marking to market. This practice results in the conversion of gains and losses on paper into actual gains and losses. As margin account balances change, holders of futures positions must maintain balances above a level called the **maintenance margin requirement**. The maintenance margin requirement is lower than the initial margin requirement. On any day in which the amount of money in the margin account at the end of the day falls below the maintenance margin requirement, the trader must deposit sufficient funds to bring the balance back up to the initial margin requirement. Alternatively, the trader can simply close out the position but is responsible for any further losses incurred if the price changes before a closing transaction can be made.

To provide a fair mark-to-market process, the clearinghouse must designate the official price for determining daily gains and losses. This price is called the **settlement price** and represents an average of the final few trades of the day. It would appear that the closing price of the day would serve as the settlement price, but the closing price is a single value that can potentially be biased high or low or perhaps even manipulated by an unscrupulous trader. Hence, the clearinghouse takes an average of all trades during the closing period (as defined by each exchange).

Exhibit 1 provides an example of the marking-to-market process that occurs over a period of six trading days. We start with the assumption that the futures price is $100 when the transaction opens, the initial margin requirement is $5, and the maintenance margin requirement is $3. In Panel A, the trader takes a long position of 10 contracts on Day 0, depositing $50 ($5 times 10 contracts) as indicated in Column 3. At the end of the day, his ending balance is $50.[9] Although the trader can withdraw any funds in excess of the initial margin requirement, we shall assume that he does not do so.[10]

The ending balance on Day 0 is then carried forward to the beginning balance on Day 1. On Day 1, the futures price moves down to 99.20, as indicated in Column 4 of Panel A. The futures price change, Column 5, is $-0.80 (99.20 - 100)$. This amount is then multiplied by the number of contracts to obtain the number in Column 6 of $-0.80 \times 10 = -\$8$. The ending balance, Column 7, is the beginning balance plus the gain or loss. The ending balance on Day 1 of $42 is above the maintenance margin requirement of $30, so no funds need to be deposited on Day 2.

On Day 2 the settlement price goes down to $96. Based on a price decrease of $3.20 per contract and 10 contracts, the loss is $32, lowering the ending balance to $10. This amount is $20 below the maintenance margin requirement. Thus, the trader will get a **margin call** the following morning and must deposit $40 to bring the balance up to the **initial margin** level of $50. This deposit is shown in Column 3 on Day 3.

Here, we must emphasize two important points. First, additional margin that must be deposited is the amount sufficient to bring the ending balance up to the initial margin requirement, not the maintenance margin requirement.[11] This

---

[9] Technically, we are assuming that the position was opened at the settlement price on Day 0. If the position is opened earlier during the day, it would be marked to the settlement price at the end of the day.

[10] Virtually all professional traders are able to deposit interest-earning assets, although many other account holders are required to deposit cash. If the deposit earns interest, there is no opportunity cost and no obvious necessity to withdraw the money to invest elsewhere.

[11] In the stock market, one must deposit only the amount necessary to bring the balance up to the maintenance margin requirement.

EXHIBIT 1	Mark-to-Market Example

Initial futures price = $100, Initial margin requirement = $5, Maintenance margin requirement = $3

A. *Holder of Long Position of 10 Contracts*

Day (1)	Beginning Balance (2)	Funds Deposited (3)	Settlement Price (4)	Futures Price Change (5)	Gain/ Loss (6)	Ending Balance (7)
0	0	50	100.00			50
1	50	0	99.20	−0.80	−8	42
2	42	0	96.00	−3.20	−32	10
3	10	40	101.00	5.00	50	100
4	100	0	103.50	2.50	25	125
5	125	0	103.00	−0.50	−5	120
6	120	0	104.00	1.00	10	130

B. *Holder of Short Position of 10 Contracts*

Day (1)	Beginning Balance (2)	Funds Deposited (3)	Settlement Price (4)	Futures Price Change (5)	Gain/ Loss (6)	Ending Balance (7)
0	0	50	100.00			50
1	50	0	99.20	−0.80	8	58
2	58	0	96.00	−3.20	32	90
3	90	0	101.00	5.00	−50	40
4	40	0	103.50	2.50	−25	15
5	15	35	103.00	−0.50	5	55
6	55	0	104.00	1.00	−10	45

additional margin is called the **variation margin**. In addition, the amount that must be deposited the following day is determined regardless of the price change the following day, which might bring the ending balance well above the initial margin requirement, as it does here, or even well below the maintenance margin requirement. Thus, another margin call could occur. Also note that when the trader closes the position, the account is marked to market to the final price at which the transaction occurs, not the settlement price that day.

Over the six-day period, the trader in this example deposited $90. The account balance at the end of the sixth day is $130—nearly a 50 percent return over six days; not bad. But look at Panel B, which shows the position of a holder of 10 short contracts over that same period. Note that the short gains when prices decrease and loses when prices increase. Here the ending balance falls below the maintenance margin requirement on Day 4, and the short must deposit $35 on Day 5. At the end of Day 6, the short has deposited $85 and the balance is $45, a loss of $40 or nearly 50 percent, which is the same $40 the long made. Both cases illustrate the leverage effect that magnifies gains and losses.

When establishing a futures position, it is important to know the price level that would trigger a margin call. In this case, it does not matter how many contracts one has. The price change would need to fall for a long position (or rise for a short position) by the difference between the initial and maintenance margin requirements. In this example, the difference between the initial and maintenance margin requirements is $5 − $3 = $2. Thus, the price would need to fall from $100 to $98 for a long position (or rise from $100 to $102 for a short position) to trigger a margin call.

As described here, when a trader receives a margin call, he is required to deposit funds sufficient to bring the account balance back up to the initial margin level. Alternatively, the trader can choose to simply close out the position as soon as possible. For example, consider the position of the long at the end of the second day when the margin balance is $10. This amount is $20 below the maintenance level, and he is required to deposit $40 to bring the balance up to the initial margin level. If he would prefer not to deposit the additional funds, he can close out the position as soon as possible the following day. Suppose, however, that the price is moving quickly at the opening on Day 3. If the price falls from $96 to $95, he has lost $10 more, wiping out the margin account balance. In fact, if it fell any further, he would have a negative margin account balance. He is still responsible for these losses. Thus, the trader could lose more than the amount of money he has placed in the margin account. The total amount of money he could lose is limited to the price per contract at which he bought, $100, times the number of contracts, 10, or $1,000. Such a loss would occur if the price fell to zero, although this is not likely. This potential loss may not seem like a lot, but it is certainly large relative to the initial margin requirement of $50. For the holder of the short position, there is no upper limit on the price and the potential loss is theoretically infinite.

EXAMPLE 1

Consider a futures contract in which the current futures price is $82. The initial margin requirement is $5, and the maintenance margin requirement is $2. You go long 20 contracts and meet all margin calls but do not withdraw any excess margin. Assume that on the first day, the contract is established at the settlement price, so there is no mark-to-market gain or loss on that day.

A. Complete the table below and provide an explanation of any funds deposited.

Day	Beginning Balance	Funds Deposited	Futures Price	Price Change	Gain/Loss	Ending Balance
0			82			
1			84			
2			78			
3			73			
4			79			
5			82			
6			84			

B. Determine the price level that would trigger a margin call.

Solution to A:

Day	Beginning Balance	Funds Deposited	Futures Price	Price Change	Gain/Loss	Ending Balance
0	0	100	82			100
1	100	0	84	2	40	140
2	140	0	78	−6	−120	20
3	20	80	73	−5	−100	0
4	0	100	79	6	120	220
5	220	0	82	3	60	280
6	280	0	84	2	40	320

On Day 0, you deposit $100 because the initial margin requirement is $5 per contract and you go long 20 contracts. At the end of Day 2, the balance is down to $20, which is $20 below the $40 maintenance margin requirement ($2 per contract times 20 contracts). You must deposit enough money to bring the balance up to the initial margin requirement of $100 ($5 per contract times 20 contracts). So on Day 3, you deposit $80. The price change on Day 3 causes a gain/loss of −$100, leaving you with a balance of $0 at the end of Day 3. On Day 4, you must deposit $100 to return the balance to the initial margin level.

Solution to B: A price decrease to $79 would trigger a margin call. This calculation is based on the fact that the difference between the initial margin requirement and the maintenance margin requirement is $3. If the futures price starts at $82, it can fall by $3 to $79 before it triggers a margin call.

Some futures contracts impose limits on the price change that can occur from one day to the next. Appropriately, these are called **price limits**. These limits are usually set as an absolute change over the previous day. Using the example above, suppose the price limit was $4. This would mean that each day, no transaction could take place higher than the previous settlement price plus $4 or lower than the previous settlement price minus $4. So the next day's settlement price cannot go beyond the price limit and thus no transaction can take place beyond the limits.

If the price at which a transaction would be made exceeds the limits, then price essentially freezes at one of the limits, which is called a **limit move**. If the price is stuck at the upper limit, it is called **limit up**; if stuck at the lower limit, it is called **limit down**. If a transaction cannot take place because the price would be beyond the limits, this situation is called **locked limit**. By the end of the day, unless the price has moved back within the limits, the settlement price will then be at one of the limits. The following day, the new range of acceptable prices is based on the settlement price plus or minus limits. The exchanges have different rules that provide for expansion or contraction of price limits under some circumstances. In addition, not all contracts have price limits.

Finally, we note that the exchanges have the power to mark contracts to market whenever they deem it necessary. Thus, they can do so during the trading day rather than wait until the end of the day. They sometimes do so when abnormally large market moves occur.

The daily settlement procedure is designed to collect losses and distribute gains in such a manner that losses are paid before becoming large enough to impose a serious risk of default. Recall that the clearinghouse guarantees to each party that it need not worry about collecting from the counterparty. The clearinghouse essentially positions itself in the middle of each contract, becoming the short counterparty to the long and the long counterparty to the short. The clearinghouse collects funds from the parties incurring losses in this daily settlement procedure and distributes them to the parties incurring gains. By doing so each day, the clearinghouse ensures that losses cannot build up. Of course, this process offers no guarantee that counterparties will not default. Some defaults do occur, but the counterparty is defaulting to the clearinghouse, which has never failed to pay off the opposite party. In the unlikely event that the clearinghouse were unable to pay, it would turn to a reserve fund or to the exchange, or it would levy a tax on exchange members to cover losses.

4 DELIVERY AND CASH SETTLEMENT

As previously described, a futures trader can close out a position before expiration. If the trader holds a long position, she can simply enter into a position to go short the same futures contract. From the clearinghouse's perspective, the trader holds both a long and short position in the same contract. These positions are considered to offset and, therefore, there is no open position in place. Most futures contracts are offset before expiration. Those that remain in place are subject to either delivery or a final cash settlement. Here we explore this process, which determines how a futures contract, terminates at expiration.

When the exchange designs a futures contract, it specifies whether the contract will terminate with delivery or cash settlement. If the contract terminates in delivery, the clearinghouse selects a counterparty, usually the holder of the oldest long contract, to accept delivery. The holder of the short position then delivers the underlying to the holder of the long position, who pays the short the necessary cash for the underlying. Suppose, for example, that two days before expiration, a party goes long one futures contract at a price of $50. The following day (the day before expiration), the settlement price is $52. The trader's margin account in then marked to market by crediting it with a gain of $2. Then suppose that the next day the contract expires with the settlement price at $53. As the end of the trading day draws near, the trader has two choices. She can attempt to close out the position by selling the futures contract. The margin account would then be marked to market at the price at which she sells. If she sells close enough to the expiration, the price she sold at would be very close to the final settlement price of $53. Doing so would add $1 to her margin account balance.

The other choice is to leave the position open at the end of the trading day. Then she would have to take delivery. If that occurred, she would be required to take possession of the asset and pay the short the settlement price of the previous day. Doing so would be equivalent to paying $52 and receiving the asset. She could then sell the asset for its price of $53, netting a $1 gain, which is equivalent to the final $1 credited to her margin account if she had terminated the position at the settlement price of $53, as described above.[12]

---

[12] The reason she pays the settlement price of the previous day is because on the previous day when her account was marked to market, she essentially created a new futures position at a price of $52. Thus, she committed to purchase the asset at expiration, just one day later, at a price of $52. The next day when the contract expires, it is then appropriate that she buy the underlying for $52.

EXHIBIT 2	Closeout versus Physical Delivery versus Cash Settlement

Closeout:
Sell contract at 53
Mark to market profit/loss:
53 − 52 = 1

or

Physical Delivery:
Pay 52, receive asset worth 53

Mark to market
profit/loss:
52 − 50 = 2

or

Cash Settlement:
Receive 53 − 52 = 1

Buy futures at 50:
Pay nothing

2 days before expiration
(futures price = 50)

1 day before expiration
(settlement price = 52)

Expiration
(settlement price = 53)

An alternative settlement procedure, which we described in Reading 62 on forward contracts, is cash settlement. The exchange designates certain futures contracts as cash-settled contracts. If the contract used in this example were cash settled, then the trader would not need to close out the position close to the end of the expiration day. She could simply leave the position open. When the contract expires, her margin account would be marked to market for a gain on the final day of $1. Cash settlement contracts have some advantages over delivery contracts, particularly with respect to significant savings in transaction costs.[13]

Exhibit 2 illustrates the equivalence of these three forms of delivery. Note, however, that because of the transaction costs of delivery, parties clearly prefer a closeout or cash settlement over physical delivery, particularly when the underlying asset is a physical commodity.

Contracts designated for delivery have a variety of features that can complicate delivery. In most cases, delivery does not occur immediately after expiration but takes place over several days. In addition, many contracts permit the short to choose when delivery takes place. For many contracts, delivery can be made any business day of the month. The delivery period usually includes the days following the last trading day of the month, which is usually in the third week of the month.

In addition, the short often has other choices regarding delivery, a major one being exactly which underlying asset is delivered. For example, a futures contract on U.S. Treasury bonds trading at the Chicago Board of Trade permits the short to deliver any of a number of U.S. Treasury bonds.[14] The wheat futures contract at the Chicago Board of Trade permits delivery of any of several types of wheat. Futures contracts calling for physical delivery of commodities often permit delivery at different locations. A given commodity delivered to one location is not the same as that commodity delivered to another because of the costs

[13] Nonetheless, cash settlement has been somewhat controversial in the United States. If a contract is designated as cash settlement, it implies that the buyer of the contract never intended to actually take possession of the underlying asset. Some legislators and regulators feel that this design is against the spirit of the law, which views a futures contract as a commitment to buy the asset at a later date. Even though parties often offset futures contracts prior to expiration, the possibility of actual delivery is still present in contracts other than those settled by cash. This controversy, however, is relatively minor and has caused no serious problems or debates in recent years.

[14] We shall cover this feature in more detail in Sections 6.2 and 7.2.3.

involved in transporting the commodity. The short holds the sole right to make decisions about what, when, and where to deliver, and the right to make these decisions can be extremely valuable. The right to make a decision concerning these aspects of delivery is called a **delivery option**.

Some futures contracts that call for delivery require delivery of the actual asset, and some use only a book entry. For example, in this day and age, no one physically handles U.S. Treasury bonds in the form of pieces of paper. Bonds are transferred electronically over the Federal Reserve's wire system. Other contracts, such as oil or wheat, do actually involve the physical transfer of the asset. Physical delivery is more common when the underlying is a physical commodity, whereas **book entry** is more common when the underlying is a financial asset.

Futures market participants use one additional delivery procedure, which is called **exchange for physicals (EFP)**. In an EFP transaction, the long and short arrange an alternative delivery procedure. For example, the Chicago Board of Trade's wheat futures contracts require delivery on certain dates at certain locations either in Chicago or in a few other specified locations in the Midwest. If the long and short agree, they could effect delivery by having the short deliver the wheat to the long in, for example, Omaha. The two parties would then report to the Chicago Board of Trade that they had settled their contract outside of the exchange's normal delivery procedures, which would be satisfactory to the exchange.

5 FUTURES EXCHANGES

A futures exchange is a legal corporate entity whose shareholders are its members. The members own memberships, more commonly called **seats**. Exchange members have the privilege of executing transactions on the exchange. Each member acts as either a **floor trader** or a **broker**. Floor traders are typically called **locals**; brokers are typically called **futures commission merchants (FCMs)**. Locals are market makers, standing ready to buy and sell by quoting a bid and an ask price. They are the primary providers of liquidity to the market. FCMs execute transactions for other parties off the exchange.

The locals on the exchange floor typically trade according to one of several distinct styles. The most common is called scalping. A **scalper** offers to buy or sell futures contracts, holding the position for only a brief period of time, perhaps just seconds. Scalpers attempt to profit by buying at the bid price and selling at the higher ask price. A **day trader** holds a position open somewhat longer but closes all positions at the end of the day.[15] A **position trader** holds positions open overnight. Day traders and position traders are quite distinct from scalpers in that they attempt to profit from the anticipated direction of the market; scalpers are trying simply to buy at the bid and sell at the ask.

Recall that futures exchanges have trading either on the floor or off the floor on electronic terminals, or in some cases, both. As previously described, floor trading in the United States takes place in pits, which are octagonal, multi-tiered areas where floor traders stand and conduct transactions. Traders wear jackets of specific colors and badges to indicate such information as what type of trader (FCM or local) they are and whom they represent.[16] As noted, to indicate a willingness to trade, a trader shouts and uses a set of standard hand signals. A

---

[15] The term "day trader" has been around the futures market for a long time but has recently acquired a new meaning in the broader financial markets. The term is now used to describe individual investors who trade stocks, often over the Internet, during the day for a living or as a hobby. In fact, the term has even been used in a somewhat pejorative manner, in that day traders are often thought of as naïve investors speculating wildly with money they can ill afford to lose.

[16] For example, an FCM or local could be trading for himself or could represent a company.

EXHIBIT 3	The World's 20 Leading Futures Exchanges

Exchange and Location	Volume in 2001 (Number of Contracts)
Eurex (Germany and Switzerland)	435,141,707
Chicago Mercantile Exchange (United States)	315,971,885
Chicago Board of Trade (United States)	209,988,002
London International Financial Futures and Options Exchange (United Kingdom)	161,522,775
Bolsa de Mercadorias & Futuros (Brazil)	94,174,452
New York Mercantile Exchange (United States)	85,039,984
Tokyo Commodity Exchange (Japan)	56,538,245
London Metal Exchange (United Kingdom)	56,224,495
Paris Bourse SA (France)	42,042,673
Sydney Futures Exchange (Australia)	34,075,508
Korea Stock Exchange (Korea)	31,502,184
Singapore Exchange (Singapore)	30,606,546
Central Japan Commodity Exchange (Japan)	27,846,712
International Petroleum Exchange (United Kingdom)	26,098,207
OM Stockholm Exchange (Sweden)	23,408,198
Tokyo Grain Exchange (Japan)	22,707,808
New York Board of Trade (United States)	14,034,168
MEFF Renta Variable (Spain)	13,108,293
Tokyo Stock Exchange (Japan)	12,465,433
South African Futures Exchange (South Africa)	11,868,242

Source: Futures Industry, January/February 2002.

trade is consummated by two traders agreeing on a price and a number of contracts. These traders might not actually say anything to each other; they may simply use a combination of hand signals and/or eye contact to agree on a transaction. When a transaction is agreed on, the traders fill out small paper forms and turn them over to clerks, who then see that the transactions are entered into the system and reported.

Each trader is required to have an account at a clearing firm. The clearing firms are the actual members of the clearinghouse. The clearinghouse deals only with the clearing firms, which then deal with their individual and institutional customers.

In electronic trading, the principles remain essentially the same but the traders do not stand in the pits. In fact, they do not see each other at all. They sit at computer terminals, which enable them to see the bids and offers of other traders. Transactions are executed by the click of a computer mouse or an entry from a keyboard.

Exhibit 3 lists the world's 20 leading futures exchanges in 2001, ranked by trading volume. Trading volume can be a misleading measure of the size of a futures markets; nonetheless, it is the measure primarily used. The structure of global futures exchanges has changed considerably in recent years. Exchanges in the United States, primarily the Chicago Board of Trade and the Chicago Mercantile Exchange, were clearly the world leaders in the past. Note that the volume leader now, however, is Eurex, the combined German–Swiss exchange. Eurex has been so successful partly because of its decision to be an all-electronic futures exchange, whereas the Chicago exchanges are still primarily pit-trading exchanges. Note the popularity of futures trading in Japan; four of the 20 leading exchanges are Japanese.

6   TYPES OF FUTURES CONTRACTS

The different types of futures contracts are generally divided into two main groups: commodity futures and financial futures. **Commodity futures** cover traditional agricultural, metal, and petroleum products. Financial futures include stocks, bonds, and currencies. Exhibit 4 gives a broad overview of the most active types of futures contracts traded on global futures exchanges. These contracts are those covered by *The Wall Street Journal* on the date indicated.

Our primary focus in this reading is on financial and currency futures contracts. Within the financials group, our main interest is on interest rate and bond futures, stock index futures, and currency futures. We may occasionally make reference to a commodity futures contract, but that will primarily be for illustrative purposes. In the following subsections, we introduce the primary contracts we shall focus on. These are U.S. contracts, but they resemble most types of futures contracts found on exchanges throughout the world. Full contract specifications for these and other contracts are available on the web sites of the futures exchanges, which are easy to locate with most Internet search engines.

6.1 Short-Term Interest Rate Futures Contracts

The primary short-term interest rate futures contracts are those on U.S. Treasury bills and Eurodollars on the Chicago Mercantile Exchange.

6.1.1 Treasury Bill Futures

The Treasury bill contract, launched in 1976, was the first interest rate futures contract. It is based on a 90-day U.S. Treasury bill, one of the most important U.S. government debt instruments (described in Reading 62, Section 3.2.1). The Treasury bill, or T-bill, is a discount instrument, meaning that its price equals the face value minus a discount representing interest. The discount equals the face value multiplied by the quoted rate times the days to maturity divided by 360. Thus, using the example from Reading 62, if a 180-day T-bill is selling at a discount of 4 percent, its price per $1 par is $1 - 0.04(180/360) = 0.98$. An investor who buys the bill and holds it to maturity would receive $1 at maturity, netting a gain of $0.02.

The futures contract is based on a 90-day $1,000,000 U.S. Treasury bill. Thus, on any given day, the contract trades with the understanding that a 90-day T-bill will be delivered at expiration. While the contract is trading, its price is quoted as 100 minus the rate quoted as a percent priced into the contract by the futures market. This value, 100 − Rate, is known as the IMM Index; IMM stands for **International Monetary Market**, a division of the Chicago Mercantile Exchange.

EXHIBIT 4   Most-Active Global Futures Contracts as Covered by *The Wall Street Journal*, 18 June 2002

Commodity Futures

Corn (CBOT)
Oats (CBOT)
Soybeans (CBOT)
Soybean Meal (CBOT)
Soybean Oil (CBOT)
Wheat (CBOT, KCBT, MGE)
Canola (WPG)
Barley (WPG)
Feeder Cattle (CME)
Live Cattle (CME)
Lean Hogs (CME)
Pork Bellies (CME)
Milk (CME)
Lumber (CME)
Cocoa (NYBOT)
Coffee (NYBOT)
World Sugar (NYBOT)
Domestic Sugar (NYBOT)
Cotton (NYBOT)

Treasury Bonds (CBOT)
Treasury Notes (CBOT)
10-Year Agency Notes (CBOT)
10-Year Interest Rate Swaps (CBOT)
2-Year Agency Notes (CBOT)
5-Year Treasury Notes (CBOT)
2-Year Treasury Notes (CBOT)
Federal Funds (CBOT)
Municipal Bond Index (CBOT)
Treasury Bills (CME)
1-Month LIBOR (CME)
Eurodollar (CME)
Euroyen (CME, SGX)
Short Sterling (LIFFE)
Long Gilt (LIFFE)
3-Month Euribor (LIFFE)
3-Month Euroswiss (LIFFE)
Canadian Bankers Acceptance (ME)
10-Year Canadian Government Bond (ME)

Financial Futures

Euro (CME)
Euro–Sterling (NYBOT)
Euro–U.S. Dollar (NYBOT)
Euro–Yen (NYBOT)
Dow Jones Industrial Average (CBOT)
Mini Dow Jones Industrial Average (CBOT)
S&P 500 Index (CME)
Mini S&P 500 Index (CME)
S&P Midcap 400 Index (CME)
Nikkei 225 (CME)
Nasdaq 100 Index (CME)
Mini Nasdaq Index (CME)
Goldman Sachs Commodity Index (CME)
Russell 1000 Index (CME)
Russell 2000 Index (CME)
NYSE Composite Index (NYBOT)
U.S. Dollar Index (NYBOT)
Share Price Index (SFE)
CAC 40 Stock Index (MATIF)

(Exhibit continued on next page …)

EXHIBIT 4   (continued)

Commodity Futures

Orange Juice (NYBOT)
Copper (NYMEX)
Gold (NYMEX)
Platinum (NYMEX)
Palladium (NYMEX)
Silver (NYMEX)
Crude Oil (NYMEX)
No. 2 Heating Oil (NYMEX)
Unleaded Gasoline (NYMEX)
Natural Gas (NYMEX)
Brent Crude Oil (IPEX)
Gas Oil (IPEX)

Financial Futures

10-Year Euro Notional Bond (MATIF)
3-Month Euribor (MATIF)
3-Year Commonwealth T-Bonds (SFE)
5-Year German Euro Government Bond (EUREX)
10-Year German Euro Government Bond (EUREX)
2-Year German Euro Government Bond (EUREX)
Japanese Yen (CME)
Canadian Dollar (CME)
British Pound (CME)
Swiss Franc (CME)
Australian Dollar (CME)
Mexican Peso (CME)
Xetra Dax (EUREX)
FTSE 200 Index (LIFFE)
Dow Jones Euro Stoxx 50 Index (EUREX)
Dow Jones Stoxx 50 Index EUREX)

Exchange codes: CBOT (Chicago Board of Trade), CME (Chicago Mercantile Exchange), LIFFE (London International Financial Futures Exchange), WPG (Winnipeg Grain Exchange), EUREX (Eurex), NYBOT (New York Board of Trade), IPEX (International Petroleum Exchange), MATIF (Marché a Terme International de France), ME (Montreal Exchange), MGE (Minneapolis Grain Exchange), SFE (Sydney Futures Exchange), SGX (Singapore Exchange), KCBT (Kansas City Board of Trade), NYMEX (New York Mercantile Exchange)

Note: These are not the only global futures contracts but are those covered in *The Wall Street Journal* on the date given and represent the most active contracts at that time.

The IMM Index is a reported and publicly available price; however, it is not the actual futures price, which is

$$100 - (\text{Rate}/100)(90/360)$$

For example, suppose on a given day the rate priced into the contract is 6.25 percent. Then the quoted price will be $100 - 6.25 = 93.75$. The actual futures price would be

$$\$1,000,000[1 - 0.0625(90/360)] = \$984,375$$

Recall, however, that except for the small **margin deposit**, a futures transaction does not require any cash to be paid up front. As trading takes place, the rate fluctuates with market interest rates and the associated IMM Index price changes accordingly. The actual futures price, as calculated above, also fluctuates according to the above formula, but interestingly, that price is not very important. The same information can be captured more easily by referencing the IMM Index than by calculating the actual price.

Suppose, for example, that a trader had his account marked to market to the above price, 6.25 in terms of the rate, 93.75 in terms of the IMM Index, and $984,375 in terms of the actual futures price. Now suppose the rate goes to 6.50, an increase of 0.25 or 25 basis points. The IMM Index declines to 93.50, and the actual futures price drops to

$$\$1,000,000[1 - 0.065(90/360)] = \$983,750$$

Thus, the actual futures price decreased by $984,375 - $983,750 = 625. A trader who is long would have a loss of $625; a trader who is short would have a gain of $625.

This $625 gain or loss can be arrived at more directly, however, by simply noting that each basis point move is equivalent to $25.[17] This special design of the contract makes it easy for floor traders to do the necessary arithmetic in their heads. For example, if floor traders observe the IMM Index move from 93.75 to 93.50, they immediately know that it has moved down 25 basis points and that 25 basis points times $25 per basis point is a loss of $625. The minimum tick size is one-half basis point or $12.50.

T-bill futures contracts have expirations of the current month, the next month, and the next four months of March, June, September, and December. Because of the small trading volume, however, only the closest expiration has much trading volume, and even that one is only lightly traded. T-bill futures expire specifically on the Monday of the week of the third Wednesday each month and settle in cash rather than physical delivery of the T-bill, as described in Section 4.

As important as Treasury bills are in U.S. financial markets, however, today this futures contract is barely active. The Eurodollar contract is considered much more important because it reflects the interest rate on a dollar borrowed by a high-quality private borrower. The rates on T-bills are considered too heavily influenced by U.S. government policies, budget deficits, government funding plans, politics, and Federal Reserve monetary policy. Although unquestionably Eurodollar rates are affected by those factors, market participants consider them much less directly influenced. But in spite of this relative inactivity, T-bill futures are useful instruments for illustrating certain principles of futures market

---

[17] Expressed mathematically, $\$1,000,000[0.0001(90/360)] = \$25$. In other words, any move in the last digit of the rate (a basis point) affects the actual futures price by $25.

pricing and trading. Accordingly, we shall use them on some occasions. For now, however, we turn to the Eurodollar futures contract.

6.1.2 Eurodollar Futures

Recall that in Reading 62, we devoted a good bit of effort to understanding Eurodollar forward contracts, known as FRAs. These contracts pay off based on LIBOR on a given day. The Eurodollar futures contract of the Chicago Mercantile Exchange is based on $1 million notional principal of 90-day Eurodollars. Specifically, the underlying is the rate on a 90-day dollar-denominated time deposit issued by a bank in London. As we described in Reading 62, this deposit is called a Eurodollar time deposit, and the rate is referred to as LIBOR (London Interbank Offer Rate). On a given day, the futures contract trades based on the understanding that at expiration, the official Eurodollar rate, as compiled by the British Bankers Association (BBA), will be the rate at which the final settlement of the contract is made. While the contract is trading, its price is quoted as 100 minus the rate priced into the contract by futures traders. Like its counterpart in the T-bill futures market, this value, 100 − Rate, is also known as the IMM Index.

As in the T-bill futures market, on a given day, if the rate priced into the contract is 5.25 percent, the quoted price will be 100 − 5.25 = 94.75. With each contract based on $1 million notional principal of Eurodollars, the actual futures price is

$$\$1,000,000[1 - 0.0525(90/360)] = \$986,875$$

Like the T-bill contract, the actual futures price moves $25 for every basis point move in the rate or IMM Index price.

As with all futures contracts, the price fluctuates on a daily basis and margin accounts are marked to market according to the exchange's official settlement price. At expiration, the final settlement price is the official rate quoted on a 90-day Eurodollar time deposit by the BBA. That rate determines the final settlement. Eurodollar futures contracts do not permit actual delivery of a Eurodollar time deposit; rather, they settle in cash, as described in Section 4.

The Eurodollar futures contract is one of the most active in the world. Because its rate is based on LIBOR, it is widely used by dealers in swaps, FRAs, and interest rate options to hedge their positions taken in dollar-denominated over-the-counter interest rate derivatives. Such derivatives usually use LIBOR as the underlying rate.

It is important to note, however, that there is a critical distinction between the manner in which the interest calculation is built into the Eurodollar futures contract and the manner in which interest is imputed on actual Eurodollar time deposits. Recall from Reading 62 that when a bank borrows $1 million at a rate of 5 percent for 90 days, the amount it will owe in 90 days is

$$\$1,000,000[1 + 0.05(90/360)] = \$1,012,500$$

Interest on Eurodollar time deposits is computed on an add-on basis to the principal. As described in this section, however, it appears that in computing the futures price, interest is deducted from the principal so that a bank borrowing $1,000,000 at a rate of 5 percent would receive

$$\$1,000,000[1 - 0.05(90/360)] = \$987,500$$

and would pay back $1,000,000. This procedure is referred to as discount interest and is used in the T-bill market.

The discount interest computation associated with Eurodollar futures is merely a convenience contrived by the futures exchange to facilitate quoting prices in a manner already familiar to its traders, who were previously trading T-bill futures. This inconsistency between the ways in which Eurodollar futures and Eurodollar spot transactions are constructed causes some pricing problems, as we shall see in Section 7.2.2.

The minimum tick size for Eurodollar futures is 1 basis point or $25. The available expirations are the next two months plus March, June, September, and December. The expirations go out about 10 years, a reflection of their use by over-the-counter **derivatives dealers** to hedge their positions in long-term interest rate derivatives. Eurodollar futures expire on the second business day on which London banks are open before the third Wednesday of the month and terminate with a cash settlement.

6.2 Intermediate- and Long-Term Interest Rate Futures Contracts

In U.S. markets, the primary interest-rate-related instruments of **intermediate** and long maturities are U.S. Treasury notes and bonds. The U.S. government issues both instruments: Treasury notes have an original maturity of 2 to 10 years, and Treasury bonds have an original maturity of more than 10 years. Futures contracts on these instruments are very actively traded on the Chicago Board of Trade. For the most part, there are no real differences in the contract characteristics for Treasury note and Treasury bond futures; the underlying bonds differ slightly, but the futures contracts are qualitatively the same. We shall focus here on one of the most active instruments, the U.S. Treasury bond futures contract.

The contract is based on the delivery of a U.S. Treasury bond with any coupon but with a maturity of at least 15 years. If the deliverable bond is callable, it cannot be callable for at least 15 years from the delivery date.[18] These specifications mean that there are potentially a large number of deliverable bonds, which is exactly the way the Chicago Board of Trade, the Federal Reserve, and the U.S. Treasury want it. They do not want a potential run on a single issue that might distort prices. By having multiple deliverable issues, however, the contract must be structured with some fairly complicated procedures to adjust for the fact that the short can deliver whatever bond he chooses from among the eligible bonds. This choice gives the short a potentially valuable option and puts the long at a disadvantage. Moreover, it complicates pricing the contract, because the identity of the underlying bond is not clear. Although when referring to a futures contract on a 90-day Eurodollar time deposit we are relatively clear about the underlying instrument, a futures contract on a long-term Treasury bond does not allow us the same clarity.

To reduce the confusion, the exchange declares a standard or hypothetical version of the deliverable bond. This hypothetical deliverable bond has a 6 percent coupon. When a trader holding a short position at expiration delivers a bond with a coupon greater (less) than 6 percent, she receives an upward (a downward) adjustment to the price paid for the bond by the long. The adjustment is done by means of a device called the **conversion factor**. In brief, the conversion factor is the price of a $1.00 par bond with a coupon and maturity equal to those of the deliverable bond and a yield of 6 percent. Thus, if the short delivers a bond with a coupon greater (less) than 6 percent, the conversion factor exceeds (is less than)

---

[18] The U.S. government no longer issues callable bonds but has done so in the past.

1.0.[19] The amount the long pays the short is the futures price at expiration multiplied by the conversion factor. Thus, delivery of a bond with coupon greater (less) than the standard amount, 6 percent, results in the short receiving an upward (a downward) adjustment to the amount received. A number of other technical considerations are also involved in determining the delivery price.[20]

The conversion factor system is designed to put all bonds on equal footing. Ideally, application of the conversion factor would result in the short finding no preference for delivery of any one bond over any other. That is not the case, however, because the complex relationships between bond prices cannot be reduced to a simple linear adjustment, such as the conversion factor method. As a result, some bonds are cheaper to deliver than others. When making the delivery decision, the short compares the cost of buying a given bond on the open market with the amount she would receive upon delivery of that bond. The former will always exceed the latter; otherwise, a clear arbitrage opportunity would be available. The most attractive bond for delivery would be the one in which the amount received for delivering the bond is largest relative to the amount paid on the open market for the bond. The bond that minimizes this loss is referred to as the **cheapest-to-deliver** bond.

At any time during the life of a Treasury bond futures contract, traders can identify the cheapest-to-deliver bond. Determining the amount received at delivery is straightforward; it equals the current futures price times the conversion factor for a given bond. To determine the amount the bond would cost at expiration, one calculates the forward price of the bond, positioned at the delivery date. Of course, this is just a forward computation; circumstances could change by the expiration date. But this forward calculation gives a picture of circumstances as they currently stand and identifies which bond is currently the cheapest to deliver. That bond is then considered the bond most likely to be delivered. Recall that one problem with this futures contract is that the identity of the underlying bond is unclear. Traders traditionally treat the cheapest to deliver as the bond that underlies the contract. As time passes and interest rates change, however, the cheapest-to-deliver bond can change. Thus, the bond underlying the futures contract can change, adding an element of uncertainty to the pricing and trading of this contract.

With this complexity associated with the U.S. Treasury bond futures contract, one might suspect that it is less actively traded. In fact, the opposite is true: Complexity creates extraordinary opportunities for gain for those who understand what is going on and can identify the cheapest bond to deliver.

The Chicago Board of Trade's U.S. Treasury bond futures contract covers $100,000 par value of U.S. Treasury bonds. The expiration months are March, June, September, and December. They expire on the seventh business day preceding the last business day of the month and call for actual delivery, through the Federal Reserve's wire system, of the Treasury bond. Prices are quoted in points and 32nds, meaning that you will see prices like 98 18/32, which equals 98.5625. For a contract covering $100,000 par value, for example, the price is $98,562.50. The minimum tick size is 1/32, which is $31.25.

In addition to the futures contract on the long-term government bond, there are also very similar futures contracts on intermediate-term government bonds. The Chicago Board of Trade's contracts on 2-, 5-, and 10-year Treasury notes are

---

[19] This statement is true regardless of the maturity of the deliverable bond. Any bond with a coupon in excess of its yield is worth more than its par value.

[20] For example, the actual procedure for delivery of U.S. Treasury bonds is a three-day process starting with the short notifying the exchange of intention to make delivery. Delivery actually occurs several days later. In addition, as is the custom in U.S. bond markets, the quoted price does not include the accrued interest. Accordingly, an adjustment must be made.

very actively traded and are almost identical to its long-term bond contract, except for the exact specification of the underlying instrument. Intermediate and long-term government bonds are important instruments in every country's financial markets. They give the best indication of the long-term default-free interest rate and are often viewed as a **benchmark bond** for various comparisons in financial markets.[21] Accordingly, futures contracts on such bonds play an important role in a country's financial markets and are almost always among the most actively traded contracts in futures markets around the world.

If the underlying instrument is not widely available and not actively traded, the viability of a futures contract on it becomes questionable. The reduction seen in U.S. government debt in the late 1990s has led to a reduction in the supply of intermediate and long-term government bonds, and some concern has arisen over this fact. In the United States, some efforts have been made to promote the long-term debt of Fannie Mae and Freddie Mac as substitute benchmark bonds.[22] It remains to be seen whether such efforts will be necessary and, if so, whether they will succeed.

6.3 Stock Index Futures Contracts

One of the most successful types of futures contracts of all time is the class of futures on stock indices. Probably the most successful has been the Chicago Mercantile Exchange's contract on the Standard and Poor's 500 Stock Index. Called the S&P 500 Stock Index futures, this contract premiered in 1982 and has benefited from the widespread acceptance of the S&P 500 Index as a stock market benchmark. The contract is quoted in terms of a price on the same order of magnitude as the S&P 500 itself. For example, if the S&P 500 Index is at 1183, a two-month futures contract might be quoted at a price of, say, 1187. We shall explain how to determine a stock index futures price in Section 7.3.

The contract implicitly contains a multiplier, which is (appropriately) multiplied by the quoted futures price to produce the actual futures price. The multiplier for the S&P 500 futures is $250. Thus, when you hear of a futures price of 1187, the actual price is 1187($250) = $296,750.

S&P 500 futures expirations are March, June, September, and December and go out about two years, although trading is active only in the nearest two to three expirations. With occasional exceptions, the contracts expire on the Thursday preceding the third Friday of the month. Given the impracticality of delivering a portfolio of the 500 stocks in the index combined according to their relative weights in the index, the contract is structured to provide for cash settlement at expiration.

The S&P 500 is not the only active stock index futures contract. In fact, the Chicago Mercantile Exchange has a smaller version of the S&P 500 contract,

---

[21] For example, the default risk of a corporate bond is often measured as the difference between the corporate bond yield and the yield on a Treasury bond or note of comparable maturity. Fixed rates on interest rate swaps are usually quoted as a spread over the rate on a Treasury bond or note of comparable maturity.

[22] Fannie Mae is the Federal National Mortgage Association, and Freddie Mac is the Federal Home Loan Mortgage Corporation. These institutions were formerly U.S. government agencies that issued debt to raise funds to buy and sell mortgages and mortgage-backed securities. These institutions are now publicly traded corporations but are considered to have extremely low default risk because of their critical importance in U.S. mortgage markets. It is believed that an implicit Federal government guarantee is associated with their debt. Nonetheless, it seems unlikely that the debt of these institutions could take over that of the U.S. government as a benchmark. The Chicago Board of Trade has offered futures contracts on the bonds of these organizations, but the contracts have not traded actively.

called the Mini S&P 500, which has a multiplier of $50 and trades only electronically. Other widely traded contracts in the United States are on the Dow Jones Industrials, the S&P **Midcap** 400, and the Nasdaq 100. Virtually every developed country has a stock index futures contract based on the leading equities of that country. Well-known stock index futures contracts around the world include the United Kingdom's FTSE 100 (pronounced "Footsic 100"), Japan's Nikkei 225, France's CAC 40, and Germany's DAX 30.

6.4 Currency Futures Contracts

In Reading 62, we described forward contracts on foreign currencies. There are also futures contracts on foreign currencies. Although the forward market for foreign currencies is much more widely used, the futures market is still quite active. In fact, currency futures were the first futures contracts not based on physical commodities. Thus, they are sometimes referred to as the first financial futures contracts, and their initial success paved the way for the later introduction of interest rate and stock index futures.

Compared with forward contracts on currencies, currency futures contracts are much smaller in size. In the United States, these contracts trade at the Chicago Mercantile Exchange with a small amount of trading at the New York Board of Trade. In addition there is some trading on exchanges outside the United States. The characteristics we describe below refer to the Chicago Mercantile Exchange's contract.

In the United States, the primary currencies on which trading occurs are the euro, Canadian dollar, Swiss franc, Japanese yen, British pound, Mexican peso, and Australian dollar. Each contract has a designated size and a quotation unit. For example, the euro contract covers €125,000 and is quoted in dollars per euro. A futures price such as $0.8555 is stated in dollars and converts to a contract price of

$$125{,}000(\$0.8555) = \$106{,}937.50$$

The Japanese yen futures price is structured somewhat differently. Because of the large number of yen per dollar, the contract covers ¥12,500,000 and is quoted without two zeroes that ordinarily precede the price. For example, a price might be stated as 0.8205, but this actually represents a price of 0.008205, which converts to a contract price of

$$12{,}500{,}000(0.008205) = \$102{,}562.50$$

Alternatively, a quoted price of 0.8205 can be viewed as $1/0.008205 = ¥121.88$ per dollar.

Currency futures contracts expire in the months of March, June, September, and December. The specific expiration is the second business day before the third Wednesday of the month. Currency futures contracts call for actual delivery, through book entry, of the underlying currency.

We have briefly examined the different types of futures contracts of interest to us. Of course there are a variety of similar instruments trading on futures exchanges around the world. Our purpose, however, is not to provide institutional details, which can be obtained at the web sites of the world's futures exchanges, but rather to enhance your understanding of the important principles necessary to function in the world of derivatives.

Until now we have made reference to prices of futures contracts. Accordingly, let us move forward and examine the pricing of futures contracts.

PRICING AND VALUATION OF FUTURES CONTRACTS

7

In Reading 62, we devoted considerable effort to understanding the pricing and valuation of forward contracts. We first discussed the notion of what it means to *price* a forward contract in contrast to what it means to *value* a forward contract. Recall that pricing means to assign a fixed price or rate at which the underlying will be bought by the long and sold by the short at expiration. In assigning a forward price, we set the price such that the value of the contract is zero at the start. A zero-value contract means that the present value of the payments promised by each party to the other is the same, a result in keeping with the fact that neither party pays the other any money at the start. The value of the contract to the long is the present value of the payments promised by the short to the long minus the present value of the payments promised by the long to the short. Although the value is zero at the start, during the life of the contract, the value will fluctuate as market conditions change; the original forward contract price, however, stays the same.

In Reading 62, we presented numerous examples of how to apply the concept of pricing and valuation when dealing with forward contracts on stocks, bonds, currencies, and interest rates. To illustrate the concepts of pricing and valuation, we started with a generic forward contract. Accordingly, we do so here in the futures reading. We assume no transaction costs.

7.1 Generic Pricing and Valuation of a Futures Contract

As we did with forward contracts, we start by illustrating the time frame within which we are working:

Today is time 0. The expiration date of the futures contract is time T. Times $t - 1$ and t are arbitrary times between today and the expiration and are the points at which the contract will be marked to market. Thus, we can think of the three periods depicted above, 0 to $t - 1$, $t - 1$ to t, and t to T, as three distinct trading days with times $t - 1$, t, and T being the end of each of the three days.

The price of the underlying asset in the spot market is denoted as S_0 at time 0, S_{t-1} at time $t - 1$, S_t at time t, and S_T at time T. We denote the futures contract price at time 0 as $f_0(T)$. This notation indicates that $f_0(T)$ is the price of a futures contract at time 0 that expires at time T. Unlike forward contract prices, however, futures prices fluctuate in an open and competitive market. The marking-to-market process results in each futures contract being terminated every day and reinitiated. Thus, we not only have a futures price set at time 0 but we also have a new one at time $t - 1$, at time t, and at time T. In other words,

$$f_0(T) = \text{price of a futures contract at time 0 that expires at time T}$$

$$f_{t-1}(T) = \text{price of a futures contract at time } t - 1 \text{ that expires at time T}$$

$$f_t(T) = \text{price of a futures contract at time t that expires at time T}$$

$$f_T(T) = \text{price of a futures contract at time T that expires at time T}$$

Note, however, that $f_{t-1}(T)$ and $f_t(T)$ are also the prices of contracts newly established at times $t - 1$ and t for delivery at time T. Futures contracts are homogeneous and fungible. Any contract for delivery of the underlying at T is equivalent to any other contract, regardless of when the contracts were created.[23]

The value of the futures contract is denoted as $v_0(T)$. This notation indicates that $v_0(T)$ is the value at time 0 of a futures contract expiring at time T. We are also interested in the values of the contract prior to expiration, such as at time t, denoted as $v_t(T)$, as well as the value of the contract at expiration, denoted as $v_T(T)$.[24]

7.1.1 The Futures Price at Expiration

Now suppose we are at time T. The spot price is S_T and the futures price is $f_T(T)$. To avoid an arbitrage opportunity, *the futures price must converge to the spot price at expiration*:

$$f_T(T) = S_T \qquad \text{(63-1)}$$

Consider what would happen if this were not the case. If $f_T(T) < S_T$, a trader could buy the futures contract, let it immediately expire, pay $f_T(T)$ to take delivery of the underlying, and receive an asset worth S_T. The trader would have paid $f_T(T)$ and received an asset worth S_T, which is greater, at no risk. If $f_T(T) > S_T$, the trader would go short the futures, buy the asset for S_T, make delivery, and receive $f_T(T)$ for the asset, for which he paid a lesser amount. Only if $f_T(T) = S_T$ does this arbitrage opportunity go away. Thus, the futures price must equal the spot price at expiration.

Another way to understand this point is to recall that by definition, a futures contract calls for the delivery of an asset at expiration at a price determined when the transaction is initiated. If expiration is right now, a futures transaction is equivalent to a spot transaction, so the futures price must equal the spot price.

7.1.2 Valuation of a Futures Contract

Let us consider how to determine the value of a futures contract. We already agreed that because no money changes hands, the value of a forward contract at the initiation date is zero. For the same reason, *the value of a futures contract at the initiation date is zero*. Thus,

$$v_0(T) = 0 \qquad \text{(63-2)}$$

Now let us determine the value of the contract during its life. Suppose we are at the end of the second day, at time t. In our diagram above, this point would be

---

[23] As an analogy from the bond markets, consider a 9 percent coupon bond, originally issued with 10 years remaining. Three years later, that bond is a 9 percent seven-year bond. Consider a newly issued 9 percent coupon bond with seven years maturity and the same issuer. As long as the coupon dates are the same and all other terms are the same, these two bonds are fungible and are perfect substitutes for each other.

[24] It is important at this point to make some comments about notation. First, note that in Reading 62 we use an uppercase F and V for forward contracts; here we use lowercase f and v for futures contracts. Also we follow the pattern of using subscripts to indicate a price or value at a particular point in time. The arguments in parentheses refer to characteristics of a contract. Thus, in Reading 62 we described the price of a forward contract as F(0,T) meaning the price of a forward contract initiated at time 0 and expiring at time T. This price does not fluctuate during the life of the contract. A futures contract, however, reprices on a daily basis. Its original time of initiation does not matter—it is reinitiated every day. Hence, futures prices are indicated by notation such as $f_0(T)$ and $f_t(T)$. We follow a similar pattern for value, using $V_0(0,T)$, $V_t(0,T)$, and $V_T(0,T)$ for forwards and $v_0(T)$, $v_t(T)$, and $v_T(T)$ for futures.

essentially at time t, but perhaps just an instant before it. So let us call it time t−. An instant later, we call the time point t+. In both cases, the futures price is $f_t(T)$. The contract was previously marked to market at the end of day $t − 1$ to a price of $f_{t-1}(T)$. An instant later when the futures account is marked to market, the trader will receive a gain of $f_t(T) − f_{t-1}(T)$. We can reasonably ignore the present value difference of receiving this money an instant later. Let us now state more formally that the value of a futures contract is

$v_{t-}(T) = f_t(T) − f_{t-1}(T)$ *an instant before the account is marked to market*

$v_{t+}(T) = 0$ *as soon as the account is marked to market*   **(63-2)**

Suppose, however, that the trader is at a time j during the second trading day, between $t − 1$ and t. The accumulated gain or loss since the account was last marked to market is $f_j(T) − f_{t-1}(T)$. If the trader closes the position out, he would receive or be charged this amount at the end of the day. So the value at time j would be $f_j(T) − f_{t-1}(T)$ discounted back from the end of the day at time t until time j—that is, a fraction of a day. It is fairly routine to ignore this intraday interest. Thus, in general we say that *the value of a futures contract before it has been marked to market is the gain or loss accumulated since the account was last marked to market.*

So to recap, the value of a futures contract is the accumulated gain or loss since the last mark to market. The holder of a futures contract has a claim or liability on this amount. Once that claim is captured or the liability paid through the mark-to-market process, the contract is repriced to its current market price and the claim or liability goes back to a value of zero. Using these results, determining the value of a futures contract at expiration is easy. An instant before expiration, it is simply the accumulated profit since the last mark to market. At expiration, the value goes back to zero. With respect to the value of the futures, expiration is no different from any other day. Exhibit 5 summarizes the principles of valuation.

In Reading 62, we devoted considerable effort toward understanding how forward contracts are valued. When holding positions in forward contracts, we are forced to assign values to instruments that do not trade in an open market with widely disseminated prices. Thus, it is important that we understand how forward contracts are valued. When dealing with futures contracts, the process is considerably simplified. Because futures contracts are generally quite actively traded, there is a market with reliable prices that provides all of the information we need. For futures contracts, we see that the value is simply the observable price change since the last mark to market.

EXHIBIT 5	The Value of a Futures Contract Before and After Marking to Market

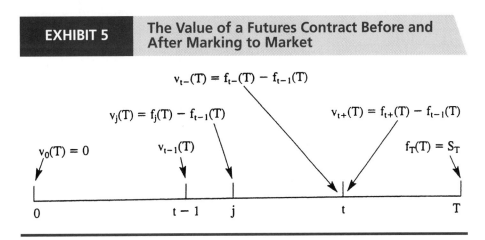

7.1.3 Forward and Futures Prices

For all financial instruments, it is important to be able to determine whether the price available in the market is an appropriate one. Hence, we engage in the process of "pricing" the financial instrument. A major objective of this reading is to determine the appropriate price of a futures contract. Given the similarity between futures and forward prices, however, we can benefit from studying forward contract pricing, which was covered in Reading 62. But first, we must look at the similarities and differences between forward and futures contracts.

Recall that futures contracts settle daily and are essentially free of default risk. Forward contracts settle only at expiration and are subject to default risk. Yet both types of contracts allow the party to purchase or sell the underlying asset at a price agreed on in advance. It seems intuitive that futures prices and forward prices would be relatively close to each other.

The issues involved in demonstrating the relationship between futures and forward prices are relatively technical and beyond the scope of this reading. We can, however, take a brief and fairly nontechnical look at the question. First let us ignore the credit risk issue. We shall assume that the forward contract participants are prime credit risks. We focus only on the technical distinction caused by the daily marking to market.

The day before expiration, both the futures contract and the forward contract have one day to go. At expiration, they will both settle. These contracts are therefore the same. At any other time prior to expiration, futures and forward prices can be the same or different. If interest rates are constant or at least known, any effect of the addition or subtraction of funds from the marking-to-market process can be shown to be neutral. If interest rates are positively correlated with futures prices, traders with long positions will prefer futures over forwards, because they will generate gains when interest rates are going up, and traders can invest those gains for higher returns. Also, traders will incur losses when interest rates are going down and can borrow to cover those losses at lower rates. Because traders holding long positions prefer the marking to market of futures over forwards when futures prices are positively correlated with interest rates, futures will carry higher prices than forwards. Conversely, when futures prices are negatively correlated with interest rates, traders will prefer not to mark to market, so forward contracts will carry higher prices.

Because interest rates and fixed-income security prices move in opposite directions, interest rate futures are good examples of cases in which forward and futures prices should be inversely related. Alternatively, when inflation is high, interest rates are high and investors oftentimes put their money in such assets as gold. Thus, gold futures prices and interest rates would tend to be positively correlated. It would be difficult to identify a situation in which futures prices are not correlated with interest rates. Zero correlation is rare in the financial world, but we can say that when the correlation is low or close to zero, the difference between forward and futures prices would be very small.

At this introductory level of treatment, we shall make the simplifying assumption that futures prices and forward prices are the same. We do so by ignoring the effects of marking a futures contract to market. In practice, some significant issues arise related to the marking-to-market process, but they detract from our ability to understand the important concepts in pricing and trading futures and forwards.

Therefore, based on the equivalence we are assuming between futures and forwards, we can assume that the value of a futures contract at expiration, before marking to market, is

$$v_T(T) = f_T(T) - f_0(T) = S_T - f_0(T)$$

with the spot price substituted for the futures price at T, given what we know about their convergence.

7.1.4 Pricing Futures Contracts

Now let us proceed to the pricing of futures contracts. As we did with forward contracts, we consider the case of a generic underlying asset priced at $100. A futures contract calls for delivery of the underlying asset in one year at a price of $108. Let us see if $108 is the appropriate price for this futures contract.

Suppose we buy the asset for $100 and sell the futures contract. We hold the position until expiration. For right now, we assume no costs are involved in holding the asset. We do, however, lose interest on the $100 tied up in the asset for one year. We assume that this opportunity cost is at the risk-free interest rate of 5 percent.

Recall that no money changes hands at the start of a futures contract. Moreover, we can reasonably ignore the rather small margin deposit that would be required. In addition, margin deposits can generally be met by putting up interest-earning securities, so there is really no opportunity cost. As discussed in the previous section, we also will assume away the daily settlement procedure; in other words, the value of the futures contract paid out at expiration is the final futures price minus the original futures price. Because the final futures price converges to the spot price, the final payout is the spot price minus the original futures price.

So at the contract expiration, we are short the futures and must deliver the asset, which we own. We do so and receive the original futures price for it. So we receive $108 for an asset purchased a year ago at $100. At a 5 percent interest rate, we lose only $5 in interest, so our return in excess of the opportunity cost is 3 percent risk free. This risk-free return in excess of the risk-free rate is clearly attractive and would induce traders to buy the asset and sell the futures. This arbitrage activity would drive the futures price down until it reaches $105.

If the futures price falls below $105, say to $102, the opposite arbitrage would occur. The arbitrageur would buy the futures, but either we would need to be able to borrow the asset and sell it short, or investors who own the asset would have to be willing to sell it and buy the futures. They would receive the asset price of $100 and invest it at 5 percent interest. Then at expiration, those investors would get the asset back upon taking delivery, paying $102. This transaction would net a clear and risk-free profit of $3, consisting of interest of $5 minus a $2 loss from selling the asset at $100 and buying it back at $102. Again, through the buying of the futures and shorting of the asset, the forces of arbitrage would cause prices to realign to $105.

Some difficulties occur with selling short certain assets. Although the financial markets make short selling relatively easy, some commodities are not easy to sell short. In such a case, it is still possible for arbitrage to occur. If investors who already own the asset sell it and buy the futures, they can reap similar gains at no risk. Because our interest is in financial instruments, we shall ignore these commodity market issues and assume that short selling can be easily executed.[25]

If the market price is not equal to the price given by the model, it is important to note that regardless of the asset price at expiration, the above arbitrage guarantees a risk-free profit. That profit is known at the time the parties enter the transaction. Exhibit 6 summarizes and illustrates this point.

---

[25] Keep in mind that there are some restrictions on the short selling of financial instruments, such as uptick rules and margin requirements, but we will not concern ourselves with these impediments here.

EXHIBIT 6	The Risk-Free Nature of Long and Short Futures Arbitrage

Asset is priced at \$100, futures is priced at $f_0(T)$ and expires in one year. Interest rate over the life of the futures is 5 percent.

Time	Long Asset, Short Futures Arbitrage	Short Asset, Long Futures Arbitrage
Today (time 0)	Buy asset at \$100 Sell futures at $f_0(T)$	Sell short asset for \$100 Buy futures for $f_0(T)$
Expiration (time T)	Asset price is S_T Futures price converges to asset price Deliver asset Profit on asset after accounting for the 5 percent (\$5) interest lost from \$100 tied up in the investment in the asset: $S_T - 100 - 5$ Profit on futures: $f_0(T) - S_T$ Total profit: $f_0(T) - 100 - 5$	Asset price is S_T Futures price converges to asset price Take delivery of asset Profit on asset after accounting for the 5 percent (\$5) interest earned on the \$100 received from the short sale of the asset: $100 + 5 - S_T$ Profit on futures: $S_T - f_0(T)$ Total profit: $100 + 5 - f_0(T)$

Conclusion: The asset price at expiration has no effect on the profit captured at expiration for either transaction. The profit is known today. To eliminate arbitrage, the futures price today, $f_0(T)$, must equal $100 + 5 = \$105$.

The transactions we have described are identical to those using forward contracts. We did note with forward contracts, however, that one can enter into an off-market forward contract, having one party pay cash to another to settle any difference resulting from the contract not trading at its arbitrage-free value up front. In the futures market, this type of arrangement is not permitted; all contracts are entered into without any cash payments up front.

So in general, through the forces of arbitrage, we say that *the futures price is the spot price compounded at the risk-free rate*:

$$f_0(T) = S_0(1 + r)$$

It is important, however, to write this result in a form we are more likely to use. In the above form, we specify r as the interest rate over the life of the futures contract. In financial markets, however, interest rates are nearly always specified as annual rates. Therefore, to compound the asset price over the life of the futures, we let r equal an annual rate and specify the life of the futures as T years. Then the futures price is found as

$$f_0(T) = S_0(1 + r)^T \qquad \textbf{(63-4)}$$

The futures price is the spot price compounded over the life of the contract, T years, at the annual risk-free rate, r. From this point on, we shall use this more general specification.

As an example, consider a futures contract that has a life of 182 days; the annual interest rate is 5 percent. Then $T = 182/365$ and $r = 0.05$. If the spot price is $100, the futures price would then be

$$f_0(T) = S_0(1 + r)^T$$
$$f_0(182/365) = 100(1.05)^{182/365}$$
$$= 102.46$$

If the futures is selling for more than $102.46, an arbitrageur can buy the asset for $100 and sell the futures for whatever its price is, hold the asset (losing interest on $100 at an annual rate of 5 percent) and deliver it to receive the futures price. The overall strategy will net a return in excess of 5 percent a year at no risk. If the futures is selling for less than $102.46, the arbitrageur can borrow the asset, sell it short, and buy the futures. She will earn interest on the funds obtained from the **short sale** and take delivery of the asset at the futures expiration, paying the original futures price. The overall transaction results in receiving $100 up front and paying back an amount less than the 5 percent risk-free rate, making the transaction like a loan that is paid back at less than the risk-free rate. If one could create such a loan, one could use it to raise funds and invest the funds at the risk-free rate to earn unlimited gains.

7.1.5 Pricing Futures Contracts When There Are Storage Costs

Except for opportunity costs, we have until now ignored any costs associated with holding the asset. In many asset markets, there are significant costs, other than the opportunity cost, to holding an asset. These costs are referred to as **storage costs** or **carrying costs** and are generally a function of the physical characteristics of the underlying asset. Some assets are easy to store; some are difficult. For example, assume the underlying is oil, which has significant storage costs but a very long storage life.[26] One would not expect to incur costs associated with a decrease in quality of the oil. Significant risks do exist, however, such as spillage, fire, or explosion. Some assets on which futures are based are at risk for damage. For example, cattle and pigs can become ill and die during storage. Grains are subject to pest damage and fire. All of these factors have the potential to produce significant storage costs, and protection such as insurance leads to higher storage costs for these assets. On the other hand, financial assets have virtually no storage costs. Of course, all assets have one significant storage cost, which is the opportunity cost of money tied up in the asset, but this effect is covered in the present value calculation.

It is reasonable to assume that the storage costs on an asset are a function of the quantity of the asset to be stored and the length of time in storage. Let us specify this cost with the variable $FV(SC,0,T)$, which denotes the value at time T (expiration) of the storage costs (excluding opportunity costs) associated with holding the asset over the period 0 to T. By specifying these costs as of time T, we are accumulating the costs and compounding the interest thereon until the end of the storage period. We can reasonably assume that when storage is initiated, these costs are known.[27]

Revisiting the example we used previously, we would buy the asset at S_0, sell a futures contract at $f_0(T)$, store the asset and accumulate costs of $FV(SC,0,T)$, and

---

[26] After all, oil has been stored by nature for millions of years.

[27] There may be reason to suggest that storage costs have an element of uncertainty in them, complicating the analysis.

deliver the asset at expiration to receive the futures price. The total payoff is $f_0(T) - FV(SC,0,T)$. This amount is risk free. To avoid an arbitrage opportunity, its present value should equal the initial outlay, S_0, required to establish the position. Thus,

$$[f_0(T) - FV(SC,0,T)]/(1 + r)^T = S_0$$

Solving for the futures price gives

$$f_0(T) = S_0(1 + r)^T + FV(SC,0,T) \qquad \text{(63-5)}$$

This result says that *the futures price equals the spot price compounded over the life of the futures contract at the risk-free rate, plus the future value of the storage costs over the life of the contract.* In the previous example with no storage costs, we saw that the futures price was the spot price compounded at the risk-free rate. With storage costs, we must add the future value of the storage costs. The logic behind this adjustment should make sense. The futures price should be higher by enough to cover the storage costs when a trader buys the asset and sells a futures to create a risk-free position.[28]

Consider the following example. The spot price of the asset is $50, the interest rate is 6.25 percent, the future value of the storage costs is $1.35, and the futures expires in 15 months. Then $T = 15/12 = 1.25$. The futures price would, therefore, be

$$f_0(T) = S_0(1 + r)^T + FV(SC,0,T)$$
$$f_0(1.25) = 50(1.0625)^{1.25} + 1.35$$
$$= 55.29$$

If the futures is selling for more than $55.29, the arbitrageur would buy the asset and sell the futures, holding the position until expiration, at which time he would deliver the asset and collect the futures price, earning a return that covers the 6.25 percent cost of the money and the storage costs of $1.35. If the futures is selling for less than $55.29, the arbitrageur would sell short the asset and buy the futures, reinvesting the proceeds from the short sale at 6.25 percent and saving the storage costs. The net effect would be to generate a cash inflow today plus the storage cost savings and a cash outflow at expiration that would replicate a loan with a rate less than the risk-free rate. Only if the futures sells for exactly $55.29 do these arbitrage opportunities go away.

7.1.6 Pricing Futures Contracts When There Are Cash Flows on the Underlying Asset

In each case we have considered so far, the underlying asset did not generate any positive cash flows to the holder. For some assets, there will indeed be positive cash flows to the holder. Recall that in Reading 62, we examined the pricing and valuation of forward contracts on stocks and bonds and were forced to recognize that stocks pay dividends, bonds pay interest, and these cash flows affect the forward price. A similar concept applies here and does so in a symmetric manner

---

[28] We did not cover assets that are storable at significant cost when we studied forward contracts because such contracts are less widely used for these assets. Nonetheless, the formula given here would apply for forward contracts as well, given our assumption of no credit risk on forward contracts.

to what we described in the previous section in which the asset incurs a cash cost. As we saw in that section, a cash cost incurred from holding the asset increases the futures price. Thus, we might expect that cash generated from holding the asset would result in a lower futures price and, as we shall see in this section, that is indeed the case. But in the next section, we shall also see that it is even possible for an asset to generate nonmonetary benefits that must also be taken into account when pricing a futures contract on it.

Let us start by assuming that over the life of the futures contract, the asset generates positive cash flows of $FV(CF,0,T)$. It is no coincidence that this notation is similar to the one we used in the previous section for the storage costs of the underlying asset over the life of the futures. Cash inflows and storage costs are just different sides of the same coin. We must remember, however, that $FV(CF,0,T)$ represents a positive flow in this case. Now let us revisit our example.

We would buy the asset at S_0, sell a futures contract at $f_0(T)$, store the asset and generate positive cash flows of $FV(CF,0,T)$, and deliver the asset at expiration, receiving the futures price. The total payoff is $f_0(T) + FV(CF,0,T)$. This amount is risk free and known at the start. To avoid an arbitrage opportunity, its present value should equal the initial outlay, S_0, required to establish the position. Thus,

$$[f_0(T) + FV(CF,0,T)]/(1 + r)^T = S_0$$

Solving for the futures price gives

$$f_0(T) = S_0(1 + r)^T - FV(CF,0,T) \qquad \text{(63-6)}$$

In the previous example that included storage costs, we saw that the futures price was the spot price compounded at the risk-free rate plus the future value of the storage costs. With positive cash flows, we must subtract the future value of these cash flows. The logic behind this adjustment should make sense. The futures price should be reduced by enough to account for the positive cash flows when a trader buys the asset and sells a futures to create a risk-free position. Otherwise, the trader would receive risk-free cash flows from the asset *and* the equivalent amount from the sale of the asset at the futures price. Reduction of the futures price by this amount avoids overcompensating the trader.

As noted, these cash flows can be in the form of dividends from a stock or coupon interest from a bond. When we specifically examine the pricing of bond and stock futures, we shall make this specification a little more precise and work an example.

7.1.7 Pricing Futures Contracts When There Is a Convenience Yield

Now consider the possibility that the asset might generate nonmonetary benefits that must also be taken into account. The notion of nonmonetary benefits that could affect futures prices might sound strange, but upon reflection, it makes perfect sense. For example, a house is a common and normally desirable investment made by individuals and families. The house generates no monetary benefits and incurs significant costs. As well as being a possible monetary investment if prices rise, the house generates some nonmonetary benefits in the form of serving as a place to live. These benefits are quite substantial; many people consider owning a residence preferable to renting, and people often sell their homes for monetary gains far less than any reasonable return on a risky asset. Clearly the notion of a nonmonetary benefit to owning an asset is one most people are familiar with.

In a futures contract on an asset with a nonmonetary gain, that gain must be taken into account. Suppose, for the purpose of understanding the effect of nonmonetary benefits on a futures contract, we create a hypothetical futures contract on a house. An individual purchases a house and sells a futures contract on it. We shall keep the arguments as simple as possible by ignoring the operating or carrying costs. What should be the futures price? If the futures is priced at the spot price plus the risk-free rate, as in the original case, the homeowner receives a guaranteed sale price, giving a return of the risk-free rate *and* the use of the home. This is clearly a good deal. Homeowners would be eager to sell futures contracts, leading to a decrease in the price of the futures. Thus, any nonmonetary benefits ought to be factored into the futures price and logically would lead to a lower futures price.

Of course, in the real world of standardized futures contracts, there are no futures contracts on houses. Nonetheless, there are futures contracts on assets that have nonmonetary benefits. Assets that are often in short supply, particularly those with seasonal and highly risky production processes, are commonly viewed as having such benefits. The nonmonetary benefits of these assets are referred to as the **convenience yield**. Formally, a convenience yield is the nonmonetary return offered by an asset when in short supply. When an asset is in short supply, its price tends to be high. Holders of the asset earn an implicit incremental return from having the asset on hand. This return enables them, as commercial enterprises, to avoid the cost and inconvenience of not having their primary product or resource input on hand. Because shortages are generally temporary, the spot price can be higher than the futures price, even when the asset incurs storage costs. If a trader buys the asset, sells a futures contract, and stores the asset, the return is risk free and will be sufficient to cover the storage costs and the opportunity cost of money, but it will be reduced by an amount reflecting the benefits of holding the asset during a period of shortage or any other nonmonetary benefits.

Now, let the notation FV(CB,0,T) represent the future value of the costs of storage minus the benefits:

$$\text{FV(CB,0,T)} = \text{Costs of storage} - \text{Nonmonetary benefits (Convenience yield)}$$

where all terms are expressed in terms of their future value at time T and are considered to be known at time 0. If the costs exceed the benefits, FV(CB,0,T) is a positive number.[29] We refer to FV(CB,0,T) as the **cost of carry**.[30] The general futures pricing formula is

$$f_0(T) = S_0(1 + r)^T + \text{FV(CB,0,T)} \qquad \textbf{(63-7)}$$

The futures price is the spot price compounded at the risk-free rate plus the cost of carry. This model is often called the **cost-of-carry model**.

Consider an asset priced at $75; the risk-free interest rate is 5.15 percent, the net of the storage costs, interest, and convenience yield is $3.20, and the futures expires in nine months. Thus, $T = 9/12 = 0.75$. Then the futures price should be

$$f_0(T) = S_0(1 + r)^T + \text{FV(CB,0,T)}$$
$$f_0(0.75) = 75(1.0515)^{0.75} + 3.20$$
$$= 81.08$$

---

[29] In other words, FV(CB,0,T) has to be positive to refer to it as a "cost."

[30] In some cases, such as in inventory storage, it is customary to include the opportunity cost in the definition of cost of carry; but we keep it separate in this reading.

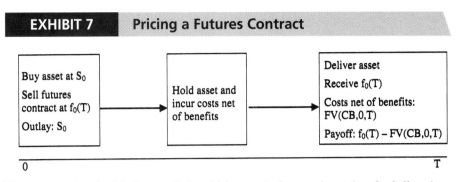

| EXHIBIT 7 | Pricing a Futures Contract |

The transaction is risk-free and should be equivalent to investing S_0 dollars in a risk-free asset that pays $f_0(T) - FV(CB,0,T)$ at time T. Therefore, the payoff at T must be the future value of the initial outlay invested at the risk-free rate. For this relationship to hold, the futures price must be given as

$$f_0(T) = S_0(1 + r)^T + FV(CB,0,T)$$

Example: An asset is selling for \$225. A futures contract expires in 150 days (T = 150/365 = 0.411). The risk-free rate is 7.5 percent, and the net cost of carry is \$5.75. The futures price will be

$$f_0(T) = f_0(0.411) = \$225(1.075)^{0.411} + \$5.75 = \$237.54$$

As we have always done, we assume that this price will prevail in the marketplace. If it does not, the forces of arbitrage will drive the market price to the model price. If the futures price exceeds \$81.08, the arbitrageur can buy the asset and sell the futures to earn a risk-free return in excess of the risk-free rate. If the futures price is less than \$81.08, the arbitrageur can either sell the asset short or sell it if he already owns it, and then also buy the futures, creating a risk-free position equivalent to a loan that will cost less than the risk-free rate. The gains from both of these transactions will have accounted for any nonmonetary benefits. This arbitrage activity will force the market price to converge to the model price.

The above equation is the most general form of the futures pricing formula we shall encounter. Exhibit 7 reviews and illustrates how we obtained this formula and provides another example.

Some variations of this general formula are occasionally seen. Sometimes the opportunity cost of interest is converted to dollars and imbedded in the cost of carry. Then we say that $f_0(T) = S_0 + FV(CB,0,T)$; the futures price is the spot price plus the cost of carry. This is a perfectly appropriate way to express the formula if the interest is imbedded in the cost of carry, but we shall not do so in this reading.

Another variation of this formula is to specify the cost of carry in terms of a rate, such as y. Then we have $f_0(T) = S_0(1 + r)^T(1 + y)^T$. Again, this variation is certainly appropriate but is not the version we shall use.[31]

Note that when we get into the specifics of pricing certain types of futures contracts, we must fine-tune the formulas a little more. First, however, we explore some general characterizations of the relationship between futures and spot prices.

---

[31] Yet another variation of this formula is to use $(1 + r + y)^T$ as an approximation for $(1 + r)^T(1 + y)^T$. We do not, however, consider this expression an acceptable way to compute the futures price as it is an approximation of a formula that is simple enough to use without approximating.

EXAMPLE 2

Consider an asset priced at $50. The risk-free interest rate is 8 percent, and a futures contract on the asset expires in 45 days. Answer the following, with questions A, B, C, and D independent of the others.

A. Find the appropriate futures price if the underlying asset has no storage costs, cash flows, or convenience yield.

B. Find the appropriate futures price if the future value of storage costs on the underlying asset at the futures expiration equals $2.25.

C. Find the appropriate futures price if the future value of positive cash flows on the underlying asset equals $0.75.

D. Find the appropriate futures price if the future value of the net overall cost of carry on the underlying asset equals $3.55.

E. Using Part D above, illustrate how an arbitrage transaction could be executed if the futures contract is trading at $60.

F. Using Part A above, determine the value of a long futures contract an instant before marking to market if the previous settlement price was $49.

Solution to A: First determine that $T = 45/365 = 0.1233$. Then the futures price is

$$f_0(0.1233) = \$50(1.08)^{0.1233} = \$50.48$$

Solution to B: Storage costs must be covered in the futures price, so we add them:

$$f_0(0.1233) = \$50(1.08)^{0.1233} + \$2.25 = \$52.73$$

Solution to C: A positive cash flow, such as interest or dividends on the underlying, reduces the futures price:

$$f_0(0.1233) = \$50(1.08)^{0.1233} - \$0.75 = \$49.73$$

Solution to D: The net overall cost of carry must be covered in the futures price, so we add it:

$$f_0(0.1233) = \$50(1.08)^{0.1233} + \$3.55 = \$54.03$$

Solution to E: Follow these steps:
- Sell the futures at $60.
- Buy the asset at $50.
- Because the asset price compounded at the interest rate is $50.48, the interest forgone is $0.48. So the asset price is effectively $50.48 by the time of the futures expiration.
- Incur costs of $3.55.
- At expiration, deliver the asset and receive $60. The net investment in the asset is $50.48 + $3.55 = $54.03. If the asset is sold for $60, the net gain is $5.97.

Solution to F: If the last settlement price was $49.00 and the price is now $50.48 (our answer in Part A), the value of a long futures contract equals the difference between these prices: $50.48 − $49.00 = $1.48.

7.1.8 Backwardation and Contango

Because the cost of carry, FV(CB,0,T), can be either positive or negative, the futures price can be greater or less than the spot price. Because the costs plus the interest tend to exceed the benefits, it is more common for the futures price to exceed the spot price, a situation called **contango**. In contrast, when the benefits exceed the costs plus the interest, the futures price will be less than the spot price, called **backwardation**. These terms are not particularly important in understanding the necessary concepts, but they are so commonly used that they are worthwhile to remember.

7.1.9 Futures Prices and Expected Spot Prices

An important concept when examining futures prices is the relationship between futures prices and expected spot prices. In order to fully understand the issue, let us first consider the relationship between spot prices and expected spot prices. Consider an asset with no risk, but which incurs carrying costs. At time 0, the holder of the asset purchases it with the certainty that she will cover her opportunity cost and carrying cost. Otherwise, she would not purchase the asset. Thus, the spot price at time 0 is the present value of the total of the spot price at time T less costs minus benefits:

$$S_0 = \frac{S_T - FV(CB,0,T)}{(1 + r)^T}$$

$$= \frac{S_T}{(1 + r)^T} - \frac{FV(CB,0,T)}{(1 + r)^T}$$

Because FV(CB,0,T) is the future value of the carrying cost, $FV(CB,0,T)/(1 + r)^T$ is the present value of the carrying cost. So on the one hand, we can say that the spot price is the future spot price minus the future value of the carrying cost, all discounted to the present. On the other hand, we can also say that the spot price is the discounted value of the future spot price minus the present value of the carrying cost.

If, however, the future price of the asset is uncertain, as it nearly always is, we must make some adjustments. For one, we do not know at time 0 what S_T will be. We must form an expectation, which we will denote as $E_0(S_T)$. But if we simply replace S_T above with $E_0(S_T)$ we would not be acting rationally. We would be paying a price today and expecting compensation only at the risk-free rate along with coverage of our carrying cost. Indeed, one of the most important and intuitive elements of all we know about finance is that risky assets require a risk premium. Let us denote this risk premium with the symbol, $\phi_0(S_T)$. It represents a discount off of the expected value that is imbedded in the current price, S_0. Specifically, the current price is now given as

$$S_0 = \frac{E_0(S_T) - FV(CB,0,T) - \phi_0(S_T)}{(1 + r)^T}$$

where we see that the risk premium lowers the current spot price. Intuitively, investors pay less for risky assets, all other things equal.

Until now, we have worked only with the spot price, but nothing we have said so far violates the rule of no arbitrage. Hence, our futures pricing formula, $f_0(T) = S_0(1 + r)^T + FV(CB,0,T)$, still applies. If we rearrange the futures pricing formula for FV(CB,0,T), substitute this result into the formula for S_0, and solve for the futures price, $f_0(T)$, we obtain $f_0(T) = E_0(S_T) - \phi_0(S_T)$. This equation says that the futures price equals the expected future spot price minus the risk premium.

An important conclusion to draw from this formula is that the futures price does not equal the expectation of the future spot price. The futures price would be biased on the low side. If one felt that the futures price were an unbiased predictor of the future spot price, $f_0(T) = E_0(S_T)$, one could expect on average to be able to predict the future spot price of oil by looking at the futures price of oil. But that is not likely to be the case.

The intuition behind this result is easy to see. We start with the assumption that all units of the asset must be held by someone. Holders of the asset incur the risk of its future selling price. If a holder of the asset wishes to transfer that risk by selling a futures contract, she must offer a futures contract for sale. But if the futures contract is offered at a price equal to the expected spot price, the buyer of the futures contract takes on the risk but expects to earn only a price equal to the price paid for the futures. Thus, the futures trader incurs the risk without an expected gain in the form of a risk premium. On the opposite side of the coin, the holder of the asset would have a risk-free position with an expected gain in excess of the risk-free rate. Clearly, the holder of the asset would not be able to do such a transaction. Thus, she must lower the price to a level sufficient to compensate the futures trader for the risk he is taking on. This process will lead to a futures price that equals the expected spot price minus the risk premium, as shown in the above equation. In effect, the risk premium transfers from the holder of the asset to the buyer of the futures contract.

In all fairness, however, we must acknowledge that this view is not without its opponents. Some consider the futures price an unbiased predictor of the future spot price. In such a case, the futures price would tend to overshoot and undershoot the future spot price but on average would be equal to it. For such a situation to exist would require the unreasonable assumption that there is no risk or that investors are risk neutral, meaning that they are indifferent to risk. There is, however, one other situation in which the risk premium could disappear or even turn negative. Suppose holders of the asset who want to hedge their holdings could find other parties who need to purchase the asset and who would like to hedge by going long. In that case, it should be possible for the two parties to consummate a futures transaction with the futures price equal to the expected spot price. In fact, if the parties going long exerted greater pressure than the parties going short, it might even be possible for the futures price to exceed the expected spot price.

When futures prices are lower than expected spot prices, the situation is called **normal backwardation**. When futures prices are higher than expected spot prices, it is called **normal contango**. Note the contrast with the terms backwardation and contango, which we encountered in Section 7.1.8. Backwardation means that the futures price is lower than the spot price; contango means that the futures price exceeds the spot price. Normal backwardation means that the futures price is lower than the expected spot price; normal contango means that the futures price exceeds the expected spot price.

Generally speaking, we should favor the notion that futures prices are biased predictors of future spot prices because of the transferal of the risk premium from holders of the asset to buyers of futures. Intuitively, this is the more likely case, but the other interpretations are possible. Fortunately, for our purposes, it is not critical to resolve the issue, but we do need to be aware of it.

7.2 Pricing Interest Rate Futures

We shall examine the pricing of three classes of interest rate futures contracts: Treasury bill futures, Eurodollar futures, and Treasury bond futures. In Section 6.1, we described the characteristics of these instruments and contracts. Now we look at their pricing, keeping in mind that we established the general foundations for pricing—the cost-of-carry model—in the previous section. Recall that in the cost-of-carry model, we buy the underlying asset, sell a futures contract, store the asset (which incurs costs and could generate benefits), and deliver the asset at expiration. To prevent arbitrage, the futures price is found in general as

Futures price = Spot price of underlying asset × Compounding factor
    + Costs net of monetary and nonmonetary benefits

When the underlying is a financial instrument, there will be no nonmonetary benefits and no costs other than the opportunity cost.

7.2.1 Pricing T-Bill Futures

Consider the following time line of our problem:

Time 0 is today, and time h is the expiration day of the futures contract. The T-bill underlying the contract is an m-day T-bill. Thus, when the futures expires, the T-bill is required to have m days to go before maturity. So from our perspective today, the underlying T-bill is an (h + m)-day T-bill.[32] As in Reading 62, for FRAs, h and m represent a particular number of days. In accordance with common practice, m is traditionally 90. We now introduce some necessary notation. First, where necessary, we use a simple expression, r, for the risk-free interest rate. But when pricing Treasury bill futures, we need a more flexible notation. Here we need the rates for T-bills maturing on day h and on day h + m. In addition, because interest rates can change from day 0 to day h, we need notation that distinguishes rates for different maturities and rates at different points in time.[33]

To find the spot price of the underlying asset, we need the discount rate on an (h + m)-day T-bill. Suppose we have

$$r_0^d(h), r_0^d(h + m) = \text{Discount rates in effect on day 0 of h-day}$$
$$\text{and (h + m)-day T-bills}$$

As described in Section 6, these are discount rates and convert to prices by the following formula: $B_0(j) = 1 - r_0^d(j)(j/360)$, where in this case j will either be h or h + m. Thus, the prices of h- and (h + m)-day spot T-bills on day 0 (assuming $1 face amounts) are

$$B_0(h) = 1 - r_0^d(h)\left(\frac{h}{360}\right)$$

$$B_0(h + m) = 1 - r_0^d(h + m)\left(\frac{h + m}{360}\right)$$

In other words, the h- or (h + m)-day discount rate is multiplied by the number of days in the life of the T-bill over 360 and subtracted from the face value of $1.

---

[32] It is common practice in the T-bill futures market to refer to the underlying as an m-day T-bill, but at time 0, the underlying must be an (h + m)-day T-bill in order for it to be an m-day T-bill at time h.

[33] When we assume that the interest rates are the same for all maturities and cannot change over time, which is considered acceptable when working with stock index and currency futures, we can use the simpler notation of r for the rate.

Now let us turn to the futures market. We define

$r_0^{df}(h)$ = implied discount rate on day 0 of futures contract expiring on day h, where the deliverable instrument is an m-day T-bill

$f_0(h)$ = price on day 0 of futures contract expiring on day h

The relationship between $r_0^{df}(h)$ and $f_0(h)$ is

$$f_0(h) = 1 - r_0^{df}(h)\left(\frac{m}{360}\right)$$

It is important to note that the futures price, not the implied discount rate, is the more important variable. Like any price, the futures price is determined in a market of buyers and sellers. Any rate is simply a way of transforming a price into a number that can be compared with rates on various other fixed-income instruments.[34] Do not think that a futures contract pays an interest rate. It is more appropriate to think of such a rate imbedded in a futures price as an *implied rate*, hence our use of the term *implied discount rate*. Although knowing this rate does not tell us any more than knowing the futures price, traders often refer to the futures contract in terms of the rate rather than the price.

Finally, let us note that at expiration, the futures price is the price of the underlying T-bill

$$f_h(h) = B_h(h + m)$$
$$= 1 - r_h^d(h + m)\left(\frac{m}{360}\right)$$

where $B_h(h + m)$ is the price on day h of the T-bill maturing on day h + m, and $r_h^d(h + m)$ is the discount rate on day h on the T-bill maturing on day h + m.

We now derive the futures price by constructing a risk-free portfolio that permits no arbitrage profits to be earned. This transaction is referred to as a cash-and-carry strategy, because the trader buys the asset in the cash (spot) market and carries (holds) it.

On day 0, we buy the (h + m)-day T-bill, investing $B_0(h + m)$. We simultaneously sell a futures contract at the price $f_0(h)$. On day h, we are required to deliver an m-day T-bill. The bill we purchased, which originally had h + m days to maturity, now has m days to maturity. We therefore deliver that bill and receive the original futures price. We can view this transaction as having paid $B_0(h + m)$ on day 0 and receiving $f_0(h)$. Because $f_0(h)$ is known on day 0, this transaction is risk free. It should thus earn the same return per dollar invested as would a T-bill purchased on day 0 that matures on day h. The return per dollar invested from the arbitrage transaction would be $f_0(h)/B_0(h + m)$, and

---

[34] To further reinforce the notion that an interest rate is just a transformation of a price, consider a zero-coupon bond selling at $95 and using 360 days as a year. The price can be transformed into a rate in the manner of $1/0.95 - 1 = 0.0526$ or 5.26 percent. But using the convention of the Treasury bill market, the rate is expressed as a discount rate. Then $0.95 = 1 - \text{Rate} \times (360/360)$, and the rate would be 0.05 or 5 percent. A price can be converted into a rate in a number of other ways, such as by assuming different compound periods. The price of any asset is determined in a market-clearing process. The rate is just a means of transforming the price so that interest rate instruments and their derivatives can be discussed in a more comparable manner.

the return per dollar invested in an h-day T-bill would be $1/B_0(h)$.[35] Consequently, we set these values equal:

$$\frac{f_0(h)}{B_0(h + m)} = \frac{1}{B_0(h)}$$

Solving for the futures price, we obtain

$$f_0(h) = \frac{B_0(h + m)}{B_0(h)}$$

In other words, the futures price is the ratio of the longer-term bill price to the shorter-term bill price. This price is, in fact, the same as the forward price from the term structure. In fact, as we noted above, futures prices and forward prices will be equal under the assumptions we have made so far and will follow throughout this book.

Recall that we previously demonstrated that the futures price should equal the spot price plus the cost of carry. Yet the above formula looks nothing like this result. In fact, however, it is consistent with the cost-of-carry formula. First, the above formula can be written as

$$f_0(h) = B_0(h + m)\left[\frac{1}{B_0(h)}\right]$$

As noted above, the expression $1/B_0(h)$ can be identified as the return per dollar invested over h days, which simplifies to $[1 + r_0(h)]^{h/365}$, which is essentially a **compound interest** factor for h days at the rate $r_0(h)$. Note that h is the number of days, assuming 365 in a year. For the period ending at day h, the above formula becomes

$$f_0(h) = B_0(h + m)[1 + r_0(h)]^{h/365} \qquad \textbf{(63-8)}$$

and the futures price is seen to equal the spot price of the underlying compounded at the interest rate, which simply reflects the opportunity cost of the money tied up for h days.

Note that what we have been doing is deriving the appropriate price for a futures contract. In a market with no arbitrage opportunities, the actual futures price would be this theoretical price. Let us suppose for a moment, however, that the actual futures price is something else, say $f_0(h)^*$. The spot price is, of course, $B_0(h + m)$. Using these two numbers, we can infer the implied rate of return from a transaction involving the purchase of the T-bill and sale of the futures. We have

$$f_0(h)^* = B_0(h + m)[1 + r_0(h)^*]^{h/365}$$

where $r_0(h)^*$ is the implied rate of return. Solving for $r_0(h)^*$ we obtain

$$r_0(h)^* = \left[\frac{f_0(h)^*}{B_0(h + m)}\right]^{365/h} - 1 \qquad \textbf{(63-9)}$$

---

[35] For example, if a one-year $1 face value T-bill is selling for $0.90, the return per dollar invested is $1/$0.90 = 1.1111.

This rate of return, $r_0(h)^*$, has a special name, the **implied repo rate**. It is the rate of return from a cash-and-carry transaction that is implied by the futures price relative to the spot price. Traders who engage in such transactions often obtain the funds to do so in the repurchase agreement (repo) market. The implied repo rate tells the trader what rate of return to expect from the strategy. If the financing rate available in the repo market is less than the implied repo rate, the strategy is worthwhile and would generate an arbitrage profit. If the trader could lend in the repo market at greater than the implied repo rate, the appropriate strategy would be to reverse the transaction—selling the T-bill short and buying the futures—turning the strategy into a source of financing that would cost less than the rate at which the funds could be lent in the repo market.[36]

The implied repo rate is the rate of return implied by the strategy of buying the asset and selling the futures. As noted above, the futures price is often expressed in terms of an implied discount rate. Remember that the buyer of a futures contract is committing to buy a T-bill at the price $f_0(h)$. In the convention of pricing a T-bill by subtracting a discount rate from par value, the implied discount rate would be

$$r_0^{df}(h) = [1 - f_0(h)]\left(\frac{360}{m}\right)$$

(63-10)

We can also determine this implied discount rate from the discount rates on the h- and (h + m)-day T-bills as follows:[37]

$$r_0^{df}(h) = \left\{1 - \left[\frac{1 - r_0^d(h + m)\left(\frac{h + m}{360}\right)}{1 - r_0^d(h)\left(\frac{h}{360}\right)}\right]\right\}\left(\frac{360}{m}\right)$$

Now let us look at an example. We are interested in pricing a futures contract expiring in 30 days. A 30-day T-bill has a discount rate of 6 percent, and a 120-day T-bill has a discount rate of 6.6 percent. With h = 30 and h + m = 120, we have

$$r_0^d(h) = r_0^d(30) = 0.06$$
$$r_0^d(h + m) = r_0^d(120) = 0.066$$

The prices of these T-bills will, therefore, be

$$B_0(h) = 1 - r_0^d(h)\left(\frac{h}{360}\right)$$

$$B_0(30) = 1 - 0.06\left(\frac{30}{360}\right) = 0.9950$$

$$B_0(h + m) = 1 - r_0^d(h + m)\left(\frac{h + m}{360}\right)$$

$$B_0(120) = 1 - 0.066\left(\frac{120}{360}\right) = 0.9780$$

---

[36] The concepts of a cash-and-carry strategy and the implied repo rate are applicable to any type of futures contract, but we cover them only with respect to T-bill futures.

[37] This formula is found by substituting $1 - r_0^d(h + m)[(h + m)/360]$ for $B_0(h + m)$ and $1 - r_0^d(h)(h/360)$ for $B_0(h)$ in the above equation for $r_0^{df}(h)$. This procedure expresses the spot prices in terms of their respective discount rates.

Using the formula we derived, we have the price of a futures expiring in 30 days as

$$f_0(h) = \frac{B_0(h+m)}{B_0(h)}$$

$$f_0(30) = \frac{B_0(120)}{B_0(30)} = \frac{0.9780}{0.9950} = 0.9829$$

The discount rate implied by the futures price would be

$$r_0^{df}(h) = [1 - f_0(h)]\left(\frac{360}{m}\right)$$

$$r_0^{df}(30) = (1 - 0.9829)\left(\frac{360}{90}\right) = 0.0684$$

In other words, in the T-bill futures market, the rate would be stated as 6.84 percent, which would imply a futures price of 0.9829.[38] Alternatively, the implied futures discount rate could be obtained from the spot discount rates as

$$r_0^{df}(h) = \left\{1 - \left[\frac{1 - r_0^d(h+m)\left(\frac{h+m}{360}\right)}{1 - r_0^d(h)\left(\frac{h}{360}\right)}\right]\right\}\left(\frac{360}{m}\right)$$

$$r_0^{df}(30) = \left\{1 - \left[\frac{1 - 0.066\left(\frac{120}{360}\right)}{1 - 0.06\left(\frac{30}{360}\right)}\right]\right\}\left(\frac{360}{90}\right) = 0.0683$$

with a slight difference due to rounding.

To verify this result, one would buy the 120-day T-bill for 0.9780 and sell the futures at a price of 0.9829. Then, 30 days later, the T-bill would be a 90-day T-bill and would be delivered to settle the futures contract. The trader would receive the original futures price of 0.9829. The return per dollar invested would be

$$\frac{0.9829}{0.9780} = 1.0050$$

If, instead, the trader had purchased a 30-day T-bill at the price of 0.9950 and held it for 30 days, the return per dollar invested would be

$$\frac{1}{0.9950} = 1.0050$$

Thus, the purchase of the 120-day T-bill with its price in 30 days hedged by the sale of the futures contract is equivalent to purchasing a 30-day T-bill and holding it to maturity. Each transaction has the same return per dollar invested and is free of risk.

---

[38] We should also probably note that the IMM Index would be $100 - 6.84 = 93.16$. Thus, the futures price would be quoted in the market as 93.16.

Suppose in the market, the futures price is 0.9850. The implied repo rate would be

$$r_0(h)* = \left[\frac{f_0(h)*}{B_0(h + m)}\right]^{365/h} - 1$$

$$= \left(\frac{0.9850}{0.9780}\right)^{365/30} - 1 = 0.0906$$

Buying the 120-day T-bill for 0.9780 and selling a futures for 0.9850 generates a rate of return of $0.9850/0.9780 - 1 = 0.007157$. Annualizing this rate, $(1.007157)^{365/30} - 1 = 0.0906$. If financing could be obtained in the repo market for less than this annualized rate, the strategy would be attractive. If the trader could lend in the repo market at higher than this rate, he should buy the futures and sell short the T-bill to implicitly borrow at 9.06 percent and lend in the repo market at a higher rate.

Let us now recap the pricing of Treasury bill futures. We buy an $(h + m)$-day bond and sell a futures expiring on day h, which calls for delivery of an m-day T-bill. The futures price should be the price of the $(h + m)$-day T-bill compounded at the h-day risk-free rate. That rate is the rate of return on an h-day bill. The futures price can also be obtained as the ratio of the price of the $(h + m)$-day T-bill to the price of the h-day T-bill. Alternatively, we can express the futures price in terms of an implied discount rate, and we can derive the price in terms of the discount rates on the $(h + m)$-day T-bill and the h-day T-bill. Finally, remember that the actual futures price in the market relative to the price of the $(h + m)$-day T-bill implies a rate of return called the implied repo rate. The implied repo rate can be compared with the rate in the actual repo market to determine the attractiveness of an arbitrage transaction.

Exhibit 8 summarizes the important formulas involved in the pricing of T-bill futures. We then turn to the pricing of another short-term interest rate futures contract, the Eurodollar futures.

EXHIBIT 8   Pricing Formulas for T-Bill Futures Contract

Futures price = Underlying T-bill price compounded at risk-free rate

Futures price in terms of spot T-bills:

$$f_0(h) = \frac{B_0(h + m)}{B_0(h)}$$

Futures price as spot price compounded at risk-free rate:

$$f_0(h) = B_0(h + m)[1 + r_0(h)]^{h/365}$$

Discount rate implied by futures price:

$$r_0^{df}(h) = [1 - f_0(h)]\left(\frac{360}{m}\right) = \left\{1 - \left[\frac{1 - r_0^d(h + m)\left(\frac{h + m}{360}\right)}{1 - r_0^d(h)\left(\frac{h}{360}\right)}\right]\right\}\left(\frac{360}{m}\right)$$

Implied repo rate:

$$r_0(h)* = \left[\frac{f_0(h)*}{B_0(h + m)}\right]^{365/h} - 1$$

EXAMPLE 3

A futures contract on a Treasury bill expires in 50 days. The T-bill matures in 140 days. The discount rates on T-bills are as follows:

50-day bill: 5.0 percent
140-day bill: 4.6 percent

A. Find the appropriate futures price by using the prices of the 50- and 140-day T-bills.

B. Find the futures price in terms of the underlying spot price compounded at the appropriate risk-free rate.

C. Convert the futures price to the implied discount rate on the futures.

D. Now assume that the futures contract is trading in the market at an implied discount rate 10 basis points lower than is appropriate, given the pricing model and the rule of no arbitrage. Demonstrate how an arbitrage transaction could be executed and show the outcome. Calculate the implied repo rate and discuss how it would be used to determine the profitability of the arbitrage.

Solution to A: First, find the prices of the 50- and 140-day bonds:

$$B_0(50) = 1 - 0.05(50/360) = 0.9931$$
$$B_0(140) = 1 - 0.046(140/360) = 0.9821$$

The futures price is, therefore,

$$f_0(50) = \frac{0.9821}{0.9931} = 0.9889$$

Solution to B: First, find the rate at which to compound the spot price of the 140-day T-bill. This rate is obtained from the 50-day T-bill:

$$[1 + r_0(h)]^{h/365} = \frac{1}{0.9931} = 1.0069$$

We actually do not need to solve for $r_0(h)$. The above says that based on the rate $r_0(h)$, every dollar invested should grow to a value of 1.0069. Thus, the futures price should be the spot price (the price of the 140-day T-bill) compounded by the factor 1.0069:

$$f_0(50) = 0.9821(1.0069) = 0.9889$$

Annualized, this rate would equal $(1.0069)^{365/50} - 1 = 0.0515$.

Solution to C: Given the futures price of 0.9889, the implied discount rate is

$$r_0^{df}(50) = (1 - 0.9889)\left(\frac{360}{90}\right)$$
$$= 0.0444$$

Solution to D: If the futures is trading for 10 basis points lower, it trades at a rate of 4.34 percent, so the futures price would be

$$f_0(50) = 1 - 0.0434 \left(\frac{90}{360} \right)$$
$$= 0.9892$$

Do the following:

▶ Buy the 140-day bond at 0.9821
▶ Sell the futures at 0.9892

This strategy provides a return per dollar invested of

$$\frac{0.9892}{0.9821} = 1.0072$$

which compares favorably with a return per dollar invested of 1.0069 if the futures is correctly priced.

The implied repo rate is simply the annualization of this rate: $(1.0072)^{365/50} - 1 = 0.0538$. The cash-and-carry transaction would, therefore, earn 5.38 percent. Because the futures appears to be mispriced, we could likely obtain financing in the repo market at less than this rate.

OPTIONAL SEGMENT

ENDS

7.2.2 Pricing Eurodollar Futures

Based on the T-bill case, it is tempting to argue that the interest rate implied by the Eurodollar futures price would be the forward rate in the term structure of LIBOR. Unfortunately, that is not quite the case. In fact, the unusual construction of the Eurodollar futures contract relative to the Eurodollar spot market means that no risk-free combination of a Eurodollar time deposit and a Eurodollar futures contract can be constructed. Recall that the Eurodollar time deposit is an add-on instrument. Using $L_0(j)$ as the rate (LIBOR) on a j-day Eurodollar time deposit on day 0, if one deposits \$1, the deposit will grow to a value of $1 + L_0(j)(j/360)$ j days later. So, the present value of \$1 in j days is $1/[1 + L_0(j)(j/360)]$. The Eurodollar futures contract, however, is structured like the T-bill contract—as though the underlying were a discount instrument. So its price is stated in the form of $1 - L_0(j)(j/360)$. If we try the same arbitrage with Eurodollars that we did with T-bills, we cannot get the LIBOR that determines the spot price of a Eurodollar at expiration to offset the LIBOR that determines the futures price at expiration.

In other words, suppose that on day 0 we buy an (h + m)-day Eurodollar deposit that pays \$1 on day (h + m) and sell a futures at a price of $f_0(h)$. On day h, the futures expiration, the Eurodollar deposit has m days to go and is worth $1/[1 + L_h(m)(m/360)]$. The futures price at expiration is $f_h(h) = 1 - L_h(m)(m/360)$. The profit from the futures is $f_0(h) - [1 - L_h(m)(m/360)]$.

Adding this amount to the value of the m-day Eurodollar deposit we are holding gives a total position value of

$$\frac{1}{1 + L_h(m)\left(\dfrac{m}{360}\right)} + f_0(h) - [1 - L_h(m)]\left(\frac{m}{360}\right)$$

Although $f_0(h)$ is known when the transaction is initiated, $L_h(m)$ is not determined until the futures expiration. There is no way for the $L_h(m)$ terms to offset. This problem does not occur in the T-bill market because the spot price is a discount instrument and the futures contract is designed as a discount instrument.[39] It is, nonetheless, common for participants in the futures market to treat the Eurodollar rate as equivalent to the implied forward rate. Such an assumption would require the ability to conduct the risk-free arbitrage, which, as we have shown, is impossible. The differences are fairly small, but we shall not assume that the Eurodollar futures rate should equal the implied forward rate. In that case, it would take a more advanced model to solve the pricing problem. The essential points in pricing interest rate futures on short-term instruments can be understood by studying the T-bill futures market.

This mismatch in the design of spot and futures instruments in the Eurodollar market would appear to make the contract difficult to use as a hedging instrument. Note that in the above equation for the payoff of the portfolio combining a spot Eurodollar time deposit and a short Eurodollar futures contract, an increase (decrease) in LIBOR lowers (raises) the value of the spot Eurodollar deposit and raises (lowers) the payoff from the short Eurodollar futures. Thus, the Eurodollar futures contract can still serve as a hedging tool. The hedge will not be perfect but can still be quite effective. Indeed, the Eurodollar futures contract is a major hedging tool of dealers in over-the-counter derivatives.

We have now completed the treatment of futures contracts on short-term interest rate instruments. Now let us look at the pricing of Treasury bond futures.

7.2.3 Pricing Treasury Note and Bond Futures

Recall that in Section 6.2, we described the bond futures contract as one in which there are a number of deliverable bonds. When a given bond is delivered, the long pays the short the futures price times an adjustment term called the conversion factor. The conversion factor is the price of a $1 bond with coupon equal to that of the deliverable bond and yield equal to 6 percent, with calculations based on semiannual compounding. Bonds with a coupon greater (less) than 6 percent will have a conversion factor greater (less) than 1. Before we delve into the complexities added by this feature, however, let us start off by assuming a fairly generic type of contract: one in which the underlying is a single, specific bond.

---

[39] It is not clear why the Chicago Mercantile Exchange designed the Eurodollar contract as a discount instrument when the underlying Eurodollar deposit is an add-on instrument. The most likely reason is that the T-bill futures contract was already trading, was successful, and its design was well understood and accepted by traders. The CME most likely felt that this particular design was successful and should be continued with the Eurodollar contract. Ironically, the Eurodollar contract became exceptionally successful and the T-bill contract now has virtually no trading volume.

When examining bond forward contracts in Reading 62, we specified a time line and notation. We return to that specific time line and notation, which differs from those we used for examining short-term interest rate futures.

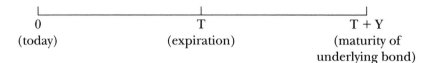

0	T	T + Y
(today)	(expiration)	(maturity of underlying bond)

Recall our notation from Reading 62:

$B_0^c(T + Y)$ = price at time 0 of coupon bond that matures at time T+Y. The bond has a maturity of Y at the futures expiration.

CI_i = coupon at time t_i, where the coupons occur at times t_1, t_2, ..., t_n. Note that we care only about coupons prior to the futures expiration at T.

$f_0(T)$ = price at time 0 of futures expiring at time T.

$B_0(T)$ = price at time 0 of zero-coupon bond maturing at T.

We also need to know at time T the accumulated value of all coupons received over the period from 0 to T. We need the compound value from 0 to T of any coupons paid during the time the futures contract is alive. This value is denoted as FV(CI,0,T). We introduced this variable in Reading 62 and showed how to compute it, so you may wish to review that material. It is traditionally assumed that the interest rate at which these coupons are reinvested is known. We also assume that this interest rate applies to the period from 0 to T for money borrowed or lent. We denote this rate as

$r_0(T)$ = Interest rate at time 0 for period until time T

As described in the section on T-bill futures pricing, this is the rate that determines the price of a zero-coupon bond maturing at T.[40] Hence,

$$B_0(T) = \frac{1}{[1 + r_0(T)]^T}$$

The futures price at expiration is the price of the deliverable bond at expiration:

$$f_T(T) = B_T(T + Y)$$

Now we are ready to price this bond futures contract. On day 0, we buy the bond at the price $B_0^c(T + Y)$ and sell the futures at the price $f_0(T)$. Because the futures does not require any cash up front, its initial value is zero. The current value of the overall transaction is, therefore, just the value of the bond, $B_0^c(T + Y)$. This value represents the amount of money we must invest to engage in this transaction.

We hold this position until the futures expiration. During this time, we collect and reinvest the coupons. On day T, the futures expires. We deliver the bond and receive the futures price, $f_0(T)$. We also have the reinvested coupons, which

---

[40] Keep in mind, however, that this rate is not the discount rate that determines the price of the zero-coupon bond maturing at T. It is the rate of return, expressed as an annual rate. When working with T-bills, the symbol "T" represented Days/365, which is consistent with its use here with T-bonds.

have a value at T of FV(CI,0,T). These two amounts, $f_0(T)$ and FV(CI,0,T), are known when the transaction was initiated at time 0, so the transaction is risk-free. Therefore, the current value of the transaction, $B_0^c(T + Y)$, should be the discounted value of its value at T of $f_0(T) + $ FV(CI,0,T):

$$B_0^c(T + Y) = \frac{f_0(T) + FV(CI,0,T)}{[1 + r_0(T)]^T}$$

Note that we are simply discounting the known future value at T of the transaction at the risk-free rate of $r_0(T)$.[41]

We are, of course, more interested in the futures price, which is the only unknown in the above equation. Solving, we obtain

$$f_0(T) = B_0^c(T + Y)[1 + r_0(T)]^T - FV(CI,0,T) \qquad \textbf{(63-11)}$$

This equation is a variation of our basic cost-of-carry formula. The spot price, $B_0^c(T + Y)$, is compounded at the risk-free interest rate. We then subtract the compound future value of the reinvested coupons over the life of the contract. The coupon interest is like a negative cost of carry; it is a positive cash flow associated with holding the underlying bond.

Now let us work an example. Consider a \$1 face value Treasury bond that pays interest at 7 percent semiannually. Thus, each coupon is \$0.035. The bond has exactly five years remaining, so during that time it will pay 10 coupons, each six months apart. The yield on the bond is 8 percent. The price of the bond is found by calculating the present value of both the 10 coupons and the face value: The price is \$0.9594.

Now consider a futures contract that expires in one year and three months: T = 1.25. The risk-free rate, $r_0(T)$, is 6.5 percent. The accumulated value of the coupons and the interest on them is

$$\$0.035(1.065)^{0.75} + \$0.035(1.065)^{0.25} = \$0.0722$$

The first coupon is paid in one-half a year and reinvests for three-quarters of a year. The second coupon is paid in one year and reinvests for one-quarter of a year.

Now the futures price is obtained as

$$f_0(T) = B_0^c(T + Y)[1 + r_0(T)]^T - FV(CI,0,T)$$
$$f_0(1.25) = \$0.9594(1.065)^{1.25} - \$0.0722 = \$0.9658$$

This is the price at which the futures should trade, given current market conditions. To verify this result, buy the five-year bond for \$0.9594 and sell the futures for \$0.9658. Hold the position for 15 months until the futures expiration. Collect and reinvest the coupons. When the futures expires, deliver the bond and receive the futures price of \$0.9658. Then add the reinvested coupons of \$0.0722 for a total of \$0.9658 + \$0.0722 = \$1.0380. If we invest \$0.9594 and end up with \$1.0380 15 months later, the return is \$1.0380/\$0.9594 = 1.0819. For comparison purposes, we should determine the annual equivalent of this rate, which is found as $(1.0819)^{1/1.25} - 1 = 0.065$. This is the same 6.5 percent risk-free rate. If the futures contract trades at a higher price, the above transaction would result

---

[41] We shall not take up the topic of the implied repo rate again, but note that if the futures is selling for $f_0(T)$, then $r_0(T)$ would be the implied repo rate.

in a return greater than 6.5 percent. The amount available at expiration would be higher, clearly leading to a rate of return higher than 6.5 percent. If the futures trades at a lower price, the arbitrageur would sell short the bond and buy the futures, which would generate a cash inflow today. The amount paid back would be at less than the risk-free rate of 6.5 percent.[42]

Unfortunately, we now must complicate the matter a little by moving to the more realistic case with a delivery option. Bond futures contracts traditionally permit the short to choose which bond to deliver. This feature reduces the possibility of unusual price behavior of the deliverable bond caused by holders of short positions scrambling to buy a single deliverable bond at expiration. By allowing more than one bond to be deliverable, such problems are avoided. The contract is structured as though there is a standard hypothetical deliverable bond, which has a given coupon rate. The Chicago Board of Trade's contract uses a 6 percent rate. If the short delivers a bond with a higher (lower) coupon rate, the price received at delivery is adjusted upward (downward). The conversion factor is defined and calculated as the price of a $1 face value bond with a coupon and maturity equal to that of the deliverable bond and a yield of 6 percent. Each deliverable bond has its own conversion factor. The short designates which bond he will deliver, and that bond's conversion factor is multiplied by the final futures price to determine the amount the long will pay the short for the bond.

The availability of numerous deliverable bonds creates some confusion in pricing the futures contract, arising from the fact that the underlying cannot be uniquely identified, at least not on the surface. This confusion has given rise to the concept that one bond is always the best one to deliver. If a trader buys a given bond and sells the futures, he creates a risk-free hedge. If there are no arbitrage opportunities, the return from that hedge cannot exceed the risk-free rate. That return can, however, be *less* than the risk-free rate. How can this be? In all previous cases, if a return from a risk-free transaction is less than the risk-free rate, it should be a simple matter to reverse the transaction and capture an arbitrage profit. In this case, however, a reverse transaction would not work. If the arbitrageur sells short the bond and buys the futures, she must be assured that the short will deliver the bond from which the potential arbitrage profit was computed. But the short makes the delivery decision and in all likelihood would not deliver that particular bond.

Thus, the short can be long a bond and short futures and earn a return less than the risk-free rate. One bond, however, results in a return closest to the risk-free rate. Clearly that bond is the best bond to deliver. The terminology in the business is that this bond is the cheapest to deliver.

The cheapest-to-deliver bond is determined by selecting a given bond and computing the rate of return from buying that bond and selling the futures to hedge its delivery at expiration. This calculation is performed for all bonds. The one with the highest rate of return is the cheapest to deliver.[43] The cheapest-to-deliver bond can change, however, which can benefit the short and not the long. We ignore the details of determining the cheapest-to-deliver bond and assume that it has been identified. From here, we proceed to price the futures.

Let $CF(T)$ be the conversion factor for the bond we have identified as the cheapest to deliver. Now we go back to the arbitrage transaction described for the case where there is only one deliverable bond. Recall that we buy the bond, sell a futures, and reinvest the coupons on the bond. At expiration, we deliver the bond, receive the futures price $f_0(T)$, and have the reinvested coupons,

---

[42] Again, as in the section on T-bill futures, this analysis could be conducted in terms of the implied repo rate.

[43] As noted, this rate of return will not exceed the risk-free rate but will be the highest rate below the risk-free rate.

which are worth $FV(CI,0,T)$. Now, in the case where the futures contract has many deliverable bonds, we must recognize that when the bond is delivered, the long pays $f_0(T)$ times $CF(T)$. This adjustment does not add any risk to this risk-free transaction. Thus, the present value of the amount received at delivery, $f_0(T)CF(T) + FV(CI,0,T)$, should still equal the original price of the bond, which was the amount we invested to initiate the transaction:

$$B_0^c(T + Y) = \frac{f_0(T)CF(T) + FV(CI,0,T)}{[1 + r_0(T)]^T}$$

Solving for the futures price, we obtain

$$f_0(T) = \frac{B_0^c(T + Y)[1 + r_0(T)]^T - FV(CI,0,T)}{CF(T)} \qquad \textbf{(63-12)}$$

Note that when we had only one deliverable bond, the formula did not have the $CF(T)$ term, but a better way to look at it is that for only one deliverable bond, the conversion factor is effectively 1, so Equation 63-12 would still apply.

Consider the same example we previously worked, but now we need a conversion factor. As noted above, the conversion factor is the price of a \$1 bond with coupon and maturity equal to that of the deliverable bond on the expiration day and yield of 6 percent, with all calculations made assuming semiannual interest payments. As noted, we shall skip the specifics of this calculation here; it is simply a present value calculation. For this example, the 7 percent bond with maturity of three and three-quarter years on the delivery day would have a conversion factor of 1.0505. Thus, the futures price would be

$$f_0(T) = \frac{B_0^c(T + Y)[1 + r_0(T)]^T - FV(CI,0,T)}{CF(T)}$$

$$f_0(1.25) = \frac{0.9594(1.065)^{1.25} - 0.0722}{1.0505} = 0.9193$$

If the futures is priced higher than 0.9193, one can buy the bond and sell the futures to earn more than the risk-free rate. If the futures price is less than 0.9193, one can sell short the bond and buy the futures to end up borrowing at less than the risk-free rate. As noted previously, however, this transaction has a complication: If one goes short the bond and long the futures, this bond must remain the cheapest to deliver. Otherwise, the short will not deliver this particular bond and the arbitrage will not be successful.

Exhibit 9 reviews the important formulas for pricing Treasury bond futures contracts.

EXAMPLE 4

Consider a three-year \$1 par Treasury bond with a 7.5 percent annual yield and 8 percent semiannual coupon. Its price is \$1.0132. A futures contract calling for delivery of this bond only expires in one year. The one-year risk-free rate is 7 percent.

A. Find the future value in one year of the coupons on this bond. Assume a reinvestment rate of 3.75 percent per six-month period.

B. Find the appropriate futures price.

> **C.** Now suppose the bond is one of many deliverable bonds. The contract specification calls for the use of a conversion factor to determine the price paid for a given deliverable bond. Suppose the bond described here has a conversion factor of 1.0372. Now determine the appropriate futures price.
>
> **Solution to A:** One coupon of 0.04 will be invested for half a year at 3.75 percent (half of the rate of 7.5 percent). The other coupon is not reinvested but is still counted. Thus, $FV(CI,0,1) = 0.04(1.0375) + 0.04 = 0.0815$.
>
> **Solution to B:** $f_0(1) = 1.0132(1.07) - 0.0815 = 1.0026$
>
> **Solution to C:** $f_0(1) = \dfrac{1.0132(1.07) - 0.0815}{1.0372} = 0.9667$

EXHIBIT 9	Pricing Formulas for Treasury Bond Futures Contract

Futures price = Underlying T-bond price compounded at risk-free rate less Compound future value of reinvested coupons.

Futures price if underlying bond is the only deliverable bond:

$$f_0(T) = B_0^c(T + Y)[1 + r_0(T)]^T - FV(CI,0,T)$$

Futures price when there are multiple deliverable bonds:

$$f_0(T) = \frac{B_0^c(T + Y)[1 + r_0(T)]^T - FV(CI,0,T)}{CF(T)}$$

7.3 Pricing Stock Index Futures

Now let the underlying be either a portfolio of stocks or an individual stock.[44] The former are normally referred to as stock index futures, in which the portfolio is identical in composition to an underlying index of stocks. In this material, we focus on the pricing of stock index futures, but the principles are the same if the underlying is an individual stock.

In pricing stock index futures, we must account for the fact that the underlying stocks pay dividends.[45] Recall that in our previous discussions about the generic pricing of futures, we demonstrated that the futures price is lower as a result of the compound future value of any cash flows paid on the asset. Such cash flows consist of coupon interest payments if the underlying is a bond, or

---

[44] Futures on individual stocks have taken a long time to develop, primarily because of regulatory hurdles. They were introduced in the United States in late 2002 and, as of the publication date of this book, have achieved only modest trading volume. They currently trade in a few other countries such as the United Kingdom and Australia.

[45] Even if not all of the stocks pay dividends, at least some of the stocks almost surely pay dividends.

storage costs if the underlying incurs costs to store.[46] Dividends work exactly like coupon interest.

Consider the same time line we used before. Today is time 0, and the futures expires at time T. During the life of the futures, there are n dividends of $D_j, j = 1, 2, \ldots, n$. We assume these dividends are all known when the futures contract is initiated. Let

FV(D,0,T) = the compound value over the period of 0 to T of all dividends collected and reinvested

We introduced this variable in Reading 62 and showed how to compute it, so you may wish to review that material. The other notation is the same we have previously used:

S_0 = current value of the stock index

$f_0(T)$ = futures price today of a contract that expires at T

r = risk-free interest rate over the period 0 to T

Now that we are no longer working with interest rate futures, we do not need the more flexible notation for interest rates on bonds of different maturities or interest rates at different time points. So we can use the simple notation of r as the risk-free interest rate, but we must keep in mind that it is the risk-free rate for the time period from 0 to T.

We undertake the following transaction: On day 0, we buy the stock portfolio that replicates the index. This transaction will require that we invest the amount S_0. We simultaneously sell the futures at the price $f_0(T)$.

On day T, the futures expires. We deliver the stock and receive the original futures price $f_0(T)$.[47] We also have the accumulated value of the reinvested dividends, FV(D,0,T) for a total of $f_0(T) + FV(D,0,T)$. Because this amount is known at time 0, the transaction is risk free. Therefore, we should discount its value at the risk-free rate and set this equal to the initial value of the portfolio, S_0, as follows:

$$S_0 = \frac{f_0(T) + FV(D,0,T)}{(1 + r)^T}$$

Solving for the futures price gives

$$f_0(T) = S_0(1 + r)^T - FV(D,0,T)$$ (63-13)

which is the cost-of-carry formula for stock index futures. Notice that it is virtually identical to that for bond futures. Ignoring the conversion factor necessitated by the delivery option, the only difference is that we use the compound future value of the dividends instead of the compound future value of the coupon interest.

Consider the following example. A stock index is at 1,452.45, and a futures contract on the index expires in three months. Thus, $T = 3/12 = 0.25$. The risk-free interest rate is 5.5 percent. The value of the dividends reinvested over the life of the futures is 7.26. The futures price should, therefore, be

$$f_0(T) = S_0(1 + r)^T - FV(D,0,T)$$
$$f_0(0.25) = 1,452.45(1.055)^{0.25} - 7.26$$
$$= 1,464.76$$

[46] We also allowed for the possibility of noncash costs, which we called the convenience yield, but there are no implicit costs or benefits associated with stock index futures.

[47] Virtually all stock index futures contracts call for cash settlement at expiration. See the explanation of the equivalence of delivery and cash settlement in Section 4 and Exhibit 2.

Thus, if the futures contract is selling for more than this price, an arbitrageur can buy the stocks and sell the futures. The arbitrageur would collect and reinvest the dividends and at expiration would receive a gain that would exceed the risk-free rate of 5.5 percent, a result of receiving more than 1,464.76 for the stocks. If the futures contract is selling for less than this price, the arbitrageur can sell short the stocks and buy the futures. After paying the dividends while holding the stocks,[48] the arbitrageur will end up buying back the stocks at a price that implies that he has borrowed money and paid it back at a rate less than the risk-free rate. The combined activities of all arbitrageurs will force the futures price to 1,464.76.

The stock index futures pricing formula has a number of variations. Suppose we define $FV(D,0,T)/(1 + r)^T$ as the present value of the dividends, $PV(D,0,T)$:

$$FV(D,0,T) = PV(D,0,T)(1 + r)^T$$

Substituting in the futures pricing formula above for $FV(D,0,T)$, we obtain

$$f_0(T) = [S_0 - PV(D,0,T)](1 + r)^T \qquad \textbf{(63-14)}$$

Notice here that the stock price is reduced by the present value of the dividends. This adjusted stock price is then compounded at the risk-free rate over the life of the futures.

In the problem we worked above, the present value of the dividends is found as

$$PV(D,0,T) = \frac{FV(D,0,T)}{(1 + r)^T}$$

$$PV(D,0,0.25) = \frac{7.26}{(1.055)^{0.25}} = 7.16$$

Then the futures price would be

$$f_0(T) = [S_0 - PV(D,0,T)](1 + r)^T$$
$$f_0(0.25) = (1,452.45 - 7.16)(1.055)^{0.25}$$
$$= 1,464.76$$

Another variation of the formula defines the yield as δ in the following manner:

$$\frac{1}{(1 + \delta)^T} = 1 - \frac{FV(D,0,T)}{S_0(1 + r)^T}$$

The exact solution for δ is somewhat complex, so we shall just leave it in the form above. Using this specification, we find that the futures pricing formula would be

$$f_0(T) = \left(\frac{S_0}{(1 + \delta)^T}\right)(1 + r)^T \qquad \textbf{(63-15)}$$

The stock price is, thus, discounted at the dividend yield, and this adjusted stock price is then compounded at the risk-free rate over the life of the futures.[49]

---

[48] Remember that a short seller must make restitution for any dividends paid while the position is short.

[49] Sometimes the futures price is written as $f_0(T) = S_0(1 + r - \delta)^T$ where the dividend yield is simply subtracted from the risk-free rate to give a net cost of carry. This formula is a rough approximation that we do not consider acceptable.

In the example above, the yield calculation is

$$\frac{1}{(1 + \delta)^T} = 1 - \frac{FV(D,0,T)}{S_0(1 + r)^T}$$

$$\frac{1}{(1 + \delta)^T} = 1 - \frac{7.26}{1,452.45(1.055)^{0.25}} = 0.9951$$

Then $(1 + \delta)^T$ is $1/0.9951 = 1.0049$ and the futures price is

$$f_0(T) = \left(\frac{S_0}{(1 + \delta)^T}\right)(1 + r)^T$$

$$f_0(0.25) = \left(\frac{1,452.45}{1.0049}\right)(1.055)^{0.25}$$

$$= 1,464.84$$

The difference between this and the answer we previously obtained is strictly caused by a rounding error.

Another variation of this formula is to express the yield as

$$\delta* = \frac{PV(D,0,T)}{S_0} = \frac{FV(D,0,T)/(1 + r)^T}{S_0}$$

This means that $FV(D,0,T) = S_0(1 + r)^T\delta*$. Substituting into our futures pricing formula for $FV(D,0,T)$, we obtain

$$f_0(T) = S_0(1 - \delta*)(1 + r)^T \qquad \textbf{(63-16)}$$

Here again, the stock price is reduced by the yield, and this "adjusted" stock price is compounded at the risk-free rate.

In the problem we worked above, the yield would be found as

$$\delta* = \frac{PV(D,0,T)}{S_0}$$

$$\delta* = \frac{7.16}{1,452.45} = 0.0049$$

Then the futures price would be

$$f_0(T) = S_0(1 - \delta*)(1 + r)^T$$

$$f_0(0.25) = 1,452.45(1 - 0.0049)(1.055)^{0.25}$$

$$= 1,464.81$$

Again, the difference between the two prices comes from rounding.

A common variation uses the assumption of continuous compounding. The continuously compounded risk-free rate is defined as $r^c = \ln(1 + r)$. The continuously compounded dividend yield is $\delta^c = \ln(1 + \delta)$. When working with discrete dividends, we obtained the relationship

$$\frac{1}{(1 + \delta)^T} = 1 - \frac{FV(D,0,T)}{S_0(1 + r)^T}$$

We calculated $(1 + \delta)^T$. To obtain δ^c, we take the natural log of this value and divide by T: $\delta^c = (1/T)\ln[(1 + \delta)^T]$. The formula for the futures price is

$$f_0(T) = S_0 e^{(r^c - \delta^c)T}$$

In the above formula, the opportunity cost, expressed as the interest rate, is reduced by the dividend yield. Thus, the formula compounds the spot price by the interest cost less the dividend benefits. An equivalent variation of the above formula is

$$f_0(T) = (S_0 e^{-\delta^c T}) e^{r^c T} \qquad \textbf{(63-17)}$$

The expression in parentheses is the stock price discounted at the dividend yield rate. The result is an adjusted stock price with the present value of the dividends removed. This adjusted stock price is then compounded at the risk-free rate. So, as we have previously seen, the stock price less the present value of the dividends is compounded at the risk-free rate to obtain the futures price.

In the previous problem, $(1 + \delta)^T = 1.0049$. Then $\delta^c = (1/0.25)\ln(1.0049)$ $= 0.0196$. The continuously compounded risk-free rate is $\ln(1.055) = 0.0535$. The futures price is, therefore, $f_0(0.25) = (1452.45 e^{-0.0196(0.25)}) e^{0.0535(0.25)}$ $= 1464.81$; again the difference comes from rounding.

Exhibit 10 summarizes the formulas for pricing stock index futures contracts. Each of these formulas is consistent with the general formula for pricing futures. They are each based on the notion that a futures price is the spot price compounded at the risk-free rate, plus the compound future value of any other costs minus any cash flows and benefits. Alternatively, one can convert the

EXHIBIT 10	**Pricing Formulas for Stock Index Futures Contract**

Futures price = Stock index compounded at risk-free rate − Future value of dividends, or (Stock index − Present value of dividends) compounded at risk-free rate.

Futures price as stock index compounded at risk-free rate − Future value of dividends:

$$f_0(T) = S_0(1 + r)^T - FV(D,0,T)$$

Futures price as stock index − Present value of dividends compounded at risk-free rate:

$$f_0(T) = [S_0 - PV(D,0,T)](1 + r)^T$$

Futures price as stock index discounted at dividend yield, compounded at risk-free rate:

$$f_0(T) = \left(\frac{S_0}{(1 + \delta)^T}\right)(1 + r)^T \qquad \text{or}$$

$$f_0(T) = S_0(1 - \delta^*)(1 + r)^T$$

Futures price in terms of continuously compounded rate and yield:

$$f_0(T) = S_0 e^{(r^c - \delta^c)T} \qquad \text{or}$$

$$f_0(T) = (S_0 e^{-\delta^c T}) e^{r^c T}$$

compound future value of the costs net of benefits or cash flows of holding the asset to their current value and subtract this amount from the spot price before compounding the spot price at the interest rate. In this manner, the spot price adjusted for any costs or benefits is then compounded at the risk-free interest rate to give the futures price. These costs, benefits, and cash flows thus represent the linkage between spot and futures prices.

EXAMPLE 5

A stock index is at 755.42. A futures contract on the index expires in 57 days. The risk-free interest rate is 6.25 percent. At expiration, the value of the dividends on the index is 3.94.

A. Find the appropriate futures price, using both the future value of the dividends and the present value of the dividends.

B. Find the appropriate futures price in terms of the two specifications of the dividend yield.

C. Using your answer in Part B, find the futures price under the assumption of continuous compounding of interest and dividends.

Solution to A: $T = 57/365 = 0.1562$

$$f_0(0.1562) = 755.42(1.0625)^{0.1562} - 3.94 = 758.67$$

Alternatively, we can find the present value of the dividends:

$$PV(D,0,0.1562) = \frac{3.94}{(1.0625)^{0.1562}} = 3.90$$

Then we can find the futures price as $f_0(0.1562) = (755.42 - 3.90)(1.0625)^{0.1562} = 758.67$.

Solution to B: Under one specification of the yield, we have

$$\frac{1}{(1 + \delta)^T} = 1 - \frac{3.94}{755.42(1.0625)^{0.1562}} = 0.9948$$

We need the inverse of this amount, which is $1/0.9948 = 1.0052$. Then the futures price is

$$f_0(0.1562) = \left(\frac{755.42}{1.0052}\right)(1.0625)^{0.1562} = 758.66$$

Under the other specification of the dividend yield, we have

$$\delta^* = \frac{3.90}{755.42} = 0.0052$$

The futures price is $f_0(0.1562) = 755.42(1 - 0.0052)(1.0625)^{0.1562} = 758.64$, with the difference caused by rounding.

Solution to C: The continuously compounded risk-free rate is $r^c = \ln(1.0625) = 0.0606$. The continuously compounded dividend yield is

$$\frac{1}{0.1562}\ln(1.0052) = 0.0332$$

The futures price would then be

$$f_0(0.1562) = 755.42e^{(0.0606 - 0.0332)(0.1562)}$$
$$= 758.66$$

7.4 Pricing Currency Futures

Given our assumptions about no marking to market, it will be a simple matter to learn how to price currency futures: We price them the same as currency forwards. Recall that in Reading 62 we described a currency as an asset paying a yield of r^f, which can be viewed as the foreign risk-free rate. Thus, in this sense, a currency futures can also be viewed like a stock index futures, whereby the dividend yield is analogous to the foreign interest rate.

Therefore, an arbitrageur can buy the currency for the spot exchange rate of S_0 and sell a futures expiring at T for $f_0(T)$, holding the position until expiration, collecting the foreign interest, and delivering the currency to receive the original futures price. An important twist, however, is that the arbitrageur must be careful to have the correct number of units of the currency on hand to deliver.

Consider a futures contract on one unit of the currency. If the arbitrageur purchases one unit of the currency up front, the accumulation of interest on the currency will result in having more than one unit at the futures expiration. To adjust for this problem, the arbitrageur should take $S_0/(1 + r^f)^T$ units of his own currency and buy $1/(1 + r^f)^T$ units of the foreign currency.[50] The arbitrageur holds this position and collects interest at the foreign rate. The accumulation of interest is accounted for by multiplying by the interest factor $(1 + r^f)^T$. At expiration, the number of units of the currency will have grown to $[1/(1 + r^f)^T][1 + r^f]^T = 1$. So, the arbitrageur would then have 1 unit of the currency. He delivers that unit and receives the futures price of $f_0(T)$.

To avoid an arbitrage opportunity, the present value of the payoff of $f_0(T)$ must equal the amount initially invested. To find the present value of the payoff, we must discount at the domestic risk-free rate, because that rate reflects the opportunity cost of the arbitrageur's investment of his own money. So, first we equate the present value of the future payoff, discounting at the domestic risk-free rate, to the amount initially invested:

$$\frac{f_0(T)}{(1 + r)^T} = \frac{S_0}{(1 + r^f)^T}$$

---

[50] In other words, if S_0 buys 1 unit, then $S_0/(1 + r^f)^T$ buys $1/(1 + r^f)^T$ units.

Then we solve for the futures price to obtain

$$f_0(T) = \left(\frac{S_0}{(1 + r^f)^T}\right)(1 + r)^T \qquad \textbf{(63-18)}$$

This formula is the same one we used for currency forwards.

An alternative variation of this formula would apply when we use continuously compounded interest rates. The adjustment is very slight. In the formula above, dividing S_0 by $(1 + r^f)^T$ finds a present value by discounting at the foreign interest rate. Multiplying by $(1 + r)^T$ is finding a future value by compounding at the domestic interest rate. The continuously compounded analogs to those rates are $r^{fc} = \ln(1 + r^f)$ and $r^c = \ln(1 + r)$. Then the formula becomes

$$f_0(T) = (S_0 e^{-r^{fc}T}) e^{r^c T} \qquad \textbf{(63-19)}$$

We also saw this formula in Reading 62.

Consider a futures contract expiring in 55 days on the euro. Therefore, $T = 55/365 = 0.1507$. The spot exchange rate is \$0.8590. The foreign interest rate is 5.25 percent, and the domestic risk-free rate is 6.35 percent. The futures price should, therefore, be

$$f_0(T) = \left(\frac{S_0}{(1 + r^f)^T}\right)(1 + r)^T$$

$$f_0(0.1507) = \left(\frac{0.8590}{(1.0525)^{0.1507}}\right)(1.0635)^{0.1507} = 0.8603$$

If the futures is selling for more than this amount, the arbitrageur can buy the currency and sell the futures. He collects the foreign interest and converts the currency back at a higher rate than 0.8603, resulting in a risk-free return that exceeds the domestic risk-free rate. If the futures is selling for less than this amount, the arbitrageur can borrow the currency and buy the futures. The end result will be to receive money at the start and pay back money at a rate less than the domestic risk-free rate.

If the above problem were structured in terms of continuously compounded rates, the domestic rate would be $\ln(1.0635) = 0.0616$ and the foreign rate would be $\ln(1.0525) = 0.0512$. The futures price would then be

$$f_0(T) = (S_0 e^{-r^{fc}T}) e^{r^c T}$$

$$f_0(0.1507) = (0.85890 e^{-0.0512(0.1507)}) e^{0.0616(0.1507)} = 0.8603$$

which, of course, is the same price we calculated above.

Exhibit 11 summarizes the formulas for pricing currency futures.

EXHIBIT 11   **Pricing Formulas for Currency Futures Contract**

Futures price = (Spot exchange rate discounted by Foreign interest rate) compounded at Domestic interest rate:

Discrete interest: $f_0(T) = \left(\dfrac{S_0}{(1 + r^f)^T}\right)(1 + r)^T$

Continuous interest: $f_0(T) = (S_0 e^{-r^{fc}T}) e^{r^c T}$

EXAMPLE 6

The spot exchange rate for the Swiss franc is $0.60. The U.S. interest rate is 6 percent, and the Swiss interest rate is 5 percent. A futures contract expires in 78 days.

A. Find the appropriate futures price.

B. Find the appropriate futures price under the assumption of continuous compounding.

C. Using Part A, execute an arbitrage resulting from a futures price of $0.62.

$$T = 78/365 = 0.2137$$

Solution to A:

$$f_0(0.2137) = \frac{\$0.60}{(1.05)^{0.2137}}(1.06)^{0.2137} = \$0.6012$$

Solution to B: The continuously compounded equivalent rates are

$$r^{fc} = \ln(1.05) = 0.0488$$
$$r^c = \ln(1.06) = 0.0583$$

The futures price is

$$f_0(0.2137) = (\$0.60e^{-0.0488(0.2137)})e^{0.0583(0.2137)}$$
$$= \$0.6012$$

Solution to C: At $0.62, the futures price is too high, so we will need to sell the futures. First, however, we must determine how many units of the currency to buy. It should be

$$\frac{1}{(1.05)^{0.2137}} = 0.9896$$

So we buy this many units, which costs 0.9896($0.60) = $0.5938. We sell the futures at $0.62. We hold the position until expiration. During that time the accumulation of interest will make the 0.9896 units of the currency grow to 1.0000 unit. We convert the Swiss franc to dollars at the futures rate of $0.62. The return per dollar invested is

$$\frac{0.62}{0.5938} = 1.0441$$

This is a return of 1.0441 per dollar invested over 78 days. At the risk-free rate of 6 percent, the return over 78 days should be $(1.06)^{0.2137} = 1.0125$. Obviously, the arbitrage transaction is much better.

7.5 Futures Pricing: A Recap

We have now examined the pricing of short-term interest rate futures, intermediate- and long-term interest rate futures, stock index futures, and currency futures. Let us recall the intuition behind pricing a futures contract and see the commonality in each of those special cases. First recall that under the assumption of no marking to market, at expiration the short makes delivery and we assume that the long pays the full futures price at that point. An arbitrageur buys the asset and sells a futures contract, holds the asset for the life of the futures, and delivers it at expiration of the futures, at which time he is paid the futures price. In addition, while holding the asset, the arbitrageur accumulates costs and accrues cash flows, such as interest, dividends, and benefits such as a convenience yield. The value of the position at expiration will be the futures price net of these costs minus benefits and cash flows. The overall value of this transaction at expiration is known when the transaction is initiated; thus, the value at expiration is risk-free. The return from a risk-free transaction should equal the risk-free rate, which is the rate on a zero-coupon bond whose maturity is the futures expiration day. If the return is indeed this risk-free rate, then the futures price must equal the spot price compounded at the risk-free rate plus the compound value of these costs net of benefits and cash flows.

It should also be noted that although we have taken the more natural approach of buying the asset and selling the futures, we could just as easily have sold short the asset and bought the futures. Because short selling is usually a little harder to do as well as to understand, the approach we take is preferable from a pedagogical point of view. It is important, nonetheless, to remember that the ability to sell short the asset or the willingness of parties who own the asset to sell it to offset the buying of the futures is critical to establishing the results we have shown here. Otherwise, the futures pricing formulas would be inequalities—limited on one side but not restricted on the other.

We should remind ourselves that this general form of the futures pricing model also applied in Reading 62 in our discussion of forward contracts. Futures contracts differ from forward contracts in that the latter are subject to credit risk. Futures contracts are marked to market on a daily basis and guaranteed against losses from default by the futures clearinghouse, which has never defaulted. Although there are certain institutional features that distinguish futures from forwards, we consider those features separately from the material on pricing. Because the general economic and financial concepts are the same, for pricing purposes, we treat futures and forwards as the same.

THE ROLE OF FUTURES MARKETS AND EXCHANGES

8

We conclude this reading with a brief look at the role that futures markets and exchanges play in global financial systems and in society. Virtually all participants in the financial markets have heard of futures markets, but many do not understand the role that futures markets play. Some participants do not understand how futures markets function in global financial systems and often look at futures with suspicion, if not disdain.

Derivative markets provide price discovery and risk management, make the markets for the underlying assets more efficient, and permit trading at low transaction costs. These characteristics are also associated with futures markets.

In fact, **price discovery** is often cited by others as the primary advantage of futures markets. Yet, all derivative markets provide these benefits. What characteristics do futures markets have that are not provided by comparable markets as forward markets?

First recall that a major distinction between futures and forwards is that futures are standardized instruments. By having an agreed-upon set of homogeneous contracts, futures markets can provide an orderly, liquid market in which traders can open and close positions without having to worry about holding these positions to expiration. Although not all futures contracts have a high degree of liquidity, an open position can nonetheless be closed on the exchange where the contract was initiated.[51] More importantly, however, futures contracts are guaranteed against credit losses. If a counterparty defaults, the clearinghouse pays and, as we have emphasized, no clearinghouse has ever defaulted. In this manner, a party can engage in a transaction to lock in a future price or rate without having to worry about the credit quality of the counterparty. Forward contracts are subject to default risk, but of course they offer the advantage of customization, the tailoring of a contract's terms to meet the needs of the parties involved.

With an open, standardized, and regulated market for futures contracts, their prices can be disseminated to other investors and the general public. Futures prices are closely watched by a vast number of market participants, many trying to discern an indication of the direction of future spot prices and some simply trying to determine what price they could lock in for future purchase or sale of the underlying asset. Although forward prices provide similar information, forward contracts are private transactions and their prices are not publicly reported. Futures markets thus provide transparency to the financial markets. They reveal the prices at which parties contract for future transactions.

Therefore, futures prices contribute an important element to the body of information on which investors make decisions. In addition, they provide opportunities to transact for future purchase or sale of an underlying asset without having to worry about the credit quality of the counterparty.

In Readings 62 and 63, we studied forward and futures contracts and showed that they have a lot in common. Both are commitments to buy or sell an asset at a future date at a price agreed on today. No money changes hands at the start of either transaction. We learned how to determine appropriate prices and values for these contracts. There are a variety of strategies and applications using forward and futures contracts. For now, however, we take a totally different approach and look at contracts that provide not the obligation but rather the right to buy or sell an asset at a later date at a price agreed on today. To obtain such a right, in contrast to agreeing to an obligation, one must pay money at the start. These instruments, called options, are the subject of Reading 64.

---

[51] Recall that there is no liquid market for previously opened forward contracts to be closed, but the holder of a forward contract can re-enter the market and establish a position opposite to the one previously established. If one holds a long forward contract to buy an asset in six months, one can then do a short forward contract to sell the asset in six months, and this transaction offsets the risk of changing market prices. The credit risk on both contracts remains. In some cases, the offsetting contract can be done with the same counterparty as in the original contract, permitting the two parties to arrange a single cash settlement to offset both contracts.

SUMMARY

▶ Futures contracts are standardized instruments that trade on a futures exchange, have a secondary market, and are guaranteed against default by means of a daily settling of gains and losses. Forward contracts are customized instruments that are not guaranteed against default and are created anywhere off of an exchange.

▶ Modern futures markets primarily originated in Chicago out of a need for grain farmers and buyers to be able to transact for delivery at future dates for grain that would, in the interim, be placed in storage.

▶ Futures transactions are standardized and conducted in a public market, are homogeneous, have a secondary market giving them an element of liquidity, and have a clearinghouse, which collects margins and settles gains and losses daily to provide a guarantee against default. Futures markets are also regulated at the federal government level.

▶ Margin in the securities markets is the deposit of money, the margin, and a loan for the remainder of the funds required to purchase a stock or bond. Margin in the futures markets is much smaller and does not involve a loan. Futures margin is more like a performance bond or down payment.

▶ Futures trading occurs on a futures exchange, which involves trading either in a physical location called a pit or via a computer terminal off of the floor of the futures exchange as part of an electronic trading system. In either case, a party to a futures contract goes long, committing to buy the underlying asset at an agreed-upon price, or short, committing to sell the underlying asset at an agreed-upon price.

▶ A futures trader who has established a position can re-enter the market and close out the position by doing the opposite transaction (sell if the original position was long or buy if the original position was short). The party has offset the position, no longer has a contract outstanding, and has no further obligation.

▶ Initial margin is the amount of money in a margin account on the day of a transaction or when a margin call is made. Maintenance margin is the amount of money in a margin account on any day other than when the initial margin applies. Minimum requirements exist for the initial and maintenance margins, with the initial margin requirement normally being less than 10 percent of the futures price and the maintenance margin requirement being smaller than the initial margin requirement. Variation margin is the amount of money that must be deposited into the account to bring the balance up to the required level. The settlement price is an average of the last few trades of the day and is used to determine the gains and losses marked to the parties' accounts.

▶ The futures clearinghouse engages in a practice called marking to market, also known as the daily settlement, in which gains and losses on a futures position are credited and charged to the trader's margin account on a daily basis. Thus, profits are available for withdrawal and losses must be paid quickly before they build up and pose a risk that the party will be unable to cover large losses.

▶ The margin balance at the end of the day is determined by taking the previous balance and accounting for any gains or losses from the day's activity, based on the settlement price, as well as any money added or withdrawn.

▶ Price limits are restrictions on the price of a futures trade and are based on a range relative to the previous day's settlement price. No trade can take place outside of the price limits. A limit move is when the price at which two parties would like to trade is at or beyond the price limit. Limit up is when the market price would be at or above the upper limit. Limit down is when the market price would be at or below the lower limit. Locked limit occurs when a trade cannot take place because the price would be above the limit up or below the limit down prices.

▶ A futures contract can be terminated by entering into an offsetting position very shortly before the end of the expiration day. If the position is still open when the contract expires, the trader must take delivery (if long) or make delivery (if short), unless the contract requires that an equivalent cash settlement be used in lieu of delivery. In addition, two participants can agree to alternative delivery terms, an arrangement called exchange for physicals.

▶ Delivery options are features associated with a futures contract that permit the short some flexibility in what to deliver, where to deliver it, and when in the expiration month to make delivery.

▶ Scalpers are futures traders who take positions for very short periods of time and attempt to profit by buying at the bid price and selling at the ask price. Day traders close out all positions by the end of the day. Position traders leave their positions open overnight and potentially longer.

▶ Treasury bill futures are contracts in which the underlying is $1,000,000 of a U.S. Treasury bill. Eurodollar futures are contracts in which the underlying is $1,000,000 of a Eurodollar time deposit. Treasury bond futures are contracts in which the underlying is $100,000 of a U.S. Treasury bond with a minimum 15-year maturity. Stock index futures are contracts in which the underlying is a well-known stock index, such as the S&P 500 or FTSE 100. Currency futures are contracts in which the underlying is a foreign currency.

▶ An expiring futures contract is equivalent to a spot transaction. Consequently, at expiration the futures price must converge to the spot price to avoid an arbitrage opportunity in which one can buy the asset and sell a futures or sell the asset and buy a futures to capture an immediate profit at no risk.

▶ The value of a futures contract just prior to marking to market is the accumulated price change since the last mark to market. The value of a futures contract just after marking to market is zero. These values reflect the claim a participant has as a result of her position in the contract.

▶ The price of a futures contract will equal the price of an otherwise equivalent forward contract one day prior to expiration, or if interest rates are known or constant, or if interest rates are uncorrelated with futures prices.

▶ A futures price is derived by constructing a combination of a long position in the asset and a short position in the futures. This strategy guarantees that the price received from the sale of the asset is known when the transaction is initiated. The futures price is then derived as the unknown value that eliminates the opportunity to earn an arbitrage profit off of the transaction.

▶ Futures prices are affected by the opportunity cost of funds tied up in the investment in the underlying asset, the costs of storing the underlying asset, any cash flows paid on the underlying asset, such as interest or dividends, and nonmonetary benefits of holding the underlying asset, referred to as the convenience yield.

▶ Backwardation describes a condition in which the futures price is lower than the spot price. Contango describes a condition in which the futures price is higher than the spot price.

► The futures price will not equal the expected spot price if the risk premium in the spot price is transferred from hedgers to futures traders. If the risk premium is transferred, then the futures price will be biased high or low relative to the expected future spot price. When the futures price is biased low (high), it is called normal backwardation (normal contango).

► T-bill futures prices are determined by going short a futures contract and going long a T-bill that will have the desired maturity at the futures expiration. At expiration, the T-bill is delivered or cash settled to a price locked in when the transaction was initiated through the sale of the futures. The correct futures price is the one that prohibits this combination from earning an arbitrage profit. Under the assumptions we make, the T-bill futures price is the same as the T-bill forward price.

► The implied repo rate is the rate of return implied by a transaction of buying a spot asset and selling a futures contract. If financing can be obtained in the repo market at less than the implied repo rate, the transaction should be undertaken. If financing can be supplied to the repo market at greater than the implied repo rate, the transaction should be reversed.

► Eurodollar futures cannot be priced as easily as T-bill futures, because the expiration price of a Eurodollar futures is based on a value computed as 1 minus a rate, whereas the value of the underlying Eurodollar time deposit is based on 1 divided by a rate. The difference is small but not zero. Hence, Eurodollar futures do not lend themselves to an exact pricing formula based on the notion of a cost of carry of the underlying.

► Treasury bond futures prices are determined by first identifying the cheapest bond to deliver, which is the bond that the short would deliver under current market conditions. Then one must construct a combination of a short futures contract and a long position in that bond. The bond is held, and the coupons are collected and reinvested. At expiration, the underlying bond is delivered and the futures price times the conversion factor for that bond is received. The correct futures price is the one that prevents this transaction from earning an arbitrage profit.

► Stock index futures prices are determined by constructing a combination of a long portfolio of stocks identical to the underlying index and a short futures contract. The stocks are held and the dividends are collected and reinvested. At expiration, the cash settlement results in the effective sale of the stock at the futures price. The correct futures price is the one that prevents this transaction from earning an arbitrage profit.

► Currency futures prices are determined by buying the underlying currency and selling a futures on the currency. The position is held, and the underlying currency pays interest at the foreign risk-free rate. At expiration, the currency is delivered and the futures price is received. The correct futures price is the one that prevents this transaction from earning an arbitrage profit.

► Futures markets serve our financial systems by making the markets for the underlying assets more efficient, by providing price discovery, by offering opportunities to trade at lower transaction costs, and by providing a means of managing risk. Futures markets also provide a homogeneous, standardized, and tradable instrument through which participants who might not have access to forward markets can make commitments to buy and sell assets at a future date at a locked-in price with no fear of credit risk. Because futures markets are so visible and widely reported on, they are also an excellent source of information, contributing greatly to the transparency of financial markets.

PRACTICE PROBLEMS FOR READING 63

1. Mary Craft is expecting large-capitalization stocks to rally close to the end of the year. She is pessimistic, however, about the performance of small-capitalization stocks. She decides to go long one December futures contract on the Dow Jones Industrial Average at a price of 9,020 and short one December futures contract on the S&P Midcap 400 Index at a price of 369.40. The multiplier for a futures contract on the Dow is $10, and the multiplier for a futures contract on the S&P Midcap 400 is $500. When Craft closes her position toward the end of the year, the Dow and S&P Midcap 400 futures prices are 9,086 and 370.20, respectively. How much is the net gain or loss to Craft?

2. **A.** The current price of gold is $300 per ounce. Consider the net cost of carry for gold to be zero. The risk-free interest rate is 6 percent. What should be the price of a gold futures contract that expires in 90 days?

   B. Using Part A above, illustrate how an arbitrage transaction could be executed if the futures contract is priced at $306 per ounce.

   C. Using Part A above, illustrate how an arbitrage transaction could be executed if the futures contract is priced at $303 per ounce.

3. Consider an asset priced at $90. A futures contract on the asset expires in 75 days. The risk-free interest rate is 7 percent. Answer the following questions, each of which is independent of the others, unless indicated otherwise.

   A. Find the appropriate futures price if the underlying asset has no storage costs, cash flows, or convenience yield.

   B. Find the appropriate futures price if the underlying asset's storage costs at the futures expiration equal $3.

   C. Find the appropriate futures price if the underlying asset has positive cash flows. The future value of these cash flows is $0.50 at the time of futures expiration.

   D. Find the appropriate futures price if the underlying asset's storage costs at the futures expiration equal $3.00 and the compound value at the time of the futures expiration of the positive cash flow from the underlying asset is $0.50.

   E. Using Part D above, illustrate how an arbitrage transaction could be executed if the futures contract is trading at $95.

   F. Using Part A above, determine the value of a long futures contract an instant before marking to market if the previous settlement price was $89.50.

   G. What happens to the value of the futures contract in Part F above as soon as it is marked to market?

4. A $1 face value bond pays an 8 percent semiannual coupon. The annual yield is 6 percent. The bond has 10 years remaining until maturity, and its price is $1.1488. Consider a futures contract calling for delivery of this bond only. The contract expires in 18 months. The risk-free rate is 5 percent.

   A. Compute the appropriate futures price.

   B. Assuming that the futures contract is appropriately priced, show the riskless strategy involving the bond and the futures contract that would earn the risk-free rate of return.

5. Consider a six-year $1 par Treasury bond. The bond pays a 6 percent semi-annual coupon, and the annual yield is 6 percent. The bond is priced at par. A futures contract expiring in 15 months calls for delivery of this bond only. The risk-free rate is 5 percent.

   A. Find the future value in 15 months of the coupons on this bond.

   B. Find the appropriate futures price.

   C. Now suppose that the above bond is only one of many deliverable bonds. The contract specification calls for the use of a conversion factor to determine the price paid for a given deliverable bond. Suppose the bond described here has a conversion factor of 1.0567. Find the appropriate futures price.

6. A stock index is at 1,521.75. A futures contract on the index expires in 73 days. The risk-free interest rate is 6.10 percent. The value of the dividends reinvested over the life of the futures is 5.36.

   A. Find the appropriate futures price.

   B. Find the appropriate futures price in terms of the two specifications of the dividend yield.

   C. Using your answer in Part B, find the futures price under the assumption of continuous compounding of interest and dividends.

7. A stock index is at 443.35. A futures contract on the index expires in 201 days. The price of the futures contract is 458.50. The risk-free interest rate is 6.50 percent. The value of the dividends reinvested over the life of the futures is 5.0.

   A. Show that the futures contract above is mispriced by computing what the price of this futures contract should be.

   B. Show how an arbitrageur could take advantage of the mispricing.

8. The spot exchange rate for the British pound is $1.4390. The U.S. interest rate is 6.3 percent, and the British interest rate is 5.8 percent. A futures contract on the exchange rate for the British pound expires in 100 days.

   A. Find the appropriate futures price.

   B. Find the appropriate futures price under the assumption of continuous compounding.

   C. Suppose the actual futures price is $1.4650. Is the future contract mispriced? If yes, how could an arbitrageur take advantage of the mispricing? Use discrete compounding as in Part A.

Use the following information to answer Questions 9–14

Uda Malquist is the chief financial officer of Axia Corporation, a global manufacturer of mobile communication devices. Axia is headquartered in Germany and reports its financial statements in euros (EUR).

Axia expects to make two major financial transactions in the coming months:

▶ The company will issue a note of 300 million U.S. dollars (USD) in three months (90 days) time. The note will have a six-month (180 days) term, and the proceeds will be used to meet the working capital needs of Axia's U.S. operations.

▶ Under a new law, Axia will have an opportunity to repatriate 900 million British pounds (GBP) of profits held in the U.K. This repatriation would be on favorable tax terms and would occur in eight months (244 days) time. Axia intends to take full advantage of this tax benefit.

Malquist must first decide whether to hedge the interest rate exposure on the U.S. borrowing with a forward rate agreement (FRA) or with futures contracts.

▶ Using the information in Exhibit 1 and a 30/360 day count, Malquist calculates the FRA rates implicit in the term structure. Stream Partners, a large brokerage house, offers Axia an FRA rate of 4.68 percent for the USD 300 million note in three months time (with settlement at initiation of the loan).

▶ Malquist believes that building a perfect hedge for the U.S. borrowing by using Eurodollar futures contracts may not be possible.

EXHIBIT 1	Current Term Structure of USD LIBOR Rates (annualized)

Term	Rate
30-day	3.10%
60-day	3.40%
90-day	3.71%
180-day	3.99%
270-day	4.12%
360-day	4.22%

Malquist must also decide whether to hedge the conversion of pounds to euros. She analyzes the GBP per euro (EUR) exchange rate using the data in Exhibit 2. She calculates the 244-day arbitrage-free forward exchange rate using a 365-day per year convention.

Malquist finds that the futures contract on the euro (quoted as GBP per EUR) is trading above the fair value and that an arbitrage opportunity exists. She also finds that the 244-day arbitrage-free futures price (GBP/EUR) is below the 244-day expected spot exchange rate, but she is confident that rates and prices will be the same in 244 days.

EXHIBIT 2	Interest Rate and Exchange Rate Data

U.K. interest rate[a]	4.17%
Euro interest rate[a]	3.28%
Spot exchange rate (GBP per EUR)	0.6892

[a] 244-day interest rates, discrete and annualized.

Malquist assumes that the interest rates in both exhibits are risk-free rates in her analysis.

9. The six-month FRA rate three months from now, implicit in the current term structure of USD LIBOR rates (Exhibit 1), is *closest* to

   A. 4.09%.

   B. 4.29%.

   C. 4.43%.

   D. 5.02%.

10. Assuming a 180-day spot rate of 4.48 percent at expiration, the payoff to Axia from the FRA offered by Stream Partners will be *closest* to

    A. $293,427.

    B. $287,136.

    C. $287,136.

    D. $293,427.

11. Which of the following most likely supports Malquist's belief about building a perfect hedge with Eurodollar futures contracts?

    A. Contango bias.

    B. Convexity bias.

    C. Normality bias.

    D. Backwardation bias.

12. Based on information provided in Exhibit 2, the arbitrage-free 244-day forward exchange rate (GBP per EUR) is *closest* to

    A. 0.6853.

    B. 0.6932.

    C. 0.6951.

    D. 0.7083.

13. With respect to the futures contract on the euro, two of the transactions necessary to exploit the arbitrage opportunity include

    A. sell euros and sell euro futures contracts.

    B. buy euros and buy euro futures contracts.

    C. sell euros and buy euro futures contracts.

    D. buy euros and sell euro futures contracts.

2006 exam

14. The difference Malquist finds between the futures price and the expected spot price for GBP in 244 days is *most likely* due to

   A. contango.

   B. backwardation.

   C. normal contango.

   D. normal backwardation.

STUDY SESSION 17
DERIVATIVE INVESTMENTS:
Options, Swaps, and Interest Rate and Credit Derivatives

This study session addresses options, swaps, interest rate derivatives, and embedded derivatives and their valuation. Because derivatives are widely used to reduce risk or generate additional income, it is imperative to understand the relative cost/benefit of derivative strategies.

READING ASSIGNMENTS

Reading 64   Option Markets and Contracts
Reading 65   Swap Markets and Contracts
Reading 66   Interest Rate Derivative Instruments
Reading 67   Using Credit Derivatives to Enhance Return and Manage Risk

LEARNING OUTCOMES

Reading 64: Option Markets and Contracts

The candidate should be able to:

a. calculate and interpret the prices of a synthetic call option, synthetic put option, synthetic bond, and synthetic underlying stock, and infer why an investor would want to create such instruments;

125

b. calculate and interpret prices of interest rate options and options on assets using one- and two-period binomial models;

c. explain the assumptions underlying the Black–Scholes–Merton model and their limitations;

d. explain how an option price, as represented by the Black–Scholes–Merton model, is affected by each of the input values (the option Greeks);

e. explain the delta of an option, and demonstrate how it is used in dynamic hedging;

f. explain the gamma effect on an option's price and delta and how gamma can affect a delta hedge;

g. discuss the effect of the underlying asset's cash flows on the price of an option;

h. demonstrate the methods for estimating the future volatility of the underlying asset (i.e., the historical volatility and the implied volatility methods);

i. illustrate how put–call parity for options on forwards (or futures) is established;

j. compare and contrast American options on forwards and futures to European options on forwards and futures, and identify the appropriate pricing model for European options.

Reading 65: Swap Markets and Contracts

The candidate should be able to:

a. distinguish between the pricing and valuation of swaps;

b. explain the equivalence of the following swaps to combinations of other instruments: interest rate swaps to a series of off market forward rate agreements (FRAs) and a plain vanilla swap to a combination of an interest rate call and interest rate put;

c. calculate and interpret the fixed rate on a plain vanilla interest rate swap and the market value of the swap during its life;

d. calculate and interpret the fixed rate, if applicable, and the foreign notional principal for a given domestic notional principal on a currency swap, and determine the market values of each of the different types of currency swaps during their lives;

e. calculate and interpret the fixed rate, if applicable, on an equity swap and the market values of the different types of equity swaps during their lives;

f. explain and interpret the characteristics and uses of swaptions, including the difference between payer and receiver swaptions;

g. identify and calculate the possible payoffs and cash flows of an interest rate swaption;

h. calculate and interpret the value of an interest rate swaption on the expiration day;

i. evaluate swap credit risk for each party and over the life of the swap, distinguish between current credit risk and potential credit risk, and illustrate how swap credit risk is reduced by both netting and marking to market;

j. define swap spread and relate it to credit risk.

Reading 66: Interest Rate Derivative Instruments

The candidate should be able to:

a. demonstrate how both a cap and a floor are packages of options on interest rates, and options on fixed income instruments;

b. compute the payoff for a cap and a floor, and explain how a collar is created.

Reading 67: Using Credit Derivatives to Enhance Return and Manage Risk

The candidate should be able to:

a. describe the characteristics of a credit default swap, and compare and contrast a credit default swap to a corporate bond;

b. explain the advantages of using credit derivatives over other credit instruments;

c. explain the use of credit derivatives by the various market participants;

d. discuss credit derivatives strategies and how they are used.

OPTION MARKETS AND CONTRACTS
by Don M. Chance

LEARNING OUTCOMES

The candidate should be able to:

a. calculate and interpret the prices of a synthetic call option, synthetic put option, synthetic bond, and synthetic underlying stock, and infer why an investor would want to create such instruments;

b. calculate and interpret prices of interest rate options and options on assets using one- and two-period binomial models;

c. explain the assumptions underlying the Black–Scholes–Merton model and their limitations;

d. explain how an option price, as represented by the Black–Scholes–Merton model, is affected by each of the input values (the option Greeks);

e. explain the delta of an option, and demonstrate how it is used in dynamic hedging;

f. explain the gamma effect on an option's price and delta and how gamma can affect a delta hedge;

g. discuss the effect of the underlying asset's cash flows on the price of an option;

h. demonstrate the methods for estimating the future volatility of the underlying asset (i.e., the historical volatility and the implied volatility methods);

i. illustrate how put–call parity for options on forwards (or futures) is established;

j. compare and contrast American options on forwards and futures to European options on forwards and futures, and identify the appropriate pricing model for European options.

INTRODUCTION

In Reading 62 we examined forward contracts, and in Reading 63 we looked at futures contracts. We noted how similar forward and futures contracts are: Both are commitments to buy an underlying asset at a fixed price at a later date. Forward contracts, however, are privately created, over-the-counter customized instruments that carry credit risk. Futures contracts are publicly traded, exchange-listed standardized instruments that effectively have no credit risk. Now we turn to options. Like forwards and futures, they are derivative instruments that provide the opportunity to buy or sell an underlying asset with a specific expiration date. But in contrast, buying an option gives the *right*, not the obligation, to buy or sell an underlying asset. And whereas forward and futures contracts involve no exchange of cash up front, options require a cash payment from the option buyer to the option seller.

Yet options contain several features common to forward and futures contracts. For one, options can be created by any two parties with any set of terms they desire. In this sense, options can be privately created, over-the-counter, customized instruments that are subject to credit risk. In addition, however, there is a large market for publicly traded, exchange-listed, standardized options, for which credit risk is essentially eliminated by the clearinghouse.

Just as we examined the pricing of forwards and futures in the last two readings, we shall examine option pricing in this reading. We shall also see that options can be created out of forward contracts, and that forward contracts can be created out of options. With some simplifying assumptions, options can be created out of futures contracts and futures contracts can be created out of options.

Finally, we note that options also exist that have a futures or forward contract as the underlying. These instruments blend some of the features of both options and forwards/futures.

As background, we discuss the definitions and characteristics of options.

BASIC DEFINITIONS AND ILLUSTRATIONS OF OPTIONS CONTRACTS

An option is a financial derivative contract that provides a party the right to buy or sell an underlying at a fixed price by a certain time in the future. The party holding the right is the option buyer; the party granting the right is the option seller. There are two types of options, a **call** and a **put**. A call is an option granting the right to buy the underlying; a put is an option granting the right to sell the underlying. With the exception of some advanced types of options, a given **option contract** is either a call, granting the right to buy, or a put, granting the right to sell, but not both.[1] We emphasize that this right to buy or sell is held by the option buyer, also called the long or option holder, and granted by the option seller, also called the short or option writer.

To obtain this right, the option buyer pays the seller a sum of money, commonly referred to as the **option price**. On occasion, this option price is called the **option premium** or just the **premium**. This money is paid when the option contract is initiated.

2.1 Basic Characteristics of Options

The fixed price at which the option holder can buy or sell the underlying is called the **exercise price, strike price, striking price**, or strike. The use of this right to buy or sell the underlying is referred to as **exercise** or **exercising the option**. Like all derivative contracts, an option has an **expiration date**, giving rise to the notion of an option's time to expiration. When the expiration date arrives, an option that is not exercised simply expires.

What happens at exercise depends on the whether the option is a call or a put. If the buyer is exercising a call, she pays the exercise price and receives either the underlying or an equivalent cash settlement. On the opposite side of the transaction is the seller, who receives the exercise price from the buyer and delivers the underlying, or alternatively, pays an equivalent cash settlement. If the buyer is exercising a put, she delivers the stock and receives the exercise price or an equivalent cash settlement. The seller, therefore, receives the underlying and must pay the exercise price or the equivalent cash settlement.

As noted in the above paragraph, cash settlement is possible. In that case, the option holder exercising a call receives the difference between the market value of the underlying and the exercise price from the seller in cash. If the option holder exercises a put, she receives the difference between the exercise price and the market value of the underlying in cash.

There are two primary exercise styles associated with options. One type of option has European-style exercise, which means that the option can be exercised only on its expiration day. In some cases, expiration could occur during that day; in others, exercise can occur only when the option has expired. In either case, such an option is called a **European option**. The other style of exercise is American-style exercise. Such an option can be exercised on any day through the expiration day and is generally called an **American option**.[2]

Option contracts specify a designated number of units of the underlying. For exchange-listed, standardized options, the exchange establishes each term, with the exception of the price. The price is negotiated by the two parties. For an over-the-counter option, the two parties decide each of the terms through negotiation.

In an over-the-counter option—one created off of an exchange by any two parties who agree to trade—the buyer is subject to the possibility of the writer defaulting. When the buyer exercises, the writer must either deliver the stock or cash if a call, or pay for the stock or pay cash if a put. If the writer cannot do so for financial reasons, the option holder faces a credit loss. Because the option holder paid the price up front and is not required to do anything else, the seller does not face any credit risk. Thus, although credit risk is bilateral in forward contracts—the long

---

[1] Of course, a party could buy both a call and a put, thereby holding the right to buy *and* sell the underlying.

[2] It is worthwhile to be aware that these terms have nothing to do with Europe or America. Both types of options are found in Europe and America. The names are part of the folklore of options markets, and there is no definitive history to explain how they came into use.

assumes the risk of the short defaulting, and the short assumes the risk of the long defaulting—the credit risk in an option is unilateral. Only the buyer faces credit risk because only the seller can default. As we discuss later, in exchange-listed options, the clearinghouse guarantees payment to the buyer.

2.2 Some Examples of Options

Consider some call and put options on Sun Microsystems (SUNW). The date is 13 June and Sun is selling for $16.25. Exhibit 1 gives information on the closing prices of four options, ones expiring in July and October and ones with exercise prices of 15.00 and 17.50. The July options expire on 20 July and the October options expire on 18 October. In the parlance of the profession, these are referred to as the July 15 calls, July 17.50 calls, October 15 calls, and October 17.50 calls, with similar terminology for the puts. These particular options are American style.

Consider the July 15 call. This option permits the holder to buy SUNW at a price of $15 a share any time through 20 July. To obtain this option, one would pay a price of $2.35. Therefore, a writer received $2.35 on 13 June and must be ready to sell SUNW to the buyer for $15 during the period through 20 July. Currently, SUNW trades above $15 a share, but as we shall see in more detail later, the option holder has no reason to exercise the option right now.[3] To justify purchase of the call, the buyer must be anticipating that SUNW will increase in price before the option expires. The seller of the call must be anticipating that SUNW will not rise sufficiently in price before the option expires.

Note that the option buyer could purchase a call expiring in July but permitting the purchase of SUNW at a price of $17.50. This price is more than the $15.00 exercise price, but as a result, the option, which sells for $1.00, is considerably cheaper. The cheaper price comes from the fact that the July 17.50 call is less likely to be exercised, because the stock has a higher hurdle to clear. A buyer is not willing to pay as much and a seller is more willing to take less for an option that is less likely to be exercised.

Alternatively, the option buyer could choose to purchase an October call instead of a July call. For any exercise price, however, the October calls would be more expensive than the July calls because they allow a longer period for the stock to make the move that the buyer wants. October options are more likely to be exercised than July options; therefore, a buyer would be willing to pay more and the seller would demand more for the October calls.

EXHIBIT 1	Closing Prices of Selected Options on SUNW, 13 June			
Exercise Price	**July Calls**	**October Calls**	**July Puts**	**October Puts**
15.00	2.35	3.30	0.90	1.85
17.50	1.00	2.15	2.15	3.20

Note: Stock price is $16.25; July options expire on 20 July; October options expire on 18 October.

---

[3] The buyer paid $2.35 for the option. If he exercised it right now, he would pay $15.00 for the stock, which is worth only $16.25. Thus, he would have effectively paid $17.35 (the cost of the option of $2.35 plus the exercise price of $15) for a stock worth $16.25. Even if he had purchased the option previously at a much lower price, the current option price of $2.35 is the opportunity cost of exercising the option—that is, he can always sell the option for $2.35. Therefore, if he exercised the option, he would be throwing away the $2.35 he could receive if he sold it.

Suppose the buyer expects the stock price to go down. In that case, he might buy a put. Consider the October 17.50 put, which would cost the buyer $3.20. This option would allow the holder to sell SUNW at a price of $17.50 any time up through 18 October.[4] He has no reason to exercise the option right now, because it would mean he would be buying the option for $3.20 and selling a stock worth $16.25 for $17.50. In effect, the option holder would part with $19.45 (the cost of the option of $3.20 plus the value of the stock of $16.25) and obtain only $17.50.[5] The buyer of a put obviously must be anticipating that the stock will fall before the expiration day.

If he wanted a cheaper option than the October 17.50 put, he could buy the October 15 put, which would cost only $1.85 but would allow him to sell the stock for only $15.00 a share. The October 15 put is less likely to be exercised than the October 17.50, because the stock price must fall below a lower hurdle. Thus, the buyer is not willing to pay as much and the seller is willing to take less.

For either exercise price, purchase of a July put instead of an October put would be much cheaper but would allow less time for the stock to make the downward move necessary for the transaction to be worthwhile. The July put is cheaper than the October put; the buyer is not willing to pay as much and the seller is willing to take less because the option is less likely to be exercised.

In observing these option prices, we have obtained our first taste of some principles involved in pricing options.

> *Call options have a lower premium the higher the exercise price.*
> *Put options have a lower premium the lower the exercise price.*
> *Both call and put options are cheaper the shorter the time to expiration.*[6]

These results should be intuitive, but later in this reading we show unequivocally why they must be true.

2.3 The Concept of Moneyness of an Option

An important concept in the study of options is the notion of an option's **moneyness**, which refers to the relationship between the price of the underlying and the exercise price. We use the terms **in-the-money**, **out-of-the-money**, and at-the-money. We explain the concept in Exhibit 2 with examples from the SUNW options. Note that in-the-money options are those in which exercising the option would produce a cash inflow that exceeds the cash outflow. Thus, calls are in-the-money when the value of the underlying exceeds the exercise price. Puts are in-the-money when the exercise price exceeds the value of the underlying. In our example, there are no at-the-money SUNW options, which would require that the stock value equal the exercise price; however, an at-the-money option can effectively be viewed as an out-of-the-money option, because its exercise would not bring in more money than is paid out.

As explained above, *one would not necessarily exercise an in-the-money option, but one would never exercise an out-of-the-money option.*

We now move on to explore how options markets are organized.

---

[4] Even if the option holder did not own the stock, he could use the option to sell the stock short.

[5] Again, even if the option were purchased in the past at a much lower price, the $3.20 current value of the option is an opportunity cost. Exercise of the option is equivalent to throwing away the opportunity cost.

[6] There is an exception to the rule that put options are cheaper the shorter the time to expiration. This statement is always true for American options but not always for European options. We explore this point later.

OPTIONAL SEGMENT

EXHIBIT 2	Moneyness of an Option		
In-the-Money		**Out-of-the-Money**	
Option	Justification	Option	Justification
July 15 call	16.25 > 15.00	July 17.50 call	16.25 < 17.50
October 15 call	16.25 > 15.00	October 17.50 call	16.25 < 17.50
July 17.50 put	17.50 > 16.25	July 15 put	15.00 < 16.25
October 17.50 put	17.50 > 16.25	October 15 put	15.00 < 16.25

Notes: Sun Microsystems options on 13 June; stock price is 16.25. See Exhibit 1 for more details. There are no options with an exercise price of 16.25, so no options are at-the-money.

3

THE STRUCTURE OF GLOBAL OPTIONS MARKETS

Although no one knows exactly how options first got started, contracts similar to options have been around for thousands of years. In fact, insurance is a form of an option. The insurance buyer pays the insurance writer a premium and receives a type of guarantee that covers losses. This transaction is similar to a put option, which provides coverage of a portion of losses on the underlying and is often used by holders of the underlying. The first true options markets were over-the-counter options markets in the United States in the 19th century.

3.1 Over-the-Counter Options Markets

In the United States, customized over-the-counter options markets were in existence in the early part of the 20th century and lasted well into the 1970s. An organization called the Put and Call Brokers and Dealers Association consisted of a group of firms that served as brokers and dealers. As brokers, they attempted to match buyers of options with sellers, thereby earning a commission. As dealers, they offered to take either side of the option transaction, usually laying off (hedging) the risk in another transaction. Most of these transactions were retail, meaning that the general public were their customers.

As we discuss in Section 3.2 below, the creation of the Chicago Board Options Exchange was a revolutionary event, but it effectively killed the Put and Call Brokers and Dealers Association. Subsequently, the increasing use of swaps facilitated a rebirth of the customized over-the-counter options market. Currency options, a natural extension to currency swaps, were in much demand. Later, interest rate options emerged as a natural outgrowth of interest rate swaps. Soon bond, equity, and **index options** were trading in a vibrant over-the-counter market. In contrast to the previous over-the-counter options market, however, the current one emerged as a largely wholesale market. Transactions are usually made with institutions and corporations and are rarely conducted directly with individuals. This market is much like the forward market described in Reading 62, with dealers offering to take either the long or short position in options and hedging that risk with transactions in other options or derivatives. There are no guarantees that the seller will perform; hence, the buyer faces credit risk. As such, option buyers must scrutinize sellers' credit risk and may require some risk reduction measures, such as collateral.

As previously noted, customized options have *all* of their terms—such as price, exercise price, time to expiration, identification of the underlying, settlement or delivery terms, size of the contract, and so on—determined by the two parties.

Like forward markets, over-the-counter options markets are essentially unregulated. In most countries, participating firms, such as banks and securities firms, are regulated by the appropriate authorities but there is usually no particular regulatory body for the over-the-counter options markets. In some countries, however, there are regulatory bodies for these markets.

Exhibit 3 on page 136 provides information on the leading dealers in over-the-counter currency and interest rate options as determined by *Risk* magazine in its annual surveys of banks and investment banks and also end users.

3.2 Exchange-Listed Options Markets

As briefly noted above, the Chicago Board Options Exchange was formed in 1973. Created as an extension of the Chicago Board of Trade, it became the first organization to offer a market for standardized options. In the United States, standardized options also trade on the Amex–Nasdaq, the Philadelphia Stock Exchange, and the Pacific Stock Exchange.[7] On a worldwide basis, standardized options are widely traded on such exchanges as LIFFE (the London International Financial Futures and Options Exchange) in London, Eurex in Frankfurt, and most other foreign exchanges. Exhibit 4 (page 137) shows the 20 largest options exchanges in the world. Note, perhaps surprisingly, that the leading options exchange is in Korea.

As described in Reading 62, on futures, the exchange fixes all terms of standardized instruments except the price. Thus, the exchange establishes the expiration dates and exercise prices as well as the minimum price quotation unit. The exchange also determines whether the option is European or American, whether the exercise is cash settlement or delivery of the underlying, and the contract size. In the United States, an option contract on an individual stock covers 100 shares of stock. Terminology such as "one option" is often used to refer to one option contract, which is really a set of options on 100 shares of stock. Index option sizes are stated in terms of a multiplier, indicating that the contract covers a hypothetical number of shares, as though the index were an individual stock. Similar specifications apply for options on other types of underlyings.

The exchange generally allows trading in exercise prices that surround the current stock price. As the stock price moves, options with exercise prices around the new stock price are usually added. The majority of trading occurs in options that are close to being at-the-money. Options that are far in-the-money or far out-of-the-money, called **deep-in-the-money** and **deep-out-of-the-money** options, are usually not very actively traded and are often not even listed for trading.

Most exchange-listed options have fairly short-term expirations, usually the current month, the next month, and perhaps one or two other months. Most of the trading takes place for the two shortest expirations. Some exchanges list options with expirations of several years, which have come to be called LEAPS, for **long-term equity anticipatory securities**. These options are fairly actively

---

[7] You may wonder why the New York Stock Exchange is not mentioned. Standardized options did trade on the NYSE at one time but were not successful, and the right to trade these options was sold to another exchange.

| | **EXHIBIT 3** | **Risk Magazine Surveys of Banks, Investment Banks, and Corporate End Users to Determine the Top Three Dealers in Over-the-Counter Currency and Interest Rate Options** |

		Respondents	
Currencies	**Banks and Investment Banks**	**Corporate End Users**

Currency Options

Currencies	**Banks and Investment Banks**	**Corporate End Users**
$/€	UBS Warburg	Citigroup
	Citigroup/Deutsche Bank	Royal Bank of Scotland
		Deutsche Bank
$/¥	UBS Warburg	Citigroup
	Credit Suisse First Boston	JP Morgan Chase
	JP Morgan Chase/Royal Bank of Scotland	UBS Warburg
$/£	Royal Bank of Scotland	Royal Bank of Scotland
	UBS Warburg	Citigroup
	Citigroup	Hong Kong Shanghai Banking Corp.
$/SF	UBS Warburg	UBS Warburg
	Credit Suisse First Boston	Credit Suisse First Boston
	Citigroup	Citigroup

Interest Rate Options

$	JP Morgan Chase	JP Morgan Chase
	Deutsche Bank	Citigroup
	Bank of America	Deutsche Bank/Lehman Brothers
€	JP Morgan Chase	JP Morgan Chase
	Credit Suisse First Boston/ Morgan Stanley	Citigroup
		UBS Warburg
¥	JP Morgan Chase/Deutsche Bank	UBS Warburg
	Bank of America	Barclays Capital
		Citigroup
£	Barclays Capital	Royal Bank of Scotland
	Societe Generale Groupe	Citigroup
	Bank of America/Royal Bank of Scotland	Hong Kong Shanghai Banking Corp.
SF	UBS Warburg	UBS Warburg
	JP Morgan Chase	JP Morgan
	Credit Suisse First Boston	Goldman Sachs

Notes: $ = U.S. dollar, € = euro, ¥ = Japanese yen, £ = U.K. pound sterling, SF = Swiss franc.

Source: Risk, September 2002, pp. 30–67, for Banks and Investment Banking dealer respondents, and June 2002, pp. 24–34, for Corporate End User respondents.

Results for Corporate End Users for Interest Rate Options are from *Risk,* July 2001, pp. 38–46. *Risk* omitted this category from its 2002 survey.

EXHIBIT 4	World's 20 Largest Options Exchanges

Exchange and Location	Volume in 2001
Korea Stock Exchange (Korea)	854,791,792
Chicago Board Options Exchange (United States)	306,667,851
MONEP (France)	285,667,686
Eurex (Germany and Switzerland)	239,016,516
American Stock Exchange (United States)	205,103,884
Pacific Stock Exchange (United States)	102,701,752
Philadelphia Stock Exchange (United States)	101,373,433
Chicago Mercantile Exchange (United States)	95,740,352
Amsterdam Exchange (Netherlands)	66,400,654
LIFFE (United Kingdom)	54,225,652
Chicago Board of Trade (United States)	50,345,068
OM Stockholm (Sweden)	39,327,619
South African Futures Exchange (South Africa)	24,307,477
MEFF Renta Variable (Spain)	23,628,446
New York Mercantile Exchange (United States)	17,985,109
Korea Futures Exchange (Korea)	11,468,991
Italian Derivatives Exchange (Italy)	11,045,804
Osaka Securities Exchange (Japan)	6,991,908
Bourse de Montreal (Canada)	5,372,930
Hong Kong Futures Exchange (China)	4,718,880

Note: Volume given is in number of contracts.

Source: Data supplied by *Futures Industry* magazine.

purchased, but most investors tend to buy and hold them and do not trade them as often as they do the shorter-term options.

The exchanges also determine on which companies they will list options for trading. Although specific requirements do exist, generally the exchange will list the options of any company for which it feels the options would be actively traded. The company has no voice in the matter. Options of a company can be listed on more than one exchange in a given country.

In Reading 63, we described the manner in which futures are traded. The procedure is very similar for exchange-listed options. Some exchanges have pit trading, whereby parties meet in the pit and arrange a transaction. Some exchanges use electronic trading, in which transactions are conducted through computers. In either case, the transactions are guaranteed by the clearinghouse. In the United States, the clearinghouse is an independent company called the **Options Clearing Corporation** or OCC. The OCC guarantees to the buyer that the clearinghouse will step in and fulfill the obligation if the seller reneges at exercise.

When the buyer purchases the option, the premium, which one might think would go to the seller, instead goes to the clearinghouse, which maintains it in a margin account. In addition, the seller must post some margin money, which is based on a formula that reflects whether the seller has a position that hedges the risk and whether the option is in- or out-of-the-money. If the price moves against the seller, the clearinghouse will force the seller to put up additional margin money. Although defaults are rare, the clearinghouse has always been successful in paying when the seller defaults. Thus, exchange-listed options are effectively free of credit risk.

Because of the standardization of option terms and participants' general acceptance of these terms, exchange-listed options can be bought and sold at any time prior to expiration. Thus, a party who buys or sells an option can re-enter the market before the option expires and offset the position with a sale or a purchase of the identical option. From the clearinghouse's perspective, the positions cancel.

As in futures markets, traders on the options exchange are generally either market makers or brokers. Some slight technical distinctions exist between different types of market makers in different options markets, but the differences are minor and do not concern us here. Like futures traders, option market makers attempt to profit by scalping (holding positions very short term) to earn the bid–ask spread and sometimes holding positions longer, perhaps closing them overnight or leaving them open for days or more.

When an option expires, the holder decides whether or not to exercise it. When the option is expiring, there are no further gains to waiting, so in-the-money options are always exercised, assuming they are in-the-money by more than the transaction cost of buying or selling the underlying or arranging a cash settlement when exercising. Using our example of the SUNW options, if at expiration the stock is at 16, the calls with an exercise price of 15 would be exercised. Most exchange-listed stock options call for actual delivery of the stock. Thus, the seller delivers the stock and the buyer pays the seller, through the clearinghouse, $15 per share. If the exchange specifies that the contract is cash settled, the seller simply pays the buyer $1. For puts requiring delivery, the buyer tenders the stock and receives the exercise price from the seller. If the option is out-of-the-money, it simply expires unexercised and is removed from the books. If the put is cash settled, the writer pays the buyer the equivalent cash amount.

Some nonstandardized exchange-traded options exist in the United States. In an attempt to compete with the over-the-counter options market, some exchanges permit some options to be individually customized and traded on the exchange, thereby benefiting from the advantages of the clearinghouse's credit guarantee. These options are primarily available only in large sizes and tend to be traded only by large institutional investors.

Like futures markets, exchange-listed options markets are typically regulated at the federal level. In the United States, federal regulation of options markets is the responsibility of the Securities and Exchange Commission; similar regulatory structures exist in other countries.

4   TYPES OF OPTIONS

Almost anything with a random outcome can have an option on it. Note that by using the word *anything*, we are implying that the underlying does not even need to be an asset. In this section, we shall discover the different types of options, identified by the nature of the underlying. Our focus in this reading is on financial options, but it is important, nonetheless, to gain some awareness of other types of options.

4.1 Financial Options

Financial options are options in which the underlying is a financial asset, an interest rate, or a currency.

4.1.1 Stock Options

Options on individual stocks, also called **equity options**, are among the most popular. Exchange-listed options are available on most widely traded stocks and an option on any stock can potentially be created on the over-the-counter market. We have already given examples of stock options in an earlier section; we now move on to index options.

4.1.2 Index Options

Stock market indices are well known, not only in the investment community but also among many individuals who are not even directly investing in the market. Because a stock index is just an artificial portfolio of stocks, it is reasonable to expect that one could create an option on a stock index. Indeed, we have already covered forward and futures contracts on stock indices; options are no more difficult in structure.

For example, consider options on the S&P 500 Index, which trade on the Chicago Board Options Exchange and have a designated index contract multiplier of 250. On 13 June of a given year, the S&P 500 closed at 1241.60. A call option with an exercise price of $1,250 expiring on 20 July was selling for $28. The option is European style and settles in cash. The underlying, the S&P 500, is treated as though it were a share of stock worth $1,241.60, which can be bought, using the call option, for $1,250 on 20 July. At expiration, if the option is in-the-money, the buyer exercises it and the writer pays the buyer the $250 contract multiplier times the difference between the index value at expiration and $1,250.

In the United States, there are also options on the Dow Jones Industrial Average, the Nasdaq, and various other indices. There are nearly always options on the best-known stock indices in most countries.

Just as there are options on stocks, there are also options on bonds.

4.1.3 Bond Options

Options on bonds, usually called **bond options**, are primarily traded in the over-the-counter markets. Options exchanges have attempted to generate interest in options on bonds, but have not been very successful. Corporate bonds are not very actively traded; most are purchased and held to expiration. Government bonds, however, are very actively traded; nevertheless, options on them have not gained widespread acceptance on options exchanges. Options exchanges generate much of their trading volume from individual investors, who have far more interest in and understanding of stocks than bonds.

Thus, bond options are found almost exclusively in the over-the-counter market and are almost always options on government bonds. Consider, for example, a U.S. Treasury bond maturing in 27 years. The bond has a coupon of 5.50 percent, a yield of 5.75 percent, and is selling for $0.9659 per $1 par. An over-the-counter options dealer might sell a put or call option on the bond with an exercise price of $0.98 per $1.00 par. The option could be European or American. Its expiration day must be significantly before the maturity date of the bond. Otherwise, as the bond approaches maturity, its price will move toward par, thereby removing much of the uncertainty in its price. The option could be specified to settle with actual delivery of the bond or with a cash settlement. The parties would also specify that the contract covered a given notional principal, expressed in terms of a face value of the underlying bond.

Continuing our example, let us assume that the contract covers $5 million face value of bonds and is cash settled. Suppose the buyer exercises a call option when the bond price is at $0.995. Then the option is in-the-money by $0.995 − $0.98 = $0.015 per $1 par. The seller pays the buyer 0.015($5,000,000) = $75,000. If instead the contract called for delivery, the seller would deliver $5 million face value of bonds, which would be worth $5,000,000($0.995) = $4,975,000. The buyer would pay $5,000,000($0.98) = $4,900,000. Because the option is created in the over-the-counter market, the option buyer would assume the risk of the seller defaulting.

Even though bond options are not very widely traded, another type of related option is widely used, especially by corporations. This family of options is called **interest rate options**. These are quite different from the options we have previously discussed, because the underlying is not a particular financial instrument.

4.1.4 Interest Rate Options

In Reading 62, we devoted considerable effort to understanding the Eurodollar spot market and forward contracts on the Eurodollar rate or LIBOR, called FRAs. In this reading, we cover options on LIBOR. Although these are not the only interest rate options, their characteristics are sufficiently general to capture most of what we need to know about options on other interest rates. First recall that a Eurodollar is a dollar deposited outside of the United States. The primary Eurodollar rate is LIBOR, and it is considered the best measure of an interest rate paid in dollars on a nongovernmental borrower. These Eurodollars represent dollar-denominated time deposits issued by banks in London borrowing from other banks in London.

Before looking at the characteristics of interest rate options, let us set the perspective by recalling that FRAs are forward contracts that pay off based on the difference between the underlying rate and the fixed rate embedded in the contract when it is constructed. For example, consider a 3 × 9 FRA. This contract expires in three months. The underlying rate is six-month LIBOR. Hence, when the contract is constructed, the underlying Eurodollar instrument matures in nine months. *When the contract expires, the payoff is made immediately,* but the rate on which it is based, 180-day LIBOR, is set in the spot market, where it is assumed that interest will be paid 180 days later. Hence, the payoff on an FRA is discounted by the spot rate on 180-day LIBOR to give a present value for the payoff as of the expiration date.

Just as an FRA is a forward contract in which the underlying is an interest rate, an **interest rate option** is an option in which the underlying is an interest rate. Instead of an exercise price, it has an **exercise rate** (or **strike rate**), which is expressed on an order of magnitude of an interest rate. At expiration, the option payoff is based on the difference between the underlying rate in the market and the exercise rate. Whereas an FRA is a *commitment* to make one interest payment and receive another at a future date, an interest rate option is the *right* to make one interest payment and receive another. And just as there are call and put options, there is also an **interest rate call** and an **interest rate put**.

An interest rate call is an option in which the holder has the right to make a known interest payment and receive an unknown interest payment. The underlying is the unknown interest rate. If the unknown underlying rate turns out to be higher than the exercise rate at expiration, the option is in-the-money and is exercised; otherwise, the option simply expires. *An interest rate put is an option in which the holder has the right to make an unknown interest payment and receive a known interest payment.* If the unknown underlying rate turns out to be lower than the exercise rate at expiration, the option is in-the-money and is exercised; otherwise, the option simply expires. All interest rate option contracts have a specified size, which, as in FRAs, is called the notional principal. An interest rate option can be European or American style, but most tend to be European style. Interest rate options are settled in cash.

As with FRAs, these options are offered for purchase and sale by dealers, which are financial institutions, usually the same ones who offer FRAs. These dealers quote rates for options of various exercise prices and expirations. When a dealer takes an option position, it usually then offsets the risk with other transactions, often Eurodollar futures.

To use the same example we used in introducing FRAs, consider options expiring in 90 days on 180-day LIBOR. The option buyer specifies whatever exercise rate he desires. Let us say he chooses an exercise rate of 5.5 percent and a notional principal of $10 million.

Now let us move to the expiration day. Suppose that 180-day LIBOR is 6 percent. Then the call option is in-the-money. The payoff to the holder of the option is

$$(\$10{,}000{,}000)\,(0.06 - 0.055)\left(\frac{180}{360}\right) = \$25{,}000$$

This money is not paid at expiration, however; it is paid 180 days later. There is no reason why the payoff could not be made at expiration, as is done with an FRA. The delay of payment associated with interest rate options actually makes more sense, because these instruments are commonly used to hedge floating-rate loans in which the rate is set on a given day but the interest is paid later.

Note that the difference between the underlying rate and the exercise rate is multiplied by 180/360 to reflect the fact that the rate quoted is a 180-day rate but is stated as an annual rate. Also, the interest calculation is multiplied by the notional principal.

In general, the payoff of an interest rate call is

$$(\text{Notional Principal})\,\text{Max}\,(0, \text{Underlying rate at expiration}$$
$$- \text{Exercise rate})\left(\frac{\text{Days in underlying rate}}{360}\right)$$

(64-1)

The expression Max(0,Underlying rate at expiration − Exercise rate) is similar to a form that we shall commonly see throughout this reading for all options. The payoff of a call option at expiration is based on the maximum of zero or the underlying minus the exercise rate. If the option expires out-of-the-money, then "Underlying rate at expiration − Exercise rate" is negative; consequently, zero is greater. Thus, the option expires with no value. If the option expires in-the-money, "Underlying rate at expiration − Exercise rate" is positive. Thus, the option expires worth this difference (multiplied by the notional principal and the Days/360 adjustment). The expression "Days in underlying rate," which we used in Reading 62, refers to the fact that the rate is specified as the rate on an instrument of a specific number of days to maturity, such as a 90-day or 180-day rate, thereby requiring that we multiply by 90/360 or 180/360 or some similar adjustment.

For an interest rate put option, the general formula is

$$(\text{Notional Principal})\,\text{Max}\!\left(0, \text{Exercise rate} - \text{Underlying rate at expiration}\right)\!\left(\frac{\text{Days in underlying rate}}{360}\right) \quad \textbf{(64-2)}$$

For an exercise rate of 5.5 percent and an underlying rate at expiration of 6 percent, an interest rate put expires out-of-the-money. Only if the underlying rate is less than the exercise rate does the put option expire in-the-money.

As noted above, borrowers often use interest rate call options to hedge the risk of rising rates on floating-rate loans. Lenders often use interest rate put options to hedge the risk of falling rates on floating-rate loans. The form we have seen here, in which the option expires with a single payoff, is not the more commonly used variety of interest rate option. Floating-rate loans usually involve multiple interest payments. Each of those payments is set on a given date. To hedge the risk of interest rates increasing, the borrower would need options expiring on each rate reset date. Thus, the borrower would require a combination of interest rate call options. Likewise, a lender needing to hedge the risk of falling rates on a multiple-payment floating-rate loan would need a combination of interest rate put options.

A combination of interest rate calls is referred to as an **interest rate cap** or sometimes just a **cap**. A combination of interest rate puts is called an **interest rate floor** or sometimes just a **floor**.[8] Specifically, *an interest rate cap is a series of call options on an interest rate, with each option expiring at the date on which the floating loan rate will be reset, and with each option having the same exercise rate.*[9] Each option is independent of the others; thus, exercise of one option does not affect the right to exercise any of the others. Each component call option is called a **caplet**. *An interest rate floor is a series of put options on an interest rate, with each option expiring at the date on which the floating loan rate will be reset, and with each option having the same exercise rate.* Each component put option is called a **floorlet**. The price of an interest rate cap or floor is the sum of the prices of the options that make up the cap or floor.

A special combination of caps and floors is called an **interest rate collar**. *An interest rate collar is a combination of a long cap and a short floor or a short cap and a long floor.* Consider a borrower in a floating rate loan who wants to hedge the risk of rising interest rates but is concerned about the requirement that this hedge must have a cash outlay up front: the option premium. A collar, which adds a short floor to a long cap, is a way of reducing and even eliminating the up-front cost of the cap. The sale of the floor brings in cash that reduces the cost of the cap. It is possible to set the exercise rates such that the price received for the sale of the floor precisely offsets the price paid for the cap, thereby completely eliminating the up-front cost. This transaction is sometimes called a **zero-cost collar**. The term is a bit misleading, however, and brings to mind the importance of noting the true cost of a collar. Although the cap allows the borrower to be paid from the call options when rates are high, the sale of the floor requires the borrower to pay the counterparty when rates are low. Thus, the cost of protection against rising rates is the loss of the advantage of falling rates. Caps, floors, and collars are popular instruments in the interest rate markets.

Although interest rate options are primarily written on such rates as LIBOR, Euribor, and Euroyen, the underlying can be any interest rate.

---

[8] It is possible to construct caps and floors with options on any other type of underlying, but they are very often used when the underlying is an interest rate.

[9] Technically, each option need not have the same exercise rate, but they generally do.

4.1.5 Currency Options

As we noted in Reading 62, the currency forward market is quite large. The same is true for the currency options market. A **currency option** allows the holder to buy (if a call) or sell (if a put) an underlying currency at a fixed exercise rate, expressed as an exchange rate. Many companies, knowing that they will need to convert a currency X at a future date into a currency Y, will buy a call option on currency Y specified in terms of currency X. For example, say that a U.S. company will be needing €50 million for an expansion project in three months. Thus, it will be buying euros and is exposed to the risk of the euro rising against the dollar. Even though it has that concern, it would also like to benefit if the euro weakens against the dollar. Thus, it might buy a call option on the euro. Let us say it specifies an exercise rate of $0.90. So it pays cash up front for the right to buy €50 million at a rate of $0.90 per euro. If the option expires with the euro above $0.90, it can buy euros at $0.90 and avoid any additional cost over $0.90. If the option expires with the euro below $0.90, it does not exercise the option and buys euros at the market rate.

Note closely these two cases:

Euro expires above $0.90
Company buys €50 million at $0.90
Euro expires at or below $0.90
Company buys €50 million at the market rate

These outcomes can also be viewed in the following manner:

Dollar expires below €1.1111, that is, €1 > $0.90
Company sells $45 million (€50 million × $0.90) at €1.1111, equivalent to buying €50 million
Dollar expires above €1.1111, that is, €1 < $0.90
Company sells sufficient dollars to buy €50 million at the market rate

This transaction looks more like a put in which the underlying is the dollar and the exercise rate is expressed as €1.1111. Thus, the call on the euro can be viewed as a put on the dollar. Specifically, a call to buy €50 million at an exercise price of $0.90 is also a put to sell €50 million × $0.90 = $45 million at an exercise price of 1/$0.90, or €1.1111.

Most foreign currency options activity occurs on the customized over-the-counter markets. Some exchange-listed currency options trade on a few exchanges, but activity is fairly low.

4.2 Options on Futures

In Reading 62 we covered futures markets. One of the important innovations of futures markets is options on futures. These contracts originated in the United States as a result of a regulatory structure that separated exchange-listed options and futures markets. The former are regulated by the Securities and Exchange Commission, and the latter are regulated by the Commodity Futures Trading Commission (**CFTC**). SEC regulations forbid the trading of options side by side with their underlying instruments. Options on stocks trade on one exchange, and the underlying trades on another or on Nasdaq.

The futures exchanges got the idea that they could offer options in which the underlying is a futures contract; no such prohibitions for side-by-side trading existed under CFTC rules. As a result, the futures exchanges were able to add an attractive instrument to their product lines. The side-by-side trading of the option and its underlying futures made for excellent arbitrage linkages between these instruments. Moreover, some of the options on futures are designed to expire on the same day the underlying futures expires. Thus, the options on the futures are effectively options on the spot asset that underlies the futures.

A call option on a futures gives the holder the right to enter into a long futures contract at a fixed futures price. A put option on a futures gives the holder the right to enter into a short futures contract at a fixed futures price. The fixed futures price is, of course, the exercise price. Consider an option on the Eurodollar futures contract trading at the Chicago Mercantile Exchange. On 13 June of a particular year, an option expiring on 13 July was based on the July Eurodollar futures contract. That futures contract expires on 16 July, a few days after the option expires.[10] The call option with exercise price of 95.75 had a price of $4.60. The underlying futures price was 96.21. Recall that this price is the IMM index value, which means that the price is based on a discount rate of $100 - 96.21 = 3.79$. The contract size is $1 million.

The buyer of this call option on a futures would pay $0.046(\$1,000,000) = \$46,000$ and would obtain the right to buy the July futures contract at a price of 95.75. Thus, at that time, the option was in the money by $96.21 - 95.75 = 0.46$ per $100 face value. Suppose that when the option expires, the futures price is 96.00. Then the holder of the call would exercise it and obtain a long futures position at a price of 95.75. The price of the underlying futures is 96.00, so the margin account is immediately marked to market with a credit of 0.25 or $625.[11] The party on the short side of the contract is immediately set up with a short futures contract at the price of 95.75. That party will be charged the $625 gain that the long made. If the option is a put, exercise of it establishes a short position. The exchange assigns the put writer a long futures position.

4.3 Commodity Options

Options in which the asset underlying the option is a commodity, such as oil, gold, wheat, or soybeans, are also widely traded. There are exchange-traded as well as over-the-counter versions. Over-the-counter options on oil are widely used.

Our focus in this reading is on financial instruments so we will not spend any time on **commodity options**, but readers should be aware of the existence and use of these instruments by companies whose business involves the buying and selling of these commodities.

---

[10] Some options on futures expire a month or so before the futures expires. Others expire very close to, if not at, the futures expiration.

[11] If the contract is in-the-money by $96 - 95.75 = 0.25$ per $100 par, it is in-the-money by $0.25/100 = 0.0025$, or 0.25 percent of the face value. Because the face value is $1 million, the contract is in the money by $(0.0025)(90/360)(\$1,000,000) = \$625$. (Note the adjustment by 90/360) Another way to look at this calculation is that the futures price at 95.75 is $1 - (0.0425)(90/360) = \$0.989375$ per $1 par, or $989,375. At 96, the futures price is $1 - 0.04(90/360) = \$0.99$ per $1 par or $990,000. The difference is $625. So, exercising this option is like entering into a futures contract at a price of $989,375 and having the price immediately go to $990,000, a gain of $625. The call holder must deposit money to meet the Eurodollar futures margin, but the exercise of the option gives him $625. In other words, assuming he meets the minimum initial margin requirement, he is immediately credited with $625 more.

4.4 Other Types of Options

As derivative markets develop, options (and even some other types of derivatives) have begun to emerge on such underlyings as electricity, various sources of energy, and even weather. These instruments are almost exclusively customized over-the-counter instruments. Perhaps the most notable feature of these instruments is how the underlyings are often instruments that cannot actually be held. For example, electricity is not considered a storable asset because it is produced and almost immediately consumed, but it is nonetheless an asset and certainly has a volatile price. Consequently, it is ideally suited for options and other derivatives trading.

Consider weather. It is hardly an asset at all but simply a random factor that exerts an enormous influence on economic activity. The need to hedge against and speculate on the weather has created a market in which measures of weather activity, such as economic losses from storms or average temperature or rainfall, are structured into a derivative instrument. Option versions of these derivatives are growing in importance and use. For example, consider a company that generates considerable revenue from outdoor summer activities, provided that it does not rain. Obviously a certain amount of rain will occur, but the more rain, the greater the losses for the company. It could buy a call option on the amount of rainfall with the exercise price stated as a quantity of rainfall. If actual rainfall exceeds the exercise price, the company exercises the option and receives an amount of money related to the excess of the rainfall amount over the exercise price.

Another type of option, which is not at all new but is increasingly recognized in practice, is the real option. A real option is an option associated with the flexibility inherent in capital investment projects. For example, companies may invest in new projects that have the option to defer the full investment, expand or contract the project at a later date, or even terminate the project. In fact, most capital investment projects have numerous elements of flexibility that can be viewed as options. Of course, these options do not trade in markets the same way as financial and commodity options, and they must be evaluated much more carefully. They are, nonetheless, options and thus have the potential for generating enormous value.

Again, our emphasis is on financial options, but readers should be aware of the growing role of these other types of options in our economy. Investors who buy shares in companies that have real options are, in effect, buying real options. In addition, commodity and other types of options are sometimes found in investment portfolios in the form of "alternative investments" and can provide significant diversification benefits.

To this point, we have examined characteristics of options markets and contracts. Now we move forward to the all-important topic of how options are priced.

PRINCIPLES OF OPTION PRICING

5

In Readings 62 and 63, we discussed the pricing and valuation of forward and futures contracts. Recall that the value of a contract is what someone must pay to buy into it or what someone would receive to sell out of it. A forward or futures contract has zero value at the start of the contract, but the value turns positive or negative as prices or rates change. A contract that has positive value to one party and negative value to the counterparty can turn around and have negative value to the former and positive value to the latter as prices or rates change. The forward or futures price is the price that the parties agree will be paid on the future date to buy and sell the underlying.

With options, these concepts are different. An option has a positive value at the start. The buyer must pay money and the seller receives money to initiate the contract. Prior to expiration, the option always has positive value to the buyer and negative value to the seller. In a forward or futures contract, the two parties agree on the fixed price the buyer will pay the seller. This fixed price is set such that the buyer and seller do not exchange any money. The corresponding fixed price at which a call holder can buy the underlying or a put holder can sell the underlying is the exercise price. It, too, is negotiated between buyer and seller but still results in the buyer paying the seller money up front in the form of an option premium or price.[12]

Thus, what we called the forward or futures price corresponds more to the exercise price of an option. The option price *is* the option value: With a few exceptions that will be clearly noted, in this reading we do not distinguish between the option price and value.

In this section of the reading, we examine the principles of option pricing. These principles are characteristics of option prices that are governed by the rationality of investors. These principles alone do not allow us to calculate the option price. We do that in Section 6.

Before we begin, it is important to remind the reader that we assume all participants in the market behave in a rational manner such that they do not throw away money and that they take advantage of arbitrage opportunities. As such, we assume that markets are sufficiently competitive that no arbitrage opportunities exist.

Let us start by developing the notation, which is very similar to what we have used previously. Note that time 0 is today and time T is the expiration.

S_0, S_T = price of the underlying asset at time 0 (today) and time T (expiration)

X = exercise price

r = risk-free rate

T = time to expiration, equal to number of days to expiration divided by 365

c_0, c_T = price of European call today and at expiration

C_0, C_T = price of American call today and at expiration

p_0, p_T = price of European put today and at expiration

P_0, P_T = price of American put today and at expiration

On occasion, we will introduce some variations of the above as well as some new notation. For example, we start off with no cash flows on the underlying, but we shall discuss the effects of cash flows on the underlying in Section 5.7.

5.1 Payoff Values

The easiest time to determine an option's value is at expiration. At that point, there is no future. Only the present matters. An option's value at expiration is called its **payoff**. We introduced this material briefly in our basic descriptions of types of options; now we cover it in more depth.

At expiration, a call option is worth either zero or the difference between the underlying price and the exercise price, whichever is greater.

$$c_T = \text{Max}(0, S_T - X)$$

$$C_T = \text{Max}(0, S_T - X)$$

(64-3)

---

[12] For a call, there is no finite exercise price that drives the option price to zero. For a put, the unrealistic example of a zero exercise price would make the put price be zero.

Note that at expiration, a European option and an American option have the same payoff because they are equivalent instruments at that point.

The expression $\text{Max}(0, S_T - X)$ means to take the greater of zero or $S_T - X$. Suppose the underlying price exceeds the exercise price, $S_T > X$. In this case, the option is expiring in-the-money and the option is worth $S_T - X$. Suppose that at the instant of expiration, it is possible to buy the option for less than $S_T - X$. Then one could buy the option, immediately exercise it, and immediately sell the underlying. Doing so would cost c_T (or C_T) for the option and X to buy the underlying but would bring in S_T for the sale of the underlying. If c_T (or C_T) $< S_T - X$, this transaction would net an immediate risk-free profit. The collective actions of all investors doing this would force the option price up to $S_T - X$. The price could not go higher than $S_T - X$, because all that the option holder would end up with an instant later when the option expires is $S_T - X$. If $S_T < X$, meaning that the call is expiring out-of-the-money, the formula says the option should be worth zero. It cannot sell for less than zero because that would mean that the option seller would have to pay the option buyer. A buyer would not pay more than zero, because the option will expire an instant later with no value.

At expiration, a put option is worth either zero or the difference between the exercise price and the underlying price, whichever is greater.

$$p_T = \text{Max}(0, X - S_T)$$
$$P_T = \text{Max}(0, X - S_T)$$

(64-4)

Suppose $S_T < X$, meaning that the put is expiring in-the-money. At the instant of expiration, suppose the put is selling for less than $X - S_T$. Then an investor buys the put for p_T (or P_T) and the underlying for S_T and exercises the put, receiving X. If p_T (or P_T) $< X - S_T$, this transaction will net an immediate risk-free profit. The combined actions of participants doing this will force the put price up to $X - S_T$. It cannot go any higher, because the put buyer will end up an instant later with only $X - S_T$ and would not pay more than this. If $S_T > X$, meaning that the put is expiring out-of-the-money, it is worth zero. It cannot be worth less than zero because the option seller would have to pay the option buyer. It cannot be worth more than zero because the buyer would not pay for a position that, an instant later, will be worth nothing.

These important results are summarized along with an example in Exhibit 5. The payoff diagrams for the short positions are also shown and are obtained as the negative of the long positions. For the special case of $S_T = X$, meaning that both call and put are expiring at-the-money, we can effectively treat the option as out-of-the-money because it is worth zero at expiration.

The value $\text{Max}(0, S_T - X)$ for calls or $\text{Max}(0, X - S_T)$ for puts is also called the option's **intrinsic value** or exercise value. We shall use the former terminology. Intrinsic value is what the option is worth to exercise it based on current conditions. In this section, we have talked only about the option at expiration. Prior to expiration, an option will normally sell for more than its intrinsic value.[13] The difference between the market price of the option and its intrinsic value is called its **time value** or speculative value. We shall use the former terminology. The time value reflects the potential for the option's intrinsic value at expiration to be greater than its current intrinsic value. At expiration, of course, the time value is zero.

---

[13] We shall later see an exception to this statement for European puts, but for now take it as the truth.

		Example (X = 50)	
Option	Value	$S_T = 52$	$S_T = 48$
European call	$c_T = \text{Max}(0, S_T - X)$	$c_T = \text{Max}(0, 52 - 50) = 2$	$c_T = \text{Max}(0, 48 - 50) = 0$
American call	$C_T = \text{Max}(0, S_T - X)$	$C_T = \text{Max}(0, 52 - 50) = 2$	$C_T = \text{Max}(0, 48 - 50) = 0$
European put	$p_T = \text{Max}(0, X - S_T)$	$p_T = \text{Max}(0, 50 - 52) = 0$	$p_T = \text{Max}(0, 50 - 48) = 2$
American put	$P_T = \text{Max}(0, X - S_T)$	$P_T = \text{Max}(0, 50 - 52) = 0$	$P_T = \text{Max}(0, 50 - 48) = 2$

EXHIBIT 5   **Option Values at Expiration (Payoffs)**

Notes: Results for the European and American calls correspond to Graph A. Results for Graph B are the negative of Graph A. Results for the European and American puts correspond to Graph C, and results for Graph D are the negative of Graph C.

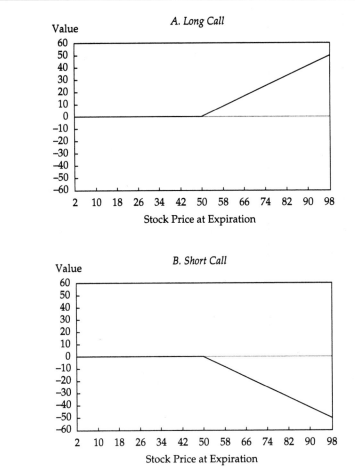

(Exhibit continued on next page ...)

EXHIBIT 5   (continued)

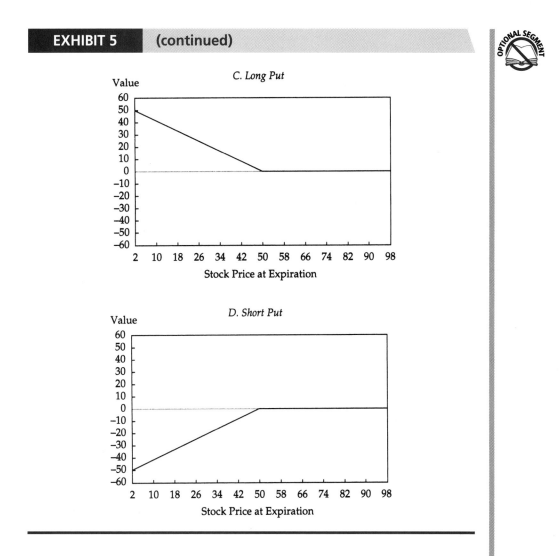

EXAMPLE 1

For Parts A through E, determine the payoffs of calls and puts under the conditions given.

A. The underlying is a stock index and is at 5,601.19 when the options expire. The multiplier is 500. The exercise price is

   i. 5,500

   ii. 6,000

B. The underlying is a bond and is at $1.035 per $1 par when the options expire. The contract is on $100,000 face value of bonds. The exercise price is

   i. $1.00

   ii. $1.05

C. The underlying is a 90-day interest rate and is at 9 percent when the options expire. The notional principal is $50 million. The exercise rate is

   i. 8 percent.

   ii. 10.5 percent.

D. The underlying is the Swiss franc and is at $0.775 when the options expire. The options are on SF500,000. The exercise price is

   i. $0.75.

   ii. $0.81.

E. The underlying is a futures contract and is at 110.5 when the options expire. The options are on a futures contract covering $1 million of the underlying. These prices are percentages of par. The exercise price is

   i. 110.

   ii. 115.

For Parts F and G, determine the payoffs of the strategies indicated and describe the payoff graph.

F. The underlying is a stock priced at $40. A call option with an exercise price of $40 is selling for $7. You buy the stock and sell the call. At expiration, the stock price is

   i. $52.

   ii. $38.

G. The underlying is a stock priced at $60. A put option with an exercise price of $60 is priced at $5. You buy the stock and buy the put. At expiration, the stock price is

   i. $68.

   ii. $50.

Solution to A:
  i. Calls: $\text{Max}(0, 5601.19 - 5500) \times 500 = 50{,}595$
     Puts: $\text{Max}(0, 5500 - 5601.19) \times 500 = 0$

  ii. Calls: $\text{Max}(0, 5601.19 - 6000) \times 500 = 0$
     Puts: $\text{Max}(0, 6000 - 5601.19) \times 500 = 199{,}405$

Solution to B:
  i. Calls: $\text{Max}(0, 1.035 - 1.00) \times \$100{,}000 = \$3{,}500$
     Puts: $\text{Max}(0, 1.00 - 1.035) \times \$100{,}000 = \$0$

  ii. Calls: $\text{Max}(0, 1.035 - 1.05) \times \$100{,}000 = \$0$
     Puts: $\text{Max}(0, 1.05 - 1.035) \times \$100{,}000 = \$1{,}500$

Solution to C:
  i. Calls: $\text{Max}(0, 0.09 - 0.08) \times (90/360) \times \$50{,}000{,}000 = \$125{,}000$
     Puts: $\text{Max}(0, 0.08 - 0.09) \times (90/360) \times \$50{,}000{,}000 = \$0$

  ii. Calls: $\text{Max}(0, 0.09 - 0.105) \times (90/360) \times \$50{,}000{,}000 = \$0$
     Puts: $\text{Max}(0, 0.105 - 0.09) \times (90/360) \times \$50{,}000{,}000 = \$187{,}500$

Solution to D: **i.** Calls: $\text{Max}(0, 0.775 - 0.75) \times \$500{,}000 = \$12{,}500$
                           Puts: $\text{Max}(0, 0.75 - 0.775) \times \$500{,}000 = \$0$

                     ii. Calls: $\text{Max}(0, 0.775 - 0.81) \times \$500{,}000 = \$0$
                           Puts: $\text{Max}(0, 0.81 - 0.775) \times \$500{,}000 = \$17{,}500$

Solution to E: **i.** Calls: $\text{Max}(0, 110.5 - 110) \times (1/100) \times \$1{,}000{,}000 = \$5{,}000$
                           Puts: $\text{Max}(0, 110 - 110.5) \times (1/100) \times \$1{,}000{,}000 = \$0$

                     ii. Calls: $\text{Max}(0, 110.5 - 115) \times (1/100) \times \$1{,}000{,}000 = \$0$
                           Puts: $\text{Max}(0, 115 - 110.5) \times (1/100) \times \$1{,}000{,}000 = \$45{,}000$

Solution to F: **i.** $52 - \text{Max}(0, 52 - 40) = 40$
                     ii. $38 - \text{Max}(0, 38 - 40) = 38$

For any value of the stock price at expiration of 40 or above, the payoff is constant at 40. For stock price values below 40 at expiration, the payoff declines with the stock price. The graph would look similar to the short put in Panel D of Exhibit 5. This strategy is known as a covered call.

Solution to G: **i.** $68 + \text{Max}(0, 60 - 68) = 68$
                     ii. $50 + \text{Max}(0, 60 - 50) = 60$

For any value of the stock price at expiration of 60 or below, the payoff is constant at 60. For stock price values above 60 at expiration, the payoff increases with the stock price at expiration. The graph will look similar to the long call in Panel A of Exhibit 5. This strategy is known as a **protective put** and is covered later in this reading.

There is no question that everyone agrees on the option's intrinsic value; after all, it is based on the current stock price and exercise price. It is the time value that we have more difficulty estimating. So remembering that *Option price = Intrinsic value + Time value,* let us move forward and attempt to determine the value of an option today, prior to expiration.

5.2 Boundary Conditions

We start by examining some simple results that establish minimum and maximum values for options prior to expiration.

5.2.1 Minimum and Maximum Values

The first and perhaps most obvious result is one we have already alluded to: *The minimum value of any option is zero.* We state this formally as

$$c_0 \geq 0, C_0 \geq 0$$
$$p_0 \geq 0, P_0 \geq 0$$

(64-5)

No option can sell for less than zero, for in that case the writer would have to pay the buyer.

Now consider the maximum value of an option. It differs somewhat depending on whether the option is a call or a put and whether it is European or American. *The maximum value of a call is the current value of the underlying:*

$$c_0 \leq S_0, C_0 \leq S_0 \qquad \textbf{(64-6)}$$

A call is a means of buying the underlying. It would not make sense to pay more for the right to buy the underlying than the value of the underlying itself.

For a put, it makes a difference whether the put is European or American. One way to see the maximum value for puts is to consider the best possible outcome for the put holder. The best outcome is that the underlying goes to a value of zero. Then the put holder could sell a worthless asset for X. For an American put, the holder could sell it immediately and capture a value of X. For a European put, the holder would have to wait until expiration; consequently, we must discount X from the expiration day to the present. Thus, *the maximum value of a European put is the present value of the exercise price. The maximum value of an American put is the exercise price,*

$$P_0 \leq X/(1 + r)^T, P_0 \leq X \qquad \textbf{(64-7)}$$

where r is the risk-free interest rate and T is the time to expiration. These results for the maximums and minimums for calls and puts are summarized in Exhibit 6, which also includes a numerical example.

EXHIBIT 6	Minimum and Maximum Values of Options		
Option	Minimum Value	Maximum Value	Example (S_0 = 52, X = 50, r = 5%, T = 1/2 year)
European call	$c_0 \geq 0$	$c_0 \leq S_0$	$0 \leq c_0 \leq 52$
American call	$C_0 \geq 0$	$C_0 \leq S_0$	$0 \leq C_0 \leq 52$
European put	$p_0 \geq 0$	$p_0 \leq X/(1 + r)^T$	$0 \leq p_0 \leq 48.80$ [$48.80 = 50/(1.05)^{0.5}$]
American put	$P_0 \geq 0$	$P_0 \leq X$	$0 \leq P_0 \leq 50$

5.2.2 *Lower Bounds*

The results we established in Section 5.2.1 do not put much in the way of restrictions on the option price. They tell us that the price is somewhere between zero and the maximum, which is either the underlying price, the exercise price, or the present value of the exercise price—a fairly wide range of possibilities. Fortunately, we can tighten the range up a little on the low side: We can establish a **lower bound** on the option price.

For American options, which are exercisable immediately, we can state that the lower bound of an American option price is its current intrinsic value:[14]

---

[14] Normally we have italicized sentences containing important results. This one, however, is a little different: We are stating it temporarily. We shall soon show that we can override one of these results with a lower bound that is higher and, therefore, is a better lower bound.

$$C_0 \geq Max(0, S_0 - X)$$
$$P_0 \geq Max(0, X - S_0)$$

(64-8)

The reason these results hold today is the same reason we have already shown for why they must hold at expiration. If the option is in-the-money and is selling for less than its intrinsic value, it can be bought and exercised to net an immediate risk-free profit.[15] The collective actions of market participants doing this will force the American option price up to at least the intrinsic value.

Unfortunately, we cannot make such a statement about European options—but we can show that the lower bound is either zero or the current underlying price minus the present value of the exercise price, whichever is greater. They cannot be exercised early; thus, there is no way for market participants to exercise an option selling for too little with respect to its intrinsic value. Fortunately, however, there is a way to establish a lower bound for European options. We can combine options with risk-free bonds and the underlying in such a way that a lower bound for the option price emerges.

First, we need the ability to buy and sell a risk-free bond with a face value equal to the exercise price and current value equal to the present value of the exercise price. This procedure is simple but perhaps not obvious. If the exercise price is X (say, 100), we buy a bond with a face value of X (100) maturing on the option expiration day. The current value of that bond is the present value of X, which is $X/(1 + r)^T$. So we buy the bond today for $X/(1 + r)^T$ and hold it until it matures on the option expiration day, at which time it will pay off X. We assume that we can buy or sell (issue) this type of bond. Note that this transaction involves borrowing or lending an amount of money equal to the present value of the exercise price with repayment of the full exercise price.

Exhibit 7 illustrates the construction of a special combination of instruments. We buy the European call and the risk-free bond and sell short the underlying asset. Recall that short selling involves borrowing the asset and selling it. At expiration, we shall buy back the asset. In order to illustrate the logic behind the lower bound for a European call in the simplest way, we assume that we can sell short without any restrictions.

In Exhibit 7 the two right-hand columns contain the value of each instrument when the option expires. The rightmost column is the case of the call

		Value at Expiration	
Transaction	**Current Value**	$S_T \leq X$	$S_T > X$
Buy call	c_0	0	$S_T - X$
Sell short underlying	$-S_0$	$-S_T$	$-S_T$
Buy bond	$X/(1 + r)^T$	X	X
Total	$c_0 - S_0 + X/(1 + r)^T$	$X - S_T \geq 0$	0

EXHIBIT 7   A Lower Bound Combination for European Calls

---

[15] Consider, for example, an in-the-money call selling for less than $S_0 - X$. One can buy the call for C_0, exercise it, paying X, and sell the underlying netting a gain of $S_0 - X - C_0$. This value is positive and represents an immediate risk-free gain. If the option is an in-the-money put selling for less than $X - S_0$, one can buy the put for P_0, buy the underlying for S_0, and exercise the put to receive X, thereby netting an immediate risk-free gain of $X - S_0 - P_0$.

expiring in-the-money, in which case it is worth $S_T - X$. In the other column, the out-of-the-money case, the call is worth zero. The underlying is worth $-S_T$ (the negative of its current value) in either case, reflecting the fact that we buy it back to cover the short position. The bond is worth X in both cases. The sum of all the positions is positive when the option expires out-of-the-money and zero when the option expires in-the-money. Therefore, in no case does this combination of instruments have a negative value. That means that we never have to pay out any money at expiration. We are guaranteed at least no loss at expiration and possibly something positive.

If there is a possibility of a positive outcome from the combination and if we know we shall never have to pay anything out from holding a combination of instruments, the cost of that combination must be positive—it must cost us something to enter into the position. We cannot take in money to enter into the position. In that case, we would be receiving money up front and never having to pay anything out. The cost of entering the position is shown in the second column, labeled the "Current Value." Because that value must be positive, we therefore require that $c_0 - S_0 + X/(1 + r)^T \geq 0$. Rearranging this equation, we obtain $c_0 \geq S_0 - X/(1 + r)^T$. Now we have a statement about the minimum value of the option, which can serve as a lower bound. This result is solid, because if the call is selling for less than $S_0 - X/(1 + r)^T$, an investor can buy the call, sell short the underlying, and buy the bond. Doing so would bring in money up front and, as we see in Exhibit 7, an investor would not have to pay out any money at expiration and might even get a little more money. Because other investors would do the same, the call price would be forced up until it is at least $S_0 - X/(1 + r)^T$.

But we can improve on this result. Suppose $S_0 - X/(1 + r)^T$ is negative. Then we are stating that the call price is greater than a negative number. But we already know that the call price cannot be negative. So we can now say that

$$c_0 \geq \text{Max}[0, S_0 - X/(1 + r)^T]$$

In other words, *the lower bound on a European call price is either zero or the underlying price minus the present value of the exercise price, whichever is greater.* Notice how this lower bound differs from the lower bound for the American call, $\text{Max}(0, S_0 - X)$. For the European call, we must wait to pay the exercise price and obtain the underlying. Therefore, the expression contains the current underlying value—the present value of its future value—as well as the present value of the exercise price. For the American call, we do not have to wait until expiration; therefore, the expression reflects the potential to immediately receive the underlying price minus the exercise price. We shall have more to say, however, about the relationship between these two values.

To illustrate the lower bound, let $X = 50$, $r = 0.05$, and $T = 0.5$. If the current underlying price is 45, then the lower bound for the European call is

$$\text{Max}[0, 45 - 50/(1.05)^{0.5}] = \text{Max}(0, 45 - 48.80) = \text{Max}(0, -3.80) = 0$$

All this calculation tells us is that the call must be worth no less than zero, which we already knew. If the current underlying price is 54, however, the lower bound for the European call is

$$\text{Max}(0, 54 - 48.80) = \text{Max}(0, 5.20) = 5.20$$

which tells us that the call must be worth no less than 5.20. With European puts, we can also see that the lower bound differs from the lower bound on American puts in this same use of the present value of the exercise price.

		Value at Expiration	
Transaction	**Current Value**	$S_T < X$	$S_T \geq X$
Buy put	p_0	$X - S_T$	0
Buy underlying	S_0	S_T	S_T
Issue bond	$-X/(1 + r)^T$	$-X$	$-X$
Total	$p_0 + S_0 - X/(1 + r)^T$	0	$S_T - X \geq 0$

EXHIBIT 8   **A Lower Bound Combination for European Puts**

Exhibit 8 constructs a similar type of portfolio for European puts. Here, however, we buy the put and the underlying and borrow by issuing the zero-coupon bond. The payoff of each instrument is indicated in the two rightmost columns. Note that the total payoff is never less than zero. Consequently, the initial value of the combination must not be less than zero. Therefore, $p_0 + S_0 - X/(1 + r)^T \geq 0$. Isolating the put price gives us $p_0 \geq X/(1 + r)^T - S_0$. But suppose that $X/(1 + r)^T - S_0$ is negative. Then, the put price must be greater than a negative number. We know that the put price must be no less than zero. So we can now formally say that

$$p_0 \geq Max[0, X/(1 + r)^T - S_0]$$

In other words, *the lower bound of a European put is the greater of either zero or the present value of the exercise price minus the underlying price.* For the American put, recall that the expression was $Max(0, X - S_0)$. So for the European put, we adjust this value to the present value of the exercise price. The present value of the asset price is already adjusted to S_0.

Using the same example we did for calls, let $X = 50$, $r = 0.05$, and $T = 0.5$. If the current underlying price is 45, then the lower bound for the European put is

$$Max(0, 50/(1.05)^{0.5} - 45) = Max(0, 48.80 - 45) = Max(0, 3.80) = 3.80$$

If the current underlying price is 54, however, the lower bound is

$$Max(0, 48.80 - 54) = Max(0, -5.20) = 0$$

At this point let us reconsider what we have found. The lower bound for a European call is $Max[0, S_0 - X/(1 + r)^T]$. We also observed that an American call must be worth at least $Max(0, S_0 - X)$. But except at expiration, the European lower bound is greater than the minimum value of the American call.[16] We could not, however, expect an American call to be worth less than a European call. Thus the lower bound of the European call holds for American calls as well. Hence, we can conclude that

$$c_0 \geq Max[0, S_0 - X/(1 + r)^T]$$
$$C_0 \geq Max[0, S_0 - X/(1 + r)^T]$$

(64-9)

---

[16] We discuss this point more formally and in the context of whether it is ever worthwhile to exercise an American call early in Section 5.6.

For European puts, the lower bound is $\text{Max}[0, X/(1+r)^T - S_0]$. For American puts, the minimum price is $\text{Max}(0, X - S_0)$. The European lower bound is lower than the minimum price of the American put, so the American put lower bound is not changed to the European lower bound, the way we did for calls. Hence,

$$p_0 \geq \text{Max}[0, X/(1+r)^T - S_0]$$
$$P_0 \geq \text{Max}(0, X - S_0)$$

(64-10)

These results tell us the lowest possible price for European and American options.

Recall that we previously referred to an option price as having an intrinsic value and a time value. For American options, the intrinsic value is the value if exercised, $\text{Max}(0, S_0 - X)$ for calls and $\text{Max}(0, X - S_0)$ for puts. The remainder of the option price is the time value. For European options, the notion of a time value is somewhat murky, because it first requires recognition of an intrinsic value. Because a European option cannot be exercised until expiration, in a sense, all of the value of a European option is time value. The notion of an intrinsic value and its **complement**, a time value, is therefore inappropriate for European options, though the concepts are commonly applied to European options. Fortunately, understanding European options does not require that we separate intrinsic value from time value. We shall include them together as they make up the option price.

EXAMPLE 2

Consider call and put options expiring in 42 days, in which the underlying is at 72 and the risk-free rate is 4.5 percent. The underlying makes no cash payments during the life of the options.

A. Find the lower bounds for European calls and puts with exercise prices of 70 and 75.

B. Find the lower bounds for American calls and puts with exercise prices of 70 and 75.

Solution to A:
70 call: $\text{Max}[0, 72 - 70/(1.045)^{0.1151}] = \text{Max}(0, 2.35) = 2.35$
75 call: $\text{Max}[0, 72 - 75/(1.045)^{0.1151}] = \text{Max}(0, -2.62) = 0$
70 put: $\text{Max}[0, 70/(1.045)^{0.1151} - 72] = \text{Max}(0, -2.35) = 0$
75 put: $\text{Max}[0, 75/(1.045)^{0.1151} - 72] = \text{Max}(0, 2.62) = 2.62$

Solution to B:
70 call: $\text{Max}[0, 72 - 70/(1.045)^{0.1151}] = \text{Max}(0, 2.35) = 2.35$
75 call: $\text{Max}[0, 72 - 75/(1.045)^{0.1151}] = \text{Max}(0, -2.62) = 0$
70 put: $\text{Max}(0, 70 - 72) = 0$
75 put: $\text{Max}(0, 75 - 72) = 3$

EXHIBIT 9	Portfolio Combination for European Calls Illustrating the Effect of Differences in Exercise Prices			
		Value at Expiration		
Transaction	**Current Value**	$S_T \leq X_1$	$X_1 < S_T < X_2$	$S_T \geq X_2$
Buy call $(X = X_1)$	$c_0(X_1)$	0	$S_T - X_1$	$S_T - X_1$
Sell call $(X = X_2)$	$-c_0(X_2)$	0	0	$-(S_T - X_2)$
Total	$c_0(X_1) - c_0(X_2)$	0	$S_T - X_1 > 0$	$X_2 - X_1 > 0$

5.3 The Effect of a Difference in Exercise Price

Now consider two options on the same underlying with the same expiration day but different exercise prices. Generally, the higher the exercise price, the lower the value of a call and the higher the price of a put. To see this, let the two exercise prices be X_1 and X_2, with X_1 being the smaller. Let $c_0(X_1)$ be the price of a European call with exercise price X_1 and $c_0(X_2)$ be the price of a European call with exercise price X_2. We refer to these as the X_1 call and the X_2 call. In Exhibit 9, we construct a combination in which we buy the X_1 call and sell the X_2 call.[17]

Note first that the three outcomes are all non-negative. This fact establishes that the current value of the combination, $c_0(X_1) - c_0(X_2)$ has to be non-negative. We have to pay out at least as much for the X_1 call as we take in for the X_2 call; otherwise, we would get money up front, have the possibility of a positive value at expiration, and never have to pay any money out. Thus, because $c_0(X_1) - c_0(X_2) \geq 0$, we restate this result as

$$c_0(X_1) \geq c_0(X_2)$$

This expression is equivalent to the statement that *a call option with a higher exercise price cannot have a higher value than one with a lower exercise price*. The option with the higher exercise price has a higher hurdle to get over; therefore, the buyer is not willing to pay as much for it. Even though we demonstrated this result with European calls, it is also true for American calls. Thus,[18]

$$C_0(X_1) \geq C_0(X_2)$$

In Exhibit 10 we construct a similar portfolio for puts, except that we buy the X_2 put (the one with the higher exercise price) and sell the X_1 put (the one with the lower exercise price).

Observe that the value of this combination is never negative at expiration; therefore, it must be non-negative today. Hence, $p_0(X_2) - p_0(X_1) \geq 0$. We restate this result as

$$p_0(X_2) \geq p_0(X_1)$$

---

[17] This transaction is also known as a **bull spread**.

[18] It is possible to use the results from this table to establish a limit on the difference between the prices of these two options, but we shall not do so here.

		Value at Expiration		
Transaction	**Current Value**	$S_T \leq X_1$	$X_1 < S_T < X_2$	$S_T \geq X_2$
Buy put $(X = X_2)$	$p_0(X_2)$	$X_2 - S_T$	$X_2 - S_T$	0
Sell put $(X = X_1)$	$-p_0(X_1)$	$-(X_1 - S_T)$	0	0
Total	$p_0(X_2) - p_0(X_1)$	$X_2 - X_1 > 0$	$X_2 - S_T > 0$	0

EXHIBIT 10 — **Portfolio Combination for European Puts Illustrating the Effect of Differences in Exercise Prices**

Thus, *the value of a European put with a higher exercise price must be at least as great as the value of a European put with a lower exercise price.* These results also hold for American puts. Therefore,

$$P_0(X_2) \geq P_0(X_1)$$

Even though it is technically possible for calls and puts with different exercise prices to have the same price, *generally we can say that the higher the exercise price, the lower the price of a call and the higher the price of a put.* For example, refer back to Exhibit 1 and observe how the most expensive calls and least expensive puts have the lower exercise prices.

5.4 The Effect of a Difference in Time to Expiration

Option prices are also affected by the time to expiration of the option. Intuitively, one might expect that the longer the time to expiration, the more valuable the option. A longer-term option has more time for the underlying to make a favorable move. In addition, if the option is in-the-money by the end of a given period of time, it has a better chance of moving even further in-the-money over a longer period of time. If the additional time gives it a better chance of moving out-of-the-money or further out-of-the-money, the limitation of losses to the amount of the option premium means that the disadvantage of the longer time is no greater. In most cases, a longer time to expiration is beneficial for an option. We will see that longer-term American and European calls and longer-term American puts are worth no less than their shorter-term counterparts.

First let us consider each of the four types of options: European calls, American calls, European puts, and American puts. We shall introduce options otherwise identical except that one has a longer time to expiration than the other. The one expiring earlier has an expiration of T_1 and the one expiring later has an expiration of T_2. The prices of the options are $c_0(T_1)$ and $c_0(T_2)$ for the European calls, $C_0(T_1)$ and $C_0(T_2)$ for the American calls, $p_0(T_1)$ and $p_0(T_2)$ for the European puts, and $P_0(T_1)$ and $P_0(T_2)$ for the American puts.

When the shorter-term call expires, the European call is worth $\text{Max}(0, S_{T1} - X)$, but we have already shown that the longer-term European call is worth *at least* $\text{Max}(0, S_{T1} - X/(1 + r)^{(T_2 - T_1)})$, which is at least as great as this amount.[19] Thus, the longer-term European call is worth at least the value of the shorter-term European

---

[19] Technically, we showed this calculation using a time to expiration of T, but here the time to expiration is $T_2 - T_1$.

call. These results are not altered if the call is American. When the shorter-term American call expires, it is worth $\text{Max}(0, S_{T1} - X)$. The longer-term American call must be worth at least the value of the European call, so it is worth *at least* $\text{Max}[0, S - X/(1 + r)^{T_2 - T_1}]$. Thus, the longer-term call, European or American, is worth no less than the shorter-term call when the shorter-term call expires. Because this statement is always true, the longer-term call, European or American, is worth no less than the shorter-term call at any time prior to expiration. Thus,

$$c_0(T_2) \geq c_0(T_1)$$
$$C_0(T_2) \geq C_0(T_1)$$

(64-11)

Notice that these statements do not mean that the longer-term call is always worth more; it means that the longer-term call can be worth no less. With the exception of the rare case in which both calls are so far out-of-the-money or in-the-money that the additional time is of no value, the longer-term call will be worth more.

For European puts, we have a slight problem. For calls, the longer term gives additional time for a favorable move in the underlying to occur. For puts, this is also true, but there is one disadvantage to waiting the additional time. When a put is exercised, the holder receives money. The lost interest on the money is a disadvantage of the additional time. For calls, there is no lost interest. In fact, a call holder earns additional interest on the money by paying out the exercise price later. Therefore, it is not always true that additional time is beneficial to the holder of a European put. It is true, however, that the additional time is beneficial to the holder of an American put. An American put can always be exercised; there is no penalty for waiting. Thus, we have

$$p_0(T_2) \text{ can be either greater or less than } p_0(T_1)$$
$$P_0(T_2) \geq P_0(T_1)$$

(64-12)

So for European puts, either the longer-term or the shorter-term option can be worth more. The longer-term European put will tend to be worth more when volatility is greater and interest rates are lower.

Referring back to Exhibit 1, observe that the longer-term put and call options are more expensive than the shorter-term ones. As noted, we might observe an exception to this rule for European puts, but these are all American options.

5.5 Put–Call Parity

So far we have been working with puts and calls separately. To see how their prices must be consistent with each other and to explore common option strategies, let us combine puts and calls with each other or with a risk-free bond. We shall put together some combinations that produce equivalent results.

5.5.1 Fiduciary Calls and Protective Puts

First we consider an option strategy referred to as a **fiduciary call**. It consists of a European call and a risk-free bond, just like the ones we have been using, that matures on the option expiration day and has a face value equal to the exercise price of the call. The upper part of the table in Exhibit 11 shows the payoffs at expiration of the fiduciary call. We see that if the price of the underlying is below X at expiration, the call expires worthless and the bond is worth X. If the price of the underlying is above X at expiration, the call expires and is worth S_T (the underlying price) $- X$. So at expiration, the fiduciary call will end up worth X or

EXHIBIT 11	Portfolio Combinations for Equivalent Packages of Puts and Calls		
		Value at Expiration	
Transaction	**Current Value**	$S_T \leq X$	$S_T > X$
Fiduciary Call			
Buy call	c_0	0	$S_T - X$
Buy bond	$X/(1 + r)^T$	X	X
Total	$c_0 + X/(1 + r)^T$	X	S_T
Protective Put			
Buy put	p_0	$X - S_T$	0
Buy underlying asset	S_0	S_T	S_T
Total	$p_0 + S_0$	X	S_T

Value of Fiduciary Call and
Protective Put at Expiration

Stock Price at Expiration

S_T, whichever is greater. This type of combination is called a fiduciary call because it allows protection against downside losses and is thus faithful to the notion of preserving capital.

Now we construct a strategy known as a **protective put**, which consists of a European put and the underlying asset. If the price of the underlying is below X at expiration, the put expires and is worth $X - S_T$ and the underlying is worth S_T. If the price of the underlying is above X at expiration, the put expires with no value and the underlying is worth S_T. So at expiration, the protective put is worth X or S_T, whichever is greater. The lower part of the table in Exhibit 11 shows the payoffs at expiration of the protective put.

Thus, the fiduciary call and protective put end up with the same value. They are, therefore, identical combinations. To avoid arbitrage, their values today must be the same. The value of the fiduciary call is the cost of the call, c_0, and the cost of the bond, $X/(1 + r)^T$. The value of the protective put is the cost of the put, p_0, and the cost of the underlying, S_0. Thus,

$$c_0 + X/(1 + r)^T = p_0 + S_0 \qquad \textbf{(64-13)}$$

This equation is called **put–call parity** and is one of the most important results in options. It does not say that puts and calls are equivalent, but it does show an equivalence (parity) of a call/bond portfolio and a put/underlying portfolio.

Put–call parity can be written in a number of other ways. By rearranging the four terms to isolate one term, we can obtain some interesting and important results. For example,

$$c_0 = p_0 + S_0 - X/(1 + r)^T$$

means that a call is equivalent to a long position in the put, a long position in the asset, and a short position in the risk-free bond. The short bond position simply means to borrow by issuing the bond, rather than lend by buying the bond as we did in the fiduciary call portfolio. We can tell from the sign whether we should go long or short. Positive signs mean to go long; negative signs mean to go short.

5.5.2 Synthetics

Because the right-hand side of the above equation is equivalent to a call, we often refer to it as a **synthetic call**. To see that the synthetic call is equivalent to the actual call, look at Exhibit 12:

EXHIBIT 12	Call and Synthetic Call		
		Value at Expiration	
Transaction	Current Value	$S_T \leq X$	$S_T > X$
Call			
Buy call	c_0	0	$S_T - X$
Synthetic Call			
Buy put	p_0	$X - S_T$	0
Buy underlying asset	S_0	S_T	S_T
Issue bond	$-X/(1 + r)^T$	$-X$	$-X$
Total	$p_0 + S_0 - X/(1 + r)^T$	0	$S_T - X$

The call produces the value of the underlying minus the exercise price or zero, whichever is greater. The synthetic call does the same thing, but in a different way. When the call expires in-the-money, the synthetic call produces the underlying value minus the payoff on the bond, which is X. When the call expires out-of-the-money, the put covers the loss on the underlying and the exercise price on the put matches the amount of money needed to pay off the bond.

Similarly, we can isolate the put as follows:

$$p_0 = c_0 - S_0 + X/(1 + r)^T$$

which says that a put is equivalent to a long call, a short position in the underlying, and a long position in the bond. Because the left-hand side is a put, it follows that the right-hand side is a **synthetic put**. The equivalence of the put and synthetic put is shown in Exhibit 13.

As you can well imagine, there are numerous other combinations that can be constructed. Exhibit 14 shows a number of the more important combinations. There are two primary reasons that it is important to understand synthetic positions in option pricing. Synthetic positions enable us to price options, because they

| EXHIBIT 13 | Put and Synthetic Put |

Transaction	Current Value	Value at Expiration $S_T \leq X$	Value at Expiration $S_T > X$
Put			
Buy put	p_0	$X - S_T$	0
Synthetic Put			
Buy call	c_0	0	$S_T - X$
Short underlying asset	$-S_0$	$-S_T$	$-S_T$
Buy bond	$X/(1+r)^T$	X	X
Total	$c_0 - S_0 + X/(1+r)^T$	$X - S_T$	0

produce the same results as options and have known prices. Synthetic positions also tell how to exploit mispricing of options relative to their underlying assets. Note that we can not only synthesize a call or a put, but we can also synthesize the underlying or the bond. As complex as it might seem to do this, it is really quite easy. First, we learn that *a fiduciary call is a call plus a risk-free bond maturing on the option expiration day with a face value equal to the exercise price of the option.* Then we learn that *a protective put is the underlying plus a put.* Then we learn the basic put–call parity equation: *A fiduciary call is equivalent to a protective put:*

$$c_0 + X/(1+r)^T = p_0 + S_0$$

Learn the put–call parity equation this way, because it is the easiest form to remember and has no minus signs.

| EXHIBIT 14 | Alternative Equivalent Combinations of Calls, Puts, the Underlying, and Risk-Free Bonds |

Strategy	Consisting Of	Worth	Equates To	Strategy	Consisting Of	Worth
Fiduciary call	Long call + Long bond	$c_0 + X/(1+r)^T$	=	Protective put	Long put + Long underlying	$p_0 + S_0$
Long call	Long call	c_0	=	Synthetic call	Long put + Long underlying + Short bond	$p_0 + S_0 - X/(1+r)^T$
Long put	Long put	p_0	=	Synthetic put	Long call + Short underlying + Long bond	$c_0 - S_0 + X/(1+r)^T$
Long underlying	Long underlying	S_0	=	Synthetic underlying	Long call + Long bond + Short put	$c_0 + X/(1+r)^T - p_0$
Long bond	Long bond	$X/(1+r)^T$	=	Synthetic bond	Long put + Long underlying + Short call	$p_0 + S_0 - c_0$

Next, we decide which instrument we want to synthesize. We use simple algebra to isolate that instrument, with a plus sign, on one side of the equation, moving all other instruments to the other side. We then see what instruments are on the other side, taking plus signs as long positions and minus signs as short positions. Finally, to check our results, we should construct a table like Exhibits 11 or 12, with the expiration payoffs of the instrument we wish to synthesize compared with the expiration payoffs of the equivalent combination of instruments. We then check to determine that the expiration payoffs are the same.

5.5.3 An Arbitrage Opportunity

In this section we examine the arbitrage strategies that will push prices to put–call parity. Suppose that in the market, prices do not conform to put–call parity. This is a situation in which price does not equal value. Recalling our basic equation, $c_0 + X/(1 + r)^T = p_0 + S_0$, we should insert values into the equation and see if the equality holds. If it does not, then obviously one side is greater than the other. We can view one side as overpriced and the other as underpriced, which suggests an arbitrage opportunity. To exploit this mispricing, we buy the underpriced combination and sell the overpriced combination.

Consider the following example involving call options with an exercise price of $100 expiring in half a year (T = 0.5). The risk-free rate is 10 percent. The call is priced at $7.50, and the put is priced at $4.25. The underlying price is $99.

The left-hand side of the basic put–call parity equation is $c_0 + X/(1 + r)^T = 7.50 + 100/(1.10)^{0.5} = 7.50 + 95.35 = 102.85$. The right-hand side is $p_0 + S_0 = 4.25 + 99 = 103.25$. So the right-hand side is greater than the left-hand side. This means that the protective put is overpriced. Equivalently, we could view this as the fiduciary call being underpriced. Either way will lead us to the correct strategy to exploit the mispricing.

We sell the overpriced combination, the protective put. This means that we sell the put and sell short the underlying. Doing so will generate a cash inflow of $103.25. We buy the fiduciary call, paying out $102.85. This series of transactions nets a cash inflow of $103.25 − $102.85 = $0.40. Now, let us see what happens at expiration.

The options expire with the underlying above 100:
  The bond matures, paying $100.
  Use the $100 to exercise the call, receiving the underlying.
  Deliver the underlying to cover the short sale.
  The put expires with no value.
  Net effect: No money in or out.
The options expire with the underlying below 100:
  The bond matures, paying $100.
  The put expires in-the-money; use the $100 to buy the underlying.
  Use the underlying to cover the short sale.
  The call expires with no value.
  Net effect: No money in or out.

So we receive $0.40 up front and do not have to pay anything out. The position is perfectly hedged and represents an arbitrage profit. The combined effects of other investors performing this transaction will result in the value of the protective put going down and/or the value of the fiduciary call going up until the two strategies are equivalent in value. Of course, it is possible that transaction costs might consume any profit, so small discrepancies will not be exploited.

It is important to note that regardless of which put–call parity equation we use, we will arrive at the same strategy. For example, in the above problem, the synthetic put (a long call, a short position in the underlying, and a long bond) is worth $7.50 - $99 + $95.35 = $3.85. The actual put is worth $4.25. Thus, we would conclude that we should sell the actual put and buy the synthetic put. To buy the synthetic put, we would buy the call, short the underlying, and buy the bond—precisely the strategy we used to exploit this price discrepancy.

In all of these examples based on put–call parity, we used only European options. Put–call parity using American options is considerably more complicated. The resulting parity equation is a complex combination of inequalities. Thus, we cannot say that a given combination exactly equals another; we can say only that one combination is more valuable than another. Exploitation of any such mispricing is somewhat more complicated, and we shall not explore it here.

EXAMPLE 3

European put and call options with an exercise price of 45 expire in 115 days. The underlying is priced at 48 and makes no cash payments during the life of the options. The risk-free rate is 4.5 percent. The put is selling for 3.75, and the call is selling for 8.00.

A. Identify the mispricing by comparing the price of the actual call with the price of the synthetic call.

B. Based on your answer in Part A, demonstrate how an arbitrage transaction is executed.

Solution to A: Using put–call parity, the following formula applies:

$$c_0 = p_0 + S_0 - X/(1 + r)^T$$

The time to expiration is $T = 115/365 = 0.3151$. Substituting values into the right-hand side:

$$c_0 = 3.75 + 48 - 45/(1.045)^{0.3151} = 7.37$$

Hence, the synthetic call is worth 7.37, but the actual call is selling for 8.00 and is, therefore, overpriced.

Solution to B: Sell the call for 8.00 and buy the synthetic call for 7.37. To buy the synthetic call, buy the put for 3.75, buy the underlying for 48.00, and issue a zero-coupon bond paying 45.00 at expiration. The bond will bring in $45.00/(1.045)^{0.3151} = 44.38$ today. This transaction will bring in $8.00 - 7.37 = 0.63$.

At expiration, the following payoffs will occur:

	$S_T < 45$	$S_T \geq 45$
Short call	0	$-(S_T - 45)$
Long put	$45 - S_T$	0
Underlying	S_T	S_T
Bond	-45	-45
Total	0	0

Thus there will be no cash in or out at expiration. The transaction will net a risk-free gain of $8.00 - 7.37 = 0.63$ up front.

5.6 American Options, Lower Bounds, and Early Exercise

As we have noted, American options can be exercised early and in this section we specify cases in which early exercise can have value. Because early exercise is never mandatory, the right to exercise early may be worth something but could never hurt the option holder. Consequently, the prices of American options must be no less than the prices of European options:

$$C_0 \geq c_0$$
$$P_0 \geq p_0$$

(64-14)

Recall that we already used this result in establishing the minimum price from the lower bounds and intrinsic value results in Section 5.2.2. Now, however, our concern is understanding the conditions under which early exercise of an American option might occur.

Suppose today, time 0, we are considering exercising early an in-the-money American call. If we exercise, we pay X and receive an asset worth S_0. But we already determined that a European call is worth at least $S_0 - X/(1 + r)^T$—that is, the underlying price minus the present value of the exercise price, which is more than $S_0 - X$. Because we just argued that the American call must be worth no less than the European call, it therefore must also be worth at least $S_0 - X/(1 + r)^T$. This means that the value we could obtain by selling it to someone else is more than the value we could obtain by exercising it. Thus, there is no reason to exercise the call early.

Some people fail to see the logic behind not exercising early. Exercising a call early simply gives the money to the call writer and throws away the right to decide at expiration if you want the underlying. It is like renewing a magazine subscription before the current subscription expires. Not only do you lose the interest on the money, you also lose the right to decide later if you want to renew. Without offering an early exercise incentive, the American call would have a price equal to the European call price. Thus, we must look at another case to see the value of the early exercise option.

If the underlying makes a cash payment, there may be reason to exercise early. If the underlying is a stock and pays a dividend, there may be sufficient reason to exercise just before the stock goes ex-dividend. By exercising, the option holder throws away the time value but captures the dividend. We shall skip the technical details of how this decision is made and conclude by stating that

▶ *When the underlying makes no cash payments, $C_0 = c_0$.*
▶ *When the underlying makes cash payments during the life of the option, early exercise can be worthwhile and C_0 can thus be higher than c_0.*

We emphasize the word *can*. It is possible that the dividend is not high enough to justify early exercise.

For puts, there is nearly always a possibility of early exercise. Consider the most obvious case, an investor holding an American put on a bankrupt company. The stock is worth zero. It cannot go any lower. Thus, the put holder would exercise immediately. As long as there is a possibility of bankruptcy, the American put will be worth more than the European put. But in fact, bankruptcy is not required for early exercise. The stock price must be very low, although we cannot say exactly how low without resorting to an analysis using option pricing models. Suffice it to say that *the American put is nearly always worth more than the European put: $P_0 > p_0$.*

5.7 The Effect of Cash Flows on the Underlying Asset

Both the lower bounds on puts and calls and the put–call parity relationship must be modified to account for cash flows on the underlying asset. In Readings 62 and 63, we discussed situations in which the underlying has cash flows. Stocks pay dividends, bonds pay interest, foreign currencies pay interest, and commodities have carrying costs. As we have done in the previous readings, we shall assume that these cash flows are either known or can be expressed as a percentage of the asset price. Moreover, as we did previously, we can remove the present value of those cash flows from the price of the underlying and use this adjusted underlying price in the results we have obtained above.

In the previous readings, we specified these cash flows in the form of the accumulated value at T of all cash flows incurred on the underlying over the life of the derivative contract. When the underlying is a stock, we specified these cash flows more precisely in the form of dividends, using the notation FV(D,0,T) as the future value, or alternatively PV(D,0,T) as the present value, of these dividends. When the underlying was a bond, we used the notation FV(CI,0,T) or PV(CI,0,T), where CI stands for "coupon interest." When the cash flows can be specified in terms of a yield or rate, we used the notation δ where $S_0/(1 + \delta)^T$ is the underlying price reduced by the present value of the cash flows.[20] Using continuous compounding, the rate can be specified as δ^c so that $S_0 e^{-\delta_c T}$ is the underlying price reduced by the present value of the dividends. For our purposes in this reading on options, let us just write this specification as PV(CF,0,T), which represents the present value of the cash flows on the underlying over the life of the options. Therefore, we can restate the lower bounds for European options as

$$c_0 \geq \text{Max} \{0,[S_0 - \text{PV}(\text{CF},0,\text{T})] - X/(1 + r)^T\}$$
$$p_0 \geq \text{Max} \{0,X/(1 + r)^T - [S_0 - \text{PV}(\text{CF},0,\text{T})]\}$$

---

[20] We actually used several specifications of the dividend yield in Reading 63, but we shall use just one here.

and put–call parity as

$$c_0 + X/(1 + r)^T = p_0 + [S_0 - PV(CF,0,T)]$$

which reflects the fact that, as we said, we simply reduce the underlying price by the present value of its cash flows over the life of the option.

5.8 The Effect of Interest Rates and Volatility

It is important to know that interest rates and volatility exert an influence on option prices. *When interest rates are higher, call option prices are higher and put option prices are lower.* This effect is not obvious and strains the intuition somewhat. When investors buy call options instead of the underlying, they are effectively buying an indirect leveraged position in the underlying. When interest rates are higher, buying the call instead of a direct leveraged position in the underlying is more attractive. Moreover, by using call options, investors save more money by not paying for the underlying until a later date. For put options, however, higher interest rates are disadvantageous. When interest rates are higher, investors lose more interest while waiting to sell the underlying when using puts. Thus, the opportunity cost of waiting is higher when interest rates are higher. Although these points may not seem completely clear, fortunately they are not critical. Except when the underlying is a bond or interest rate, interest rates do not have a very strong effect on option prices.

Volatility, however, has an extremely strong effect on option prices. *Higher volatility increases call and put option prices because it increases possible upside values and increases possible downside values of the underlying.* The upside effect helps calls and does not hurt puts. The downside effect does not hurt calls and helps puts. The reasons calls are not hurt on the downside and puts are not hurt on the upside is that when options are out-of-the-money, it does not matter if they end up more out-of-the-money. But when options are in-the-money, it does matter if they end up more in-the-money.

Volatility is a critical variable in pricing options. It is the only variable that affects option prices that is not directly observable either in the option contract or in the market. It must be estimated. We shall have more to say about volatility later in this reading.

5.9 Option Price Sensitivities

Later in this reading, we will study option price sensitivities in more detail. These sensitivity measures have Greek names:

▶ *Delta* is the sensitivity of the option price to a change in the price of the underlying.

▶ *Gamma* is a measure of how well the delta sensitivity measure will approximate the option price's response to a change in the price of the underlying.

▶ *Rho* is the sensitivity of the option price to the risk-free rate.

▶ *Theta* is the rate at which the time value decays as the option approaches expiration.

▶ *Vega* is the sensitivity of the option price to volatility.

6

DISCRETE-TIME OPTION PRICING: THE BINOMIAL MODEL

Until now, we have looked only at some basic principles of option pricing. Other than put–call parity, all we examined were rules and conditions, often suggesting limitations, on option prices. With put–call parity, we found that we could price a put or a call based on the prices of the combinations of instruments that make up the synthetic version of the instrument. If we wanted to determine a call price, we had to have a put; if we wanted to determine a put price, we had to have a call. What we need to be able to do is price a put or a call without the other instrument. In this section, we introduce a simple means of pricing an option. It may appear that we oversimplify the situation, but we shall remove the simplifying assumptions gradually, and eventually reach a more realistic scenario.

The approach we take here is called the **binomial model**. The word "binomial" refers to the fact that there are only two outcomes. In other words, we let the underlying price move to only one of two possible new prices. As noted, this framework oversimplifies things, but the model can eventually be extended to encompass all possible prices. In addition, we refer to the structure of this model as **discrete time**, which means that time moves in distinct increments. This is much like looking at a calendar and observing only the months, weeks, or days. Even at its smallest interval, we know that time moves forward at a rate faster than one day at a time. It moves in hours, minutes, seconds, and even fractions of seconds, and fractions of fractions of seconds. When we talk about time moving in the tiniest increments, we are talking about **continuous time**. We will see that the discrete time model can be extended to become a continuous time model. Although we present the continuous time model (Black–Scholes–Merton) in Section 7, we must point out that the binomial model has the advantage of allowing us to price American options. In addition, the binomial model is a simple model requiring a minimum of mathematics. Thus it is worthy of study in its own right.

6.1 The One-Period Binomial Model

We start off by having only one binomial period. This means that the underlying price starts off at a given level, then moves forward to a new price, at which time the option expires. Here we need to change our notation slightly from what we have been using previously. We let S be the current underlying price. One period later, it can move up to S^+ or down to S^-. Note that we are removing the time subscript, because it will not be necessary here. We let X be the exercise price of the option and r be the one period risk-free rate. The option is European style.

6.1.1 The Model

We start with a call option. If the underlying goes up to S^+, the call option will be worth c^+. If the underlying goes down to S^-, the option will be worth c^-. We know that if the option is expiring, its value will be the intrinsic value. Thus,

$$c^+ = \text{Max}(0, S^+ - X)$$
$$c^- = \text{Max}(0, S^- - X)$$

EXHIBIT 15   One-Period Binomial Model

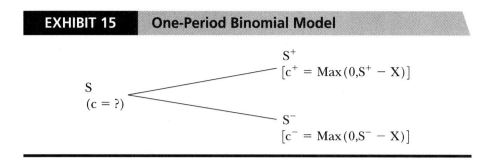

Exhibit 15 illustrates this scenario with a diagram commonly known as a **binomial tree**. Note how we indicate that the current option price, c, is unknown.

Now let us specify how the underlying moves. We identify a factor, u, as the up move on the underlying and d as the down move:

$$u = \frac{S^+}{S}$$

$$d = \frac{S^-}{S}$$

so that u and d represent 1 plus the rate of return if the underlying goes up and down, respectively. Thus, $S^+ = Su$ and $S^- = Sd$. To avoid an obvious arbitrage opportunity, we require that[21]

$$d < 1 + r < u$$

We are now ready to determine how to price the option. We assume that we have all information except for the current option price. In addition, we do not know in what direction the price of the underlying will move. We start by constructing an arbitrage portfolio consisting of one short call option. Let us now purchase an unspecified number of units of the underlying. Let that number be n. Although at the moment we do not know the value of n, we can figure it out quickly. We call this portfolio a hedge portfolio. In fact, n is sometimes called the **hedge ratio**. Its current value is H, where

$$H = nS - c$$

This specification reflects the fact that we own n units of the underlying worth S and we are short one call.[22] One period later, this portfolio value will go to either H^+ or H^-:

$$H^+ = nS^+ - c^+$$

$$H^- = nS^- - c^-$$

---

[21] This statement says that if the price of the underlying goes up, it must do so at a rate better than the risk-free rate. If it goes down, it must do so at a rate lower than the risk-free rate. If the underlying always does better than the risk-free rate, it would be possible to buy the underlying, financing it by borrowing at the risk-free rate, and be assured of earning a greater return from the underlying than the cost of borrowing. This would make it possible to generate an unlimited amount of money. If the underlying always does worse than the risk-free rate, one can buy the risk-free asset and finance it by shorting the underlying. This would also make it possible to earn an unlimited amount of money. Thus, the risky underlying asset cannot dominate or be dominated by the risk-free asset.

[22] Think of this specification as a plus sign indicating assets and a minus sign indicating liabilities.

Because we can choose the value of n, let us do so by setting H^+ equal to H^-. This specification means that regardless of which way the underlying moves, the portfolio value will be the same. Thus, the portfolio will be hedged. We do this by setting

$H^+ = H^-$, which means that

$nS^+ - c^+ = nS^- - c^-$

We then solve for n to obtain

$$n = \frac{c^+ - c^-}{S^+ - S^-}$$ **(64-15)**

Because the values on the right-hand side are known, we can easily set n according to this formula. If we do so, the portfolio will be hedged. A hedged portfolio should grow in value at the risk-free rate.

$H^+ = H(1 + r)$, or

$H^- = H(1 + r)$

We know that $H^+ = nS^+ - c^+$, $H^- = nS^- - c^-$, and $H = nS - c$. We know the values of n, S^+, S^-, c^+, and c^-, as well as r. We can substitute and solve either of the above for c to obtain

$$c = \frac{\pi c^+ + (1 - \pi)c^-}{1 + r}$$ **(64-16)**

where

$$\pi = \frac{1 + r - d}{u - d}$$ **(64-17)**

We see that the call price today, c, is a weighted average of the next two possible call prices, c^+ and c^-. The weights are π and $1 - \pi$. This weighted average is then discounted one period at the risk-free rate.

It might appear that π and $1 - \pi$ are probabilities of the up and down movements, but they are not. In fact, the probabilities of the up and down movements are not required. It is important to note, however, that π and $1 - \pi$ are the probabilities that would exist if investors were risk neutral. Risk-neutral investors value assets by computing the expected future value and discounting that value at the risk-free rate. Because we are discounting at the risk-free rate, it should be apparent that π and $1 - \pi$ would indeed by the probabilities if the investor were **risk neutral**. In fact, we shall refer to them as **risk-neutral probabilities** and the process of valuing an option is often called **risk-neutral valuation**.[23]

---

[23] It may be helpful to contrast risk neutrality with risk aversion, which characterizes nearly all individuals. People who are risk neutral value an asset, such as an option or stock, by discounting the expected value at the risk-free rate. People who are risk averse discount the expected value at a higher rate, one that consists of the risk-free rate plus a risk premium. In the valuation of options, we are not making the assumption that people are risk neutral, but the fact that options can be valued by finding the expected value, using these special probabilities, and discounting at the risk-free rate creates the *appearance* that investors are assumed to be risk neutral. We emphasize the word "appearance," because no such assumption is being made. The terms "risk neutral probabilities" and "risk neutral valuation" are widely used in options valuation, although they give a misleading impression of the assumptions underlying the process.

6.1.2 One-Period Binomial Example

Suppose the underlying is a non-dividend-paying stock currently valued at $50. It can either go up by 25 percent or go down by 20 percent. Thus, u = 1.25 and d = 0.80.

$$S^+ = Su = 50(1.25) = 62.50$$
$$S^- = Sd = 50(0.80) = 40$$

Assume that the call option has an exercise price of 50 and the risk-free rate is 7 percent. Thus, the option values one period later will be

$$c^+ = \text{Max}(0, S^+ - X) = \text{Max}(0, 62.50 - 50) = 12.50$$
$$c^- = \text{Max}(0, S^- - X) = \text{Max}(0, 40 - 50) = 0$$

Exhibit 16 depicts the situation.

EXHIBIT 16   **One-Period Binomial Example**

First we calculate π:

$$\pi = \frac{1 + r - d}{u - d} = \frac{1.07 - 0.80}{1.25 - 0.80} = 0.6$$

and, hence, $1 - \pi = 0.4$. Now, we can directly calculate the option price:

$$c = \frac{0.6(12.50) + 0.4(0)}{1.07} = 7.01$$

Thus, the option should sell for $7.01.

6.1.3 One-Period Binomial Arbitrage Opportunity

Suppose the option is selling for $8. If the option should be selling for $7.01 and it is selling for $8, it is overpriced—a clear case of price not equaling value. Investors would exploit this opportunity by selling the option and buying the underlying. The number of units of the underlying purchased for each option sold would be the value n:

$$n = \frac{c^+ - c^-}{S^+ - S^-} = \frac{12.50 - 0}{62.50 - 40} = 0.556$$

Thus, for every option sold, we would buy 0.556 units of the underlying. Suppose we sell 1,000 calls and buy 556 units of the underlying. Doing so would require an initial outlay of H = 556($50) − 1,000($8) = $19,800. One period later, the portfolio value will be either

$$H^+ = nS^+ - c^+ = 556(\$62.50) - 1,000(\$12.50) = \$22,250, \text{ or}$$
$$H^- = nS^- - c^- = 556(\$40) - 1,000(\$0) = \$22,240$$

These two values are not exactly the same, but the difference is due only to rounding the hedge ratio, n. We shall use the $22,250 value. If we invest $19,800 and end up with $22,250, the return is

$$\frac{\$22,250}{\$19,800} - 1 = 0.1237$$

that is, a risk-free return of more than 12 percent in contrast to the actual risk-free rate of 7 percent. Thus we could borrow $19,800 at 7 percent to finance the initial net cash outflow, capturing a risk-free profit of (0.1237 − 0.07) × $19,800 = $1,063 (to the nearest dollar) without any net investment of money. Other investors will recognize this opportunity and begin selling the option, which will drive down its price. When the option sells for $7.01, the initial outlay would be H = 556($50) − 1,000($7.01) = $20,790. The payoffs at expiration would still be $22,250. This transaction would generate a return of

$$\frac{\$22,250}{\$20,790} - 1 \approx 0.07$$

Thus, *when the option is trading at the price given by the model, a hedge portfolio would earn the risk-free rate,* which is appropriate because the portfolio would be risk free.

If the option sells for less than $7.01, investors would buy the option and sell short the underlying, which would generate cash up front. At expiration, the investor would have to pay back an amount less than 7 percent. All investors would perform this transaction, generating a demand for the option that would push its price back up to $7.01.

EXAMPLE 4

Consider a one-period binomial model in which the underlying is at 65 and can go up 30 percent or down 22 percent. The risk-free rate is 8 percent.

A. Determine the price of a European call option with exercise prices of 70.

B. Assume that the call is selling for 9 in the market. Demonstrate how to execute an arbitrage transaction and calculate the rate of return. Use 10,000 call options.

Solution to A: First find the underlying prices in the binomial tree. We have u = 1.30 and d = 1 − 0.22 = 0.78.

$$S^+ = Su = 65(1.30) = 84.50$$
$$S^- = Sd = 65(0.78) = 50.70$$

Then find the option values at expiration:

$$c^+ = \text{Max}(0, 84.50 - 70) = 14.50$$
$$c^- = \text{Max}(0, 50.70 - 70) = 0$$

The risk-neutral probability is

$$\pi = \frac{1.08 - 0.78}{1.30 - 0.78} = 0.5769$$

and $1 - \pi = 0.4231$. The call's price today is

$$c = \frac{0.5769(14.50) + 0.4231(0)}{1.08} = 7.75$$

Solution to B: We need the value of n for calls:

$$n = \frac{c^+ - c^-}{S^+ - S^-} = \frac{14.50 - 0}{84.50 - 50.70} = 0.4290$$

The call is overpriced, so we should sell 10,000 call options and buy 4,290 units of the underlying.

Sell 10,000 calls at 9	+90,000
Buy 4,290 units of the underlying at 65	−278,850
Net cash flow	−188,850

So we invest 188,850. The value of this combination at expiration will be

If $S_T = 84.50$,

$$4,290(84.50) - 10,000(14.50) = 217,505$$

If $S_T = 50.70$,

$$4,290(50.70) - 10,000(0) = 217,503$$

These values differ by only a rounding error.
The rate of return is

$$\frac{217,505}{188,850} - 1 = 0.1517$$

Thus, we receive a risk-free return almost twice the risk-free rate. We could borrow the initial outlay of $188,850 at the risk-free rate and capture a risk-free profit without any net investment of money.

6.2 The Two-Period Binomial Model

In the example above, the movements in the underlying were depicted over one period, and there were only two outcomes. We can extend the model and obtain more-realistic results with more than two outcomes. Exhibit 17 shows how to do so with a two-period binomial tree.

EXHIBIT 17	Two-Period Binomial Model

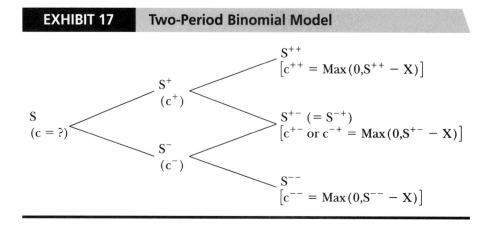

In the first period, we let the underlying price move from S to S^+ or S^- in the manner we did in the one-period model. That is, if u is the up factor and d is the down factor,

$$S^+ = Su$$
$$S^- = Sd$$

Then, with the underlying at S^+ after one period, it can either move up to S^{++} or down to S^{+-}. Thus,

$$S^{++} = S^+u$$
$$S^{+-} = S^+d$$

If the underlying is at S^- after one period, it can either move up to S^{-+} or down to S^{--}.

$$S^{-+} = S^-u$$
$$S^{--} = S^-d$$

We now have three unique final outcomes instead of two. Actually, we have four final outcomes, but S^{+-} is the same as S^{-+}. We can relate the three final outcomes to the starting price in the following manner:

$$S^{++} = S^+u = Suu = Su^2$$
$$S^{+-} \text{ (or } S^{-+}) = S^+d \text{ (or } S^-u) = Sud \text{ (or } Sdu)$$
$$S^{--} = S^-d = Sdd = Sd^2$$

Now we move forward to the end of the first period. Suppose we are at the point where the underlying price is S^+. Note that now we are back into the one-period model we previously derived. There is one period to go and two outcomes. The call price is c^+ and can go up to c^{++} or down to c^{+-}. Using what we know from the one-period model, the call price must be

$$c^+ = \frac{\pi c^{++} + (1 - \pi)c^{+-}}{1 + r}$$

(64-18)

where again we see that the call price is a weighted average of the next two possible call prices, then discounted back one period. If the underlying price is at S^-, the call price would be

$$c^- = \frac{\pi c^{-+} + (1 - \pi)c^{--}}{1 + r}$$

(64-19)

where in both cases the formula for π is still Equation 64-17:

$$\pi = \frac{1 + r - d}{u - d}$$

Now we step back to the starting point and find that the option price is still given as Equation 64-16:

$$c = \frac{\pi c^+ + (1 - \pi)c^-}{1 + r}$$

again, using the general form that the call price is a weighted average of the next two possible call prices, discounted back to the present. Other than requiring knowledge of the formula for π, the call price formula is simple and intuitive. It is an average, weighted by the risk-neutral probabilities, of the next two outcomes, then discounted to the present.[24]

Recall that the hedge ratio, n, was given as the difference in the next two call prices divided by the difference in the next two underlying prices. This will be true in all cases throughout the binomial tree. Hence, we have different hedge ratios at each time point:

$$n = \frac{c^+ - c^-}{S^+ - S^-}$$
$$n^+ = \frac{c^{++} - c^{+-}}{S^{++} - S^{+-}}$$
$$n^- = \frac{c^{-+} - c^{--}}{S^{-+} - S^{--}}$$

(64-20)

6.2.1 Two-Period Binomial Example

We can continue with the example presented in Section 6.1.2 in which the underlying goes up 25 percent or down 20 percent. Let us, however, alter the example a little. Suppose the underlying goes up 11.8 percent and down 10.56 percent, and we extend the number of periods to two. So, the up factor is 1.118 and the down factor is $1 - 0.1056 = 0.8944$. If the underlying goes up for two consecutive periods, it rises by a factor of $1.118(1.118) = 1.25$ (25 percent). If it goes down in both periods, it falls by a factor of $(0.8944)(0.8944) = 0.80$ (20 percent). This specification makes the highest and lowest prices unchanged. Let the risk-free rate be 3.44 percent per period. The π becomes $(1.0344 - 0.8944)/(1.118 - 0.8944) = 0.6261$. The underlying prices at expiration will be

---

[24] It is also possible to express the price today as a weighted average of the three final option prices discounted two periods, thereby skipping the intermediate step of finding c^+ and c^-; but little is gained by doing so and this approach is somewhat more technical.

| EXHIBIT 18 | Two-Period Binomial Example |

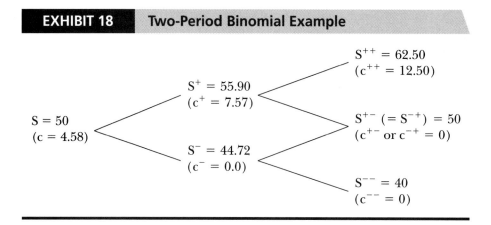

$$S^{++} = Su^2 = 50(1.118)(1.118) = 62.50$$
$$S^{+-} = Sud = 50(1.118)(0.8944) = 50$$
$$S^{--} = Sd^2 = 50(0.8944)(0.8944) = 40$$

When the options expire, they will be worth

$$c^{++} = Max(0, S^{++} - 50) = Max(0, 62.50 - 50) = 12.50$$
$$c^{+-} = Max(0, S^{+-} - 50) = Max(0, 50 - 50) = 0$$
$$c^{--} = Max(0, S^{--} - 50) = Max(0, 40 - 50) = 0$$

The option values after one period are, therefore,

$$c^+ = \frac{\pi c^{++} + (1 - \pi)c^{+-}}{1 + r} = \frac{0.6261(12.50) + 0.3739(0)}{1.0344} = 7.57$$

$$c^- = \frac{\pi c^{-+} + (1 - \pi)c^{--}}{1 + r} = \frac{0.6261(0) + 0.3739(0)}{1.0344} = 0.0$$

So the option price today is

$$c = \frac{\pi c^+ + (1 - \pi)c^-}{1 + r} = \frac{0.6261(7.57) + 0.3739(0)}{1.0344} = 4.58$$

These results are summarized in Exhibit 18.

We shall not illustrate an arbitrage opportunity, because doing so requires a very long and detailed example that goes beyond our needs. Suffice it to say that if the option is mispriced, one can construct a hedged portfolio that will capture a return in excess of the risk-free rate.

EXAMPLE 5

Consider a two-period binomial model in which the underlying is at 30 and can go up 14 percent or down 11 percent each period. The risk-free rate is 3 percent per period.

A. Find the value of a European call option expiring in two periods with an exercise price of 30.

B. Find the number of units of the underlying that would be required at each point in the binomial tree to construct a risk-free hedge using 10,000 calls.

Solution to A: First find the underlying prices in the binomial tree: We have u = 1.14 and d = 1 − 0.11 = 0.89.

$$S^+ = Su = 30(1.14) = 34.20$$
$$S^- = Sd = 30(0.89) = 26.70$$
$$S^{++} = Su^2 = 30(1.14)^2 = 38.99$$
$$S^{+-} = Sud = 30(1.14)(0.89) = 30.44$$
$$S^{--} = Sd^2 = 30(0.89)^2 = 23.76$$

Then find the option prices at expiration:

$$c^{++} = Max(0,38.99 - 30) = 8.99$$
$$c^{+-} = Max(0,30.44 - 30) = 0.44$$
$$c^{--} = Max(0,23.76 - 30) = 0$$

We will need the value of π:

$$\pi = \frac{1.03 - 0.89}{1.14 - 0.89} = 0.56$$

and $1 - \pi = 0.44$. Then step back and find the option prices at time 1:

$$c^+ = \frac{0.56(8.99) + 0.44(0.44)}{1.03} = 5.08$$

$$c^- = \frac{0.56(0.44) + 0.44(0)}{1.03} = 0.24$$

The price today is

$$c = \frac{0.56(5.08) + 0.44(0.24)}{1.03} = 2.86$$

Solution to B: The number of units of the underlying at each point in the tree is found by first computing the values of n.

$$n = \frac{5.08 - 0.24}{34.20 - 26.70} = 0.6453$$

$$n^+ = \frac{8.99 - 0.44}{38.99 - 30.44} = 1.00$$

$$n^- = \frac{0.44 - 0}{30.44 - 23.76} = 0.0659$$

The number of units of the underlying required for 10,000 calls would thus be 6,453 today, 10,000 at time 1 if the underlying is at 34.20, and 659 at time 1 if the underlying is at 26.70.

6.3 Binomial Put Option Pricing

In Section 6.2, the option was a call. It is a simple matter to make the option a put. We could step back through the entire example, changing all c's to p's and using the formulas for the payoff values of a put instead of a call. We should note, however, that if the same formula used for a call is used to calculate the hedge ratio, the minus sign should be ignored as it would suggest being long the stock (put) and short the put (stock) when the hedge portfolio should actually be long both instruments or short both instruments. The put moves opposite to the stock in the first place; hence, long or short positions in both instruments are appropriate.

EXAMPLE 6

Repeating the data from Example 4, consider a one-period binomial model in which the underlying is at 65 and can go up 30 percent or down 22 percent. The risk-free rate is 8 percent. Determine the price of a European put option with exercise price of 70.

Solution: First find the underlying prices in the binomial tree. We have $u = 1.30$ and $d = 1 - 0.22 = 0.78$.

$$S^+ = Su = 65(1.30) = 84.50$$
$$S^- = Sd = 65(0.78) = 50.70$$

Then find the option values at expiration:

$$p^+ = \text{Max}(0, 70 - 84.50) = 0$$
$$p^- = \text{Max}(0, 70 - 50.70) = 19.30$$

The risk-neutral probability is

$$\pi = \frac{1.08 - 0.78}{1.30 - 0.78} = 0.5769$$

and $1 - \pi = 0.4231$. The put price today is

$$p = \frac{0.5769(0) + 0.423(19.30)}{1.08} = 7.56$$

6.4 Binomial Interest Rate Option Pricing

In the examples above, the applications were appropriate for options on a stock, currency, or commodity.[25] Now we take a brief look at options on bonds and interest rates. A model for pricing these options must start with a model for the one-period interest rate and the prices of zero-coupon bonds.

We look at such a model in Exhibit 19. Note that this binomial tree is the first one we have seen with more than two time periods. At each point in the tree, we see a group of numbers. The first number is the one-period interest rate. The

---

[25] We have also been assuming that there are no cash flows on the underlying.

EXHIBIT 19	Binomial Interest Rate Tree

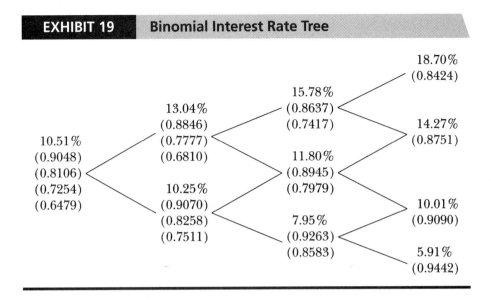

second set of numbers, which are in parentheses, represents the prices of $1 face value zero-coupon bonds of various maturities. At time 0, 0.9048 is the price of a one-period zero-coupon bond, 0.8106 is the price of a two-period zero-coupon bond, 0.7254 is the price of a three-period zero-coupon bond, and 0.6479 is the price of a four-period zero-coupon bond. The one-period bond price can be determined from the one-period rate—that is, $0.9048 = 1/1.1051$, subject to some rounding off. The other prices cannot be determined solely from the one-period rate; we would have to see a tree of the two-, three-, and four-period rates. As we move forward in time, we lose one bond as the one-period bond matures.[26] Thus, at time 1, when the one-period rate is 13.04 percent, the two-period bond from the previous period, whose price was 0.8106, is now a one-period bond whose price is $1/1.1304 = 0.8846$. Although we present these prices and rates here without derivation, they were determined using a model that prevents arbitrage opportunities in buying and selling bonds. We do not cover the actual derivation of the model here.

Now let us price a European option on a zero-coupon bond. First note that we need the option to expire before the bond matures, and it should have a reasonable exercise price. We shall work with the four-period zero-coupon bond. Exhibit 20 contains its price and the price of a two-period call option with an exercise price of $0.80 per $1 of par, as well as the one-period interest rate. The binomial interest rate tree in Exhibit 20 is based on the data in Exhibit 19. In parentheses in Exhibit 20 are the prices of the call option expiring at time 2.

First note that in binomial term structure models, the models are usually fit such that the risk-neutral probability, π, is 0.5. Thus we do not have to calculate π, as in the examples above. We must, however, do one thing quite differently. Whereas we have used a constant interest rate, we must now discount at a different interest rate, the one-period rate, given in Exhibit 19, depending on where we are in the tree.

---

[26] Technically we could show the bond we are losing as a bond with a price of $1.00, its face value, at its point of maturity.

| | | | EXHIBIT 20 | Four-Period Zero-Coupon Bond and Two-Period Call Option with Exercise Price of 0.80 |

The payoff values at time 2 of the call with exercise price of 0.80 are

$$c^{++} = \text{Max}(0, 0.7417 - 0.80) = 0$$
$$c^{+-} = \text{Max}(0, 0.7979 - 0.80) = 0$$
$$c^{--} = \text{Max}(0, 0.8583 - 0.80) = 0.0583$$

These numbers appear in Exhibit 20 at time 2 along with the underlying bond prices and the one-period interest rates. Stepping back to time 1, we find the option prices as follows:

$$c^{+} = \frac{0.5(0) + 0.5(0)}{1.1304} = 0$$
$$c^{-} = \frac{0.5(0) + 0.5(0.0583)}{1.1025} = 0.0264$$

Note how we discount by the appropriate one-period rate, which is 10.25 percent for the bottom outcome at time 1 and 13.04 percent for the top outcome at time 1. Stepping back to time 0, the option price is, therefore,

$$c = \frac{0.5(0) + 0.5(0.0264)}{1.1051} = 0.0119$$

using the one-period rate of 10.51 percent. The call option is thus worth $0.0119 when the underlying zero-coupon bond paying $1 at time 4 is currently worth $0.6479.

Now let us price an option on a coupon bond. First, however, we must construct the tree of coupon bond prices. Exhibit 21 illustrates the price of a $1 face value, 11 percent coupon bond maturing at time 4 along with a call option expiring at time 2 with an exercise price of $0.95 per $1 of par.

We obtain the prices of the coupon bond from the prices of zero-coupon bonds. For example, at time 0, a four-period 11 percent coupon bond is equivalent to a combination of zero-coupon bonds with face value of 0.11 maturing at times 1, 2, and 3, and a zero-coupon bond with face value of 1.11 maturing at time 4. Thus,

	Four-Period 11 Percent Coupon Bond and
EXHIBIT 21	**Two-Period Call Option with Exercise Price of 0.95**

its price can be found by multiplying these face values by the prices of one-, two-, three-, and four-period zero-coupon bonds respectively, the prices of which are taken from Exhibit 19.

$$0.11(0.9048) + 0.11(0.8106) + 0.11(0.7254) + 1.11(0.6479) = 0.9877$$

At any other point in the tree, we use the same procedure, but of course fewer coupons remain.[27] Of course, pricing a coupon bond by decomposing it into a combination of zero-coupon bonds is basic fixed income material, which you have learned elsewhere in the CFA curriculum.

Now let us find the option prices. At time 2, the prices are

$$c^{++} = Max(0, 0.9183 - 0.95) = 0$$
$$c^{+-} = Max(0, 0.9840 - 0.95) = 0.0340$$
$$c^{--} = Max(0, 1.0546 - 0.95) = 0.1046$$

Stepping back to time 1, the prices are

$$c^+ = \frac{0.5(0.0) + 0.5(0.0340)}{1.1304} = 0.0150$$

$$c^- = \frac{0.5(0.0340) + 0.5(0.1046)}{1.1025} = 0.0629$$

Stepping back to time 0, the option price is

$$c = \frac{0.5(0.0150) + 0.5(0.0629)}{1.1051} = 0.0352$$

Now let us look at options on interest rates. Recall that in Section 4.1.4, we illustrated how these options work. Their payoffs are based on the difference between the interest rate and an exercise rate. When the option expires, the payoff

---

[27] For example, consider the middle node at time 2. The coupon bond is now a two-period bond. The one- and two-period zero-coupon bond prices are 0.8945 and 0.7979, respectively (from Exhibit 19). Thus, the coupon bond price is $0.11(0.8945) + 1.11(0.7979) = 0.9840$ as shown in Exhibit 21.

EXHIBIT 22	Two-Period Cap on One-Period Interest Rate with Exercise Rate of 10.5 Percent

A. Pricing the Two-Period Caplet

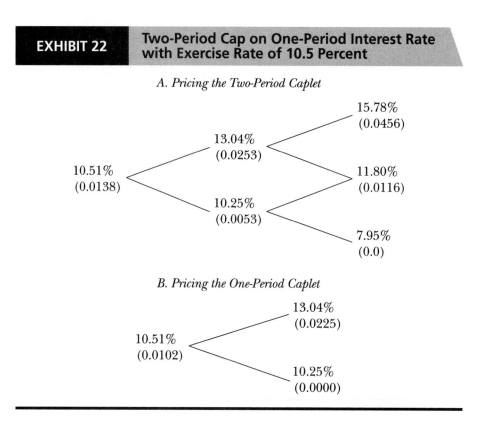

B. Pricing the One-Period Caplet

does not occur for one additional period. Thus, we have to discount the intrinsic value at expiration by the one-period interest rate. Recall that an interest rate cap is a set of interest rate call options expiring at various points in the life of a loan. The cap is generally set up to hedge the interest rate risk on a floating rate loan.

Exhibit 22 illustrates the pricing of a two-period cap with an exercise rate of 10.5 percent. This contract consists of two caplets: a one-period call option on the one-period interest rate with an exercise rate of 10.5 percent, and a two-period call option on the one-period interest rate with an exercise rate of 10.5 percent. We price the cap by pricing these two component options.

In Panel A, we price the two-period caplet. The values at time 2 are

$$c^{++} = \frac{Max(0,0.1578 - 0.105)}{1.1578} = 0.0456$$

$$c^{+-} = \frac{Max(0,0.1180 - 0.105)}{1.1180} = 0.0116$$

$$c^{--} = \frac{Max(0,0.0795 - 0.105)}{1.0795} = 0.0$$

Note especially that we discount the payoff one period at the appropriate one-period rate, because the payoff does not occur until one period later. Stepping back to time 1:

$$c^{+} = \frac{0.5(0.0456) + 0.5(0.0116)}{1.1304} = 0.0253$$

$$c^{-} = \frac{0.5(0.0116) + 0.5(0.0)}{1.1025} = 0.0053$$

At time 0, the option price is

$$c = \frac{0.5(0.0253) + 0.5(0.0053)}{1.1051} = 0.0138$$

Panel B illustrates the same procedure for the one-period caplet. We shall omit the details because they follow precisely the pattern above. The one-period caplet price is 0.0102; thus the cap costs 0.0138 + 0.0102 = 0.0240.

If the option is a floor, the procedure is precisely the same but the payoffs are based on the payoffs of a put instead of a call. Pricing a zero-cost collar, however, is considerably more complex. Remember that a zero-cost collar is a long cap and a short floor with the exercise rates set such that the premium on the cap equals the premium on the floor. We can arbitrarily choose the exercise rate on the cap or the floor, but the exercise rate on the other would have to be found by trial and error so that the premium offsets the premium on the other instrument.

EXAMPLE 7

The diagram below is a two-period binomial tree containing the one-period interest rate and the prices of zero-coupon bonds. The first price is a one-period zero-coupon bond, the second is a two-period zero-coupon bond, and the third is a three-period zero-coupon bond. As we move forward, one bond matures and its price is removed. The maturity of each bond is then shorter by one period.

A. Find the price of a European put expiring in two periods with an exercise price of 1.01 on a three-period 6 percent coupon bond with $1.00 face value.

B. Find the price of a European put option expiring at time 2 with an exercise rate of 6 percent where the underlying is the one-period rate.

Solution to A: First we have to find the price of the three-period $1.00 par, 6 percent coupon bond at expiration of the option (t = 2). We break the coupon bond up into zero-coupon bonds of one, two, and three periods to maturity. The face values of these zero-coupon bonds are 0.06, 0.06, and 1.06, respectively. The bond price at t = 2 is $1.06 discounted one period at the appropriate discount rate:

Bond prices at time 2:

$++$ outcome: 1.06(0.9210) = 0.9763
$+-$ outcome: 1.06(0.9443) = 1.0010
$--$ outcome: 1.06(0.9682) = 1.0263

Now compute the put option values at expiration:

$++$ outcome: Max(0,1.01 − 0.9763) = 0.0337
$+-$ outcome: Max(0,1.01 − 1.0010) = 0.0090
$--$ outcome: Max(0,1.01 − 1.0263) = 0.0000

Now step back and compute the option values at time 1:

$+$ outcome: $\dfrac{0.5(0.0337) + 0.5(0.0090)}{1.064} = 0.0201$

$-$ outcome: $\dfrac{0.5(0.0090) + 0.5(0.0000)}{1.0429} = 0.0043$

Now step back and compute the option values at time 0:

$$\frac{0.5(0.201) + 0.5(0.0043)}{1.0513} = 0.0116$$

Solution to B: First compute the put option values at expiration:

$$p^{++} = \frac{Max(0,0.06 - 0.0858)}{1.0858} = 0.0000$$

$$p^{+-} = \frac{Max(0,0.06 - 0.0590)}{1.059} = 0.0009$$

$$p^{--} = \frac{Max(0,0.06 - 0.0328)}{1.0328} = 0.0263$$

Step back to time 2 and compute the option values:

$$p^{+} = \frac{0.5(0.0000) + 0.5(0.0009)}{1.064} = 0.0004$$

$$p^{-} = \frac{0.5(0.0009) + 0.5(0.0263)}{1.0429} = 0.0130$$

Now step back to time 0 and compute the option price as

$$p = \frac{0.5(0.0004) + 0.5(0.0130)}{1.0513} = 0.0064$$

6.5 American Options

The binomial model is also well suited for handling American-style options. At any point in the binomial tree, we can see whether the calculated value of the option is exceeded by its value if exercised early. If that is the case, we replace the calculated value with the exercise value.[28]

6.6 Extending the Binomial Model

In the examples in this reading, we divided an option's life into a given number of periods. Suppose we are pricing a one-year option. If we use only one binomial period, it will give us only two prices for the underlying, and we are unlikely to get a very good result. If we use two binomial periods, we will have three prices for the underlying at expiration. This result would probably be better but still not very good. But as we increase the number of periods, the result should become more accurate. In fact, in the limiting case, we are likely to get a very good result. By increasing the number of periods, we are moving from discrete time to continuous time.

Consider the following example of a one-period binomial model for a nine-month option. The asset is priced at 52.75. It can go up by 35.41 percent or down by 26.15 percent, so u = 1.3541 and d = 1 − 0.2615 = 0.7385. The risk-free rate is 4.88 percent. A call option has an exercise price of 50 and expires in nine months. Using a one-period binomial model would obtain an option price of 10.0259. Exhibit 23 shows the results we obtain if we divide the nine-month option life into an increasing number of periods of smaller and smaller length. The manner in which we fit the binomial tree is not arbitrary, however, because

EXHIBIT 23	Binomial Option Prices for Different Numbers of Time Periods
Number of Time Periods	**Option Price**
1	10.0259
2	8.4782
5	8.8305
10	8.6983
25	8.5862
50	8.6438
100	8.6160
500	8.6162
1000	8.6190

Notes: Call option with underlying price of 52.75, up factor of 1.3541, down factor of 0.7385, risk-free rate of 4.88 percent, and exercise price of 50. The variables u, d, and r are altered accordingly as the number of time periods increases.

---

[28] See Chapter 4 of *An Introduction to Derivatives and Risk Management*, 6th edition, Don M. Chance (South-Western College Publishing, 2004) for a treatment of this topic.

we have to alter the values of u, d, and the risk-free rate so that the underlying price move is reasonable for the life of the option. How we alter u and d is related to the volatility, a topic we cover in the next section. In fact, we need not concern ourselves with exactly how to alter any of these values. We need only to observe that our binomial option price appears to be converging to a value of around 8.62.

In the same way a sequence of rapidly taken still photographs converges to what appears to be a continuous sequence of a subject's movements, the binomial model converges to a continuous-time model, the subject of which is in our next section.

7 CONTINUOUS-TIME OPTION PRICING: THE BLACK–SCHOLES–MERTON MODEL

When we move to a continuous-time world, we price options using the famous Black–Scholes–Merton model. Named after its founders Fischer Black, Myron Scholes, and Robert Merton, this model resulted in the award of a Nobel Prize to Scholes and Merton in 1997.[29] (Fischer Black had died in 1995 and thus was not eligible for the prize.) The model can be derived either as the continuous limit of the binomial model, or through taking expectations, or through a variety of highly complex mathematical procedures. We are not concerned with the derivation here and instead simply present the model and its applications. First, however, let us briefly review its underlying assumptions.

7.1 Assumptions of the Model

7.1.1 The Underlying Price Follows a Geometric Lognormal Diffusion Process

This assumption is probably the most difficult to understand, but in simple terms, *the underlying price follows a lognormal probability distribution as it evolves through time.* A lognormal probability distribution is one in which the log return is normally distributed. For example, if a stock moves from 100 to 110, the return is 10 percent but the log return is $\ln(1.10) = 0.0953$ or 9.53 percent. Log returns are often called **continuously compounded returns**. If the log or continuously compounded return follows the familiar normal or bell-shaped distribution, the return is said to be lognormally distributed. The distribution of the return itself is skewed, reaching further out to the right and truncated on the left side, reflecting the limitation that an asset cannot be worth less than zero.

The lognormal distribution is a convenient and widely used assumption. It is almost surely not an exact measure in reality, but it suffices for our purposes.

7.1.2 The Risk-Free Rate Is Known and Constant

The Black–Scholes–Merton model does not allow interest rates to be random. Generally, we assume that *the risk-free rate is constant.* This assumption becomes a

---

[29] The model is more commonly called the Black–Scholes model, but we choose to give Merton the credit he is due that led to his co-receipt of the Nobel Prize.

problem for pricing options on bonds and interest rates, and we will have to make some adjustments then.

7.1.3 The Volatility of the Underlying Asset Is Known and Constant

The volatility of the underlying asset, specified in the form of the standard deviation of the log return, is assumed to be known at all times and does not change over the life of the option. This assumption is the most critical, and we take it up again in a later section. In reality, the volatility is definitely not known and must be estimated or obtained from some other source. In addition, volatility is generally not constant. Obviously, the stock market is more volatile at some times than at others. Nonetheless, the assumption is critical for this model. Considerable research has been conducted with the assumption relaxed, but this topic is an advanced one and does not concern us here.

7.1.4 There Are No Taxes or Transaction Costs

We have made this assumption all along in pricing all types of derivatives. Taxes and transaction costs greatly complicate our models and keep us from seeing the essential financial principles involved in the models. It is possible to relax this assumption, but we shall not do so here.

7.1.5 There Are No Cash Flows on the Underlying

We have discussed this assumption at great length in pricing futures and forwards and earlier in this reading in studying the fundamentals of option pricing. The basic form of the Black–Scholes–Merton model makes this assumption, but it can easily be relaxed. We will show how to do this in Section 7.4.

7.1.6 The Options Are European

With only a few very advanced variations, the Black–Scholes–Merton model does not price American options. Users of the model must keep this in mind, or they may badly misprice these options. For pricing American options, the best approach is the binomial model with a large number of time periods.

7.2 The Black–Scholes–Merton Formula

Although the mathematics underlying the Black–Scholes–Merton formula are quite complex, the formula itself is not difficult, although it may appear so at first glance. The input variables are some of those we have already used: S_0 is the price of the underlying, X is the exercise price, r^c is the continuously compounded risk-free rate, and T is the time to expiration. The one other variable we need is the standard deviation of the log return on the asset. We denote this as σ and refer to it as the volatility. Then, the Black–Scholes–Merton formulas for the prices of call and put options are

$$c = S_0 N(d_1) - Xe^{-r^cT} N(d_2)$$

$$p = Xe^{-r^cT} [1 - N(d_2)] - S_0[1 - N(d_1)]$$

(64-21)

where

$$d_1 = \frac{\ln(S_0/X) + [r^c + (\sigma^2/2)]T}{\sigma\sqrt{T}}$$

$$d_2 = d_1 - \sigma\sqrt{T}$$

(64-22)

σ = the annualized standard deviation of the continuously compounded return on the stock

r^c = the continuously compounded risk-free rate of return

Of course, we have already seen the term "ln" and "e" in previous readings. We do, however, introduce two new and somewhat unusual looking terms, $N(d_1)$ and $N(d_2)$. These terms represent normal probabilities based on the values of d_1 and d_2. We compute the normal probabilities associated with values of d_1 and d_2 using the second equation above and insert these values into the formula as $N(d_1)$ and $N(d_2)$. Exhibit 24 presents a brief review of the normal probability distribution and explains how to obtain a probability value. Once we know how to look up a number in a normal probability table, we can then easily calculate d_1 and d_2, look them up in the table to obtain $N(d_1)$ and $N(d_2)$, and then insert the values of $N(d_1)$ and $N(d_2)$ into the above formula.

Consider the following example. The underlying price is 52.75 and has a volatility of 0.35. The continuously compounded risk-free rate is 4.88 percent. The option expires in nine months; therefore, T = 9/12 = 0.75. The exercise price is 50. First we calculate the values of d_1 and d_2:

$$d_1 = \frac{\ln(52.75/50) + (0.0488 + (0.35)^2/2)0.75}{0.35\sqrt{0.75}} = 0.4489$$

$$d_2 = 0.4489 - 0.35\sqrt{0.75} = 0.1458$$

To use the normal probability table in Appendix 64A, we must round off d_1 and d_2 to two digits to the right of the decimal. Thus we have d_1 = 0.45 and d_2 = 0.15. From the table, we obtain

N(0.45) = 0.6736

N(0.15) = 0.5596

Then we plug everything into the equation for c:

c = 52.75(0.6736) − 50$e^{-0.0488(0.75)}$(0.5596) = 8.5580

The value of a put with the same terms would be

p = 50$e^{-0.0488(0.75)}$(1 − 0.5596) − 52.75(1 − 0.6736) = 4.0110

At this point, we should note that the Black–Scholes–Merton model is extremely sensitive to rounding errors. In particular, the process of looking up values in the normal probability table is a major source of error. A number of other way exist to obtain $N(d_1)$ and $N(d_2)$, such as using Microsoft Excel's function "=normsdist()". Using a more precise method, such as Excel, the value of the call would be 8.619. Note that this is the value to which the binomial option price converged in the example we showed with 1,000 time periods in Exhibit 23. Indeed, the Black–Scholes–Merton model is said to be the continuous limit of the binomial model.

EXHIBIT 24   **The Normal Probability Distribution**

The normal probability distribution, or bell-shaped curve, gives the probability that a standard normal random variable will be less than or equal to a given value. The graph below shows the normal probability distribution; note that the curve is centered around zero. The values on the horizontal axis run from $-\infty$ to $+\infty$. If we were interested in a value of x of positive infinity, we would have $N(+\infty) = 1$. This expression means that the probability is 1.0 that we would obtain a value less than $+\infty$. If we were interested in a value of x of negative infinity, then $N(-\infty) = 0.0$. This expression means that there is zero probability of a value of x of less than negative infinity. Below, we are interested in the probability of a value less than x, where x is not infinite. We want $N(x)$, which is the area under the curve to the left of x.

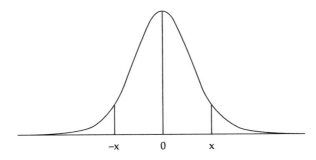

We obtain the values of $N(x)$ by looking them up in a table. Below is an excerpt from a table of values of x (the full table is given as Appendix 64A). Suppose x = 1.12. Then we find the row containing the value 1.1 and move over to the column containing 0.02. The sum of the row value and the column value is the value of x. The corresponding probability is seen as the value 0.8686. Thus, $N(1.12) = 0.8686$. This means that the probability of obtaining a value of less than 1.12 in a normal distribution is 0.8686.

x	0	0.01	0.02	0.03	0.04	0.05	0.06	0.07	0.08	0.09
0.60	0.7257	0.7291	0.7324	0.7357	0.7389	0.7422	0.7454	0.7486	0.7517	0.7549
0.70	0.7580	0.7611	0.7642	0.7673	0.7704	**0.7734**	0.7764	0.7794	0.7823	0.7852
0.80	0.7881	0.7910	0.7939	0.7967	0.7995	0.8023	0.8051	0.8078	0.8106	0.8133
0.90	0.8159	0.8186	0.8212	0.8238	0.8264	0.8289	0.8315	0.8340	0.8365	0.8389
1.00	0.8413	0.8438	0.8461	0.8485	0.8508	0.8531	0.8554	0.8577	0.8599	0.8621
1.10	0.8643	0.8665	**0.8686**	0.8708	0.8729	0.8749	0.8770	0.8790	0.8810	0.8830
1.20	0.8849	0.8869	0.8888	0.8907	0.8925	0.8944	0.8962	0.8980	0.8997	0.9015

Now, suppose the value of x is negative. Observe in the figure above that the area to the left of $-x$ is the same as the area to the right of $+x$. Therefore, if x is a negative number, $N(x)$ is found as $1 - N(-x)$. For example, let x = -0.75. We simply look up $N(-x) = N[-(-0.75)] = N(0.75) = 0.7734$. Then $N(-0.75) = 1 - 0.7734 = 0.2266$.

EXAMPLE 8

Use the Black–Scholes–Merton model to calculate the prices of European call and put options on an asset priced at 68.5. The exercise price is 65, the continuously compounded risk-free rate is 4 percent, the options expire in 110 days, and the volatility is 0.38. There are no cash flows on the underlying.

Solutions: The time to expiration will be T = 110/365 = 0.3014. Then d_1 and d_2 are

$$d_1 = \frac{ln(68.5/65) + (0.04 + (0.38)^2/2)(0.3014)}{0.38\sqrt{0.3014}} = 0.4135$$

$$d_2 = 0.4135 - 0.38\sqrt{0.3014} = 0.2049$$

Looking up in the normal probability table, we have

N(0.41) = 0.6591
N(0.20) = 0.5793

Plugging into the option price formula,

$$c = 68.5(0.6591) - 65e^{-0.04(0.3014)}(0.5793) = 7.95$$
$$p = 65e^{-0.04(0.3014)}(1 - 0.5793) - 68.5(1 - 0.6591) = 3.67$$

Let us now take a look at the various inputs required in the Black–Scholes–Merton model. We need to know where to obtain the inputs and how the option price varies with these inputs.

7.3 Inputs to the Black–Scholes–Merton Model

The Black–Scholes–Merton model has five inputs: the underlying price, the exercise price, the risk-free rate, the time to expiration, and the volatility.[30] As we have previously seen, call option prices should be higher the higher the underlying price, the longer the time to expiration, the higher the volatility, and the higher the risk-free rate. They should be lower the higher the exercise price. Put option prices should be higher the higher the exercise price and the higher the volatility. They should be lower the higher the underlying price and the higher the risk-free rate. As we saw, European put option prices can be either higher or lower the longer the time to expiration. American put option prices are always higher the longer the time to expiration, but the Black–Scholes–Merton model does not apply to American options.

These relationships are general to any European and American options and do not require the Black–Scholes–Merton model to understand them. Nonetheless, the Black–Scholes–Merton model provides an excellent opportunity to examine these relationships more closely. We can calculate and plot

---

[30] Later we shall add one more input, cash flows on the underlying.

relationships such as those mentioned, which are usually called the option Greeks, because they are often referred to with Greek names. Let us now look at each of the inputs and the various option Greeks.

7.3.1 The Underlying Price: Delta and Gamma

The price of the underlying is generally one of the easiest sources of input information. Suffice it to say that if an investor cannot obtain the price of the underlying, then she should not even be considering the option. The price should generally be obtained as a quote or trade price from a liquid, open market.

The relationship between the option price and the underlying price has a special name: It is called the **option delta**. In fact, the delta can be obtained approximately from the Black–Scholes–Merton formula as the value of $N(d_1)$ for calls and $N(d_1) - 1$ for puts. More formally, the delta is defined as

$$\text{Delta} = \frac{\text{Change in option price}}{\text{Change in underlying price}} \qquad \textbf{(64-23)}$$

The above definition for delta is exact; the use of $N(d_1)$ for calls and $N(d_1) - 1$ for puts is approximate. Later in this section, we shall see why $N(d_1)$ and $N(d_2)$ are approximations and when they are good or bad approximations.

Let us consider the example we previously worked, where S = 52.75, X = 50, r^c = 0.0488, T = 0.75, and σ = 0.35. Using a computer to obtain a more precise Black–Scholes–Merton answer, we get a call option price of 8.6186 and a put option price of 4.0717. $N(d_1)$, the call delta, is 0.6733, so the put delta is 0.6733 − 1 = −0.3267. Given that Delta = (Change in option price/Change in underlying price), we should expect that

Change in option price = Delta × Change in underlying price.

Therefore, for a $1 change in the price of the underlying, we should expect

Change in call option price = 0.6733(1) = 0.6733

Change in put option price = −0.3267(1) = −0.3267

This calculation would mean that

Approximate new call option price = 8.6186 + 0.6733 = 9.2919

Approximate new put option price = 4.0717 − 0.3267 = 3.7450

To test the accuracy of this approximation, we let the underlying price move up $1 to $53.75 and re-insert these values into the Black–Scholes–Merton model. We would then obtain

Actual new call option price = 9.3030

Actual new put option price = 3.7560

The delta approximation is fairly good, but not perfect.

Delta is important as a risk measure. *The delta defines the sensitivity of the option price to a change in the price of the underlying.* Traders, especially dealers in options, use delta to construct hedges to offset the risk they have assumed by buying and selling options. For example, recall from Reading 62 that FRA dealers offer to take either side of an FRA transaction. They then usually hedge the risk they have assumed by entering into other transactions. These same types of dealers offer to buy and sell options, hedging that risk with other transactions. For example, suppose we are a dealer offering to sell the call option we have been working with above. A customer buys 1,000 options for 8.619. We now are short 1,000 call options, which exposes us to considerable risk if the underlying goes up. So we must buy a certain number of units of the underlying to hedge this risk. We previously showed that the delta is 0.6733, so we would buy 673 units of the underlying at 52.75.[31] Assume for the moment that the delta tells us precisely the movement in the option for a movement in the underlying. Then suppose the underlying moves up $1:

Change in value of 673 long units of the underlying: $673(+\$1) = \$673$

Change in value of 1,000 short options: $1,000(+\$1)(0.6733) \approx \$673$

Because we are long the underlying and short the options, these values offset. At this point, however, the delta has changed. If we recalculate it, we would find it to be 0.6953. This would require that we have 695 units of the underlying, so we would need to buy an additional 22 units. We would borrow the money to do this. In some cases, we would need to sell off units of the underlying, in which case we would invest the money in the risk-free asset.

Let us consider how changes in the underlying price will change the delta. In fact, even if the underlying price does not change, the delta would still change as the option moves toward expiration. For a call, the delta will increase toward 1.0 as the underlying price moves up and will decrease toward 0.0 as the underlying price moves down. For a put, the delta will decrease toward −1.0 as the underlying price moves down and increase towards 0.0 as the underlying price moves up.[32] If the underlying price does not move, a call delta will move toward 1.0 if the call is in-the-money or 0.0 if the call is out-of-the-money as the call moves toward the expiration day. A put delta will move toward −1.0 if the put is in-the-money or 0.0 if the put is out-of-the-money as it moves toward expiration.

So the delta is constantly changing, which means that delta hedging is a dynamic process. In fact, delta hedging is often referred to as **dynamic hedging**. In theory, the delta is changing continuously and the hedge should be adjusted continuously, but continuous adjustment is not possible in reality. When the hedge is not adjusted continuously, we are admitting the possibility of much larger moves in the price of the underlying. Let us see what happens in that case.

Using our previous example, we allow an increase in the underlying price of $10 to $62.75. Then the call price should change by $0.6733(10) = 6.733$, and the put option price should change by $−0.3267(10) = −3.267$. Thus, the approximate prices would be

Approximate new call option price $= 8.619 + 6.733 = 15.3520$

Approximate new put option price $= 4.0717 - 3.267 = 0.8047$

The actual prices are obtained by recalculating the option values using the Black–Scholes–Merton model with an underlying price of 62.75. Using a computer for greater precision, we find that these prices are

---

[31] This transaction would require $673(\$52.75) = \$35,500$, less the $1,000(\$8.619) = \$8,619$ received from the sale of the option, for a total investment required of $26,881. We would probably borrow this money.

[32] Remember that the put delta is negative; hence, its movement is down toward −1.0 or up toward 0.0.

Actual new call option price $= 16.3026$

Actual new put option price $= 1.7557$

The approximations based on delta are not very accurate. In general, the larger the move in the underlying, the worse the approximation. This will make delta hedging less effective.

Exhibit 25 shows the relationship between the option price and the underlying price. Panel A depicts the relationship for calls and Panel B shows the corresponding relationship for puts. Notice the curvature in the relationship between the option price and the underlying price. Call option values definitely increase the greater the underlying value, and put option values definitely decrease. But the amount of change is not the same in each direction. $N(d_1)$ measures the slope of this line at a given point. As such, it measures only the slope for a very small change in the underlying. When the underlying changes by more than a very small amount, the curvature of the line comes into play and distorts the relationship between the option price and underlying price that is explained by the delta. The problem here is much like the relationship between a bond price and its yield. This first-order relationship between a bond price and its yield is called the duration; therefore, duration is similar to delta.

The curvature or second-order effect is known in the fixed income world as the convexity. In the options world, this effect is called **gamma**. Gamma is a numerical measure of how sensitive the delta is to a change in the underlying—in other words, how much the delta changes. When gamma is large, the delta

| EXHIBIT 25 | The Relationship between Option Price and Underlying Price X = 50, r^c = 0.0488, T = 0.75, σ = 0.35 |

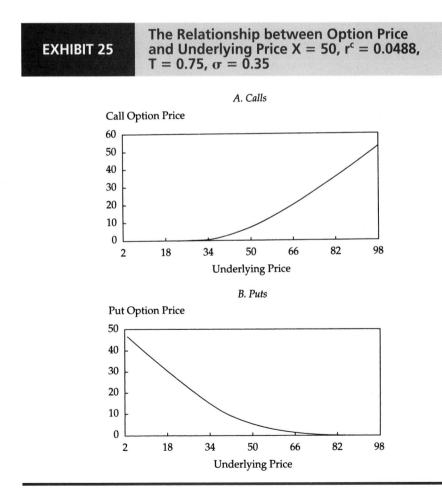

A. Calls

Call Option Price

B. Puts

Put Option Price

changes rapidly and cannot provide a good approximation of how much the option moves for each unit of movement in the underlying. We shall not concern ourselves with measuring and using gamma, but we should know a few things about the gamma and, therefore, about the behavior of the delta.

Gamma is larger when there is more uncertainty about whether the option will expire in- or out-of-the-money. This means that *gamma will tend to be large when the option is at-the-money and close to expiration.* In turn, this statement means that delta will be a poor approximation for the option's price sensitivity when it is at-the-money and close to the expiration day. Thus, a **delta hedge** will work poorly. When the gamma is large, we may need to use a gamma-based hedge, which would require that we add a position in another option to the delta-hedge position of the underlying and the option. We shall not take up this advanced topic here.

7.3.2 The Exercise Price

The exercise price is easy to obtain. It is specified in the option contract and does not change. Therefore, it is not worthwhile to speak about what happens when the exercise price changes, but we can talk about how the option price would differ if we choose an option with a different exercise price. As we have previously seen, the call option price will be lower the higher the exercise price and the put option price will be higher. This relationship is confirmed for our sample option in Exhibit 26.

EXHIBIT 26	The Relationship between Option Price and Exercise Price S = 52.75, r^c = 0.0488, T = 0.75, σ = 0.35

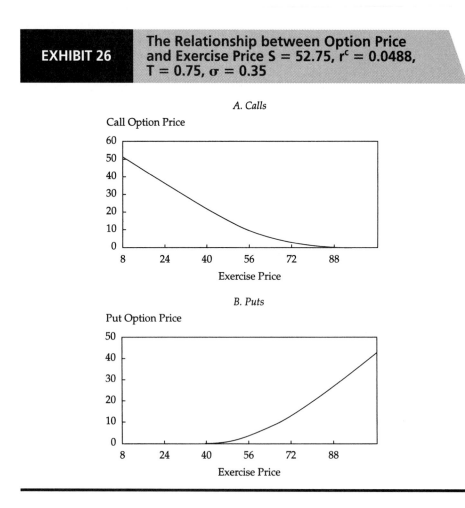

A. Calls

Call Option Price

B. Puts

Put Option Price

7.3.3 The Risk-Free Rate: Rho

The risk-free rate is the continuously compounded rate on the risk-free security whose maturity corresponds to the option's life. We have used the risk-free rate in previous readings; sometimes we have used the discrete version and sometimes the continuous version. As we have noted, the continuously compounded risk-free rate is the natural log of 1 plus the discrete risk-free rate.

For example, suppose the discrete risk-free rate quoted in annual terms is 5 percent. Then the continuous rate is

$$r^c = \ln(1 + r) = \ln(1.05) = 0.0488$$

Let us recall the difference in these two specifications. Suppose we want to find the present value of $1 in six months using both the discrete and continuous risk-free rates.

$$\text{Present value using discrete rate} = \frac{1}{(1 + r)^T} = \frac{1}{(1.05)^{0.5}} = 0.9759$$

$$\text{Present value using continuous rate} = e^{-r^c T} = e^{-0.0488(0.5)} = 0.9759$$

Obviously either specification will work. Because of how it uses the risk-free rate in the calculation of d_1, however, the Black–Scholes–Merton model requires the continuous risk-free rate.

The sensitivity of the option price to the risk-free rate is called the **rho**. We shall not concern ourselves with the calculation of rho. Technically, the Black–Scholes–Merton model assumes a constant risk-free rate, so it is meaningless to talk about the risk-free rate changing over the life of the option. We can, however, explore how the option price would differ if the current rate were different. Exhibit 27 on page 196 depicts this effect. Note how little change occurs in the option price over a very broad range of the risk-free rate. Indeed, *the price of a European option on an asset is not very sensitive to the risk-free rate.*[33]

7.3.4 Time to Expiration: Theta

Time to expiration is an easy input to determine. An option has a definite expiration date specified in the contract. We simply count the number of days until expiration and divide by 365, as we have done previously with forward and futures contracts.

Obviously, the time remaining in an option's life moves constantly towards zero. Even if the underlying price is constant, the option price will still change. We noted that American options have both an intrinsic value and a time value. For European options, all of the price can be viewed as time value. In either case, time value is a function of the option's moneyness, its time to expiration, and its volatility. The more uncertainty there is, the greater the time value. As expiration approaches, the option price moves toward the payoff value of the option at expiration, a process known as **time value decay**. The rate at which the time value decays is called the option's **theta**. We shall not concern ourselves with calculating the specific value of theta, but be aware that if the option price decreases as time moves forward, the theta will be negative. Exhibit 28 shows the time value decay for our sample option.

---

[33] When the underlying is an interest rate, however, there is a strong relationship between the option price and interest rates.

EXHIBIT 27	The Relationship between Option Price and Risk-Free Rate S = 52.75, X = 50, T = 0.75, σ = 0.35

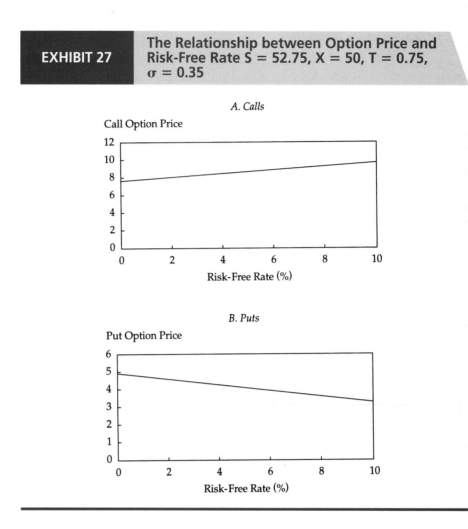

Note that both call and put values decrease as the time to expiration decreases. We previously noted that European put options do not necessarily do this. For some cases, European put options can increase in value as the time to expiration decreases, the case of a positive theta, but that is not so for our put.[34] *Most of the time, option prices are higher the longer the time to expiration. For European puts, however, some exceptions exist.*

7.3.5 Volatility: Vega

As we have previously noted, volatility is the standard deviation of the continuously compounded return on the stock. We have also noted that the volatility is an extremely important variable in the valuation of an option. It is the only variable that cannot be obtained easily and directly from another source. In addition, as we illustrate here, option prices are extremely sensitive to the volatility. We take up the subject of estimating volatility in Section 7.5.

---

[34] Positive put thetas tend to occur when the put is deep in-the-money, the volatility is low, the interest rate is high, and the time to expiration is low.

EXHIBIT 28	The Relationship between Option Price and Time to Expiration S = 52.75, X = 50, r^c = 0.0488, σ = 0.35. T Starts at 0.75 and Goes toward 0.0

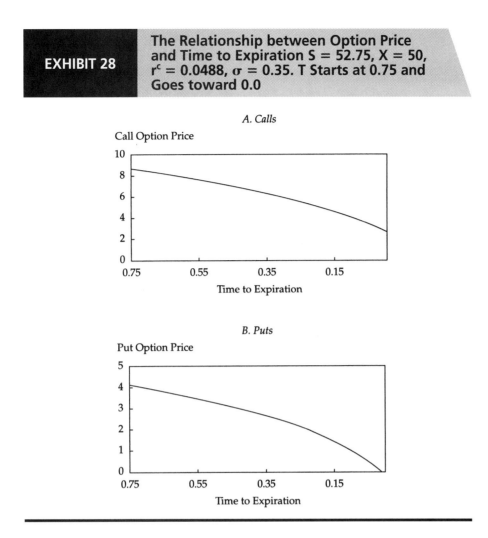

A. Calls

Call Option Price

B. Puts

Put Option Price

The relationship between option price and volatility is called the **vega**, which—albeit considered an option Greek—is not actually a Greek word.[35] We shall not concern ourselves with the actual calculation of the vega, but know that the vega is positive for both calls and puts, meaning that if the volatility increases, both call and put prices increase. Also, the vega is larger the closer the option is to being at-the-money.

In the problem we previously worked (S_0 = \$52.75, X = \$50, r^c = 0.0488, T = 0.75), at a volatility of 0.35, the option price was 8.619. Suppose we erroneously use a volatility of 0.40. Then the call price would be 9.446. An error in the volatility of this magnitude would not be difficult to make, especially for a variable that is not directly observable. Yet the result is a very large error in the option price.

Exhibit 29 displays the relationship between the option price and the volatility. Note that this relationship is nearly linear and that the option price varies over a very wide range, although this near-linearity is not the case for all options.

---

[35] So that all of these effects ("the Greeks") be named after Greek words, the term *kappa* is sometimes used to represent the relationship between an option price and its volatility. As it turns out, however, vega is used far more often than kappa and is probably easier to remember, given the "v" in vega and the "v" in volatility. Vega, however, is a star, not a letter, and its origin is Latin.

	The Relationship between Option Price and
EXHIBIT 29	**Volatility S = 52.75, X = 50, r^c = 0.0488, T = 0.75**

A. Calls

Call Option Price

B. Puts

Put Option Price

7.4 The Effect of Cash Flows on the Underlying

As we saw in Readings 62 and 63, cash flows on the underlying affect the prices of forward and futures contracts. It should follow that they would affect the prices of options. In studying the option boundary conditions and put–call parity earlier in this reading, we noted that we subtract the present value of the dividends from the underlying price and use this adjusted price to obtain the boundary conditions or to price the options using put–call parity. We do the same using the Black–Scholes–Merton model. Specifically, we introduced the expression PV(CF,0,T) for the present value of the cash flows on the underlying over the life of the option. So, we simply use S_0 − PV(CF,0,T) in the Black–Scholes–Merton model instead of S_0.

Recall that in previous readings, we also used continuous compounding to express the cash flows. For stocks, we used a continuously compounded dividend yield; for currencies, we used a continuously compounded interest rate. In the case of stocks, we let δ^c represent the continuously compounded dividend rate. Then we substituted for $S_0 e^{-\delta_c T}$ for S_0 in the Black–Scholes–Merton formula. For a foreign currency, we let S_0 represent the exchange rate, which we discount using r^{fc}, the continuously compounded foreign risk-free rate. Let us work an example involving a foreign currency option.

Let the exchange rate of U.S. dollars for euros be $0.8475. The continuously compounded U.S. risk-free rate, which in this example is r^c, is 5.10 percent. The continuously compounded euro risk-free rate, r^{fc}, is 4.25 percent. A call option expires in 125 days (T = 125/365 = 0.3425) and has an exercise price of $0.90. The volatility of the continuously compounded exchange rate is 0.055.

The first thing we do is obtain the adjusted price of the underlying: $0.8475e^{-0.0425(0.3425)} = 0.8353$. We then use this value as S_0 in the formula for d_1 and d_2:

$$d_1 = \frac{ln(0.8353/0.90) + [0.051 + (0.055)^2/2](0.3425)}{0.055\sqrt{0.3425}} = -1.7590$$

$$d_2 = -1.7590 - 0.055\sqrt{0.3425} = -1.7912$$

Using the normal probability table, we find that

$$N(d_1) = N(-1.76) = 1 - 0.9608 = 0.0392$$
$$N(d_2) = N(-1.79) = 1 - 0.9633 = 0.0367$$

In discounting the exercise rate to evaluate the second term in the Black–Scholes–Merton expression, we use the domestic (here, U.S.) continuously compounded risk-free rate. The call option price would thus be

$$c = 0.8353(0.0392) - 0.90e^{-0.051(0.3425)}(0.0367) = 0.0003$$

Therefore, this call option on an asset worth $0.8475 would cost $0.0003.

EXAMPLE 9

Use the Black–Scholes–Merton model adjusted for cash flows on the underlying to calculate the price of a call option in which the underlying is priced at 225, the exercise price is 200, the continuously compounded risk-free rate is 5.25 percent, the time to expiration is three years, and the volatility is 0.15. The effect of cash flows on the underlying is indicated below for two alternative approaches:

A. The present value of the cash flows over the life of the option is 19.72.

B. The continuously compounded dividend yield is 2.7 percent.

Solution to A: Adjust the price of the underlying to $S_0 = 225 - 19.72 = 205.28$. Then insert into the Black–Scholes–Merton formula as follows:

$$d_1 = \frac{\ln(205.28/200) + [0.0525 + (0.15)^2/2]3.0}{0.15\sqrt{3.0}} = 0.8364$$
$$d_2 = 0.8364 - 0.15\sqrt{3.0} = 0.5766$$
$$N(0.84) = 0.7995$$
$$N(0.58) = 0.7190$$
$$c = 205.28(0.7995) - 200e^{-0.0525(3.0)}(0.7190) = 41.28$$

Solution to B: Adjust the price of the underlying to $S_0 = 225e^{-0.027(3.0)}$ $= 207.49$

$$d_1 = \frac{\ln(207.49/200) + [0.0525 + (0.15)^2/2]3.0}{0.15\sqrt{3.0}} = 0.8776$$

$$d_2 = 0.8776 - 0.15\sqrt{3.0} = 0.6178$$

$$N(0.88) = 0.8106$$

$$N(0.62) = 0.7324$$

$$c = 207.49(0.8106) - 200e^{-0.0525(3.0)}(0.7324) = 43.06$$

7.5 The Critical Role of Volatility

As we have previously stressed, volatility is an extremely important variable in the pricing of options. In fact, with the possible exception of the cash flows on the underlying, it is the only variable that cannot be directly observed and easily obtained. It is, after all, the volatility over the life of the option; therefore, it is not past or current volatility but rather the future volatility. Differences in opinion on option prices nearly always result from differences of opinion about volatility. But how does one obtain a number for the future volatility?

7.5.1 Historical Volatility

The most logical starting place to look for an estimate of future volatility is past volatility. When the underlying is a publicly traded asset, we usually can collect some data over a recent past period and estimate the standard deviation of the continuously compounded return.

Exhibit 30 illustrates this process for a sample of 12 monthly prices of a particular stock. We convert these prices to returns, convert the returns to continuously compounded returns, find the variance of the series of continuously compounded returns, and then convert the variance to the standard deviation. In this example, the data are monthly returns, so we must annualize the variance by multiplying it by 12. Then we take the square root to obtain the historical estimate of the annual standard deviation or volatility.

The historical estimate of the volatility is based only on what happened in the past. To get the best estimate, we must use a lot of prices, but that means going back farther in time. The farther back we go, the less current the data become, and the less reliable our estimate of the volatility. We now look at a way of obtaining a more current estimate of the volatility, but one that raises questions as well as answers them.

7.5.2 Implied Volatility

In a market in which options are traded actively, we can reasonably assume that the market price of the option is an accurate reflection of its true value. Thus, by setting the Black–Scholes–Merton price equal to the market price, we can work backwards to infer the volatility. This procedure enables us to determine the volatility that option traders are using to price the option. This volatility is called the **implied volatility**.

Unfortunately, determining implied volatility is not a simple task. We cannot simply solve the Black–Scholes–Merton equation for the volatility. It is a complicated function with the volatility appearing several times, in some cases as σ^2.

EXHIBIT 30		Estimating Historical Volatility		
Month	Price	Return	Log Return	(Log Return − Average)²
0	100			
1	102	0.020000	0.019803	0.000123
2	99	−0.029412	−0.029853	0.001486
3	97	−0.020202	−0.020409	0.000847
4	89	−0.082474	−0.086075	0.008982
5	103	0.157303	0.146093	0.018878
6	104	0.009709	0.009662	0.000001
7	102	−0.019231	−0.019418	0.000790
8	99	−0.029412	−0.029853	0.001486
9	104	0.050505	0.049271	0.001646
10	102	−0.019231	−0.019418	0.000790
11	105	0.029412	0.028988	0.000412
12	111	0.057143	0.055570	0.002197
		Sum	0.104360	0.037639
		Average	0.008697	

The variance is estimated as follows:

$$\sigma^2 = \frac{\sum_{i=1}^{N} (R_i^c - \overline{R^c})^2}{N - 1}$$

where R_i^c is the continuously compounded return for observation i (shown above in the fourth column and calculated as $\ln(1 + R_i)$, where i goes from 1 to 12) and R_i is the ith return, $\overline{R^c}$ is the average return over the entire sample, and N is the number of observations in the sample (here, N = 12). Then

$$\sigma^2 = \frac{0.037639}{11} = 0.003422$$

Because this sample consists of monthly returns, to obtain the annual variance, we must multiply this number by 12 (or 52 for weekly, or 250—the approximate number of trading days in a year—for daily). Thus

$$\sigma^2 = 12(0.003422) = 0.041064$$

The annual standard deviation or volatility is, therefore,

$$\sigma = \sqrt{0.041064} = 0.2026$$

So the historical volatility estimate is 20.26 percent.

There are some mathematical techniques that speed up the estimation of the implied volatility. Here, however, we shall look at only the most basic method: trial and error.

Recall the option we have been working with. The underlying price is 52.75, the exercise price is 50, the risk-free rate is 4.88 percent, and the time to expiration is 0.75. In our previous examples, the volatility was 0.35. Using these values in the Black–Scholes–Merton model, we obtained a call option price of 8.619. Suppose we observe the option selling in the market for 9.25. What volatility would produce this price?

We have already calculated a price of 8.619 at a volatility of 0.35. Because the call price varies directly with the volatility, we know that it would take a volatility greater than 0.35 to produce a price higher than 8.619. We do not know how much higher, so we should just take a guess. Let us try a volatility of 0.40. Using the Black–Scholes–Merton formula with a volatility of 0.40, we obtain a price of 9.446. This is too high, so we try a lower volatility. We keep doing this in the following manner:

Volatility	Black–Scholes–Merton Price
0.35	8.619
0.40	9.446
0.39	9.280
0.38	9.114

So now we know that the correct volatility lies between 0.38 and 0.39, closer to 0.39. In solving for the implied volatility, we must decide either how close to the option price we want to be or how many significant digits we want in the implied volatility. If we choose four significant digits in the implied volatility, a value of 0.3882 would produce the option price of 9.2500. Alternatively, if we decide that we want to be within 0.01 of the option price, we would find that the implied volatility is in the range of 38.76 to 38.88 percent.

Thus, if the option is selling for about 9.25, we say that the market is pricing it at a volatility of 0.3882. This number represents the market's best estimate of the true volatility of the underlying asset; it can be viewed as a more current source of volatility information than the past volatility. Unfortunately, a circularity exists in the argument. If one uses the Black–Scholes–Merton model to determine if an option is over- or underpriced, the procedure for extracting the implied volatility assumes that the market correctly prices the option. The only way to use the implied volatility in identifying mispriced options is to interpret the implied volatility as either too high or too low, which would require an estimate of true volatility. Nonetheless, the implied volatility is a source of valuable information on the uncertainty in the underlying, and option traders use it routinely.

All of this material on continuous-time option pricing has been focused on options in which the underlying is an asset. As we described earlier in this reading, there are also options on futures. Let us take a look at the pricing of options on futures, which will pave the way for a continuous-time pricing model for options on interest rates, another case in which the underlying is not an asset.

PRICING OPTIONS ON FORWARD AND FUTURES CONTRACTS AND AN APPLICATION TO INTEREST RATE OPTION PRICING

Earlier in this reading, we discussed how options on futures contracts are active, exchange-traded options in which the underlying is a futures contract. In addition, there are over-the-counter options in which the underlying is a forward contract. In our treatment of these instruments, we assume constant interest rates. As we learned in Readings 62 and 63, this assumption means that futures and forward contracts will have the same prices. European options on futures and forward contracts will, therefore, have the same prices. American options on forwards will differ in price from American options on futures, and we discuss this later.

First we take a quick look at the basic rules that we previously developed for options on underlying assets. If the underlying asset is a futures contract, the payoff values of the options at expiration are

$$
\begin{aligned}
c_T &= \text{Max}[0, f_T(T) - X] \\
p_T &= \text{Max}[0, X - f_T(T)]
\end{aligned}
$$

(64-24)

where $f_T(T)$ is the price of a futures contract at T in which the contract expires at T. Thus, $f_T(T)$ is the futures price at expiration. These formulas are, of course, the same as for options when the underlying is an asset, with the futures price substituted for the asset price. When the option and the futures expire simultaneously, the futures price at expiration, $f_T(T)$, converges to the asset price, S_T, making the above payoffs precisely the same as those of the option on the underlying asset.

The minimum and maximum values for options on forwards or futures are the same as those we obtained for options on assets, substituting the futures price for the asset price. Specifically,

$$
\begin{aligned}
0 &\le c_0 \le f_0(T) \\
0 &\le C_0 \le f_0(T) \\
0 &\le p_0 \le X/(1 + r)^T \\
0 &\le P_0 \le X
\end{aligned}
$$

(64-25)

We also established lower bounds for European options and intrinsic values for American options and used these results to establish the minimum prices of these options. For options on futures, the lower bounds are

$$
\begin{aligned}
c_0 &\ge \text{Max}\{0, [f_0(T) - X]/(1 + r)^T\} \\
p_0 &\ge \text{Max}\{0, [X - f_0(T)]/(1 + r)^T\}
\end{aligned}
$$

(64-26)

where $f_0(T)$ is the price at time 0 of a futures contract expiring at T. Therefore, the price of a European call or put on the futures is either zero or the difference between the futures price and exercise price, as formulated above, discounted to the present. For American options on futures, early exercise is possible. Thus, we express their lowest prices as the intrinsic values:

$$
\begin{aligned}
C_0 &\ge \text{Max}[0, f_0(T) - X] \\
P_0 &\ge \text{Max}[0, X - f_0(T)]
\end{aligned}
$$

(64-27)

Because these values are greater than the lower bounds, we maintain these values as the minimum prices of American calls.[36]

As we have previously pointed out, with the assumption of constant interest rates, futures prices and forward prices are the same. We can treat European options on futures the same way as options on forwards. American options on futures will differ from American options on forwards. Now we explore how put–call parity works for options on forwards.

8.1 Put–Call Parity for Options on Forwards

In an earlier section, we examined put–call parity. Now we take a look at the parity between puts and calls on forward contracts and their underlying forward contracts. First recall the notation: $F(0,T)$ is the price established at time 0 for a forward contract expiring at time T. Let c_0 and p_0 be the prices today of calls and puts on the forward contract. We shall assume that the puts and calls expire when the forward contract expires. The exercise price of the options is X. The payoff of the call is $\text{Max}(0, S_T - X)$, and the payoff of the put is $\text{Max}(0, X - S_T)$.[37] We construct a combination consisting of a long call and a long position in a zero-coupon bond with face value of $X - F(0,T)$. We construct another combination consisting of a long position in a put and a long position in a forward contract. Exhibit 31 shows the results.

As the exhibit demonstrates, both combinations produce a payoff of either $X - F(0,T)$ or $S_T - F(0,T)$, whichever is greater. The call and bond combination is thus equivalent to the put and forward contract combination. Hence, to prevent an arbitrage opportunity, the initial values of these combinations must be the same. The initial value of the call and bond combination is $c_0 + [X - F(0,T)]/(1 + r)^T$. The forward contract has zero initial value, so the initial value

EXHIBIT 31	Portfolio Combinations for Equivalent Packages of Puts, Calls, and Forward Contracts (Put–Call Parity for Forward Contracts)		
		Value at Expiration	
Transaction	Current Value	$S_T \leq X$	$S_T > X$
Call and Bond			
Buy call	c_0	0	$S_T - X$
Buy bond	$[X - F(0,T)]/(1 + r)^T$	$X - F(0,T)$	$X - F(0,T)$
Total	$c_0 + [X - F(0,T)]/(1 + r)^T$	$X - F(0,T)$	$S_T - F(0,T)$
Put and Forward			
Buy put	p_0	$X - S_T$	0
Buy forward contract	0	$S_T - F(0,T)$	$S_T - F(0,T)$
Total	p_0	$X - F(0,T)$	$S_T - F(0,T)$

---

[36] In other words, we cannot use the European lower bound as the lowest price of an American call or put, as we could with calls when the underlying was an asset instead of a futures.

[37] Recall that the option payoffs are given by the underlying price at expiration, because the forward contract expires when the option expires. Therefore, the forward price at expiration is the underlying price at expiration.

of the put and forward contract combination is only the initial value of the put, p_0. Therefore,

$$c_0 + [X - F(0,T)]/(1 + r)^T = p_0 \qquad \textbf{(64-28)}$$

This equation is **put–call parity** for options on forward contracts.

Note that we seem to have implied that the bond is a long position, but that might not be the case. The bond should have a face value of $X - F(0,T)$. We learned in Reading 62 that $F(0,T)$ is determined in the market as the underlying price compounded at the risk-free rate.[38] Because there are a variety of options with different exercise prices, any one of which could be chosen, it is clearly possible for X to exceed or be less than $F(0,T)$. If $X > F(0,T)$, we are long the bond, because the payoff of $X - F(0,T)$ is greater than zero, meaning that we get back money from the bond. If $X < F(0,T)$, we issue the bond, because the payoff of $X - F(0,T)$ is less than zero, meaning that we must pay back money. Note the special case when $X = F(0,T)$. The bond is effectively out of the picture. Then $c_0 = p_0$.

Now recall from Reading 62 that with discrete interest compounding and no storage costs, the forward price is the spot price compounded at the risk-free rate. So,

$$F(0,T) = S_0(1 + r)^T$$

If we substitute this result for $F(0,T)$ in the put–call parity equation for options on forwards, we obtain

$$p_0 + S_0 = c_0 + X/(1 + r)^T$$

which is the put–call parity equation for options on the underlying that we learned earlier in this reading. Indeed, put–call parity for options on forwards and put–call parity for options on the underlying asset are the same. The only difference is that in the former, the forward contract and the bond replace the underlying. Given the equivalence of options on the forward contract and options on the underlying, we can refer to put–call parity for options on forwards as **put–call–forward parity**. The equation

$$c_0 + [X - F(0,T)]/(1 + r)^T = p_0$$

expresses the relationship between the forward price and the prices of the options on the underlying asset, or alternatively between the forward price and the prices of options on the forward contract. We can also rearrange the equation to isolate the forward price and obtain

$$F(0,T) = (c_0 - p_0)(1 + r)^T + X$$

which shows how the forward price is related to the put and call prices and to the exercise price.

Now observe in Exhibit 32 how a synthetic forward contract can be created out of options.

In the top half of the exhibit is a forward contract. Its payoff at expiration is $S_T - F(0,T)$. In the bottom half of the exhibit is a **synthetic forward contract**, which consists of a long call, a short put, and a long risk-free bond with a face

---

[38] We are, of course, assuming no cash flows or costs on the underlying asset.

EXHIBIT 32	Forward Contract and Synthetic Forward Contract		
		Value at Expiration	
Transaction	**Current Value**	$S_T \leq X$	$S_T > X$
Forward Contract			
Long forward contract	0	$S_T - F(0,T)$	$S_T - F(0,T)$
Synthetic Forward Contract			
Buy call	c_0	0	$S_T - X$
Sell put	$-p_0$	$-(X - S_T)$	0
Buy (or sell) bond	$[X - F(0,T)]/(1 + r)^T$	$X - F(0,T)$	$X - F(0,T)$
Total	$c_0 - p_0 + [X - F(0,T)]/(1 + r)^T$	$S_T - F(0,T)$	$S_T - F(0,T)$

value equal to the exercise price minus the forward price. Note that this bond can actually be short if the exercise price of these options is lower than the forward price. The forward contract and synthetic forward contract have the same payoffs, so their initial values must be equal. The initial value of the forward contract is zero, so the initial value of the synthetic forward contract must be zero. Thus,

$$c_0 - p_0 + [X - F(0,T)]/(1 + r)^T = 0$$

Solving for $F(0,T)$, we obtain the equation for the forward price in terms of the call, put, and bond that was given previously. So a synthetic forward contract is a combination consisting of a long call, a short put, and a zero-coupon bond with face value of $X - F(0,T)$.

Consider the following example: The options and a forward contract expire in 50 days, so $T = 50/365 = 0.1370$. The risk-free rate is 6 percent, and the exercise price is 95. The call price is 5.50, the put price is 10.50, and the forward price is 90.72. Substituting in the above equation, we obtain

$$5.50 - 10.50 + \frac{95 - 90.72}{(1.06)^{0.1370}} = -0.7540$$

which is supposed to be zero. The left-hand side replicates a forward contract. Thus, the synthetic forward is underpriced. We buy it and sell the actual forward contract. So if we buy the call, sell the put, and buy the bond with face value $95 - 90.72 = 4.28$, we bring in 0.7540. At expiration, the payoffs are as follows.

> *The options and forward expire with the underlying above 95:*
> The bond matures and pays off $95 - 90.72 = 4.28$.
> Exercise the call, paying 95 and obtaining the underlying.
> Deliver the underlying and receive 90.72 from the forward contract.
> The put expires with no value.
> Net effect: No money in or out.

> *The options and forward expire with the underlying at or below 95:*
> The bond matures and pays off $95 - 90.72 = 4.28$.
> Buy the underlying for 95 with the short put.
> Deliver the underlying and receive 90.72 from the forward contract.
> The call expires with no value.
> Net effect: No money in or out.

So we take in 0.7540 up front and never have to pay anything out. The pressure of other investors doing this will cause the call price to increase and the put price to decrease until the above equation equals zero or is at least equal to the transaction costs that would be incurred to exploit any discrepancy from zero.

Similarly, an option can be created from a forward contract. If a long forward contract is equivalent to a long call, short put, and zero-coupon bond with face value of $X - F(0,T)$, then a long call is a long forward, long put, and a zero-coupon bond with face value of $F(0,T) - X$. A long put is a long call, short forward, and a bond with face value of $X - F(0,T)$. These results are obtained just by rearranging what we learned here about forwards and options.

These results hold strictly for European options; some additional considerations exist for American options, but we do not cover them here.

EXAMPLE 10

Determine if a forward contract is correctly priced by using put–call–forward parity. The option exercise price is 90, the risk-free rate is 5 percent, the options and the forward contract expire in two years, the call price is 15.25, the put price is 3.00, and the forward price is 101.43.

Solution: First note that the time to expiration is $T = 2.0$. There are many ways to express put–call–forward parity. We use the following specification:

$$p_0 = c_0 + [X - F(0,T)]/(1 + r)^T$$

The right-hand side is the synthetic put and consists of a long call, a short forward contract, and a bond with face value of $X - F(0,T)$. Substituting the values into the right-hand side, we obtain

$$p_0 = 15.25 + (90 - 101.43)/(1.05)^{2.0} = 4.88$$

Because the actual put is selling for 3.00, it is underpriced. So we should buy the put and sell the synthetic put. To sell the synthetic put we should sell the call, buy the forward contract, and hold a bond with face value $F(0,T) - X$. Doing so will generate the following cash flow up front:

Buy put:	-3.00
Sell call:	$+15.25$
Buy bond:	$-(101.43 - 90)/(1.05)^{2.0} = -10.37$
Total:	$+1.88$

Thus the transaction brings in 1.88 up front. The payoffs at expiration are

	$S_T < 90$	$S_T \geq 90$
Long put	$90 - S_T$	0
Short call	0	$-(S_T - 90)$
Long bond	$101.43 - 90$	$101.43 - 90$
Long forward	$S_T - 101.43$	$S_T - 101.43$
Total	0	0

Therefore, no money flows in or out at expiration.

8.2 Early Exercise of American Options on Forward and Futures Contracts

As we noted earlier, the holder of an American put option may want to exercise it early. For American call options on underlying assets that make no cash payments, however, there is no justification for exercising the option early. If the underlying asset makes a cash payment, such as a dividend on a stock or interest on a bond, it may be justifiable to exercise the call option early.

For American options on futures, it may be worthwhile to exercise both calls and puts early. Even though early exercise is never justified for American calls on underlying assets that make no cash payments, early exercise can be justified for American call options on futures. Deep-in-the money American call options on futures behave almost identically to the underlying, but the investor has money tied up in the call. If the holder exercises the call and establishes a futures position, he earns interest on the futures margin account. A similar argument holds for deep-in-the-money American put options on futures. The determination of the timing of early exercise is a specialist topic so we do not explore it here.

If the option is on a forward contract instead of a futures contract, however, these arguments are overshadowed by the fact that a forward contract does not pay off until expiration, in contrast to the mark-to-market procedure of futures contracts. Thus, if one exercised either a call or a put on a forward contract early, doing so would only establish a long or short position in a forward contract. This position would not pay any cash until expiration. No justification exists for exercising early if one cannot generate any cash from the exercise. Therefore, an American call on a forward contract is the same as a European call on a forward contract, but American calls on futures are different from European calls on futures and carry higher prices.

8.3 The Black Model

The usual model for pricing European options on futures is called the Black model, named after Fischer Black of Black–Scholes–Merton fame. The formula is

$$c = e^{-r^cT}[f_0(T)N(d_1) - XN(d_2)]$$
$$p = e^{-r^cT}(X[1 - N(d_2)] - f_0(T)[1 - N(d_1)])$$

where

$$d_1 = \frac{\ln(f_0(T)/X) + (\sigma^2/2)T}{\sigma\sqrt{T}}$$
$$d_2 = d_1 - \sigma\sqrt{T}$$
$$f_0(T) = \text{the futures price}$$

and the other terms are those we have previously used. The volatility, σ, is the volatility of the continuously compounded change in the futures price.[39]

---

[39] If we were using the model to price options on forward contracts, we would insert F(0,T), the forward price, instead of the futures price. Doing so would produce some confusion because we have never subscripted the forward price, arguing that it does not change. Therefore, although we could use the formula to price options on forwards at time 0, how could we use the formula to price options on forwards at a later time, say time t, prior to expiration? In that case, we would have to use the price of a newly constructed forward contract that expires at T, F(t,T). Of course, with constant interest rates, these forward prices, F(0,T) and F(t,T), would be identical to the analogous futures price, $f_0(T)$ and $f_t(T)$. So, for ease of exposition we use the futures price.

Although the Black model may appear to give a somewhat different formula, it can be obtained directly from the Black–Scholes–Merton formula. Recall that the futures price in terms of the underlying spot price would be $f_0(T) = S_0 e^{r^c T}$. If we substitute the right-hand-side for $f_0(T)$ in the Black formula for d_1, we obtain the Black–Scholes–Merton formula for d_1.[40] Then if we substitute the right-hand side of the above for $f_0(T)$ in the Black formula for c_0 and p_0, we obtain the Black–Scholes–Merton formula for c_0 and p_0. These substitutions should make sense: The prices of options on futures equal the prices of options on the asset when the options and futures expire simultaneously.

The procedure should be straightforward if you have mastered substituting the asset price and other inputs into the Black–Scholes–Merton formula. Also, note that as with the Black–Scholes–Merton formula, the formula applies only to European options. As we noted in the previous section, early exercise of American options on futures is often justified, so we cannot get away with using this formula for American options on futures. We can, however, use the formula for American options on forwards, because they are never exercised early.

EXAMPLE 11

The price of a forward contract is 139.19. A European option on the forward contract expires in 215 days. The exercise price is 125. The continuously compounded risk-free rate is 4.25 percent. The volatility is 0.15.

A. Use the Black model to determine the price of the call option.

B. Determine the price of the underlying from the above information and use the Black–Scholes–Merton model to show that the price of an option on the underlying is the same as the price of the option on the forward.

The time to expiration is $T = 215/365 = 0.5890$.

Solution to A: First find d_1 and d_2, then $N(d_1)$ and $N(d_2)$, and then the call price:

$$d_1 = \frac{ln(139.19/125) + [(0.15)^2/2]\,0.5890}{0.15\sqrt{0.5890}} = 0.9916$$

$$d_2 = 0.9916 - 0.15\sqrt{0.5890} = 0.8765$$

$$N(0.99) = 0.8389$$

$$N(0.88) = 0.8106$$

$$c = e^{-0.0425(0.5890)}[139.19(0.8389) - 125(0.8106)] = 15.06$$

Solution to B: We learned in Reading 62 that if there are no cash flows on the underlying and the interest is compounded continuously, the forward price is given by the formula $F(0, T) = S_0 e^{r^c T}$. We can thus find the spot price as

$$S_0 = F(0,T)e^{-r^c T} = 139.19 e^{-0.0425(0.5890)} = 135.75$$

---

[40] This action requires us to recognize that $ln(S_0 e^{r^c T}/X) = ln(S_0/X) + r^c T$.

Then we simply use the Black–Scholes–Merton formula:

$$d_1 = \frac{ln(135.75/125) + (0.0425 + (0.15)^2/2)(0.5890)}{0.15\sqrt{0.5890}} = 0.9916$$

$$d_2 = 0.9916 - 0.15\sqrt{0.5890} = 0.8765$$

These are the same values as in Part A, so $N(d_1)$ and $N(d_2)$ will be the same. Plugging into the formula for the call price gives

$$c = 135.75(0.8389) - 125e^{-0.0425(0.5890)}(0.8106) = 15.06$$

This price is the same as in Part A.

8.4 Application of the Black Model to Interest Rate Options

Earlier in this reading, we described options on interest rates. These derivative instruments parallel the FRAs that we covered in Reading 62, in that they are derivatives in which the underlying is not a bond but rather an interest rate. Pricing options on interest rates is a challenging task. We showed how this is done using binomial trees. It would be nice if the Black–Scholes–Merton model could be easily used to price interest rate options, but the process is not so straightforward. Pricing options on interest rates requires a sophisticated model that prohibits arbitrage among interest-rate related instruments and their derivatives. The Black–Scholes–Merton model is not sufficiently general to use in this manner. Nonetheless, practitioners often employ the Black model to price interest rate options. Somewhat remarkably, perhaps, it is known to give satisfactory results. Therefore, we provide a quick overview of this practice here.

Suppose we wish to price a one-year interest rate cap, consisting of three caplets. One caplet expires in 90 days, one 180 days, and one in 270 days.[41] The exercise rate is 9 percent. To use the Black model, we use the forward rate as though it were $f_0(T)$. Therefore, we also require its volatility and the risk-free rate for the period to the option's expiration.[42] Recalling that there are three caplets and we have to price each one individually, let us first focus on the caplet expiring in 90 days. We first specify that $T = 90/365 = 0.2466$. Then we need the forward rate today for the period day 90 to day 180. Let this rate be 9.25 percent. We shall assume its volatility is 0.03. We then need the continuously compounded

---

[41] A one-year cap will have three individual caplets. The first expires in 90 days and pays off in 180 days, the second expires in 180 days and pays off in 270 days, and the third expires in 270 days and pays off in 360 days. The tendency to think that a one-year cap using quarterly periods should have four caplets is incorrect because there is no caplet expiring right now and paying off in 90 days. It would make no sense to create an option that expires immediately. Also, in a one-year loan, the rate is set at the start and reset only three times; hence, only three caplets are required.

[42] It is important to note here that the Black model requires that all inputs be in continuous compounding format. Therefore, the forward rate and risk-free rate would need to be the continuously compounded analogs to the discrete rates. Because the underlying is usually LIBOR, which is a discrete rate quoted on the basis of a 360-day year, some adjustments must be made to convert to a continuous rate quoted on the basis of a 365-day year. We will not address these adjustments here.

risk-free rate for 90 days, which we assume to be 9.60 percent. So now we have the following input variables:

$$T = 0.2466$$
$$f_0(T) = 0.0925$$
$$\sigma = 0.03$$
$$X = 0.09$$
$$r^c = 0.096$$

Inserting these inputs into the Black model produces

$$d_1 = \frac{ln(0.0925/0.09) + [(0.03)^2/2](0.2466)}{0.03\sqrt{0.2466}} = 1.8466$$

$$d_2 = 1.8466 - 0.03\sqrt{0.2466} = 1.8317$$

$$N(1.85) = 0.9678$$

$$N(1.83) = 0.9664$$

$$c_0 = e^{-0.096(0.2466)}[0.0925(0.9678) - 0.09(0.9664)] = 0.00248594$$

(Because of the order of magnitude of the inputs, we carry the answer out to eight decimal places.) But this answer is not quite what we need. The formula gives the answer under the assumption that the option payoff occurs at the option expiration. As we know, interest rate options pay off later than their expirations. This option expires in 90 days and pays off 90 days after that. Therefore, we need to discount this result back from day 180 to day 90 using the forward rate of 9.25 percent.[43] We thus have

$$0.00248594e^{-0.0925(0.2466)} = 0.00242988$$

Another adjustment is necessary. Because the underlying price and exercise price are entered as rates, the resulting answer is a rate. Moreover, the underlying rate and exercise rate are expressed as annual rates, so the answer is an annual rate. Interest rate option prices are always quoted as **periodic rates** (which are prices for $1 notional principal). We would adjust this rate by multiplying by 90/360.[44] The price would thus be

$$0.00242988(90/360) = 0.00060747$$

Finally, we should note that this price is valid for a $1 notional principal option. If the notional principal were $1 million, the option price would be

$$\$1,000,000(0.00060747) = \$607.47$$

We have just priced the first caplet of this cap. To price the second caplet, we need the forward rate for the period 180 days to 270 days, we would use $180/365 = 0.4932$ as the time to expiration, and we need the risk-free rate for 180 days. To price the third caplet, we need the forward rate for the period 270 days to 360 days,

---

[43] Be very careful in this discounting procedure. The exponent in the exponential should have a time factor of the number of days between the option expiration and its payoff. Because there are 90 days between days 90 and 180, we use $90/365 = 0.2466$. This value is not quite the same as the time until the option expiration, which today is 90 but which will count down to zero.

[44] It is customary in the interest rate options market to use 360 in the denominator to make this adjustment, even though we have used 365 in other places.

we would use $270/365 = 0.7397$ as the time to expiration, and we need the risk-free rate for 270 days. The price of the cap would be the sum of the prices of the three component caplets. If we were pricing a floor, we would price the component floorlets using the Black model for puts.

Although the Black model is frequently used to price interest rate options, binomial models, as we illustrated earlier, are somewhat more widely used in this area. These models are more attuned to deriving prices that prohibit arbitrage opportunities using any of the diverse instruments whose prices are given by the term structure. When you use the Black model to price interest rate options, there is some risk, perhaps minor, of having a counterparty be able to do arbitrage against you. Yet somehow the Black model is used often, and professionals seem to agree that it works remarkably well.

EXAMPLE 12

Use the Black model to price an interest rate put that expires in 280 days. The forward rate is currently 6.8 percent, the 280-day continuously compounded risk-free rate is 6.25 percent, the exercise rate is 7 percent, and the volatility is 0.02. The option is based on a 180-day underlying rate, and the notional principal is $10 million.

Solution: The time to expiration is $T = 280/365 = 0.7671$. Calculate the value of d_1, d_2, and $N(d_1)$, $N(d_2)$, and p_0 using the Black model:

$$d_1 = \frac{ln(0.068/0.07) + [(0.02)^2/2]0.7671}{0.02\sqrt{0.7671}} = -1.6461$$

$d_2 = -1.6461 - 0.02\sqrt{0.7671} = -1.6636$

$N(-1.65) = 1 - N(1.65) = 1 - 0.9505 = 0.0495$

$N(-1.66) = 1 - N(1.66) = 1 - 0.9515 = 0.0485$

$p_0 = e^{-0.0625(0.7671)}[0.07(1 - 0.0485) - 0.068(1 - 0.0495)]$

$\quad = 0.00187873$

This formula assumes the option payoff is made at expiration. For an interest rate option, that assumption is false. This is a 180-day rate, so the payoff is made 180 days later. Therefore, we discount the payoff over 180 days using the forward rate:

$$e^{-0.068(180/365)}(0.00187873) = 0.00181677$$

Interest rate option prices must reflect the fact that the rate used in the formula is quoted as an annual rate. So, we must multiply by 180/360 because the transaction is based on a 180-day rate:

$$0.00181677(180/360) = 0.00090839$$

Then we multiply by the notional principal:

$$\$10,000,000(0.00090839) = \$9,084$$

THE ROLE OF OPTIONS MARKETS

As we did with futures markets, we conclude the reading by looking at the important role options markets play in the financial system. Derivative markets provide price discovery and risk management, make the markets for the underlying assets more efficient, and permit trading at low transaction costs. These features are also associated with options markets. Yet, options offer further advantages that some other derivatives do not offer.

For example, forward and futures contracts have bidirectional payoffs. They have the potential for a substantial gain in one direction and a substantial loss in the other direction. The advantage of taking such a position lies in the fact that one need pay no cash up front. In contrast, options offer the feature that, if one is willing to pay cash up front, one can limit the loss in a given direction. In other words, options have unidirectional payoffs. This feature can be attractive to the holder of an option. To the writer, options offer the opportunity to be paid cash up front for a willingness to assume the risk of the unidirectional payoff. An option writer can assume the risk of potentially a large loss unmatched by the potential for a large gain. In fact, the potential gain is small. But for this risk, the option writer receives money up front.

Options also offer excellent devices for managing the risk of various exposures. An obvious one is the protective put, which we saw earlier and which can protect a position against loss by paying off when the value of the underlying is down.

Recall that futures contracts offer price discovery, the revelation of the prices at which investors will contract today for transactions to take place later. Options, on the other hand, provide volatility discovery. Through the implied volatility, investors can determine the market's assessment of how volatile it believes the underlying asset is. This valuable information can be difficult to obtain from any other source.

Futures offer advantages over forwards, in that futures are standardized, tend to be actively traded in a secondary market, and are protected by the exchange's clearinghouse against credit risk. Although some options, such as interest rate options, are available only in over-the-counter forms, many options exist in both over-the-counter and exchange-listed forms. Hence, one can often customize an option if necessary or trade it on an exchange.

In Reading 62, we covered forward contracts; in Reading 63, we covered futures contracts; and in this reading we covered option contracts. We have one more major class of derivative instruments, swaps, which we now turn to in Reading 65.

SUMMARY

▶ Options are rights to buy or sell an underlying at a fixed price, the exercise price, for a period of time. The right to buy is a call; the right to sell is a put. Options have a definite expiration date. Using the option to buy or sell is the action of exercising it. The buyer or holder of an option pays a price to the seller or writer for the right to buy (a call) or sell (a put) the underlying instrument. The **writer of an option** has the corresponding potential obligation to sell or buy the underlying.

▶ European options can be exercised only at expiration; American options can be exercised at any time prior to expiration. Moneyness refers to the characteristic that an option has positive intrinsic value. The payoff is the value of the option at expiration. An option's intrinsic value is the value that can be captured if the option is exercised. Time value is the component of an option's price that reflects the uncertainty of what will happen in the future to the price of the underlying.

▶ Options can be traded as standardized instruments on an options exchange, where they are protected from default on the part of the writer, or as customized instruments on the over-the-counter market, where they are subject to the possibility of the writer defaulting. Because the buyer pays a price at the start and does not have to do anything else, the buyer cannot default.

▶ The underlying instruments for options are individual stocks, stock indices, bonds, interest rates, currencies, futures, commodities, and even such random factors as the weather. In addition, a class of options called real options is associated with the flexibility in capital investment projects.

▶ Like FRAs, which are forward contracts in which the underlying is an interest rate, interest rate options are options in which the underlying is an interest rate. However, FRAs are commitments to make one interest payment and receive another, whereas interest rate options are rights to make one interest payment and receive another.

▶ Option payoffs, which are the values of options when they expire, are determined by the greater of zero or the difference between underlying price and exercise price, if a call, or the greater of zero or the difference between exercise price and underlying price, if a put. For interest rate options, the exercise price is a specified rate and the underlying price is a variable interest rate.

▶ Interest rate options exist in the form of caps, which are call options on interest rates, and floors, which are put options on interest rates. Caps consist of a series of call options, called caplets, on an underlying rate, with each option expiring at a different time. Floors consist of a series of put options, called floorlets, on an underlying rate, with each option expiring at a different time.

▶ The minimum value of European and American calls and puts is zero. The maximum value of European and American calls is the underlying price. The maximum value of a European put is the present value of the exercise price. The maximum value of an American put is the exercise price.

▶ The lower bound of a European call is established by constructing a portfolio consisting of a long call and risk-free bond and a short position in the underlying asset. This combination produces a non-negative value at expiration, so its current value must be non-negative. For this situation to occur, the call price has to be worth at least the underlying price minus the present value of the exercise price. The lower bound of a European put is established by constructing a portfolio consisting of a long put, a long position in the underlying, and the issuance of a zero-coupon bond. This combination produces a non-negative value at expiration so its current value must be non-negative. For this to occur, the put price has to be at least as much as the present value of the exercise price minus the underlying price. For both calls and puts, if this lower bound is negative, we invoke the rule that an option price can be no lower than zero.

▶ The lowest price of a European call is referred to as the lower bound. The lowest price of an American call is also the lower bound of a European call. The lowest price of a European put is also referred to as the lower bound. The lowest price of an American put, however, is its intrinsic value.

▶ Buying a call with a given exercise price and selling an otherwise identical call with a higher exercise price creates a combination that always pays off with a non-negative value. Therefore, its current value must be non-negative. For this to occur, the call with the lower exercise price must be worth at least as much as the other call. A similar argument holds for puts, except that one would buy the put with the higher exercise price. This line of reasoning shows that the put with the higher exercise price must be worth at least as much as the one with the lower exercise price.

▶ A longer-term European or American call must be worth at least as much as a corresponding shorter-term European or American call. A longer-term American put must be worth at least as much as a shorter-term American put. A longer-term European put, however, can be worth more or less than a shorter-term European put.

▶ A fiduciary call, consisting of a European call and a zero-coupon bond, produces the same payoff as a protective put, consisting of the underlying and a European put. Therefore, their current values must be the same. For this equivalence to occur, the call price plus bond price must equal the underlying price plus put price. This relationship is called put–call parity and can be used to identify combinations of instruments that synthesize another instrument by rearranging the equation to isolate the instrument you are trying to create. Long positions are indicated by positive signs, and short positions are indicated by negative signs. One can create a synthetic call, a synthetic put, a synthetic underlying, and a synthetic bond, as well as synthetic short positions in these instruments for the purpose of exploiting mispricing in these instruments.

▶ Put–call parity violations exist when one side of the equation does not equal the other. An arbitrageur buys the lower-priced side and sells the higher-priced side, thereby earning the difference in price, and the positions offset at expiration. The combined actions of many arbitrageurs performing this set of transactions would increase the demand and price for the underpriced instruments and decrease the demand and price for the overpriced instruments, until the put–call parity relationship is upheld.

▶ American option prices must always be no less than those of otherwise equivalent European options. American call options, however, are never exercised early unless there is a cash flow on the underlying, so they can sell for the same as their European counterparts in the absence of such a cash flow. American put options nearly always have a possibility of early exercise, so they ordinarily sell for more than their European counterparts.

▶ Cash flows on the underlying affect an option's boundary conditions and put–call parity by lowering the underlying price by the present value of the cash flows over the life of the option.

▶ A higher interest rate increases a call option's price and decreases a put option's price.

▶ In a one-period binomial model, the underlying asset can move up to one of two prices. A portfolio consisting of a long position in the underlying and a short position in a call option can be made risk-free and, therefore, must return the risk-free rate. Under this condition, the option price can be obtained by inferring it from a formula that uses the other input values. The option price is a weighted average of the two option prices at expiration, discounted back one period at the risk-free rate.

▶ If an option is trading for a price higher than that given in the binomial model, one can sell the option and buy a specific number of units of the underlying, as given by the model. This combination is risk free but will earn a return higher than the risk-free rate. If the option is trading for a price lower than the price given in the binomial model, a short position in a specific number of units of the underlying and a long position in the option will create a risk-free loan that costs less than the risk-free rate.

▶ In a two-period binomial model, the underlying can move to one of two prices in each of two periods; thus three underlying prices are possible at the option expiration. To price an option, start at the expiration and work backward, following the procedure in the one-period model in which an option price at any given point in time is a weighted average of the next two possible prices discounted at the risk-free rate.

▶ To calculate the price of an option on a zero-coupon bond or a coupon bond, one must first construct a binomial tree of the price of the bond over the life of the option. To calculate the price of an option on an interest rate, one should use a binomial tree of interest rates. Then the option price is found by starting at the option expiration, determining the payoff and successively working backwards by computing the option price as the weighted average of the next two option prices discounted back one period. For the case of options on bonds or interest rates, a different discount rate is used at different parts of the tree.

▶ For an option of a given expiration, a greater pricing accuracy is obtained by dividing the option's life into a greater number of time periods in a binomial tree. As more time periods are added, the discrete-time binomial price converges to a stable value as though the option is being modeled in a continuous-time world.

▶ The assumptions under which the Black–Scholes–Merton model is derived state that the underlying asset follows a geometric lognormal diffusion process, the risk-free rate is known and constant, the volatility of the underlying asset is known and constant, there are no taxes or transaction costs, there are no cash flows on the underlying, and the options are European.

▶ To calculate the value of an option using the Black–Scholes–Merton model, enter the underlying price, exercise price, risk-free rate, volatility, and time to expiration into a formula. The formula will require you to look up two normal probabilities, obtained from either a table or preferably a computer routine.

▶ The change in the option price for a change in the price of the underlying is called the delta. The change in the option price for a change in the risk-free rate is called the rho. The change in the option price for a change in the time to expiration is called the theta. The change in the option price for a change in the volatility is called the vega.

▶ The delta is defined as the change in the option price divided by the change in the underlying price. The option price change can be approximated by the delta times the change in the underlying price. To construct a delta-hedged position, a short (long) position in each call is matched with a long (short) position in delta units of the underlying. Changes in the underlying price will generate offsetting changes in the value of the option position, provided the changes in the underlying price are small and occur over a short time period. A delta-hedged position should be adjusted as the delta changes and time passes.

▶ If changes in the price of the underlying are large or the delta hedge is not adjusted over a longer time period, the hedge may not be effective. This effect is due to the instability of the delta and is called the gamma effect. If the gamma effect is large, option price changes will not be very close to the changes as approximated by the delta times the underlying price change.

▶ Cash flows on the underlying are accommodated in option pricing models by reducing the price of the underlying by the present value of the cash flows over the life of the option.

▶ Volatility can be estimated by calculating the standard deviation of the continuously compounded returns from a sample of recent data for the underlying. This is called the historical volatility. An alternative measure, called the implied volatility, can be obtained by setting the Black–Scholes–Merton model price equal to the market price and inferring the volatility. The implied volatility is a measure of the volatility the market is using to price the option.

▶ The payoffs of a call on a forward contract and an appropriately chosen zero-coupon bond are equivalent to the payoffs of a put on the forward contract and the forward contract. Thus, their current values must be the same. For this equality to occur, the call price plus the bond price must equal the put price. The appropriate zero-coupon bond is one with a face value equal to the exercise price minus the forward price. This relationship is called put–call–forward (or futures) parity.

▶ There is no justification for exercising American options on forward contracts early, so they are equivalent to European options on forwards. American options on futures, both calls and puts, can sometimes be exercised early, so they are different from European options on futures and carry a higher price.

▶ The Black model can be used to price European options on forwards or futures by entering the forward price, exercise price, risk-free rate, time to expiration, and volatility into a formula that will also require the determination of two normal probabilities.

▶ The Black model can be used to price European options on interest rates by entering the **forward interest rate** into the model for the forward or futures price and the exercise rate for the exercise price.

▶ Options are useful in financial markets because they provide a way to limit losses to the premium paid while permitting potentially large gains. They can be used for hedging purposes, especially in the case of puts, which can be used to limit the loss on a long position in an asset. Options also provide information on the volatility of the underlying asset. Options can be standardized and exchange-traded or customized in the over-the-counter market.

APPENDIX 64A

Cumulative Probabilities for a Standard Normal Distribution
$P(X \leq x) = N(x)$ for ≥ 0 or $1 - N(-x)$ for $x < 0$

x	0	0.01	0.02	0.03	0.04	0.05	0.06	0.07	0.08	0.09
0.00	0.5000	0.5040	0.5080	0.5120	0.5160	0.5199	0.5239	0.5279	0.5319	0.5359
0.10	0.5398	0.5438	0.5478	0.5517	0.5557	0.5596	0.5636	0.5675	0.5714	0.5753
0.20	0.5793	0.5832	0.5871	0.5910	0.5948	0.5987	0.6026	0.6064	0.6103	0.6141
0.30	0.6179	0.6217	0.6255	0.6293	0.6331	0.6368	0.6406	0.6443	0.6480	0.6517
0.40	0.6554	0.6591	0.6628	0.6664	0.6700	0.6736	0.6772	0.6808	0.6844	0.6879
0.50	0.6915	0.6950	0.6985	0.7019	0.7054	0.7088	0.7123	0.7157	0.7190	0.7224
0.60	0.7257	0.7291	0.7324	0.7357	0.7389	0.7422	0.7454	0.7486	0.7517	0.7549
0.70	0.7580	0.7611	0.7642	0.7673	0.7704	0.7734	0.7764	0.7794	0.7823	0.7852
0.80	0.7881	0.7910	0.7939	0.7967	0.7995	0.8023	0.8051	0.8078	0.8106	0.8133
0.90	0.8159	0.8186	0.8212	0.8238	0.8264	0.8289	0.8315	0.8340	0.8365	0.8389
1.00	0.8413	0.8438	0.8461	0.8485	0.8508	0.8531	0.8554	0.8577	0.8599	0.8621
1.10	0.8643	0.8665	0.8686	0.8708	0.8729	0.8749	0.8770	0.8790	0.8810	0.8830
1.20	0.8849	0.8869	0.8888	0.8907	0.8925	0.8944	0.8962	0.8980	0.8997	0.9015
1.30	0.9032	0.9049	0.9066	0.9082	0.9099	0.9115	0.9131	0.9147	0.9162	0.9177
1.40	0.9192	0.9207	0.9222	0.9236	0.9251	0.9265	0.9279	0.9292	0.9306	0.9319
1.50	0.9332	0.9345	0.9357	0.9370	0.9382	0.9394	0.9406	0.9418	0.9429	0.9441
1.60	0.9452	0.9463	0.9474	0.9484	0.9495	0.9505	0.9515	0.9525	0.9535	0.9545
1.70	0.9554	0.9564	0.9573	0.9582	0.9591	0.9599	0.9608	0.9616	0.9625	0.9633
1.80	0.9641	0.9649	0.9656	0.9664	0.9671	0.9678	0.9686	0.9693	0.9699	0.9706
1.90	0.9713	0.9719	0.9726	0.9732	0.9738	0.9744	0.9750	0.9756	0.9761	0.9767
2.00	0.9772	0.9778	0.9783	0.9788	0.9793	0.9798	0.9803	0.9808	0.9812	0.9817
2.10	0.9821	0.9826	0.9830	0.9834	0.9838	0.9842	0.9846	0.9850	0.9854	0.9857
2.20	0.9861	0.9864	0.9868	0.9871	0.9875	0.9878	0.9881	0.9884	0.9887	0.9890
2.30	0.9893	0.9896	0.9898	0.9901	0.9904	0.9906	0.9909	0.9911	0.9913	0.9916
2.40	0.9918	0.9920	0.9922	0.9925	0.9927	0.9929	0.9931	0.9932	0.9934	0.9936
2.50	0.9938	0.9940	0.9941	0.9943	0.9945	0.9946	0.9948	0.9949	0.9951	0.9952
2.60	0.9953	0.9955	0.9956	0.9957	0.9959	0.9960	0.9961	0.9962	0.9963	0.9964
2.70	0.9965	0.9966	0.9967	0.9968	0.9969	0.9970	0.9971	0.9972	0.9973	0.9974
2.80	0.9974	0.9975	0.9976	0.9977	0.9977	0.9978	0.9979	0.9979	0.9980	0.9981
2.90	0.9981	0.9982	0.9982	0.9983	0.9984	0.9984	0.9985	0.9985	0.9986	0.9986
3.00	0.9987	0.9987	0.9987	0.9988	0.9988	0.9989	0.9989	0.9989	0.9990	0.9990

PRACTICE PROBLEMS FOR READING 64

1. Consider the following information on put and call options on a stock:

Call price, c_0 = $4.50

Put price, p_0 = $6.80

Exercise price, X = $70

Days to option expiration = 139

Current stock price, S_0 = $67.32

Risk-free rate, r = 5 percent

   A. Use put–call parity to calculate prices of the following:

     i. Synthetic call option

     ii. Synthetic put option

     iii. Synthetic bond

     iv. Synthetic underlying stock

   B. For each of the synthetic instruments in Part A, identify any mispricing by comparing the actual price with the synthetic price.

   C. Based on the mispricing in Part B, illustrate an arbitrage transaction using a synthetic call.

   D. Based on the mispricing in Part B, illustrate an arbitrage transaction using a synthetic put.

2. A stock currently trades at a price of $100. The stock price can go up 10 percent or down 15 percent. The risk-free rate is 6.5 percent.

   A. Use a one-period binomial model to calculate the price of a call option with an exercise price of $90.

   B. Suppose the call price is currently $17.50. Show how to execute an arbitrage transaction that will earn more than the risk-free rate. Use 100 call options.

   C. Suppose the call price is currently $14. Show how to execute an arbitrage transaction that replicates a loan that will earn less than the risk-free rate. Use 100 call options.

3. Suppose a stock currently trades at a price of $150. The stock price can go up 33 percent or down 15 percent. The risk-free rate is 4.5 percent.

   A. Use a one-period binomial model to calculate the price of a put option with exercise price of $150.

   B. Suppose the put price is currently $14. Show how to execute an arbitrage transaction that will earn more than the risk-free rate. Use 10,000 put options.

   C. Suppose the put price is currently $11. Show how to execute an arbitrage transaction that will earn more than the risk-free rate. Use 10,000 put options.

4. Consider a two-period binomial model in which a stock currently trades at a price of $65. The stock price can go up 20 percent or down 17 percent each period. The risk-free rate is 5 percent.

   A. Calculate the price of a call option expiring in two periods with an exercise price of $60.

B. Based on your answer in Part A, calculate the number of units of the underlying stock that would be needed at each point in the binomial tree to construct a risk-free hedge. Use 10,000 calls.

C. Calculate the price of a call option expiring in two periods with an exercise price of $70.

D. Based on your answer in Part C, calculate the number of units of the underlying stock that would be needed at each point in the binomial tree to construct a risk-free hedge. Use 10,000 calls.

5. Consider a two-period binomial model in which a stock currently trades at a price of $65. The stock price can go up 20 percent or down 17 percent each period. The risk-free rate is 5 percent.

A. Calculate the price of a put option expiring in two periods with exercise price of $60.

B. Based on your answer in Part A, calculate the number of units of the underlying stock that would be needed at each point in the binomial tree in order to construct a risk-free hedge. Use 10,000 puts.

C. Calculate the price of a put option expiring in two periods with an exercise price of $70.

D. Based on your answer in Part C, calculate the number of units of the underlying stock that would be needed at each point in the binomial tree in order to construct a risk-free hedge. Use 10,000 puts.

SWAP MARKETS AND CONTRACTS
by Don M. Chance

LEARNING OUTCOMES

The candidate should be able to:

a. distinguish between the pricing and valuation of swaps;

b. explain the equivalence of the following swaps to combinations of other instruments: interest rate swaps to a series of off market forward rate agreements (FRAs) and a plain vanilla swap to a combination of an interest rate call and interest rate put;

c. calculate and interpret the fixed rate on a plain vanilla interest rate swap and the market value of the swap during its life;

d. calculate and interpret the fixed rate, if applicable, and the foreign notional principal for a given domestic notional principal on a currency swap, and determine the market values of each of the different types of currency swaps during their lives;

e. calculate and interpret the fixed rate, if applicable, on an equity swap and the market values of the different types of equity swaps during their lives;

f. explain and interpret the characteristics and uses of swaptions, including the difference between payer and receiver swaptions;

g. identify and calculate the possible payoffs and cash flows of an interest rate swaption;

h. calculate and interpret the value of an interest rate swaption on the expiration day;

i. evaluate swap credit risk for each party and over the life of the swap, distinguish between current credit risk and potential credit risk, and illustrate how swap credit risk is reduced by both netting and marking to market;

j. define swap spread and relate it to credit risk.

OPTIONAL SEGMENT BEGINS

1

INTRODUCTION

This reading completes the survey of the main types of derivative instruments. Preceding readings covered forward contracts, futures contracts, and options. This reading covers swaps. Although swaps were the last of the main types of derivatives to be invented, they are clearly not the least important. In fact, judging by the size of the swap market, they are probably the most important. The Bank for International Settlements estimated the notional principal of the global over-the-counter derivatives market as of 30 June 2001 at $100 trillion. Of that amount, interest rate and currency swaps account for about $61 trillion, with interest rate swaps representing about $57 trillion of that total.[1] Indeed, interest rate swaps have had overwhelming success as a derivative product. They are widely used by corporations, financial institutions, and governments.

Recall first that *a swap is an agreement between two parties to exchange a series of future cash flows*. For most types of swaps, one party makes payments that are determined by a random outcome, such as an interest rate, a currency rate, an equity return, or a commodity price. These payments are commonly referred to as variable or *floating*. The other party either makes variable or floating payments determined by some other random factor or makes fixed payments. At least one type of swap involves both parties making fixed payments, but the values of those payments vary due to random factors.

In forwards, futures, and options, the terminology of *long* and *short* has been used to describe buyers and sellers. These terms are not used as often in swaps. The preferred terminology usually designates a party as being the floating- (or variable-) rate payer or the fixed-rate payer. Nonetheless, in swaps in which one party receives a floating rate and the other receives a fixed rate, the former is usually said to be long and the latter is said to be short. This usage is in keeping with the fact that parties who go long in other instruments pay a known amount and receive a claim on an unknown amount. In some swaps, however, both sides are floating or variable, and this terminology breaks down.

1.1 Characteristics of Swap Contracts

Although technically a swap can have a single payment, most swaps involve multiple payments. Thus, we refer to a swap as a *series* of payments. In fact, we have already covered a swap with one payment, which is just a forward contract. Hence, a swap is basically a series of forward contracts. We will elaborate further in Section 4.1.2, but with this idea in mind, we can see that a swap is like an agreement to buy something over a period of time. We might be paying a variable price or a price that has already been fixed: we might be paying an uncertain price, or we might already know the price we shall pay.

---

[1] Equity and commodity swaps account for less than the notional principal of currency swaps.

When a swap is initiated, neither party pays any amount to the other. Therefore, a swap has zero value at the start of the contract. Although it is not absolutely necessary for this condition to be true, swaps are typically done in this fashion. Neither party pays anything up front. There is, however, a technical exception to this point in regard to currency swaps. Each party pays the notional principal to the other, but the amounts exchanged are equivalent, though denominated in two different currencies.

Each date on which the parties make payments is called a **settlement date**, sometimes called a payment date, and the time between settlement dates is called the **settlement period**. On a given settlement date when payments are due, one party makes a payment to the other, which in turn makes a payment to the first party. With the exception of currency swaps and a few variations associated with other types of swaps, both sets of payments are made in the same currency. Consequently, the parties typically agree to exchange only the net amount owed from one party to the other, a practice called **netting**. In currency swaps and a few other special cases, the payments are not made in the same currency; hence, the parties usually make separate payments without netting. Note the implication that swaps are generally settled in cash. It is quite rare for swaps to call for actual physical delivery of an underlying asset.

A swap always has a **termination date**, the date of the final payment. We can think of this date as its expiration date, as we do with other derivatives. The original time to maturity is sometimes called the **tenor** of a swap.

The swap market is almost exclusively an over-the-counter market, so swaps contracts are customized to the parties' specific needs. Several of the leading futures exchanges have created futures contracts on swaps. These contracts allow participants to hedge and speculate on the rates that will prevail in the swap market at future dates. Of course, these contracts are not swaps themselves but, as derivatives of swaps, they can in some ways serve as substitutes for swaps. These futures contracts have been moderately successful, but their volume is insignificant compared with the over-the-counter market for swaps.

As we have discussed in previous readings, over-the-counter instruments are subject to default risk. Default is possible whenever a payment is due. When a series of payments is made, there is default risk potential throughout the life of the contract, depending on the financial condition of the two parties. But default can be somewhat complicated in swaps. Suppose, for example, that on a settlement date, Party A owes Party B a payment of $50,000 and Party B owes Party A a payment of $12,000. Agreeing to net, Party A owes Party B $38,000 for that particular payment. Party A may be illiquid, or perhaps even bankrupt, and unable to make the payment. But it may be the case that the market value of the swap, which reflects the present value of the remaining payments, could be positive from the perspective of Party A and negative from the perspective of Party B. In that case, Party B owes Party A more for the remaining payments. We will learn how to determine the market value of a swap in Section 4.2 of this reading.

The handling of default in swaps can be complicated, depending on the contract specifications and the applicable laws under which the contract was written. In most cases, the above situation would be resolved by having A be in default but possessing an asset, the swap, that can be used to help settle its other liabilities. We shall discuss the default risk of swaps in more detail in Section 7.

1.2 Termination of a Swap

As we noted earlier, a swap has a termination or expiration date. Sometimes, however, a party could want to terminate a swap before its formal expiration. This scenario is much like a party selling a bond before it matures or selling an exchange-traded option or futures contract before its expiration. With swaps, early termination can take place in several ways.

As we mentioned briefly and will cover in more detail later, a swap has a market value that can be calculated during its life. If a party holds a swap with a market value of $125,000, for example, it can settle the swap with the counterparty by having the counterparty pay it $125,000 in cash. This payment terminates the transaction for both parties. From the opposite perspective, a party holding a swap with a negative market value can terminate the swap by paying the market value to the counterparty. Terminating a swap in this manner is possible only if the counterparties specify in advance that such a transaction can be made, or if they reach an agreement to do so without having specified in advance. In other words, this feature is not automatically available and must be agreed to by both parties.

Many swaps are terminated early by entering into a separate and offsetting swap. For example, suppose a corporation is engaged in a swap to make fixed payments of 5 percent and receive floating payments based on LIBOR, with the payments made each 15 January and 15 July. Three years remain on the swap. That corporation can offset the swap by entering into an entirely new swap in which it makes payments based on LIBOR and receives a fixed rate with the payments made each 15 January and 15 July for three years. The swap fixed rate is determined by market conditions at the time the swap is initiated. Thus, the fixed rate on the new swap is not likely to match the fixed rate on the old swap, but the effect of this transaction is simply to have the floating payments offset; the fixed payments will net out to a known amount. Hence, the risk associated with the floating rate is eliminated. The default risk, however, is not eliminated because both swaps remain in effect.

Another way to terminate a swap early is sell the swap to another counterparty. Suppose a corporation holds a swap worth $75,000. If it can obtain the counterparty's permission, it can find another party to take over its payments. In effect, it sells the swap for $75,000 to that party. This procedure, however, is not commonly used.

A final way to terminate a swap early is by using a swaption. This instrument is an option to enter into a swap at terms that are established in advance. Thus, a party could use a swaption to enter into an offsetting swap, as described above. We shall cover swaptions in more detail in Section 6.

2   THE STRUCTURE OF GLOBAL SWAP MARKETS

The global swaps market is much like the global forward and over-the-counter options markets, which we covered in some detail in Readings 62 and 64. It is made up of dealers, which are banks and investment banking firms. These dealers make markets in swaps, quoting bid and ask prices and rates, thereby offering to take either side of a swap transaction. Upon taking a position in a swap, the dealer generally offsets the risk by making transactions in other markets. The counterparties to swaps are either end users or other dealers. The end users are often corporations with risk management problems that can be solved by engaging in a swap—a corporation or other end user is usually exposed to or needs an exposure to some type of risk that arises from interest rates, exchange rates, stock prices, or commodity prices. The end user contacts a dealer that makes a market in swaps. The two engage in a transaction, at which point the dealer assumes some risk from the end user. The dealer then usually lays off the risk by engaging in a transaction with another party. That transaction could be something as simple as a futures contract, or it could be an over-the-counter transaction with another dealer.

Risk magazine conducts annual surveys of participants in various derivative products. Exhibit 1 presents the results of those surveys for currency and interest

EXHIBIT 1	Risk Magazine Surveys of Banks, Investment Banks, and Corporate End Users to Determine the Top Three Dealers in Currency and Interest Rate Swaps

	Respondents	
Currencies	**Banks and Investment Banks**	**Corporate End Users**
Currency Swaps		
$/€	UBS Warburg	Citigroup
	JP Morgan Chase	Royal Bank of Scotland
	Deutsche Bank	Bank of America
$/¥	JP Morgan Chase	Citigroup
	UBS Warburg	Bank of America
	Credit Suisse First Boston/ Deutsche Bank	JP Morgan Chase
$/£	Royal Bank of Scotland	Royal Bank of Scotland
	JP Morgan Chase	Citigroup
	Goldman Sachs	Deutsche Bank
$/SF	UBS Warburg	UBS Warburg
	Goldman Sachs	Citigroup
	Credit Suisse First Boston	Credit Suisse First Boston
Interest Rate Swaps (2–10 years)		
$	JP Morgan Chase	JP Morgan Chase
	Bank of America	Bank of America
	Morgan Stanley	Royal Bank of Scotland
€	JP Morgan Chase	Royal Bank of Scotland
	Deutsche Bank	Deutsche Bank
	Morgan Stanley	Citigroup
¥	JP Morgan Chase	Royal Bank of Scotland
	Deutsche Bank	Barclays Capital
	Bank of America	Citigroup/JP Morgan Chase
£	Royal Bank of Scotland	Royal Bank of Scotland
	Barclays Capital	Barclays Capital
	UBS Warburg	Deutsche Bank
SF	UBS Warburg	UBS Warburg
	Credit Suisse First Boston	Credit Suisse First Boston
	Zürcher Kantonalbank	Zürcher Kantonalbank

Note: $ = U.S. dollar, € = euro, ¥ = Japanese yen, £ = U.K. pound sterling, SF = Swiss franc.

Source: Risk, September 2002, pp. 30–67 for banks and investment banking dealer respondents, and June 2002, pp. 24–34 for corporate end user respondents. Ratings for swaps with maturities less than 2 years and greater than 10 years are also provided in the September 2002 issue of *Risk.*

OPTIONAL SEGMENT

rate swaps. One survey provides opinions of banks and investment banks that are swaps dealers. In the other survey, the respondents are end users. The results give a good idea of the major players in this market. It is interesting to note the disagreement between how dealers view themselves and how end users view them. Also, note that the rankings change, sometimes drastically, from year to year.

TYPES OF SWAPS

We alluded to the fact that the underlying asset in a swap can be a currency, interest rate, stock, or commodity. We now take a look at these types of swaps in more detail.

3.1 Currency Swaps

In a currency swap, each party makes interest payments to the other in different currencies.[2] Consider this example. The U.S. retailer Target Corporation (NYSE: TGT) does not have an established presence in Europe. Let us say that it has decided to begin opening a few stores in Germany and needs €9 million to fund construction and initial operations. TGT would like to issue a fixed-rate euro-denominated bond with face value of €9 million, but the company is not very well known in Europe. European investment bankers have given it a quote for such a bond. Deutsche Bank, AG (NYSE: DB), however, tells TGT that it should issue the bond in dollars and use a swap to convert it into euros.

Suppose TGT issues a five-year US$10 million bond at a rate of 6 percent. It then enters into a swap with DB in which DB will make payments to TGT in U.S. dollars at a fixed rate of 5.5 percent and TGT will make payments to DB in euros at a fixed rate of 4.9 percent each 15 March and 15 September for five years. The payments are based on a notional principal of 10 million in dollars and 9 million in euros. We assume the swap starts on 15 September of the current year. The swap specifies that the two parties exchange the notional principal at the start of the swap and at the end. Because the payments are made in different currencies, netting is not practical, so each party makes its respective payments.[3]

Thus, the swap is composed of the following transactions:
15 September:

▶ DB pays TGT €9 million

▶ TGT pays DB $10 million

---

[2] It is important at this point to clear up some terminology confusion. Foreign currency is often called *foreign exchange* or sometimes *FX*. There is another transaction called an *FX swap*, which sounds as if it might be referring to a currency swap. In fact, an FX swap is just a long position in a forward contract on a foreign currency and a short position in a forward contract on the same currency with a different expiration. Why this transaction is called a swap is not clear, but this transaction existed before currency swaps were created. In futures markets, the analogous transaction is called a *spread*, reflecting as it does the risk associated with the spread between the prices of futures contracts with different expirations.

[3] In this example, we shall assume 180 days between payment dates. In practice, exact day counts are usually used, leading to different fixed payment amounts in one six-month period from those of another. In the example here, we are only illustrating the idea behind swap cash flows, so it is convenient to keep the fixed payments the same. Later in the reading, we shall illustrate situations in which the exact day count is used, leading to fixed payments that vary slightly.

Each 15 March and 15 September for five years:

▶ DB pays TGT 0.055(180/360)$10 million = $275,000

▶ TGT pays DB 0.049(180/360) €9 million = €220,500

15 September five years after initiation:

▶ DB pays TGT $10 million

▶ TGT pays DB €9 million

Note that we have simplified the interest calculations a little. In this example, we calculated semiannual interest using the fraction 180/360. Some parties might choose to use the exact day count in the six-month period divided by 365 days. LIBOR and Euribor transactions, the predominant rates used in interest rate swaps, nearly always use 360 days, as mentioned in previous readings. Exhibit 2 shows the stream of cash flows from TGT's perspective.

EXHIBIT 2	Cash Flows to TGT on Swap with DB

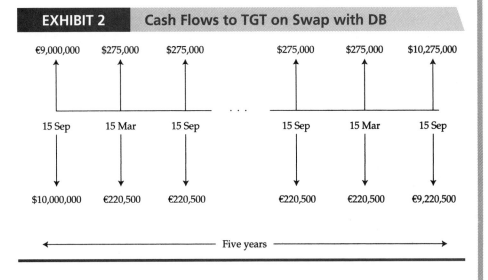

Note that the Target–Deutsche Bank transaction looks just like TGT is issuing a bond with face value of €9 million and that bond is purchased by DB. TGT converts the €9 million to $10 million and buys a dollar-denominated bond issued by DB. Note that TGT, having issued a bond denominated in euros, accordingly makes interest payments to DB in euros. DB, appropriately, makes interest payments in dollars to TGT. At the end, they each pay off the face values of the bonds they have issued. We emphasize that the Target–Deutsche Bank transaction *looks like* what we have just described. In fact, neither TGT nor DB actually issues or purchases a bond. They exchange only a series of cash flows that replicated the issuance and purchase of these bonds.

Exhibit 3 illustrates how such a combined transaction would work. TGT issues a bond in dollars (Exhibit 3, Panel A). It takes the dollars and passes them through to DB, which gives TGT the €9 million it needs. On the interest payment dates, the swap generates $275,000 of the $300,000 in interest TGT needs to pay its bondholders (Panel B). In turn, TGT makes interest payments in euros. Still, small dollar interest payments are necessary because TGT cannot issue a dollar bond at the swap rate. At the end of the transaction, TGT receives $10 million back from DB and passes it through to its bondholders (Panel C). TGT pays DB €9 million, thus effectively paying off a euro-denominated bond.

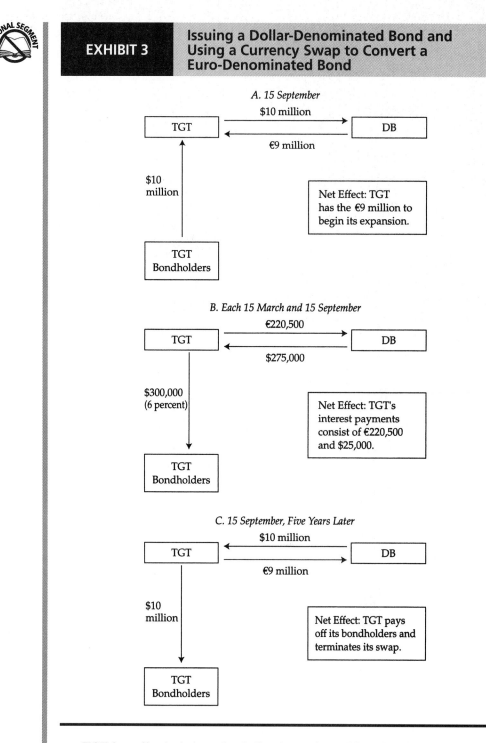

| EXHIBIT 3 | Issuing a Dollar-Denominated Bond and Using a Currency Swap to Convert a Euro-Denominated Bond |

A. 15 September

B. Each 15 March and 15 September

C. 15 September, Five Years Later

TGT has effectively issued a dollar-denominated bond and converted it to a euro-denominated bond. In all likelihood, it can save on interest expense by funding its need for euros in this way, because TGT is better known in the United States than in Europe. Its swap dealer, DB, knows TGT well and also obviously has a strong presence in Europe. Thus, DB can pass on its advantage in euro bond markets to TGT. In addition, had TGT issued a euro-denominated bond, it would have assumed no credit risk. By entering into the swap, TGT assumes a remote possibility of DB defaulting. Thus, TGT saves a little money by assuming some credit risk.

EXAMPLE 1

Consider a currency swap in which the domestic party pays a fixed rate in the foreign currency, the British pound, and the counterparty pays a fixed rate in U.S. dollars. The notional principals are $50 million and £30 million. The fixed rates are 5.6 percent in dollars and 6.25 percent in pounds. Both sets of payments are made on the basis of 30 days per month and 365 days per year, and the payments are made semiannually.

A. Determine the initial exchange of cash that occurs at the start of the swap.

B. Determine the semiannual payments.

C. Determine the final exchange of cash that occurs at the end of the swap.

D. Give an example of a situation in which this swap might be appropriate.

Solution to A: At the start of the swap:
Domestic party pays counterparty $50 million
Counterparty pays domestic party £30 million

Solution to B: Semiannually:
Domestic party pays counterparty £30,000,000(0.0625)(180/365)
= £924,658
Counterparty pays domestic party $50,000,000(0.056)(180/365)
= $1,380,822

Solution to C: At the end of the swap:
Domestic party pays counterparty £30,000,000
Counterparty pays domestic party $50,000,000

Solution to D: This swap would be appropriate for a U.S. company that issues a dollar-denominated bond but would prefer to borrow in British pounds.

Returning to the Target swap, recall that Target effectively converted a fixed-rate loan in dollars to a fixed-rate loan in euros. Suppose instead that TGT preferred to borrow in euros at a floating rate. It then would have specified that the swap required it to make payments to DB at a floating rate. Had TGT preferred to issue the dollar-denominated bond at a floating rate, it would have specified that DB pay it dollars at a floating rate.

Although TGT and DB exchanged notional principal, some scenarios exist in which the notional principals are not exchanged. For example, suppose many years later, TGT is generating €10 million in cash semi annually and converting it back to dollars on 15 January and 15 July. It might then wish to lock in the conversion rate by entering into a currency swap that would require it to pay a dealer €10 million and receive a fixed amount of dollars. If the euro fixed rate were 5 percent, a notional principal of €400 million would generate a payment of 0.05(180/360)€400 million = €10 million. If the exchange rate is, for example, $0.85, the equivalent dollar notional principal would be $340 million. If the dollar fixed rate is 6 percent, TGT would receive 0.06(180/360)$340 million =

$10.2 million.[4] These payments would occur twice a year for the life of the swap. TGT might then lock in the conversion rate by entering into a currency swap with notional principal amounts that would allow it to receive a fixed amount of dollars on 15 January and 15 July. There would be not reason to specify an exchange of notional principal. As we previously described, there are four types of currency swaps. Using the original Target–Deutsche Bank swap as an example, the semiannual payments would be

  A. TGT pays euros at a fixed rate; DB pays dollars at a fixed rate.

  B. TGT pays euros at a fixed rate; DB pays dollars at a floating rate.

  C. TGT pays euros at a floating rate; DB pays dollars at a floating rate.

  D. TGT pays euros at a floating rate; DB pays dollars at a fixed rate.

Or, reversing the flow, TGT could be the payer of dollars and DB could be the payer of euros:

  E. TGT pays dollars at a fixed rate; DB pays euros at a fixed rate.

  F. TGT pays dollars at a fixed rate; DB pays euros at a floating rate.

  G. TGT pays dollars at a floating rate; DB pays euros at a floating rate.

  H. TGT pays dollars at a floating rate; DB pays euros at a fixed rate.

Suppose we combine Swap A with Swap H. With TGT paying euros at a fixed rate and DB paying euros at a fixed rate, the euro payments wash out and the net effect is

  I. TGT pays dollars at a floating rate; DB pays dollars at a fixed rate.

Suppose we combine Swap B with Swap E. Similarly, the euro payments again wash out, and the net effect is

  J. TGT pays dollars at a fixed rate; DB pays dollars at a floating rate.

Suppose we combine Swap C with Swap F. Likewise, the euro floating payments wash out, and the net effect is

  K. TGT pays dollars at a fixed rate; DB pays dollars at a floating rate.

Lastly, suppose we combine Swap D with Swap G. Again, the euro floating payments wash out, and the net effect is

  L. TGT pays dollars at a floating rate; DB pays dollars at a fixed rate.

Of course, the net results of I and L are equivalent, and the net results of J and K are equivalent. What we have shown here, however, is that combinations of currency swaps eliminate the currency flows and leave us with transactions in only one currency. A swap in which both sets of interest payments are made in the same currency is an interest rate swap.

---

[4] It might appear that TGT has somehow converted cash flows worth €10 million($0.085) = $8.5 million into cash flows worth $10.2 million. Recall, however, that the €10 million cash flows are generated yearly and $0.85 is the *current* exchange rate. We cannot apply the current exchange rate to a series of cash flows over various future dates. We would apply the respective forward exchange rates, not the spot rate, to the series of future euro cash flows.

3.2 Interest Rate Swaps

As we discovered in the above paragraph, an interest rate swap can be created as a combination of currency swaps. Of course, no one would create an interest rate swap that way; doing so would require two transactions when only one would suffice. Interest rate swaps evolved into their own market. In fact, the interest rate swap market is much bigger than the currency swap market, as we have seen in the notional principal statistics.

As previously noted, one way to look at an interest rate swap is that it is a currency swap in which both currencies are the same. Consider a swap to pay Currency A fixed and Currency B floating. Currency A could be dollars, and B could be euros. But what if A and B are both dollars, or A and B are both euros? The first case is a dollar-denominated plain vanilla swap; the second is a euro-denominated plain vanilla swap. A **plain vanilla swap** *is simply an interest rate swap in which one party pays a fixed rate and the other pays a floating rate, with both sets of payments in the same currency.* In fact, the plain vanilla swap is probably the most common derivative transaction in the global financial system.

Note that because we are paying in the same currency, there is no need to exchange notional principals at the beginning and at the end of an interest rate swap. In addition, the interest payments can be, and nearly always are, netted. If one party owes $X and the other owes $Y, the party owing the greater amount pays the net difference, which greatly reduces the credit risk (as we discuss in more detail in Section 7). Finally, we note that there is no reason to have both sides pay a fixed rate. The two streams of payments would be identical in that case. So in an interest rate swap, either one side always pays fixed and the other side pays floating, or both sides paying floating, but never do both sides pay fixed.[5]

Thus, in a plain vanilla interest rate swap, one party makes interest payments at a fixed rate and the other makes interest payments at a floating rate. Both sets of payments are on the same notional principal and occur on regularly scheduled dates. For each payment, the interest rate is multiplied by a fraction representing the number of days in the settlement period over the number of days in a year. In some cases, the settlement period is computed assuming 30 days in each month; in others, an exact day count is used. Some cases assume a 360-day year; others use 365 days.

Let us now illustrate an interest rate swap. Suppose that on 15 December, General Electric Company (NYSE: GE) borrows money for one year from a bank such as Bank of America (NYSE: BAC). The loan is for $25 million and specifies that GE will make interest payments on a quarterly basis on the 15th of March, June, September, and December for one year at the rate of LIBOR plus 25 basis points. At the end of the year, it will pay back the principal. On the 15th of December, March, June, and September, LIBOR is observed and sets the rate for that quarter. The interest is then paid at the end of the quarter.[6]

GE believes that it is getting a good rate, but fearing a rise in interest rates, it would prefer a fixed-rate loan. It can easily convert the floating-rate loan to a fixed-rate loan by engaging in a swap. Suppose it approaches JP Morgan Chase (NYSE: JPM), a large dealer bank, and requests a quote on a swap to pay a fixed rate and receive LIBOR, with payments on the dates of its loan payments. The bank prices the swap (a procedure we cover in Section 4) and quotes a fixed rate

---

[5] The case of both sides paying floating is called a basis swap, which we shall cover in Section 5.

[6] Again, we assume 90 days in each interest payment period for this example. The exact payment dates are not particularly important for illustrative purposes.

of 6.2 percent.[7] The fixed payments will be made based on a day count of 90/365, and the floating payments will be made based on 90/360. Current LIBOR is 5.9 percent. Therefore, the first fixed payment, which GE makes to JPM, is $25,000,000(0.062)(90/365) = $382,192. This is also the amount of each remaining fixed payment.

The first floating payment, which JPM makes to GE, is $25,000,000(0.059) (90/360) = $368,750. Of course, the remaining floating payments will not be known until later. Exhibit 4 shows the pattern of cash flows on the swap from GE's perspective.

EXHIBIT 4	Cash Flows to GE on Swap with JPM

To GE   \$368,750   \$[a]   \$[a]   \$[a]

15 Dec   15 Mar   15 Jun   15 Sep   15 Dec

To JPM   \$382,192   \$382,192   \$382,192   \$382,192

[a] Computed as $25,000,000(L)90/360, where L is LIBOR on the previous settlement date.

EXAMPLE 2

Determine the upcoming payments in a plain vanilla interest rate swap in which the notional principal is €70 million. The end user makes semiannual fixed payments at the rate of 7 percent, and the dealer makes semiannual floating payments at Euribor, which was 6.25 percent on the last settlement period. The floating payments are made on the basis of 180 days in the settlement period and 360 days in a year. The fixed payments are made on the basis of 180 days in the settlement period and 365 days in a year. Payments are netted, so determine which party pays which and what amount.

Solution: The fixed payments are €70,000,000(0.07)(180/365) = €2,416,438.
The upcoming floating payment is €70,000,000(0.0625)(180/360) = €2,187,500.
The net payment is that the party paying fixed will pay the party paying floating

$$€2,416,438 - €2,187,500 = €228,938.$$

---

[7] Typically the rate is quoted as a spread over the rate on a U.S. Treasury security with a comparable maturity. Suppose the yield on a two-year Treasury note is 6 percent. Then the swap would be quoted as 20 basis points over the two-year Treasury rate. By quoting the rate in this manner, GE knows what it is paying over the Treasury rate, a differential called the swap spread, which is a type of credit risk premium we discuss in Section 7. In addition, a quote in this form protects the bank from the rate changing drastically either during the phone conversation or shortly thereafter. Thus, the quote can stay in effect for a reasonable period of time while GE checks out quotes from other dealers.

Note in Exhibit 4 that we did not show the notional principal, because it was not exchanged. We could implicitly show that GE received $25 million from JPM and paid $25 million to JPM at the start of the swap. We could also show that the same thing happens at the end. If we look at it that way, it appears as if GE has issued a $25 million fixed-rate bond, which was purchased by JPM, which in turn issued a $25 million floating-rate bond, which was in turn purchased by GE. We say that *it appears* as if this is what happened: In fact, neither party actually issued a bond, but they have generated the cash flows that would occur if GE had issued such a fixed-rate bond, JPM had issued such a **floating-rate bond**, and each purchased the bond of the other. In other words, we could include the principals on both sides to make each set of cash flows look like a bond, yet the overall cash flows would be the same as on the swap.

So let us say that GE enters into this swap. Exhibit 5 shows the net effect of the swap and the loan. GE pays LIBOR plus 25 basis points to Bank of America on its loan, pays 6.2 percent to JPM, and receives LIBOR from JPM. The net effect is that GE pays $6.2 + 0.25 = 6.45$ percent fixed.

EXHIBIT 5	GE's Conversion of a Floating-Rate Loan to a Fixed-Rate Loan Using an Interest Rate Swap with JPM

Now, JPM is engaged in a swap to pay LIBOR and receive 6.2 percent. It is exposed to the risk of LIBOR increasing. It would, therefore, probably engage in some other type of transaction to offset this risk. One transaction commonly used in this situation is to sell Eurodollar futures. As discussed in Reading 63, Eurodollar futures prices move $25 in value for each basis point move in LIBOR. JPM will determine how sensitive its position is to a move in LIBOR and sell an appropriate number of futures to offset the risk. Note that Bank of America is exposed to LIBOR as well, but in the banking industry, floating-rate loans are often made because the funding that the bank obtained to make the loan was probably already at LIBOR or a comparable floating rate.

It is possible but unlikely that GE could get a fixed-rate loan at a better rate. The swap involves some credit risk: the possibility, however small, that JPM will default. In return for assuming that risk, GE in all likelihood would get a better rate than it would if it borrowed at a fixed rate. JPM is effectively a wholesaler of risk, using its powerful position as one of the world's leading banks to facilitate the buying and selling of risk for companies such as GE. Dealers profit from the spread between the rates they quote to pay and the rates they quote to receive. The swaps market is, however, extremely competitive and the spreads have been squeezed very tight, which makes it very challenging for dealers to make a profit. Of course, this competition is good for end users, because it gives them more attractive rates.

3.3 Equity Swaps

By now, it should be apparent that a swap requires at least one variable rate or price underlying it. So far, that rate has been an interest rate.[8] In an equity swap, the rate is the return on a stock or stock index. This characteristic gives the equity swap two features that distinguish it from interest rate and currency swaps.

First, the party making the fixed-rate payment could also have to make a variable payment based on the equity return. Suppose the end user pays the equity payment and receives the fixed payment, i.e., it pays the dealer the return on the S&P 500 Index, and the dealer pays the end user a fixed rate. If the S&P 500 increases, the return is positive and the end user pays that return to the dealer. If the S&P 500 goes down, however, its return is obviously negative. In that case, the end user would pay the dealer the *negative return on the S&P 500*, which means that it would receive that return from the dealer. For example, if the S&P 500 falls by 1 percent, the dealer would pay the end user 1 percent, in addition to the fixed payment the dealer makes in any case. So the dealer, or in general the party receiving the equity return, could end up making *both* a fixed-rate payment and an equity payment.

The second distinguishing feature of an equity swap is that the payment is not known until the end of the settlement period, at which time the return on the stock is known. In an interest rate or currency swap, the floating interest rate is set at the beginning of the period.[9] Therefore, one always knows the amount of the upcoming floating interest payment.[10]

Another important feature of some equity swaps is that the rate of return is often structured to include both dividends and capital gains. In interest rate and currency swaps, capital gains are not paid.[11] Finally, we note that in some equity swaps, the notional principal is indexed to change with the level of the stock, although we will not explore such swaps in this reading.[12]

Equity swaps are commonly used by asset managers. Let us consider a situation in which an asset manager might use such a swap. Suppose that the Vanguard Asset Allocation Fund (Nasdaq: VAAPX) is authorized to use swaps. On the last day of December, it would like to sell $100 million in U.S. large-cap equities and invest the proceeds at a fixed rate. It believes that a swap allowing it to pay the total return on the S&P 500, while receiving a fixed rate, would achieve this objective. It would like to hold this position for one year, with payments to be made on the last day of March, June, September, and December. It enters into such a swap with Morgan Stanley (NYSE: MWD).

Specifically, the swap covers a notional principal of $100 million and calls for VAAPX to pay MWD the return on the S&P 500 Total Return Index and for MWD to pay VAAPX a fixed rate on the last day of March, June, September, and December for one year. MWD prices the swap at a fixed rate of 6.5 percent. The fixed payments will be made using an actual day count/365 days convention. There are 90 days between 31 December and 31 March, 91 days between

---

[8] Currency swaps also have the element that the exchange rate is variable.

[9] Technically, there are interest rate swaps in which the floating rate is set at the end of the period, at which time the payment is made. We shall briefly mention these swaps in Section 5.

[10] In a currency swap, however, one does not know the exchange rate until the settlement date.

[11] In some kinds of interest rate swaps, the total return on a bond, which includes dividends and capital gains, is paid. This instrument is called a **total return swap** and is a common variety of a credit derivative.

[12] Some interest rate swaps also have a notional principal that changes, which we shall briefly discuss in Section 5.

31 March and 30 June, 92 days between 30 June and 30 September, and 92 days between 30 September and 31 December. Thus, the fixed payments will be

31 March:	$100,000,000(0.065)(90/365) = \$1,602,740$
30 June:	$100,000,000(0.065)(91/365) = \$1,620,548$
30 September:	$100,000,000(0.065)(92/365) = \$1,638,356$
31 December:	$100,000,000(0.065)(92/365) = \$1,638,356$

Exhibit 6 shows the cash flow stream to VAAPX.

EXHIBIT 6	Cash Flows to VAAPX on Equity Swap with MWD

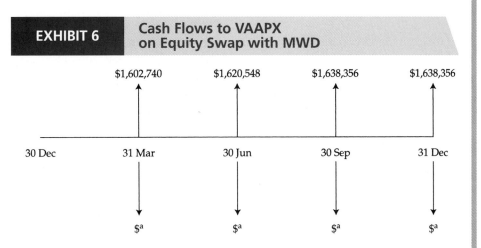

[a] Computed as $100,000,000R$, where R is the return on the S&P 500 Total Return Index from the previous settlement date.

Suppose that on the day the swap is initiated, 31 December, the S&P 500 Total Return Index is at 3,517.76. Now suppose that on 31 March, the index is at 3,579.12. The return on the index is

$$\frac{3,579.12}{3,517.76} - 1 = 0.0174$$

Thus, the return is 1.74 percent. The equity payment that VAAPX would make to MWD would be $100,000,000(0.0174) = \$1,740,000$.

Of course, this amount would not be known until 31 March, and only the difference between this amount and the fixed payment would be paid. Then on 31 March, the index value of 3,579.12 would be the base for the following period. Suppose that on 30 June, the index declines to 3,452.78. Then the return for the second quarter would be

$$\frac{3,452.78}{3,579.12} - 1 = -0.0353$$

Therefore, the loss is 3.53 percent, requiring a payment of $100,000,000(0.0353) = \$3,530,000$.

Because this amount represents a loss on the S&P 500, MWD would make a payment to VAAPX. In addition, MWD would also owe VAAPX the fixed payment of $1,620,548. It is as though VAAPX sold out of its position in stock, thereby avoiding the loss of about $3.5 million, and moved into a fixed-income position, thereby picking up a gain of about $1.6 million.

EXAMPLE 3

A mutual fund has arranged an equity swap with a dealer. The swap's notional principal is $100 million, and payments will be made semi-annually. The mutual fund agrees to pay the dealer the return on a small-cap stock index, and the dealer agrees to pay the mutual fund based on one of the two specifications given below. The small-cap index starts off at 1,805.20; six months later, it is at 1,796.15.

A. The dealer pays a fixed rate of 6.75 percent to the mutual fund, with payments made on the basis of 182 days in the period and 365 days in a year. Determine the first payment for both parties and, under the assumption of netting, determine the net payment and which party makes it.

B. The dealer pays the return on a large-cap index. The index starts off at 1155.14 and six months later is at 1148.91. Determine the first payment for both parties and, under the assumption of netting, determine the net payment and which party makes it.

Solution to A: The fixed payment is $100,000,000(0.0675)182/365 = $3,365,753. The equity payment is

$$\left(\frac{1796.15}{1805.20} - 1\right)\$100,000,000 = -\$501,329$$

Because the fund pays the equity return and the equity return is negative, the dealer must pay the equity return. The dealer also pays the fixed return, so the dealer makes both payments, which add up to $3,365,753 + $501,329 = $3,867,082. The net payment is $3,867,082, paid by the dealer to the mutual fund.

Solution to B: The large-cap equity payment is

$$\left(\frac{1148.91}{1155.14} - 1\right)\$100,000,000 = -\$539,329$$

The fund owes −$501,329, so the dealer owes the fund $501,329. The dealer owes −$539,329, so the fund owes the dealer $539,329. Therefore, the fund pays the dealer the net amount of $539,329 − $501,329 = $38,000.

Exhibit 7 illustrates what VAAPX has accomplished. It is important to note that the conversion of its equity assets into fixed income is not perfect. VAAPX does not hold a portfolio precisely equal to the S&P 500 Total Return Index. To the extent that VAAPX's portfolio generates a return that deviates from the index, some mismatching can occur, which can be a problem. As an alternative, VAAPX can request that MWD give it a swap based on the precise portfolio that VAAPX wishes to sell off. In that case, however, MWD would assess a charge by lowering the fixed rate it pays or raising the rate VAAPX pays to it.[13]

---

[13] Note, however, that VAAPX is converting not its entire portfolio but simply a $100 million portion of it.

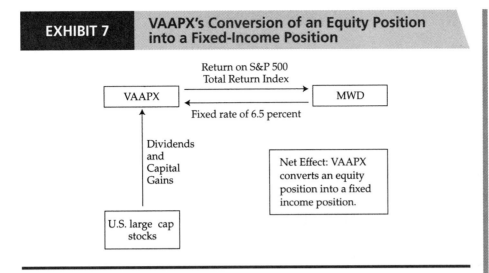

| EXHIBIT 7 | VAAPX's Conversion of an Equity Position into a Fixed-Income Position |

In our previous VAAPX example, the fund wanted to move some money out of a large-cap equity position and invest the proceeds at a fixed rate. Suppose instead that they do not want to move the proceeds into a fixed-rate investment. VAAPX could structure a swap to pay it a floating rate or the return on some other equity index. For example, an asset allocation from U.S. large-cap stocks to U.S. small-cap stocks could be accomplished by having MWD pay the return on the S&P 500 Small Cap 600 Index.

Suppose VAAPX wanted to move out of a position in U.S. stocks and into a position in U.K. large-cap stocks. It could structure the swap to have MWD pay it the return on the FTSE (Financial Times Stock Exchange) 100 Index. Note, however, that this index is based on the prices of U.K. stocks as quoted in pounds sterling. If VAAPX wanted the exposure in pounds—that is, it wanted the currency risk as well as the risk of the U.K. stock market—the payments from MWD to VAAPX would be made in pounds. VAAPX could, however, ask for the payments in dollars. In that case, MWD would hedge the currency risk and make payments in dollars.

Although our focus is on currency, interest rate, and equity products, we shall take a very brief look at some other types of swaps.

3.4 Commodity and Other Types of Swaps

Just as currencies, interest rates, and equities can be used to structure swaps, so too can commodities and just about anything that has a random outcome and to which a corporation, financial institution, or even an individual is exposed. **Commodity swaps** are very commonly used. For example, airlines enter into swaps to hedge their future purchases of jet fuel. They agree to make fixed payments to a swap dealer on regularly scheduled dates and receive payments determined by the price of jet fuel. Gold mining companies use swaps to hedge future deliveries of gold. Other parties dealing in such commodities as natural gas and precious metals often use swaps to lock in prices for future purchases and sales. In addition, swaps can be based on non-storable commodities, like electricity and the weather. In the case of the weather, payments are made based on a measure of a particular weather factor, such as amounts of rain, snowfall, or weather-related damage.

We have now introduced and described the basic structure of swaps. We have made many references to the pricing and valuation of swaps, and we now move on to explore how this is done.

OPTIONAL SEGMENT
ENDS

| **4** | # PRICING AND VALUATION OF SWAPS |

In Reading 62, we took our first look at the concepts of pricing and valuation when we examined forward contracts on assets and FRAs, which are essentially forward contracts on interest rates. Recall that a forward contract requires no cash payment at the start and commits one party to buy and another to sell an asset at a later date. An FRA commits one party to make a single fixed-rate interest payment and the other to make a single floating-rate interest payment. A swap extends that concept by committing one party to making a series of floating payments. The other party commits to making a series of fixed or floating payments. For swaps containing any fixed terms, such as a fixed rate, pricing the swap means to determine those terms at the start of the swap. Some swaps do not contain any fixed terms; we explore examples of both types of swaps.

All swaps have a market value. Valuation of a swap means to determine the market value of the swap based on current market conditions. The fixed terms, such as the fixed rate, are established at the start to give the swap an initial market value of zero. As we have already discussed, a zero market value means that neither party pays anything to the other at the start. Later during the life of the swap, as market conditions change, the market value will change, moving from zero from both parties' perspective to a positive value for one party and a negative value for the other. When a swap has zero value, it is neither an asset nor a liability to either party. When the swap has positive value to one party, it is an asset to that party; from the perspective of the other party, it thus has negative value and is a liability.

We begin the process of pricing and valuing swaps by learning how swaps are comparable to other instruments. If we know that one financial instrument is equivalent to another, we can price one instrument if we know or can determine the price of the other instrument.

4.1 Equivalence of Swaps and Other Instruments

In this section, we look at how swaps are similar to other instruments. Because our focus is on currency, interest rate, and equity swaps, we do not discuss commodity swaps here.

4.1.1 Swaps and Assets

We have already alluded to the similarity between swaps and assets. For example, a currency swap is identical to issuing a fixed- or floating-rate bond in one currency, converting the proceeds to the other currency, and using the proceeds to purchase a fixed- or floating-rate bond denominated in the other currency. An interest rate swap is identical to issuing a fixed- or floating-rate bond and using the proceeds to purchase a floating- or fixed-rate bond. The notional principal is equivalent to the face value on these hypothetical bonds.

Equity swaps appear to be equivalent to issuing one type of security and using the proceeds to purchase another, where at least one of the types of securities is a stock or stock index. For example, a pay-fixed, receive-equity swap looks like issuing a fixed-rate bond and using the proceeds to buy a stock or index portfolio. As it turns out, however, these two transactions are not exactly the same, although they are close. The stock position in the transaction is not the same as a buy-and-hold position; some adjustments are required on the settlement dates to replicate the cash flows of a swap. We shall take a look at this process of replicating an equity swap in Section 4.2.3. For now, simply recognize that an equity swap is like issuing bonds and buying stock, but not buying and holding stock.

The equivalence of a swap to transactions we are already familiar with, such as owning assets, is important because it allows us to price and value the swap using simple instruments, such as the underlying currency, interest rate, or stock. We do not require other derivatives to replicate the cash flows of a swap. Nonetheless, other derivatives can be used to replicate the cash flows of a swap, and it is worth seeing why this is true.

4.1.2 Swaps and Forward Contracts

Recall that a forward contract, whether on an interest rate, a currency, or an equity, is an agreement for one party to make a fixed payment to the other, while the latter party makes a variable payment to the former. A swap extends this notion by combining a series of forward contracts into a single transaction. There are, however, some subtle differences between swaps and forward contracts. For example, swaps are a series of equal fixed payments, whereas the component contracts of a series of forward contracts would almost always be priced at different fixed rates.[14] In this context we often refer to a swap as a series of off-market forward contracts, reflecting the fact that the implicit forward contracts that make up the swap are all priced at the swap fixed rate and not at the rate at which they would normally be priced in the market. In addition, in interest rate swaps, the next payment that each party makes is known. That would obviously not be the case for a single forward contract. Other subtleties distinguish currency swaps from a series of currency forwards and equity swaps from a series of equity forwards, but in general, it is acceptable to view a swap as a series of forward contracts.

4.1.3 Swaps and Futures Contracts

It is a fairly common practice to equate swaps to futures contracts. This practice is partially correct, but only to the extent that futures contracts can be equated to forward contracts. We saw in Reading 63 that futures contracts are equivalent to forward contracts only when future interest rates are known. Obviously this condition can never truly be met, and because swaps are often used to manage uncertain interest rates, the equivalence of futures with swaps is not always appropriate. Moreover, swaps are highly customized contracts, whereas futures are standardized with respect to expiration and the underlying instrument. Although it is common to equate a swap with a series of futures contracts, this equality holds true only in very limited cases.[15]

4.1.4 Swaps and Options

Finally, we note that swaps can be equated to combinations of options. Buying a call and selling a put would force the transacting party to make a net payment if the underlying is below the exercise rate at expiration, and would result in receipt of a payment if the underlying is above the exercise rate at expiration.

---

[14] For example, a series of FRAs would have different fixed rates unless the term structure is flat.

[15] It is possible only in extremely rare circumstances for futures expirations to line up with swap settlement dates and thereby provide perfect equivalence. That does not mean, however, that futures cannot be used to hedge in a delta-hedging sense, as described in Reading 64. A futures price has a given sensitivity to the underlying, and futures are often highly liquid. A dealer, having entered into a swap, can determine the swap's sensitivity to the underlying and execute the appropriate number of futures transactions to balance the volatility of the swap to that of the futures. Indeed, this method is standard for hedging plain vanilla swaps using the Eurodollar futures contract.

This payment will be equivalent to a swap payment if the exercise rate is set at the fixed rate on the swap. Therefore, a swap is equivalent to a combination of options with expirations at the swap payment dates. The connection between swaps and options is relatively straightforward for interest rate instruments, but less so for currency and equity instruments. Nonetheless, we can generally consider swaps as equivalent to combinations of options.

In this section, we have learned that swaps can be shown to be equivalent to combinations of assets, combinations of forward contracts, combinations of futures contracts, and combinations of options. Thus, to price and value swaps we can choose any of these approaches. We choose the simplest: swaps and assets.

4.2 Pricing and Valuation

As in previous readings, our goal is to determine the market value of the derivative transaction of interest, in this case, swaps. At the start of a swap, the market value is set to zero. The process of pricing the swap involves finding the terms that force that market value to zero. To determine the market value of a swap, we replicate the swap using other instruments that produce the same cash flows. Knowing the values of these other instruments, we are able to value the swap. This value can be thought of as what the swap is worth if we were to sell it to someone else. In addition, we can think of the value as what we might assign to it on our balance sheet. The swap can have a positive value, making it an asset, or a negative value, making it a liability.

As we noted in Section 4.1, swaps are equivalent to a variety of instruments, but we prefer to use the simplest instruments to replicate the swap. The simplest instruments are the underlying assets: bonds, stocks, and currencies. Therefore, we shall use these underlying instruments to replicate the swap.

To understand the pricing of currency, interest rate, and equity swaps, we shall have to first take a brief digression to examine an instrument that plays an important role in their pricing. We shall see that the floating-rate security will have a value of 1.0, its par, at the start and on any coupon reset date. Recall that we have made numerous references to floating rates and floating payments. Accordingly, we must first obtain a solid understanding of floating-rate notes.

As we did in Reading 62, let us first set up a time line that indicates where we are and where the interest payments on the floating-rate note will occur:

We start at time 0. The interest payments will occur on days $h_1, h_2, \ldots, h_{n-1}$, and h_n, so there are n interest payments in all. Day h_n is the maturity date of the floating-rate note. The time interval between payments is m days. The underlying rate is an m-day interest rate.

For simplicity, we will use LIBOR as the underlying rate and denote it with the symbol we have previously used, $L_i(m)$, which stands for the m-day LIBOR on day i. If i = 1, we are referring to day h_1, which might, for example, be 180 days after day 0. Thus, $h_1 = 180$. $L_0(180)$ is the 180-day LIBOR on day 0. Then h_2 would likely be 360 and $L_0(2m) = L_0(360)$, the 360-day LIBOR on day 0. We denote $B_0(h_j)$ as the present value factor on a zero-coupon instrument paying \$1 at its maturity date. As an example, to discount payments 180 and 360 days later, we multiply the payment amount by the following respective factors:

$$B_0(180) = \frac{1}{1 + L_0(180) \times (180/360)}$$

$$B_0(360) = \frac{1}{1 + L_0(360) \times (360/360)}$$

We can think of these **discount factors** as the values of spot LIBOR deposits that pay \$1 at maturity, 180 and 360 days later.

On day 0, the floating rate is set for the first period and the interest to be paid at that rate is paid on day h_1. Then on day h_1, the rate is set for the second period and the interest is paid on day h_2. This process continues so that on day h_{n-1} the rate is set for the last period, and the final interest payment and the principal are paid on day h_n. Let the principal be 1.0.

Suppose today is day h_{n-1} and LIBOR on that day is $L_{n-1}(m)$. Remember that this rate is the m-day LIBOR in the market at that time. Therefore, looking ahead to day h_n, we anticipate receiving 1.0, the final principal payment, plus $L_{n-1}(m) \times (m/360)$. What is the value of this amount on day h_{n-1}? We would discount it by the appropriate m-day LIBOR in the following manner:

Value at h_{n-1} = (Payment at h_n) (One-period discount factor)

$$= \left[1.0 + L_{n-1}(m) \times (m/360)\right] \left[\frac{1}{1.0 + L_{n-1}(m) \times (m/360)}\right] = 1.0$$

The value is 1.0, its par value. Now step back to day h_{n-2}, at which time the rate is $L_{n-2}(m)$. Looking ahead to day h_{n-1} we shall receive an interest payment of $L_{n-2}(m) \times (m/360)$. We do not receive the principal on day h_{n-1}, but it is appropriate to discount the market value on day h_{n-1}, which we just determined is 1.0.[16] Thus, the value of the floating-rate security will be

Value at h_{n-2} = (Payment at h_{n-1})(One-period discount factor)

$$= \left[1.0 + L_{n-2}(m) \times (m/360)\right] \left[\frac{1}{1.0 + L_{n-2}(m) \times (m/360)}\right] = 1.0$$

We continue this procedure, stepping back until we reach time 0. The floating-rate security will have a value of 1.0, its par, at the start and on any coupon reset date.[17] We shall use this result to help us price and value swaps.

In previous material in this reading, we have covered currency swaps first. We did so because we showed that an interest rate swap is just a currency swap in which both currencies are the same. A currency swap is thus the more general instrument of the two. For the purposes of this section, however, it will be easier to price and value a currency swap if we first price and value an interest rate swap.

---

[16] All we are doing here is discounting the upcoming cash flow and the market value of the security on the next payment date. This procedure is not unique to floating-rate securities; it is standard valuation procedure for any type of security. What is special and different for floating-rate securities is that the market value goes back to par on each payment date.

[17] Floating-rate securities are designed to allow the coupon to catch up with market interest rates on a regularly scheduled basis. The price can deviate from par during the period between reset dates. In addition, if there is any credit risk and that risk changes during the life of the security, its price can deviate from par at any time, including at the coupon reset date. We are assuming no credit risk here.

4.2.1 Interest Rate Swaps

Pricing an interest rate swap means finding the fixed rate that equates the present value of the fixed payments to the present value of the floating payments, a process that sets the market value of the swap to zero at the start. Using the time line illustrated earlier, the swap cash flows will occur on days $h_1, h_2, \ldots, h_{n-1}$, and h_n, so there are n cash flows in the swap. Day h_n is the expiration date of the swap. The time interval between payments is m days. We can thus think of the swap as being on an m-day interest rate, which will be LIBOR in our examples.

As previously mentioned, the payments in an interest rate swap are a series of fixed and floating interest payments. They do not include an initial and final exchange of notional principals. As we already observed, such payments would be only an exchange of the same money. But if we introduce the notional principal payments as though they were actually made, we have not done any harm. The cash flows on the swap are still the same. The advantage of introducing the notional principal payments is that we can now treat the fixed and floating sides of the swap as though they were fixed- and floating-rate bonds.

So we introduce a hypothetical final notional principal payment of $1 on a swap starting at day 0 and ending on day h_n, in which the underlying is an m-day rate. The fixed swap interest payment *rate*, FS(0,n,m), gives the fixed payment *amount* corresponding to the $1 notional principal. Thus, the present value of a series of fixed interest payments at the swap rate FS(0,n,m) plus a final principal payment of 1.0 is

$$\sum_{j=1}^{n} FS(0, n, m) B_0(h_j) + \$1 \times B_0(h_n), \text{ or}$$

$$FS(0, n, m) \sum_{j=1}^{n} B_0(h_j) + B_0(h_n)$$

Here the summation simply represents the sum of the present value factors for each payment. The expression $B_0(h_n)$ is the present value factor for the final hypothetical notional principal payment of 1.0.

Now we must find the present value of the floating payments, and here we use what we learned about floating-rate notes. Remember that a floating-rate note with $1 face will have a value of $1 at the start and at any coupon reset date. If the swap's floating payments include a final principal payment, we can treat them like a floating-rate note. Hence, we know their value is $1.

Now all we have to do is equate the present value of the fixed payments to the present value of the floating payments

$$FS(0, n, m) \sum_{j=1}^{n} B_0(h_j) + B_0(h_n) = 1.0$$

and solve for the fixed rate FS(0,n,m) that will result in equality of these two streams of payments. The solution is as follows:

$$FS(0, n, m) = \frac{1.0 - B_0(h_n)}{\sum_{j=1}^{n} B_0(h_j)} \qquad \textbf{(65-1)}$$

The swap fixed payment is 1.0 minus the last present value factor divided by the sum of the present value factors for each payment. Thus, we have priced the swap.

One can use several other ways to find the fixed payment on a swap, but this method is unquestionably the simplest. In fact, this formulation shows that the fixed rate on a swap is simply the coupon rate on a par bond whose payments coincide with those on the swap.[18]

Let us now work a problem. Consider a one-year swap with quarterly payments on days 90, 180, 270, and 360. The underlying is 90-day LIBOR. The annualized LIBOR spot rates today are

$$L_0(90) = 0.0345$$

$$L_0(180) = 0.0358$$

$$L_0(270) = 0.0370$$

$$L_0(360) = 0.0375$$

The present value factors are obtained as follows:

$$B_0(90) = \frac{1}{1 + 0.0345(90/360)} = 0.9914$$

$$B_0(180) = \frac{1}{1 + 0.0358(180/360)} = 0.9824$$

$$B_0(270) = \frac{1}{1 + 0.0370(270/360)} = 0.9730$$

$$B_0(360) = \frac{1}{1 + 0.0375(360/360)} = 0.9639$$

The fixed payment is found as

$$FS(0, n, m) = FS(0,4,90) = \frac{1 - 0.9639}{0.9914 + 0.9824 + 0.9730 + 0.9639} = 0.0092$$

Therefore, the quarterly fixed payment will be 0.0092 for each $1 notional principal. Of course, this rate is quarterly; it is customary to quote it as an annual rate. We would thus see the rate quoted as $0.0092 \times (360/90) = 0.0368$, or 3.68 percent. We would also have to adjust our payment by multiplying by the actual notional principal. For example, if the actual notional principal were $30 million, the payment would be (0.0092)$30 million = $276,000.

In determining the fixed rate on the swap, we have essentially found the fixed payment that sets the present value of the floating payments plus a hypothetical notional principal of 1.0 equal to the present value of the fixed payments plus a hypothetical notional principal of 1.0. We have thus made the market value of the swap equal to zero at the start of the transaction. This equality makes sense, because neither party pays any money to the other.

Now suppose we have entered into the swap. Let us move forward into the life of the swap, at which time interest rates have changed, and determine its market value. Rather than present mathematical equations for determining its value, we shall work through this example informally. We shall see that the procedure is simple and intuitive. Suppose we have now moved 60 days into the life of the swap. At day 60, we face a new term structure of LIBORs. Because the

---

[18] Technically, bond interest payments are usually found by dividing the annual rate by 2 if the payments are semiannual, whereas swap payments do, on occasion, use day counts such as 181/365 to determine semiannual payments. When we refer to a par bond, we are assuming the payments are structured exactly like those on the swap.

upcoming payments occur in 30, 120, 210, and 300 days, we want the term structure for 30, 120, 210, and 300 days, which is given as follows:

$$L_{60}(30) \quad = 0.0425$$

$$L_{60}(120) = 0.0432$$

$$L_{60}(210) = 0.0437$$

$$L_{60}(300) = 0.0444$$

The new set of discount factors is

$$B_{60}(30) \quad = \frac{1}{1 + 0.0425(30/360)} = 0.9965$$

$$B_{60}(120) = \frac{1}{1 + 0.0432(120/360)} = 0.9858$$

$$B_{60}(210) = \frac{1}{1 + 0.0437(210/360)} = 0.9751$$

$$B_{60}(300) = \frac{1}{1 + 0.0444(300/360)} = 0.9643$$

We must value the swap from the perspective of one of the parties. Let us look at it as though we were the party paying fixed and receiving floating. Finding the present value of the remaining fixed payments of 0.0092 is straightforward. This present value, including the hypothetical notional principal, is 0.0092(0.9965 + 0.9858 + 0.9751 + 0.9643) + 1.0(0.9643) = 1.0004.

Now we must find the present value of the floating payments. Recall that on day 0, the 90-day LIBOR was 3.45 percent. Thus, the first floating payment will be 0.0345(90/360) = 0.0086. We know that we should discount this payment back 30 days, but what about the remaining floating payments? Remember that we know that the market value of the remaining payments on day 90, including the hypothetical final notional principal, is 1.0. So, we can discount 1.00 + 0.0086 = 1.0086 back 30 days to obtain 1.0086(0.9965) = 1.0051.

The present value of the remaining floating payments, plus the hypothetical notional principal, is 1.0051, and the present value of the remaining fixed payments, plus the hypothetical notional principal, is 1.0004. Therefore, the value of the swap is 1.0051 − 1.0004 = 0.0047 per \$1 notional principal. If, for example, the actual swap were for a notional principal of \$30 million, the market value would be \$30 million(0.0047) = \$141,000.

EXAMPLE 4

Consider a one-year interest rate swap with semiannual payments.

A. Determine the fixed rate on the swap and express it in annualized terms. The term structure of LIBOR spot rates is given as follows:

Days	Rate
180	7.2%
360	8.0%

B. Ninety days later, the term structure is as follows:

Days	Rate
90	7.1%
270	7.4%

Determine the market value of the swap from the perspective of the party paying the floating rate and receiving the fixed rate. Assume a notional principal of $15 million.

Solution to A: First calculate the present value factors for 180 and 360 days:

$$B_0(180) = \frac{1}{1 + 0.072(180/360)} = 0.9653$$

$$B_0(360) = \frac{1}{1 + 0.08(360/360)} = 0.9259$$

The fixed rate is $\frac{1 - 0.9259}{0.9653 + 0.9259} = 0.0392$. The fixed payment would, therefore, be 0.0392 per $1 notional principal. The annualized rate would be $0.0392(360/180) = 0.0784$.

Solution to B: Calculate the new present value factors for 90 and 270 days:

$$B_{90}(90) = \frac{1}{1 + 0.071(90/360)} = 0.9826$$

$$B_{90}(270) = \frac{1}{1 + 0.0074(270/360)} = 0.9474$$

The present value of the remaining fixed payments plus hypothetical $1 notional principal is $0.0392(0.9826 + 0.9474) + 1.0(0.9474) = 1.0231$.

The 180-day rate at the start was 7.2 percent, so the first floating payment would be $0.072(180/360) = 0.036$. The present value of the floating payments plus hypothetical $1 notional principal will be $1.036(0.9826) = 1.0180$. The market value of a pay-floating, receive-fixed swap is, therefore, $1.0231 - 1.0180 = 0.0051$. For a notional principal of $15 million, the market value is $15,000,000(0.0051) = \$76,500$.

Note that we valued the swap from the perspective of the party paying the fixed rate. From the counterparty's perspective, the value of the swap would be the negative of the value to the fixed-rate payer.

Although an interest rate swap is like a series of FRAs, or a long position in an interest rate cap and a short position in an interest rate floor with the exercise rate set at the fixed rate on a swap, pricing and valuing an interest rate swap as either of these instruments is more difficult than what we have done here. To price the swap as a series of FRAs, we would need to calculate the forward rates, which is not difficult but would add another step. If we priced a swap as a combination of caps and floors, we would need to price these options. As we saw in Reading 64, interest rate option pricing can be somewhat complex. In addition, we would have to find the exercise rate on the cap and floor that equated their values, which would require trial and error. What we have seen here is the trick that if we add the notional principal to both sides of an interest rate swap, we do not change the swap payments, but we make the cash flows on each side of the swap equivalent to those of a bond. Then we can price the swap as though it were a pair of bonds, one long and the other short. One side is like a floating-rate bond, which we know is priced at par value at the time of issuance as well as on any reset date. The other side is like a fixed-rate bond. Because the value of the fixed-rate bond must equal that of the floating-rate bond at the start, we know that the coupon on a par value bond is the fixed rate on the swap.

Having discussed the pricing and valuation of interest rate swaps, we can now move on to currency swaps, taking advantage of what we know about pricing interest rate swaps. As we have already noted, an interest rate swap is just like a currency swap in which both currencies are the same.

4.2.2 Currency Swaps

Recall the four types of currency swaps: (1) pay one currency fixed, receive the other fixed, (2) pay one currency fixed, receive the other floating, (3) pay one currency floating, receive the other fixed, and (4) pay one currency floating, receive the other floating. In determining the fixed rate on a swap, we must keep in mind one major point: The fixed rate is the rate that makes the present value of the payments made equal the present value of the payments received. In the fourth type of currency swap mentioned here, both sides pay floating so there is no need to find a fixed rate. But all currency swaps have two notional principals, one in each currency. We can arbitrarily set the notional principal in the domestic currency at one unit. We then must determine the equivalent notional principal in the other currency. This task is straightforward: We simply convert the one unit of domestic currency to the equivalent amount of foreign currency, dividing 1.0 by the exchange rate.

Consider the first type of currency swap, in which we pay the foreign currency at a fixed rate and receive the domestic currency at a fixed rate. What are the two fixed rates? We will see that they are the fixed rates on plain vanilla interest rate swaps in the respective countries.

Because we know that the value of a floating-rate security with $1 face value is $1, we know that the fixed rate on a plain vanilla interest rate swap is the rate on a $1 par bond in the domestic currency. That rate results in the present value of the interest payments and the hypothetical notional principal being equal to 1.0 unit of the domestic currency. Moreover, for a currency swap, the notional principal is typically paid, so we do not even have to call it hypothetical. We know that the fixed rate on the domestic leg of an interest rate swap is the appropriate domestic fixed rate for a currency swap in which the domestic notional principal is 1.0 unit of the domestic currency.

What about the fixed rate for the foreign payments on the currency swap? To answer that question, let us assume the point of view of a resident of the foreign country. Given the term structure in the foreign country, we might be interested in first pricing plain vanilla interest rate swaps in that country. So, we know that the fixed rate on interest rate swaps in that country would make the present value of the interest and principal payments equal 1.0 unit of that currency.

Now let us return to our domestic setting. We know that the fixed rate on interest rate swaps in the foreign currency makes the present value of the foreign interest and principal payments equal to 1.0 unit of the foreign currency. We multiply by the spot rate, S_0, to obtain the value of those payments in our domestic currency: 1.0 times S_0 equals S_0, which is now in terms of the domestic currency. This amount does not equal the present value of the domestic payments, but if we set the notional principal on the foreign side of the swap equal to $1/S_0$, then the present value of the foreign payments will be $S_0(1/S_0) = 1.0$ unit of our domestic currency, which is what we want.

Let us now summarize this argument:

▶ The fixed rate on plain vanilla swaps in our country makes the present value of the domestic interest and principal payments equal 1.0 unit of the domestic currency.

▶ The fixed rate on plain vanilla swaps in the foreign country makes the present value of the foreign interest and principal payments equal 1.0 unit of the foreign currency.

▶ A notional principal of $1/S_0$ units of foreign currency makes the present value of the foreign interest and principal payments equal $1/S_0$ units of the foreign currency.

▶ Conversion of $1/S_0$ units of foreign currency at the current exchange rate of S_0 gives 1.0 unit of domestic currency.

▶ Therefore, the present value of the domestic payments equals the present value of the foreign payments.

▶ The fixed rates on a currency swap are, therefore, the fixed rates on plain vanilla interest rate swaps in the respective countries.

Of course, if the domestic notional principal is any amount other than 1.0, we multiply the domestic notional principal by $1/S_0$ to obtain the foreign notional principal. Then the actual swap payments are calculated by multiplying by the overall respective notional principals.

The second and third types of currency swaps each involve one side paying fixed and the other paying floating. The rate on the fixed side of each of these swaps is, again, just the fixed rate on an interest rate swap in the given country. The payments on the floating side automatically have the same present value as the payments on the fixed side. We again use 1.0 unit of domestic currency and $1/S_0$ units of foreign currency as the notional principal.

For the last type of currency swap, in which both sides pay floating, we do not need to price the swap because both sides pay a floating rate. Again, the notional principals are 1.0 unit of domestic currency and $1/S_0$ units of foreign currency.

In the example we used in pricing interest rate swaps, we were given a term structure for a one-year swap with quarterly payments. We found that the fixed payment was 0.0092, implying an annual rate of 3.68 percent. Let us now work through a currency swap in which the domestic currency is the dollar and the foreign currency is the Swiss franc. The current exchange rate is $0.80.

We shall use the same term structure used previously for the domestic term structure: $L_0(90) = 0.0345$, $L_0(180) = 0.0358$, $L_0(270) = 0.0370$, and $L_0(360) = 0.0375$. The Swiss term structure, denoted with a superscript SF, is

$$L_0^{SF}(90) \quad = 0.0520$$

$$L_0^{SF}(180) = 0.0540$$

$$L_0^{SF}(270) = 0.0555$$

$$L_0^{SF}(360) = 0.0570$$

The present value factors are

$$B_0^{SF}(90) \quad = \frac{1}{1 + 0.0520(90/360)} = 0.9872$$

$$B_0^{SF}(180) = \frac{1}{1 + 0.0540(180/360)} = 0.9737$$

$$B_0^{SF}(270) = \frac{1}{1 + 0.0555(270/360)} = 0.9600$$

$$B_0^{SF}(360) = \frac{1}{1 + 0.0570(360/360)} = 0.9461$$

The fixed payment is easily found as

$$FS^{SF}(0, n, m) = FS^{SF}(0,4,90) = \frac{1 - 0.9461}{0.9872 + 0.9737 + 0.9600 + 0.9461} = 0.0139$$

The quarterly fixed payment is thus SF0.0139 for each SF1.00 of notional principal. This translates into an annual rate of $0.0139(360/90) = 0.0556$ or 5.56 percent, so in Switzerland we would quote the fixed rate on a plain vanilla interest rate swap in Swiss francs as 5.56 percent.

Our currency swap involving dollars for Swiss francs would have a fixed rate of 3.68 percent in dollars and 5.56 percent in Swiss francs. The notional principal would be $1.0 and 1/$0.80 = SF1.25. Summarizing, we have the following terms for the four swaps:

Swap 1: Pay dollars fixed at 3.68 percent, receive SF fixed at 5.56 percent.
Swap 2: Pay dollars fixed at 3.68 percent, receive SF floating.
Swap 3: Pay dollars floating, receive SF fixed at 5.56 percent.
Swap 4: Pay dollars floating, receive SF floating.

In each case, the notional principal is $1 and SF1.25, or more generally, SF1.25 for every dollar of notional principal.

As we did with interest rate swaps, we move 60 days forward in time. We have a new U.S. term structure, given in the interest rate swap problem, and a new Swiss franc term structure, which is given below:

$$L_{60}^{SF}(30) \quad = 0.0600$$

$$L_{60}^{SF}(120) = 0.0615$$

$$L_{60}^{SF}(210) = 0.0635$$

$$L_{60}^{SF}(300) = 0.0653$$

The new set of discount factors is

$$B_{60}^{SF}(30) = \frac{1}{1 + 0.0600(30/360)} = 0.9950$$

$$B_{60}^{SF}(120) = \frac{1}{1 + 0.0615(120/360)} = 0.9799$$

$$B_{60}^{SF}(210) = \frac{1}{1 + 0.0635(210/360)} = 0.9643$$

$$B_{60}^{SF}(300) = \frac{1}{1 + 0.0653(300/360)} = 0.9484$$

The new exchange rate is $0.82. Now let us value each swap in turn, taking advantage of what we already know about the values of the U.S. dollar interest rate swaps calculated in the previous section. Recall we found that

Present value of dollar fixed payments = 1.0004
Present value of dollar floating payments = 1.0051

Let us find the comparable numbers for the Swiss franc payments. In other words, we position ourselves as a Swiss resident or institution and obtain the values of the fixed and floating streams of Swiss franc payments per SF1 notional principal. The present value of the remaining Swiss fixed payments is

$$0.0139(0.9950 + 0.9799 + 0.9643 + 0.9484) + 1.0(0.9484) = 1.0024$$

Recall that in finding the present value of the floating payments, we simply recognize that on the next payment date, we shall receive a floating payment of $0.052(90/360) = 0.013$, and the market value of the remaining payments will be 1.0.[19] Thus, we can discount 1.0130 back 30 days to obtain 1.0130(0.9950) = 1.0079.

These two figures are based on SF1 notional principal. We convert them to the actual notional principal in Swiss francs by multiplying by SF1.25. Thus,

Present value of SF fixed payments = 1.0024(1.25) = SF1.2530
Present value of SF floating payments = 1.0079(1.25) = SF1.2599

Now we need to convert these figures to dollars by multiplying by the current exchange rate of $0.82. Thus,

Present value of SF fixed payments in dollars = 1.2530($0.82) = $1.0275
Present value of SF floating payments in dollars = 1.2599($0.82) = $1.0331

Now we can value the four currency swaps:

Value of swap to receive SF fixed, pay $ fixed
$$= +\$1.0275 - \$1.0004 = +\$0.0271$$
Value of swap to receive SF floating, pay $ fixed
$$= +\$1.0331 - \$1.0004 = +\$0.0327$$

---

[19] The first floating payment was set when the swap was initiated at the 90-day rate of 5.2 percent times 90/360.

Value of swap to receive SF fixed, pay $ floating
$$= +\$1.0275 - \$1.0051 = +\$0.0224$$
Value of swap to receive SF floating, pay $ floating
$$= +\$1.0331 - \$1.0051 = +\$0.0280$$

Note that all of these numbers are positive. Therefore, our swaps are showing gains as a result of the combination of interest rate changes in the two countries as well as the exchange rate change. To the counterparty, the swaps are worth these same numerical amounts, but the signs are negative.

EXAMPLE 5

Consider a one-year currency swap with semiannual payments. The two currencies are the U.S. dollar and the euro. The current exchange rate is $0.75.

A. The term structure of interest rates for LIBOR and Euribor are

Days	LIBOR	Euribor
180	7.2%	6.0%
360	8.0%	6.6%

Determine the fixed rate in euros and express it in annualized terms. Note that the LIBOR rates are the same as in Example 4, in which we found that the fixed payment in dollars was 0.0392.

B. Ninety days later, the term structure is as follows:

Days	LIBOR	Euribor
90	7.1%	5.5%
270	7.4%	6.0%

The new exchange rate is $0.70. Determine the market values of swaps to pay dollars and receive euros. Consider all four swaps that are covered in the reading. Assume a notional principal of $20 million and the appropriate amount for euros. Note that the LIBOR rates are the same as in Example 4, in which we found that the present value of the fixed payments (floating payments) plus the hypothetical $1 notional principal was $1.0231 ($1.0180).

Solution to A: The fixed payment in dollars is the same as in Example 4: 0.0392. To determine the fixed rate in euros, we first compute the discount factors:

$$B_0^{\euro}(180) = \frac{1}{1 + 0.06(180/360)} = 0.9709$$

$$B_0^\euro(360) = \frac{1}{1 + 0.066(360/360)} = 0.9381$$

The fixed rate in euros is, therefore, $\dfrac{1 - 0.9381}{0.9709 + 0.9381} = 0.0324$.

On an annual basis, this rate would be $0.0324(360/180) = 0.0648$.

Solution to B: Recalculate the euro discount factors:

$$B_{90}^\euro(90) = \frac{1}{1 + 0.055(90/360)} = 0.9864$$

$$B_{90}^\euro(270) = \frac{1}{1 + 0.060(270/360)} = 0.9569$$

The present value of the fixed payments plus hypothetical €1 notional principal is €$0.0324(0.9864 + 0.9569) + €1.0(0.9569) = €1.0199$.

The 180-day rate at the start of the swap was 6 percent, so the first floating payment would be $0.06(180/360) = 0.03$. The present value of the floating payments plus hypothetical notional principal of €1 is €$1.03(0.9864) = €1.0160$.

The euro notional principal, established at the start of the swap, is $1/\$0.75 = €1.3333$. Converting the euro payments to dollars at the new exchange rate and multiplying by the euro notional principal, we obtain the following values for the four swaps (where we use the present values of U.S. dollar fixed and floating payments as found in Example 4, repeated in the statement of Part B above).

- Pay \$ fixed, receive € fixed $= -\$1.0231 + €1.3333(\$0.70)1.0199$
  $= -\$0.0712$
- Pay \$ fixed, receive € floating $= -\$1.0231 + €1.3333(\$0.70)1.0160$
  $= -\$0.0749$
- Pay \$ floating, receive € fixed $= -\$1.0180 + €1.3333(\$0.70)1.0199$
  $= -\$0.0661$
- Pay \$ floating, receive € floating $= -\$1.0180 + €1.3333(\$0.70)1.0160$
  $= -\$0.0698$

Now we turn to equity swaps. It is tempting to believe that we will not use any more information regarding the term structure in pricing and valuing equity swaps. In fact, for equity swaps in which one side pays either a fixed or floating rate, the results we have obtained for interest rate swaps will be very useful.

4.2.3 Equity Swaps

In this section, we explore how to price and value three types of equity swaps: (1) a swap to pay a fixed rate and receive the return on the equity, (2) a swap to pay a floating rate and receive the return on the equity, and (3) a swap to pay the return on one equity and receive the return on another.

To price or value an equity swap, we must determine a combination of stock and bonds that replicates the cash flows on the swap. As we saw with interest rate and currency swaps, such a replication is not difficult to create. We issue a bond and buy a bond, with one being a fixed-rate bond and the other being a floating-rate bond. If we are dealing with a currency swap, we require that one of the bonds be denominated in one currency and the other be denominated in the other currency. With an equity swap, it would appear that a replicating strategy would involve issuing a bond and buying the stock or vice versa, but this is not exactly how to replicate an equity swap. Remember that in an equity swap, we receive cash payments representing the return on the stock, and that is somewhat different from payments based on the price.

Pricing a Swap to Pay a Fixed Rate and Receive the Return on the Equity   By example, we will demonstrate how to price an n-payment m-day rate swap to pay a fixed rate and receive the return on equity. Suppose the notional principal is $1, the swap involves annual settlements and lasts for two years (n = 2), and the returns on the stock for each of the two years are 10 percent for the first year and 15 percent for the second year. The equity payment on the swap would be $0.10 the first year and $0.15 the second. If, however, we purchased the stock instead of doing the equity swap, we would have to sell the stock at the end of the first year or we would not generate any cash. Suppose at the end of the first year, the stock is at $1.10. We sell the stock, withdraw $0.10, and reinvest $1.00 in the stock. At the end of the second year the stock would be at $1.15. We then sell the stock, taking cash of $0.15. But we have $1.00 left over. To get rid of, or offset, this cash flow, suppose that when we purchased the stock we borrowed the present value of $1.00 for two years. Then two years later, we would pay back $1.00 on that loan. This procedure would offset the $1.00 in cash we have from the stock. The fixed payments on the swap can be easily replicated. If the fixed payment is denoted as FS(0,n,m), we simply borrow the present value of FS(0,n,m) for one year and also borrow the present value of FS(0,n,m) for two years. When we pay those loans back, we will have replicated the fixed payments on the swap.

For the more general case of n payments, we do the following to replicate the swap whose fixed payments are FS(0,n,m):

1. Invest $1.00 in the stock.

2. Borrow the present value of $1.00 to be paid back at the swap expiration, day h_n. This is the amount $B_0(h_n)$.

3. Take out a series of loans requiring that we pay back FS(0,n,m) at time h_1, and also at time h_2, and at all remaining times through time h_n.

Note that this transaction is like issuing debt and buying stock. The amount of money required to do this is

$$\$1 - B_0(h_n) - FS(0, n, m) \sum_{j=1}^{n} B_0(h_j)$$

Because no money changes hands at the start, the initial value of the swap is zero. We set the expression above to zero and solve for the fixed payment FS(0,n,m) to obtain

$$FS(0, n, m) = \frac{1.0 - B_0(h_n)}{\sum_{j=1}^{n} B_0(h_j)}$$

This is precisely the formula (Equation 65-1) for the fixed rate on an interest rate swap or a currency swap.

Pricing a Swap to Pay a Floating Rate and Receive the Return on the Equity If, instead, the swap involves the payment of a floating rate for the equity return, no further effort is needed because there is no fixed rate for which we must solve. We know from our understanding of interest rate swaps that the present value of the floating payments equals the present value of the fixed payments, which equals the notional principal of 1.0. The market value of the swap is zero at the start, as it should be.

Pricing a Swap to Pay the Return on One Equity and Receive the Return on Another Equity Let $S_0(1)$ and $S_1(1)$ be the level of Stock Index 1 at times 0 and 1, and let $S_0(2)$ and $S_1(2)$ be the level of Stock Index 2 at times 0 and 1. Assume we pay the return on Index 2 and receive the return on Index 1. We need to replicate the cash flows on this swap by investing in these two stocks using some type of strategy. Suppose we sell short $1.00 of Index 2, taking the proceeds and investing in $1.00 of Index 1. Then at time 1, we liquidate the position in Index 1, as described above, withdrawing the cash and reinvesting the $1.00 back into Index 1. We cover the short position in Index 2, taking the proceeds and re-shorting Index 2. We continue in this manner throughout the life of the swap. This strategy replicates the cash flows on the swap. Thus, going long one stock and short the other replicates this swap. Of course, there is no fixed rate and thus no need to price the swap. The market value at the start is zero as it should be.

Now let us look at how to determine the market values of each of these swaps during their lives. In other words, after the swap has been initiated, we move forward in time. We must take into account where we are in the life of the swap and how interest rates and the equity price have changed.

Valuing a Swap to Pay the Fixed Rate and Receive the Return on the Equity Let us use the same U.S. term structure we have already been using for interest rate and currency swaps. Our equity swap is for one year and will involve fixed quarterly payments. Recall that the fixed payment on the interest rate swap is 0.0092, corresponding to an annual rate of 3.68 percent. This will be the rate on the swap to pay fixed and receive the equity payment.

Now let us move 60 days into the life of the swap, at which time we have a new term structure as given in the interest rate swap example. We started off with a stock price of S_0, and now the stock price is S_{60}. The stock payment we will receive at the first settlement in 30 days is $S_{90}/S_0 - 1$. Let us write this amount as

$$\left(\frac{1}{S_0}\right)S_{90} - 1$$

Sixty days into the life of the swap, we could replicate this payment by purchasing $1/S_0$ shares of stock, currently at S_{60}. Doing so will cost $(1/S_0)S_{60}$. Then at the first settlement, we shall have stock worth $(1/S_0)S_{90}$. We sell that stock, withdrawing cash of $(1/S_0)S_{90} - 1$. We then take the $1 left over and roll it into the stock again, which will replicate the return the following period, as described above. This procedure will leave $1 left over at the end. Thus, sixty days into the swap, to replicate the remaining cash flows, we do the following:

1. Invest $(1/S_0)S_{60}$ in the stock.
2. Borrow the present value of $1.00 to be paid back at the swap expiration, time h_n. This is the amount $B_{60}(h_n)$.
3. Take out a series of loans requiring that we pay back $FS(0,n,m)$ at time h_1, and also at time h_2, and at all remaining times through time h_n.

For the general case of day t, the market value of the swap is

$$\left(\frac{S_t}{S_0}\right) - B_t(h_n) - FS(0,n,m) \sum_{j=1}^{n} B_t(h_j) \tag{65-2}$$

The first term reflects the investment in the stock necessary to replicate the equity return. The second term is the loan for the present value of $1.00 due at the expiration date of the swap. The third term is the series of loans of the amount FS(0,n,m) due at the various swap settlement dates. Note that all discounting is done using the new term structure. Of course, the overall market value figure would then be multiplied by the notional principal.

Let us calculate these results for our pay-fixed, receive-equity swap 60 days into its life. Suppose the stock index was at 1405.72 when the swap was initiated. Now it is at 1436.59. We use the same term structure at 60 days that we used for the interest rate swap example. The market value of the swap is

$$\left(\frac{1436.59}{1405.72}\right) - 0.9643 - (0.0092)(0.9965 + 0.9858 + 0.9751 + 0.9643)$$
$$= 0.0216$$

Thus, 60 days into its life, the market value of this fixed-for-equity swap is positive at $0.0216 per $1 notional principal.

Valuing a Swap to Pay a Floating Rate and Receive the Return on the Equity
We can value this swap in two ways. The first will require that we discount the next floating rate and the par value, as we did with interest rate swaps. We can do this because we recognize that a floating-rate security is worth its par value on the payment date. As long as we add the notional principal, we can assume the floating payments are those of a floating-rate bond. The notional principal offsets the $1 left over at the end from holding the stock and withdrawing all of the profits on each settlement date. The calculation of the market value of this swap is simple. We just determine the value of $1 invested in the stock since the last settlement period, minus the present value of the floating leg. With the upcoming floating payment being 0.0086, the market value of the swap is, therefore,

$$\left(\frac{1436.59}{1405.72}\right) - (1.0086)(0.9965) = 0.0169$$

Another, and probably easier, way to arrive at this answer is to recognize that:

▶ a swap to pay fixed and receive the equity return is worth 0.0216; and
▶ a swap to pay floating and receive fixed is worth −0.0047.[20]

If we did both of these swaps, the fixed payments would offset and would leave the equivalent of the equity swap. The value would then be 0.0216 − 0.0047 = 0.0169.

Valuing a Swap to Pay One Equity Return and Receive Another   Now we need to value the swap to pay the return on Index 2 and receive the return on Index 1, 60 days into the swap's life. Let the following be the values of the indices on days 0 and 60.

---

[20] In Section 4.2.1, we found the value of a swap to pay fixed and receive floating to be 0.0047. Therefore, a swap to pay floating and receive fixed is worth −0.0047.

	Day 0	Day 60
Index 1	1405.72	1436.59
Index 2	5255.18	5285.73

As we previously described, this swap can be replicated by going long Index 1 and short Index 2. The market value calculation is simple: We find the value of $1 invested in Index 1 since the last settlement day minus the value of $1 invested in Index 2 since the last settlement day. Thus, the market value of the position is

$$\left(\frac{1436.59}{1405.72}\right) - \left(\frac{5285.73}{5255.18}\right) = 0.0161$$

Of course, all of these results are per $1 notional principal, so we would have to multiply by the actual notional principal to get the overall market value of this equity-for-equity swap.

EXAMPLE 6

Consider an equity swap that calls for semiannual payments for one year. The party will receive the return on the Dow Jones Industrial Average (DJIA), which starts off at 10033.27. The current LIBOR term structure is

Days	Rate
180	7.2%
360	8.0%

A. In Example 4, we determined that the fixed rate for a one-year interest rate swap given the above term structure was 0.0392. Given this term structure data, what is the fixed rate in an equity swap calling for the party to pay a fixed rate and receive the return on the DJIA?

B. Find the market value of the swap 90 days later if the new term structure is

Days	Rate
90	7.1%
270	7.4%

The notional principal of the swap is $60 million. The DJIA is at 9955.14. Again, these are the same rates as in Example 4, for which we computed $B_{90}(90) = 0.9826$ and $B_{90}(270) = 0.9474$.

C. Recompute the market value under the assumption that the counterparty pays a floating rate instead of a fixed rate.

D. Recompute the market value under the assumption that the counterparty pays the return on the Dow Jones Transportation Index, which started off at 2835.17 and 90 days later is 2842.44.

Solution to A: Because this term structure is the same as in Example 4, the fixed rate is the same at 0.0392. The fact that the party here receives an equity return rather than a floating interest rate does not affect the magnitude of the fixed payment.

Solution to B: Using the 180- and 360-day discount factors at 90 days from Example 4, the market value of the swap to pay a fixed rate and receive the equity return is

$$\left(\frac{9955.14}{10033.27}\right) - 0.9474 - 0.0392(0.9826 + 0.9474) = -0.0309$$

Multiplying by the notional principal of $60 million, we obtain a market value of $60,000,000(-0.0309) = -$1,854,000.

Solution to C: Because the first floating payment would be at the rate of 7.2 percent and is, therefore, 0.036, the market value of the swap to pay a floating rate and receive the equity return is

$$\left(\frac{9955.14}{10033.27}\right) - 1.036(0.9826) = -0.0258$$

Adjusting for the notional principal, the market value is $60,000,000(-0.0258) = -$1,548,000.

Solution to D: The market value of the swap to pay the return on the Dow Jones Transportation Average and receive the return on the DJIA is

$$\left(\frac{9955.14}{10033.27}\right) - \left(\frac{2842.44}{2835.17}\right) = -0.0104$$

Adjusting for the notional principal, the market value is $60,000,000(-0.0104) = -$624,000.

4.3 Some Concluding Comments on Swap Valuation

Let us review some important results on swap valuation and pricing. Because the market value of the swap when initiated is zero, pricing the swap means to find the terms of the swap that will make its market value be zero. If the swap pays a fixed rate, we must find the fixed rate that makes the present value of the fixed payments equal the present value of the floating payments. If both sides of the swap involve floating payments, there are no terms to determine. For currency swaps, we also have to determine the notional principal in one currency that is equivalent to a given notional principal in another currency.

The market value of a swap starts off at zero but changes to either a positive or negative value as the swap evolves through its life and market conditions change. To determine the market value of a swap, we must determine the present value of the remaining stream of payments, netting one against the other.

The market value of a swap gives a number that represents what the swap is worth to each party. If the market value is positive, the swap is like an asset. The amount due to one party is worth more than the amount that party owes. If it is negative, the swap is like a liability. The amount that party owes is worth more than the amount owed to it. The market value of a swap is also sometimes known as the **replacement value**. This notion views the swap as an instrument whose value can potentially be lost through default. If a party is holding a positive value swap and the other party defaults, that value is lost and would require that amount of money to replace it. We discuss this point further in Section 7.

VARIATIONS OF SWAPS   5

So far we have covered the most common types of swaps: fixed-for-floating interest rate swaps, various combinations of fixed and floating currency swaps, and equity swaps involving fixed payments, floating payments, or the returns on another equity. We must also mention some other types of swaps.

We briefly referred to the **basis swap**, in which both sides pay a floating rate. A typical basis swap involves one party paying LIBOR and the other paying the T-bill rate. As we learned in Reading 63, the term *basis* refers to the spread between two prices, usually the spot and futures prices. Here it is simply the spread between two rates, LIBOR and the T-bill rate. Because LIBOR is always more than the T-bill rate, the two parties negotiate a fixed spread such that the party paying LIBOR actually pays LIBOR minus the spread.[21] LIBOR is the borrowing rate of high-quality London banks, and the T-bill rate is the default-free borrowing rate of the U.S. government. The difference between LIBOR and the T-bill rate is thus a reflection of investors' perception of the general level of credit risk in the market. Basis swaps are usually employed for speculative purposes by end users who believe the spread between LIBOR and the T-bill rate will change.[22] A basis swap of this type is, therefore, usually a position taken in anticipation of a change in the relative level of credit risk in the market. As noted, both sides are floating, and typically both sides use 360-day years in their calculations.[23]

Another type of swap we sometimes encounter is not all that different from a plain vanilla or basis swap. In a **constant maturity swap**, one party pays a fixed rate, or a short-term floating rate such as LIBOR, and the other party pays a floating rate that is the rate on a security known as a **constant maturity treasury (CMT)** security. The transaction is also sometimes known as a CMT swap. This underlying instrument is a hypothetical U.S. Treasury note, meaning that its maturity is in the 2- to 10-year range, with a constant maturity. Obviously the reference to a particular CMT cannot be referring to a single note, because the maturity of any security decreases continuously. As mentioned, the note is hypothetical. For example, for a

---

[21] Alternatively, the counterparty could pay the T-bill rate plus the spread.

[22] The spread between LIBOR and the T-bill rate is called the **TED spread**. It is considered an indicator of the relative state of credit risk in the markets. LIBOR represents the rate on a private borrower (London banks); the T-bill rate is the U.S. government borrowing rate. When the global economy weakens, the TED spread tends to widen because rates based on the credit risk of private borrowers will increase while the U.S. government remains a risk-free borrower.

[23] Of course, a basis swap need not be based on LIBOR and the T-bill rate, so other conventions can be used.

two-year CMT security, when there is an actual two-year note, that note is the CMT security. Otherwise, the yield on a CMT security is interpolated from the yields of securities with surrounding maturities. The distinguishing characteristic of a constant maturity swap is that the maturity of the underlying security exceeds the length of the settlement period. For example, a CMT swap might call for payments every six months, with the rate based on the one-year CMT security. In contrast, a standard swap settling every six months would nearly always be based on a six-month security. Otherwise, however, a constant maturity swap possesses the general characteristics of a plain vanilla swap.

One interesting variant of an interest rate swap is an **overnight index swap (OIS)**. This instrument commits one party to paying a fixed rate as usual. The floating rate, however, is the cumulative value of a single unit of currency invested at an overnight rate during the settlement period. The overnight rate changes daily. This instrument is used widely in Europe but not in the United States.

Amortizing and **accreting swaps** are those in which the notional principal changes according to a formula related to the underlying. The more common of the two is the amortizing swap, sometimes called an **index amortizing swap**. In this type of interest rate swap, the notional principal is indexed to the level of interest rates. The notional principal declines with the level of interest rates according to a predefined schedule. This feature makes the swap similar to certain asset-backed securities, such as mortgage-backed securities, which prepay some of their principal as rates fall. An index amortizing swap is often used to hedge this type of security.

Diff swaps combine elements of interest rate, currency, and equity swaps. In a typical diff swap, one party pays the floating interest rate of one country and the other pays the floating interest rate of another country. Both sets of payments, however, are made in a single currency. So one set of payments is based on the interest rate of one country, but the payment is made in the currency of another country. This swap is a pure play on the interest rate differential between two countries and is basically a currency swap with the currency risk hedged. Alternatively, in equity diff swaps, the return on a foreign stock index is paid in the domestic currency.

An **arrears swap** is a special type of interest rate swap in which the floating payment is set at the end of the period and the interest is paid at that same time. This procedure stands in contrast to the typical interest rate swap, in which the payment is set on one settlement date and the interest is paid on the next settlement date.

In a **capped swap**, the floating payments have a limit as to how high they can be. Similarly, a **floored swap** has a limit on how low the floating payments can be.

There is no limit to the number of variations that can be found in swaps, and it is not worthwhile to examine them beyond the basic, most frequently used types. We must, however, cover an important variation of a swap that combines elements of both swaps and options.

6   SWAPTIONS

A **swaption** *is an option to enter into a swap.* Although swaptions can be designed in a variety of ways, we shall focus exclusively on the most widely used swaption, the plain vanilla interest rate swaption. This is a swaption to pay the fixed rate and receive the floating rate or the other way around. It allows the holder to establish a fixed rate on the underlying swap in advance and have the option of entering into the swap with that fixed rate or allowing the swaption to expire and entering into the swap at the fixed rate that prevails in the market.

6.1 Basic Characteristics of Swaptions

The two types of swaptions are a **payer swaption** and a **receiver swaption**. A payer swaption allows the holder to enter into a swap as the fixed-rate payer and floating-rate receiver. A receiver swaption allows the holder to enter into a swap as the fixed-rate receiver and floating-rate payer. Therefore, these terms refer to the fixed rate and are comparable to the terms *call* and *put* used for other types of options. Although it is not apparent at this point, a payer swaption is a put and a receiver swaption is a call.

Swaptions have specific expiration dates. Like ordinary options, swaptions can be European style (exercisable only at expiration) or American style (exercisable at any time prior to expiration). A swaption is based on a specific underlying swap. For example, consider a European payer swaption that expires in two years and allows the holder to enter into a three-year swap with semiannual payments every 15 January and 15 July. The payments will be made at the rate of 6.25 percent and will be computed using the 30/360 adjustment. The underlying swap is based on LIBOR, and the notional principal is $10 million. Of course, a swaption has a price or premium, which is an amount paid by the buyer to the seller up front.

Note that this swaption expires in two years and the underlying swap expires three years after that. This arrangement is called a 2 × 5 swaption, a terminology we used in explaining FRAs. The underlying can be viewed as a five-year swap at the time the swaption is initiated and will be a three-year swap when the swaption expires.

Finally, there are a number of ways to settle a swaption at expiration. Recall that ordinary options can allow for either physical delivery or cash settlement. We will explore the comparable concepts for swaptions in Section 6.3.

6.2 Uses of Swaptions

Swaptions have a variety of purposes. Now, however, we take a brief glance at why swaptions exist.

Swaptions are used by parties who anticipate the need for a swap at a later date but would like to establish the fixed rate today, while providing the flexibility to not engage in the swap later or engage in the swap at a more favorable rate in the market. These parties are often corporations that expect to need a swap later and would like to hedge against unfavorable interest rate moves while preserving the flexibility to gain from favorable moves.

Swaptions are used by parties entering into a swap to give them the flexibility to terminate the swap. In Section 1.2, we discussed why a party engaged in a swap might wish to terminate it before expiration. Suppose the party in a swap is paying fixed and receiving floating. If it owned a receiver swaption, it could exercise the swaption, thereby entering into a swap to receive a fixed rate and pay a floating rate. It would then have offset the floating parts of the swap, effectively removing any randomness from the position.[24] But the only way the party could do so would require having previously purchased a swaption. Similarly, parties engaged in a receive-fixed, pay-floating swap can effectively offset it by exercising a payer swaption.

Swaptions are used by parties to speculate on interest rates. As with any interest rate sensitive instrument, swaptions can be used to speculate. Their prices move with interest rates and, like all options, they contain significant leverage. Thus, they are appropriate instruments for interest rate speculators.

---

[24] Note, however, that both swaps are still in effect even though the floating sides offset. Because both swaps remain in effect, there is credit risk on the two transactions.

6.3 Swaption Payoffs

When a swaption is exercised, it effectively creates a stream of equivalent payments, commonly referred to in the financial world as an annuity. This stream is a series of interest payments equal to the difference between the exercise rate and the market rate on the underlying swap when the swaption is exercised.

Consider a European payer swaption that expires in two years and is exercisable into a one-year swap with quarterly payments, using 90/360 as the day-count adjustment. The exercise rate is 3.60 percent. The notional principal is $20 million. Now, suppose we are at the swaption expiration and the term structure is the one we obtained when pricing the interest rate swap earlier in this reading. We repeat that information here:

Maturity	Rate	Discount Factor
90 days	3.45%	0.9914
180 days	3.58%	0.9824
270 days	3.70%	0.9730
360 days	3.75%	0.9639

Under these conditions, we found that the swap fixed payment is 0.0092, equating to an annual fixed rate of 3.68 percent.

The holder of the swaption has the right to enter into a swap to pay 3.60 percent, whereas in the market such a swap would require payment at a rate of 3.68 percent. Therefore, here at expiration this swaption does appear to offer an advantage over the market rate. Let us consider the three possible ways to exercise this swaption.

The holder can exercise the swaption, thereby entering into a swap to pay 3.60 percent. The quarterly payment at the rate of 3.60 percent would be $20,000,000(0.0360) (90/360) = $180,000. The swaption holder would then be engaged in a swap to pay $180,000 quarterly and receive LIBOR. The first floating payment would be at 3.45 percent[25] and would be $20,000,000(0.0345)(90/360) = $172,500. The remaining floating payments would, of course, be determined later. The payment stream is illustrated in Exhibit 8, Panel A.

Alternatively, the holder can exercise the swaption, thereby entering into a swap to pay 3.60 percent, and then enter into a swap in the market to receive fixed and pay floating. The fixed rate the holder would receive is 3.68 percent, the market-determined fixed rate at the time the swaption expires. The quarterly fixed payment at 3.68 percent would be $20,000,000(0.0368)(90/360) = $184,000. Technically, the LIBOR payments are still made, but the same amount is paid and received. Hence, they effectively offset. Panel B illustrates this payment stream. This arrangement would be common if the counterparty to the second swap is not the same as the counterparty to the swaption.

The holder can arrange to receive a net payment stream of $184,000 − $180,000 = $4,000. Panel C illustrates this payment stream. In this case, the counterparty to the second swap is probably the same as the counterparty to the swap created by exercising the swaption, who would be the counterparty to the swaption. Because the floating payments are eliminated, the amount of cash passing between the parties is reduced, which mitigates the credit risk.

---

[25] The first floating payment is at 3.45 percent because this is the 90-day rate in effect at the time the swap is initiated.

EXHIBIT 8	Cash Flows from Swaptions

A. Exercise of Payer Swaption, Entering into a Pay-Fixed, Receive-Floating Swap

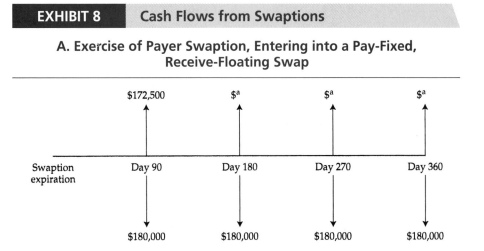

^a Computed as $\$20,000,000(L)90/360$, where L is LIBOR on the previous settlement date.

B. Exercise of Payer Swaption, Entering into a Pay-Fixed, Receive-Floating Swap and Entering into a Receive-Fixed, Pay-Floating Swap at the Market Rate

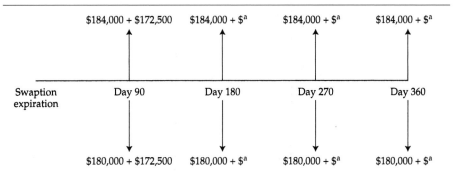

^a Computed as $\$20,000,000(L)90/360$, where L is LIBOR on the previous settlement date.

C. Exercise of Swaption with Offsetting Swap Netted

D. Cash Settlement

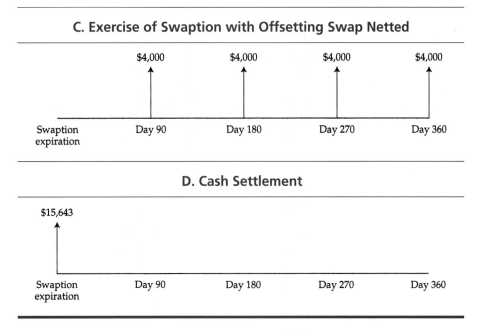

The holder can receive an up-front cash payment. We can easily determine the amount. It is simply the present value of the payment stream shown in Panel C, which we can obtain using the discount factors shown above:

$$\$4,000(0.9914 + 0.9824 + 0.9730 + 0.9639) = \$15,643$$

This pure cash settlement is illustrated in Panel D.

Other than transaction costs and the credit risk associated with the newly created swaps, each of these means of exercising a swaption has the same value. Of course, the two parties would have to agree up front which of these means to use at expiration. Cash settlement is the most common.

Therefore, the payoff of a payer swaption in which the exercise rate is x and the market rate on the underlying swap is FS(0,n,m) is

$$\text{Max}[0, \text{FS}(0, n, m) - x]\sum_{j=1}^{n} B_0(h_j) \qquad \textbf{(65-3)}$$

Similarly, the payoff of a receiver swaption would be

$$\text{Max}[0, x - \text{FS}(0, n, m)]\sum_{j=1}^{n} B_0(h_j) \qquad \textbf{(65-4)}$$

Of course, these figures would be multiplied by the actual notional principal. So we see that a swaption effectively creates an annuity. The present value factors are not relevant in determining whether the swaption will be exercised. Exercise is determined solely on the relationship between the swap rate at expiration and the exercise rate. The present value factors are used to convert the stream of net payments obtained upon exercise of the swap into a current value. Now, let us take a brief look at how a swaption is priced.

6.4 Pricing and Valuation of Swaptions

We shall show here, perhaps somewhat surprisingly, that an interest rate swaption is like an option on a coupon bond. Restating our result given about, the payoff of a payer swaption is

$$\text{Max}[0, \text{FS}(0, n, m) - x]\sum_{j=1}^{n} B_0(h_j)$$

This expression finds the present value of the difference between the fixed rate on the swap and the exercise rate on the swaption if that difference is positive. Otherwise, the payoff is zero. Recall from Section 4.2.1 (Equation 65-1) that the fixed rate on an interest rate swap is

$$\text{FS}(0, n, m) = \frac{1.0 - B_0(h_n)}{\sum_{j=1}^{n} B_0(h_j)}$$

Substituting the fixed rate into the payoff equation, we obtain

$$\text{Max}\left[0, \frac{1.0 - B_0(h_n)}{\sum_{j=1}^{n} B_0(h_j)} - x\right]\sum_{j=1}^{n} B_0(h_j)$$

which can be rewritten as

$$\text{Max}\left\{0, 1.0 - \left[x\sum_{j=1}^{n} B_0(h_j) + B_0(h_N)\right]\right\}$$

Note the term in brackets,

$$x\sum_{j=1}^{n} B_0(h_j) + B_0(h_N)$$

which is the same as the market value at the swaption expiration of a coupon bond of \$1.00 par value, in which the coupon is x. Thus, the swaption payoff is effectively $\text{Max}(0, 1.0 - \text{Market value of coupon bond})$. This amount is the payoff of a put option on a coupon bond with coupon of x, a face value of 1.0, and a maturity of the swap expiration date. The exercise price is the par value of 1.0, and the exercise rate of the swaption is the coupon rate on the bond. Hence, we can value the swaption as though it were simply a put on a bond. In a similar manner, the payoff of a receiver swaption can be shown to be that of a call option on this coupon bond.

Now you can see why, as we stated earlier, a payer swaption is a put option and a receiver swaption is a call option. More specifically, a payer swaption is a put option on a bond and a receiver swaption is a call option on a bond.

EXAMPLE 7

Calculate the market value of a receiver swaption at the expiration if the exercise rate is 4 percent and the term structure is given below:

Days	Rate
180	7.2%
360	8.0%

These are the same rates as in Example 4. The swaption is on a swap that will make payments in 180 and 360 days, and the notional principal is \$25 million. Also, show that this payoff is equivalent to that of a call option on a bond.

Solution: Based on a fixed rate of 0.0392 from Example 4, the market value is $\text{Max}(0, 0.04 - 0.0392)(0.9653 + 0.9259) = 0.0015$.

Based on a notional principal of \$25 million, this is a market value of $25,000,000(0.0015) = \$37,500$.

This payoff is equivalent to that of a call option on a bond with an exercise price of 1.0, its par value. At this point in time, the expiration of the option, the bond on which this call is based would have a market value of $0.04(0.9653 + 0.9259) + 1.0(0.9259) = 1.0015$.

Therefore, the payoff of a call on this bond is $\text{Max}(0, 1.0015 - 1.0) = 0.0015$—the same as that of the swaption.

With that result in mind, we could value the swaption using any of a number of approaches to valuing bond options. We shall not take up the pricing of swaptions here, as it is a somewhat advanced topic and the issues are somewhat complicated. It is not a straightforward matter to apply the Black–Scholes–Merton or Black models to pricing bond options. We discussed the valuation of options on bonds in Reading 64, noting that the binomial model is probably the best way to do so.

6.5 Forward Swaps

We have seen in this volume that options represent rights and forward contracts represent commitments. Just as there are options to enter swaps, there are also forward contracts to enter into swaps, called **forward swaps**. They are not as widely used as swaptions but do offer the advantage, as is always the case with forwards, that one does not have to pay any cash up front as with an option premium. Forward swaps are priced by pricing the swap off of the forward term structure instead of the spot term structure.

7   CREDIT RISK AND SWAPS

In this reading, we have mentioned on a few occasions that swaps are subject to credit risk. Indeed, as we have emphasized throughout the volume, *all* over-the-counter derivatives are subject to credit risk. In this section, we examine some of the issues involved in the credit risk of swaps.

Recall that a swap has zero market value at the start. It starts off as neither an asset nor a liability. Once the swap is engaged and market conditions change, the market value becomes positive for one party and negative for the other. The party holding the positive value swap effectively owns an asset, which represents a claim against the counterparty. This claim is a netting of the amount owed by the counterparty and the amount that the party owes, with the former exceeding the latter. The party holding the positive-value swap thus assumes credit risk. The counterparty could declare bankruptcy, leaving the party holding the positive-value swap with a claim that is subject to the legal process of bankruptcy. In most swap arrangements, netting is legally recognized, so the claim has a value based on the net amount. Of course, as we described in the reading, currency swaps are generally not netted so the credit risk is greater on currency swaps.

The party to which the swap has a negative value is not subject to credit risk. It owes more than is owed to it, so the other party faces the risk.

During the life of the swap, however, the market value to a given party can change from positive to negative or vice versa. Hence, the party not facing credit risk at a given moment is not entirely free of risk, because the swap value could turn positive for it later.

The timing of credit risk is in the form of immediate or **current credit risk** and deferred or **potential credit risk**. The former arises when a payment is immediately due and cannot be made by one party. The latter reflects the ever-present possibility that, although a counterparty may currently be able to make payments, it may be unable to make future payments.

Let us work through an example illustrating these points. Consider two parties A and B who are engaged in a swap. At a given payment date, the payment of Party A to Party B is $100,000 and the payment of Party B to Party A is $35,000. As is customarily the case, Party A must pay $65,000 to Party B. Once the payment is made, we shall assume that the market value of the swap is $1,250,000, which is an asset to A and a liability to B.

Suppose Party A is unable to pay and declares bankruptcy. Then Party B does not make any payment to Party A. Party A is bankrupt, but the swap is an asset to A. Given the $65,000 owed by A to B, the claim of A against B is $1,250,000 − $65,000 = $1,185,000. We emphasize in this example that A is the bankrupt party, but the swap is an asset to A, representing its claim against B. If B were holding the positive market value of the swap, it would have a claim of $1,250,000 + $65,000 = $1,315,000 on A as A enters into the bankruptcy process.

Let us change the example a little by having A not be bankrupt on the payment date. It makes its payment of $65,000 to B and moves forward. But a few months later, before the next payment, A declares bankruptcy. Its payment is not immediately due, but it has essentially stated that it will not make its next payment or any payments thereafter. To determine the financial implications of the event, the two parties must compute the market value of the swap. Suppose the value is now $1,100,000 and is positive to A. Then A, the bankrupt party, holds a claim against B of $1,100,000. The fact that A is bankrupt does not mean that it cannot have a claim against someone else, just as a bankrupt corporation can be owed money for inventory it has sold but on which it has not yet collected payment.

Of course, A could be bankrupt and B's claim against A could be the greater. In fact, with A bankrupt, there is a very good possibility that this scenario would be the case. Then, of course, B would simply be another of A's many creditors.

Exactly what happens to resolve these claims in each of these situations is a complex legal issue and is beyond the scope of our level of treatment. In addition, the bankruptcy laws vary somewhat around the world, so the potential exists for different treatments of the same situation. Most countries do recognize the legality of netting, however, so it would be rare that a party would be able to claim the full amount owed it without netting out the amount it owes.

The credit risk in a swap varies during its life. An interest rate or equity swap has no final principal payments. The credit risk in either of these swap types is greater during the middle of its life. This occurs because near the end of the life of the swap, not many payments remain, so there is not much money at risk. And at the beginning of the life of the swap, the credit risk is usually low because the parties would probably not engage in the swap if a great deal of credit risk already were present at the start. Therefore, the greatest potential for credit losses is during the middle of the life of the swap. For currency swaps, in which the notional principals are typically exchanged at the end of the life of the swap, the credit risk is concentrated between the middle and the end of its life.

The parties that engage in swaps are generally of good credit quality, but the fear of default is still a significant concern. Yet, perhaps surprisingly, the rates that all parties pay on swaps are the same, regardless of either party's credit quality. As we have illustrated here, a plain vanilla swap, in which one party pays a floating rate and the other pays a fixed rate, has the fixed rate determined by the term structure for that underlying rate. Therefore, if a party wanted to engage in a swap to pay LIBOR and receive a fixed rate, it would get the fixed rate based on the LIBOR term structure, regardless of its credit quality or that of the counterparty, provided that the two parties agreed to do the transaction. Implicit in the fixed rate, however, is the spread between LIBOR and the default-free rate. As we described earlier in the reading, swap rates are quoted with respect to a spread over the equivalent default-free rate. Thus, a one-year swap rate of 3.68 percent as in our example might be quoted as 50 basis points over the rate on a one-year U.S. Treasury note, implying that the one-year U.S. Treasury note rate was 3.18 percent. This differential is called the **swap spread**.

It is important to note that the swap spread is not a measure of the credit risk on a given swap but rather a reflection of the general level of credit risk in the global economy. The LIBOR term structure reflects the borrowing rate for London banks, which are generally highly rated but not default free. Whenever a recession approaches or credit concerns arise, this spread widens and fixed-rate payers on swaps end up paying more. Of course, floating-rate payers end up paying more as well, but the additional cost to them is less obvious up front because the floating rates change over the life of the swap.

So all parties pay the same rate, but clearly some parties are better credit risks than others. In addition, virtually no parties are default free, and many are of lower credit quality than the typical London bank on which LIBOR is based. How do parties manage the credit risk in swaps? There are a number of methods, which we shall discuss in more detail in Reading 67. For right now, however, we cover one such method that we have seen before with respect to forward contracts and that is routinely used in the futures market: marking to market.

Reconsider the interest rate swap we covered earlier in the reading in which the payments are made quarterly in the amount of 0.0092 per $1 notional principal. The swap lasts for one year, so there are four payments. Suppose the parties agree to mark the contract to market halfway through its life—that is, in six months, immediately after the payment is made. Suppose we are at that point and the term structure is as follows:

$$L_{180}(90) = 0.0390$$
$$L_{180}(180) = 0.0402$$

Note that we are at day 180, and the upcoming payments occur in 90 and 180 days. We thus need to calculate $B_{180}(270)$ and $B_{180}(360)$. These present value factors are

$$B_{180}(270) = \frac{1}{1 + 0.039(90/360)} = 0.9903$$

$$B_{180}(360) = \frac{1}{1 = 0.0402(180/360)} = 0.9803$$

Now we can compute the market value of the swap. The present value of the remaining fixed payments, plus the hypothetical notional principal, is $0.0092(0.9903 + 0.9803) + 1.0(0.9803) = 0.9984$.

Because the 90-day floating rate is 3.90 percent, the next floating payment will be $0.0390(90/360) = 0.00975$. Of course, we do not know the last floating payment, but it does not matter because the present value of the remaining floating payments, plus hypothetical notional principal, is automatically 1.0 because we are on the coupon reset date. Therefore, the market value of the swap to the party receiving floating and paying fixed is the present value of the floating payments, 1.0, minus the present value of the fixed payments, 0.9984, or $1.0 - 0.9984 = 0.0016$.

If the two parties marked this swap to market, the party paying floating and receiving fixed would pay the other party a lump sum cash payment of $0.0016 per $1 notional principal. The two parties would then reprice the swap. The new payment would be

$$FS(0, n, m) = FS(0,2,90) = \frac{1 - 0.9803}{0.9903 + 0.9803} = 0.01$$

Thus, the fixed payment would be 0.01 for the rest of the swap.

EXAMPLE 8

Consider a two-year swap to pay a fixed rate and receive a floating rate with semiannual payments. The fixed rate is 0.0462. Now, 360 days later, the term structure is

Days	Rate
180	10.1%
360	10.4%

The next floating payment will be 0.045. The swap calls for marking to market after 180 days, and, therefore, will now be marked to market. Determine the market value, identify which party pays which, and calculate the new fixed rate.

Solution: First find the discount factors:

$$B_{360}(540) = \frac{1}{1 + 0.101(180/360)} = 0.9519$$

$$B_{360}(720) = \frac{1}{1 + 0.104(360/360)} = 0.9058$$

The market value of the fixed payments plus $1 hypothetical notional principal is $0.0462(0.9519 + 0.9058) + 1.0(0.9058) = 0.9916$.

The market value of the floating payments plus $1 hypothetical notional principal is $1.045(0.9519) = 0.9947$.

Therefore, the market value to the party paying fixed and receiving floating is $0.9947 - 0.9916 = 0.0031$.

This amount would be paid by the party paying floating and receiving fixed. The new fixed rate would then be

$$\frac{1 - 0.9058}{0.9519 + 0.9058} = 0.0507$$

This rate would be quoted as an annual rate of $5.07\%(360/180) = 10.14\%$.

As in the futures market, marking a swap contract to market results in the two parties terminating the contract and automatically engaging in a new swap. In essence, the arrangement commits the two parties to terminating the swap and re-establishing it on a predetermined schedule. This process reduces the credit risk by requiring one party to pay the other any amount due at a time prior to the expiration date of the swap. The effect is to reduce the extent to which the swap can go deeply underwater to one of the parties, who may be facing financial problems.

8   THE ROLE OF SWAP MARKETS

In each of the preceding three readings, we have discussed the role played by the markets represented by the various derivative instruments. The swap market is extremely large, consisting of dealers and end users engaging in customized transactions that involve a series of payments. As we showed in this reading, swaps can be equivalent to various other derivative instruments. Moreover, we used transactions in assets to replicate swaps. Hence, an obvious question is why swaps exist when the same results can be obtained using other instruments.

First let us ignore the obvious counter-question of why other instruments exist when swaps serve the same purpose. In the race to see which derivative instrument is more popular, swaps have clearly won. We can only surmise the reason why.

The tremendous popularity of swaps results largely from the popularity of interest rate swaps. For several reasons, these instruments have been embraced by corporations as tools for managing interest rate risk. One is that interest rate swaps, certainly the plain vanilla type, are simple instruments, rarely requiring technology, computational skills, or financial know-how beyond what exists in most corporate treasury offices. In short, they are easy to understand. In addition, interest rate swaps can easily be viewed as a pair of loans. Borrowing and lending money is second nature to corporations. Corporations view engaging in swaps as nothing more than an extension of their regular practice of borrowing and lending money. Many corporations are restricted in their use of options and futures, but they can usually justify swaps as nothing more than variations of loans. Also, swaps are so easily tailored to alter the interest rate patterns on most corporate loans that they seem to go hand in hand with the typical fixed- and floating-rate loans that corporations take out. Many corporations borrow money and combine the loan with a swap right from the start. Finally, we should note that some dealer firms have exploited the attractions of swaps by aggressive selling. In some cases, corporations entered into ill-advised and occasionally complex, exotic swaps. We do not suggest that most dealers have engaged in unethical actions (although some certainly have) but rather that, as in all sales-oriented activities, customers do not always get impartial advice from sales personnel. In some cases, corporations have used swaps to step over the line from good risk management into speculation on risks they know nothing about. In short, at least part of the success of swaps has probably not been for the right reasons.

But using swaps for the wrong reason does not sufficiently explain the success of these instruments. If it were the primary motivation for their use, swaps would die out as a risk management tool. Instead, swaps have grown in popularity. Swaps provide a mechanism for managing the risks associated with a series of payments. Although forward contracts and other instruments can manage that risk, a swap is more of a portfolio approach to managing risk—a package of risk management tools all rolled up into one. Given that risk often exists in a series, swaps are ideal instruments for managing it. Other instruments may be able to do the job, but they must be carefully constructed with a certain amount of financial ingenuity.

SUMMARY

▶ Swaps are over-the-counter contracts in which two parties agree to pay a series of cash flows to each other. At least one series is floating or variable and related to an interest rate, exchange rate, equity price, or commodity price; the other can be fixed or floating. Swaps have zero value at the start and have payments made on scheduled payment or settlement dates and a final termination or expiration date. When swap payments are made in the same currency, the payments are usually netted. Swaps are subject to default on the part of either party.

▶ Swaps can be terminated by having one party pay the market value of the swap to the other party, by entering into a swap in which the variable payments offset, by selling the swap to another party, or by exercising a swaption to enter into an offsetting swap.

▶ In a currency swap, each party makes payments to the other in different currencies. A currency swap can have one party pay a fixed rate in one currency and the other pay a fixed rate in the other currency; have both pay a floating rate in their respective currencies; have the first party pay a fixed rate in one currency and the second party pay a floating rate in the other currency; or have the first party pay a floating rate in one currency and the second pay a fixed rate in the other currency. In currency swaps, the notional principal is usually exchanged at the beginning and at the end of the life of the swap, although this exchange is not mandatory.

▶ The payments on a currency swap are calculated by multiplying the notional principal by the fixed or floating interest rate times a day-count adjustment. This procedure is done in each currency, and the respective parties make their separate payments to each other. The payments are not netted.

▶ In a plain vanilla interest rate swap, one party makes payments at a fixed rate and the other makes payments at a floating rate, with no exchange of notional principal. A typical plain vanilla swap involves one party paying a fixed rate and the other paying a floating rate such as LIBOR. Swaps are often done by a party borrowing floating at a rate tied to LIBOR; that party then uses a pay-fixed, receive-floating swap to offset the risk of its exposure to LIBOR and effectively convert its loan to a fixed-rate loan.

▶ The payments on an interest rate swap are calculated by multiplying the notional principal by the fixed or floating interest rate times a day-count adjustment. The respective amounts are netted so that the party owing the greater amount makes a net payment to the other.

▶ The three types of equity swaps involve one party paying a fixed rate, a floating rate, or the return on another equity, while the other party pays an equity return. Therefore, an equity swap is a swap in which at least one party pays the return on a stock or stock index.

▶ The equity payment (or payments, if both sides of the swap are related to an equity return) on an equity swap is calculated by multiplying the return on the stock over the settlement period by the notional principal. If there is a fixed or floating payment, it is calculated in the same manner as in an interest rate swap. With payments in a single currency, the two sets of payments are netted.

▶ Swap pricing means to determine the fixed rate and any relevant terms, such as the foreign notional principal on a currency swap, at the start of the swap. Valuation means to determine the market value of the swap, which is the present value of one stream of payments less the present value of the other stream of payments. The market value of a swap is zero at the start but will change to positive for one party and negative for the other during the life of the swap, as market conditions change and time passes.

▶ Swaps can be viewed as combinations of assets. Currency swaps are like issuing a bond denominated in one currency and using the proceeds to buy a bond denominated in another currency. Interest rate swaps are like issuing a fixed-rate bond and using the proceeds to buy a floating-rate bond or vice versa. Equity swaps are like issuing a bond and using the proceeds to buy stock or vice versa. Equity swaps with both sides paying an equity return are like selling short one stock and using the proceeds to buy another stock. The stock position is not, however, a buy-and-hold position and requires some rebalancing.

▶ An interest rate swap is like a series of off-market FRAs, meaning that the rate on each FRA is set at the swap rate, not at the rate it would be set at if priced as an FRA with zero market value at the start. In addition, the first payment on a swap is just an exchange of known amounts of cash. Currency swaps and equity swaps are similar to forward contracts, but the connection is not as straightforward as in interest rate swaps.

▶ Interest rate swaps are like being long (short) interest rate calls and short (long) interest rate puts. Currency swaps and equity swaps are also similar to combinations of options, but the connection is not as straightforward.

▶ The fixed rate on an interest rate swap equates the present value of the fixed payments plus a hypothetical notional principal to the present value of the floating payments plus a hypothetical notional principal. The notional principals offset but permit these swaps to be treated like bonds. The fixed rate is then equivalent to the fixed rate on a par bond with the same payments as on the swap. The market value of the swap during its life is found by determining the difference in the market values of the floating- and fixed-rate bonds later during their lives under the new term structure.

▶ The fixed rates on a currency swap are the same as the fixed rates on plain vanilla interest rate swaps in the given countries. The foreign notional principal for a domestic notional principal of one unit is the inverse of the exchange rate. In other words, it is the foreign currency equivalent of the domestic notional principal. Because a currency swap is like issuing a bond in one currency and using the proceeds to buy a bond in another currency, the market value of a currency swap during its life is found by determining the difference in the market values of the two bonds during their lives using the new term structures in the two countries. The **foreign bond** value must be converted to its domestic equivalent by using the new exchange rate.

▶ The fixed rate on an equity swap is the same as the fixed rate on a plain vanilla interest rate swap. The market value of an equity swap involving fixed or floating payments during its life is found as the present value of the equity payments less the present value of the fixed or floating payments necessary to replicate the equity swap payment. The market value of an equity swap in which both sides make equity payments is the market value of a long position in one equity and a short position in the other, assuming the positions are liquidated at each settlement date and gains and losses are paid out.

▶ A swaption is an option to enter into a swap. The two types of interest rate swaptions are payer swaptions, which allow the holder to enter into a swap to pay the fixed rate and receive the floating rate, and receiver swaptions, which allow the holder to enter into a swap to receive the fixed rate and pay the floating rate. Swaptions are based on a specific underlying swap and have an exercise rate and an expiration date. At expiration, they can be exercised to enter into the underlying swap. Swaptions require an up-front premium.

▶ Swaptions exist to allow users the flexibility to enter into swaps at later dates but establish the terms in advance. If market conditions are not favorable to exercising a swaption, the holder can allow the swaption to expire and obtain more favorable terms by entering into a swap at the market rate. Swaptions are used by parties who anticipate a need to enter into a swap at a later date, who anticipate the need to terminate an already-existing swap, or who wish to speculate on interest rates.

▶ The payoffs of an interest rate swaption are like those of an option on a coupon-bearing bond. The option has an exercise price of par value, and the coupon rate is the exercise rate on the swaption. A payer swaption is like a put on the bond, and a receiver swaption is like a call on the bond.

▶ At expiration, an interest rate payer swaption is worth the maximum of zero or the present value of the difference between the market swap rate and the exercise rate, valued as an annuity extending over the remaining life of the underlying swap. To value a receiver swaption at expiration, we take the difference between the exercise rate and the market swap rate, adjusted for its present value over the life of the underlying swap. These figures must be multiplied by the notional principal.

▶ The market value of a swaption at expiration can be received in one of four ways: by exercising the swaption to enter into the underlying swap, by exercising the swaption and entering into an offsetting swap that keeps both swaps in force, by exercising the swaption and entering into an offsetting swap that eliminates both swaps and pays a series of payments equal to the net difference in the fixed rates on the two swaps, or by exercising the swaption and receiving a lump sum cash payment.

▶ A forward swap is a forward contract to enter into a swap. It commits both parties to entering into a swap at a later date at a fixed rate agreed on today. In contrast to a swaption, which is the right to enter into a swap, a forward swap is a binding commitment to enter into a swap.

▶ Credit risk arises in a swap due to the possibility that a party will not be able to make its payments. Current credit risk is the risk of a party being unable to make the upcoming payment. Potential credit risk is the risk of a party being unable to make future payments. Credit risk is faced only by the party that is owed the greater amount.

▶ The credit risk in an interest rate or equity swap is greatest during the middle of the swap's life. The risk is small at the beginning of the swap because the parties would not engage in the swap if the credit risk were significant at the start. The risk is low at the end of the life of the swap because of the small number of remaining payments. For currency swaps, the payment of notional principal shifts the credit risk more toward the end of the life of the swap. In addition, because the payments are typically not netted, the credit risk on currency swaps is greater than on interest rate swaps.

▶ The swap spread is the difference between the fixed rate on a swap and the yield on a default-free security of the same maturity as the swap. The spread indicates the average credit risk in the global economy but not the credit risk in a given swap.

▶ Netting reduces the credit risk in a swap by reducing the amount of money passing from any one party to another. The amount owed by a party is deducted from the amount due to a party, and only the net is paid. Marking a swap to market is a process in which the parties agree to periodically calculate the market value of the swap and have the party owing the greater amount pay the market value to the other party. The fixed rate is then reset on the swap until it is marked to market again or terminates. This procedure forces the party to which the swap is losing money to pay the other party before getting too deeply in debt.

▶ Swaps play an important role in the financial system by providing a simple means of managing a series of risks. Their popularity has arisen largely from corporate use in managing interest rate exposure.

PRACTICE PROBLEMS FOR READING 65

1. Consider a two-year interest rate swap with semiannual payments. Assume a notional principal of $25 million.

A. Calculate the annualized fixed rate on the swap. The current term structure of LIBOR interest rates is as follows:

$$L_0(180) = 0.0585$$
$$L_0(360) = 0.0605$$
$$L_0(540) = 0.0624$$
$$L_0(720) = 0.0665$$

B. Calculate the market value of the swap 120 days later 1) from the point of view of the party paying the floating rate and receiving the fixed rate and 2) from the point of view of the party paying the fixed rate and receiving the floating rate. The term structure 120 days later is as follows:

$$L_{120}(60) = 0.0613$$
$$L_{120}(240) = 0.0629$$
$$L_{120}(420) = 0.0653$$
$$L_{120}(600) = 0.0697$$

2. Consider a one-year interest rate swap with quarterly payments. Assume a notional principal of $15 million.

A. Calculate the annualized fixed rate on the swap. The current term structure of LIBOR interest rates is as follows:

$$L_0(90) = 0.0656$$
$$L_0(180) = 0.0640$$
$$L_0(270) = 0.0621$$
$$L_0(360) = 0.0599$$

B. Calculate the market value of the swap 30 days later 1) from the point of view of the party paying the floating rate and receiving the fixed rate and 2) from the point of view of the party paying the fixed rate and receiving the floating rate. The term structure 30 days later is as follows:

$$L_{30}(60) = 0.0384$$
$$L_{30}(150) = 0.0379$$
$$L_{30}(240) = 0.0382$$
$$L_{30}(330) = 0.0406$$

3. Consider a two-year currency swap with semiannual payments. The domestic currency is the U.S. dollar, and the foreign currency is the U.K. pound. The current exchange rate is $1.41 per pound.

A. Calculate the annualized fixed rates for dollars and pounds. The current U.S. term structure is the same as in Problem 8, Part A:

$$L_0(180) = 0.0585$$
$$L_0(360) = 0.0605$$
$$L_0(540) = 0.0624$$
$$L_0(720) = 0.0665$$

The U.K. term structure is

$$L_0^£(180) = 0.0493$$
$$L_0^£(360) = 0.0505$$
$$L_0^£(540) = 0.0519$$
$$L_0^£(720) = 0.0551$$

B. Now move forward 120 days. The new exchange rate is $1.35 per pound, and the new U.S. term structure is the same as in Problem 8, Part B:

$$L_{120}(60) = 0.0613$$
$$L_{120}(240) = 0.0629$$
$$L_{120}(420) = 0.0653$$
$$L_{120}(600) = 0.0697$$

The new U.K. term structure is

$$L_{120}{}^£(60) = 0.0517$$
$$L_{120}{}^£(240) = 0.0532$$
$$L_{120}{}^£(420) = 0.0568$$
$$L_{120}{}^£(600) = 0.0583$$

Assume that the notional principal is $1 or the corresponding amount in British pounds. Calculate the market values of the following swaps:

  i. Pay £ fixed and receive $ fixed.

  ii. Pay £ floating and receive $ fixed.

  iii. Pay £ floating and receive $ floating.

  iv. Pay £ fixed and receive $ floating.

4. Consider a one-year currency swap with quarterly payments. The domestic currency is the U.S. dollar, and the foreign currency is the euro. The current exchange rate is $0.86 per euro.

  A. Calculate the annualized fixed rates for dollars and euros. The current U.S. term structure is the same as in Problem 9, Part A:

$$L_0(90) = 0.0656$$
$$L_0(180) = 0.0640$$
$$L_0(270) = 0.0621$$
$$L_0(360) = 0.0599$$

The Euribor term structure is

$$L_0(90) = 0.0682$$
$$L_0(180) = 0.0673$$
$$L_0(270) = 0.0661$$
$$L_0(360) = 0.0668$$

  B. Now move forward 30 days. The new exchange rate is $0.82 per euro, and the new U.S. term structure is the same as in Problem 9, Part B:

$$L_{30}(60) = 0.0384$$
$$L_{30}(150) = 0.0379$$
$$L_{30}(240) = 0.0382$$
$$L_{30}(330) = 0.0406$$

The new Euribor term structure is

$$L_{30}^{€}(60) = 0.0583$$
$$L_{30}^{€}(150) = 0.0605$$
$$L_{30}^{€}(240) = 0.0613$$
$$L_{30}^{€}(330) = 0.0651$$

Assume that the notional principal is \$1 or the corresponding amount in euros. Calculate the market values of the following swaps:

i. Pay € fixed and receive \$ fixed.

ii. Pay € floating and receive \$ fixed.

iii. Pay € floating and receive \$ floating.

iv. Pay € fixed and receive \$ floating.

5. Consider a one-year currency swap with semiannual payments. The two currencies are the U.K. pound and the euro. The current exchange rate is £0.61 per euro.

   A. Calculate the annualized fixed rates for pounds and euros. The current U.K. term structure is

   $$L_0^{€}(180) = 0.0623$$
   $$L_0^{€}(360) = 0.0665$$

   The Euribor term structure is

   $$L_0^{€}(180) = 0.0563$$
   $$L_0^{€}(360) = 0.0580$$

   B. Now move forward 60 days. The new exchange rate is £0.57 per euro, and the new British term structure is

   $$L_{60}^{£}(120) = 0.0585$$
   $$L_{60}^{£}(300) = 0.0605$$

   The new Euribor term structure is

   $$L_{60}^{£}(120) = 0.0493$$
   $$L_{60}^{£}(300) = 0.0505$$

   Assume that the notional principal is £1 or the corresponding amount in euros. Calculate the market values in pounds of the following swaps:

   i. Pay £ fixed and receive € fixed.

   ii. Pay £ floating and receive € fixed.

   iii. Pay £ floating and receive € floating.

   iv. Pay £ fixed and receive € floating.

6. An asset manager wishes to enter into a two-year equity swap in which he will receive the rate of return on the S&P 500 Index in exchange for paying a fixed interest rate. The S&P 500 stock index is at 1150.89 at the beginning of the swap. The swap calls for semiannual payments.

   A. Calculate the annualized fixed rate on the swap. The current term structure of interest rates is as follows:

   $$L_0(180) = 0.0458$$
   $$L_0(360) = 0.0528$$
   $$L_0(540) = 0.0624$$
   $$L_0(720) = 0.0665$$

B. Calculate the market value of the swap 160 days later if the new term structure is

$$L_{160}(20) = 0.0544$$
$$L_{160}(200) = 0.0629$$
$$L_{160}(380) = 0.0679$$
$$L_{160}(560) = 0.0697$$

The S&P 500 is at 1204.10. The notional principal of the swap is $100 million.

7. Assume an asset manager enters into a one-year equity swap in which he will receive the return on the Nasdaq 100 Index in return for paying a floating interest rate. The swap calls for quarterly payments. The Nasdaq 100 is at 1561.27 at the beginning of the swap. Ninety days later, the rate $L_{90}(90)$ is 0.0432. Calculate the market value of the swap 100 days from the beginning of the swap if the Nasdaq 100 is at 1595.72 and the term structure is

$$L_{100}(80) = 0.0427$$
$$L_{100}(170) = 0.0481$$
$$L_{100}(260) = 0.0544$$

The notional principal of the swap is $50 million.

8. Consider an equity swap in which the asset manager receives the return on the Russell 2000 Index in return for paying the return on the DJIA. At the inception of the equity swap, the Russell 2000 is at 478.19 and the DJIA is at 9867.33. Calculate the market value of the swap a few months later when the Russell 2000 is at 524.29 and the DJIA is at 10016. The notional principal of the swap is $15 million.

9. Consider a European receiver swaption that expires in one year and is on a two-year swap that will make semiannual payments. The swaption has an exercise rate of 7 percent. The notional principal is $50 million. At expiration, the term structure of interest rates is as follows:

$$L_0(180) = 0.0420$$
$$L_0(360) = 0.0474$$
$$L_0(540) = 0.0544$$
$$L_0(720) = 0.0661$$

A. List the four possible ways this swaption could be exercised, and indicate the relevant cash flows in each case.

B. Show that the payoff on the swaption is equivalent to that of a call option on a bond with exercise price of $1 (the par value of the bond).

10. Consider a European payer swaption that expires in one year and is on a two-year swap that will make semiannual payments. The swaption has an exercise rate of 5 percent. The notional principal is $10 million. At expiration, the term structure of interest rates is as follows:

$$L_0(180) = 0.0583$$
$$L_0(360) = 0.0605$$
$$L_0(540) = 0.0614$$
$$L_0(720) = 0.0651$$

A. List the four possible ways this swaption could be exercised, and indicate the relevant cash flows in each case.

B. Show that the payoff on the swaption is equivalent to that of a put option on a bond with exercise price of $1 (the par value of the bond).

11. Consider a European receiver swaption that expires in two years and is on a one-year swap that will make quarterly payments. The swaption has an exercise rate of 6.5 percent. The notional principal is $100 million. At expiration, the term structure of interest rates is as follows:

$$L_0(90) = 0.0373$$
$$L_0(180) = 0.0429$$
$$L_0(270) = 0.0477$$
$$L_0(360) = 0.0538$$

   A. Calculate the market value of the swaption at expiration.

   B. Show that the payoff is equivalent to that of a call option on a bond with exercise price of $1 (the par value of the bond).

12. A two-year swap with semiannual payments pays a floating rate and receives a fixed rate. The term structure at the beginning of the swap is

$$L_0(180) = 0.0583$$
$$L_0(360) = 0.0616$$
$$L_0(540) = 0.0680$$
$$L_0(720) = 0.0705$$

In order to mitigate the credit risk of the parties engaged in the swap, the swap will be marked to market in 180 days. Suppose it is now 180 days later and the swap is being marked to market. The new term structure is

$$L_{180}(180) = 0.0429$$
$$L_{180}(360) = 0.0538$$
$$L_{180}(540) = 0.0618$$

   A. Calculate the market value of the swap per $1 notional principal and indicate which party pays which.

   B. Calculate the new fixed rate on the swap at which the swap would proceed after marking to market.

13. A one-year swap with quarterly payments pays a fixed rate and receives a floating rate. The term structure at the beginning of the swap is

$$L_0(90) = 0.0252$$
$$L_0(180) = 0.0305$$
$$L_0(270) = 0.0373$$
$$L_0(360) = 0.0406$$

In order to mitigate the credit risk of the parties engaged in the swap, the swap will be marked to market in 90 days. Suppose it is now 90 days later and the swap is being marked to market. The new term structure is

$$L_{90}(90) = 0.0539$$
$$L_{90}(180) = 0.0608$$
$$L_{90}(270) = 0.0653$$

   A. Calculate the market value of the swap per $1 notional principal and indicate which party pays which.

   B. Calculate the new fixed rate on the swap at which the swap would proceed after marking to market.

Use the following information to answer Questions 14–19

Meredith Gale, an analyst at a money management firm, is preparing for a meeting with clients to discuss using equity options and interest rate swaptions as investment and hedging vehicles. Gale plans to focus on three major issues: (1) the implications of put–call parity for identifying and exploiting arbitrage opportunities, (2) valuing options by using binomial pricing models, and (3) the application and pricing of interest rate swaptions.

Allison Burke, a summer intern, is helping Gale prepare for the meeting. Based on her research on put–call parity and swaption valuation, Burke makes the following statements:

1. "Based on put–call parity, an arbitrage opportunity is indicated when the price of the protective put is greater than the price of the fiduciary call."

2. "Using put–call parity, you can create a long position in a synthetic underlying asset by combining long positions in a call option, a risk-free bond, and a put option."

3. "Using put–call parity, you can also create synthetic options on forward contracts. The data in Exhibit 1 can be used to establish the price of such a synthetic put."

EXHIBIT 1	Market Data for Options on Forward Contracts
Call price	$7.50
Put price	$18.00
Exercise price	$55.00
Days to option expiration	175
Days in year	365
Forward price	$46.00
Annualized risk-free rate	4.00%
Market value of forward contract	$0.00

Burke also examines the valuation of call options with a one-period binomial pricing model. She uses the information in Exhibit 2, which applies to a non-dividend-paying stock whose price could rise by 12 percent or fall by 15 percent over one year. Based on a one-period binomial model, she calculates the price of a call option on this stock to be $7.44 and concludes that an arbitrage opportunity is available.

EXHIBIT 2	Market Data for Option on Non-Dividend-Paying Stock
Annualized risk-free rate	4.00%
Exercise price	$45
Current stock market price	$50
Current call option market price	$7.75

Note: One call is exercisable for one share.

In addition, Gale must address the following situations of two clients:

Client 1 has asked Gale to value the following European-style, interest rate payer swaption:

▶ The payer swaption was entered into one year ago and is maturing today.

▶ The payer swaption is on a two-year swap that will make semi-annual payments.

▶ The payer swaption has an exercise rate of 5.10 percent and a notional principal of $15 million.

▶ Based on the data in Exhibit 3, the annualized fixed payment on the swap underlying the payer swaption is 6.20 percent.

EXHIBIT 3	Term Structure of Interest Rates at Expiration of Swaptions	
Days	**Rate**	**Discount Factor**
180	0.0583	0.9717
360	0.0605	0.9430
540	0.0614	0.9157
720	0.0651	0.8848

Finally, Gale meets with Client 2, who last year purchased an interest rate swap in which he pays fixed and receives floating. Now, Client 2 would like to know the type of interest rate swaption contract to buy in order to have the flexibility to remove interest rate uncertainty from his interest rate swap position.

---

14. To exploit the arbitrage condition described in Burke's statement #1, two of the actions that are necessary, but not sufficient, are

    A. sell the put and sell the underlying asset.

    B. sell the put and sell the appropriate risk-free bond.

    C. buy the call and buy the underlying asset.

    D. buy the call and sell the appropriate risk-free bond.

2006 exam

15. Is Burke's statement #2 correct?

    A. Yes.

    B. No, because the appropriate combination is a long position in a call option, a long position in a risk-free bond, and a short position in a put option.

    C. No, because the appropriate combination is a long position in a put option, a short position in a risk-free bond, and a short position in a call option.

    D. No, because the appropriate combination is a long position in a put option, a long position in a risk-free bond, and a short position in a call option.

2006 exam

16. The price of the synthetic put in statement #3 is closest to

    A. $15.48.

    B. $16.33.

    C. $17.36.

    D. $18.00.

2006 exam

2006 exam

17. Based on Exhibit 2 and Burke's valuation of the call option, an appropriate set of arbitrage transactions is to

   A. sell 1,000 calls and buy 815 shares.

   B. sell 815 calls and buy 1,000 shares.

   C. buy 1,000 calls and sell 815 shares.

   D. buy 815 calls and sell 1,000 shares.

2006 exam

18. Based on the data in Exhibit 3, the market value of the European-style, interest rate payer swaption at expiration is *closest* to

   A. $219,000.

   B. $307,000.

   C. $330,000.

   D. $465,000.

2006 exam

19. To remove Client 2's interest rate uncertainty, Gale is *most likely* to recommend buying a

   A. payer swaption that would allow Client 2 the option to enter into a swap to pay floating and receive fixed.

   B. payer swaption that would allow Client 2 the option to enter into a swap to pay fixed and receive floating.

   C. receiver swaption that would allow Client 2 the option to enter into a swap to receive floating and pay fixed.

   D. receiver swaption that would allow Client 2 the option to enter into a swap to receive fixed and pay floating.

INTEREST RATE DERIVATIVE INSTRUMENTS

by Frank J. Fabozzi

LEARNING OUTCOMES

The candidate should be able to:

a. demonstrate how both a cap and a floor are packages of options on interest rates, and options on fixed income instruments;

b. compute the payoff for a cap and a floor, and explain how a collar is created.

INTRODUCTION   1

OPTIONAL SEGMENT BEGINS

In this reading we turn our attention to financial contracts that are popularly referred to as interest rate derivative instruments because they derive their value from some cash market instrument or reference interest rate. These instruments include futures, forwards, options, swaps, caps, and floors. In this reading we will discuss the basic features of these instruments and in the next we will see how they are valued.

Why would a portfolio manager be motivated to use interest rate derivatives rather than the corresponding cash market instruments? There are three principal reasons for doing this when there is a well-developed interest rate derivatives market for a particular cash market instrument. First, typically it costs less to execute a transaction or a strategy in the interest rate derivatives market in order to alter the interest rate risk exposure of a portfolio than to make the adjustment in the corresponding cash market. Second, portfolio adjustments typically can be accomplished faster in the interest rate derivatives market than in the corresponding cash market. Finally, interest rate derivative may be able to absorb a greater dollar transaction amount without an adverse effect on the price of the derivative

281

instrument compared to the **price effect** on the cash market instrument; that is, the interest rate derivative may be more liquid than the cash market. To summarize: There are three potential advantages that motivate the use of interest rate derivatives: cost, speed, and liquidity.

2 INTEREST RATE FUTURES

A **futures contract** is an agreement that requires a party to the agreement either to buy or sell something at a designated future date at a predetermined price. Futures contracts are products created by exchanges. Futures contracts based on a financial instrument or a financial index are known as **financial futures**. Financial futures can be classified as (1) stock index futures, (2) interest rate futures, and (3) currency futures. Our focus in this reading is on interest rate futures.

A. Mechanics of Futures Trading

A futures contract is an agreement between a buyer (seller) and an established exchange or its clearinghouse in which the buyer (seller) agrees to take (make) delivery of something (the **underlying**) at a specified price at the end of a designated period of time. The price at which the parties agree to transact in the future is called the **futures price**. The designated date at which the parties must transact is called the **settlement date** or delivery date.

1. Liquidating a Position

Most financial futures contracts have settlement dates in the months of March, June, September, and December. This means that at a predetermined time in the contract settlement month the contract stops trading, and a price is determined by the exchange for settlement of the contract. The contract with the closest settlement date is called the nearby futures contract. The next futures contract is the one that settles just after the nearby futures contract. The contract farthest away in time from settlement is called the most distant futures contract.

A party to a futures contract has two choices on liquidation of the position. First, the position can be liquidated prior to the settlement date. For this purpose, the party must take an offsetting position in the same contract. For the buyer of a futures contract, this means selling the same number of the identical futures contracts; for the seller of a futures contract, this means buying the same number of identical futures contracts.

The alternative is to wait until the settlement date. At that time the party purchasing a futures contract accepts delivery of the underlying at the agreed-upon price; the party that sells a futures contract liquidates the position by delivering the underlying at the agreed-upon price. For some interest rate futures contracts, settlement is made in cash only. Such contracts are referred to as cash settlement contracts.

2. The Role of the Clearinghouse

Associated with every futures exchange is a clearinghouse, which performs several functions. One of these functions is to guarantee that the two parties to the transaction will perform.

When an investor takes a position in the futures market, the clearinghouse takes the opposite position and agrees to satisfy the terms set forth in the contract.

Because of the clearinghouse, the investor need not worry about the financial strength and integrity of the party taking the opposite side of the contract. After initial execution of an order, the relationship between the two parties ends. The clearinghouse interposes itself as the buyer for every sale and the seller for every purchase. Thus investors are free to liquidate their positions without involving the other party in the original contract, and without worrying that the other party may default. This is the reason that we define a futures contract as an agreement between a party and a clearinghouse associated with an exchange. Besides its guarantee function, the clearinghouse makes it simple for parties to a futures contract to unwind their positions prior to the settlement date.

3. Margin Requirements

When a position is first taken in a futures contract, the investor must deposit a minimum dollar amount per contract as specified by the exchange. This amount is called **initial margin** and is required as deposit for the contract. The initial margin may be in the form of an interest-bearing security such as a Treasury bill. As the price of the futures contract fluctuates, the value of the margin account changes. Marking to market means effectively replacing the initiation price with a current settlement price. The contract thus has a new settlement price. At the end of each trading day, the exchange determines the current settlement price for the futures contract. This price is used to mark to market the investor's position, so that any gain or loss from the position is reflected in the margin account.[1]

Maintenance margin is the minimum level (specified by the exchange) to which the margin account may fall to as a result of an unfavorable price movement before the investor is required to deposit additional margin. The additional margin deposited is called **variation margin**, and it is an amount necessary to bring the account back to its initial margin level. This amount is determined from the process of marking the position to market. Unlike initial margin, variation margin must be in cash, not interest-bearing instruments. Any excess margin in the account may be withdrawn by the investor. If a party to a futures contract who is required to deposit variation margin fails to do so within 24 hours, the futures position is closed out.

Although there are initial and maintenance margin requirements for buying securities on margin, the concept of margin differs for securities and futures. When securities are acquired on margin, the difference between the price of the security and the initial margin is borrowed from the broker. The security purchased serves as collateral for the loan, and the investor pays interest. For futures contracts, the initial margin, in effect, serves as "good faith" money, an indication that the investor will satisfy the obligation of the contract.

B. Forward Contracts

A **forward contract**, just like a futures contract, is an agreement for the future delivery of something at a specified price at the end of a designated period of time. Futures contracts are standardized agreements as to the delivery date (or month) and quality of the deliverable, and are traded on organized exchanges. A forward contract differs in that it is usually non-standardized (that is, the terms

---

[1] For a further discussion of margin requirements and illustrations of how the margin account changes as the futures price changes, see Don M. Chance, *Analysis of Derivatives for the CFA Program* (Charlottesville, VA: Association for Investment Management and Research, 2003), pp. 86–91.

of each contract are negotiated individually between buyer and seller), there is no clearinghouse, and secondary markets are often non-existent or extremely thin. Unlike a futures contract, which is an exchange-traded product, a forward contract is an over-the-counter instrument.

Futures contracts are marked to market at the end of each trading day. Consequently, futures contracts are subject to interim cash flows as additional margin may be required in the case of adverse price movements, or as cash is withdrawn in the case of favorable price movements. A forward contract *may* or *may not be marked to market*, depending on the wishes of the two parties. For a forward contract that is *not* marked to market, there are no interim cash flow effects because no additional margin is required.

Finally, the parties in a forward contract are exposed to credit risk because either party may default on its obligation. This risk is called counterparty risk. This risk is minimal in the case of futures contracts because the clearinghouse associated with the exchange guarantees the other side of the transaction. In the case of a forward contract, both parties face counterparty risk. Thus, there exists bilateral counterparty risk.

Other than these differences, most of what we say about futures contracts applies equally to forward contracts.

C. Risk and Return Characteristics of Futures Contracts

When an investor takes a position in the market by buying a futures contract, the investor is said to be in a **long position** or to be long futures. The buyer of the futures contract is also referred to as the "long." If, instead, the investor's opening position is the sale of a futures contract, the investor is said to be in a **short position** or to be short futures. The seller of the futures contract is also referred to as the "short." The buyer of a futures contract will realize a profit if the futures price increases; the seller of a futures contract will realize a profit if the futures price decreases.

When a position is taken in a futures contract, the party need not put up the entire amount of the investment. Instead, only initial margin must be put up. Consequently, an investor can effectively create a leveraged position by using futures. At first, the leverage available in the futures market may suggest that the market benefits only those who want to speculate on price movements. This is not true. As we shall see in Level III, futures markets can be used to control interest rate risk. Without the effective leverage possible in futures transactions, the cost of reducing price risk using futures would be too high for many market participants.

D. Exchange-Traded Interest Rate Futures Contracts

Interest rate futures contracts can be classified by the maturity of their underlying security. Short-term interest rate futures contracts have an underlying security that matures in less than one year. Examples of these are futures contracts in which the underlying is a 3-month Treasury bill and a 3-month Eurodollar **certificate of deposit**. The maturity of the underlying security of long-term futures contracts exceeds one year. Examples of these are futures contracts in which the underlying is a Treasury coupon security, a 10-year agency note, and a municipal bond index. Our focus will be on futures contracts in which the underlying is a Treasury coupon security (a Treasury bond or a Treasury note). These contracts are the most widely used by managers of bond portfolios and we begin with the specifications of the Treasury bond futures contract. We will also discuss the agency note futures contracts.

There are futures contracts on non-U.S. government securities traded throughout the world. Many of them are modeled after the U.S. Treasury futures contracts and consequently, the concepts discussed below apply directly to those futures contracts.

1. Treasury Bond Futures

The Treasury bond futures contract is traded on the Chicago Board of Trade (CBOT). The underlying instrument for a Treasury bond futures contract is $100,000 par value of a hypothetical 20-year coupon bond. The coupon rate on the hypothetical bond is called the **notional coupon**.

The futures price is quoted in terms of par being 100. Quotes are in 32nds of 1%. Thus a quote for a Treasury bond futures contract of 97-16 means 97 and $\frac{16}{32}$ or 97.50. So, if a buyer and seller agree on a futures price of 97-16, this means that the buyer agrees to accept delivery of the hypothetical underlying Treasury bond and pay 97.50% of par value and the seller agrees to accept 97.50% of par value. Since the par value is $100,000, the futures price that the buyer and seller agree to for this hypothetical Treasury bond is $97,500.

The minimum price fluctuation for the Treasury bond futures contract is $\frac{1}{32}$ of 1%, which is referred to as "a 32nd." The dollar value of a 32nd for $100,000 par value (the par value for the underlying Treasury bond) is $31.25. Thus, the minimum price fluctuation is $31.25 for this contract.

We have been referring to the underlying as a hypothetical Treasury bond. The seller of a Treasury bond futures contract who decides to make delivery rather than liquidate the position by buying back the contract prior to the settlement date must deliver some Treasury bond issue. But what Treasury bond issue? The CBOT allows the seller to deliver one of several Treasury bonds that the CBOT designates as acceptable for delivery. The specific issues that the seller may deliver are published by the CBOT for all contracts by settlement date. The CBOT makes its determination of the Treasury bond issues that are acceptable for delivery from all outstanding Treasury bond issues that have at least 15 years to maturity from the date of delivery.

Exhibit 1 shows the Treasury bond issues that the seller could have selected to deliver to the buyer of the CBOT Treasury bond futures contract as of May 29, 2002. Should the U.S. Department of the Treasury issue any Treasury bonds that meet the CBOT criteria for eligible delivery, those issues would be added to the list. Notice that for the Treasury bond futures contract settling (i.e., maturing) in March 2005, notice that there are 25 eligible issues. For contracts settling after March 2005, there are fewer than 25 eligible issues due to the shorter maturity of each previous eligible issue that results in a maturity of less than 15 years.

Although the underlying Treasury bond for this contract is a hypothetical issue and therefore cannot itself be delivered into the futures contract, the contract is not a cash settlement contract. The only way to close out a Treasury bond futures contract is to either initiate an offsetting futures position, or to deliver a Treasury bond issue satisfying the above-mentioned criteria into the futures contract.

a. Conversion Factors   The delivery process for the Treasury bond futures contract makes the contract interesting. At the settlement date, the seller of a futures contract (the short) is now required to deliver to the buyer (the long) $100,000 par value of a 6% 20-year Treasury bond. Since no such bond exists, the seller

EXHIBIT 1	U.S. Treasury Bond Issues Acceptable for Delivery and Conversion Factors

Eligible for Delivery as of May 29, 2002.

		Conversion Factors									
Issue		Mar. 2005	Jun. 2005	Sep. 2005	Dec. 2005	Mar. 2006	Jun. 2006	Sep. 2006	Dec. 2006	Mar. 2007	Jun. 2007
5¼	11/15/28	0.9062	0.9065	0.9071	0.9075	0.9081	0.9084	0.9090	0.9095	0.9101	0.9105
5¼	02/15/29	0.9056	0.9062	0.9065	0.9071	0.9075	0.9081	0.9084	0.9090	0.9095	0.9101
5⅜	02/15/31	0.9185	0.9189	0.9191	0.9196	0.9198	0.9203	0.9206	0.9210	0.9213	0.9218
5	08/15/28	0.9376	0.9381	0.9383	0.9387	0.9389	0.9394	0.9396	0.9400	0.9403	0.9407
6	02/15/26	0.9999	1.0000	0.9999	1.0000	0.9999	1.0000	0.9999	1.0000	0.9999	1.0000
6⅛	11/15/27	1.0153	1.0151	1.0152	1.0150	1.0150	1.0148	1.0148	1.0146	1.0146	1.0144
6⅛	08/15/29	1.0158	1.0158	1.0156	1.0156	1.0154	1.0155	1.0153	1.0153	1.0151	1.0152
6¼	08/15/23	1.0274	1.0273	1.0270	1.0269	1.0265	1.0264	1.0261	1.0260	1.0256	1.0255
6¼	05/15/30	1.0322	1.0319	1.0319	1.0316	1.0316	1.0313	1.0313	1.0310	1.0310	1.0307
6⅜	08/15/27	1.0456	1.0455	1.0451	1.0450	1.0446	1.0444	1.0441	1.0439	1.0435	1.0433
6	11/15/26	1.0600	1.0595	1.0593	1.0588	1.0585	1.0580	1.0578	1.0573	1.0570	1.0565
6⅜	02/15/27	1.0752	1.0749	1.0744	1.0741	1.0735	1.0732	1.0726	1.0722	1.0716	1.0713
6¾	08/15/26	1.0893	1.0889	1.0882	1.0878	1.0871	1.0867	1.0860	1.0855	1.0848	1.0843
6⅞	08/15/25	1.1017	1.1011	1.1003	1.0998	1.0990	1.0984	1.0976	1.0970	1.0961	1.0955
7⅛	02/15/23	1.1217	1.1209	1.1197	1.1189	1.1177	1.1168	1.1156	1.1147	1.1135	1.1125
7¼	08/15/22	1.1331	1.1321	1.1308	1.1298	1.1285	1.1274	1.1261	1.1250	1.1236	1.1225
7	11/15/24	1.1711	1.1697	1.1687	1.1673	1.1663	1.1649	1.1637	1.1623	1.1612	1.1597
7⅜	11/15/22	1.1746	1.1730	1.1717	1.1701	1.1687	1.1671	1.1657	1.1640	1.1625	1.1607
7⅝	02/15/25	1.1864	1.1853	1.1839	1.1828	1.1813	1.1801	1.1786	1.1774	1.1759	1.1746
7⅞	02/15/21	1.1892	1.1875	1.1855	1.1838	—	—	—	—	—	—
8	11/15/21	1.2077	1.2056	1.2039	1.2018	1.2000	1.1979	1.1960	—	—	—
8⅛	05/15/21	1.2166	1.2144	1.2125	1.2102	1.2083	—	—	—	—	—
8⅛	08/15/21	1.2185	1.2166	1.2144	1.2125	1.2102	1.2083	—	—	—	—
8¾	05/15/20	1.2695	—	—	—	—	—	—	—	—	—
8¾	08/15/20	1.2721	1.2695	—	—	—	—	—	—	—	—
No. of Eligible issues		25	24	23	23	22	21	20	19	19	19

Source: Chicago Board of Trade.

must choose from one of the acceptable deliverable Treasury bonds that the CBOT has specified. Suppose the seller is entitled to deliver $100,000 of a 5% 20-year Treasury bond to settle the futures contract. The value of this bond is less than the value of a 6% 20-year bond. If the seller delivers the 5% 20-year bond, this would be unfair to the buyer of the futures contract who contracted to receive $100,000 of a 6% 20-year Treasury bond. Alternatively, suppose the seller delivers $100,000 of a 7% 20-year Treasury bond. The value of a 7% 20-year Treasury bond is greater than that of a 6% 20-year bond, so this would be a disadvantage to the seller.

How can this problem be resolved? To make delivery equitable to both parties, the CBOT has introduced **conversion factors** for adjusting the price of each Treasury issue that can be delivered to satisfy the Treasury bond futures contract. The conversion factor is determined by the CBOT before a contract with a specific settlement date begins trading.[2] The adjusted price is found by multiplying the conversion factor by the futures price. The adjusted price is called the converted price.

Exhibit 1 shows conversion factors as of May 29, 2002. The conversion factors are shown by contract settlement date. Note that the conversion factor depends not only on the issue delivered but also on the settlement date of the contract. For example, look at the first issue in Exhibit 1, the 5¼% coupon bond maturing 11/15/28. For the Treasury bond futures contract settling (i.e., maturing) in March 2005, the conversion factor is 0.9062. For the December 2005 contract, the conversion factor is 0.9075.

The price that the buyer must pay the seller when a Treasury bond is delivered is called the invoice price. The invoice price is the futures settlement price plus accrued interest. However, as just noted, the seller can deliver one of several acceptable Treasury issues and to make delivery fair to both parties, the invoice price must be adjusted based on the actual Treasury issue delivered. It is the conversion factors that are used to adjust the invoice price. The invoice price is:

invoice price = contract size × futures settlement price × conversion factor + accrued interest

Suppose the Treasury March 2006 futures contract settles at 105-16 and that the issue delivered is the 8% of 11/15/21. The futures contract settlement price of 105-16 means 105.5% of par value or 1.055 times par value. As indicated in Exhibit 1, the conversion factor for this issue for the March 2006 contract is 1.2000. Since the contract size is $100,000, the invoice price the buyer pays the seller is:

$100,000 × 1.055 × 1.2000 + accrued interest = $126,600 + accrued interest

b. Cheapest-to-Deliver Issue   As can be seen in Exhibit 1, there can be more than one issue that is permitted to be delivered to satisfy a futures contract. In fact, for the March 2005 contract, there are 25 deliverable or eligible bond issues. It is the short that has the option of selecting which one of the deliverable bond issues if he decides to deliver.[3] The decision of which one of the

---

PRACTICE QUESTION 1

Suppose that the June 200X Treasury bond futures contract settles at 97-24 and the issue delivered has a conversion factor of 1.17. Assume that the accrued interest for the issue delivered is $3,800 per $100,000 par value. What is the invoice price the buyer pays the seller?

---

[2] The conversion factor is based on the price that a deliverable bond would sell for at the beginning of the delivery month if it were to yield 6%.

[3] Remember that the short can always unwind his position by buying the same futures contract before the settlement date.

bond issues a short will elect to deliver is *not* made arbitrarily. There is an economic analysis that a short will undertake in order to determine the best bond issue to deliver. In fact, as we will see, all of the elements that go into the economic analysis will be the same for all participants in the market who are either electing to deliver or who are anticipating delivery of one of the eligible bond issues. In this section, how the best bond issue to deliver is determined will be explained.

The economic analysis is not complicated. The basic principle is as follows. Suppose that an investor enters into the following two transactions *simultaneously*:

1. buys one of the deliverable bond issues today with borrowed money and

2. sells a futures contract

The two positions (i.e., the long position in the deliverable bond issue purchased and the short position in the futures contract) will be held to the delivery date. At the delivery date, the bond issue purchased will be used to satisfy the short's obligation to deliver an eligible bond issue. The simultaneous transactions above and the delivery of the acceptable bond issue purchased to satisfy the short position in the futures contract is called a **cash and carry** trade.

Let's look at the economics of this cash and carry trade. The investor (who by virtue of the fact that he sold a futures contract is the short), has synthetically created a short-term investment vehicle. The reason is that the investor has purchased a bond issue (one of the deliverable bond issues) and at the delivery date delivers that bond issue and receives the futures price. So, the investor knows the cost of buying the bond issue and knows how much will be received from the investment. The amount received is the coupon interest until the delivery date, any reinvestment income from reinvesting coupon payments, and the futures price at the delivery date. (Remember that the futures price at the delivery date for a given deliverable bond issue will be its converted price.) Thus, the investor can calculate the rate of return that will be earned on the investment. In the futures market, this rate of return is called the **implied repo rate**.

An implied repo rate can be calculated for *every* deliverable bond issue. For example, suppose that there are N deliverable bond issues that can be delivered to satisfy a bond futures contract. Market participants who want to know either the best issue to deliver or what issue is likely to be delivered will calculate an implied repo rate for all N eligible bond issues. Which would be the best issue to deliver by a short? Since the implied repo rate is the rate of return on an investment, the best bond issue is the one that has the *highest* implied repo rate (i.e., the highest rate of return). The bond issue with the highest implied repo rate is called the **cheapest-to-deliver** issue.

Now that we understand the economic principle for determining the best bond issue to deliver (i.e., the cheapest-to-deliver issue), let's look more closely at how one calculates the implied repo rate for each deliverable bond issue. This rate is computed using the following information for a given deliverable bond issue:

1. the price plus accrued interest at which the Treasury issue could be purchased

2. the converted price plus the accrued interest that will be received upon delivery of that Treasury bond issue to satisfy the short futures position

3. the coupon payments that will be received between today and the date the issue is delivered to satisfy the futures contract.

4. the reinvestment income that will be realized on the coupon payments between the time the interim coupon payment is received and the date that the issue is delivered to satisfy the Treasury bond futures contract.

The first three elements are known. The last element will depend on the reinvestment rate that can be earned. While the reinvestment rate is unknown, typically this is a small part of the rate of return and not much is lost by assuming that the implied repo rate can be predicted with certainty.

The general formula for the implied repo rate is as follows:

$$\text{implied repo rate} = \frac{\text{dollar return}}{\text{cost of the investment}} \times \frac{360}{\text{days}_1}$$

where days_1 is equal to the number of days until settlement of the futures contract. Below we will explain the other components in the formula for the implied repo rate.

Let's begin with the dollar return. The dollar return for an issue is the difference between the proceeds received and the cost of the investment. The proceeds received are equal to the proceeds received at the settlement date of the futures contract and any interim coupon payment plus interest from reinvesting the interim coupon payment. The proceeds received at the settlement date include the converted price (i.e., futures settlement price multiplied by the conversion factor for the issue) and the accrued interest received from delivery of the issue. That is,

$$\begin{aligned}
\text{proceeds received} = {} &\text{converted price} + \text{accrued interest received} \\
&+ \text{interim coupon payment} + \text{interest from reinvesting} \\
&\text{the interim coupon payment}
\end{aligned}$$

As noted earlier, all of the elements are known except the interest from reinvesting the interim coupon payment. This amount is estimated by assuming that the coupon payment can be reinvested at the term repo rate. At Level III we describe the repo market and the term repo rate. The term **repo** rate is not only a borrowing rate for an investor who wants to borrow in the repo market but also the rate at which an investor can invest proceeds on a short-term basis. For how long is the reinvestment of the interim coupon payment? It is the number of days from when the interim coupon payment is received and the actual delivery date to satisfy the futures contract. The reinvestment income is then computed as follows:

$$\begin{aligned}
\text{interest from reinvesting the interim coupon payment} = {} &\text{interim coupon} \\
\times \text{term repo rate} \times (\text{days}_2/360)
\end{aligned}$$

where

days_2 = number of days between when the interim coupon payment is received and the actual delivery date of the futures contract

The reason for dividing days_2 by 360 is that the ratio represents the number of days the interim coupon is reinvested as a percentage of the number of days in a year as measured in the money market.

The cost of the investment is the amount paid to purchase the issue. This cost is equal to the purchase price plus accrued interest paid. That is,

$$\text{cost of the investment} = \text{purchase price} + \text{accrued interest paid}$$

Thus, the dollar return for the numerator of the formula for the implied repo rate is equal to

dollar return = proceeds received − cost of the investment

The dollar return is then divided by the cost of the investment.[4]

So, now we know how to compute the numerator and the denominator in the formula for the implied repo rate. The second ratio in the formula for the implied repo rate simply involves annualizing the return using a convention in the money market for the number of days. (Recall that in the money market the convention is to use a 360 day year.) Since the investment resulting from the cash and carry trade is a synthetic money market instrument, 360 days are used.

Let's compute the implied repo rate for a hypothetical issue that may be delivered to satisfy a hypothetical Treasury bond futures contract. Assume the following for the deliverable issue and the futures contract:

Futures contract

    futures price = 96

    days to futures delivery date ($days_1$) = 82 days

Deliverable issue

    price of issue = 107

    accrued interest paid = 3.8904

    coupon rate = 10%

    days remaining before interim coupon paid = 40 days

    interim coupon = $5

    number of days between when the interim coupon payment is received
       and the actual delivery date of the futures contract ($days_2$) = 42

    conversion factor = 1.1111

    accrued interest received at futures settlement date = 1.1507

Other information:

    42-day term repo rate = 3.8%

Let's begin with the proceeds received. We need to compute the converted price and the interest from reinvesting the interim coupon payment. The converted price is:

$$\text{converted price} = \text{futures price} \times \text{conversion factor}$$
$$= 96 \times 1.1111 = 106.6656$$

The interest from reinvesting the interim coupon payment depends on the term repo rate. The term repo rate is assumed to be 3.8%. Therefore,

$$\text{interest from reinvesting the interim coupon payment} = \$5 \times 0.038$$
$$\times \left(\frac{42}{360}\right)$$
$$= 0.0222$$

---

[4] Actually, the cost of the investment should be adjusted because the amount that the investor ties up in the investment is reduced if there is an interim coupon payment. We will ignore this adjustment here.

To summarize:

converted price	= 106.6656
accrued interest received at futures settlement date	= 1.1507
interim coupon payment	= 5.0000
interest from reinvesting the interim coupon payment	= 0.0222
proceeds received	= 112.8385

The cost of the investment is the purchase price for the issue plus the accrued interest paid, as shown below:

$$\text{cost of the investment} = 107 + 3.8904 = 110.8904$$

The implied repo rate is then:

$$\text{implied repo rate} = \frac{112.8385 - 110.8904}{110.8904} \times \frac{360}{82} = 0.0771 = 7.71\%$$

Once the implied repo rate is calculated for each deliverable issue, the cheapest-to-deliver issue will be the one that has the highest implied repo rate (i.e., the issue that gives the maximum return in a cash-and-carry trade). As explained in the next reading, this issue plays a key role in the pricing of a Treasury bond futures contract.

While an eligible bond issue may be the cheapest to deliver today, changes in factors may cause some other eligible bond issue to be the cheapest to deliver at a future date. A sensitivity analysis can be performed to determine how a change in yield affects the cheapest to deliver.

PRACTICE QUESTION 2

Calculate the implied repo rate for a hypothetical issue that is deliverable for a Treasury bond futures contract assuming the following for the deliverable issue and the futures contract:

Futures contract
Futures price = 97
days to futures delivery date (days$_1$) = 62 days

Deliverable issue
price of issue = 95
accrued interest paid = 3.0110
coupon rate = 7%
days remaining before interim coupon made = 25 days
interim coupon = $3.50
number of days between when the interim coupon payment is received and the actual delivery date of the futures contract (day$_2$) = 37 days
conversion factor = 0.9710
accrued interest received at futures settlement date = 0.7096

Other information:
37-day repo rate = 4.7%

c. Other Delivery Options   In addition to the choice of which acceptable Treasury issue to deliver—sometimes referred to as the quality option or swap option—the short has at least two more options granted under CBOT delivery guidelines. The short is permitted to decide when in the delivery month delivery actually will take place. This is called the timing option. The other option is the right of the short to give notice of intent to deliver up to 8:00 p.m. Chicago time after the closing of the exchange (3:15 p.m. Chicago time) on the date when the futures settlement price has been fixed. This option is referred to as the wild card option. The quality option, the timing option, and the wild card option (in sum referred to as the **delivery options**), mean that the long position can never be sure which Treasury bond will be delivered or when it will be delivered. These three delivery options are summarized in Exhibit 2.

d. Delivery Procedure   For a short who wants to deliver, the delivery procedure involves three days. The first day is the position day. On this day, the short notifies the CBOT that it intends to deliver. The short has until 8:00 p.m. central standard time to do so. The second day is the notice day. On this day, the short specifies which particular issue will be delivered. The short has until 2:00 p.m. central standard time to make this declaration. (On the last possible notice day in the delivery month, the short has until 3:00 p.m.) The CBOT then selects the long to whom delivery will be made. This is the long position that has been outstanding for the greatest period of time. The long is then notified by 4:00 p.m. that delivery will be made. The third day is the delivery day. By 10:00 a.m. on this day the short must have in its account the Treasury issue that it specified on the notice day and by 1:00 p.m. must deliver that bond to the long that was assigned by the CBOT to accept delivery. The long pays the short the invoice price upon receipt of the bond.

2. Treasury Note Futures

The three Treasury note futures contracts are 10-year, 5-year, and 2-year note contracts. All three contracts are modeled after the Treasury bond futures contract and are traded on the CBOT.

The underlying instrument for the 10-year Treasury note futures contract is $100,000 par value of a hypothetical 10-year, 6% Treasury note. Several acceptable Treasury issues may be delivered by the short. An issue is acceptable if the maturity is not less than 6.5 years and not greater than 10 years from the first day of the delivery month. Delivery options are granted to the short position.

EXHIBIT 2	Delivery Options Granted to the Short (Seller) of a CBOT Treasury Bond Futures Contract
Delivery Option	**Description**
Quality or swap option	Choice of which acceptable Treasury issue to deliver
Timing option	Choice of when in delivery month to deliver
Wild card option	Choice to deliver after the closing price of the futures contract is determined

For the 5-year Treasury note futures contract, the underlying is $100,000 par value of a 6% notional coupon U.S. Treasury note that satisfies the following conditions: (1) an original maturity of not more than 5 years and 3 months, (2) a remaining maturity no greater than 5 years and 3 months, and (3) a remaining maturity not less than 4 years and 2 months.

The underlying for the 2-year Treasury note futures contract is $200,000 par value of a 6% notional coupon U.S. Treasury note with a remaining maturity of not more than 2 years and not less than 1 year and 9 months. Moreover, the original maturity of the note delivered to satisfy the 2-year futures cannot be more than 5 years and 3 months.

3. Agency Note Futures Contract

In 2000, the CBOT and the Chicago Mercantile Exchange (CME) began trading in futures contracts in which the underlying is a Fannie Mae or Freddie Mac agency debenture security. (Agency debentures are explained at Level I.) The underlying for the CBOT 10-year agency note futures contract is a Fannie Mae benchmark note or Freddie Mac reference note having a par value of $100,000 and a notional coupon of 6%. The 10-year agency note futures contract of the CME is similar to that of the CBOT, but has a notional coupon of 6.5% instead of 6%.

As with the Treasury futures contract, more than one issue is deliverable for both the CBOT and CME agency note futures contract. The contract delivery months are March, June, September, and December. As with the Treasury futures contract a conversion factor applies to each eligible issue for each contract settlement date. Because many issues are deliverable, one issue is the cheapest-to-deliver issue. This issue is found in exactly the same way as with the Treasury futures contract.

INTEREST RATE OPTIONS   **3**

An **option** is a contract in which the writer of the option grants the buyer of the option the right, but not the obligation, to purchase from or sell to the writer something at a specified price within a specified period of time (or at a specified date). The writer, also referred to as the seller, grants this right to the buyer in exchange for a certain sum of money, called the **option price** or **option premium**. The price at which the underlying for the contract may be bought or sold is called the **exercise price** or **strike price**. The date after which an option is void is called the **expiration date**. Our focus is on options where the "something" underlying the option is an interest rate instrument or an interest rate.

When an option grants the buyer the right to purchase the designated instrument from the writer (seller), it is referred to as a **call option**, or **call**. When the option buyer has the right to sell the designated instrument to the writer, the option is called a **put option**, or **put**.

An option is also categorized according to when the option buyer may exercise the option. There are options that may be exercised at any time up to and including the expiration date. Such an option is referred to as an **American option**. There are options that may be exercised only at the expiration date. An option with this feature is called a **European option**. An option that can be exercised prior to maturity but only on designated dates is called a modified American, Bermuda, or Atlantic option.

A. Risk and Return Characteristics of Options

The maximum amount that an option buyer can lose is the option price. The maximum profit that the option writer can realize is the option price at the time of sale. The option buyer has substantial upside return potential, while the option writer has substantial downside risk.

It is assumed in this reading that the reader has an understanding of the basic positions that can be created with options. These positions include:

1. long call position (buying a call option)

2. short call position (selling a call option)

3. long put position (buying a put option)

4. short put position (selling a put option)

Exhibit 3 shows the payoff profile for these four option positions *assuming that each option position is held to the expiration date and not exercised early.*

B. Differences between Options and Futures Contracts

Unlike a futures contract, one party to an option contract is not obligated to transact. Specifically, the option buyer has the right, but not the obligation, to transact. The option writer does have the obligation to perform. In the case of a futures contract, both buyer and seller are obligated to perform. Of course, a futures buyer does not pay the seller to accept the obligation, while an option buyer pays the option seller an option price.

Consequently, the risk/reward characteristics of the two contracts are also different. In the case of a futures contract, the buyer of the contract realizes a dollar-for-dollar gain when the price of the futures contract increases and suffers a dollar-for-dollar loss when the price of the futures contract drops. The opposite occurs for the seller of a futures contract. Options do not provide this symmetric risk/reward relationship. The most that the buyer of an option can lose is the

EXHIBIT 3	Payoff of Basic Option Positions if Held to Expiration Date

A. Long Call Position

(Exhibit continued on next page ...)

EXHIBIT 3   **(continued)**

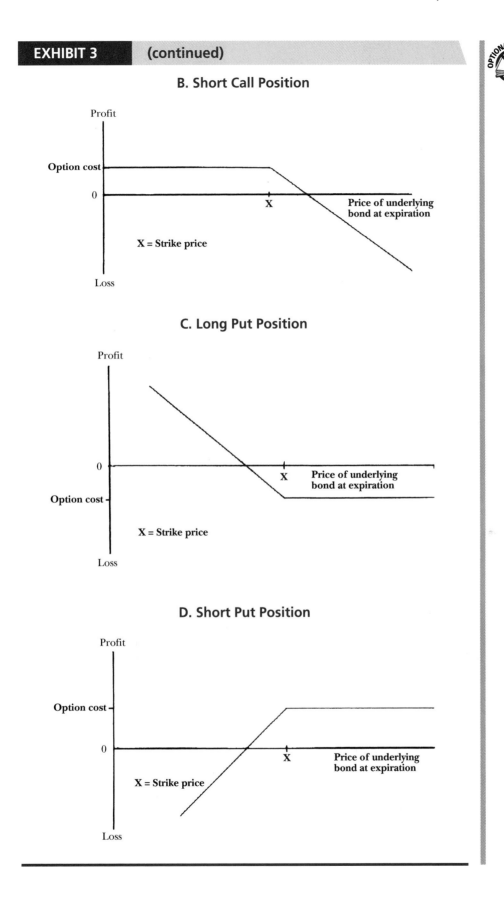

B. Short Call Position

X = Strike price

C. Long Put Position

X = Strike price

D. Short Put Position

X = Strike price

option price. While the buyer of an option retains all the potential benefits, the gain is always reduced by the amount of the option price. The maximum profit that the writer may realize is the option price; this is compensation for accepting substantial downside risk.

Both parties to a futures contract are required to post margin. There are no margin requirements for the buyer of an option once the option price has been paid in full. Because the option price is the maximum amount that the investor can lose, no matter how adverse the price movement of the underlying, there is no need for margin. Because the writer of an option has agreed to accept all of the risk (and none of the reward) of the position in the underlying, the writer is generally required to put up the option price received as margin. In addition, as price changes occur that adversely affect the writer's position, the writer is required to deposit additional margin (with some exceptions) as the position is marked to market.

C. Exchange-Traded versus OTC Options

Options, like other financial instruments, may be traded either on an organized exchange or in the over-the-counter (OTC) market. An exchange that wants to create an options contract must obtain approval from regulators. Exchange-traded options have three advantages. First, the strike price and expiration date of the contract are standardized.[5] Second, as in the case of futures contracts, the direct link between buyer and seller is severed after the order is executed because of the interchangeability of exchange-traded options. The clearinghouse performs the same guarantor function in the options market that it does in the futures market. Finally, transaction costs are lower for exchange-traded options than for OTC options.

The higher cost of an OTC option reflects the cost of customizing the option for the many situations where an institutional investor needs to have a tailor-made option because the standardized exchange-traded option does not satisfy its investment objectives. Investment banking firms and commercial banks act as principals as well as brokers in the OTC options market. While an OTC option is less liquid than an exchange-traded option, this is typically not of concern to an institutional investor—most institutional investors use OTC options as part of an asset/liability strategy and intend to hold them to expiration.

Exchange-traded interest rate options can be written on a fixed income security or an interest rate futures contract. The former options are called *options on physicals*. For reasons to be explained later, options on interest rate futures are more popular than options on physicals. However, portfolio managers have made increasingly greater use of OTC options.

1. Exchange-Traded Futures Options

There are futures options on all the interest rate futures contracts mentioned earlier in this reading. An option on a futures contract, commonly referred to as a **futures option**, gives the buyer the right to buy from or sell to the writer a designated futures contract at the strike price at any time during the life of the option. If the futures option is a call option, the buyer has the right to purchase

---

[5] Exchanges have developed put and call options issued by their clearinghouse that are customized with respect to expiration date, exercise style, and strike price. These options are called *flexible exchange options* and are nicknamed "Flex" options.

one designated futures contract at the strike price. That is, the buyer has the right to acquire a long futures position in the underlying futures contract. If the buyer exercises the call option, the writer acquires a corresponding short position in the same futures contract.

A put option on a futures contract grants the buyer the right to sell one designated futures contract to the writer at the strike price. That is, the option buyer has the right to acquire a short position in the designated futures contract. If the put option is exercised, the writer acquires a corresponding long position in the designated futures contract.

As the parties to the futures option will realize a position in a futures contract when the option is exercised, the question is: what will the futures price be? What futures price will the long be required to pay for the futures contract, and at what futures price will the short be required to sell the futures contract?

Upon exercise, the futures price for the futures contract will be set equal to the strike price. The position of the two parties is then immediately marked-to-market in terms of the then-current futures price. Thus, the futures position of the two parties will be at the prevailing futures price. At the same time, the option buyer will receive from the option seller the economic benefit from exercising. In the case of a call futures option, the option writer must pay the difference between the current futures price and the strike price to the buyer of the option. In the case of a put futures option, the option writer must pay the option buyer the difference between the strike price and the current futures price.

For example, suppose an investor buys a call option on some futures contract in which the strike price is 85. Assume also that the futures price is 95 and that the buyer exercises the call option. Upon exercise, the call buyer is given a long position in the futures contract at 85 and the call writer is assigned the corresponding short position in the futures contract at 85. The futures positions of the buyer and the writer are immediately marked-to-market by the exchange. Because the prevailing futures price is 95 and the strike price is 85, the long futures position (the position of the call buyer) realizes a gain of 10, while the short futures position (the position of the call writer) realizes a loss of 10. The call writer pays the exchange 10 and the call buyer receives from the exchange 10. The call buyer, who now has a long futures position at 95, can either liquidate the futures position at 95 or maintain a long futures position. If the former course of action is taken, the call buyer sells his futures contract at the prevailing futures price of 95. There is no gain or loss from liquidating the position. Overall, the call buyer realizes a gain of 10 (less the option purchase price). The call buyer who elects to hold the long futures position will face the same risk and reward of holding such a position, but still realizes a gain of 10 from the exercise of the call option.

Suppose instead that the futures option with a strike price of 85 is a put rather than a call, and the current futures price is 60 rather than 95. Then, if the buyer of this put option exercises it, the buyer would have a short position in the futures contract at 85; the option writer would have a long position in the futures contract at 85. The exchange then marks the position to market at the then-current futures price of 60, resulting in a gain to the put buyer of 25 and a loss to the put writer of the same amount. The put buyer now has a short futures position at 60 and can either liquidate the short futures position by buying a futures contract at the prevailing futures price of 60 or maintain the short futures position. In either case the put buyer realizes a gain of 25 (less the option purchase price) from exercising the put option.

There are no margin requirements for the buyer of a futures option once the option price has been paid in full. Because the option price is the maximum amount that the buyer can lose regardless of how adverse the price movement of the underlying instrument, there is no need for margin. Because the writer (seller) of a futures option has agreed to accept all of the risk (and none of the reward) of the position in the underlying instrument, the writer (seller) is required to deposit not only the margin required on the interest rate futures contract position but also (with certain exceptions) the option price that is received from writing the option.

The price of a futures option is quoted in 64ths of 1% of par value. For example, a price of 24 means $24/64$ of 1% of par value. Since the par value of a Treasury bond futures contract is $100,000, an option price of 24 means: $[(24/64)/100] \times \$100,000 = \$375$. In general, the price of a futures option quoted at Q is equal to:

$$\text{Option price} = \left[\frac{Q/64}{100} \right] \times \$100,000$$

There are three reasons that futures options have largely supplanted options on fixed income securities as the options vehicle of choice for institutional investors who want to use exchange-traded options. First, unlike options on fixed income securities, options on Treasury coupon futures do not require payments for accrued interest to be made. Consequently, when a futures option is exercised, the call buyer and the put writer need not compensate the other party for accrued interest. Second, futures options are believed to be "cleaner" instruments because of the reduced likelihood of delivery squeezes. Market participants who must deliver an instrument are concerned that at the time of delivery the instrument to be delivered will be in short supply, resulting in a higher price to acquire the instrument. As the deliverable supply of futures contracts is infinite for futures options currently traded, there is no concern about a delivery squeeze. Finally, in order to price any option, it is imperative to know at all times the price of the underlying instrument. In the bond market, current prices are not as easily available as price information on the futures contract. The reason is that as bonds trade in the OTC market there is no single reporting system with recent price information. Thus, an investor who wanted to purchase an option on a Treasury bond would have to call several dealer firms to obtain a price. In contrast, futures contracts are traded on an exchange and, as a result, price information is reported.

2. Over-the-Counter Options

Institutional investors who want to purchase an option on a specific Treasury security or a Ginnie Mae passthrough security can do so on an over-the-counter basis. There are government and mortgage-backed securities dealers who make a

---

PRACTICE QUESTION 3

A. Suppose an investor purchases a call option on a Treasury bond futures contract with a strike price of 98. Also assume that at the expiration date the price of the Treasury bond futures contract is 103. Will the investor exercise the call option and, if so, what will the investor and the writer of the call option receive?

B. Suppose an investor purchases a put option on a Treasury bond futures contract with a strike price of 105. Also assume that at the expiration date the price of the Treasury bond futures contract is 96. Will the investor exercise the put option and, if so, what will the investor and the writer of the put option receive?

market in options on specific securities. OTC options, also called dealer options, usually are purchased by institutional investors who want to hedge the risk associated with a specific security. For example, a thrift may be interested in hedging its position in a specific mortgage passthrough security. Typically, the maturity of the option coincides with the time period over which the buyer of the option wants to hedge, so the buyer is not concerned with the option's liquidity.

In the absence of a clearinghouse the parties to any over-the-counter contract are exposed to counterparty risk.[6] In the case of forward contracts where both parties are obligated to perform, both parties face counterparty risk. In contrast, in the case of an option, once the option buyer pays the option price, it has satisfied its obligation. It is only the seller that must perform if the option is exercised. Thus, the option buyer is exposed to counterparty risk—the risk that the option seller will fail to perform.

OTC options can be customized in any manner sought by an institutional investor. Basically, if a dealer can reasonably hedge the risk associated with the opposite side of the option sought, it will create the option desired by a customer. OTC options are not limited to European or American type. Dealers also create modified American (Bermuda or Atlantic) type options.

INTEREST RATE SWAPS

4

In an interest rate swap, two parties agree to exchange periodic interest payments. The dollar amount of the interest payments exchanged is based on some predetermined dollar principal, which is called the **notional principal** or notional amount. The dollar amount each counterparty pays to the other is the agreed-upon periodic interest rate times the notional principal. The only dollars that are exchanged between the parties are the interest payments, not the notional principal. In the most common type of swap, one party agrees to pay the other party fixed interest payments at designated dates for the life of the contract. This party is referred to as the fixed-rate payer. The fixed rate that the fixed-rate payer must make is called the swap rate. The other party, who agrees to make interest rate payments that float with some reference rate, is referred to as the fixed-rate receiver.

The reference rates that have been used for the floating rate in an interest rate swap are those on various money market instruments: Treasury bills, the London interbank offered rate, commercial paper, bankers acceptances, certificates of deposit, the **federal funds rate**, and the prime rate. The most common is the **London interbank offered rate (LIBOR)**. LIBOR is the rate at which prime banks offer to pay on Eurodollar deposits available to other prime banks for a given maturity. Basically, it is viewed as the global cost of bank borrowing. There is not just one rate but a rate for different maturities. For example, there is a 1-month LIBOR, 3-month LIBOR, 6-month LIBOR, etc.

To illustrate an interest rate swap, suppose that for the next five years party X agrees to pay party Y 6% per year (the swap rate), while party Y agrees to pay party X 6-month LIBOR (the reference rate). Party X is the fixed-rate payer, while party Y is the fixed-rate receiver. Assume that the notional principal is $50

---

[6] There are well-established institutional arrangements for mitigating counterparty risk in not only OTC options but also the other OTC derivatives described in this reading (swaps, caps, and floors). These arrangement include limiting exposure to a specific counterparty, marking to market positions, collateralizing trades, and netting arrangement. For a discussion of these arrangements, see Chance, *Analysis of Derivatives for the CFA Program*, pp. 595–598.

PRACTICE QUESTION 4

Suppose that party G and party H enter into a 4-year interest rate swap. The notional amount for the swap is $100 million and the reference rate is 3-month LIBOR. Suppose that the payments are made quarterly by both the fixed-rate payer and the fixed-rate receiver. Also assume that the swap rate is 4.4%.

A. What are the payments that must be made by the fixed-rate payer every quarter?

B. Suppose for the first floating-rate payment 3-month LIBOR is 7.2%. What is the amount of the first floating-rate payment that must be made by the fixed-rate receiver?

million, and that payments are exchanged every six months for the next five years. This means that every six months, party X (the fixed-rate payer) will pay party Y $1.5 million (6% times $50 million divided by 2). The amount that party Y (the fixed-rate receiver) will pay party X will be 6-month LIBOR times $50 million divided by 2. If 6-month LIBOR is 5% at the beginning of the 6-month period, party Y will pay party X $1.25 million (5% times $50 million divided by 2). Mechanically, the floating-rate is determined at the beginning of a period and paid in arrears—that is, it is paid at the end of the period. The two payments are actually netted out so that $0.25 million will be paid from party X to party Y. Note that we divide by two because one-half year's interest is being paid. This is illustrated in panel A of Exhibit 4.

The convention that has evolved for quoting a swap rate is that a dealer sets the floating rate equal to the reference rate and then quotes the fixed rate that will apply. The fixed rate is the swap rate and reflects a "spread" above the Treasury yield curve with the same term to maturity as the swap. This spread is called the **swap spread**.

A. Entering into a Swap and Counterparty Risk

Interest rate swaps are OTC instruments. This means that they are not traded on an exchange. An institutional investor wishing to enter into a swap transaction can do so through either a securities firm or a commercial bank that transacts in swaps.[7] These entities can do one of the following. First, they can arrange or broker a swap between two parties that want to enter into an interest rate swap. In this case, the securities firm or commercial bank is acting in a brokerage capacity. The broker is not a party to the swap.

The second way in which a securities firm or commercial bank can get an institutional investor into a swap position is by taking the other side of the swap. This means that the securities firm or the commercial bank is a dealer rather than a broker in the transaction. Acting as a dealer, the securities firm or the commercial bank must hedge its swap position in the same way that it hedges its position in other securities that it holds. Also it means that the dealer (which we refer to as a swap dealer) is the counterparty to the transaction. If an

---

[7] Don't get confused here about the role of commercial banks. A bank can use a swap in its asset/liability management. Or, a bank can transact (buy and sell) swaps to clients to generate fee income. It is in the latter sense that we are discussing the role of a commercial bank in the swap market here.

EXHIBIT 4	Summary of How the Value of a Swap to Each Counterparty Changes When Interest Rates Change

A. Initial Position

Swap rate   = 6%   Settlement   = semiannual
Reference rate   = 6-month LIBOR   Term of swap   = 5 years
Notional amount = $50 million   Payment by   = $1.5 million
                                             fixed-rate payer

Every six months

```
                        $1.5 million
 ┌─────────────────┐  ───────────────▶  ┌─────────────────┐
 │ Fixed-rate payer │                    │Fixed-rate receiver│
 │                 │  ◀───────────────  │                 │
 └─────────────────┘   (6-month LIBOR)/2 └─────────────────┘
                         × $50 million
```

B. Interest Rates Increase Such that Swap Rate is 7% for New Swaps

Fixed-rate payer pays initial swap rate of 6% to obtain 6-month LIBOR
    Advantage to fixed-rate payer: pays only 6% not 7% to obtain 6-month LIBOR

Fixed-rate receiver pays 6-month LIBOR
    Disadvantage to fixed-rate receiver: receives only 6% in exchange for 6-month LIBOR, not 7%

Results of a rise in interest rates:

Party	Value of Swap
Fixed-rate payer	Increases
Fixed-rate receiver	Decreases

C. Interest Rates Decrease Such that Swap Rate Is 5% for New Swaps

Fixed-rate payer pays initial swap rate of 6% to obtain 6-month LIBOR
    Disadvantage to fixed-rate payer: must pay 6% not 5% to obtain 6-month LIBOR

Fixed-rate receiver pays 6-month LIBOR
    Advantage to fixed-rate receiver: receives 6% in exchange for 6-month LIBOR, not 5%

Results of a decrease in interest rates:

Party	Value of Swap
Fixed-rate payer	Decreases
Fixed-rate receiver	Increases

institutional investor entered into a swap with a swap dealer, the institutional investor will look to the swap dealer to satisfy the obligations of the swap; similarly, that same swap dealer looks to the institutional investor to fulfill its obligations as set forth in the swap.

The risk that the two parties take on when they enter into a swap is that the other party will fail to fulfill its obligations as set forth in the swap agreement. That is, each party faces default risk and therefore there is bilateral counterparty risk.

B. Risk/Return Characteristics of an Interest Rate Swap

The value of an interest rate swap will fluctuate with market interest rates. As interest rates rise, the fixed-rate payer is receiving a higher 6-month LIBOR (in our illustration). He would need to pay more for a new swap. Let's consider our hypothetical swap. Suppose that interest rates change immediately after parties X and Y enter into the swap. Panel A in Exhibit 4 shows the transaction. First, consider what would happen if the market demanded that in any 5-year swap the fixed-rate payer must pay 7% in order to receive 6-month LIBOR. If party X (the fixed-rate payer) wants to sell its position to party A, then party A will benefit by having to pay only 6% (the original swap rate agreed upon) rather than 7% (the current swap rate) to receive 6-month LIBOR. Party X will want compensation for this benefit. Consequently, the value of party X's position has increased. Thus, if interest rates increase, the fixed-rate payer will realize a profit and the fixed-rate receiver will realize a loss. Panel B in Exhibit 4 summarizes the results of a rise in interest rates.

Next, consider what would happen if interest rates decline to, say, 5%. Now a 5-year swap would require a new fixed-rate payer to pay 5% rather than 6% to receive 6-month LIBOR. If party X wants to sell its position to party B, the latter would demand compensation to take over the position. In other words, if interest rates decline, the fixed-rate payer will realize a loss, while the fixed-rate receiver will realize a profit. Panel C in Exhibit 4 summarizes the results of a decline in interest rates.

C. Interpreting a Swap Position

There are two ways that a swap position can be interpreted: (1) a package of forward (futures) contracts and (2) a package of cash flows from buying and selling cash market instruments.

1. Package of Forward (Futures) Contracts

Contrast the position of the counterparties in an interest rate swap summarized above to the position of the long and short interest rate futures (forward) contract. The long futures position gains if interest rates decline and loses if interest rates rise—this is similar to the risk/return profile for a floating-rate payer. The risk/return profile for a fixed-rate payer is similar to that of the short futures position: a gain if interest rates increase and a loss if interest rates decrease. By taking a closer look at the interest rate swap we can understand why the risk/return relationships are similar.

Consider party X's position in our previous swap illustration. Party X has agreed to pay 6% and receive 6-month LIBOR. More specifically, assuming a $50 million notional principal, X has agreed to buy a commodity called "6-month LIBOR" for $1.5 million. This is effectively a 6-month forward contract where X agrees to pay $1.5 million in exchange for delivery of 6-month LIBOR. If interest rates increase to 7%, the price of that commodity (6-month LIBOR) is higher, resulting in a gain for the fixed-rate payer, who is effectively long a 6-month forward contract on 6-month LIBOR. The floating-rate payer is effectively short a 6-month forward contract on 6-month LIBOR. There is therefore an implicit forward contract corresponding to each exchange date.

Now we can see why there is a similarity between the risk/return relationship for an interest rate swap and a forward contract. If interest rates increase to, say, 7%, the price of that commodity (6-month LIBOR) increases to $1.75 million (7% times $50 million divided by 2). The long forward position (the fixed-rate payer) gains, and the short forward position (the floating-rate payer) loses. If interest rates decline to, say, 5%, the price of our commodity decreases to $1.25 million (5% times $50 million divided by 2). The short forward position (the floating-rate payer) gains, and the long forward position (the fixed-rate payer) loses.

Consequently, interest rate swaps can be viewed as a package of more basic interest rate derivatives, such as forwards.[8] The pricing of an interest rate swap will then depend on the price of a package of forward contracts with the same settlement dates in which the underlying for the forward contract is the same reference rate. We will make use of this principle in the next reading when we explain how to value swaps.

While an interest rate swap may be nothing more than a package of forward contracts, it is not a redundant contract for several reasons. First, maturities for forward or futures contracts do not extend out as far as those of an interest rate swap; an interest rate swap with a term of 15 years or longer can be obtained. Second, an interest rate swap is a more transactionally efficient instrument. By this we mean that in one transaction an entity can effectively establish a payoff equivalent to a package of forward contracts. The forward contracts would each have to be negotiated separately. Third, the interest rate swap market has grown in liquidity since its introduction in 1981; interest rate swaps now provide more liquidity than forward contracts, particularly long-dated (i.e., long-term) forward contracts.

2. Package of Cash Market Instruments

To understand why a swap can also be interpreted as a package of cash market instruments, consider an investor who enters into the transaction below:

▶ buy $50 million par of a 5-year floating-rate bond that pays 6-month LIBOR every six months

▶ finance the purchase by borrowing $50 million for five years on terms requiring a 6% annual interest rate payable every six months

As a result of this transaction, the investor

▶ receives a floating rate every six months for the next five years

▶ pays a fixed rate every six months for the next five years

---

[8] More specifically, an interest rate swap is equivalent to a package of **forward rate agreements**. A forward rate agreement (FRA) is the over-the-counter equivalent of the exchange-traded futures contracts on short-term rates. Typically, the short-term rate is LIBOR. The elements of an FRA are the contract rate, reference rate, settlement rate, notional amount, and settlement date.

EXHIBIT 5	Cash Flow for the Purchase of a 5-Year Floating-Rate Bond Financed by Borrowing on a Fixed-Rate Basis

Transaction:

▶ Purchase for $50 million a 5-year floating-rate bond: floating rate = LIBOR, semiannual payments

▶ Borrow $50 million for five years: fixed rate = 6%, semiannual payments

Six Month Period	Cash Flow (in Millions of Dollars) from:		
	Floating-Rate Bond[a]	Borrowing at 5%	Net = Same as Swap
0	−$50	+$50.0	$0
1	+(LIBOR$_1$/2) × 50	−1.5	+(LIBOR$_1$/2) × 50 − 1.5
2	+(LIBOR$_2$/2) × 50	−1.5	+(LIBOR$_2$/2) × 50 − 1.5
3	+(LIBOR$_3$/2) × 50	−1.5	+(LIBOR$_3$/2) × 50 − 1.5
4	+(LIBOR$_4$/2) × 50	−1.5	+(LIBOR$_4$/2) × 50 − 1.5
5	+(LIBOR$_5$/2) × 50	−1.5	+(LIBOR$_5$/2) × 50 − 1.5
6	+(LIBOR$_6$/2) × 50	−1.5	+(LIBOR$_6$/2) × 50 − 1.5
7	+(LIBOR$_7$/2) × 50	−1.5	+(LIBOR$_7$/2) × 50 − 1.5
8	+(LIBOR$_8$/2) × 50	−1.5	+(LIBOR$_8$/2) × 50 − 1.5
9	+(LIBOR$_9$/2) × 50	−1.5	+(LIBOR$_9$/2) × 50 − 1.5
10	+(LIBOR$_{10}$/2) × 50 + 50	−51.5	+(LIBOR$_{10}$/2) × 50 − 1.5

[a] The subscript for LIBOR indicates the 6-month LIBOR as per the terms of the floating-rate bond at time t.

The cash flows for this transaction are set forth in Exhibit 5. The second column of the exhibit shows the cash flow from purchasing the 5-year floating-rate bond. There is a $50 million cash outlay and then ten cash inflows. The amount of the cash inflows is uncertain because they depend on future LIBOR. The next column shows the cash flow from borrowing $50 million on a fixed-rate basis. The last column shows the net cash flow from the entire transaction. As the last column indicates, there is no initial cash flow (no cash inflow or cash outlay). In all ten 6-month periods, the net position results in a cash inflow of LIBOR and a cash outlay of $1.5 million. This net position, however, is identical to the position of a fixed-rate payer/floating-rate receiver.

It can be seen from the net cash flow in Exhibit 5 that a fixed-rate payer has a cash market position that is equivalent to a long position in a floating-rate bond and a short position in a fixed-rate bond—the short position being the equivalent of borrowing by issuing a fixed-rate bond.

What about the position of a floating-rate payer? It can be easily demonstrated that the position of a floating-rate payer is equivalent to purchasing a fixed-rate bond and financing that purchase at a floating rate, where the floating rate is the reference rate for the swap. That is, the position of a floating-rate payer is equivalent to a long position in a fixed-rate bond and a short position in a floating-rate bond.

EXHIBIT 6	Describing the Parties to a Swap Agreement

Fixed-Rate Payer	**Fixed-Rate Receiver**
▶ pays fixed rate in the swap	▶ pays floating rate in the swap
▶ receives floating in the swap	▶ receives fixed in the swap
▶ is short the bond market	▶ is long the bond market
▶ has bought a swap	▶ has sold a swap
▶ is long a swap	▶ is short a swap
▶ has established the price sensitivities of a longer-term fixed-rate liability and a floating-rate asset	▶ has established the price sensitivities of a longer-term fixed-rate asset and a floating-rate liability

D. Describing the Counterparties to a Swap Agreement

The terminology used to describe the position of a party in the swap markets combines cash market jargon and futures market jargon, given that a swap position can be interpreted as a position in a package of cash market instruments or a package of futures/forward positions. As we have said, the counterparty to an interest rate swap is either a fixed-rate payer or floating-rate payer.

Exhibit 6 lists how the counterparties to an interest rate swap agreement are described.[9] To understand why the fixed-rate payer is viewed as "short the bond market," and the floating-rate payer is viewed as "long the bond market," consider what happens when interest rates change. Those who borrow on a fixed-rate basis will benefit if interest rates rise because they have locked in a lower interest rate. But those who have a short bond position will also benefit if interest rates rise. Thus, a fixed-rate payer can be said to be short the bond market. A floating-rate payer benefits if interest rates fall. A long position in a bond also benefits if interest rates fall, so terminology describing a floating-rate payer as long the bond market is not surprising. From our discussion of the interpretation of a swap as a package of cash market instruments, describing a swap in terms of the sensitivities of long and short cash positions follows naturally.[10]

OPTIONAL SEGMENT ENDS

INTEREST RATE CAPS AND FLOORS

There are agreements between two parties whereby one party for an upfront premium agrees to compensate the other at specific time periods if the reference rate is different from a predetermined level. If one party agrees to pay the other when the reference rate exceeds a predetermined level, the agreement is referred to as an **interest rate cap** or ceiling. The agreement is referred to as an **interest rate floor** if one party agrees to pay the other when the reference rate

---

[9] Robert F. Kopprasch, John Macfarlane, Daniel R. Ross, and Janet Showers, "The Interest Rate Swap Market: Yield Mathematics, Terminology, and Conventions," Chapter 58 in Frank J. Fabozzi and Irving M. Pollack (eds.), *The Handbook of Fixed Income Securities* (Homewood, IL: Dow Jones-Irwin, 1987).

[10] It is common for market participants to refer to one leg of a swap as the "funding leg" and the other as the "asset leg." This jargon is the result of the interpretation of a swap as a leveraged position in the asset. The payment of the floating-rate is referred to as the "funding leg" and the fixed-rate side is referred to as the "asset side."

falls below a predetermined level. The predetermined level is called the strike rate. The strike rate for a cap is called the cap rate; the strike rate for a floor is called the floor rate.

The terms of a cap and **floor agreement** include:

1. the reference rate
2. the strike rate (cap rate or floor rate) that sets the ceiling or floor
3. the length of the agreement
4. the frequency of settlement
5. the notional principal

For example, suppose that C buys an interest rate cap from D with the following terms:

1. the reference rate is 3-month LIBOR.
2. the strike rate is 6%.
3. the agreement is for four years.
4. settlement is every three months.
5. the notional principal is $20 million.

Under this agreement, every three months for the next four years, D will pay C whenever 3-month LIBOR exceeds 6% at a settlement date. The payment will equal the dollar value of the difference between 3-month LIBOR and 6% times the notional principal divided by 4. For example, if three months from now 3-month LIBOR on a settlement date is 8%, then D will pay C 2% (8% minus 6%) times $20 million divided by 4, or $100,000. If 3-month LIBOR is 6% or less, D does not have to pay anything to C.

In the case of an interest rate floor, assume the same terms as the interest rate cap we just illustrated. In this case, if 3-month LIBOR is 8%, C receives nothing from D, but if 3-month LIBOR is less than 6%, D compensates C for the difference. For example, if 3-month LIBOR is 5%, D will pay C $50,000 (6% minus 5% times $20 million divided by 4).[11]

A. Risk/Return Characteristics

In an interest rate agreement, the buyer pays an upfront fee which represents the maximum amount that the buyer can lose and the maximum amount that the seller (writer) can gain. The only party that is required to perform is the seller of the interest rate agreement. The buyer of an interest rate cap benefits if the reference rate rises above the strike rate because the seller must compensate the buyer. The buyer of an interest rate floor benefits if the reference rate falls below the strike rate, because the seller must compensate the buyer.

The seller of an interest rate cap or floor does not face counterparty risk once the buyer pays the fee. In contrast, the buyer faces counterparty risk. Thus, as with options, there is unilateral counterparty risk.

---

[11] Interest rate caps and floors can be combined to create an *interest rate collar*. This is done by buying an interest rate cap and selling an interest rate floor. The purchase of the cap sets a maximum rate; the sale of the floor sets a minimum rate. The range between the maximum and minimum rate is called the collar.

PRACTICE QUESTION 5

Suppose that a 4-year cap has a cap rate of 7% and a notional amount of $100 million. The frequency of settlement is quarterly and the reference rate is 3-month LIBOR. Assume that 3-month LIBOR for the next four quarters is as shown below. What is the payoff for each quarter?

Period	3-Month LIBOR
1	6.7%
2	7.0%
3	7.4%
4	7.6%

B. Interpretation of a Cap and Floor Position

In an interest rate cap and floor, the buyer pays an upfront fee, which represents the maximum amount that the buyer can lose and the maximum amount that the seller of the agreement can gain. The only party that is required to perform is the seller of the interest rate agreement. The buyer of an interest rate cap benefits if the reference rate rises above the strike rate because the seller must compensate the buyer. The buyer of an interest rate floor benefits if the reference rate falls below the strike rate because the seller must compensate the buyer.

How can we better understand interest rate caps and interest rate floors? In essence these contracts are equivalent to a *package of interest rate options* at different time periods. As with a swap, a complex contract can be seen to be a package of basic contracts—options in the case of caps and floors. Each of the interest rate options comprising a cap are called **caplets**; similarly, each of the interest rate options comprising a floor are called **floorlets**.

The question is what type of package of options is a cap and a floor. Note the following very carefully! It depends on whether the underlying is a rate or a fixed-income instrument. If the underlying is considered a fixed-income instrument, its value changes inversely with interest rates. Therefore:

▶ for a call option on a fixed-income instrument:

1. interest rates increase → fixed-income instrument's price decreases → call option value decreases

and

2. interest rates decrease → fixed-income instrument's price increases → call option value increases

▶ for a put option on a fixed-income instrument:

1. interest rates increase → fixed-income instrument's price decreases → put option value increases

and

2. interest rates decrease → fixed-income instrument's price increases → put option value decreases

To summarize the situation for call and put options on a fixed-income instrument:

	When Interest Rates	
Value Of	**Increase**	**Decrease**
long call	decrease	increase
short call	increase	decrease
long put	increase	decrease
short put	decrease	increase

For a cap and floor, the situation is as follows:

	When Interest Rates	
Value Of	**Increase**	**Decrease**
short cap	decrease	increase
long cap	increase	decrease
short floor	increase	decrease
long floor	decrease	increase

Therefore, buying a cap (long cap) is equivalent to buying a package of puts on a fixed-income instrument and buying a floor (long floor) is equivalent to buying a package of calls on a fixed-income instrument.

Caps and floors can also be seen as packages of options on interest rates. In the over-the-counter market one can purchase an option on an interest rate. These options work as follows in terms of their payoff. There is a strike rate. For a call option on an interest rate, there is a payoff if the reference rate is greater than the strike rate. This means that when interest rates increase, the call option's value increases and when interest rates decrease, the call option's value decreases. As can be seen from the payoff for a cap and a floor summarized above, this is the payoff of a long cap. Consequently, a cap is equivalent to a package of call options on an interest rate. For a put option on an interest rate, there is a payoff when the reference rate is less than the strike rate. When interest rates increase, the value of the put option on an interest rate decreases, as does the value of a long floor position (see the summary above); when interest rates decrease, the value of the put on an interest rate increases, as does the value of a long floor position (again, see the summary above). Thus, a floor is equivalent to a package of put options on an interest rate.

When market participants talk about the equivalency of caps and floors in terms of put and call options, they must specify the underlying. For example, a long cap is equivalent to a package of call options on interest rates or a package of put options on a fixed-income instrument.

C. Creation of an Interest Rate Collar

Interest rate caps and floors can be combined by borrowers to create an **interest rate collar**. This is done by buying an interest rate cap and selling an interest rate floor. The purchase of the cap sets a maximum interest rate that a borrower would have to pay if the reference rate rises. The sale of a floor sets the minimum interest rate that a borrower can benefit from if the reference rate declines. Therefore, there is a range for the interest rate that the borrower must pay if the reference rate changes. The net premium that a borrower who wants to create a collar must pay is the difference between the premium paid to purchase the cap and the premium received to sell the floor.

For example, consider the following collar created by a borrower: a cap purchased with a strike rate of 7% and a floor sold with a strike rate of 4%. If the reference rate exceeds 7%, the borrower receives a payment; if the reference rate is less than 4%, the borrower makes a payment. Thus, the borrower's cost will have a range from 4% to 7%. Note, however, that the borrower's effective interest cost is adjusted by the net premium that the borrower must pay.

SUMMARY

▶ A futures contract is an agreement between a buyer (seller) and an established exchange or its clearinghouse in which the buyer (seller) agrees to take (make) delivery of something at a specified price at the end of a designated period of time.

▶ A forward contract is an agreement for the future delivery of something at a specified price at a designated time, but differs from a futures contract in that it is usually non-standardized and traded in the over-the-counter market.

▶ An investor who takes a long futures position realizes a gain when the futures price increases; an investor who takes a short futures position realizes a gain when the futures price decreases.

▶ The parties to a futures contract are required to satisfy margin requirements.

▶ Parties to over-the-counter interest rate contracts are exposed to counterparty risk which is the risk that the counterparty will not satisfy its contractual obligations.

▶ For the Treasury bond futures contract the underlying instrument is $100,000 par value of a hypothetical 20-year 6% coupon Treasury bond.

▶ Conversion factors are used to adjust the invoice price of a Treasury bond futures contract to make delivery equitable to both parties.

▶ The short in a Treasury bond futures contract has several delivery options: quality option (or swap option), timing option, and wildcard option.

▶ For all the issues that may be delivered to satisfy a Treasury futures contract, a rate of return can be computed in a cash and carry trade; the rate of return is called the implied repo rate.

▶ For all the issues that may be delivered to satisfy a Treasury futures contract, the cheapest-to-deliver issue is the one with the highest implied repo rate.

▶ By varying the yield on Treasury bonds, it can be determined which issue will become the new cheapest-to-deliver issue.

▶ There are futures contracts in which the underlying is a Fannie Mae and Freddie Mac debenture.

▶ An option is a contract in which the writer of the option grants the buyer of the option the right, but not the obligation, to purchase from or sell to the writer something at a specified price within a specified period of time (or at a specified date).

▶ The option buyer pays the option writer (seller) a fee, called the option price (or premium).

▶ A call option allows the option buyer to purchase the underlying from the option writer at the strike price; a put option allows the option buyer to sell the underlying to the option writer at the strike price.

▶ Interest rate options include options on fixed income securities and options on interest rate futures contracts; the latter, called futures options, are the preferred exchange-traded vehicle for implementing investment strategies.

▶ Because of the difficulties of hedging particular fixed income securities, some institutional investors have found over-the-counter options more useful.

▶ An interest rate swap is an agreement specifying that the parties exchange interest payments at designated times, with a generic or vanilla swap calling for one party to make fixed-rate payments and the other to make floating-rate payments based on a notional principal.

- The swap rate is the interest rate paid by the fixed-rate payer.
- The swap spread is the spread paid by the fixed-rate payer over the on-the-run Treasury rate with the same maturity as the swap agreement.
- The convention in quoting swaps is to quote the payments made by the floating-rate payer flat (that is, without a spread) and the fixed-rate payer payments as a spread to the on-the-run Treasury with the same maturity as the swap (the swap spread).
- A swap position can be interpreted as either a package of forward/futures contracts or a package of cash flows from buying and selling cash market instruments.
- An interest rate cap specifies that one party receive a payment if the reference rate is above the cap rate; an interest rate floor specifies that one party receive a payment if a reference rate is below the floor rate.
- The terms of a cap and floor set forth the reference rate, the strike rate, the length of the agreement, the frequency of reset, and the notional amount.
- In an interest rate cap and floor, the buyer pays an upfront fee, which represents the maximum amount that the buyer can lose and the maximum amount that the seller of the agreement can gain.
- Buying a cap is equivalent to buying a package of puts on a fixed income security and buying a floor is equivalent to buying a package of calls on a fixed income security.
- If an option is viewed as one in which the underlying is an interest rate, then buying a cap is equivalent to buying a package of calls on interest rates and buying a floor is equivalent to buying a package of puts on interest rates.
- An interest collar is created by buying an interest rate cap and selling an interest rate floor.
- Forward contracts and swaps expose the parties to bilateral counterparty risk while buyers of OTC options, caps, and floors face unilateral counterparty risk.

PRACTICE PROBLEMS FOR READING 66

1. Suppose that a 1-year cap has a cap rate of 8% and a notional amount of $10 million. The frequency of settlement is quarterly and the reference rate is 3-month LIBOR. Assume that 3-month LIBOR for the next four quarters is as shown below. What is the payoff for each quarter?

Period	3-Month LIBOR
1	8.7%
2	8.0%
3	7.8%
4	8.2%

2. Suppose that a 1-year floor has a floor rate of 4% and a notional amount of $20 million. The frequency of settlement is quarterly and the reference rate is 3-month LIBOR. Assume that 3-month LIBOR for the next four quarters is as shown below. What is the payoff for each quarter?

Period	3-Month LIBOR
1	4.7%
2	4.4%
3	3.8%
4	3.4%

3. What counterparty risk is the seller of an interest rate floor exposed to?

4. A. What is an interest rate cap or floor equivalent to?

   B. What is a caplet and a floorlet?

USING CREDIT DERIVATIVES TO ENHANCE RETURN AND MANAGE RISK

by George Spentzos

LEARNING OUTCOMES

The candidate should be able to:

a. describe the characteristics of a credit default swap, and compare and contrast a credit default swap to a corporate bond;

b. explain the advantages of using credit derivatives over other credit instruments;

c. explain the use of credit derivatives by the various market participants;

d. discuss credit derivatives strategies and how they are used.

INTRODUCTION 1

The credit derivatives market is growing rapidly in size as well as importance. Credit default swaps, the building blocks in the market, have several advantages over corporate bonds and asset swaps—not least of which is the ability to disaggregate the interest rate component from the credit component. The predominant strategies that hedge funds and other managers use to optimize credit portfolios are basis trades, curve trades, index trades, options trades, capital structure trades, and correlation trades.

Credit derivatives have generated significant interest over the past few years. In this reading, I will address some of the topics and questions that people might have regarding this growing part of the capital markets. I will first briefly discuss the background and evolution of the credit derivatives market and then address the specific strategies used by hedge funds and other institutional managers to enhance return and manage risk.

George Spentzos is a Portfolio Manager at Brevan Howard Asset Management LLP, London. This reading was presented at the Fixed-Income Management 2005 conference held in Boston on 6–7 October 2005.

EVOLUTION OF THE CREDIT DERIVATIVES MARKET

Credit default swaps (CDS) are the building blocks in the credit derivatives market and represent about half of its volume. A CDS is a bilateral contract between a protection buyer and a protection seller that exchanges the credit risk of a specific issuer (reference entity). The protection buyer (short the credit) pays a premium to the protection seller (long) to assume the risk associated with a particular credit event. Credit events are typically defined to include bankruptcy, a material default, and debt restructuring for a specified reference asset. For example, an investor might take a long position in Volkswagen (VW)—notional amount of €10 million with a maturity of five years. The protection seller will receive a premium from the protection buyer of 60 bps a year. On €10 million notional, that premium is €60,000 a year normally paid on a quarterly basis (20 March, 20 June, 20 September, and 20 December). If a credit event does not occur, the arrangement will continue for the full five years.

In the case of a credit event, most single-name CDS physically settle. That is, the protection buyer delivers the reference obligation, either a bond or a loan, to the protection seller, and the protection seller returns the notional amount (€10 million in the Volkswagen example) to the protection buyer.

Some single-name CDS are settled on a cash basis, such as those in the synthetic collateralized debt obligation (CDO) market. In that case, the protection buyer receives the par amount (€10 million in the Volkswagen example) minus the market value, which is the recovery rate determined by dealer quotes after the credit event. If the recovery rate for Volkswagen is determined to be 40 percent, the protection seller will give the protection buyer €6 million. Figure 1 summarizes these exchanges.

Similar to bonds, yield spreads on CDS widen when markets reflect more credit risk and tighten when markets reflect less credit risk. But a CDS is clearly different from a corporate bond or an asset swap. Corporate bond yields are composed of the risk-free rate, funding risk (swap spread), and credit risk (the

FIGURE 1   CDS: The Building Block

Before Credit Event

After Credit Event (physical settlement)

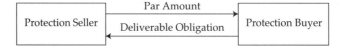

After Credit Event (cash settlement)

FIGURE 2   CDS: Pure Credit Risk

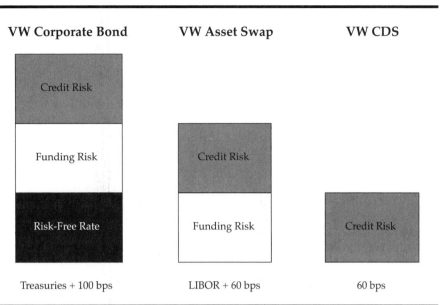

idiosyncratic default risk associated with the company), as shown in Figure 2. An investor might be paid 100 bps over five-year Treasuries on a five-year Volkswagen bond. If an investor swaps fixed cash flows for floating cash flows, she will be left with an asset swap that is essentially the funding risk plus the credit risk (in the Volkswagen case it would be LIBOR plus 60 bps). Where the CDS differentiates itself is that it is not spread over anything; it is simply the credit risk (60 bps in this example). It is an unfunded contract between two counterparties and thus is the purest form of credit risk in the market.

Advantages

Credit derivatives have several advantages over other credit instruments. As mentioned, the portability of pure risk (i.e., the ability to independently manage default risk and interest rate risk) is the key advantage. Buying protection is an efficient way to short credit because shorting corporate bonds can be difficult. If an investor wanted to short a bond that was in high demand in the repo market (i.e., trading special), the cost of shorting could vastly reduce the economics of the trade.

Liquidity has been growing in the credit derivatives market to the extent that many names are more readily traded in the CDS market than in the underlying corporate bond market. Ten years ago, the five-year CDS contract was by far the most liquid maturity. Activity from various market participants with diversified interests has resulted in increased trading in the 3-, 7-, and 10-year maturities, and other off-the-run dates are now relatively liquid. Default swaps enable one to create maturity, currency, and credit exposures that are not readily available in the underlying cash market. For example, if an investor wants exposure to an issuer with a 7-year maturity but only 2-year and 10-year securities are trading in the secondary market, then a customized credit default swap can be created to suit the investor's requirements. With credit derivatives, the transfer of credit risk is done on a confidential basis. Unlike loans, where the referenced entity is party to the transaction, a CDS is an over-the-counter bilateral contract.

FIGURE 3   Credit Derivatives Volume, 1997–2005

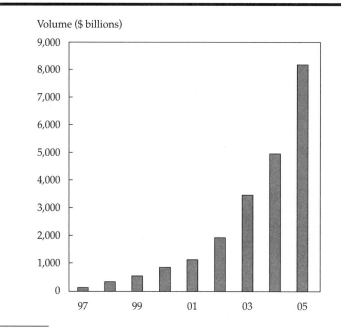

Source: Based on data from the British Bankers' Association.

Market Growth

Largely as a result of these advantages, the growth in the credit derivatives market has been impressive, similar to the growth in the interest rate derivatives market, which started in the 1980s. The credit derivatives market began in the mid-1990s and progressed relatively slowly, as seen in Figure 3. A lot of the early concerns centered on **legal risk** and the interpretation of contracts. The first contract took about six months to actually settle, but now the CDS market is very liquid, and volumes have actually overtaken volumes in the underlying corporate bond market. Current estimates of the size of the credit derivatives market are between $8 trillion and $12 trillion, depending on the source. Global issuance of corporate bonds in 2004 was in the $2 trillion to $3 trillion range.

Part of this growth came from some key developments in the standardization of documentation. The ISDA (**International Swaps and Derivatives Association**) came out in 1999 and 2003 with standardized documents specifying key contract items, such as maturity, premium, reference name, credit events, business calendars, legal jurisdiction, day-count convention, and so on. The resulting reduction in legal risk has enhanced liquidity in the credit derivatives market and has also sped up the confirmation process. Market participants have seen the development and rapid acceptance of indices over the past few years. The active indices in Europe are the Dow Jones iTraxx indices, and in North America, the Dow Jones CDX indices. These indices have contributed greatly to the growth in the market. Also fueling the growth has been the increase in product innovation, not only in the CDS market but also in the synthetic CDO market, which uses CDS as its underlying collateral.

Market Participants

The number of market participants, shown in Figure 4, continues to grow. Although the market has become broader over the past few years, it is still

FIGURE 4   Participants in the Credit Derivatives Market, 2003–2004

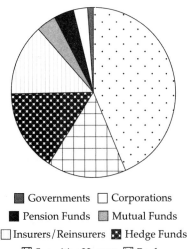

Governments ☐ Corporations
■ Pension Funds ■ Mutual Funds
☐ Insurers/Reinsurers ■ Hedge Funds
⊞ Securities Houses ⠿ Banks

Source: Based on data from the British Bankers' Association.

essentially dominated by several major groups: banks, securities houses (or investment banks), hedge funds, and insurance companies. Banks have traditionally been buyers of credit protection to hedge their risk (i.e., loan portfolios) and to obtain regulatory capital relief. They once represented about half of the volume in the markets, but that share has since declined to 35–40 percent in a maturing market. As market makers, investment banks are major players. They use credit derivatives to hedge their underlying corporate bond portfolios and provide access and liquidity to the rest of the participants in the market. Additionally, they tend to have proprietary trading desks, which behave similarly to hedge funds.

Hedge funds represent about 15 percent of the market and are the largest growing segment. Five years ago, very few pure credit hedge funds existed. The hedge funds that did use credit derivatives were primarily the convertible bond players and the distressed players. Now, credit hedge funds have emerged and opportunistically trade a number of different strategies. They are motivated by relative-value opportunities and are active traders of most credit derivatives products. By nature, they are risk takers and add essential liquidity to the marketplace.

Insurance companies play a major role, particularly as sellers of protection (going long). Life insurers, property and casualty companies, monolines, and reinsurers also use a number of structured products to enhance yield and provide diversification in their portfolios. Traditional fund managers have started to focus on credit derivatives products for relative-value purposes, whereas corporations have been more focused on credit derivatives products for risk management and for enhancing their pension assets and managing their balance sheets.

Structured Credit Market

Structured credit represents about 15 percent of the total credit derivatives market and is the fastest growing segment. As shown in Figure 5, the recent growth has been significant.

A synthetic CDO takes a reference portfolio of CDS and redistributes the risk among a number of tranches with varying amounts of subordination, spread, and risk. Synthetic CDOs can be either customized or index transactions.

FIGURE 5   Synthetic CDO Issuance, 2002–2004

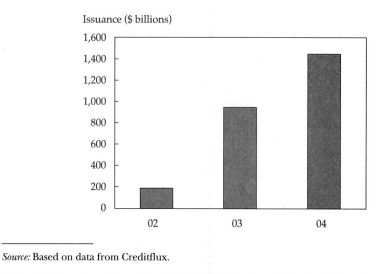

Source: Based on data from Creditflux.

The advantage of customized tranches is that one can precisely select the individual underlying credits as well as the attachment and detachment points (the lower and upper bounds of risk in a tranche). The advantage of index tranches is that they are standardized and have much better liquidity than the customized tranches. For example, the Dow Jones iTraxx Europe is composed of 125 names and currently yields 37 bps, illustrated in Figure 6. That risk can be redistributed among a number of different tranches, ranging from the super senior tranche (yielding only a few basis points) to the equity tranche (yielding about 15 percent). The equity tranche is the most junior tranche and typically absorbs the first 3 percent of losses. Once losses exceed the notional of the equity tranche, the next tranche (i.e., junior mezzanine) absorbs further losses, and so on.

FIGURE 6   iTraxx Europe Tranches, Five Year

Throughout the capital structure, different players are typically involved. The banks and securities houses are generally active in all parts of the capital structure; however, the insurance companies and reinsurers are generally more interested in investment-grade products and invest in mezzanine and senior tranches. Hedge funds are more interested in the higher-yielding and riskier tranches.

CREDIT DERIVATIVES STRATEGIES **3**

The main strategies that hedge funds and other managers use to optimize portfolios are basis trades, curve trades, index trades, options trades, capital structure trades, and correlation trades.

Basis Trades

The cash-default basis is simply defined as the difference between the CDS premium and the asset swap spread on a bond. If the CDS premium is higher than the asset swap spread, the basis is said to be positive. If the CDS is tighter, the basis is negative and can represent an arbitrage opportunity. The investor, however, needs a strong balance sheet to fund long positions cheaply, and it is generally not worthwhile to execute for just a couple of basis points. Typically, investors look for 10–20 bps of upside.

The problem with this type of strategy is that it can quickly get arbitraged away and can have some residual risk attached to it because the long and the short segments of the trade might not exactly match. Also, opportunities can be limited by the available bond supply.

An example of this strategy is to buy a five-year British American Tobacco bond at LIBOR plus 60 bps and short five-year CDS at 46 bps, resulting in a negative-basis package of 14 bps.

Curve Trades

CDS curve trades allow investors to express views on how a company's credit profile will change over time. A curve trade can be constructed in two ways. The first way is to match the notional of the long and short trades. In this case, the investor is default neutral but is not duration neutral. The second way is to be duration neutral, so the investor weights both sides of the trade by adjusting for duration.

One example of a curve transaction is a flattener—buying short protection and selling long protection to establish forward exposure. The investor might believe that a company is basically a good credit but has some short-term uncertainty. For instance, an investor might have a view that Ahold, the Dutch retailer, is an improving BB credit that is likely to come back to investment grade at some point in the next five to seven years. The investor, however, also sees some volatility associated with the credit in the next couple of years. The investor could then sell seven-year CDS at 170 bps and buy two-year CDS at 70 bps to temper the short-term volatility.

The opposite trade is a steepener, where the investor sells the short protection and buys the long protection. The investor might have a bearish long-term view but wants to reduce the immediate negative carry. For instance, an investor might argue that Fiat, the Italian automobile manufacturer, is a declining business but has good short-term liquidity. In this case, the investor could buy five-year CDS at 400 bps and then partially fund that position by selling two-year CDS at 225 bps.

Index Trades

Credit indices are an efficient and inexpensive way to take a macro view on credit as an asset class. They also provide diversification and are very liquid. A typical index is the Dow Jones iTraxx Europe. The 125 issuers represented in the index are decided by market-making volumes and are equally weighted—0.8 percent per name. The maturities are 5.5 years and 10.5 years at inception, and the constituents are readjusted every six months.

A number of strategies can be used with credit indices. One strategy is to establish an outright short in a particular index, where the investor has a negative view or wants to temporarily protect a credit portfolio from market volatility.

An investor could also go long an index versus a subsector or versus specific credits (e.g., long the investment-grade European index and short European automobile manufacturers for which the investor has a negative view.) Also, an investor could use an intersector relative-value strategy (e.g., automobiles index versus telecommunications index) or use a macro capital structure strategy in which the investor goes long a credit index and short an equity index.

Options Trades

Options on CDS have begun to gain acceptance but still have a way to go to catch up to their equity brethren. Although most trading in credit options is based on the major indices, liquidity in single-name credit default options will likely increase in the future when the underlying CDS is actively traded.

Two types of options are generally available, similar to puts and calls. A receiver option is the right to sell protection at a specified level at some date in the future, and a payer option is the right to buy protection. Buying a receiver option implies a bullish view on credit and will make money when spreads tighten. Buying a payer option implies a bearish view on credit and will make money if spreads widen. In the credit derivatives market, these options are European style and are the building blocks for creating options strategies, such as **straddles**, **strangles**, or other exotic strategies. These products may be used to leverage existing cash positions, provide a temporary downside hedge, or reflect a view on future credit market volatility.

Capital Structure Trades

A variety of ways exist to take advantage of a perceived mispricing in a company's capital structure. An investor might have a view on the relative value between a holding company and an operating company or financial subsidiary. For example, if an investor thought that Ford Motor Company was going to deteriorate but that its financial subsidiary was in better shape, the investor could sell five-year CDS of Ford Motor Credit at 400 bps and buy five-year CDS of the holding company at 525 bps with the expectation that the spread would widen from 125 bps.

Alternatively, one could examine the relationship between senior and subordinated debt for a given company. With banks and insurance companies, an investor might have a view on recovery rates. If an investor has a bullish outlook on U.S. housing, he might sell five-year Fannie Mae subordinated CDS at 30 bps and buy senior protection at 15 bps for a positive carry of 15 bps.

Recently, a popular strategy has been credit versus equity trades. Structural models have been developed to relate credit risk to equity. The most common model is the Merton model, which assesses the credit risk of a company by characterizing the company's equity as a call option on its assets. If an investor wanted to reflect a view on potential event risk, a variety of instruments could be used for the credit leg (CDS, corporate bonds, asset swaps, and loans) and the equity leg (stocks, stock options, and equity default swaps). For example, an investor might believe that the Dutch publishing company VNU would be an ideal leveraged buyout candidate. (A leveraged buyout is a mechanism in which the controlling interest of a corporation is acquired by purchasing a majority of its stock using borrowed money.) The investor could then buy five-year protection on the expectation that spreads would widen from 50 bps and at the same time purchase equity calls with the expectation that the stock price would increase in value.

Correlation Trades

To understand correlation trading, one must understand the concept of default correlation. Default correlation, a key model input for synthetic CDOs, is the likelihood that any two credits in a portfolio will default together. If names are uncorrelated, the default of one credit will have no impact on the other credits. In a CDO with low correlation, most of the risk is concentrated in the equity tranche and the least is in the senior tranches. Correlations can be derived from historical data or implied from actively traded tranches on CDS indices in much the same way that implied volatilities for equity options can be derived from the Black–Scholes model.

First-to-default baskets represent a relatively simple way to leverage a view on a number of credits. Typically, a first-to-default basket has five names, but it could contain any number of names. The premium is determined by several factors, including the number of basket components, the absolute spread levels, and the default correlation. More credits in the basket infer a greater likelihood of default and a higher premium. Higher premiums are also associated with higher absolute spread levels, lower dispersion of spreads, and lower default correlations.

Figure 7 illustrates the difference between a €10 million five-year first-to-default (FTD) swap basket. In the CDS example, the five names all trade around

FIGURE 7   First-to-Default Example

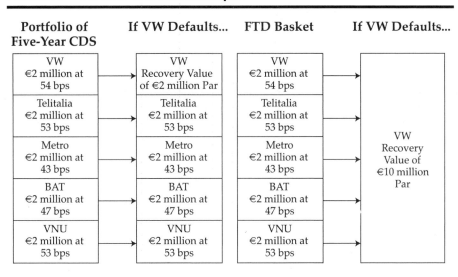

Premium = 50 bps   Premium = 175 bps

Note: BAT = British American Tobacco.

FIGURE 8   **Equity vs. Mezzanine Trade Example**

Transaction	Premium	Leverage	Notional (millions)	Annual Carry	DV01[a]
Sell 0–3% 3-year CDX	500 bps + 11.75%	26x	$ 10	$940,000	$68,000
Buy 3–7% 3-year CDX	24 bps	2	130	(310,000)	(68,000)
Net trade				630,000	0

[a]Dollar value of 1 bp change.

50 bps, so the portfolio premium is 50 bps. Suppose one of the names (VW) defaults and it has a 50 percent recovery rate. The investor is left with €1 million from the VW trade but continues to receive the premium on the four other trades in the portfolio.

Alternatively, the investor could invest in a FTD basket where she could take a leveraged view on the same five names and the premium would typically be 60–80 percent of the aggregate spread. Instead of getting paid 50 bps like in the previous example, the investor might receive 175 bps. If VW defaults in this scenario, the contract immediately ceases and the protection buyer delivers the notional amount of the basket in VW bonds or loans to the investor. The investor then pays the protection buyer the trade notional amount in cash; it is as if the investor had written a contract only on VW.

Another strategy that has been popular over the past couple of years with hedge funds and proprietary trading desks is trading different parts of the synthetic CDO capital structure. For example, assume that an investor thinks that default rates will go up in five to seven years but that for the next three years they will be benign. The investor could go long $10 million notional of three-year CDX 0–3 percent equity tranche and get an annual carry of $940,000, as illustrated in Figure 8. The investor could then hedge that out on a delta basis with a corresponding amount of three-year CDX mezzanine tranche exposure (3–7 percent). The investor is 26 times levered on the equity and 2 times levered on the mezzanine. To hedge out that $10 million of equity notional, the investor must short $130 million notional of mezzanine. Even after hedging out the delta exposure, the investor is left with a net annual carry of $630,000.

Rather than trading different parts of the capital structure against each other, the investor could simply go long the 0–3 percent equity tranche and delta hedge with single-name default swaps. With the equity tranche, the investor is getting significant positive carry, and by buying a basket of single-name CDS, the investor could eliminate the idiosyncratic default risk associated with select names.

4   CONCLUSION

I foresee continued growth in credit derivatives for managing default risk. Ten years ago, the risks were concentrated in the hands of a few large banks. Now, that risk is distributed among a large number of counterparties. Standardization of documentation has been one of the major forces in developing this market, and further product innovation will be a key driver in the future.

APPENDIX 67A

Question and Answer Session with George Spentzos

Question: With the rapid growth of the market, is a crisis brewing?

Spentzos: The main risks in the credit derivatives market are potential defaults, widening spreads, and correlation. Defaults are a given, and having Delphi Corporation default or having a cluster of defaults will not bring down the system; we have weathered numerous defaults without adverse consequences in the past.

Regulators have been more concerned that a crisis could arise if there were confirmation backlogs and problems with contracts not being processed in a timely manner. Is it realistic to assume that we could have a significant logjam in the future? The ISDA has recently developed a new protocol that will create a new communication process to manage that counterparty risk and potential confirmation backlog, which is a step in the right direction.

Question: Is the correlation risk a real risk?

Spentzos: Definitely. A popular correlation trade among hedge fund investors has been to sell protection (go long) on the equity tranche and either buy protection on the underlying index or on the junior mezzanine tranche as a delta hedge. These trades are profitable if spreads move together or if implied equity correlation increases, but they lose money if there is idiosyncratic volatility or implied equity correlation decreases.

Correlation is driven by both fundamental and technical factors. Fundamental factors could involve credit deterioration isolated to a few names in one sector, which could result in increased dispersion and, therefore, shift risk from the mezzanine to equity tranches. Technical factors include dealer flows, investor preferences, and market attitudes to risk. Although correlation risk was heightened because of General Motors Corporation (GM) and Ford downgrades in 2005, which resulted in market aversion to risk, I believe default rates will start to pick up in the next few years and that this will be the primary risk that we will have to manage going forward.

Question: What is the credit derivatives market like in emerging markets, such as Asia?

Spentzos: The problem with the Asian market is that it lacks maturity, even though it represents about 10 percent of the global market. Asian credits are more difficult to trade because they generally lack liquidity, and the ones that are liquid trade at very tight levels. One of the barriers is the regulatory environment, although this has been helped somewhat by relaxation of regulations, particularly in South Korea and Thailand. In the future, I would expect reasonable growth in emerging market credits.

Question: What would the impact be of a Ford or GM default on the synthetic CDO market?

Spentzos: It would be very significant because Ford and GM have been two of the most prevalent names in global CDO tranches. If either GM or Ford were to default, most deals would be subject to at least one credit event. That impact was seen on a smaller scale earlier in 2005 as those credits were downgraded from investment grade to junk.

If certain mezzanine tranches get downgraded, there could be forced sellers of these tranches in the marketplace. For example, if a BBB rated mezzanine tranche incurred several defaults and was subsequently downgraded to BB, you could have forced sellers of this mezzanine risk in the market, which would be advantageous for owners of other parts of the capital structure, including equity.

Question: Has the CDS market pulled liquidity away from the cash market?

Spentzos: It has taken some liquidity away from the corporate bond market, but the two have worked side by side in a relatively efficient manner. The corporate bond market isn't going to disappear, and the CDS market facilitates a more transparent pricing of corporate bonds. If someone is looking for exposure to a particular credit for a particular maturity and there are no relevant bonds, the CDS market will become a natural avenue to customize a solution.

Question: Does anyone other than the providers make consistent money in CDS strategies and instruments?

Spentzos: Flow desks at investment banks have traditionally made money from the bid–offer spreads in credit derivatives. As markets have matured, these margins have decreased, thus allowing market participants to inexpensively reflect views and construct optimized portfolios.

Question: Is there opportunity to exploit inefficiencies in this market?

Spentzos: One could argue that credit markets are less efficient than equity markets because of technical effects and exaggerated spread movements. With lower transaction costs and the advancement of the synthetic structured credit market, it is becoming easier to exploit these inefficiencies.

PORTFOLIO MANAGEMENT

STUDY SESSION

Study Session 18 Capital Market Theory and
the Portfolio Management Process

TOPIC LEVEL LEARNING OUTCOME

The candidate should be able to estimate the return and determine
the risk of various securities and apply the basic principles of the
portfolio management process to specific scenarios.

PORTFOLIO MANAGEMENT:
Capital Market Theory and the Portfolio Management Process

The first reading in this study session reintroduces CAPM (the capital asset pricing model)—a foundation for this study session and one of the first rigorous models for the expected returns on risky assets in equilibrium. Readings 69 through 71 extend the first reading, introducing further capital market theory and practical approaches to capital asset pricing, including capital asset pricing in a global marketplace. The final reading summarizes the portfolio management process, introducing topics that will be covered in more detail at Level III.

READING ASSIGNMENTS

Reading 68   Portfolio Concepts
Reading 69   A Note on Harry M. Markowitz's "Market Efficiency: A Theoretical Distinction and So What?"
Reading 70   International Asset Pricing
Reading 71   The Theory of Active Portfolio Management
Reading 72   The Portfolio Management Process and the Investment Policy Statement

LEARNING OUTCOMES

Reading 68: Portfolio Concepts

The candidate should be able to:

a. discuss mean–variance analysis and its assumptions; and calculate the expected return and the standard deviation of return for a portfolio of two or three assets;

b. explain the minimum variance and the efficient frontiers; and discuss the steps to solve for the minimum–variance frontier;

c. discuss diversification benefits, and explain how 1) the correlation in a two-asset portfolio and 2) the number of assets in a multi-asset portfolio affect the diversification benefits;

d. calculate the variance of an equally-weighted portfolio of n stocks; explain the capital allocation and the capital market lines (CAL and CML), explain the relation between them, and calculate the values of one of the variables given the values of the remaining variables;

327

e. explain the capital asset pricing model (CAPM), including its underlying assumptions and the resulting conclusions;

f. discuss the security market line (SML), the beta coefficient, the market risk premium, and the Sharpe ratio, and calculate the values of one of these variables given the values of the remaining variables;

g. explain the market model, and state and interpret the market model's predictions with respect to asset returns, variances, and covariances;

h. calculate an adjusted beta, and discuss the use of adjusted and historical betas as predictors of future betas;

i. discuss reasons for and problems related to instability in the minimum-variance frontier;

j. discuss and compare macroeconomic factor models, fundamental factor models, and statistical factor models;

k. calculate the expected return on a portfolio of two stocks, given the estimated macroeconomic factor model for each stock;

l. discuss the arbitrage pricing theory (APT), including its underlying assumptions and its relation to the multifactor models, calculate the expected return on an asset given an asset's factor sensitivities and the factor risk premiums, and determine whether an arbitrage opportunity exists, including how to exploit the opportunity;

m. explain the sources of active risk, and define and interpret tracking error, tracking risk, and the information ratio, and explain factor portfolio and tracking portfolio;

n. compare and contrast the conclusions and the underlying assumptions of the CAPM and the APT models, and explain why an investor can possibly earn a substantial premium for exposure to dimensions of risk unrelated to market movements.

Reading 69: A Note on Harry M. Markowitz's "Market Efficiency: A Theoretical Distinction and So What?"

The candidate should be able to:

a. discuss the efficiency of the market portfolio in the CAPM and the relationship between the expected return and beta of an asset when there are restrictions on borrowing at the risk-free rate and on short selling;

b. discuss the practical consequences that follow when there are restrictions on borrowing at the risk-free rate and on short selling.

Reading 70: International Asset Pricing

The candidate should be able to:

a. explain international market integration and segmentation, discuss the impediments to international capital mobility, and discuss the factors that favor international market integration;

b. state the assumptions of the domestic capital asset pricing model (CAPM), explain the extension of the domestic CAPM to an international context (the extended CAPM), and describe the additional assumptions needed to justify the extended CAPM;

  c. determine whether the real exchange rate has changed in a period, given the beginning-of-period (nominal) exchange rate, the inflation rates in the period, and the end-of-period (nominal) exchange rate;

  d. calculate the expected 1) exchange rate and 2) domestic-currency holding period return on a foreign bond (security), given expected, predictable inflation rates, the beginning-of-period nominal exchange rate, and the constant real exchange rate;

  e. calculate the end-of-period real exchange rate and the domestic-currency ex-post return on a foreign bond (security), given the end-of-period exchange rate, the beginning-of-period real exchange rate, and the inflation rates during the period;

  f. calculate a foreign currency risk premium, and explain a foreign currency risk premium in terms of interest rate differentials and forward rates;

  g. state the assumptions, the risk pricing relation, and the formula for the international capital asset pricing model (ICAPM);

  h. calculate the expected return on a stock, given its world market beta and currency exposure as well as the appropriate risk-free rates and risk premiums;

  i. explain the effect of market segmentation on the ICAPM;

  j. define currency exposure and explain exposures in terms of correlations;

  k. discuss the likely exchange rate exposure of a company based on a description of the company's activities, and explain the impact of both real and nominal exchange rate changes on the valuation of the company;

  l. discuss the currency exposures of national economies, equity markets, and bond markets;

  m. contrast the traditional trade approach and the money demand approach to modeling the relationship between real exchange rate changes and domestic economic activity.

Reading 71: The Theory of Active Portfolio Management

The candidate should be able to:

  a. justify the need for a theory of active portfolio management;

  b. discuss the steps and the approach of the Treynor-Black model for security selection;

  c. describe how an analyst's accuracy in forecasting alphas can be measured and how estimates of forecasting can be incorporated into the Treynor-Black approach.

Note:
Candidates are not responsible, within Reading 71, for deriving or memorizing the formulas introduced in Sections 4–6.

Reading 72: The Portfolio Management Process and the Investment Policy Statement

The candidate should be able to:

  a. explain the importance of the portfolio perspective;

  b. describe the steps of the portfolio management process and the components of those steps;

  c. define investment objectives and constraints and explain and distinguish among the types of investment objectives and constraints;

  d. discuss the role of the investment policy statement in the portfolio management process and explain the elements of an investment policy statement;

e. explain how capital market expectations and the investment policy statement help influence the strategic asset allocation decision and discuss how an investor's investment time horizon may influence the investor's strategic asset allocation;

f. contrast the types of investment time horizons, determine the time horizon for a particular investor, and evaluate the effects of this time horizon on portfolio choice;

g. justify ethical conduct as a requirement for managing investment portfolios.

PORTFOLIO CONCEPTS

by Richard A. DeFusco, Dennis W. McLeavey,
Jerald E. Pinto, and David E. Runkle

LEARNING OUTCOMES

The candidate should be able to:

a. discuss mean–variance analysis and its assumptions; and calculate the expected return and the standard deviation of return for a portfolio of two or three assets;

b. explain the minimum variance and the efficient frontiers; and discuss the steps to solve for the minimum–variance frontier;

c. discuss diversification benefits, and explain how 1) the correlation in a two-asset portfolio and 2) the number of assets in a multi-asset portfolio affect the diversification benefits;

d. calculate the variance of an equally-weighted portfolio of *n* stocks; explain the capital allocation and the capital market lines (CAL and CML), explain the relation between them, and calculate the values of one of the variables given the values of the remaining variables;

e. explain the capital asset pricing model (CAPM), including its underlying assumptions and the resulting conclusions;

f. discuss the security market line (SML), the beta coefficient, the market risk premium, and the Sharpe ratio, and calculate the values of one of these variables given the values of the remaining variables;

g. explain the market model, and state and interpret the market model's predictions with respect to asset returns, variances, and covariances;

h. calculate an adjusted beta, and discuss the use of adjusted and historical betas as predictors of future betas;

i. discuss reasons for and problems related to instability in the minimum-variance frontier;

j. discuss and compare macroeconomic factor models, fundamental factor models, and statistical factor models;

k. calculate the expected return on a portfolio of two stocks, given the estimated macroeconomic factor model for each stock;

Quantitative Methods for Investment Analysis, Second Edition, by Richard A. DeFusco, Dennis W. McLeavey, Jerald E. Pinto, and David E. Runkle. Copyright © 2004 by CFA Institute. Reprinted with permission.

l. discuss the arbitrage pricing theory (APT), including its underlying assumptions and its relation to the multifactor models, calculate the expected return on an asset given an asset's factor sensitivities and the factor risk premiums, and determine whether an arbitrage opportunity exists, including how to exploit the opportunity;

m. explain the sources of active risk, and define and interpret tracking error, tracking risk, and the information ratio, and explain factor portfolio and tracking portfolio;

n. compare and contrast the conclusions and the underlying assumptions of the CAPM and the APT models, and explain why an investor can possibly earn a substantial premium for exposure to dimensions of risk unrelated to market movements.

1   INTRODUCTION

No aspect of quantitative investment analysis is as widely studied or as vigorously debated as portfolio theory. Issues that portfolio managers have studied during the last 50 years include the following:

► What characteristics of a portfolio are important, and how may we quantify them?

► How do we model risk?

► If we could know the distribution of asset returns, how would we select an optimal portfolio?

► What is the optimal way to combine risky and risk-free assets in a portfolio?

► What are the limitations of using historical return data to predict a portfolio's future characteristics?

► What risk factors should we consider in addition to market risk?

In this reading, we present key quantitative methods to support the management of portfolios. In Section 2, we focus on mean–variance analysis and related models and issues. Then in Section 3, we address some of the problems encountered using mean–variance analysis and how we can respond to them. We introduce a **single-factor model**, the market model, which explains the return on assets in terms of a single variable, a market index. In Section 4, we present models that explain the returns on assets in terms of multiple factors, and we illustrate some important applications of these models in current practice.

2   MEAN–VARIANCE ANALYSIS

When does portfolio diversification reduce risk? Are there some portfolios that all risk-averse investors would avoid? These are some of the questions that Harry Markowitz addressed in the research for which he shared the 1990 Nobel Prize in Economics.

Mean–variance portfolio theory, the oldest and perhaps most accepted part of modern portfolio theory, provides the theoretical foundation for examining the roles of risk and return in portfolio selection. In this section, we describe Markowitz's theory, illustrate the principles of portfolio diversification with several examples, and discuss several important issues in implementation.

Mean–variance portfolio theory is based on the idea that the value of investment opportunities can be meaningfully measured in terms of mean return and variance of return. Markowitz called this approach to portfolio formation **mean–variance analysis**. Mean–variance analysis is based on the following assumptions:

1. All investors are risk averse; they prefer less risk to more for the same level of expected return.[1]

2. Expected returns for all assets are known.

3. The variances and covariances of all asset returns are known.

4. Investors need only know the expected returns, variances, and covariances of returns to determine optimal portfolios. They can ignore skewness, kurtosis, and other attributes of a distribution.[2]

5. There are no transaction costs or taxes.

Note that the first assumption does not mean that all investors have the same tolerance for risk. Investors differ in the level of risk they are willing to accept; however, risk-averse investors prefer as little risk as possible for a given level of expected return. In practice, expected returns and variances and covariances of returns for assets are not known but rather estimated. The estimation of those quantities may be a source of mistakes in decision-making when we use mean–variance analysis.

The fourth assumption is a key one, as it says that we may rely on certain summary measures of assets' return distributions—expected returns, variances, and covariances—to determine which combinations of assets make an optimal portfolio.

2.1 The Minimum-Variance Frontier and Related Concepts

An investor's objective in using a mean–variance approach to portfolio selection is to choose an efficient portfolio. An **efficient portfolio** is one offering the highest expected return for a given level of risk as measured by variance or standard deviation of return. Thus if an investor quantifies her tolerance for risk using standard deviation, she seeks the portfolio that she expects will deliver the greatest return for the standard deviation of return consistent with her risk tolerance. We begin the exploration of portfolio selection by forming a portfolio from just two asset classes, government bonds and large-cap stocks.

Table 1 shows the assumptions we make about the expected returns of the two assets, along with the standard deviation of return for the two assets and the correlation between their returns.

To begin the process of finding an efficient portfolio, we must identify the portfolios that have minimum variance for each given level of expected return.

---

[1] For more on risk aversion and its role in portfolio theory, see, for example, Sharpe, Alexander, and Bailey (1999) or Reilly and Brown (2003).

[2] This assumption could follow either from assuming that returns follow a normal distribution or from assuming that investors' attitudes toward risk and return can be mathematically represented in terms of mean and variance only.

TABLE 1	Assumed Expected Returns, Variances, and Correlation: Two-Asset Case	
	Asset 1 **Large-Cap Stocks**	**Asset 2** **Government Bonds**
Expected return	15%	5%
Variance	225	100
Standard deviation	15%	10%
Correlation	0.5	

Such portfolios are called **minimum-variance portfolios**. As we shall see, the set of efficient portfolios is a subset of the set of minimum variance portfolios.

We see from Table 1 that the standard deviation of the return to large-cap stocks (Asset 1) is 15 percent, the standard deviation of the return to government bonds (Asset 2) is 10 percent, and the correlation between the two assets returns is 0.5. Therefore, we can compute the variance of a portfolio's returns as a function of the fraction of the portfolio invested in large-cap stocks (w_1) and the fraction of the portfolio invested in government bonds (w_2). Because the portfolio contains only these two assets, we have the relationship $w_1 + w_2 = 1$. When the portfolio is 100 percent invested in Asset 1, w_1 is 1.0 and w_2 is 0; and when w_2 is 1.0, then w_1 is 0 and the portfolio is 100 percent invested in Asset 2. Also, when w_1 is 1.0, we know that our portfolio's expected return and variance of return are those of Asset 1. Conversely, when w_2 is 1.0, the portfolio's expected return and variance are those of Asset 2. In this case, the portfolio's maximum expected return is 15 percent if 100 percent of the portfolio is invested in large-cap stocks; its minimum expected return is 5 percent if 100 percent of the portfolio is invested in government bonds.

Before we can determine risk and return for all portfolios composed of large-cap stocks and government bonds, we must know how the expected return, variance, and standard deviation of the return for any two-asset portfolio depend on the expected returns of the two assets, their variances, and the correlation between the two assets' returns.

For any portfolio composed of two assets, the expected return to the portfolio, $E(R_p)$, is

$$E(R_p) = w_1 E(R_1) + w_2 E(R_2)$$

where

$E(R_1)$ = the expected return on Asset 1
$E(R_2)$ = the expected return on Asset 2

The portfolio variance of return is

$$\sigma_p^2 = w_1^2 \sigma_1^2 + w_2^2 \sigma_2^2 + 2w_1 w_2 \rho_{1,2} \sigma_1 \sigma_2$$

where

σ_1 = the standard deviation of return on Asset 1
σ_2 = the standard deviation of return on Asset 2
$\rho_{1,2}$ = the correlation between the two assets' returns

and $\mathrm{Cov}(R_1, R_2) = \rho_{1,2}\sigma_1\sigma_2$ is the covariance between the two returns, recalling the definition of correlation as the covariance divided by the individual standard deviations. The portfolio standard deviation of return is

$$\sigma_p = (w_1^2\sigma_1^2 + w_2^2\sigma_2^2 + 2w_1w_2\rho_{1,2}\sigma_1\sigma_2)^{1/2}$$

In this case, the expected return to the portfolio is $E(R_p) = w_1(0.15) + w_2(0.05)$, and the portfolio variance is $\sigma_p^2 = w_1^2 0.15^2 + w_2^2 0.10^2 + 2w_1w_2(0.5)(0.15)(0.10)$.

Given our assumptions about the expected returns, variances, and return correlation for the two assets, we can determine both the variance and the expected return of the portfolio as a function of the proportion of assets invested in large-cap stocks and government bonds. Table 2 shows the portfolio expected return, variance, and standard deviation as the weights on large-cap stocks rise from 0 to 1.0.

TABLE 2   Relation between Expected Return and Risk for a Portfolio of Stocks and Bonds

Expected Return	Portfolio Variance	Portfolio Standard Deviation	Large-Cap Stocks (w_1)	Government Bonds (w_2)
5%	100.00	10.00%	0	1.0
6%	96.75	9.84%	0.1	0.9
7%	97.00	9.85%	0.2	0.8
8%	100.75	10.04%	0.3	0.7
9%	108.00	10.39%	0.4	0.6
10%	118.75	10.90%	0.5	0.5
11%	133.00	11.53%	0.6	0.4
12%	150.75	12.28%	0.7	0.3
13%	172.00	13.11%	0.8	0.2
14%	196.75	14.03%	0.9	0.1
15%	225.00	15.00%	1.0	0

As Table 2 shows, when the weight on large-cap stocks is 0.1, the expected portfolio return is 6 percent and the portfolio variance is 96.75.[3] That portfolio has a higher expected return and lower variance than a portfolio with a weight of 0 on stocks—that is, a portfolio fully invested in government bonds. This improvement in risk–return characteristics illustrates the power of diversification: Because the returns to large-cap stocks are not perfectly correlated with the returns to government bonds (they do not have a correlation of 1), by putting some of the portfolio into large-cap stocks, we increase the expected return and reduce the variance of return. Furthermore, there is no cost to improving the risk–return characteristics of the portfolio in this way.

Figure 1 graphs the possible combinations of risk and return for a portfolio composed of government bonds and large-cap stocks. Figure 1 plots the expected portfolio return on the y-axis and the portfolio variance on the x-axis.

---

[3] Note that the 96.75 is in units of percent squared. In decimals, the expected portfolio return is 0.06 and the portfolio variance is 0.009675.

FIGURE 1 Minimum-Variance Frontier: Large-Cap Stocks and Government Bonds

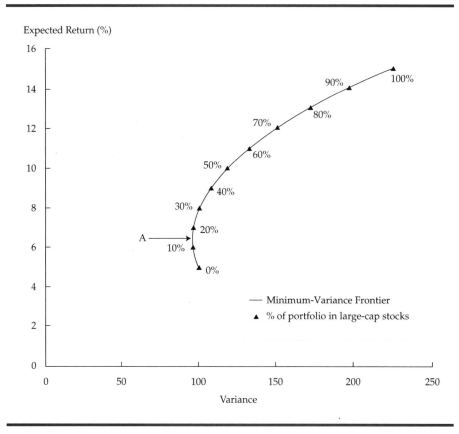

The two-asset case is special because all two-asset portfolios plot on the curve illustrated (there is a unique combination of two assets that provides a given level of expected return). This is the **portfolio possibilities curve**—a curve plotting the expected return and risk of the portfolios that can be formed using two assets. We can also call the curve in Figure 1 the **minimum-variance frontier** because it shows the minimum variance that can be achieved for a given level of expected return. The minimum-variance frontier is a more useful concept than the portfolio possibilities curve because it also applies to portfolios with more than two assets. In the general case of more than two assets, any portfolios plotting on an imaginary horizontal line at any expected return level have the same expected return, and as we move left on that line, we have less variance of return. The attainable portfolio farthest to the left on such a line is the minimum-variance portfolio for that level of expected return and one point on the minimum-variance frontier. With three or more assets, the minimum-variance frontier is a true frontier: It is the border of a region representing all combinations of expected return and risk that are possible (the border of the feasible region). The region results from the fact that with three or more assets, an unlimited number of portfolios can provide a given level of expected return.[4] In the case of three or more assets, if we move to the right from a point on the minimum-variance frontier, we reach another portfolio but one with more risk.

---

[4] For example, if we have three assets with expected returns of 5 percent, 12 percent, and 20 percent and we want an expected return of 11 percent on the portfolio, we would use the following equation to solve for the portfolio weights (using the fact that portfolio weights must sum to 1): $11\% = (5\% \times w_1) + (12\% \times w_2) + [20\% \times (1 - w_1 - w_2)]$. This single equation with two unknowns, w_1 and w_2, has an unlimited number of possible solutions, each solution representing a portfolio.

From Figure 1, note that the variance of the global minimum-variance portfolio (the one with the smallest variance) appears to be close to 96.43 (Point A) when the expected return of the portfolio is 6.43. This global minimum-variance portfolio has 14.3 percent of assets in large-cap stocks and 85.7 percent of assets in government bonds. Given these assumed returns, standard deviations, and correlation, a portfolio manager should not choose a portfolio with less than 14.3 percent of assets in large-cap stocks because any such portfolio will have both a higher variance and a lower expected return than the global minimum-variance portfolio. All of the points on the minimum-variance frontier below Point A are inferior to the global minimum-variance portfolio, and they should be avoided.

Financial economists often say that portfolios located below the global minimum-variance portfolio (Point A in Figure 1) are dominated by others that have the same variances but higher expected returns. Because these dominated portfolios use risk inefficiently, they are inefficient portfolios. The portion of the minimum-variance frontier beginning with the global minimum-variance portfolio and continuing above it is called the **efficient frontier**. Portfolios lying on the efficient frontier offer the maximum expected return for their level of variance of return. Efficient portfolios use risk efficiently: Investors making portfolio choices in terms of mean return and variance of return can restrict their selections to portfolios lying on the efficient frontier. This reduction in the number of portfolios to be considered simplifies the selection process. If an investor can quantify his risk tolerance in terms of variance or standard deviation of return, the efficient portfolio for that level of variance or standard deviation will represent the optimal mean–variance choice.

Because standard deviation is easier to interpret than variance, investors often plot the expected return against standard deviation rather than variance.[5] Figure 2 plots the expected portfolio return for this example on the *y*-axis and

FIGURE 2   Minimum-Variance Frontier: Large-Cap Stocks and Government Bonds

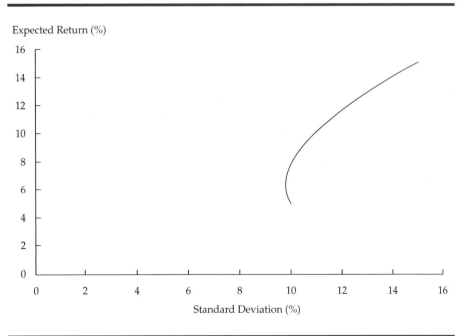

---

[5] Expected return and standard deviation are measured in the same units, percent.

the portfolio standard deviation of return on the *x*-axis.[6] The curve graphed is still called the minimum-variance frontier.

Example 1 illustrates the process of determining a historical minimum-variance frontier.

EXAMPLE 1

A Two-Asset Minimum-Variance Frontier Using Historical U.S. Return Data

Susan Fitzsimmons has decided to invest her retirement plan assets in a U.S. small-cap equity index fund and a U.S. long-term government bond index fund. Fitzsimmons decides to use mean–variance analysis to help determine the fraction of her funds to invest in each fund. Assuming that expected returns and variances can be estimated accurately using monthly historical returns from 1970 through 2002, she computes the average returns, variances of returns, and correlation of returns for the indexes that the index funds attempt to track. Table 3 shows those historical statistics.

TABLE 3   Average Returns and Variances of Returns (Annualized, Based on Monthly Data, January 1970–December 2002)

Asset Class	Average Return	Variance
U.S. small-cap stocks	14.63%	491.8
U.S. long-term government bonds	9.55%	109.0
Correlation	0.138	

Source: Ibbotson Associates.

Given these statistics, Fitzsimmons can determine the allocation of the portfolio between the two assets using the expected return and variance. To do so, she must calculate

▶ the range of possible expected returns for the portfolio (minimum and maximum),

▶ the proportion of each of the two assets (asset weights) in the minimum-variance portfolio for each possible level of expected return, and

▶ the variance[7] for each possible level of expected return.

---

[6] For the remainder of this reading, we will plot the expected return against standard deviation of return.

[7] In the two-asset case, as previously stated, there is a unique combination of the two assets that provides a given level of expected return, so there is a unique variance for a given level of expected return. Thus the portfolio variance calculated for each level of expected return is trivially the minimum-variance portfolio for that level of expected return.

Because U.S. government bonds have a lower expected return than U.S. small-cap stocks, the minimum expected return portfolio has 100 percent weight in U.S. long-term government bonds, 0 percent weight in U.S. small-cap stocks, and an expected return of 9.55 percent. In contrast, the maximum expected return portfolio has 100 percent weight in U.S. small-cap stocks, 0 percent weight in U.S. long-term government bonds, and an expected return of 14.63 percent. Therefore, the range of possible expected portfolio returns is 9.55 percent to 14.63 percent.

Fitzsimmons now determines the asset weights of the two asset classes at different levels of expected return, starting at the minimum expected return of 9.55 percent and concluding at the maximum level of expected return of 14.63 percent. The weights at each level of expected return determine the variance for the portfolio consisting of these two asset classes. Table 4 shows the composition of portfolios for various levels of expected return.

TABLE 4	Points on the Minimum-Variance Frontier for U.S. Small-Cap Stocks and U.S. Long-Term Government Bonds			
Expected Return	Variance	Standard Deviation	Small-Cap Stocks, w_1	Government Bonds, w_2
9.55%	109.0	10.4%	0.000	1.000
9.65%	106.2	10.3%	0.020	0.980
9.95%	100.2	10.0%	0.079	0.921
10.25%	98.0	9.9%	0.138	0.862
10.55%	99.5	10.0%	0.197	0.803
10.75%	102.6	10.1%	0.236	0.764
14.63%	491.8	22.2%	1.000	0.000

Table 4 illustrates what happens to the weights in the individual asset classes as we move from the minimum expected return to the maximum expected return. When the expected return is 9.55 percent, the weight for the long-term government bonds is 100 percent. As we increase the expected return, the weight in long-term government bonds decreases; at the same time, the weight for U.S. small stocks increases. This result makes sense because we know that the maximum expected return of 14.63 percent must have a weight of 100 percent in U.S. small stocks. The weights in Table 4 reflect that property. Note that the global minimum-variance portfolio (which is also the global minimum-standard-deviation portfolio) contains some of both assets. A portfolio consisting only of bonds has more risk and a lower expected return than the global minimum-variance portfolio because diversification can reduce total portfolio risk, as we discuss shortly.

Figure 3 illustrates the minimum-variance frontier (in the two-asset-class case, merely a portfolio possibilities curve) over the period

FIGURE 3   Minimum-Variance Frontier: U.S. Small-Cap Stocks and Government Bonds

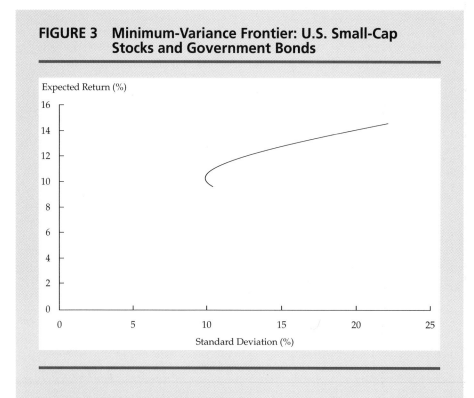

1970 to 2002 by graphing expected return as a function of standard deviation.

If Fitzsimmons quantifies her risk tolerance as a standard deviation of 10 percent, for example, mean–variance analysis suggests that she choose a portfolio with an approximate weighting of 0.20 in small-cap stocks and 0.80 in long-term government bonds. One major caution that we shall discuss later in this reading is that even small changes in inputs can have a significant effect on the minimum-variance frontier, and the future may obviously be very different from the past. The historical record is only a starting point in developing inputs for calculating the minimum-variance frontier.[8]

The trade-off between risk and return for a portfolio depends not only on the expected asset returns and variances but also on the correlation of asset returns. Returning to the case of large-cap stocks and government bonds, we assumed that the correlation was 0.5. The risk-return trade-off is quite different for other correlation values. Figure 4 shows the minimum-variance frontiers for portfolios containing large-cap stocks and government bonds for varying weights.[9] The weights go from 100 percent in government bonds and 0 percent in large-cap stocks to 0 percent in government bonds and 100 percent in large-cap stocks, for

---

[8] Note also that the historical data are monthly, corresponding to a monthly investment horizon. The minimum-variance frontier could be quite different if we used data with a different horizon (say quarterly).

[9] Recall from Table 1 that large-cap stocks have an assumed expected return and standard deviation of return of 15 percent, while government bonds have an assumed expected return and standard deviation of return of 5 percent and 10 percent, respectively.

FIGURE 4   Minimum-Variance Frontier for Varied Correlations: Large-Cap Stocks and Government Bonds

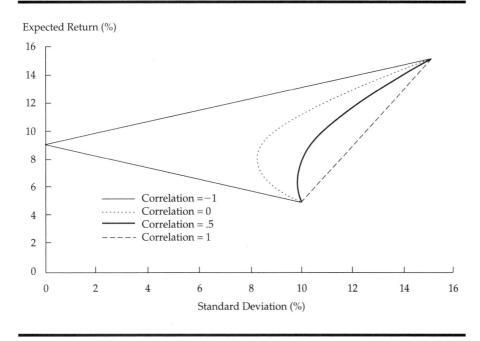

four different values of the correlation coefficient. The correlations illustrated in Figure 4 are −1, 0, 0.5, and 1.

Figure 4 illustrates a number of interesting characteristics about minimum-variance frontiers and diversification:[10]

▶ The endpoints for all of the frontiers are the same. This fact should not be surprising, because at one endpoint all of the assets are in government bonds and at the other endpoint all of the assets are in large-cap stocks. At each endpoint, the expected return and standard deviation are simply the return and standard deviation for the relevant asset (stocks or bonds).

▶ When the correlation is +1, the minimum-variance frontier is an upward-sloping straight line. If we start at any point on the line, for each one percentage point increase in standard deviation we achieve the same constant increment in expected return. With a correlation of +1, the return (not just the expected return) on one asset is an exact positive linear function of the return on the other asset.[11] Because fluctuations in the returns on the two assets track each other in this way, the returns on one asset cannot dampen or smooth out the fluctuations in the returns on the other asset. For a correlation of +1, diversification has no potential benefits.

---

[10] We are examining, and our observations generally pertain to, the case in which neither of the two assets is dominated. In mean–variance analysis, an asset A is dominated by an asset B if (1) the mean return on B is equal to or larger than that on A, but B has a smaller standard deviation of return than A; or (2) the mean return on B is strictly larger than that on A, but A and B have the same standard deviation of return. The slope of a straight line connecting two assets, neither of which is dominated, is positive.

[11] If the correlation is +1, $R_1 = a + bR_2$, with $b > 0$.

▶ When we move from a correlation of +1 to a correlation of 0.5, the minimum-variance frontier bows out to the left, in the direction of smaller standard deviation. With any correlation less than +1, we can achieve any feasible level of expected return with a smaller standard deviation of return than for the +1 correlation case. As we move from a correlation of 0.5 to each smaller value of correlation, the minimum-variance frontier bows out farther to the left.

▶ The frontiers for correlation of 0.5, 0, and −1 have a negatively sloped part.[12] This means that if we start at the lowest point (100 percent in government bonds) and shift money into stocks until we reach the global minimum-variance portfolio, we can get more expected return with less risk. Therefore, relative to an initial position fully invested in government bonds, there are diversification benefits in each of these correlation cases. A diversification benefit is a reduction in portfolio standard deviation of return through diversification without an accompanying decrease in expected return. Because the minimum-variance frontier bows out further to the left as we lower correlation, we can also conclude that as we lower correlation, holding all other values constant, there are increasingly larger potential benefits to diversification.

▶ When the correlation is −1, the minimum-variance frontier has two linear segments. The two segments join at the global minimum-variance portfolio, which has a standard deviation of 0. With a correlation of −1, portfolio risk can be reduced to zero, if desired.

▶ Between the two extreme correlations of +1 and −1, the minimum-variance frontier has a bullet-like shape. Thus the minimum-variance frontier is sometimes called the "bullet."

▶ The efficient frontier is the positively sloped part of the minimum-variance frontier. Holding all other values constant, as we lower correlation, the efficient frontier improves in the sense of offering a higher expected return for a given feasible level of standard deviation of return.

In summary, when the correlation between two portfolios is less than +1, diversification offers potential benefits. As we lower the correlation coefficient toward −1, holding other values constant, the potential benefits to diversification increase.

2.2 Extension to the Three-Asset Case

Earlier we considered forming a portfolio composed of two assets: large-cap stocks and government bonds. For investors in our example who want to maximize expected return for a given level of risk (hold an efficient portfolio), the optimal portfolio combination of two assets contains some of each asset, unless the portfolio is placed entirely in stocks.

---

[12] For positive correlations (between 0 and 1), a negatively sloped part is present when correlation is less than the standard deviation of the less risky asset divided by the standard deviation of the riskier asset. In our case, this ratio is equal to the standard deviation of long-term government bonds to large-cap stocks, or $10/15 = 0.6667$. Because 0.5 is less than 0.6667, the minimum-variance frontier for 0.5 has a negatively sloped part. We have not allowed short sales (negative asset weights). If we allow short sales, frontiers for any positive correlation will have a negatively sloped part, which may involve the short sale of the more risky asset. For details, see Elton, Gruber, Brown, and Goetzmann (2003).

Now we may ask, would adding another asset to the possible investment choices improve the available trade-offs between risk and return? The answer to this question is very frequently yes. A fundamental economic principle states that one is never worse off for having additional choices. At worst, an investor can ignore the additional choices and be no worse off than initially. Often, however, a new asset permits us to move to a superior minimum-variance frontier. We can illustrate this common result by contrasting the minimum-variance frontier for two assets (here, large-cap stocks and government bonds) with the minimum-variance frontier for three assets (large-cap stocks, government bonds, and small-cap stocks).

In our initial two-asset case shown in Table 1, we assumed expected returns, variances, and correlations for large-cap stocks and government bonds. Now suppose we have an additional investment option, small-cap stocks. Can we achieve a better trade-off between risk and return than when we could choose between only two assets, large-cap stocks and government bonds?

Table 5 shows our assumptions about the expected returns of all three assets, along with the standard deviations of the asset returns and their correlations.

TABLE 5	Assumed Expected Returns, Variances, and Correlations: Three-Asset Case		
	Asset 1 Large-Cap Stocks	Asset 2 Government Bonds	Asset 3 Small-Cap Stocks
Expected return	15%	5%	15%
Variance	225	100	225
Standard deviation	15%	10%	15%
Correlations			
Large-cap stocks and bonds	0.5		
Large-cap stocks and small-cap stocks	0.8		
Bonds and small-cap stocks	0.5		

Now we can consider the relation between these statistics and the expected return and variance for the portfolio. For any portfolio composed of three assets with portfolio weights w_1, w_2, and w_3, the expected return on the portfolio, $E(R_p)$, is

$$E(R_p) = w_1 E(R_1) + w_2 E(R_2) + w_3 E(R_3)$$

where

$E(R_1)$ = the expected return on Asset 1 (here, large-cap stocks)
$E(R_2)$ = the expected return on Asset 2 (government bonds)
$E(R_3)$ = the expected return on Asset 3 (small-cap stocks)

The portfolio variance is

$$\sigma_p^2 = w_1^2 \sigma_1^2 + w_2^2 \sigma_2^2 + w_3^2 \sigma_3^2 + 2 w_1 w_2 \rho_{1,2} \sigma_1 \sigma_2 + 2 w_1 w_3 \rho_{1,3} \sigma_1 \sigma_3 + 2 w_2 w_3 \rho_{2,3} \sigma_2 \sigma_3$$

where

σ_1 = the standard deviation of the return on Asset 1
σ_2 = the standard deviation of the return on Asset 2
σ_3 = the standard deviation of the return on Asset 3
$\rho_{1,2}$ = the correlation between returns on Asset 1 and Asset 2
$\rho_{1,3}$ = the correlation between returns on Asset 1 and Asset 3
$\rho_{2,3}$ = the correlation between returns on Asset 2 and Asset 3

The portfolio standard deviation is

$$\sigma_p = [w_1^2\sigma_1^2 + w_2^2\sigma_2^2 + w_3^2\sigma_3^2 + 2w_1w_2\rho_{1,2}\sigma_1\sigma_2 + 2w_1w_3\rho_{1,3}\sigma_1\sigma_3 + 2w_2w_3\rho_{2,3}\sigma_2\sigma_3]^{1/2}$$

Given our assumptions, the expected return on the portfolio is

$$E(R_p) = w_1(0.15) + w_2(0.05) + w_3(0.15)$$

The portfolio variance is

$$\sigma_p^2 = w_1^2 0.15^2 + w_2^2 0.10^2 + w_3^2 0.15^2 + 2w_1w_2(0.5)(0.15)(0.10)$$
$$+ 2w_1w_3(0.8)(0.15)(0.15) + 2w_2w_3(0.5)(0.10)(0.15)$$

The portfolio standard deviation is

$$\sigma_p = [w_1^2 0.15^2 + w_2^2 0.10^2 + w_3^2 0.15^2 + 2w_1w_2(0.5)(0.15)(0.10)$$
$$+ 2w_1w_3(0.8)(0.15)(0.15) + 2w_2w_3(0.5)(0.10)(0.15)]^{1/2}$$

In this three-asset case, however, determining the optimal combinations of assets is much more difficult than it was in the two-asset example. In the two-asset case, the percentage of assets in large-cap stocks was simply 100 percent minus the percentage of assets in government bonds. But with three assets, we need a method to determine what combination of assets will produce the lowest variance for any particular expected return. At least we know the minimum expected return (the return that would result from putting all assets in government bonds, 5 percent) and the maximum expected return (the return from putting no assets in government bonds, 15 percent). For any level of expected return between the minimum and maximum levels, we must solve for the portfolio weights that will result in the lowest risk for that level of expected return. We use an **optimizer** (a specialized computer program or a spreadsheet with this capability) to provide these weights.[13]

Notice that the new asset, small-cap stocks, has a correlation of less than +1 with both large-cap stocks and bonds, suggesting that small-cap stocks may be useful in diversifying risk.

Table 6 shows the portfolio expected return, variance, standard deviation, and portfolio weights for the minimum-variance portfolio as the expected return rises from 5 percent to 15 percent.

As Table 6 shows, the proportion of the portfolio in large-cap stocks and small-cap stocks is the same in all the minimum-variance portfolios. This proportion results from the simplifying assumption in Table 5 that large-cap stocks and small-cap stocks have identical expected returns and standard deviations of

---

[13] These programs use a solution method called quadratic programming.

TABLE 6	Points on the Minimum-Variance Frontier for the Three-Asset Case				
Expected Return	Portfolio Variance	Portfolio Standard Deviation	Large-Cap Stocks (w_1)	Government Bonds (w_2)	Small-Cap (w_3)
5%	100.00	10.00%	0	1.00	0
6%	96.53	9.82%	0.05	0.90	0.05
7%	96.10	9.80%	0.10	0.80	0.10
8%	98.72	9.94%	0.15	0.70	0.15
9%	104.40	10.22%	0.20	0.60	0.20
10%	113.13	10.64%	0.25	0.50	0.25
11%	124.90	11.18%	0.30	0.40	0.30
12%	139.73	11.82%	0.35	0.30	0.35
13%	157.60	12.55%	0.40	0.20	0.40
14%	178.53	13.36%	0.45	0.10	0.45
15%	202.50	14.23%	0.50	0	0.50

return, as well as the same correlation with government bonds. With a different, more realistic combination of returns, variances, and correlations, the minimum-variance portfolios in this example would contain different proportions of the large-cap stocks and small-cap stocks, but we would reach a similar conclusion about the possibility of improving the available risk-return trade-offs.

How does the minimum variance for each level of expected return in the three-asset case compare with the minimum variance for each level of expected return in the two-asset case? Figure 5 shows the comparison.

FIGURE 5   Comparing Minimum-Variance Frontiers: Three Assets versus Two Assets

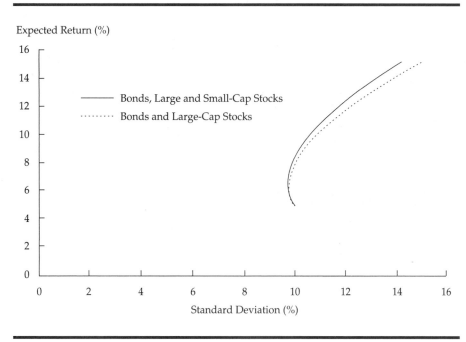

When 100 percent of the portfolio is invested in government bonds, the minimum-variance portfolio has the same expected return (5 percent) and standard deviation (10 percent) in both cases. For every other level of expected return, however, the minimum-variance portfolio in the three-asset case has a lower standard deviation than the minimum-variance portfolio in the two-asset case for the same expected return. Note also that the efficient frontier with three assets dominates the efficient frontier with two assets (we would choose our optimal portfolio from those on the superior efficient frontier).

From this three-asset example, we can draw two conclusions about the theory of portfolio diversification. First, we generally can improve the risk-return trade-off by expanding the set of assets in which we can invest. Second, the composition of the minimum-variance portfolio for any particular level of expected return depends on the expected returns, the variances and correlations of those returns, and the number of assets.

2.3 Determining the Minimum-Variance Frontier for Many Assets

We have shown examples of mean–variance analysis with two and three assets. Typically, however, portfolio managers form optimal portfolios using a larger number of assets. In this section, we show how to determine the minimum-variance frontier for a portfolio composed of many assets.

For a portfolio of n assets, the expected return on the portfolio is[14]

$$E(R_p) = \sum_{j=1}^{n} w_j E(R_j) \tag{68-1}$$

The variance of return on the portfolio is[15]

$$\sigma_p^2 = \sum_{i=1}^{n} \sum_{j=1}^{n} w_i w_j \mathrm{Cov}(R_i, R_j) \tag{68-2}$$

Before determining the optimal portfolio weights, remember that the weights of the individual assets in the portfolio must sum to 1:

$$\sum_{j=1}^{n} w_j = 1$$

To determine the minimum-variance frontier for a set of n assets, we must first determine the minimum and maximum expected returns possible with the set of assets (these are the minimum, r_{min}, and the maximum, r_{max}, expected returns for the individual assets). Then we must determine the portfolio weights that will create the minimum-variance portfolio for values of expected return between r_{min} and r_{max}. In mathematical terms, we must solve the following problem for specified values of z, $r_{min} \le z \le r_{max}$:

$$\underset{\text{by choice of } w\text{'s}}{\text{Minimize }} \sigma_p^2 = \sum_{i=1}^{n} \sum_{j=1}^{n} w_i w_j \mathrm{Cov}(R_i, R_j) \tag{68-3}$$

---

[14] The summation notation says that we set j equal to 1 through n, and then we sum the resulting terms.

[15] The double summation notation says that we set i equal to 1 and let j run from 1 through n, then we set i equal to 2 and let j run from 1 through n, and so forth until i equals n; then we sum all the terms.

subject to $E(R_p) = \sum_{j=1}^{n} w_j E(R_j) = z$ and subject to $\sum_{j=1}^{n} w_j = 1$

This optimization problem says that we solve for the portfolio weights (w_1, w_2, w_3, ..., w_n) that minimize the variance of return for a given level of expected return z, subject to the constraint that the weights sum to 1. The weights define a portfolio, and the portfolio is the minimum-variance portfolio for its level of expected return. Equation 68-3 shows the simplest case in which the only constraint on portfolio weights is that they sum to 1; this case allows assets to be sold short. A constraint against short sales would require adding a further constraint that $w_j \geq 0$. We trace out the minimum-variance frontier by varying the value of expected return from the minimum to the maximum level. For example, we could determine the optimal portfolio weights for a small set of z values by starting with $z = r_{min}$, then increasing z by 10 basis points (0.10 percent) and solving for the optimal portfolio weights until we reach $z = r_{max}$.[16] We use an optimizer to actually solve the optimization problem. Example 2 shows a minimum-variance frontier that results from using historical data for non-U.S. stocks and three U.S. asset classes.

EXAMPLE 2

A Minimum-Variance Frontier Using International Historical Return Data

In this example, we examine a historical minimum-variance frontier with four asset classes. The three U.S. asset classes are the S&P 500 Index, U.S. small-cap stocks, and U.S. long-term government bonds. To these we add non-U.S. stocks (MSCI World ex-United States). We estimate the minimum-variance frontier based on historical monthly return data from January 1970 to December 2002. Table 7 presents the mean returns, variances, and correlations of these four assets for the entire sample period.

Table 7 shows that the minimum average historical return from these four asset classes was 9.6 percent a year (bonds) and the maximum average historical return was 14.6 percent (U.S. small-cap stocks). To trace out the minimum-variance frontier, we use the optimization model. The optimization program with a short sales constraint solves for the mean–variance frontier using the following equations:

$$\text{Min } \sigma_p^2(R) = w_1^2\sigma_1^2 + w_2^2\sigma_2^2 + w_3^2\sigma_3^2 + w_4^2\sigma_4^2 + 2w_1w_2\rho_{1,2}\sigma_1\sigma_2$$
$$+ 2w_1w_3\rho_{1,3}\sigma_1\sigma_3 + 2w_1w_4\rho_{1,4}\sigma_1\sigma_4 + 2w_2w_3\rho_{2,3}\sigma_2\sigma_3$$
$$+ 2w_2w_4\rho_{2,4}\sigma_2\sigma_4 + 2w_3w_4\rho_{3,4}\sigma_3\sigma_4$$

subject to $E(R_p) = w_1E(R_1) + w_2E(R_2) + w_3E(R_3) + w_4E(R_4) = z$ (repeated for specified values of z, $0.096 \leq z \leq 0.146$), $w_1 + w_2 + w_3 + w_4 = 1$, and $w_j \geq 0$.

---

[16] There is a shortcut in the case of no constraints against short sales. According to Black's (1972) two-fund theorem, all portfolios on the minimum-variance frontier of risky assets are a linear combination of any two other minimum-variance portfolios, assuming that short sales are allowed. The implication is that we can trace out the minimum-variance frontier if we have calculated the portfolio weights of two minimum-variance portfolios. The procedure in the reading, however, works even when we add the constraint against short sales, which many investors face.

TABLE 7   Mean Annual Returns, Standard Deviations, and Correlation Matrix for Four Asset Classes, January 1970–December 2002

	S&P 500	U.S. Small-Cap Stocks	MSCI World ex-United States	U.S. Long-Term Government Bonds
Mean Annual Returns	11.6%	14.6%	11.1%	9.6%
Standard deviation	15.83%	22.18%	17.07%	10.44%
Correlations				
S&P 500	1			
U.S. small-cap stocks	0.731	1		
MSCI World ex-U.S.	0.573	0.475	1	
U.S. long-term bonds	0.266	0.138	0.155	1

Source: Ibbotson Associates.

The weights w_1, w_2, w_3, and w_4 represent the four asset classes in the order listed in Table 7. The optimizer chooses the weights (allocations to the four asset classes) that result in the minimum-variance portfolio for each level of average return as we move from the minimum level (r_{min} = 9.6 percent) to the maximum level (r_{max} = 14.6 percent). In this example, $E(R_j)$ is represented by the sample mean return on asset class j, and the variances and covariances are also sample statistics. Unless we deliberately chose to use these historical data as our forward-looking estimates, we would not interpret the results of the optimization as a prediction about the future.

Figure 6 shows the minimum-variance frontier for these four asset classes based on the historical means, variances, and covariances from 1970 to 2002. The figure also shows the means and standard deviations of the four asset classes separately.

Although U.S. government bonds lie on the minimum-variance frontier, they are dominated by other asset classes that offer a better mean return for the same level of risk. Note that the points representing S & P 500 and the MSCI World ex-U.S. stocks plotted off and to the right of the minimum-variance frontier. If we move directly to the left from either the S & P 500 or MSCI ex-U.S. stock portfolio, we reach a portfolio on the efficient frontier that has smaller risk without affecting the mean return. If we move directly up from either, we reach a portfolio that has greater mean return with the same level of risk. After the fact, at least, these two portfolios were not efficient for an investor who could invest in all four asset classes. Despite the fact that MSCI World ex-U.S. stocks is itself a very broad index, for example, there were benefits to further diversifying. Of the four asset classes, only U.S. small-cap stocks

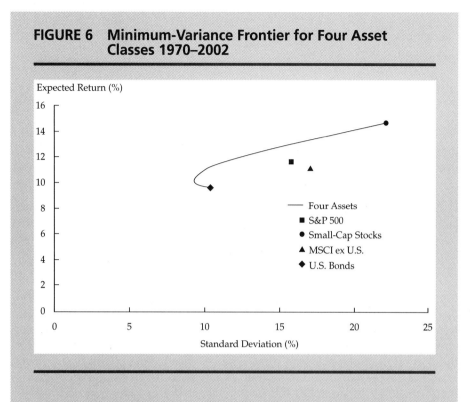

FIGURE 6 Minimum-Variance Frontier for Four Asset Classes 1970–2002

as the highest-mean-return portfolio plotted on the efficient frontier; in general, the highest-mean-return portfolio appears as an endpoint of the efficient frontier in an optimization with a constraint against short sales, as in this case.

In this section, we showed the process for tracing out a minimum-variance frontier. We also analyzed a frontier generated from actual data. In the next section, we address the relationship between portfolio size and diversification.

2.4 Diversification and Portfolio Size

Earlier, we illustrated the diversification benefits of adding a third asset to a two-asset portfolio. That discussion opened a question of practical interest that we explore in this section: How many different stocks must we hold in order to have a well-diversified portfolio? How does covariance or correlation interact with portfolio size in determining a portfolio's risk?

We address these questions using the example of an investor who holds an equally weighted portfolio. Suppose we purchase a portfolio of n stocks and put an equal fraction of the value of the portfolio into each of the stocks ($w_i = 1/n$, $i = 1, 2, \ldots, n$). The variance of return is

$$\sigma_p^2 = \sum_{i=1}^{n} \sum_{j=1}^{n} w_i w_j \mathrm{Cov}(R_i, R_j) = \frac{1}{n^2} \sum_{i=1}^{n} \sum_{j=1}^{n} \mathrm{Cov}(R_i, R_j) \qquad \textbf{(68-4)}$$

Suppose we call the average variance of return across all stocks $\overline{\sigma}^2$ and the average covariance between all pairs of two stocks $\overline{\text{Cov}}$. It is possible to show[17] that Equation 68-4 simplifies to

$$\sigma_p^2 = \frac{1}{n}\overline{\sigma}^2 + \frac{n-1}{n}\overline{\text{Cov}}$$

(68-5)

As the number of stocks, n, increases, the contribution of the variance of the individual stocks becomes very small because $(1/n)\overline{\sigma}^2$ has a limit of 0 as n becomes large. Also, the contribution of the average covariance across stocks to the portfolio variance stays nonzero because $\dfrac{n-1}{n}\overline{\text{Cov}}$ has a limit of $\overline{\text{Cov}}$ as n becomes large. Therefore, as the number of assets in the portfolio becomes large, portfolio variance approximately equals average covariance. In large portfolios, average covariance—capturing how assets move together—becomes more important than average individual risk or variance.

In addition to this insight, Equation 68-5 allows us to gauge the reduction in portfolio variance from the completely undiversified position of holding only one stock. If the portfolio contained only one stock, then of course its variance would be the individual stock's variance, which is the position of maximum variance.[18] If the portfolio contained a very large number of stocks, the variance of the portfolio would be close to the average covariance of any two of the stocks, known as the position of minimum variance. How large is the difference between these two levels of variance, and how much of the maximum benefit can we obtain with a relatively small number of stocks?

The answers depend on the sizes of the average variance and the average covariance. Because correlation is easier to interpret than covariance, we will work with correlation. Suppose, for simplicity's sake, that the correlation between the returns for any two stocks is the same and that all stocks have the same standard deviation. Chan, Karceski, and Lakonishok (1999) found that for U.S. NYSE and Amex stocks over the 1968–98 period, the average correlation of small-stock returns was 0.24, the average correlation of large-stock returns was 0.33, and the average correlation of stock returns across the entire sample of stocks was 0.28. Assume that the common correlation is 0.30, which is in the approximate range for the average correlation of U.S. equities for many time periods. The covariance of two random variables is the correlation of those variables multiplied by the standard deviations of the two variables, so $\overline{\text{Cov}} = 0.30\sigma^2$ (using our assumption that all stocks have the same standard deviation of returns, denoted σ).

Look back at Equation 68-5 and replace $\overline{\text{Cov}}$ with $0.30\sigma^2$:

$$\sigma_p^2 = \frac{1}{n}\sigma^2 + \frac{n-1}{n}(0.30\sigma^2)$$

$$= \frac{\sigma^2}{n}[1 + 0.30(n-1)]$$

$$= \frac{\sigma^2}{n}(0.70 + 0.30n)$$

$$= \sigma^2\left(\frac{0.70}{n} + 0.30\right)$$

---

[17] See Bodie, Kane, and Marcus (2001).

[18] For realistic values of correlation, average variance is greater than average covariance.

which provides an example of the more general expression (assuming stocks have the same standard deviation of returns)

$$\sigma_p^2 = \sigma^2 \left(\frac{1 - \rho}{n} + \rho \right)$$

(68-6)

If the portfolio contains one stock, the portfolio variance is σ^2. As n increases, portfolio variance drops rapidly. In our example, if the portfolio contains 15 stocks, the portfolio variance is $0.347\sigma^2$, or only 34.7 percent of the variance of a portfolio with one stock. With 30 stocks, the portfolio variance is 32.3 percent of the variance of a single-stock portfolio. The smallest possible portfolio variance in this case is 30 percent of the variance of a single stock, because $\sigma_p^2 = 0.30\,\sigma^2$ when n is extremely large. With only 30 stocks, for example, the portfolio variance is only approximately 8 percent larger than minimum possible value $(0.323\sigma^2/0.30\sigma^2 - 1 = 0.077)$, and the variance is 67.7 percent smaller than the variance of a portfolio that contains only one stock.

For a reasonable assumed value of correlation, the previous example shows that a portfolio composed of many stocks has far less total risk than a portfolio composed of only one stock. In this example, we can diversify away 70 percent of an individual stock's risk by holding many stocks. Furthermore, we may be able to obtain a large part of the risk reduction benefits of diversification with a surprisingly small number of securities.

What if the correlation among stocks is higher than 0.30? Suppose an investor wanted to be sure that his portfolio variance was only 110 percent of the minimum possible portfolio variance of a diversified portfolio. How many stocks would the investor need? If the average correlation among stocks were 0.5, he would need only 10 stocks for the portfolio to have 110 percent of the minimum possible portfolio variance. With a higher correlation, the investor would need fewer stocks to obtain the same percentage of minimum possible portfolio variance. What if the correlation is lower than 0.30? If the correlation among stocks were 0.1, the investor would need 90 stocks in the portfolio to obtain 110 percent of the minimum possible portfolio variance.

One common belief among investors is that almost all of the benefits of diversification can be achieved with a portfolio of only 30 stocks. In fact, Fisher and Lorie (1970) showed that 95 percent of the benefits of diversification among NYSE-traded stocks from 1926 to 1965 were achieved with a portfolio of 32 stocks.

As shown above, the number of stocks needed to achieve a particular diversification gain depends on the average correlation among stock returns: The lower the average correlation, the greater the number of stocks needed. Campbell, Lettau, Malkiel, and Xu (2001) showed that although overall market volatility has not increased since 1963, individual stock returns have been more volatile recently (1986–97) and individual stock returns have been less correlated with each other. Consequently, to achieve the same percentage of the risk-reducing benefits of diversification during the more recent period, more stocks were needed in a portfolio than in the period studied by Fisher and Lorie. Campbell et al. conclude that during the 1963–85 period, "a portfolio of 20 stocks reduced annualized excess standard deviation to about five percent, but in the 1986–1997 subsample, this level of excess standard deviation required almost 50 stocks."[19]

---

[19] Campbell et al. defined "excess standard deviation" as the standard deviation of a randomly selected portfolio of a given size minus the standard deviation of an equally weighted market index.

EXAMPLE 3

Diversification at Berkshire Hathaway

Berkshire Hathaway's highly successful CEO, Warren Buffett, is one of the harshest critics of modern portfolio theory and diversification. Buffett has said, for example, that "[I]f you are a know-something investor, able to understand business economics, and find 5 to 10 sensibly priced companies that possess important long-term competitive advantages, conventional diversification makes no sense for you. It is apt simply to hurt your results and increase your risk."[20]

Does Buffett avoid diversification altogether? Certainly his investment record is phenomenal, but even Buffett engages in diversification to some extent. For example, consider Berkshire Hathaway's top three investment holdings at the end of 2002.[21]

American Express Company	$ 5.6 billion (32%)
The Coca-Cola Company	$ 8.8 billion (51%)
The Gillette Company	$ 2.9 billion (17%)
Total	$ 17.3 billion

How much diversification do these three stocks provide? How much lower is this portfolio's standard deviation than that of a portfolio consisting only of Coca-Cola stock? To answer these questions, assume that the historical mean returns, return standard deviations, and return correlations of these stocks are the best estimates of the future expected returns, return standard deviations, and return correlations. Table 8 shows these historical statistics, based on monthly return data from 1990 through 2002.

TABLE 8 Historical Returns, Variances, and Correlations: Berkshire Hathaway's Largest Equity Holdings (Monthly Data, January 1990–December 2002)

	American Express	Coca-Cola	Gillette
Mean annual return	16.0%	16.1%	17.6%
Standard deviation	29.0%	24.7%	27.3%
Correlations			
American Express and Coca-Cola	0.361		
American Express and Gillette	0.317		
Coca-Cola and Gillette	0.548		

Source: FactSet.

---

[20] Buffett (1993).

[21] We consider only the top three holdings in order to simplify the computations in this example. Also for simplicity, we rounded the percentage allocations in the portfolio. The weights shown here are the relative weights among these three stocks, not their actual weights in the Berkshire Hathaway portfolio.

Table 8 shows that for Coca-Cola's stock during this period, the mean annual return was 16.1 percent and the annualized standard deviation of the return was 24.7 percent. In contrast, a portfolio consisting of 32 percent American Express stock, 51 percent Coca-Cola stock, and 17 percent Gillette stock had an expected return of $0.32(0.16) + 0.51(0.161) + 0.17(0.176) = 0.163$, or 16.3 percent.

The portfolio's expected standard deviation, based on these weights and the statistics in Table 8, was

$$\sigma_p = [w_1^2\sigma_1^2 + w_2^2\sigma_2^2 + w_3^2\sigma_3^2 + 2w_1w_2\rho_{1,2}\sigma_1\sigma_2 + 2w_1w_3\rho_{1,3}\sigma_1\sigma_3 + 2w_2w_3\rho_{2,3}\sigma_2\sigma_3]^{1/2}$$

or

$$\sigma_p = [(0.32^2)(0.290^2) + (0.51^2)(0.247^2) + (0.17^2)(0.273^2)$$
$$+ 2(0.32)(0.51)(0.361)(0.290)(0.247)$$
$$+ 2(0.32)(0.17)(0.317)(0.290)(0.273)$$
$$+ 2(0.51)(0.17)(0.548)(0.247)(0.273)]^{1/2}$$
$$= 0.210 \text{ or } 21.0 \text{ percent}$$

The standard deviation of a portfolio with these three stocks is only $21.0/24.7 = 85.0$ percent of the standard deviation of a portfolio composed exclusively of Coca-Cola stock. Therefore, Berkshire Hathaway actually achieved substantial diversification in the sense of risk reduction, even considering only its top three holdings.

2.5 Portfolio Choice with a Risk-Free Asset

So far, we have considered only portfolios of risky securities, implicitly assuming that investors cannot also invest in a risk-free asset. But investors can hold their own government's securities such as Treasury bills, which are virtually risk-free in nominal terms over appropriate time horizons. For example, the purchaser of a one-year Treasury bill knows his nominal return if he holds the bill to maturity. What is the trade-off between risk and return when we can invest in a risk-free asset?

A risk-free asset's standard deviation of return is 0 because the return is certain and there is no risk of default. Suppose, for example, that the return to the risk-free asset is 4 percent a year. If we take the Treasury bill as risk-free, then 4 percent is the actual return, known in advance; it is not an expected return.[22] Because the risk-free asset's standard deviation of return is 0, the covariance between the return of the risk-free asset and the return of any other asset must also be 0. These observations help us understand how adding a risk-free asset to a portfolio can affect the mean–variance trade-off among assets.

2.5.1 The Capital Allocation Line

The **capital allocation line (CAL)** describes the combinations of expected return and standard deviation of return available to an investor from combining her

---

[22] We assume here that the maturity of the T-bills is the same as the investment horizon so that there is no interest rate risk.

optimal portfolio of risky assets with the risk-free asset. Thus the CAL describes the expected results of the investor's decision on how to optimally allocate her capital among risky and risk-free assets.

What graph in mean return-standard deviation space satisfies the definition of the CAL? The CAL must be the line from the risk-free rate of return that is tangent to the efficient frontier of risky assets; of all lines we could extend from the risk-free rate to the efficient frontier of risky assets, the tangent line has the maximum slope and best risk–return tradeoff ("tangent" means touching without intersecting). The tangency portfolio is the investor's optimal portfolio of risky assets. The investor's risk tolerance determines which point on the line he or she will choose. Example 4 and the ensuing discussion clarify and illustrate these points.

EXAMPLE 4

An Investor's Trade-Off between Risk and Return with a Risk-Free Asset

Suppose that we want to determine the effect of including a risk-free asset in addition to large-cap stocks and government bonds in our portfolio. Table 9 shows the hypothetical expected returns and correlations for the three asset classes.

TABLE 9 Expected Returns, Variances, and Correlations: Three-Asset Case with Risk-Free Asset

	Large-Cap Stocks	Government Bonds	Risk-Free Asset
Expected return	15%	5%	4%
Variance	225	100	0
Standard deviation	15%	10%	0%

Correlations

Large-cap stocks and government bonds	0.5
Large-cap stocks and risk-free asset	0
Government bonds and risk-free asset	0

Suppose we decide to invest the entire portfolio in the risk-free asset with a return of 4 percent. In this case, the expected return to the portfolio is 4 percent and the expected standard deviation is 0. Now assume that we put the entire portfolio into large-cap stocks. The expected return is now 15 percent, and the standard deviation of the portfolio is 15 percent. What will happen if we divide the portfolio between the risk-free asset and large-cap stocks? If the proportion of assets in large-cap stocks is w_1 and the proportion of assets in the risk-free asset is $(1 - w_1)$, then the expected portfolio return is

$$E(R_p) = w_1(0.15) + (1 - w_1)(0.04)$$

FIGURE 7   Portfolios of the Risk-Free Asset and Large-Cap Stocks

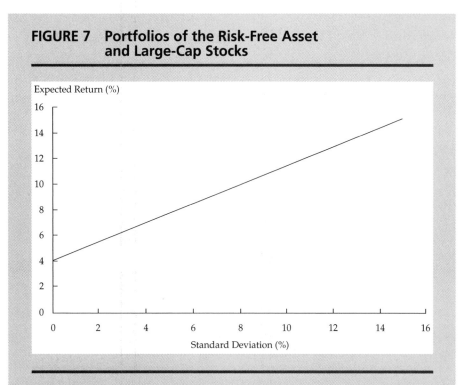

and the portfolio standard deviation is

$$\sigma_p = [w_1^2(0.15)^2 + (1 - w_1)^2(0)^2]^{1/2} = w_1(0.15)$$

Note that both the expected return and the standard deviation of return are linearly related to w_1, the percentage of the portfolio in large-cap stocks. Figure 7 illustrates the trade-off between risk and return for the risk-free asset and large-cap stocks in this example.

Now let us consider the trade-off between risk and return for a portfolio containing the risk-free asset and U.S. government bonds. Suppose we decide to put the entire portfolio in the risk-free asset. In this case, the expected return to the portfolio is 4 percent and the expected standard deviation of the portfolio is 0. Now assume that we put the the entire portfolio into U.S. government bonds. The expected return is now 5 percent, and the standard deviation of the portfolio is 10 percent. What will happen if we divide the portfolio between the risk-free asset and government bonds? If the proportion of assets in government bonds is w_1 and the proportion of assets in the risk-free asset is $(1 - w_1)$, then the expected portfolio return is

$$E(R_p) = w_1(0.05) + (1 - w_1)(0.04)$$

and the portfolio standard deviation is

$$\sigma_p = [w_1^2(0.10)^2 + (1 - w_1)^2(0)^2]^{1/2} = w_1(0.10)$$

Note that both the expected return and the standard deviation of return are linearly related to w_1, the percentage of the portfolio in the government bonds. Figure 8 shows the trade-off between risk and

FIGURE 8   Portfolios of the Risk-Free Asset and Government Bonds

return for the risk-free asset and government bonds in this example.

We have just seen the trade-off between risk and return for two different portfolios: one with the risk-free asset and large-cap stocks, the other with the risk-free asset and government bonds. How do these trade-offs between risk and return compare with the original risk-return trade-off between government bonds and large-cap stocks? Figure 9 illustrates the risk-return trade-off for all three portfolios.

FIGURE 9   Portfolios of the Risk-Free Asset, Large-Cap Stocks, and Government Bonds

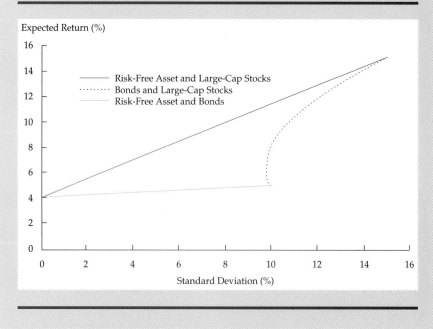

Notice that the line describing portfolios of the risk-free asset and government bonds touches the minimum-variance frontier for bonds and stocks at the point of lowest return on the bond-stock minimum-variance frontier—that is, the point where 100 percent of the portfolio is invested in bonds. Some points on the risk-free asset–bond line have lower risk and return than points on the bond-stock frontier; however, we can find no point where, for a given level of risk, the expected return is higher on the risk-free asset–bond line than on the bond-stock frontier. In this case, if we draw the line with the highest slope from the risk-free asset to the bond-stock frontier, that line is tangent to the bond-stock frontier at a point representing a portfolio 100 percent invested in stocks.[23] This CAL is labeled Risk-Free Asset and Large-Cap Stocks in Figure 9. For given assumptions about expected returns, variances, and covariances, that capital allocation line identifies portfolios with the maximum expected return for a given level of risk, if we can spread our money between an **optimal risky portfolio** and a risk-free asset. Of all lines we could extend from the risk-free rate to the minimum-variance frontier of risky assets, the CAL has maximum slope. Slope defined as rise (expected return) over run (standard deviation) measures the expected risk-return trade-off. The CAL is the line of maximum slope that touches the minimum-variance frontier; consequently, the capital allocation line offers the best risk-return trade-off achievable, given our expectations.

The previous example showed three important general principles concerning the risk-return trade-off in a portfolio containing a risk-free asset:

▶ If we can invest in a risk-free asset, then the CAL represents the best risk-return trade-off achievable.
▶ The CAL has a y-intercept equal to the risk-free rate.
▶ The CAL is tangent to the efficient frontier of risky assets.[24]

EXAMPLE 5A

The CAL with Multiple Assets

In Example 4, the CAL was tangent to the efficient frontier for all risky assets. We now illustrate how the efficient frontier changes depending on the **opportunity set** (the set of assets available for investment) and whether the investor wants to borrow to leverage his investments. We can illustrate this point by reconsidering our earlier example (Example 2) of optimal portfolio choice among the S&P 500, U.S. small-cap

---

[23] In a typical case with many assets, however, the point where the line with maximum slope from the risk-free asset touches the minimum-variance frontier of risky assets does not represent a portfolio composed of only the highest expected return asset. In such typical cases, the CAL represents combinations of the risk-free asset and a broad combination of risky assets.

[24] Note that when we expand the set of assets to include the risk-free asset, an investor's CAL becomes the efficient frontier defined in relation to the expanded set of assets. The efficient frontier of risky assets is the efficient frontier considering risky assets alone. It is critical to understand that the efficient frontier is always defined in relationship to a specified set of assets.

stocks, non-U.S. stocks (the MSCI World ex-U.S.), and U.S. government bonds, adding a risk-free asset.

We now assume that the risk-free rate is 5 percent. The standard deviation of the risk-free rate of return is 0, because the return is certain; the covariance between returns to the risk-free asset and returns to the other assets is also 0. We demonstrate the following principles:

▶ The point of maximum expected return is not the point of tangency between the CAL and the efficient frontier of risky assets.
▶ The point of tangency between the CAL and the efficient frontier for risky assets represents a portfolio containing risky assets and none of the risk-free asset.
▶ If we rule out borrowing at the risk-free rate, then the efficient frontier for all the assets (including the risk-free asset) cannot be completely linear.

Figure 10 shows the mean–variance frontier for all five assets (the original four plus the risk-free asset), assuming borrowing at the risk-free rate is not possible.

As the figure shows, the efficient frontier is linear from the *y*-intercept (the combination of risk and return for placing the entire portfolio in the risk-free asset) to the point of tangency. If the investor wants additional return (and risk) beyond the point of tangency without borrowing, however, the investor's efficient frontier is the portion of the efficient frontier for the four risky assets that lies to the right of the point of tangency. The investor's efficient frontier has linear and curved portions.[25]

FIGURE 10   The Effect of Adding a Risk-Free Asset to a Risky Portfolio

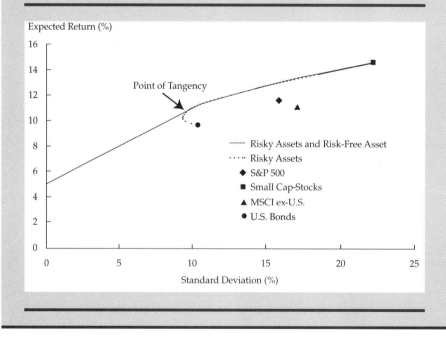

---

[25] If borrowing at the risk-free rate were possible (equivalent to buying on margin at the risk-free rate), the efficient frontier would be the straight line from the risk-free rate, now continued past the point of tangency.

2.5.2 *The Capital Allocation Line Equation*

In the previous section, we discussed the graph of the CAL and illustrated how the efficient frontier can change depending on the set of assets available for investment as well as the portfolio manager's expectations. We now provide the equation for this line.

Suppose that an investor, given expectations about means, variances, and covariances for risky assets, plots the efficient frontier of risky assets. There is a risk-free asset offering a risk-free rate of return, R_F. If w_T is the proportion of the portfolio the investor places in the tangency portfolio, then the expected return for the entire portfolio is

$$E(R_p) = (1 - w_T)R_F + w_T E(R_T)$$

and the standard deviation of the portfolio is

$$\sigma_p = \left[(1 - w_T)^2 \sigma_{R_F}^2 + w_T^2 \sigma_{R_T}^2 + 2(1 - w_T)w_T \sigma_{R_F}\sigma_{R_T}\rho_{R_F,R_T}\right]^{1/2}$$
$$= \left[(1 - w_T)^2 (0) + w_T^2 \sigma_{R_T}^2 + 2(1 - w_T)w_T (0)(\sigma_{R_T})(0)\right]^{1/2}$$
$$= (w_T^2 \sigma_{R_T}^2)^{1/2}$$
$$= w_T \sigma_{R_T}$$

An investor can choose to invest any fraction of his assets in the risk-free asset or in the tangency portfolio; therefore, he can choose many combinations of risk and return. If he puts the entire portfolio in the risk-free asset, then

$$w_T = 0$$
$$E(R_p) = (1 - 0)R_F + 0E(R_T) = R_F, \text{ and}$$
$$\sigma_p = 0\sigma_{R_T}$$
$$= 0$$

If he puts his entire portfolio in the tangency portfolio, then

$$w_T = 1$$
$$E(R_p) = (1 - 1)R_F + 1E(R_T) = E(R_T), \text{ and}$$
$$\sigma_p = 1\sigma_{R_T} = \sigma_{R_T}$$

In general, if he puts w_T percent of his portfolio in the tangency portfolio, his portfolio standard deviation will be $\sigma_p = w_T \sigma_{R_T}$.

To see how the portfolio weights, expected return, and risk are related, we use the relationship $w_T = \sigma_p/\sigma_{R_T}$. If we substitute this value of w_T back into the expression for expected return, $E(R_p) = (1 - w_T)R_F + w_T E(R_T)$, we get

$$E(R_p) = \left(1 - \frac{\sigma_p}{\sigma_{R_T}}\right)R_F + \frac{\sigma_p}{\sigma_{R_T}}E(R_T)$$

or

$$E(R_p) = R_F + \frac{E(R_T) - R_F}{\sigma_{R_T}}\sigma_p \qquad \textbf{(68-7)}$$

This equation shows the best possible trade-off between expected risk and return, given this investor's expectations. The term $[E(R_T) - R_F]/\sigma_{R_T}$ is the return that the investor demands in order to take on an extra unit of risk. Example 5B illustrates how to calculate the investor's price of risk and other aspects of his investment using the capital allocation line.

EXAMPLE 5B

CAL Calculations

Suppose that the risk-free rate, R_F, is 5 percent; the expected return to an investor's tangency portfolio, $E(R_T)$, is 15 percent; and the standard deviation of the tangency portfolio is 25 percent.

1. How much return does this investor demand in order to take on an extra unit of risk?

2. Suppose the investor wants a portfolio standard deviation of return of 10 percent. What percentage of the assets should be in the tangency portfolio, and what is the expected return?

3. Suppose the investor wants to put 40 percent of the portfolio in the risk-free asset. What is the portfolio expected return? What is the standard deviation?

4. What expected return should the investor demand for a portfolio with a standard deviation of 35 percent?

5. What combination of the tangency portfolio and the risk-free asset does the investor need to hold in order to have a portfolio with an expected return of 19 percent?

6. If the investor has $10 million to invest, how much must she borrow at the risk-free rate to have a portfolio with an expected return of 19%?

Solution to 1: In this case, $[E(R_T) - R_F]/\sigma_{R_T} = (0.15 - 0.05)/0.25 = 0.4$. The investor demands an additional 40 basis points of expected return of the portfolio for every 1 percentage point increase in the standard deviation of portfolio returns.

Solution to 2: Because $\sigma_p = w_T \sigma_{R_T}$, then $w_T = 0.1/0.25 = 0.4$, or 40 percent. In other words, 40 percent of the assets are in the tangency portfolio and 60 percent are in the risk-free asset. The expected return for the portfolio is $E(R_p) = R_F + \dfrac{E(R_T) - R_F}{\sigma_{R_T}} \sigma_p = 0.05 + (0.4)(0.1)$

$= 0.09$, or 9 percent.

Solution to 3: In this case, $w_T = 1 - 0.4 = 0.6$. Therefore, the expected portfolio return is $E(R_P) = (1 - w_T)R_F + w_T E(R_T) = (1 - 0.6)(0.05) + (0.6)(0.15) = 0.11$, or 11 percent. The portfolio standard deviation is $\sigma_P = w_T \sigma_{R_T} \sigma R_T = (0.6)(0.25) = 0.15$ or 15 percent.

Solution to 4: We know that the relation between risk and expected return for this portfolio is $E(R_p) = R_F + \dfrac{E(R_T) - R_F}{\sigma_{R_T}} \sigma_p = 0.05 + [(0.15 - 0.05)/0.25]\sigma_p = 0.05 + 0.4\sigma_p$. If the standard deviation for

---

the portfolio's returns is 35 percent, then the investor can demand an expected return of $E(R_P) = 0.05 + 0.4\sigma_p = 0.05 + 0.4(0.35) = 0.19$, or 19 percent.

Solution to 5: With an expected return of 19 percent, the asset allocation must be as follows:

$$E(R_p) = (1 - w_T)R_F + w_T E(R_T) \text{ or}$$
$$0.19 = (1 - w_T)(0.05) + w_T(0.15) = 0.05 + 0.10w_T$$
$$w_T = 1.4$$

How can the weight on the tangency portfolio be 140 percent? The interpretation of $w_T = 1.4$ is that the investment in the tangency portfolio consists of (1) the entire amount of initial wealth and (2) an amount equal to 40 percent of initial wealth that has been borrowed at the risk-free rate. We can confirm that the expected return is $(-0.4)(0.05) + (1.4)(0.15) = 0.19$ or 19 percent.

Solution to 6: The investor must borrow $4 million dollars at the risk-free rate to increase the holdings of the tangency-asset portfolio to $14 million dollars. Therefore, the net value of the portfolio will be $14 million − $4 million = $10 million.

In this section, we have assumed that investors may have different views about risky assets' mean returns, variances of returns, and correlations. Thus each investor may perceive a different efficient frontier of risky assets and have a different tangency portfolio, the optimal portfolio of risky assets which the investor may combine with risk-free borrowing or lending. In the next two sections, we examine the consequences when mean–variance investors share identical expectations.

2.5.3 The Capital Market Line

When investors share identical expectations about the mean returns, variance of returns, and correlations of risky assets, the CAL for all investors is the same and is known as the **capital market line (CML)**. With identical expectations, the tangency portfolio must be the same portfolio for all investors. In equilibrium, this tangency portfolio must be a portfolio containing all risky assets in proportions reflecting their market value weights; the tangency portfolio is the market portfolio of all risky assets. The CML is a capital allocation line with the market portfolio as the tangency portfolio. The equation of the CML is

$$E(R_p) = R_F + \frac{E(R_M) - R_F}{\sigma_M}\sigma_p \tag{68-8}$$

where

$E(R_p)$ = the expected return of portfolio p lying on the capital market line
R_F = the risk-free rate
$E(R_M)$ = the expected rate of return on the market portfolio
σ_M = the standard deviation of return on the market portfolio
σ_p = the standard deviation of return on portfolio p

The slope of the CML, $[E(R_M) - R_F]/\sigma_M$, is called the **market price of risk** because it indicates the market risk premium for each unit of market risk. As noted, the CML describes the expected return of only efficient portfolios. The implication of the capital market line is that all mean–variance investors, whatever their risk tolerance, can satisfy their investment needs by combining the risk-free asset with a single risky portfolio, the market portfolio of all risky assets.

In the next section we present a mean–variance theory describing the expected return of any asset or portfolio, efficient or inefficient.

2.6 The Capital Asset Pricing Model

The capital asset pricing model (CAPM) has played a pivotal role in the development of quantitative investment management since its introduction in the early 1960s. In this section, we review some of its key aspects.

The CAPM makes the following assumptions:[26]

▶ Investors need only know the expected returns, the variances, and the covariances of returns to determine which portfolios are optimal for them. (This assumption appears throughout all of mean–variance theory.)

▶ Investors have identical views about risky assets' mean returns, variances of returns, and correlations.

▶ Investors can buy and sell assets in any quantity without affecting price, and all assets are marketable (can be traded).

▶ Investors can borrow and lend at the risk-free rate without limit, and they can sell short any asset in any quantity.

▶ Investors pay no taxes on returns and pay no transaction costs on trades.

The CML represents the efficient frontier when the assumptions of the CAPM hold. In a CAPM world, therefore, all investors can satisfy their investment needs by combining the risk-free asset with the identical tangency portfolio, which is the market portfolio of all risky assets (no risky asset is excluded).

The following equation describes the expected returns on all assets and portfolios, whether efficient or not:

$$E(R_i) = R_F + \beta_i[E(R_M) - R_F] \tag{68-9}$$

where

$$E(R_i) = \text{the expected return on asset } i$$
$$R_F = \text{the risk-free rate of return}$$
$$E(R_M) = \text{the expected return on the market portfolio}$$
$$\beta_i = \text{Cov}(R_i, R_M)/\text{Var}(R_M)$$

Equation 68-9 itself is referred to as the **capital asset pricing model**, and its graph is called the **security market line** (SML). The CAPM is an equation describing the expected return on any asset (or portfolio) as a linear function of its **beta**, β_i, which is a measure of the asset's sensitivity to movements in the market. The CAPM says that expected return has two components: first, the risk-free rate, R_F, and second, an extra return equal to $\beta_i[E(R_M) - R_F]$. The term $[E(R_M) - R_F]$ is the expected excess return on the market. This amount is the

---

[26] For a complete list of assumptions, see Elton, Gruber, Brown, and Goetzmann (2003).

market risk premium; if we are 100 percent invested in the market, the market risk premium is the extra return we expect to obtain, on average, compared with the risk-free rate of return.

The market risk premium is multiplied by the asset's beta. A beta of 1 represents average market sensitivity, and we expect an asset with that beta to earn the market risk premium exactly.[27] A beta greater than 1 indicates greater than average market risk and, according to the CAPM, earns a higher expected excess return. Conversely, a beta less than 1 indicates less than average market risk and, according to the CAPM, earns a smaller expected excess return. Expected excess returns are related only to market risk, represented by beta. Sensitivity to the market return is the only source of difference in expected excess returns across assets.[28]

Like all theory-based models, the CAPM comes from a set of assumptions. The CAPM describes a financial market equilibrium in the sense that, if the model is correct and any asset's expected return differs from its expected return as given by the CAPM, market forces will come into play to restore the relationships specified by the model. For example, a stock that offers a higher expected return than justified by its beta will be bid up in price, lowering the stock's expected return; investors would expect that a broad-based portfolio would offset any non-market risk the stock might carry.

Because it is all-inclusive, the market portfolio defined in the CAPM is unobservable. In practice, we must use some broad index to represent it. The CAPM has been used primarily to value equities, so a common choice for the market portfolio is a broad value-weighted stock index or market proxy. The straight-line relationship between expected return and beta results from the **efficiency** of the market portfolio. As a result, the CAPM theory is equivalent to saying that the unobservable market portfolio is efficient, but not that any particular proxy for the market is efficient.[29] Of more interest to practitioners than the strict truth of CAPM as a theory is whether beta computed using available market proxies is useful for evaluating the expected mean returns to various investment strategies. The evidence now favors the existence of multiple sources of systematic risk affecting the mean returns to investment strategies.

2.7 Mean–Variance Portfolio Choice Rules: An Introduction

In this section, we introduce some of the principles of portfolio choice from a mean–variance perspective. One of the most basic portfolio choice decisions is the selection of an optimal asset allocation starting from a set of permissible asset classes. A second kind of decision involves modifying an existing portfolio. This type of decision is easier because we may be able to conclude that one portfolio represents a mean–variance improvement on another without necessarily establishing that the better portfolio is optimal. We begin with a brief discussion of this second decision type.

---

[27] The market portfolio itself has a beta of 1, as $\beta_M = \text{Cov}(R_M, R_M)/\text{Var}(R_M) = \text{Var}(R_M)/\text{Var}(R_M) = 1$. Because the market portfolio includes all assets, the average asset must have a beta of 1. The same argument applies if we compute the betas of assets in an index, using the index to represent the market.

[28] One intuition for this idea is that the market is the perfectly diversified portfolio. We can cancel out any other risk by holding the market portfolio, and we can costlessly hold the market portfolio (by the no-transaction-costs assumption). Even risk with respect to personal assets such as human capital (representing earning power) can be diversified away (all assets are tradable). Investors should not require extra return for risks they can costlessly hedge.

[29] See Bodie, Kane, and Marcus (2001) for more on this topic.

2.7.1 Decisions Related to Existing Portfolios

We examine two kinds of decisions related to existing portfolios in which mean–variance analysis may play a role.

Comparisons of Portfolios as Stand-Alone Investments
The **Markowitz decision rule** provides the principle by which a mean–variance investor facing the choice of putting all her money in Asset A or all her money in Asset B can sometimes reach a decision. This investor prefers A to B if either

▶ the mean return on A is equal to or larger than that on B, but A has a smaller standard deviation of return than B; or

▶ the mean return on A is strictly larger than that on B, but A and B have the same standard deviation of return.

When A is preferred to B by the Markowitz decision rule, we say that A *mean–variance dominates* B: Asset A clearly makes more efficient use of risk than B does. For example, if an investor is presented with a choice between (1) an asset allocation A with a mean return of 9 percent and a standard deviation of return of 12 percent and (2) a second asset allocation B with a mean return of 8 percent and a standard deviation of return of 15 percent, a mean–variance investor will prefer alternative A because it is expected to provide a higher mean return with less risk. A point to note is that when asset allocation has both higher mean return and higher standard deviation, the Markowitz decision rule does not select one asset allocation as superior; rather, the preference depends on the individual investor's risk tolerance.

We can identify an expanded set of mean–variance dominance relationships if we admit borrowing and lending at the risk-free rate. Then we can use the risk-free asset to match risk among the portfolios being compared. The Sharpe ratio (the ratio of mean return in excess of the risk-free rate of return to the standard deviation of return) serves as the appropriate metric.

▶ If a portfolio p has a higher positive Sharpe ratio than portfolio q, then p mean–variance dominates q if borrowing and lending at the risk-free rate is possible.[30]

Suppose asset allocation A is as before but now B has a mean of 6 percent and a standard deviation of 10 percent. Allocation A has higher mean return than B (9 percent versus 6 percent) but also higher risk (12 percent versus 10 percent), so the Markowitz decision rule is inconclusive about which allocation is better. Suppose we can borrow and lend at a risk-free rate of 3 percent. The Sharpe ratio of A, $(9 - 3)/12 = 0.50$, is higher than the Sharpe ratio of B, $(6 - 3)/10 = 0.30$, so we can conclude that A mean–variance dominates B. Note that a portfolio 83.3 percent invested in A and 16.7 percent invested in the risk-free asset has the same standard deviation as B, because $0.833(12) = 10$ percent, with mean return of $0.833(9) + 0.167(3) = 8$ percent, versus 6 percent for B. In short, we combined the higher Sharpe ratio portfolio p with the risk-free asset to achieve a portfolio with the same risk as portfolio q but with higher mean return. As B was originally defined (mean return of 8 percent and standard deviation of 15 percent), B had a Sharpe ratio of 0.33 and, as expected, the decision based on Sharpe ratios is consistent with that based on the Markowitz decision rule.

---

[30] The reverse of the proposition is also true: If a portfolio p mean–variance dominates a portfolio q, then p has a higher Sharpe ratio than q. The proof of these propositions is in Dybvig and Ross (1985b). Note that we assume a positive Sharpe ratio for the higher Sharpe ratio portfolio to rule out some counterintuitive results when negative-Sharpe-ratio portfolios are compared.

Practically, the above decision-making approach is most reliable when we are considering choices among well-diversified portfolios and when the return distributions of the choices are at least approximately normal.

The Decision to Add an Investment to an Existing Portfolio We described an approach for choosing between two asset allocations as an either/or proposition. We now discuss an approach to deciding whether to add a new asset class to an existing portfolio, or more generally to further diversify an existing portfolio.

Suppose you hold a portfolio p with expected or mean return $E(R_p)$ and standard deviation of return σ_p. Then you are offered the opportunity to add another investment to your portfolio, for example, a new asset class. Will you effect a mean–variance improvement by expanding your portfolio to include a positive position in the new investment? To answer this question, you need three inputs:

- the Sharpe ratio of the new investment,
- the Sharpe ratio of the existing portfolio, and
- the correlation between the new investment's return and portfolio p's return, $\mathrm{Corr}(R_{new}, R_p)$.

Adding the new asset to your portfolio is optimal if the following condition is met:[31]

$$\frac{E(R_{new}) - R_F}{\sigma_{new}} > \left(\frac{E(R_p) - R_F}{\sigma_p}\right) \mathrm{Corr}(R_{new}, R_p) \qquad \textbf{(68-10)}$$

This expression says that in order to gain by adding the new investment to your holdings, the Sharpe ratio of the new investment must be larger than the product of the Sharpe ratio of your existing portfolio and the correlation of the new investment's returns with the returns of your current portfolio. If Equation 68-10 holds, we can combine the new investment with the prior holdings to achieve a superior efficient frontier of risky assets (one in which the tangency portfolio has a higher Sharpe ratio). Note that although the expression may indicate that we effect a mean–variance improvement at the margin by adding a positive amount of a new asset, it does not indicate how much of the new asset we might want to add, or more broadly, what the efficient frontier including the new asset may be—to determine it, we would need to conduct an optimization. An insight from Equation 68-10 is that, in contrast to the case in which we considered investments as stand-alone and needed to consider only Sharpe ratios (from a mean–variance perspective) in choosing among them, in the case in which we can combine two investments, we must also consider their correlation. Example 6 illustrates how to use Equation 68-10 in deciding whether to add an asset class.

EXAMPLE 6

The Decision to Add an Asset Class

Jim Regal is chief investment officer of a Canadian pension fund invested in Canadian equities, Canadian bonds, Canadian real estate, and U.S. equities. The portfolio has a Sharpe ratio of 0.25. The investment

---

[31] See Blume (1984) and Elton, Gruber, and Rentzler (1987).

committee is considering adding one or the other (but not both) of the following asset classes:

▶ Eurobonds: predicted Sharpe ratio = 0.10; predicted correlation with existing portfolio = 0.42.

▶ Non-North American developed market equities, as represented in the MSCI EAFE (Europe, Australasia, Far East) index: predicted Sharpe ratio = 0.30; predicted correlation with existing portfolio = 0.67.

1. Explain whether the investment committee should add Eurobonds to the existing portfolio.

2. Explain whether the committee should add non-North American developed market equities to the portfolio.

Solution to 1: (Sharpe ratio of existing portfolio) × (Correlation of Eurobonds with existing portfolio) = 0.25(0.42) = 0.105. We should add Eurobonds if their predicted Sharpe ratio exceeds 0.105. Because the investment committee predicts a Sharpe ratio of 0.10 for Eurobonds, the committee should not add them to the existing portfolio.

Solution to 2: (Sharpe ratio of existing portfolio) × (Correlation of new equity class with existing portfolio) = 0.25(0.67) = 0.1675. Because the predicted Sharpe ratio of 0.30 for non-North American equities exceeds 0.1675, the investment committee should add them to the existing portfolio.

In Example 6, even if the correlation between the pension fund's existing portfolio and the proposed new equity class were +1, so that adding the new asset class had no potential risk reduction benefits, Equation 68–10 would indicate that the class should be added because the condition for adding the asset class would be satisfied, as 0.30 > 0.25(1.0). For any portfolio, we can always effect a mean–variance improvement at the margin by adding an investment with a higher Sharpe ratio than the existing portfolio. This result is intuitive, because the higher Sharpe ratio investment would mean–variance dominate the existing portfolio in a pairwise comparison. Again, we emphasize that the assumptions of mean–variance analysis must be fulfilled for these results to be reliable.

2.7.2 Determining an Asset Allocation

Our objective in this section is to summarize the mean–variance perspective on asset allocation. In a prior section, we gave the mathematical objective and constraints for determining the minimum-variance frontier of risky assets in the simplest case in which the only constraint on portfolio weights is that they sum to 1. Determining the efficient frontier using Equation 68-3 plus a constraint $w_i \geq 0$ to reflect no short sales is a starting point for many institutional investors in determining an asset allocation.[32] Mean–variance theory then points to choosing

---

[32] See Grinblatt and Titman (1998) and Elton, Gruber, Brown, and Goetzmann (2003) for discussions of solution methods and mechanics. In practice, investors often place additional constraints, such as constraints on maximum percentages, to assure plausible solutions. We discuss this approach further in the section on instability of the minimum-variance frontier.

the asset allocation represented by the perceived tangency portfolio if the investor can borrow or lend at the risk-free rate. The manager can combine the tangency portfolio with the risk-free asset to achieve an efficient portfolio at a desired level of risk. Because the tangency portfolio represents the highest-Sharpe-ratio portfolio of risky assets, it is a logical baseline for an asset allocation.

This theoretical perspective, however, views the investment in a risk-free asset as a readily available risk-adjustment variable. In practice, investors may be constrained against using margin (borrowing), may face constraints concerning minimum and maximum positive investments in a risk-free asset, or may have other reasons for not adopting the perspective of theory.[33] In such a case, the investor may establish an asset allocation among risky asset classes that differs from the tangency portfolio. Quantifying his risk tolerance in terms of standard deviation of returns, the investor could choose the portfolio on the efficient frontier of risky assets that corresponds to the chosen level of standard deviation.

The CAPM framework provides even more-narrowly focused choices because it adds the assumption that investors share the same views about mean returns, variances of returns, and correlations. Then all investors would agree on the identity of the tangency portfolio, which is the market portfolio of all risky assets held in proportion to their market values. This portfolio represents the highest possible degree of diversification. The exact identity of such an all-inclusive portfolio cannot be established, of course. Practically, however, investors can own highly diversified passively managed portfolios invested in major asset classes worldwide that approximately reflect the relative market values of the included classes. This asset allocation can be adapted to account for differential expectations. For example, the Black-Litterman (1991, 1992) asset allocation model takes a well-diversified market-value-weighted asset allocation as a neutral starting point for investors. The model incorporates a procedure for deviating from market capitalization weights in directions reflecting an investor's different-from-equilibrium model (CAPM) views concerning expected returns.

Mean–variance theory in relation to portfolio construction and asset allocation has been intensively examined, and researchers have recognized a number of its limitations. We will discuss an important limitation related to the sensitivity of the optimization procedure—the instability of the efficient frontier—in a later section. We must recognize that as a single-period model, mean–variance analysis ignores the liquidity and tax considerations that arise in a multiperiod world in which investors rebalance portfolios. Relatedly, the time horizon associated with the optimization, often one year, may be shorter than an investor's actual time horizon due to difficulties in developing inputs for long horizons.[34] Mean–variance analysis takes into account the correlation of returns across asset classes over single time periods but does not address serial correlation (long and short-term dependencies) in returns for a given asset class. Monte Carlo simulation is sometimes used in asset allocation to address such multiperiod issues.[35] Despite its limitations, mean–variance analysis provides an objective and fairly adaptable procedure for narrowing the unlimited set of choices we face in selecting an asset allocation.[36]

---

[33] For example, a risk-free asset may not be readily available if the analysis is conducted in real terms. Only short-term inflation-protected securities, if available, are potentially risk free in such a context.

[34] See Swenson (2000). For example, if the investor's time horizon is five years, developing an efficient frontier involves estimating the correlations of five-year returns. Many assets have a limited number of independent five-year observations for correlation that we might use to develop estimates.

[35] See the readings on probability distributions for more information about Monte Carlo simulation.

[36] For example, Chow (1995) adapted mean–variance optimization to address managers' concerns about performance relative to a benchmark, and Chow, Jacquier, Kritzman, and Lowry (1999) adapted optimization to account for correlations that may change in times of stress.

3

PRACTICAL ISSUES IN MEAN–VARIANCE ANALYSIS

We now discuss practical issues that arise in the application of mean–variance analysis in choosing portfolios. The two areas of focus are

▶ estimating inputs for mean–variance optimization, and

▶ the instability of the minimum-variance frontier, which results from the optimization process's sensitivity to the inputs.

Relative to the first area, we must ask two principal questions concerning the prediction of expected returns, variances, and correlations. First, which methods are feasible? Second, which are most accurate? Relative to sensitivity of the optimization process, we need to ask first, what is the source of the problem, and second, what corrective measures are available to address it.

3.1 Estimating Inputs for Mean–Variance Optimization

In this section, we compare the feasibility and accuracy of several methods for computing the inputs for mean–variance optimization. These methods use one of the following:

▶ historical means, variances, and correlations,

▶ historical betas estimated using the market model, or

▶ adjusted betas.

3.1.1 Historical Estimates

This approach involves calculating means, variances, and correlations directly from historical data. The historical method requires estimating a very large number of parameters when we are optimizing for even a moderately large number of assets. As a result, it is more feasible for asset allocation than for portfolio formation involving a large number of stocks.

The number of parameters a portfolio manager needs to estimate to determine the minimum-variance frontier depends on the number of potential stocks in the portfolio. If a portfolio manager has n stocks in a portfolio and wants to use mean–variance analysis, she must estimate

▶ n parameters for the expected returns to the stocks,

▶ n parameters for the variances of the stock returns, and

▶ $n(n-1)/2$ parameters for the covariances of all the stock returns with each other.

Together, the parameters total $n^2/2 + 3n/2$.

The two limitations of the historical approach involve the quantity of estimates needed and the quality of historical estimates of inputs.

The quantity of estimates needed may easily be very large, mainly because the number of covariances increases in the square of the number of securities. If the portfolio manager wanted to compute the minimum-variance frontier for a portfolio of 100 stocks, she would need to estimate $100^2/2 + 3(100)/2 = 5,150$ parameters. If she wanted to compute the minimum-variance frontier for 1,000 stocks, she would need to estimate 501,500 parameters. Not only is this task unappealing, it might be impossible.[37]

The second limitation is that historical estimates of return parameters typically have substantial estimation error. The problem is least severe for estimates of variances.[38] The problem is acute with historical estimates of mean returns because the variability of risky asset returns is high relative to the mean, and the problem cannot be ameliorated by increasing the frequency of observations. Estimation error is also serious with historical estimates of covariances. The intuition in the case of covariances is that the historical method essentially tries to capture every random feature of a historical data set, reducing the usefulness of the estimates in a predictive mode. In a study based on monthly returns for U.S. stocks over the period 1973–1997, Chan, Karceski, and Lakonishok (1999) found that the correlation between past and future sample covariances was 0.34 at the 36-month horizon but only 0.18 at the 12-month horizon.

In current industry practice, the historical sample **covariance matrix** is not used without adjustment in mean–variance optimization. Adjusted values of variance and covariance may be weighted averages of the raw sample values and the average variance or covariance, respectively. For example, if a stock's variance of monthly returns is 0.0210 and the average stock's variance of monthly returns is 0.0098, the procedure might adjust 0.0210 downward, in the direction of the mean. Adjusting values in the direction of the mean reduces the dispersion in the estimates that may be caused by **sampling error**.[39]

In estimating mean returns, analysts use a variety of approaches. They may adjust historical mean returns to reflect perceived contrasts between current market conditions and past average experience. They frequently use valuation models, such as models based on expected future cash flows, or equilibrium models, such as the CAPM, to develop forward-looking mean return estimates. Their use of these approaches reflects not only the technical issue of estimation error but also the risk in assuming that future performance will mirror past average performance.

3.1.2 Market Model Estimates: Historical Beta (Unadjusted)

A simpler way to compute the variances and covariances of asset returns involves the insight that asset returns may be related to each other through their correlation with a limited set of variables or factors. The simplest such model is the market model, which describes a regression relationship between the returns on an asset and the returns on the market portfolio. For asset i, the return to the asset can be modeled as

$$R_i = \alpha_i + \beta_i R_M + \epsilon_i \tag{68-11}$$

---

[37] The number of time-series observations must exceed the number of securities for the covariances (including variances) to be estimated.

[38] See Chan, Karceski, and Lakonishok (1999) for empirical evidence that future variances are relatively more predictable from past variances than is the case for future covariances.

[39] For more information on this approach, called shrinkage estimators, see Michaud (1998) and Ledoit and Wolf (2004).

where

R_i = the return on asset i

R_M = the return on the market portfolio

α_i = average return on asset i unrelated to the market return

β_i = the sensitivity of the return on asset i to the return on the market portfolio

ϵ_i = an error term

Consider first how to interpret β_i. If the market return increases by one percentage point, the market model predicts that the return to asset i will increase by β_i percentage points. (Recall that β_i is the slope in the market model.)

Now consider how to interpret α_i. If the market return is 0, the market model predicts that the return to asset i will be α_i, the intercept in the market model.

The market model makes the following assumptions about the terms in Equation 68-11:

▶ The expected value of the error term is 0, so $E(\epsilon_i) = 0$.

▶ The market return (R_M) is uncorrelated with the error term, $\text{Cov}(R_M, \epsilon_i) = 0$.

▶ The error terms, ϵ_i, are uncorrelated among different assets. For example, the error term for asset i is uncorrelated with the error term for asset j. Consequently, $E(\epsilon_i \epsilon_j) = 0$ for all i not equal to j.[40]

Note that some of these assumptions are very similar to those we made about the single-variable linear regression model in the reading on correlation and regression. The market model, however, does not assume that the error term is normally distributed or that the variance of the error term is identical across assets.

Given these assumptions, the market model makes the following predictions about the expected returns of assets as well as the variances and covariances of asset returns.[41]

First, the expected return for asset i depends on the expected return to the market, $E(R_M)$, the sensitivity of the return on asset i to the return on the market, B_i, and the part of returns on asset i that are independent of market returns, α_i.

$$E(R_i) = \alpha_i + \beta_i E(R_M) \tag{68-12}$$

Second, the variance of the return to asset i depends on the variance of the return to the market, σ_M^2, the variance of the error for the return of asset i in the market model, $\sigma_{\epsilon_i}^2$, and the sensitivity, β_i.

$$\text{Var}(R_i) = \beta_i^2 \sigma_M^2 + \sigma_{\epsilon_i}^2 \tag{68-13}$$

In the context of a model in which the market portfolio is the only source of risk, the first term in Equation 68-13, $\beta_i^2 \sigma_M^2$, is sometimes referred to as the

---

[40] $\text{Cov}(\epsilon_i, \epsilon_j) = E\{[\epsilon_i - E(\epsilon_i)][\epsilon_j - E(\epsilon_j)]\} = E[(\epsilon_i - 0)(\epsilon_j - 0)] = E(\epsilon_i \epsilon_j) = 0$. The assumption of uncorrelated errors is not innocuous. If we have more than one factor that affects returns for assets, then this assumption will be incorrect and single-factor models will produce inaccurate estimates for the covariance of asset returns.

[41] See Elton, Gruber, Brown, and Goetzmann (2003) for derivations of these results.

systematic risk of asset i. The error variance term in Equation 68-13, $\sigma^2_{\epsilon_i}$, is sometimes referred to as the **nonsystematic risk** of asset i.

Third, the covariance of the return to asset i and the return to asset j depends on the variance of the return to the market, σ^2_M, and on the sensitivities β_i and β_j.

$$\text{Cov}(R_i, R_j) = \beta_i \beta_j \sigma^2_M \tag{68-14}$$

We can use the market model to greatly reduce the computational task of providing the inputs to a mean–variance optimization. For each of the n assets, we need to know α_i, β_i, $\sigma^2_{\epsilon_i}$, as well as the expected return and variance for the market. Because we need to estimate only $3n + 2$ parameters with the market model, we need far fewer parameters to construct the minimum-variance frontier than we would if we estimated the historical means, variances, and covariances of asset returns. For example, if we estimated the minimum-variance frontier for 1,000 assets (say, 1,000 different stocks), the market model would use 3,002 parameters for computing the minimum-variance frontier, whereas the historical estimates approach would require 501,500 parameters, as discussed earlier.

We do not know the parameters of the market model, so we must estimate them. But what method do we use? The most convenient way is to estimate a linear regression using **time-series data** on the returns to the market and the returns to each asset.

We can use the market model to estimate α_i and β_i by using a separate linear regression for each asset, using historical data on asset returns and market returns.[42] The regression output produces an estimate, $\hat{\beta}_i$, of β_i; we call this estimate an unadjusted beta. Later we will introduce an adjusted beta. We can use these estimates to compute the expected returns and the variances and covariances of those returns for mean–variance optimization.

EXAMPLE 7

Computing Stock Correlations Using the Market Model

You are estimating the correlation of returns between Cisco Systems (Nasdaq: CSCO) and Microsoft (Nasdaq: MSFT) as of late 2003. You run a market-model regression for each of the two stocks based on monthly returns, using the S&P 500 to represent the market. You obtain the following regression results:

▶ The estimated beta for Cisco, $\hat{\beta}_{\text{CSCO}}$, is 2.09, and the residual standard deviation, $\hat{\sigma}_{\epsilon_{\text{CSCO}}}$, is 11.52.

▶ The estimated beta for Microsoft, $\hat{\beta}_{\text{MSFT}}$, is 1.75, and the residual standard deviation, $\hat{\sigma}_{\epsilon_{\text{MSFT}}}$, is 11.26.

---

[42] One common practice is to use 60 monthly returns to estimate this model. The default setting on Bloomberg terminals uses two years of weekly data to estimate this model.

Your estimate of the variance of monthly returns on the S&P 500 is $\hat{\sigma}_M^2 = 29.8$, which corresponds to an annual standard deviation of returns of about 18.9 percent. Using the data given, estimate the correlation of returns between Cisco and Microsoft.

Solution: We compute $\hat{\sigma}_{\epsilon_{CSCO}}^2 = 132.71$ and $\hat{\sigma}_{\epsilon_{MSFT}}^2 = 126.79$. Using the definition of correlation as covariance divided by the individual standard deviations, and using Equations 68-13 and 68-14, we have

$$
\frac{\text{Cov}(R_{CSCO}, R_{MSFT})}{\text{Var}(R_{CSCO})^{1/2} \text{Var}(R_{MSFT})^{1/2}}
$$

$$
= \frac{\hat{\beta}_{CSCO}\hat{\beta}_{MSFT}(\hat{\sigma}_M^2)}{[\hat{\beta}_{CSCO}^2(\hat{\sigma}_M^2) + \hat{\sigma}_{\epsilon_{CSCO}}^2]^{1/2}[\hat{\beta}_{MSFT}^2(\hat{\sigma}_M^2) + \hat{\sigma}_{\epsilon_{MSFT}}^2]^{1/2}}
$$

$$
= \frac{(2.09)(1.75)(29.8)}{[(2.09)^2(29.8) + 132.71]^{1/2}[(1.75)^2(29.8) + 126.79]^{1/2}} = 0.4552
$$

Thus the market model predicts that the correlation between the two asset returns is 0.4552.

One difficulty with using the market model is determining an appropriate index to represent the market. Typically, analysts who use the market model to determine the risk of individual domestic equities use returns on a domestic equity market index. In the United States, such an index might be the S&P 500 or the Wilshire 5000 Index; in the United Kingdom, the Financial Times Stock Exchange 100 Index might be used. Using returns on an equity market index may create a reasonable market model for equities, but it may not be reasonable for modeling the risk of other asset classes.[43]

3.1.3 Market Model Estimates: Adjusted Beta

Should we use historical betas from a market model for mean–variance optimization? Before we can answer this question, we need to restate our goal: We want to predict expected returns for a set of assets and the variances and covariances of those returns so that we can estimate the minimum-variance frontier for those assets. Estimates based on historical beta depend on the crucial assumption that the historical beta for a particular asset is the best predictor of the future beta for that asset. If beta changes over time, then this assumption is untrue. Therefore, we may want to use some other measure instead of historical beta to estimate an asset's future beta. These other forecasts are known by the general term **adjusted beta**. Researchers have shown that adjusted beta is often a better forecast of future beta than is historical beta. As a consequence, practitioners often use adjusted beta.

Suppose, for example, we are in period t and we want to estimate the minimum-variance frontier for period $t + 1$ for a set of stocks. We need to use data available in period t to predict the expected stock returns and the variances and

---

[43] Using this model to estimate the risk of other asset classes may violate two assumptions of single-factor models discussed earlier: The market return, R_M, is independent of the error term, ϵ_i; and the error terms, ϵ_i, are independent across assets. If either of these assumptions is violated, the market model will not produce accurate predictions of expected returns or the variances and covariances of returns.

covariances of those returns in period $t + 1$. Note, however, that the historical estimate of beta in period t for a particular stock may not be the best estimate we can make in period t of beta in period $t + 1$ for that stock. And the minimum-variance frontier for period $t + 1$ must be based on the forecast of beta for period $t + 1$.

If beta for each stock were a random walk from one period to the next, then we could write the relation between the beta for stock i in period t and the beta for stock i in period $t + 1$ as

$$\beta_{i,t+1} = \beta_{i,t} + \epsilon_{i,t+1}$$

where $\epsilon_{i,t+1}$ is an error term. If beta followed a random walk, the best predictor of $\beta_{i,t+1}$ would be $\beta_{i,t}$ because the error term has a mean value of 0. The historical beta would be the best predictor of the future beta, and the historical beta need not be adjusted.

In reality, beta for each stock often is not a random walk from one period to the next, and therefore, historical beta is not necessarily the best predictor of the future beta. For example, if beta can be represented as a first-order autoregression, then

$$\beta_{i,t+1} = \alpha_0 + \alpha_1\beta_{i,t} + \epsilon_{i,t+1} \qquad \textbf{(68-15)}$$

If we estimate Equation 68-15 using time-series data on historical betas, the best predictor of $\beta_{i,t+1}$ is $\hat{\alpha}_0 + \hat{\alpha}_1\beta_{i,t}$. In this case, the historical beta needs to be adjusted because the best prediction of beta in the next period is $\hat{\alpha}_0 + \hat{\alpha}_1\beta_{i,t}$, not $\beta_{i,t}$.

Adjusted betas predict future betas better than historical betas do because betas are, on average, mean reverting.[44] Therefore, we should use adjusted, rather than historical, betas. One common method that practitioners use to adjust historical beta is to assume that $\alpha_0 = 0.333$ and $\alpha_1 = 0.667$. With this adjustment,

- if the historical beta equals 1.0, then the adjusted beta will be $0.333 + 0.667(1.0) = 1.0$.
- if the historical beta equals 1.5, then adjusted beta will be $0.333 + 0.667(1.5) = 1.333$.
- if the historical beta equals 0.5, then adjusted beta will be $0.333 + 0.667(0.5) = 0.667$.

Thus the mean-reverting level of beta is 1.0. If the historical beta is above 1.0, then adjusted beta will be below historical beta; if historical beta is below 1.0, then adjusted beta will be above historical beta.[45]

3.2 Instability in the Minimum-Variance Frontier

Although standard mean–variance optimization, as represented by Equation 68-3, is a convenient and objective procedure for portfolio formation, we must use care when interpreting its results in practice. In this section, we discuss

---

[44] See, for example, Klemkosky and Martin (1975).

[45] Although practitioners regularly use this method for computing adjusted beta, we are unaware of any published research suggesting that $\alpha_0 = 0.333$ and $\alpha_1 = 0.667$ are the best coefficient values to use in computing adjusted beta. Some researchers suggest an additional adjustment to historical betas called fundamental betas. **Fundamental betas** predict beta based on fundamental data for a company (price–earnings ratio, earnings growth, market capitalization, volatility, and so forth). Consulting firms such as BARRA sell estimates of fundamental betas.

cautions regarding the use of mean–variance optimization. The problems that can arise have been widely studied, and remedies for them have been developed. With this knowledge, mean–variance optimization can still be a useful tool.

The chief problem with mean–variance optimization is that small changes in input assumptions can lead to large changes in the minimum-variance (and efficient) frontier. This problem is called **instability in the minimum-variance frontier**. It arises because, in practice, uncertainty exists about the expected returns, variances, and covariances used in tracing out the minimum-variance frontier.

Suppose, for example, that we use historical data to compute estimates to be used in an optimization. These means, variances, and covariances are sample quantities that are subject to random variation. Recall that the sample mean has a probability distribution, called its **sampling distribution**. The sample mean is only a point estimate of the underlying or population mean.[46] The optimization process attempts to maximally exploit differences among assets. When these differences are statistically (and economically) insignificant (e.g., representing random variation), the resulting minimum-variance frontiers are misleading and not practically useful. Mean–variance optimization then overfits the data: It does too much with differences that are actually not meaningful. In an optimization with no limitation on short sales, assets can appear with very large negative weights, reflecting this overfitting (a negative weight for an asset means that the asset is sold short). Portfolios with very large short positions are of little practical interest.[47] Because of sensitivity to small changes in inputs, mean–variance optimizations may suggest too-frequent portfolio rebalancing, which is costly. Responses to instability include the following:

▶ Adding constraints against short sales (which is sometimes an institutional investment policy constraint as well). In Equation 68-3, we can add a no-short-sales constraint specifying that all asset weights must be positive: $w_j \geq 0, j = 1, 2, 3, \ldots, n$.[48]

▶ Improving the statistical quality of inputs to optimization.

▶ Using a statistical concept of the efficient frontier, reflecting the fact that the inputs to the optimization are random variables rather than constants.[49]

We stated above that mean–variance optimizations can recommend too-frequent portfolio rebalancing. Similarly, we find that the minimum-variance frontier is generally unstable when calculated using historical data for different time periods. One possible explanation is that the different frontiers reflect shifts in the parameters of asset return distribution between sample time periods. Time instability of the minimum-variance frontier can also result from random variation in means, variances, and covariances, when the underlying parameters are actually unchanged. Small differences in sample periods used for mean–variance optimization may greatly affect a model even if the distribution of asset returns is stationary. Example 8 illustrates time instability with the data used for optimization.

---

[46] The underlying means of asset returns are particularly difficult to estimate accurately. See Luenberger (1998) for an introduction to this problem, as well as Black (1993).

[47] In practice, few investors that engage in short sales would take a large short position as a result of an analysis restricted to means, variances, and correlations. Unlimited losses are possible in a short position.

[48] In practice, other ad hoc constraints on the size of positions are sometimes used as well.

[49] For example, Michaud (1998) defines a region of efficient portfolios that are statistically equivalent at a given confidence level. A portfolio falling in the region is consistent with being efficient and does not need to be rebalanced.

EXAMPLE 8

Time Instability of the Minimum-Variance Frontier

In Example 2, we calculated a minimum-variance frontier for four asset classes for the period 1970 through 2002. What variation would we find among minimum-variance frontiers for subperiods of 1970 to 2002? To find out, we take the data for decades within the entire period, calculate the sample statistics, and then trace out the minimum-variance frontier for each decade. Table 10 shows the sample statistics of the monthly asset returns to these four asset classes for 1970 to 1979, 1980 to 1989, 1990 to 2002, and the combined sample period.

| TABLE 10 | Average Returns, Standard Deviations, and Correlation Matrixes | | | |

	S&P 500	U.S. Small-Cap Stocks	MSCI World ex-U.S.	U.S. Long-Term Government Bonds
Average Returns				
Time Period				
1970–1979	7.0%	14.4%	11.8%	5.7%
1980–1989	17.6%	16.7%	21.1%	12.9%
1990–2002	10.4%	13.2%	2.7%	9.9%
Overall period	11.6%	14.6%	11.1%	9.6%
Standard Deviations				
Time Period				
1970–1979	15.93%	26.56%	16.68%	8.25%
1980–1989	16.41%	19.17%	17.32%	14.19%
1990–2002	15.27%	20.71%	16.93%	8.31%
Overall period	15.83%	22.18%	17.07%	10.44%
Correlation Matrixes				
1970–1979				
S&P 500	1			
U.S. Small-cap	0.787	1		
MSCI ex-U.S.	0.544	0.490	1	
U.S. LT Bonds	0.415	0.316	0.218	1

(Table continued on next page . . .)

TABLE 10   (continued)

	S&P 500	U.S. Small-Cap Stocks	MSCI World ex-U.S.	U.S. Long-Term Government Bonds
1980–1989				
S&P 500	1			
U.S. Small-cap	0.844	1		
MSCI ex-U.S.	0.512	0.483	1	
U.S. LT Bonds	0.310	0.171	0.229	1
1990–1999				
S&P 500	1			
U.S. Small-cap	0.611	1		
MSCI ex-U.S.	0.647	0.473	1	
U.S. LT Bonds	0.097	−0.047	0.017	1
Overall Period				
S&P 500	1			
U.S. Small-cap	0.731	1		
MSCI ex-U.S.	0.573	0.475	1	
U.S. LT Bonds	0.266	0.138	0.155	1

Source: Ibbotson Associates.

As we might expect, variation occurs within subperiods in the sample means, variances, and covariances for all asset classes. Initially, the correlations offer the impression of relative stability over time. For example, the correlation of the S&P 500 with the MSCI World ex-U.S. was 0.544, 0.512, and 0.647 for 1970 to 1979, 1980 to 1989, and 1990 to 2002, respectively. In contrast to ranking by mean returns, the ranking of asset classes by standard deviation was the same in each decade, with U.S. small-cap stocks the riskiest asset class and bonds the least risky. We could use **statistical inference** to explore interperiod differences. With these initial impressions in mind, however, let us view the decades' minimum-variance frontiers.

Figure 11 shows the minimum-variance frontiers computed using the historical return statistics shown in Table 10 for 1970 to 1979, 1980 to 1989, 1990 to 2002, and the entire sample period. As this figure shows, the minimum-variance frontiers can differ dramatically in different periods. For example, note that the minimum-variance frontiers based on data from 1970 to 1979 and 1980 to 1989 do not overlap at all.

**FIGURE 11   Historical Minimum-Variance Frontier
Comparison**

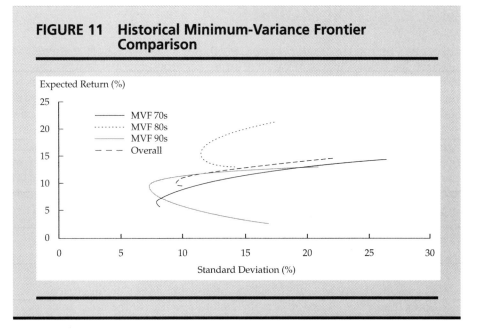

As mentioned, researchers have developed various methods to address portfolio managers' concerns about the issue of instability.

EXAMPLE 9

How Yale University's Endowment Fund Uses Mean-Variance Analysis

David Swensen, Yale University's chief investment officer (who also teaches portfolio management at Yale), wrote that "unconstrained mean–variance [optimization] usually provide[s] solutions unrecognizable as reasonable portfolios. . . . Because the process involves material simplifying assumptions, adopting the unconstrained asset allocation point estimates produced by mean–variance optimization makes little sense."[50]

Swensen's remarks highlight practitioners' concerns about the usefulness of standard mean–variance optimization. Among the most important simplifying assumptions of mean–variance analysis is that the means, variances, and covariances of assets in a portfolio are known. Because the optimization process tries to make much of small differences, and the true values of the means and other parameters are uncertain, this simplifying assumption has a large impact. As mentioned earlier, responses to instability include adding constraints on asset weights and modifying historical sample estimates of the inputs. Despite Swensen's criticism, Yale uses mean–variance analysis for allocating its portfolio; however, the Yale Investment Office adds constraints on weights and does not use raw historical inputs.

---

[50] Swensen (2000).

4   MULTIFACTOR MODELS

Earlier we discussed the market model, which was historically the first attempt to describe the process that drives asset returns. The market model assumes that all explainable variation in asset returns is related to a single factor, the return to the market. Yet asset returns may be related to factors other than market return, such as interest rate movements, inflation, or industry-specific returns. For many years, investment professionals have used multifactor models in portfolio management, risk analysis, and the evaluation of portfolio performance.

Multifactor models have gained importance for the practical business of portfolio management for two main reasons. First, multifactor models explain asset returns better than the market model does.[51] Second, multifactor models provide a more detailed analysis of risk than does a single factor model. That greater level of detail is useful in both passive and active management.

▶ *Passive management.* In managing a fund that seeks to track an index with many component securities, portfolio managers may need to select a sample of securities from the index. Analysts can use multifactor models to match an index fund's factor exposures to the factor exposures of the index tracked.

▶ *Active management.* Multifactor models are used in portfolio formation to model the expected returns and risks of securities and portfolio. Many quantitative investment managers rely on multifactor models in predicting alpha (excess risk-adjusted returns) or relative return (the return on one asset or asset class relative to that of another) as part of a variety of active investment strategies. In evaluating portfolios, analysts use multi-factor models to understand the sources of active managers' returns and assess the risks assumed relative to the manager's **benchmark** (comparison portfolio).

In the following sections, we explain the basic principles of factor models and discuss various types of models and their application. We also present the arbitrage pricing theory developed by Ross (1976), which relates the expected return of investments to their risk with respect to a set of factors.

4.1 Factors and Types of Multifactor Models

To begin by defining terms, a **factor** is a common or underlying element with which several variables are correlated. For example, the market factor is an underlying element with which individual share returns are correlated. We search for **systematic factors**, which affect the average returns of a large number of different assets. These factors represent **priced risk**, risk for which investors require an additional return for bearing. Systematic factors should thus help explain returns.

Many varieties of multifactor models have been proposed and researched. We can categorize most of them into three main groups, according to the type of factor used:

▶ In **macroeconomic factor models**, the factors are surprises in macroeconomic variables that significantly explain equity returns. The factors can be understood as affecting either the expected future cash flows of companies or the interest rate used to discount these cash flows back to the present.

---

[51] See, for example, Burmeister and McElroy (1988). These authors show that at the 1 percent significance level, the CAPM can be rejected in favor of an arbitrage pricing theory model with several factors. We discuss arbitrage pricing theory later in the reading.

▶ In **fundamental factor models**, the factors are attributes of stocks or companies that are important in explaining cross-sectional differences in stock prices. Among the fundamental factors that have been used are the book-value-to-price ratio, market capitalization, the price–earnings ratio, and financial leverage.

▶ In **statistical factor models**, statistical methods are applied to a set of historical returns to determine portfolios that explain historical returns in one of two senses. In factor analysis models, the factors are the portfolios that best explain (reproduce) historical return covariances. In principal-components models, the factors are portfolios that best explain (reproduce) the historical return variances.

Some practical factor models have the characteristics of more than one of the above categories. We can call such models **mixed factor models**.

Our discussion concentrates on macroeconomic factor models and fundamental factor models. Industry use has generally favored fundamental and macroeconomic models, perhaps because such models are much more easily interpreted; nevertheless, statistical factor models have proponents and are used in practical applications.

4.2 The Structure of Macroeconomic Factor Models

The representation of returns in macroeconomic factor models assumes that the returns to each asset are correlated with only the surprises in some factors related to the aggregate economy, such as inflation or real output.[52] We can define **surprise** in general as the actual value minus predicted (or expected) value. A factor's surprise is the component of the factor's return that was unexpected, and the factor surprises constitute the model's independent variables. This idea contrasts to the representation of independent variables as returns (as opposed to the surprise in returns) in fundamental factor models, or for that matter in the market model.

Suppose that K factors explain asset returns. Then in a macroeconomic factor model, the following equation expresses the return of asset i:

$$R_i = a_i + b_{i1}F_1 + b_{i2}F_2 + \ldots + b_{iK}F_K + \epsilon_i \qquad \textbf{(68-16)}$$

where

R_i = the return to asset i
a_i = the expected return to asset i
F_k = the surprise in the factor k, $k = 1, 2, \ldots, K$
b_{ik} = the sensitivity of the return on asset i to a surprise in factor k,
$\qquad k = 1, 2, \ldots, K$
ϵ_i = an error term with a zero mean that represents the portion of the
$\qquad$ return to asset i not explained by the factor model

What exactly do we mean by the surprise in a macroeconomic factor? Suppose we are analyzing monthly returns for stocks. At the beginning of each month, we have a prediction of inflation for the month. The prediction may come from an econometric model or a professional economic forecaster, for example. Suppose our forecast at the beginning of the month is that inflation will be 0.4 percent

---

[52] See, for example, Burmeister, Roll, and Ross (1994).

during the month. At the end of the month, we find that inflation was actually 0.5 percent during the month. During any month,

Actual inflation = Predicted inflation + Surprise inflation

In this case, actual inflation was 0.5 percent and predicted inflation was 0.4 percent. Therefore, the surprise in inflation was 0.5 − 0.4 = 0.1 percent.

What is the effect of defining the factors in terms of surprises? Suppose we believe that inflation and gross domestic product (GDP) growth are priced risk. (GDP is a money measure of the goods and services produced within a country's borders.) We do not use the predicted values of these variables because the predicted values are already reflected in stock prices and thus in their expected returns. The intercept a_i, the expected return to asset i, reflects the effect of the predicted values of the macroeconomic variables on expected stock returns. The surprise in the macroeconomic variables during the month, on the other hand, contains new information about the variable. As a result, this model structure analyzes the return to an asset into three components: the asset's expected return, its unexpected return resulting from new information about the factors, and an error term.

Consider a factor model in which the returns to each asset are correlated with two factors. For example, we might assume that the returns for a particular stock are correlated with surprises in interest rates and surprises in GDP growth. For stock i, the return to the stock can be modeled as

$$R_i = a_i + b_{i1}F_{INT} + b_{i2}F_{GDP} + \epsilon_i \qquad \textbf{(68-17)}$$

where

R_i = the return to stock i

a_i = the expected return to stock i

b_{i1} = the sensitivity of the return to stock i to interest rate surprises

F_{INT} = the surprise in interest rates

b_{i2} = the sensitivity of the return to stock i to GDP growth surprises

F_{GDP} = the surprise in GDP growth

ϵ_i = an error term with a zero mean that represents the portion of the return to asset i not explained by the factor model

Consider first how to interpret b_{i1}. The factor model predicts that a one percentage point surprise in interest rates will contribute b_{i1} percentage points to the return to stock i. The slope coefficient b_{i2} has a similar interpretation relative to the GDP growth factor. Thus slope coefficients are naturally interpreted as the factor sensitivities of the asset.[53] A **factor sensitivity** is a measure of the response of return to each unit of increase in a factor, holding all other factors constant.

Now consider how to interpret the intercept a_i. Recall that the error term has a mean or average value of 0. If the surprises in both interest rates and GDP growth are 0, the factor model predicts that the return to asset i will be a_i. Thus a_i is the expected value of the return to stock i.

Finally, consider the error term ϵ_i. The intercept a_i represents the asset's expected return. The amount $(b_{i1}F_{INT} + b_{i2}F_{GDP})$ represents the return resulting from factor surprises, and we have interpreted these as the sources of risk shared with other assets. The term ϵ_i is the part of return that is unexplained by

---

[53] Factor sensitivities are sometimes called **factor betas** or **factor loadings**.

expected return or the factor surprises. If we have adequately represented the sources of common risk (the factors), then ϵ_i must represent an asset-specific risk. For a stock, it might represent the return from an unanticipated company-specific event.

We will discuss expected returns further when we present the arbitrage pricing theory. In macroeconomic factor models, the time series of factor surprises are developed first. We use regression analysis to estimate assets' sensitivities to the factors. In our discussion, we assume that you do not estimate sensitivities and intercepts yourself; instead you use estimates from another source (for example, one of the many consulting companies that specialize in factor models).[54] When we have the parameters for the individual assets in a portfolio, we can calculate the portfolio's parameters as a weighted average of the parameters of individual assets. An individual asset's weight in that calculation is the proportion of the total market value of the portfolio that the individual asset represents.

EXAMPLE 10

Factor Sensitivities for a Two-Stock Portfolio

Suppose that stock returns are affected by two common factors: surprises in inflation and surprises in GDP growth. A portfolio manager is analyzing the returns on a portfolio of two stocks, Manumatic (MANM) and Nextech (NXT). The following equations describe the returns for those stocks, where the factors F_{INFL} and F_{GDP} represent the surprise in inflation and GDP growth, respectively:

$$R_{MANM} = 0.09 - 1F_{INFL} + 1F_{GDP} + \epsilon_{MANM}$$
$$R_{NXT} = 0.12 + 2F_{INFL} + 4F_{GDP} + \epsilon_{NXT}$$

In evaluating the equations for surprises in inflation and GDP, amounts stated in percent terms need to be converted to decimal form. One-third of the portfolio is invested in Manumatic stock, and two-thirds is invested in Nextech stock.

1. Formulate an expression for the return on the portfolio.

2. State the expected return on the portfolio.

3. Calculate the return on the portfolio given that the surprises in inflation and GDP growth are 1 percent and 0 percent, respectively, assuming that the error terms for MANM and NXT both equal 0.5 percent.

Solution to 1: The portfolio's return is the following weighted average of the returns to the two stocks:

$$R_P = (1/3)(0.09) + (2/3)(0.12) + [(1/3)(-1) + (2/3)(2)]F_{INFL}$$
$$+ [(1/3)(1) + (2/3)(4)]F_{GDP} + (1/3)\epsilon_{MANM} + (2/3)\epsilon_{NXT}$$
$$= 0.11 + 1F_{INFL} + 3F_{GDP} + (1/3)\epsilon_{MANM} + (2/3)\epsilon_{NXT}$$

---

[54] If you want to estimate your own macroeconomic factor model, follow these steps. First, estimate a time series for each macroeconomic surprise (for example, you could use the residuals from a time-series model for each different macroeconomic series). Then, use time-series data to regress the returns for a particular asset on the surprises to the different macroeconomic factors.

> **Solution to 2:** The expected return on the portfolio is 11 percent, the value of the intercept in the expression obtained in Part 1.
>
> **Solution to 3:**
>
> $$R_P = 0.11 + 1F_{INFL} + 3F_{GDP} + (1/3)\epsilon_{MANM} + (2/3)\epsilon_{NXT}$$
> $$= 0.11 + 1(0.01) + 3(0) + (1/3)(0.005) + (2/3)(0.005)$$
> $$= 0.125 \text{ or } 12.5 \text{ percent}$$

4.3 Arbitrage Pricing Theory and the Factor Model

In the 1970s, Stephen Ross developed the arbitrage pricing theory (APT) as an alternative to the CAPM. APT describes the expected return on an asset (or portfolio) as a linear function of the risk of the asset (or portfolio) with respect to a set of factors. Like the CAPM, the APT describes a financial market equilibrium. However, the APT makes less-strong assumptions than the CAPM. The APT relies on three assumptions:

1. A factor model describes asset returns.
2. There are many assets, so investors can form well-diversified portfolios that eliminate asset-specific risk.
3. No arbitrage opportunities exist among well-diversified portfolios.

Arbitrage is a risk-free operation that earns an expected positive net profit but requires no net investment of money.[55] An **arbitrage opportunity** is an opportunity to conduct an arbitrage—an opportunity to earn an expected positive net profit without risk and with no net investment of money.

In the first assumption, the number of factors is not specified. The second assumption allows us to form portfolios with factor risk but without asset-specific risk. The third assumption is the condition of financial market equilibrium.

Empirical evidence indicates that Assumption 2 is reasonable. When a portfolio contains many stocks, the asset-specific or nonsystematic risk of individual stocks makes almost no contribution to the variance of portfolio returns. Roll and Ross (2001) found that only 1 percent to 3 percent of a well-diversified portfolio's variance comes from the non-systematic variance of the individual stocks in the portfolio, as Figure 12 shows.

According to the APT, if the above three assumptions hold, the following equation holds:[56]

$$E(R_p) = R_F + \lambda_1\beta_{p,1} + \ldots + \lambda_K\beta_{p,K} \tag{68-18}$$

---

[55] As we will see, arbitrage typically involves funding the investment in assets with proceeds from the short sale of other assets, so that net, no money is invested. A short sale is the sale of a borrowed asset. Note that the word "arbitrage" is also sometimes used to describe investment operations in which significant risk is present.

[56] A risk-free asset is assumed. If no risk-free asset exists, in place of R_F we write λ_0 to represent the expected return on a risky portfolio with zero sensitivity to all the factors. The number of factors is not specified but must be much lower than the number of assets, a condition fulfilled in practice.

**FIGURE 12   Sources of Volatility: The Case of a Well-Diversified
Portfolio**

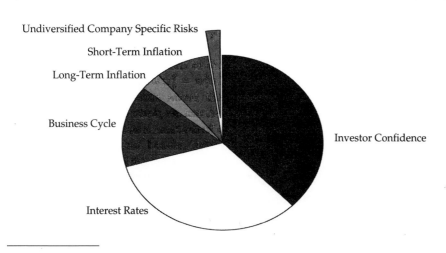

where

$E(R_p)$ = the expected return to portfolio p
R_F = the risk-free rate
λ_j = the risk premium for factor j
$\beta_{p,j}$ = the sensitivity of the portfolio to factor j
K = the number of factors

The APT equation, Equation 68-18, says that the expected return on any well-diversified portfolio is linearly related to the factor sensitivities of that portfolio.[57]

The **factor risk premium** (or **factor price**) λ_j represents the expected return in excess of the risk-free rate for a portfolio with a sensitivity of 1 to factor j and a sensitivity of 0 to all other factors. Such a portfolio is called a **pure factor portfolio** for factor j.

For example, suppose we have a portfolio with a sensitivity of 1 with respect to Factor 1 and a sensitivity of 0 to all other factors. With E_1 being the expected return on this portfolio, Equation 68-18 shows that the expected return on this portfolio is $E_1 = R_F + \lambda_1 \times 1$, so $\lambda_1 = E_1 - R_F$. Suppose that $E_1 = 0.12$ and $R_F = 0.04$. Then the risk premium for Factor 1 is $\lambda_1 = 0.12 - 0.04 = 0.08$ or 8 percent. We obtain an eight percentage point increase in expected return for an increase of 1 in the sensitivity to first factor.

What is the relationship between the APT equation and the equation for a multifactor model, Equation 68-17. In discussing the multifactor model, we stated that the intercept term is the investment's expected return. The APT equation explains what an investment's expected return is in equilibrium. Thus if the APT holds, it places a restriction on the intercept term in the multifactor model in the sense that the APT model tells us what the intercept's value should be. For instance, in Example 10, the APT would explain the intercept of 0.09 in

---

[57] The APT equation can also describe (at least approximately) the expected return on investments with asset-specific risk, under certain conditions.

the model for MANM returns as the expected return on MANM given the stock's sensitivities to the inflation and GDP factors and the risk premiums of the those factors. We can in fact substitute the APT equation into the multifactor model to produce what is known as an APT model in returns form.[58]

To use the APT equation, we need to estimate its parameters. The parameters of the APT equation are the risk-free rate and the factor risk-premiums (the factor sensitivities are specific to individual investments). Example 11 shows how the expected returns and factor sensitivities of a set of portfolios can determine the parameters of the APT model assuming a single factor.

EXAMPLE 11

Determining the Parameters in a One-Factor APT Model

Suppose we have three well-diversified portfolios that are each sensitive to the same single factor. Table 11 shows the expected returns and factor sensitivities of these portfolios. Assume that the expected returns reflect a one-year investment horizon.

TABLE 11   Sample Portfolios for a One-Factor Model

Portfolio	Expected Return	Factor Sensitivity
A	0.075	0.5
B	0.150	2.0
C	0.070	0.4

We can use these data to determine the parameters of the APT equation. According to Equation 68-18, for any well-diversified portfolio and assuming a single factor explains returns, we have $E(R_p) = R_F + \lambda_1 \beta_{p,1}$. The factor sensitivities and expected returns are known; thus there are two unknowns, the parameters R_F and λ_1. Because two points define a straight line, we need to set up only two equations. Selecting Portfolios A and B, we have

$$E(R_A) = 0.075 = R_F + 0.5\lambda_1$$

and

$$E(R_B) = 0.150 = R_F + 2\lambda_1$$

---

[58] An interesting issue is the relationship between the APT and the CAPM. If the market is the factor in a single-factor model, APT (Equation 68-18) is consistent with the CAPM. The CAPM can also be consistent with multiple factors in an APT model, if the risk premiums in the APT model satisfy certain restrictions; these CAPM-related restrictions have been repeatedly rejected in statistical tests. See Burmeister and McElroy (1988), for example.

From the equation for Portfolio A, we have $R_F = 0.075 - 0.5\lambda_1$. Substituting this expression for the risk-free rate into the equation for Portfolio B gives

$$0.15 = 0.075 - 0.5\lambda_1 + 2\lambda_1$$
$$0.15 = 0.075 + 1.5\lambda_1$$

So we have $\lambda_1 = (0.15 - 0.075)/1.5 = 0.05$. Substituting this value for λ_1 back into the equation for the expected return to Portfolio A yields

$$0.075 = R_F + 0.05 \times 0.5$$
$$R_F = 0.05$$

So the risk-free rate is 0.05 or 5 percent, and the factor premium for the common factor is also 0.05 or 5 percent. The APT equation is

$$E(R_p) = 0.05 + 0.05\beta_{p,1}$$

Portfolio C has a factor sensitivity of 0.4. Accordingly, $0.05 + (0.05 \times 0.4) = 0.07$ or 7 percent if no arbitrage opportunity exists. The expected return for Portfolio C given in Table 11 is 7 percent. Therefore, in this example no arbitrage opportunity exists.

EXAMPLE 12

Checking Whether Portfolio Returns Are Consistent with No Arbitrage

In this example, we demonstrate how to tell whether a set of expected returns for well-diversified portfolios is consistent with the APT by testing whether an arbitrage opportunity exists. In Example 11, we had three portfolios with expected returns and factor sensitivities that were consistent with the one-factor APT model $E(R_p) = 0.05 + 0.05\beta_{p,1}$. Suppose we expand the set of portfolios to include a fourth well-diversified portfolio, Portfolio D. Table 12 repeats the data given in Table 11 for Portfolios A, B, and C, in addition to providing data on Portfolio D and a portfolio we form using A and C.

TABLE 12 Sample Portfolios for a One-Factor Model

Portfolio	Expected Return	Factor Sensitivity
A	0.0750	0.50
B	0.1500	2.00
C	0.0700	0.40
D	0.0800	0.45
0.5A + 0.5C	0.0725	0.45

The expected return and factor sensitivity of a portfolio is the weighted average of the expected returns and factor sensitivities of the assets in the portfolio. Suppose we construct a portfolio consisting of 50 percent Portfolio A and 50 percent Portfolio C. Table 12 shows that the expected return of this portfolio is $(0.50)(0.0750) + (0.50)(0.07) = 0.0725$, or 7.25 percent. The factor sensitivity of this portfolio is $(0.50)(0.50) + (0.50)(0.40) = 0.45$.

Arbitrage pricing theory assumes that well-diversified portfolios present no arbitrage opportunities. If the initial investment is 0 and we bear no risk, the final expected cash flow should be 0. In this case, the configuration of expected returns in relation to factor risk presents an arbitrage opportunity involving Portfolios A, C, and D. Portfolio D offers too high an expected rate of return given its factor sensitivity. According to the APT model estimated in Example 11, an arbitrage opportunity exists unless $E(R_D) = 0.05 + 0.05\beta_{D,1} = 0.05 + (0.05 \times 0.45) = 0.0725$, so that the expected return on D is 7.25 percent. In fact, the expected return on D is 8 percent. Portfolio D is undervalued relative to its factor risk. We will buy D (hold it long) in the portfolio that exploits the arbitrage opportunity (the **arbitrage portfolio**). We purchase D using the proceeds from selling short a portfolio consisting of A and C with exactly the same 0.45 factor sensitivity as D. As we showed above, an equally weighted portfolio of A and C has a factor sensitivity of 0.45.

The arbitrage thus involves the following strategy: Invest $10,000 in Portfolio D and fund that investment by selling short an equally weighted portfolio of Portfolios A and C; then close out the investment position at the end of one year (the investment horizon for expected returns). Table 13 demonstrates the arbitrage profits to the arbitrage strategy. The final row of the table shows the net cash flow to the arbitrage portfolio.

TABLE 13   Arbitrage Opportunity within Sample Portfolios

	Initial Cash Flow	Final Cash Flow	Factor Sensitivity
Portfolio D	−$10,000.00	$10,800.00	0.45
Portfolios A and C	$10,000.00	−$10,725.00	−0.45
Sum	$0.00	$75.00	0.00

As Table 13 shows, if we buy $10,000 of Portfolio D and sell $10,000 of an equally weighted portfolio of Portfolios A and C, we have an initial net cash flow of $0. The expected value of our investment in Portfolio D at the end of one year is $10,000(1 + 0.08) = $10,800. The expected value of our short position in Portfolios A and C at the end of one year is −$10,000(1.0725) = −$10,725. So the combined expected cash flow from our investment position in one year is $75.

What about the risk? Table 13 shows that the factor risk has been eliminated: Purchasing D and selling short an equally weighted portfolio of A and C creates a portfolio with a factor sensitivity of 0.45 − 0.45 = 0.

The portfolios are well diversified, and we assume any asset-specific risk is negligible.

Because the arbitrage is possible, Portfolios A, C, and D cannot all be consistent with the same equilibrium. A unique set of parameters for the APT model does not describe the returns on these three portfolios. If Portfolio D actually had an expected return of 8 percent, investors would bid up its price until the expected return fell and the arbitrage opportunity vanished. Thus arbitrage restores equilibrium relationships among expected returns.

In Example 11, we illustrated how the parameters of a single-factor APT model can be determined from data. Example 13 shows how to determine the model parameters in a model with more than one factor.

EXAMPLE 13

Determining the Parameters in a Two-Factor Model

Suppose that two factors, surprise in inflation (Factor 1) and surprise in GDP growth (Factor 2), explain returns. According to the APT, an arbitrage opportunity exists unless

$$E(R_p) = R_F + \lambda_1\beta_{p,1} + \lambda_2\beta_{p,2}$$

Our goal is to estimate the three parameters of the model, R_F, λ_1, and λ_2. We also have hypothetical data on three well-diversified portfolios, J, K, and L, given in Table 14.

TABLE 14   Sample Portfolios for a Two-Factor Model

Portfolio	Expected Return	Sensitivity to Inflation Factor	Sensitivity to GDP Factor
J	0.14	1.0	1.5
K	0.12	0.5	1.0
L	0.11	1.3	1.1

If the market is in equilibrium (no arbitrage opportunities exist), the expected returns to the three portfolios should be described by the two-factor APT with the same set of parameters. Using the expected returns and the return sensitivities shown in Table 14 yields

$$E(R_J) = 0.14 = R_F + 1.0\lambda_1 + 1.5\lambda_2$$
$$E(R_K) = 0.12 = R_F + 0.5\lambda_1 + 1.0\lambda_2$$
$$E(R_L) = 0.11 = R_F + 1.3\lambda_1 + 1.1\lambda_2$$

We have three equations with three unknowns, so we can solve for the parameters using the method of substitution. We first want to get two equations with two unknowns. Solving the equation for $E(R_J)$ for the risk-free rate,

$$R_F = 0.14 - 1.0\lambda_1 - 1.5\lambda_2$$

Substituting this expression for the risk-free rate into the equation for $E(R_K)$, we find, after simplification, that $\lambda_1 = 0.04 - \lambda_2$. Using $\lambda_1 = 0.04 - \lambda_2$ to eliminate λ_1 in the equation for $E(R_J)$,

$$0.10 = R_F + 0.5\lambda_2$$

Using $\lambda_1 = 0.04 - \lambda_2$ to eliminate λ_1 in the equation for $E(R_L)$,

$$0.058 = R_F - 0.2\lambda_2$$

Using the two equations in R_F and λ_2 immediately above, we find that $\lambda_2 = 0.06$ (we solved for the risk-free rate in the first of these two equations and used the expression in the second equation). Because $\lambda_1 = 0.04 - \lambda_2$, $\lambda_1 = -0.02$. Finally, $R_F = 0.14 - 1.0 \times (-0.02) - 1.5 \times (0.06) = 0.07$. To summarize:

> $R_F = 0.07$ (The risk-free rate is 7 percent.)
> $\lambda_1 = -0.02$ (The inflation risk premium is -2 percent per unit of sensitivity.)
> $\lambda_2 = 0.06$ (The GDP risk premium is 6 percent per unit of sensitivity.)

So, the APT equation for these three portfolios is

$$E(R_p) = 0.07 - 0.02\beta_{p,1} + 0.06\beta_{p,2}$$

This example illustrates the calculations for determining the parameters of an APT model. It also shows that the risk premium for a factor can actually be negative.

In Example 13, we computed a *negative* risk premium for the inflation factor. One explanation for a negative inflation risk premium is that most equities have negative sensitivities to inflation risk (their returns tend to decrease with a positive inflation surprise). An asset with a positive inflation sensitivity would be in demand as an inflation-hedging asset; the premium associated with a **factor portfolio** for inflation risk could be negative as a result.

4.4 The Structure of Fundamental Factor Models

Earlier we gave the equation of a macroeconomic factor model as

$$R_i = a_i + b_{i1}F_1 + b_{i2}F_2 + \cdots + b_{iK}F_K + \epsilon_i$$

We can also represent the structure of fundamental factor models with this equation, but we need to interpret the terms differently.

In fundamental factor models, the factors are stated as returns rather than return surprises in relation to predicted values, so they do not generally have expected values of zero. This approach changes the interpretation of the intercept, which we no longer interpret as the expected return.[59]

We also interpret the factor sensitivities differently in most fundamental factor models. In fundamental factor models, the factor sensitivities are attributes of the security. Consider a fundamental model for equities with a dividend yield factor. An asset's sensitivity to the dividend factor is the value of the attribute itself, its dividend yield; the sensitivity is typically standardized. Specifically, an asset i's sensitivity to a given factor would be calculated as the value of the attribute for the asset minus the average value of the attribute across all stocks, divided by the standard deviation of the attribute across all stocks. The **standardized beta** is

$$b_{ij} = \frac{\text{Asset } i\text{'s attribute value} - \text{Average attribute value}}{\sigma(\text{Attribute values})} \qquad \textbf{(68-19)}$$

Continuing with the dividend yield example, after standardization a stock with an average dividend yield will have a factor sensitivity of 0, a stock with a dividend yield one standard deviation above the average will have a factor sensitivity of 1, and a stock with a dividend yield one standard deviation below the average will have a factor sensitivity of -1. Suppose, for example, that an investment has a dividend yield of 3.5 percent and that the average dividend yield across all stocks being considered is 2.5 percent. Further, suppose that the standard deviation of dividend yields across all stocks is 2 percent. The investment's sensitivity to dividend yield is $(3.5\% - 2.5\%)/2\% = 0.50$, or one-half standard deviation above average. The scaling permits all factor sensitivities to be interpreted similarly, despite differences in units of measure and scale in the variables. The exception to this interpretation is factors for binary variables such as industry membership. A company either participates in an industry or it does not. The industry factor sensitivities would be $0 - 1$ dummy variables; in models that recognize that companies frequently operate in multiple industries, the value of the sensitivity would be 1 for each industry in which a company operated.[60]

A second distinction between macroeconomic multifactor models and fundamental factor models is that with the former, we develop the factor (surprise) series first and then estimate the factor sensitivities through regressions; with the latter, we generally specify the factor sensitivities (attributes) first and then estimate the factor returns through regressions.[61]

---

[59] If the coefficients were not standardized as described in the following paragraph, the intercept could be interpreted as the risk-free rate, because it would be the return to an asset with no factor risk (zero factor betas) and no asset-specific risk. With standardized coefficients, the intercept is not interpreted beyond being an intercept in a regression included so that the expected asset-specific risk equals 0.

[60] To further explain $0 - 1$ variables, industry membership is measured on a **nominal scale** because we can name the industry to which a company belongs but no more. A nominal variable can be represented in a regression by a dummy variable (a variable that takes on the value of 0 or 1).

[61] In some models that may be classed as fundamental, the factor sensitivities are regression coefficients and are not specified first.

4.5 Multifactor Models in Current Practice

In the previous sections, we explained the basic concepts of multifactor models and the APT. We now describe some models in actual industry use.

4.5.1 Macroeconomic Factor Models

Chen, Roll, and Ross (1986) pioneered the development of macroeconomic factor models. Following statistically based research suggesting that more than one factor was important in explaining the average returns on U.S. stocks, Chen et al. suggested that a relatively small set of macro factors was the primary influence on the U.S. stock market. The factors in the Chen et al. study were (1) inflation, including **unanticipated inflation** and changes in expected inflation, (2) a factor related to the term structure of interest rates, represented by long-term government bond returns minus one-month Treasury-bill rates, (3) a factor reflecting changes in market risk and investors' risk aversion, represented by the difference between the returns on low-rated and high-rated bonds, and (4) changes in industrial production.

The usefulness of any factor for explaining asset returns is generally evaluated using historical data. Our confidence that a factor will explain future returns increases if we can give an economic explanation of why a factor should be important in explaining average returns. We can plausibly explain all of Chen et al.'s four factors. For example, inflation affects the cash flows of businesses as well as the level of the discount rate applied to these cash flows by investors. Changes in industrial production affect the cash flows of businesses and the opportunities faced by investors. Example 14 details a current macroeconomic factor model that expanded on the model of Chen et al.

EXAMPLE 14

Expected Return in a Macroeconomic Factor Model

Burmeister, Roll, and Ross (1994) presented a macroeconomic factor model to explain the returns on U.S. equities. The model is known as the BIRR model for short. The BIRR model includes five factors:

1. Confidence risk: the unanticipated change in the return difference between risky corporate bonds and government bonds, both with maturities of 20 years. Risky corporate bonds bear greater default risk than does government debt. Investors' attitudes toward this risk should affect the average returns on equities. To explain the factor's name, when their confidence is high, investors are willing to accept a smaller reward for bearing this risk.

2. Time horizon risk: the unanticipated change in the return difference between 20-year government bonds and 30-day Treasury bills. This factor reflects investors' willingness to invest for the long term.

3. Inflation risk: the unexpected change in the inflation rate. Nearly all stocks have negative exposure to this factor, as their returns decline with positive surprises in inflation.

---

4. Business cycle risk: the unexpected change in the level of real business activity. A positive surprise or unanticipated change indicates that the expected growth rate of the economy, measured in constant dollars, has increased.

5. Market timing risk: the portion of the S&P 500's total return that remains unexplained by the first four risk factors.[62] Almost all stocks have positive sensitivity to this factor.

The first four factors are quite similar to Chen et al.'s factors with respect to the economic influences they seek to capture. The fifth factor acknowledges the uncertainty surrounding the correct set of underlying variables for asset pricing; this factor captures influences on the returns to the S&P 500 not explained by the first four factors.

The S&P 500 is a widely used index of 500 U.S. stocks of leading companies in leading industries. Burmeister et al. used the S&P 500 to gauge the influence of their five factors on the mean excess returns (above the Treasury bill rate) to the S&P 500. Table 15 shows their results.

TABLE 15	Explaining the Annual Expected Excess Return for the S&P 500		
Risk Factor	**Factor Sensitivity**	**Risk Premium**	**Effect of Factor on Expected Return**
Confidence risk	0.27	2.59%	0.70%
Time horizon risk	0.56	−0.66%	−0.37%
Inflation risk	−0.37	−4.32%	1.60%
Business cycle risk	1.71	1.49%	2.55%
Market timing risk	1.00	3.61%	3.61%
Expected excess return			8.09%

Source: Burmeister et al.

The estimated APT model is $E(R_p) =$ T-bill rate $+ 2.59$(Confidence risk) $- 0.66$(Time horizon risk) $- 4.32$(Inflation risk) $+ 1.49$(Business cycle risk) $+ 3.61$(Market timing risk). The table shows that the S&P 500 had positive exposure to every risk factor except inflation risk. The two largest contributions to excess return came from market timing risk and business cycle risk. According to the table, this model predicts that the S&P 500 will have an expected excess return of 8.09 percent above the T-bill rate. Therefore, if the 30-day Treasury bill rate were 4 percent, for example, the forecasted return for the S&P 500 would be $4 + 8.09 = 12.09$ percent a year.

---

[62] Because of the way the factor is constructed, the S&P 500 itself has a sensitivity of 1 to market timing risk.

In Example 15, we illustrate how we might use the Burmeister et al. factor model to assess the factor bets placed by a portfolio manager managing a U.S. active core equity portfolio (an actively managed portfolio invested in large-cap stocks).

EXAMPLE 15

Exposures to Economy-Wide Risks

William Hughes is the portfolio manager of a U.S. core equity portfolio that is being evaluated relative to its benchmark, the S&P 500. Because Hughes's performance will be evaluated relative to this benchmark, it is useful to understand the active factor bets that Hughes took relative to the S&P 500. With a focus on exposures to economy-wide risk, we use the Burmeister et al. model already presented. Table 16 displays Hughes's data.

TABLE 16   Excess Factor Sensitivities for a Core Equity Portfolio

Risk Factor	Core Portfolio's Factor Sensitivity	S&P 500 Factor Sensitivity	Core Portfolio's Excess Factor Sensitivity
Confidence risk	0.27	0.27	0.00
Time horizon risk	0.56	0.56	0.00
Inflation risk	−0.12	−0.37	0.25
Business cycle risk	2.25	1.71	0.54
Market timing risk	1.10	1.00	0.10

We see that the portfolio manager tracks the S&P 500 exactly on confidence and time horizon risk but tilts toward greater business cycle risk. The portfolio also has a small positive excess exposure to the market timing factor.

We can use the excess exposure to business cycle risk to illustrate the numerical interpretation of the excess sensitivities. Ignoring nonsystematic risk and holding the values of the other factors constant, if there is a + 1 percent surprise in the business cycle factor, we expect the return on the portfolio to be $0.01 \times 0.54 = 0.0054$ or 0.54 percent higher than the return on the S&P 500. Conversely, we expect the return on the portfolio to be lower than the S&P 500's return by an equal amount for a − 1 percent surprise in business cycle risk.

Because of the excess exposure of 0.54, the portfolio manager appears to be placing a bet on economic expansion, relative to the benchmark. If the factor bet is inadvertent, Hughes is perhaps assuming an unwanted risk. If he is aware of the bet, what are the reasons for the bet?

Care must be taken in interpreting the portfolio manager's excess sensitivity of 0.25 to the inflation factor. The S&P 500 has a negative inflation factor exposure. The value of 0.25 represents a smaller negative exposure to inflation for the core portfolio—that is, less rather than more exposure to inflation risk. Note from Table 16 that because the risk premium for inflation risk is negative, Hughes is giving up expected return relative to the benchmark by his bet on inflation. Again, what are his reasons for the inflation factor bet?

The market timing factor has an interpretation somewhat similar to that of the CAPM beta about how a stock tends to respond to changes in the broad market, with a higher value indicating higher sensitivity to market returns, all else equal. But the market timing factor reflects only the portion of the S&P 500's returns not explained by the other four factors, and the two concepts are distinct. Whereas we would expect S&P 500 returns to be correlated with one or more of the first four factors, the market timing factor is constructed to be uncorrelated with the first four factors. Because the market timing factor and the S&P 500 returns are distinct, we would not expect market timing factor sensitivity to be proportional to CAPM beta computed relative to the S&P 500, in general.

Another major macroeconomic factor model is the Salomon Smith Barney U.S. Equity Risk Attribute Model, or Salomon RAM, for short.

EXAMPLE 16

Expected Return in the Salomon RAM

The Salomon RAM model explains returns to U.S. stocks in terms of nine factors: six macroeconomic factors, a residual market factor, a residual size factor, and a residual sector factor:

1. Economic growth: the monthly change in industrial production.
2. Credit quality: the monthly change in the yield of the Salomon Smith Barney High-Yield Market 10+ year index, after removing the component of the change that is correlated with the monthly changes in the yields of 30-year Treasury bonds.
3. Long rates: the monthly change in the yield of the 30-year Treasury bond.
4. Short rates: the monthly change in the yield of the 3-month Treasury bill.
5. Inflation shock: the unexpected component of monthly change in the consumer price index (CPI).
6. Dollar: the monthly change in the trade-weighted dollar.
7. Residual market: the monthly return on the S&P 500 after removing the effects of the six factors above.
8. Small-cap premium: the monthly difference between the return on the Russell 2000 Index and the S&P 500, after removing the effect of the seven factors above.

9. Residual sector: the monthly return on a sector membership index after removing the effect of the eight factors above.

Some noteworthy points concerning this model are as follows:[63]

▶ In contrast to the BIRR model and the general model (Equation 68-16), all the factors except inflation are stated in terms of returns rather than surprises.

▶ Factors 7, 8, and 9 attempt to isolate the net or unique contribution of the factor by removing the component of the factor return that is correlated with the group of preceding factors. Factors 7, 8, and 9 are each uncorrelated among themselves and with the other factors; they are said to be **orthogonal** (uncorrelated) factors. In addition, the credit quality factor is constructed to be uncorrelated with the long-rate factor.

▶ Based on the explanatory power of the model, each stock receives a RAM ranking that reflects its coefficient of determination, with 1 the highest and 5 the lowest rank.

▶ The factor sensitivities are presented in standardized form.

In Table 17, the factor sensitivities are standardized with the same interpretation as Equation 68-19.

TABLE 17	Factor Sensitivities for Four Stocks			
	Bank	Cable TV Provider	Department Store	Computer Manufacturer
Economic growth	1.48	−1.30	−0.88	0.88
Credit quality	−1.62	−0.77	−3.19	0.12
Long rates	−0.01	−1.65	1.83	0.78
Short rates	1.00	1.53	1.10	1.17
Inflation shock	−0.97	−1.99	−1.57	0.80
Dollar	0.82	1.47	0.87	−1.63
Residual market	0.06	0.30	0.13	0.26
Small-cap premium	0.13	1.44	0.92	−1.19
Residual sector	0.02	0.00	−0.03	0.00

Note: Entries are standardized factor sensitivities.

The bank and the computer manufacturer have investment-grade debt. The cable TV provider and department store are relatively heavy users of debt that is rated below investment grade. The computer manufacturer

---

[63] See Sorenson, Samak, and Miller (1998) for more information on this model.

uses little debt in its capital structure. Based only on the information given, answer the following questions.

1. Contrast the factor sensitivities of the cable TV provider stock to those of the average stock.

2. State which stocks are expected to do well in an economy showing strong economic growth coupled with an improving credit environment, all else equal.

3. Explain a possible business reason or a reason related to company fundamentals to explain negative sensitivity of the cable TV provider's stock to the credit quality factor.

Solution to 1: The factor sensitivities to short rates, the trade-weighted dollar, the residual market factor, and the small-cap premium factor are above average, as indicated by positive factor sensitivities. The sensitivity to the residual sector factor is average, as indicated by zero factor sensitivity. By contrast, the cable TV provider's stock has below-average sensitivity to the economic growth, credit quality, long-rate, and inflation factors, as indicated by negative factor sensitivities.

Solution to 2: Both the bank and the computer manufacturer have positive sensitivity to the economic growth factor, which is the monthly change in industrial production. As the factor and factor sensitivity are defined, the positive sensitivity implies above-average returns for these two stocks in an environment of strong economic growth, all else equal. The bank has a negative coefficient on the credit quality factor, whereas the computer manufacturer has a positive sensitivity. An improving credit environment means that the yields of high-yield bonds are declining. Thus we would observe a negative value for the credit quality factor in that environment. Of the two stocks, we expect that only the bank stock with a negative sensitivity should give above-average returns in an improving credit environment. Thus the bank stock is expected to do well in the stated scenario.

Solution to 3: The credit quality factor essentially measures the change in the premium for bearing default risk. A negative coefficient on the credit quality factor means that the stock should do well when the premium for bearing default risk declines (an improving credit environment). One explanation for the negative sensitivity of the cable TV provider's stock to the credit quality factor is that the company is a heavy borrower with less than investment-grade debt. The cost of such debt reflects a significant default premium. The cable TV provider's borrowing costs should decline in an improving credit environment; that decline should positively affect its stock price.

4.5.2 Fundamental Factor Models

Financial analysts frequently use fundamental factor models for a variety of purposes, including portfolio performance attribution and risk analysis.[64]

---

[64] **Portfolio performance attribution** analyzes the performance of portfolios in terms of the contributions from various sources of risk.

Fundamental factor models focus on explaining the returns to individual stocks using observable fundamental factors that describe either attributes of the securities themselves or attributes of the securities' issuers. Industry membership, price-earnings ratio, book value-to-price ratio, size, and financial leverage are examples of fundamental factors.

Example 17 reports a study that examined macroeconomic, fundamental, and statistical factor models.

EXAMPLE 17

Alternative Factor Models

Connor (1995) contrasted a macroeconomic factor model with a fundamental factor model to compare how well the models explain stock returns.[65]

Connor reported the results of applying a macroeconomic factor model to the returns for 779 large-cap U.S. stocks based on monthly data from January 1985 through December 1993. Using five macroeconomic factors, Connor was able to explain approximately 11 percent of the variance of return on these stocks.[66] Table 18 shows his results.

TABLE 18   The Explanatory Power of the Macroeconomic Factors

Factor	Explanatory Power from Using Each Factor Alone	Increase in Explanatory Power from Adding Each Factor to All the Others
Inflation	1.3%	0.0%
Term structure	1.1%	7.7%
Industrial production	0.5%	0.3%
Default premium	2.4%	8.1%
Unemployment	−0.3%	0.1%
All factors		10.9%

Source: Connor (1995).

Connor also reported a fundamental factor analysis of the same companies for which he conducted a macroeconomic factor analysis. The factor model employed was the BARRA US-E2 model (the current version is E3). Table 19 shows these results. In the table, "variability in markets" represents the stock's volatility, "success" is a price momentum variable,

---

[65] We do not discuss results for statistical factor models also reported in Connor (1995).

[66] The explanatory power of a given model was computed as $1 - [$ (Average asset-specific variance of return across stocks)/(Average total variance of return across stocks)$]$. The variance estimates were corrected for degrees of freedom, so the marginal contribution of a factor to explanatory power can be 0 or negative. Explanatory power captures the proportion of the total variance of return that a given model explains for the average stock.

"trade activity" distinguishes stocks by how often their shares trade, and "growth" distinguishes stocks by past and anticipated earnings growth.[67]

TABLE 19 The Explanatory Power of the Fundamental Factors

Factor	Explanatory Power from Using Each Factor Alone	Increase in Explanatory Power from Adding Each Factor to All the Others
Industries	16.3%	18.0%
Variability in markets	4.3%	0.9%
Success	2.8%	0.8%
Size	1.4%	0.6%
Trade activity	1.4%	0.5%
Growth	3.0%	0.4%
Earnings to price	2.2%	0.6%
Book to price	1.5%	0.6%
Earnings variability	2.5%	0.4%
Financial leverage	0.9%	0.5%
Foreign investment	0.7%	0.4%
Labor intensity	2.2%	0.5%
Dividend yield	2.9%	0.4%
All factors		42.6%

Source: Connor (1995).

As Table 19 shows, the most important fundamental factor is "industries," represented by 55 industry dummy variables. The fundamental factor model explained approximately 43 percent of the variation in stock returns, compared with approximately 11 percent for the macroeconomic factor model. Connor's article does not provide tests of the statistical significance of the various factors in either model; however, Connor did find strong evidence for the usefulness of fundamental factor models, and this evidence is mirrored by the wide use of those models in the investment community. Fundamental factor models are frequently used in portfolio performance attribution, for example. We shall illustrate this use later in the reading. Typically, fundamental factor models employ many more factors than macroeconomic factor models, giving a more detailed picture of the sources of a portfolio manager's results.

We cannot conclude from this study that fundamental factor models are inherently superior to macroeconomic factors, however. Each of the major types of models has its uses. The factors in various macroeconomic factor models are individually backed by statistical evidence that

---

[67] The explanations of the variables are from Grinold and Kahn (1994); Connor did not supply definitions.

they represent systematic risk (i.e., risk that cannot be diversified away). In contrast, a portfolio manager can easily construct a portfolio that excludes a particular industry, so exposure to a particular industry is not systematic risk. The two types of factors, macroeconomic and fundamental, have different implications for measuring and managing risk, in general. The macroeconomic factor set is parsimonious (five variables). The fundamental factor set is large (67 variables including the 55 industry dummy variables), and at the expense of greater complexity, it can give a more detailed picture of risk in terms that are easily related to company and security characteristics. Connor found that the macroeconomic factor model had no marginal explanatory power when added to the fundamental factor model, implying that the fundamental risk attributes capture all the risk characteristics represented by the macroeconomic factor betas. Because the fundamental factors supply such a detailed description of the characteristics of a stock and its issuer, however, this finding is not necessarily surprising.

We encounter a range of distinct representations of risk in the fundamental models that are currently used in practical applications. Diversity exists in both the identity and exact definition of factors as well as in the underlying functional form and estimation procedures. Despite the diversity, we can place the factors of most fundamental factor models for equities into three broad groups:

▶ **Company fundamental factors.** These are factors related to the company's internal performance. Examples are factors relating to earnings growth, earnings variability, earnings momentum, and financial leverage.

▶ **Company share-related factors.** These factors include valuation measures and other factors related to share price of the trading characteristics of the shares. In contrast to the previous category, these factors directly incorporate investors' expectations concerning the company. Examples include price multiples such as earnings yield, dividend yield, and book-to-market. Market capitalization falls under this heading. Various models incorporate variables relating to share price momentum, share price volatility, and trading activity that fall in this category.

▶ **Macroeconomic factors.** Sector or industry membership factors come under this heading. Various models include factors such as CAPM beta, other similar measures of systematic risk, and yield curve level sensitivity, all of which can be placed in this category.

4.6 Applications

The following sections present some of the major applications of multifactor models in investment practice.

We begin by discussing portfolio performance attribution and risk analysis. We could frame the discussion in terms of raw returns or in terms of returns relative to a portfolio's benchmark. Because they provide a reference standard for risk and return, benchmarks play an important role in many institutional investors' plans for quantitatively risk-controlled returns. We shall thus focus on analyzing returns relative to a benchmark.

Multifactor models can also help portfolio managers from portfolios with specific desired risk characteristics. After discussing **performance attribution** and risk analysis, we explain the use of multifactor models in creating a portfolio with risk exposures that are similar to those of another portfolio.

4.6.1 *Analyzing Sources of Returns*

Multifactor models can help us understand in detail the sources of a manager's returns relative to a benchmark. For simplicity, in this section we analyze the sources of the returns of a portfolio fully invested in the equities of a single national equity market.[68]

Analysts frequently favor fundamental multifactor models in decomposing (separating into basic elements) the sources of returns. In contrast to statistical factor models, fundamental factor models allow the sources of portfolio performance to be described by name. Also, in contrast to macroeconomic factor models, fundamental models suggest investment style choices and security characteristics more directly, and often in greater detail.

We first need to understand the objectives of active managers. As mentioned, managers are commonly evaluated relative to a specified benchmark. Active portfolio managers hold securities in different-from-benchmark weights in an attempt to add value to their portfolios relative to a passive investment approach. Securities held in different-from-benchmark weights reflect portfolio manager expectations that differ from consensus expectations. For an equity manager, those expectations may relate to common factors driving equity returns or to considerations unique to a company. Thus when we evaluate an active manager, we want to ask questions such as "Did the manager have insights that were valuable in the sense of adding value above a **passive strategy**?" Analyzing the sources of returns using multifactor models can help answer these questions.

The return on a portfolio, R_p, can be viewed as the sum of the benchmark's return, R_B, and the **active return** (portfolio return minus benchmark return):

$$\text{Active return} = R_p - R_B \qquad \textbf{(68-20)}$$

With a factor model in hand, we can analyze a portfolio manager's active return as the sum of two components. The first component is the product of portfolio manager's factor tilts (active factor sensitivities) and the factor returns; we may call that component the return from factor tilts. The second component is the part of active return reflecting the manager's skill in individual asset selection; we may call that component asset selection. Equation 68-21 shows the decomposition of active return into those two components:

$$\text{Active return} = \sum_{j=1}^{K} [(\text{Portfolio sensitivity})_j - (\text{Benchmark sensitivity})_j]$$

$$\textbf{(68-21)}$$

$$\times (\text{Factor return})_j + \text{Asset selection}$$

In Equation 68-21, we measure the portfolio's and benchmark's sensitivities to each factor in our risk model at the beginning of an evaluation period.

Example 18 illustrates the use of a relatively parsimonious fundamental factor model in decomposing and interpreting returns.

---

[68] The assumption allows us to ignore the roles of country selection, asset allocation, market timing, and currency hedging, greatly simplifying the analysis. Even in a more general context, however, we can perform similar analyses using multifactor models.

EXAMPLE 18

Active Return Decomposition of an Equity Portfolio Manager

As an equity analyst at a pension fund sponsor, Ronald Service uses the following multifactor model to evaluate U.S. equity portfolios:

$$R_p - R_F = a_p + b_{p1}RMRF + b_{p2}SMB + b_{p3}HML + b_{p4}WML + \epsilon_p \quad \text{(68-22)}$$

where

R_p and R_F = the return on the portfolio and the risk-free rate of return, respectively

RMRF = the return on a value-weighted equity index in excess of the one-month T-bill rate

SMB = small minus big, a size (market capitalization) factor. SMB is the average return on three small-cap portfolios minus the average return on three large-cap portfolios.

HML = high minus low, the average return on two high book-to-market portfolios minus the average return on two low book-to-market portfolios

WML = winners minus losers, a momentum factor. WML is the return on a portfolio of the past year's winners minus the return on a portfolio of the past year's losers.[69]

In Equation 68-22, the sensitivities are interpreted as regression coefficients and are not standardized.

Service's current task is evaluating the performance of the most recently hired U.S. equity manager. That manager's benchmark is the Russell 1000, an index representing the performance of U.S. large-cap stocks. The manager describes herself as a "stock picker" and points to her performance in beating the benchmark as evidence that she is successful. Table 20 presents an analysis based on Equation 68-21 of the sources of that manager's active return during the year. In Table 20, "A. Return from Factor Tilts," equal to 2.1241 percent, sums the four numbers above it in the column; the return from factor tilts is the first component of the Equation 68-21. Table 20 lists asset selection as equal to −0.05 percent. Active return is found as 2.1241% + (−0.05%) = 2.0741%.

From his previous work, Service knows that the returns to growth-style portfolios often have a positive sensitivity to the momentum factor (WML) in Equation 68-22. By contrast, the returns to certain value-style portfolios, such as those following a contrarian strategy, often have low or negative sensitivity to the momentum factor.

Using the information given, address the following:

1. Determine the manager's investment style mandate.

2. Evaluate the sources of the manager's active return for the year.

3. What concerns might Service discuss with the manager as a result of the return decomposition?

---

[69] WML is an equally weighted average of the stocks with the highest 30 percent 11-month returns lagged 1 month minus the equally weighted average of the stocks with the lowest 30 percent 11-month returns lagged 1 month. The model is based on Carhart (1997); WML is Carhart's PR1YR factor.

	Factor Sensitivity				**Contribution to Active Return**	
Factor	**Portfolio (1)**	**Benchmark (2)**	**Difference (3) = (1) − (2)**	**Factor Return (4)**	**Absolute (3) × (4)**	**Proportion of Total Active**
RMRF	0.85	0.90	−0.05	5.52%	−0.2760	−13.3%
SMB	0.05	0.10	−0.05	−3.35%	0.1675	8.1%
HML	1.40	1.00	0.40	5.10%	2.0400	98.4%
WML	0.08	0.06	0.02	9.63%	0.1926	9.3%
			A. Return from Factor Tilts =		2.1241	102.4%
			B. Asset Selection =		−0.0500	−2.4%
			C. Active Return (A + B) =		2.0741	100.0%

TABLE 20 Active Return Decomposition

Solution to 1: The benchmark's sensitivities reflect the baseline risk characteristics of a manager's investment opportunity set. We can infer the manager's anticipated style by examining the characteristics of the benchmark selected for her. We then confirm these inferences by examining the portfolio's actual factor exposures:

▶ Stocks with high book-to-market are generally viewed as value stocks. Because the pension sponsor selected a benchmark with a high sensitivity (1.0) to HML (the high book-to-market minus low book-to-market factor), we can infer that the manager has a value orientation. The actual sensitivity of 1.4 to HML indicates that the manager had even more exposure to high book-to-market stocks than the benchmark.

▶ The benchmark's and portfolio's approximate neutrality to the momentum factor is consistent with a value orientation.

▶ The benchmark's and portfolio's low exposure to SMB suggests essentially no net exposure to small-cap stocks.

The above considerations as a group suggest that the manager has a large-cap value orientation.

Solution to 2: The dominant source of the manager's positive active return was her positive active exposure to the HML factor. The bet contributed $(1.40 - 1.00)(5.10\%) = 2.04\%$ or approximately 98 percent of the realized active return of about 2.07 percent. During the evaluation period, the manager sharpened her value orientation, and that bet paid off. The manager's active exposure to the overall market (RMRF) was unprofitable, but her active exposures to small stocks (SMB) and to momentum (WML) were profitable; however, the magnitudes of the manager's active exposures to RMRF, SMB, and WML were relatively small, so the effects of those bets on active return was minor compared with her large and successful bet on HML.

> **Solution to 3:** Although the manager is a self-described "stock picker," her active return from asset selection in this period was actually negative. Her positive active return resulted from the concurrence of a large active bet on HML and a high return to that factor during the period. If the market had favored growth rather than value without the manager doing better in individual asset selection, the manager's performance would have been unsatisfactory. Can the manager supply evidence that she can predict changes in returns to the HML factor? Is she overconfident about her stock selection ability? Service may want to discuss these concerns with the manager. The return decomposition has helped Service distinguish between the return from positioning along the value-growth spectrum and return from insights into individual stocks within the investment approach the manager has chosen.

4.6.2 *Analyzing Sources of Risk*

Continuing with our focus on active returns, in this section we explore analysis of active risk. **Active risk** is the standard deviation of active returns. Many terms in use refer to exactly the same concept, so we need to take a short detour to mention them. A traditional synonym is **tracking error** (TE), but the term may be confusing unless *error* is associated by the reader with *standard deviation*; tracking-error volatility (TEV) has been used (where *error* is understood as a *difference*); and **tracking risk** is now in common use (but the natural abbreviation TR could be misunderstood to refer to total return). We will use the abbreviation TE for the concept of tracking risk, and we will refer to it usually as tracking risk:

$$\text{TE} = s(R_p - R_B) \tag{68-23}$$

In Equation 68-23, $s(R_p - R_B)$ indicates that we take the sample standard deviation (indicated by s) of the time series of differences between the portfolio return, R_p, and the benchmark return, R_B. We should be careful that active return and tracking risk are stated on the same time basis.[70]

As a broad indication of ranges for tracking risk, in U.S. equity markets a well-executed **passive investment strategy** can often achieve tracking risk on the order of 1 percent or less per annum. A semi-active or enhanced index investment strategy, which makes tightly controlled use of managers' expectations, often has a tracking risk goal of 2 percent per annum. A diversified active U.S. large-cap equity strategy that might be benchmarked on the S&P 500 would commonly have tracking risk in the range of 2 percent to 6 percent per annum. An aggressive active equity manager might have tracking risk in the range of 6 percent to 9 percent or more.

Somewhat analogous to use of the traditional Sharpe measure in evaluating absolute returns, the ratio of mean active return to active risk, the **information ratio (IR)**, is a tool for evaluating mean active returns per unit of active risk. The historical or *ex post* IR has the form

$$\text{IR} = \frac{\overline{R}_p - \overline{R}_B}{s(R_p - R_B)} \tag{68-24}$$

---

[70] To annualize a daily TE based on daily returns, we multiply daily TE by $(250)^{1/2}$ based on 250 trading days in a year; to annualize a monthly TE based on monthly returns, we multiply monthly TE by $(12)^{1/2}$.

In the numerator of Equation 68-24, $\overline{R}_p$ and $\overline{R}_B$ stand for the sample mean return on the portfolio and the sample mean return on the benchmark, respectively. To illustrate the calculation, if a portfolio achieved a mean return of 9 percent during the same period that its benchmark earned a mean return of 7.5 percent, and the portfolio's tracking risk was 6 percent, we would calculate an information ratio of $(9\% - 7.5\%)/6\% = 0.25$. Setting guidelines for acceptable active risk or tracking risk is one of the ways that some institutional investors attempt to assure that the overall risk and style characteristics of their investments are in line with those desired.

EXAMPLE 19

Communicating with Investment Managers

The framework of active return and active risk is appealing to investors who want to closely control the risk of investments. The benchmark serves as a known and continuously observable reference standard in relation to which quantitative risk and return objectives may be stated and communicated. For example, a U.S. public employee retirement system issued a solicitation (or request for proposal) to prospective investment managers for a "risk-controlled U.S. large-cap equity fund" that included the following requirements:

► Shares must be components of the S&P 500.

► The portfolio should have a minimum of 200 issues. At time of purchase, the maximum amount that may be invested in any one issuer is 5 percent of the portfolio at market value or 150 percent of the issuers' weight within the S&P 500 Index, whichever is greater.

► The portfolio must have a minimum 0.30 percent information ratio either since inception or over the last seven years.

► The portfolio must also have tracking risk of less than 4.0 percent with respect to the S&P 500 either since inception or over the last seven years.

Analysts use multifactor models to understand in detail a portfolio manager's risk exposures. In decomposing active risk, the analyst's objective is to measure the portfolio's active exposure along each dimension of risk—in other words, to understand the sources of tracking risk.[71] Among the questions analysts will want to answer are the following:

► What active exposures contributed most to the manager's tracking risk?

► Was the portfolio manager aware of the nature of his active exposures, and if so, can he articulate a rationale for assuming them?

► Are the portfolio's active risk exposures consistent with the manager's stated investment philosophy?

► Which active bets earned adequate returns for the level of active risk taken?

---

[71] The portfolio's active risks are weighted averages of the component securities' active risk. Therefore, we may also perform the analysis at the level of individual holdings. A portfolio manager may find this approach useful in making adjustments to his active risk profile.

In addressing these questions, analysts often choose fundamental factor models because they can be used to relate active risk exposures to a manager's portfolio decisions in a fairly direct and intuitive way. In this section, we explain how to decompose or explain a portfolio's active risk using a multifactor model.

We previously addressed the decomposition of active return; now we address the decomposition of active risk. In analyzing risk, it is convenient to use variances rather than standard deviations because the variances of uncorrelated variables are additive. We refer to the variance of active risk as **active risk squared**:

$$\text{Active risk squared} = s^2(R_p - R_B) \tag{68-25}$$

We can separate a portfolio's active risk squared into two components:

► **Active factor risk** is the contribution to active risk squared resulting from the portfolio's different-than-benchmark exposures relative to factors specified in the risk model.[72]

► **Active specific risk** or **asset selection risk** is the contribution to active risk squared resulting from the portfolio's active weights on individual assets as those weights interact with assets' residual risk.[73]

When applied to an investment in a single asset class, active risk squared has two components. The decomposition of active risk squared into two components is

$$\text{Active risk squared} = \text{Active factor risk} + \text{Active specific risk} \tag{68-26}$$

Active factor risk represents the part of active risk squared explained by the portfolio active factor exposures. Active factor risk can be found indirectly as the difference between active risk squared and active specific risk, which has the expression[74]

$$\text{Active specific risk} = \sum_{i=1}^{n} w_i^a \sigma_{\epsilon_i}^2$$

where w_i^a is the ith asset's active weight in the portfolio (that is, the difference between the asset's weight in the portfolio and its weight in the benchmark) and $\sigma_{\epsilon_i}^2$ is the residual risk of the ith asset (the variance of the ith asset's returns left unexplained by the factors).[75] Active specific risk identifies the active non-factor or residual risk assumed by the manager. We should look for a positive average return from asset selection as compensation for bearing active specific risk.

---

[72] Throughout this discussion, "active" means "different than benchmark."

[73] As we use the terms, "active specific risk" and "active factor risk" refer to variances rather than standard deviations.

[74] The direct procedure for calculating active factor risk is as follows. A portfolio's active factor exposure to a given factor j, b_j^a, is found by weighting each asset's sensitivity to factor j by its active weight and summing the terms $b_j^a = \sum_{i=1}^{n} w_i^a b_{ji}$. Then active factor risk equals $\sum_{i=1}^{K} \sum_{j=1}^{K} b_i^a b_j^a \text{Cov}(F_i, F_j)$.

[75] The residual returns of the assets are assumed to be uncorrelated with each other and with the factor returns.

EXAMPLE 20

A Comparison of Active Risk

Richard Gray is comparing the risk of four U.S. equity managers who share the same benchmark. He uses a fundamental factor model, the BARRA US-E3 model, which incorporates 13 risk indexes and a set of 52 industrial categories. The risk indexes measure various fundamental aspects of companies and their shares such as size, leverage, and dividend yield. In the model, companies have nonzero exposures to all industries in which the company operates. Table 21 presents Gray's analysis of the active risk squared of the four managers, based on Equation 68-26[76]. In Table 21, the column labeled "Industry" gives the portfolio's active factor risk associated with the industry exposures of its holdings; the column "Risk Indexes" gives the portfolio's active factor risk associated with the exposures of its holdings to the 13 risk indexes.

TABLE 21   Active Risk Squared Decomposition

| | Active Factor | | | | |
Portfolio	Industry	Risk Indexes	Total Factor	Active Specific	Active Risk Squared
A	12.25	17.15	29.40	19.60	49
B	1.25	13.75	15.00	10.00	25
C	1.25	17.50	18.75	6.25	25
D	0.03	0.47	0.50	0.50	1

Note: Entries are percent squared.

Using the information in Table 21, address the following:

1. Contrast the active risk decomposition of Portfolios A and B.

2. Contrast the active risk decomposition of Portfolios B and C.

3. Characterize the investment approach of Portfolio D.

Solution to 1: Table 22 restates the information in Table 21 to show the proportional contributions of the various sources of active risk. In the last column of Table 22, we now give the square root of active risk squared—that is, active risk or tracking risk. To explain the middle set of columns in Table 22, Portfolio A's value of 25 percent under the Industry column is found as $12.25/49 = 0.25$. So Portfolio A's active risk related to industry exposures is 25 percent of active risk squared.

---

[76] There is a covariance term in active factor risk, reflecting the correlation of industry membership and the risk indexes, which we assume is negligible in this example.

TABLE 22   Active Risk Decomposition (Re-Stated)

| Portfolio | Active Factor (% of total active) | | | Active Specific (% of total active) | Active Risk |
	Industry	Risk Indexes	Total Factor		
A	25%	35%	60%	40%	7%
B	5%	55%	60%	40%	5%
C	5%	70%	75%	25%	5%
D	3%	47%	50%	50%	1%

Portfolio A has assumed a higher level of active risk than B (tracking risk of 7 percent versus 5 percent). Portfolios A and B assumed the same proportions of active factor and active specific risk, but a sharp contrast exists between the two in terms of type of active factor risk exposure. Portfolio A assumed substantial active industry risk, whereas Portfolio B was approximately industry neutral relative to the benchmark. By contrast, Portfolio B had higher active bets on the risk indexes representing company and share characteristics.

Solution to 2: Portfolios B and C were similar in their absolute amounts of active risk. Furthermore, both Portfolios B and C were both approximately industry neutral relative to the benchmark. Portfolio C assumed more active factor risk related to the risk indexes, but B assumed more active specific risk. We can also infer from the second point that B is somewhat less diversified than C.

Solution to 3: Portfolio D appears to be a passively managed portfolio, judging by its negligible level of active risk. Referring to Table 21, Portfolio D's active factor risk of 0.50, equal to 0.707 percent expressed as a standard deviation, indicates that the portfolio very closely matches the benchmark along the dimensions of risk that the model identifies as driving average returns.

Example 20 presented a set of hypothetical portfolios with differing degrees of tracking risk in which active factor risk tended to be larger than active specific risk. Given a well-constructed multifactor model and a well-diversified portfolio, this relationship is fairly commonplace. For well-diversified portfolios, managing active factor risk is typically the chief task in managing tracking risk.

Example 20 presented an analysis of active risk at an aggregated level; a portfolio's active factor risks with respect to the multifactor model's 13 risk indexes was aggregated into a single number. In appraising performance, an analyst may be interested in a much more detailed analysis of a portfolio's active risk. How can an analyst appraise the individual contributions of a manager's active factor exposures to active risk squared?

Whatever the set of factors, the procedure for evaluating the contribution of an active factor exposure to active risk squared is the same. This quantity has been called a factor's marginal contribution to active risk squared (FMCAR). With K factors, the marginal contribution to active risk squared for a factor j, $FMCAR_j$ is

$$FMCAR_j = \frac{b_j^a \sum_{i=1}^{K} b_i^a Cov(F_j, F_i)}{\text{Active risk squared}}$$

(68-27)

where b_j^a is the portfolio's active exposure to factor j. The numerator is the active factor risk for factor j.[77] The numerator is similar to expressions involving beta that we encountered earlier in discussing the market model, but with multiple factors, factor covariances as well as variances are relevant. To illustrate Equation 68-27 in a simple setting, suppose we have a two-factor model:

▶ The manager's active exposure to the first factor is 0.50; that is, $b_1^a = 0.50$. The other active factor exposure is $b_2^a = 0.15$.

▶ The variance–covariance matrix of the factors is described by $Cov(F_1, F_1) = \sigma^2(F_1) = 225$, $Cov(F_1, F_2) = 12$, and $Cov(F_2, F_2) = \sigma^2(F_2) = 144$.

▶ Active specific risk is 53.71.

We first compute active factor risk for each factor; that calculation is the numerator in Equation 68-27. Then we find active risk squared by summing the active factor risks and active specific risk, and form the ratio indicated in Equation 68-27. For the first factor, we calculate the numerator of $FMCAR_1$ as

$$b_1^a \sum_{i=1}^{2} b_i^a Cov(F_1, F_i) = 0.50[0.50(225) + 0.15(12)] = 57.15$$

For the second factor, we have

$$b_2^a \sum_{i=1}^{2} b_i^a Cov(F_2, F_i) = 0.15[0.50(12) + 0.15(144)] = 4.14$$

Active factor risk is $57.15 + 4.14 = 61.29$. Adding active specific risk, we find that active risk squared is $61.29 + 53.71 = 115$. Thus we have $FMCAR_1 = 57.15/115 = 0.497$ or 49.7 percent, and $FMCAR_2 = 4.14/115 = 0.036$ or 3.6 percent. Active factor risk as a fraction of total risk is $FMCAR_1 + FMCAR_2 = 49.7\% + 3.6\% = 53.3\%$. Active specific risk contributes $100\% - 53.3\% = 46.7\%$ to active risk squared. Example 21 illustrates the application of these concepts.

EXAMPLE 21

An Analysis of Individual Active Factor Risk

William Whetzell is responsible for a monthly internal performance attribution and risk analysis of a domestic core equity fund managed internally by his organization, a Canadian endowment. In his monthly analyses, Whetzell uses a risk model incorporating the following factors:

▶ Log of market cap

▶ E/P, the earnings yield

---

[77] If we summed the numerator over $j = 1$ to K, we would have the expression for active factor risk given in Footnote 74.

▶ B/P, the book-to-price ratio
▶ Earnings growth
▶ Average dividend yield
▶ D/A, the long-term debt-to-asset ratio
▶ Volatility of return on equity (ROE)
▶ Volatility of EPS

The factor sensitivities in the model have the standard interpretation of factor sensitivities in fundamental factor models.

Having determined that he earned an active return of 0.75 percent during the last fiscal year, Whetzell turns to the task of analyzing the portfolio's risk. At the start of the fiscal year, the investment committee made the following decisions:

▶ to tactically tilt the portfolio in the direction of small-cap stocks;
▶ to implement an "earnings growth at a reasonable price" (GARP) bias in security selection;
▶ to keep any active factor risk, expressed as a standard deviation, under 5 percent per annum;
▶ to keep active specific risk at no more than 50 percent of active risk squared; and
▶ to achieve an information ratio of 0.15 or greater.

Before Whetzell presented his report, one investment committee member reviewing his material commented that the investment committee should adopt a passive investment strategy for domestic equities if the equity fund continues to perform as it did during the last fiscal year.

Table 23 presents information on the equity fund. The factor returns were constructed to be approximately mutually uncorrelated.

TABLE 23   Risk Analysis Data

	Sensitivity		
Factor	**Portfolio**	**Benchmark**	**Factor Variance**
Log of market cap	0.05	0.25	225
E/P	−0.05	0.05	144
B/P	−0.25	−0.02	100
Earnings growth	0.25	0.10	196
Dividend yield	0.01	0.00	169
D/A	0.03	0.03	81
Vol of ROE	−0.25	0.02	121
Vol of EPS	−0.10	0.03	64

Active specific risk =	29.9406
Active specific return =	−0.5%
Active return =	0.75%

Based on the information in Table 23, address the following:

1. For each factor, calculate (A) the active factor risk and (B) the marginal contribution to active risk squared.
2. Discuss whether the data are consistent with the objectives of the investment committee having been met.
3. Appraise the endowment's risk-adjusted performance for the year.
4. Explain two pieces of evidence supporting the committee member's statement concerning a passive investment strategy.

Solution to 1:
(A) Active factor risk for a factor = (Active sensitivity to the factor)^2 (Factor variance) in Equation 68-27 with zero factor correlations.

Log of market cap = $(0.05 - 0.25)^2(225) = 9.0$
E/P = $(-0.05 - 0.05)^2(144) = 1.44$
B/P = $[-0.25 - (-0.02)]^2(100) = 5.29$
Earnings growth = $(0.25 - 0.10)^2(196) = 4.41$
Dividend yield = $(0.01 - 0.00)^2(169) = 0.0169$
D/A = $(0.03 - 0.03)^2(81) = 0.0$
Volatility of ROE = $(-0.25 - 0.02)^2(121) = 8.8209$
Volatility of EPS = $(-0.10 - 0.03)^2(64) = 1.0816$

(B) The sum of the individual active factor risks equals 30.0594. We add active specific risk to this sum to obtain active risk squared of 30.0594 + 29.9406 = 60. Thus FMCAR for the factors is as follows:

Log of market cap = 9/60 = 0.15
E/P = 1.44/60 = 0.024
B/P = 5.29/60 = 0.0882
Earnings growth = 4.41/60 = 0.0735
Dividend yield = 0.0169/60 = 0.0003
D/A = 0.0/60 = 0.0
Volatility of ROE = 8.8209/60 = 0.1470
Volatility of EPS = 1.0816/60 = 0.0180

Solution to 2: We consider each investment committee objective in turn. The first objective was *to tactically tilt the portfolio in the direction of small-cap stocks.* A zero sensitivity to the log market cap factor would indicate average exposure to size. An exposure of 1 would indicate a positive exposure to returns to increasing size that is one standard deviation above the mean, given the standard interpretation of factor sensitivities in fundamental factor models. Although the equity fund's exposure to size is positive, the *active* exposure is negative. This result is consistent with tilting toward small-cap stocks.

The second objective was *to implement an "earnings growth at a reasonable price" bias in security selection.* The equity fund has a positive active exposure to earnings growth consistent with seeking companies with high earnings growth rates. It is questionable, however, whether the "reasonable price" part of the approach is being satisfied. The fund's absolute E/P and B/P sensitivities are negative, indicating below-average earning yield and B/P (higher than average P/E and P/B). The active exposures to these factors are also negative. If above-average earnings growth is priced in the marketplace, the fund may need to bear negative active exposures, so we cannot reach a final conclusion. We can say, however, that none of the data positively supports a conclusion that the GARP strategy was implemented.

The third objective was *to keep any active factor risk, expressed as a standard deviation, under 5 percent per annum.* The largest active factor risk was on the log of market cap factor. Expressed as a standard deviation, that risk was $(9)^{1/2} = 3$ percent per annum, so this objective was met.

The fourth objective was *to keep active specific risk at no more than 50 percent of active risk squared.* Active specific risk as a fraction of active risk squared was $29.9406/60 = 0.4990$ or 49.9 percent, so this objective was met.

The fifth objective was *to achieve an information ratio of 0.15 or greater.* The information ratio is active return divided by active risk (tracking risk). Active return was given as 0.75 percent. Active risk is the square root of active risk squared: $(60)^{1/2} = 7.7460\%$. Thus IR = $0.75\%/7.7460\% = 0.0968$ or approximately 0.10, which is short of the stated objective of 0.15.

Solution to 3: The endowment's realized information ratio of 0.10 means its risk-adjusted performance for the year was inadequate.

Solution to 4: The active specific return for the year was negative, although the fund incurred substantial active specific risk. Therefore, specific risk had a negative reward. Furthermore, the realized information ratio fell short of the investment committee's objective. With the qualification that this analysis is based on only one year, these facts would argue for the cost-efficient alternative of indexing.

In our discussion of performance attribution and risk analysis, we have given examples related to common stock. Multifactor models have also been used in similar roles for portfolios of bonds and other asset classes.

We have illustrated the use of multifactor models in analyzing a portfolio's active returns and active risk. At least equally important is the use of multifactor models in portfolio construction. At that stage of the portfolio management process, multifactor models permit the portfolio manager to make focused bets or to control portfolio risk relative to her benchmark's risk. In the remaining sections, we discuss these uses of multifactor models.

4.6.3 Factor Portfolios

A portfolio manager can use multifactor models to establish a specific desired risk profile for his portfolio. For example, he may want to create and use a factor portfolio. A factor portfolio for a particular factor has a sensitivity of 1 for that factor and a sensitivity of 0 for all other factors. It is thus a portfolio with exposure to only one risk factor and exactly represents the risk of that factor. As a pure bet on a source of risk, factor portfolios are of interest to a portfolio manager who wants to hedge that risk (offset it) or speculate on it. Example 22 illustrates the use of factor portfolios.

EXAMPLE 22

Factor Portfolios

Analyst Wanda Smithfield has constructed six portfolios for possible use by portfolio managers in her firm. The portfolios are labeled A, B, C, D, E, and F in Table 24.

TABLE 24 Factor Portfolios

	Portfolios					
Risk Factor	A	B	C	D	E	F
Confidence risk	0.50	0.00	1.00	0.00	0.00	0.80
Time horizon risk	1.92	0.00	1.00	1.00	1.00	1.00
Inflation risk	0.00	0.00	1.00	0.00	0.00	−1.05
Business cycle risk	1.00	1.00	0.00	0.00	1.00	0.30
Market timing risk	0.90	0.00	1.00	0.00	0.00	0.75

Note: Entries are factor sensitivities.

1. A portfolio manager wants to place a bet that real business activity will increase.
   A. Determine and justify the portfolio among the six given that would be most useful to the manager.
   B. What type of position would the manager take in the portfolio chosen in Part A?
2. A portfolio manager wants to hedge an existing positive exposure to time horizon risk.
   A. Determine and justify the portfolio among the six given that would be most useful to the manager.
   B. What type of position would the manager take in the portfolio chosen in Part A?

Solution to 1A: Portfolio B is the most appropriate choice. Portfolio B is the factor portfolio for business cycle risk because it has a sensitivity of 1 to business cycle risk and a sensitivity of 0 to all other risk factors. Portfolio B is thus efficient for placing a pure bet on an increase in real business activity.

Solution to 1B: The manager would take a long position in Portfolio B to place a bet on an increase in real business activity.

Solution to 2A: Portfolio D is the appropriate choice. Portfolio D is the factor portfolio for time horizon risk because it has a sensitivity of 1 to time horizon risk and a sensitivity of 0 to all other risk factors.

> Portfolio D is thus efficient for hedging an existing positive exposure to time horizon risk.
>
> **Solution to 2B:** The manager would take a short position in Portfolio D to hedge the positive exposure to time horizon risk.

The next section illustrates the procedure for constructing a portfolio with a desired configuration of factor sensitivities.

4.6.4 Creating a Tracking Portfolio

In the previous section, we discussed the use of multifactor models to speculate on or hedge a specific factor risk. Perhaps even more commonly, portfolio managers use multifactor models to control the risk of portfolios relative to their benchmarks. For example, in a risk-controlled active or enhanced index strategy, the portfolio manager may attempt to earn a small incremental return relative to her benchmark while controlling risk by matching the factor sensitivities of her portfolio to her benchmark. That portfolio would be an example of a tracking portfolio. A **tracking portfolio** is a portfolio having factor sensitivities that are matched to those of a benchmark or other portfolio.

The technique of constructing a portfolio with a target set of factor sensitivities involves the solution of a system of equations using algebra.

▶ Count the number of constraints. Each target value of beta represents a constraint on the portfolio, and another constraint is that the weights of the investments in the portfolio must sum to one. *As many investments are needed as there are constraints.*

▶ Set up an equation for the weights of the portfolio's investments reflecting each constraint on the portfolio. We have an equation stating that the portfolio weights sum to 1. We have an equation for each target factor sensitivity; on the left-hand side of the equal sign, we have a weighted average of the factor sensitivities of the investments to the factor, and on the right-hand side of the equal sign we have the target factor sensitivity.

▶ Solve the system of equations for the weights of the investments in the portfolio.

In Example 23, we illustrate how a tracking portfolio can be created.

EXAMPLE 23

Creating a Tracking Portfolio

Suppose that a pension plan sponsor wants to be fully invested in U.S. common stocks. The plan sponsor has specified an equity benchmark for a portfolio manager, who has decided to create a tracking portfolio for the benchmark. For the sake of using familiar data, let us continue with the three portfolios J, K, and L, as well as the same two-factor model from Example 13.

The portfolio manager determines that the benchmark has a sensitivity of 1.3 to the surprise in inflation and a sensitivity of 1.975 to the surprise in GDP. There are three constraints. One constraint is that portfolio weights sum to 1, a second is that the weighted sum of sensitivities to the inflation factor equals 1.3 (to match the benchmark), and a third is that the weighted sum of sensitivities to the GDP factor equals 1.975 (to match the benchmark). Thus we need three investments to form the portfolio, which we take to be Portfolios J, K, and L. We repeat Table 14 below.

TABLE 14   Sample Portfolios for a Two-Factor Model (Repeated)

Portfolio	Expected Return	Sensitivity to Inflation Factor	Sensitivity to GDP Factor
J	0.14	1.0	1.5
K	0.12	0.5	1.0
L	0.11	1.3	1.1

As mentioned, we need three equations to determine the portfolio weights w_J, w_K, and w_L in the tracking portfolio.

▶ *Equation 1*. This equation states that portfolio weights must sum to 1.

$$w_J + w_K + w_L = 1$$

▶ *Equation 2*. The second equation states that the weighted average of the sensitivities of J, K, and L to the surprise in inflation must equal the benchmark's sensitivity to the surprise in inflation, 1.3. This requirement ensures that the tracking portfolio has the same inflation risk as the benchmark.

$$1.0w_J + 0.5w_K + 1.3w_L = 1.3$$

▶ *Equation 3*. The third equation states that the weighted average of the sensitivities of J, K, and L to the surprise in GDP must equal the benchmark's sensitivity to the surprise in GDP, 1.975. This requirement ensures that the tracking portfolio has the same GDP risk as the benchmark.

$$1.5w_J + 1.0w_K + 1.1w_L = 1.975$$

We can solve for the weights as follows. From Equation 1, $w_L = (1 - w_J - w_K)$. We substitute this result in the other two equations to find

$$1.0w_J + 0.5w_K + 1.3(1 - w_J - w_K) = 1.3, \text{ simplifying to } w_K = -0.375w_J$$

and

$$1.5w_J + 1.0w_K + 1.1(1 - w_J - w_K) = 1.975, \text{ simplifying to }$$
$$0.4w_J - 0.1w_K = 0.875$$

We next substitute $w_K = -0.375w_J$ into $0.4w_J - 0.1w_K = 0.875$, obtaining $0.4w_J - 0.1(-0.375w_J) = 0.875$ or $0.4w_J + 0.0375w_J = 0.875$, so $w_J = 2$.

Using $w_K = -0.375w_J$ obtained earlier, $w_K = -0.375 \times 2 = -0.75$. Finally, from $w_L = (1 - w_J - w_K) = [1 - 2 - (-0.75)] = -0.25$. To summarize,

$$w_J = 2$$
$$w_K = -0.75$$
$$w_L = -0.25$$

The tracking has an expected return of $0.14w_J + 0.12w_K + 0.11w_L = 0.14(2) + (0.12)(-0.75) + 0.11(-0.25) = 0.28 - 0.09 - 0.0275 = 0.1625$. In Example 13 using the same inputs, we calculated the APT model as $E(R_p) = 0.07 - 0.02\beta_{p,1} + 0.06\beta_{p,2}$. For the tracking portfolio, $\beta_{p,1} = 1.3$ and $\beta_{p,2} = 1.975$. As $E(R_p) = 0.07 - 0.02(1.3) + 0.06(1.975) = 0.1625$, we have confirmed the expected return calculation.

4.7 Concluding Remarks

In earlier sections, we showed how models with multiple factors can help portfolio managers solve practical tasks in measuring and controlling risk. We now draw contrasts between the CAPM and the APT, providing additional insight into why some risks may be priced and how, as a result, the portfolio implications of a multifactor world differ from those of the world described by the CAPM. An investor may be able to make better portfolio decisions with a multifactor model than with a single-factor model.

The CAPM provides investors with useful and influential concepts for thinking about investments. Considerable evidence has accumulated, however, that shows that the CAPM provides an incomplete description of risk.[78] What is the portfolio advice of CAPM, and how can we improve on it when more than one source of systematic risk drives asset returns? An investor who believes that the CAPM explains asset returns would hold a portfolio consisting only of the risk-free asset and the market portfolio of risky assets. If the investor had a high tolerance for risk, she would put a greater proportion in the market portfolio. But to the extent the investor held risky assets, she would hold them in amounts proportional to their market-value weights, without consideration for any other dimension of risk. In reality, of course, not everyone holds the same portfolio of risky assets. Practically speaking, this CAPM-oriented investor might hold a money market fund and a portfolio indexed on a broad market index.[79]

With more than one source of systematic risk, the average investor might still want to hold a broadly based portfolio and the risk-free asset. Other investors, however, may find it appropriate to tilt away from an index fund after considering dimensions of risk ignored by the CAPM. To make this argument, let us explore why, for example, the business cycle is a source of systematic risk, as in the Burmeister et al. model discussed earlier. There is an economic intuition for why this risk is systematic:[80] Most investors hold jobs and are thus sensitive to

[78] See Bodie, Kane, and Marcus (2001) for an introduction to the empirical evidence.

[79] Passive management is a distinct issue from holding a single portfolio. There are efficient-markets arguments for holding indexed investments that are separate from the CAPM. An index fund is reasonable for this investor, however.

[80] This discussion follows Cochrane (1999a) and (1999b).

recessions. Suppose, for example, that a working investor faces the risk of a recession. If this investor compared two stocks with the same CAPM beta, given his concern about recession risk, he would accept a lower return from the countercyclical stock and require a risk premium on the procyclical one. In contrast, an investor with independent wealth and no job-loss concerns would be willing to accept the recession risk.

If the average investor holding a job bids up the price of the countercyclical stocks, then recession risk will be priced. In addition, procyclical stocks would have lower prices than if the recession factor were not priced. Investors can thus, as Cochrane (1999a) notes, "earn a substantial premium for holding dimensions of risk unrelated to market movements."

This view of risk has portfolio implications. The average investor is exposed to and negatively affected by cyclical risk, which is a priced factor. (Risks that do not affect the average investor should not be priced.) Investors who hold jobs (and thus receive labor income) want lower cyclical risk and create a cyclical risk premium, whereas investors without labor income will accept more cyclical risk to capture a premium for a risk that they do not care about. As a result, an investor who faces lower-than-average recession risk optimally tilts towards greater-than-average exposure to the business cycle factor, all else equal.

In summary, investors should know which priced risks they face and analyze the extent of their exposure. Compared with single-factor models, multifactor models offer a rich context for investors to search for ways to improve portfolio selection.

SUMMARY

In this reading, we have presented a set of concepts, models, and tools that are key ingredients to quantitative portfolio management today.

Mean–Variance Analysis

▶ Mean–variance analysis is a part of modern portfolio theory that deals with the trade-offs between risk, as represented by variance or standard deviation of return, and expected return.

▶ Mean–variance analysis assumes the following:

  ▶ Investors are risk averse.

  ▶ Assets' expected returns, variances of returns, and covariances of returns are known.

  ▶ Investors need to know only the expected returns, the variances of returns, and covariances between returns in order to determine which portfolios are optimal.

  ▶ There are no transaction costs or taxes.

▶ For any portfolio composed of two assets, the expected return to the portfolio, $E(R_p)$, is $E(R_p) = w_1 E(R_1) + w_2 E(R_2)$, where $E(R_1)$ is the expected return to Asset 1 and $E(R_2)$ is the expected return to Asset 2. In general, the expected return on a portfolio is a weighted average of the expected returns on the individual assets, where the weight applied to each asset's return is the fraction of the portfolio invested in that asset.

▶ The variance of return on a two-asset portfolio and a three-asset portfolio are, respectively,

$$\sigma_p^2 = w_1^2 \sigma_1^2 + w_2^2 \sigma_2^2 + 2 w_1 w_2 \rho_{1,2} \sigma_1 \sigma_2$$

and

$$\sigma_p^2 = w_1^2 \sigma_1^2 + w_2^2 \sigma_2^2 + w_3^2 \sigma_3^2 + 2 w_1 w_2 \rho_{1,2} \sigma_1 \sigma_2 + 2 w_1 w_3 \rho_{1,3} \sigma_1 \sigma_3$$
$$+ 2 w_2 w_3 \rho_{2,3} \sigma_2 \sigma_3$$

where

  σ_i = the standard deviation of return on asset i, i = 1, 2, 3
  $\rho_{i,j}$ = the correlation between the returns on asset i and asset j

▶ In mean–variance analysis, the investment attributes of individual assets and portfolios are represented by points in a figure having standard deviation or variance of return as the x-axis and expected return as the y-axis.

▶ The minimum-variance frontier graphs the smallest variance of return attainable for each level of expected return.

▶ The global minimum-variance portfolio is the portfolio of risky assets having the minimum variance.

▶ An efficient portfolio is one providing the maximum expected return for a given level of variance or standard deviation of return.

▶ The efficient frontier represents all combinations of mean return and variance or standard deviation of return that can be attained by holding efficient portfolios (portfolios giving maximum expected return for their levels of standard deviation of return). The efficient frontier is the upper portion of the minimum-variance frontier (the global minimum-variance portfolio and points above).

▶ According to mean–variance analysis, investors optimally select a portfolio from portfolios that lie on the efficient frontier. By restricting attention to the efficient portfolios, the investor's portfolio selection task is greatly simplified.

▶ When the correlation between the returns on two assets is less than +1, the potential exists for diversification benefits. Diversification benefits occur when portfolio standard deviation of return can be reduced through diversification without decreasing expected return.

▶ For the two-asset case, the potential benefits from diversifying increase as we lower the correlation between the two portfolios towards −1, holding all else constant. For a correlation of −1, a portfolio of the two assets exists that eliminates risk. As we lower correlation, the efficient frontier improves in the sense of offering a higher expected return for a given feasible level of standard deviation of return, holding all other values constant.

▶ In general, to determine the minimum-variance frontier for a set of n assets, we first determine the minimum expected return and the maximum expected return among all the expected returns offered by the n assets. We then choose the individual asset weights that minimize portfolio variance of return for different levels of expected return, subject to the constraint that the individual asset weights sum to 1.

▶ The introduction of a risk-free asset into the portfolio selection problem results in the efficient frontier having a linear portion that is tangent to the efficient frontier defined using only risky assets. This line is called the capital allocation line (CAL). Portfolios on the CAL represent combinations of the risk-free asset and the tangency portfolio.

▶ When all investors share identical expectations about mean returns, variance of returns, and correlations, the CAL for all investors is the same and is known as the capital market line (CML). The tangency portfolio is the market portfolio of risky assets held in market value weights. The implication of the CML for portfolio choice is that all mean–variance investors, whatever their risk tolerance, can satisfy their investment needs using the risk-free asset and a single risky portfolio, the market portfolio of all risky assets held in market value weights.

▶ The assumptions of the capital asset pricing model (CAPM) are that investors have identical views about the expected returns, the variances, and the covariances of assets, and only need to know these characteristics to determine which portfolios are optimal for them. Furthermore, investors can buy and sell assets in any quantity without affecting price, and all assets are marketable (can be traded); they can borrow and lend at the risk-free rate without limit and can sell short any asset in any quantity; and they pay no taxes on returns or transaction costs on trades.

▶ The CAPM equation describes the expected return on an asset or portfolio (whether efficient or not) as a linear function of its beta (a measure of the sensitivity of an asset's returns to the return on the market portfolio). The CAPM equation is

$$E(R_i) = R_F + \beta_i[E(R_M) - R_F]$$

where

$E(R_i)$ = the expected return on asset i
R_F = the risk-free rate of return
$E(R_M)$ = the expected return on the market portfolio
β_i = $\text{Cov}(R_i, R_M)/\sigma_M^2$, called beta.

▶ The CAPM implies that the expected excess rate of return on an asset is directly proportional to its covariance with the market return.

▶ The Markowitz decision rule states that an investor should prefer Investment A to Investment B if A's expected return is higher than that of B with no more risk than B, or if A has the same expected return as B with strictly less risk.

▶ Adding a new asset to a portfolio is optimal if the asset's Sharpe ratio is greater than the product (Sharpe ratio of existing portfolio p) × (Correlation of new investment with p).

▶ To trace out the minimum-variance frontier with n assets, we need n expected returns, n variances, and $n(n-1)/2$ covariances. If we use historical values as inputs of mean–variance optimization, then for realistic values of n, the number of parameters that needs to be estimated is very large, owing mostly to the number of covariances needed. Historical estimates are also critically subject to estimation error.

▶ The market model explains the return on a risky asset as a linear regression with the return on the market as the independent variable.

▶ According to the market model,

$$\text{Var}(R_i) = \beta_i^2\sigma_M^2 + \sigma_{\epsilon_i}^2 \text{ and } \text{Cov}(R_i, R_j) = \beta_i\beta_j\sigma_M^2$$

▶ We can use the expression for covariance from the market model to greatly simplify the calculational task of estimating the covariances needed to trace out the minimum-variance frontier.

▶ Using the parameters of the market model, we can express the correlation between the returns on two assets as

$$\text{Corr}(R_1, R_2) = \frac{\beta_1\beta_2\sigma_M^2}{(\beta_1^2\sigma_M^2 + \sigma_{\epsilon_1}^2)^{1/2}(\beta_2^2\sigma_M^2 + \sigma_{\epsilon_2}^2)^{1/2}}$$

▶ Adjusted beta is a historical beta adjusted to reflect the tendency of beta to be mean reverting. For example, one common adjustment is

Adjusted Beta = 0.33 + 0.67 Historical Beta

An adjusted beta tends to predict future beta better than historical beta does.

▶ A problem with standard mean–variance optimization is that small changes in inputs frequently lead to large changes in the weights of portfolios that appear on the minimum-variance frontier. This is the problem of instability.

The problem of instability is practically important because the inputs to mean–variance optimization are often based on sample statistics, which are subject to random variation. Relatedly, the minimum-variance frontier is not stable over time. Besides the estimation error in means, variances, and covariance, shifts in the distribution of asset returns between sample time periods can give rise to this time instability of the minimum-variance frontier.

Multifactor Models

▶ Multifactor models describe the return on an asset in terms of the risk of the asset with respect to a set of factors. Such models generally include systematic factors, which explain the average returns of a large number of risky assets. Such factors represent priced risk, risk which investors require an additional return for bearing.

▶ Multifactor models are categorized as macroeconomic factor models, fundamental factor models, and statistical factor models, according to the type of factor used.

▶ In macroeconomic factor models, the factors are surprises in macroeconomic variables that significantly explain equity returns. Surprise is defined as actual minus forecasted value and has an expected value of zero. The factors can be understood as affecting either the expected future cash flows of companies or the interest rate used to discount these cash flows back to the present.

▶ In fundamental factor models, the factors are attributes of stocks or companies that are important in explaining cross-sectional differences in stock prices. Among the fundamental factors are book-value-to-price ratio, market capitalization, price-earnings ratio, and financial leverage.

▶ In statistical factor models, statistical methods are applied to a set of historical returns to determine portfolios that explain historical returns in one of two senses. In factor analysis models, the factors are the portfolios that best explain (reproduce) historical return covariances. In principal-components models, the factors are portfolios that best explain (reproduce) the historical return variances.

▶ Arbitrage pricing theory (APT) describes the expected return on an asset (or portfolio) as a linear function of the risk of the asset with respect to a set of factors. Like the CAPM, the APT describes a financial market equilibrium, but the APT makes less-strong assumptions.

▶ The major assumptions of the APT are as follows:

   ▶ Asset returns are described by a factor model.

   ▶ There are many assets, so asset-specific risk can be eliminated.

   ▶ Assets are priced so that there are no arbitrage opportunities.

▶ APT explains the intercept term in the equation of a multifactor model, in which the factors are surprises, as an expected return.

▶ In contrast to macroeconomic factor models, in fundamental models the factors are stated as returns rather than surprises. In fundamental factor models, we generally specify the factor sensitivities (attributes) first and then estimate the factor returns through regressions, in contrast to macroeconomic factor models, in which we first develop the factor (surprise) series and then estimate the factor sensitivities through regressions. The factors of most fundamental factor models may be classified as company fundamental factors, company share-related factors, or macroeconomic factors.

▶ Active return is return in excess of the return on the benchmark.

▶ Active risk is the standard deviation of active returns. Active risk is also called tracking risk. Active risk squared can be decomposed as the sum of active factor risk and active specific risk.

▶ The information ratio (IR) is mean active return divided by active risk (tracking risk). The IR measures the increment in mean active return per unit of active risk.

▶ Factor j's marginal contribution to active risk squared is

$$\text{FMCAR}_j = \frac{b_j^a \sum_{i=1}^{K} b_i^a \text{Cov}(F_j, F_i)}{\text{Active risk squared}}$$

where b_j^a is the portfolio's active exposure to factor j. The numerator is the active factor risk for factor j. The concept explains how factor tilts away from the benchmark explain a portfolio's tracking risk.

▶ A factor portfolio is a portfolio with unit sensitivity to a factor and zero sensitivity to other factors. A tracking portfolio is a portfolio with factor sensitivities that match those of **benchmark portfolio** or other portfolio. Factor and tracking portfolios can be constructed using as many assets as there are constraints on the portfolio.

▶ Multifactor models permit a nuanced view of risk that may contrast with a single-factor perspective. From a CAPM perspective, investors should allocate their money between the risk-free asset and a broad-based index fund. With multiple sources of systematic risk, when an investor's factor risk exposures to other sources of income and risk aversion differ from the average investor's, a tilt away from an indexed investment may be optimal.

PRACTICE PROBLEMS FOR READING 68

Mean–Variance Analysis

1. Given the large-cap stock index and the government bond index data in the following table, calculate the expected mean return and standard deviation of return for a portfolio 75 percent invested in the stock index and 25 percent invested in the bond index.

Assumed Returns, Variances, and Correlations

	Large-Cap Stock Index	Government Bond Index
Expected return	15%	5%
Variance	225	100
Standard deviation	15%	10%
Correlation	0.5	

For Problems 2 and 3, assume the following:

▶ Each stock has the same variance of return, denoted σ^2.

▶ The correlation between all pairs of stocks is the same, ρ.

▶ Stocks are equally weighted.

2. Suppose 0.3 is the common correlation of returns between any two stocks in a portfolio containing 100 stocks. Also, suppose the average variance of stocks in the portfolio is 625 (corresponding to a standard deviation of return of 25 percent). Calculate the portfolio standard deviation of return.

3. Suppose the average variance of return of all stocks in a portfolio is 625 and the correlation between the returns of any two stocks is 0.3. Calculate the variance of return of an equally weighted portfolio of 24 stocks. Then state that variance as a percent of the portfolio variance achievable given an unlimited number of stocks, holding stock variance and correlation constant.

4. Suppose a risk-free asset has a 5 percent return and a second asset has an expected return of 13 percent with a standard deviation of 23 percent. Calculate the expected portfolio return and standard deviation of a portfolio consisting 10 percent of the risk-free asset and 90 percent of the second asset.

5. Suppose you have a $100,000 investment in an S&P 500 index fund. You then replace 10 percent of your investment in the index fund with an investment in a stock having a beta of 2 with respect to the index. Why is it impossible for your new portfolio, consisting of the index fund and the stock, to have a lower standard deviation of return than the original portfolio?

6. Suppose that the risk-free rate is 6 percent and the expected return on the investor's tangency portfolio is 14 percent, with a standard deviation of 24 percent.

   A. Calculate the investor's expected risk premium per unit of risk.

   B. Calculate the portfolio's expected return if the portfolio's standard deviation of return is 20 percent.

7. Eduardo Martinez is evaluating the following investments:

   Portfolio A: $E(R_A) = 12$ percent, $\sigma(R_A) = 15$

   Portfolio B: $E(R_B) = 10$ percent, $\sigma(R_B) = 8$

   Portfolio C: $E(R_C) = 10$ percent, $\sigma(R_C) = 9$

   A. Explain the choice among Portfolios A, B, and C using the Markowitz decision rule.

   B. Explain the choice among Portfolios A, B, and C assuming that borrowing and lending at a risk-free rate of $R_F = 2$ percent is possible.

8. Gita Subramaniam is the chief investment officer of an Indian pension scheme invested in Indian equities, Indian government bonds, and U.S. equities. Her current portfolio has a Sharpe ratio of 0.15, and she is considering adding U.S. bonds to this portfolio. The predicted Sharpe ratio of U.S. bonds is 0.10, and their predicted correlation with the existing portfolio is 0.20. Explain whether Subramaniam should add U.S. bonds to the pension fund.

9. Suppose that the risk-free rate is 5 percent and the expected return on the market portfolio of risky assets is 13 percent. An investor with $1 million to invest wants to achieve a 17 percent rate of return on a portfolio combining a risk-free asset and the market portfolio of risky assets. Calculate how much this investor would need to borrow at the risk-free rate in order to establish this target expected return.

10. Two assets have betas of 1.5 and 1.2, respectively. The residual standard deviation from the market model is 2 for the first asset and 4 for the second. The market standard deviation is 8. What is the correlation between the two assets?

11. Suppose that the best predictor for a stock's future beta is determined to be Expected beta = 0.33 + 0.67 (Historical beta). The historical beta is calculated as 1.2. The risk-free rate is 5 percent, and the market risk premium is 8.5 percent. Calculate the expected return on the stock using expected (adjusted) beta in the CAPM.

Multifactor Models

12. Suppose that the expected return on the stock in the following table is 11 percent. Using a two-factor model, calculate the stock's return if the company-specific surprise for the year is 3 percent.

Variable	Actual Value	Expected Value	Stock's Factor Sensitivity
Change in interest rate	2.0%	0.0%	−1.5
Growth in GDP	1.0%	4.0%	2.0

13. A portfolio manager plans to create a portfolio from two stocks, Manumatic (MANM) and Nextech (NXT). The following equations describe the returns for those stocks:

$$R_{MANM} = 0.09 - 1F_{INFL} + 1F_{GDP} + \epsilon_{MANM}$$
$$R_{NXT} = 0.12 + 2F_{INFL} + 4F_{GDP} + \epsilon_{NXT}$$

You form a portfolio with market value weights of 50 percent Manumatic and 50 percent Nextech. Calculate the sensitivity of the portfolio to a 1 percent surprise in inflation.

14. Suppose we have the three portfolios with factor sensitivities given in the table below. Using the information in the following table, create an arbitrage portfolio using a short position in A and B and a long position in C. Calculate the expected cash flow on the arbitrage portfolio for a $10,000 investment in C.

Expected Returns and Factor Sensitivities (One-Factor Model)		
Portfolio	**Expected Return**	**Factor Sensitivity**
A	0.1500	2.00
B	0.0700	0.40
C	0.0800	0.45

15. Suppose that an institution holds Portfolio K. The institution wants to use Portfolio L to hedge its exposure to inflation. Specifically, it wants to combine K and L to reduce its inflation exposure to 0. Portfolios K and L are well diversified, so the manager can ignore the risk of individual assets and assume that the only source of uncertainty in the portfolio is the surprises in the two factors. The returns to the two portfolios are

$$R_K = 0.12 + 0.5F_{INFL} + 1.0F_{GDP}$$
$$R_L = 0.11 + 1.5F_{INFL} + 2.5F_{GDP}$$

Calculate the weights that a manager should have on K and L to achieve this goal.

16. Portfolio A has an expected return of 10.25 percent and a factor sensitivity of 0.5. Portfolio B has an expected return of 16.2 percent and a factor sensitivity of 1.2. The risk-free rate is 6 percent, and there is one factor. Determine the factor's price of risk.

17. A portfolio manager uses the multifactor model shown in the following table:

Risk Factor	Portfolio A Factor Sensitivity	Portfolio B Factor Sensitivity	S&P 500 Factor Sensitivity	Portfolio A Excess Factor Sensitivity
Confidence risk	0.27	0.27	0.27	0.00
Time horizon risk	0.56	0.56	0.56	0.00
Inflation risk	−0.12	−0.45	−0.37	0.25
Business cycle risk	2.25	1.00	1.71	0.54
Market timing risk	1.00	1.00	1.00	0.00

The S&P 500 is the benchmark Portfolios A and B. Calculate the weights the manager would put on Portfolios A and B to have zero excess business cycle factor sensitivity (relative to the business cycle sensitivity of the S&P 500). Then calculate the inflation factor sensitivity of the resulting portfolio.

18. A wealthy investor has no other source of income beyond her investments. Her investment advisor recommends that she tilt her portfolio to cyclical stocks and high-yield bonds because the average investor holds a job and is recession sensitive. Explain the advisor's advice.

A NOTE ON HARRY M. MARKOWITZ'S "MARKET EFFICIENCY: A THEORETICAL DISTINCTION AND SO WHAT?"

by Adam Kobor

READING

69

LEARNING OUTCOMES

The candidate should be able to:

a. discuss the efficiency of the market portfolio in the CAPM and the relationship between the expected return and beta of an asset when there are restrictions on borrowing at the risk-free rate and on short selling;

b. discuss the practical consequences that follow when there are restrictions on borrowing at the risk-free rate and on short selling.

In this article, Markowitz makes several important observations about the capital asset pricing model (CAPM) and its implications when two alternative assumptions do not hold. To get to Markowitz's observations, the starting point is the striking implications of the CAPM when its assumptions do hold:

▶ the market portfolio is an efficient portfolio; and

▶ there is a linear relationship between the expected return of an asset and its beta.

The major assumptions of the CAPM are:

▶ A1 transaction costs and other illiquidities can be ignored;

▶ A2 all investors hold mean–variance efficient portfolios (i.e., portfolios with the highest expected return for a given level of variance);

▶ A3 all investors hold the same (correct) beliefs about means, variances and covariances of securities; and *either* A4 *or* A4′:

▶ A4 every investor can lend or borrow any desired amount at the risk-free rate.

▶ A4′ investors can sell short without limit and use the proceeds of the sale to buy long positions.

Copyright © 2007 by CFA Institute. Reprinted with permission.

425

The key point of the Markowitz article is that if neither assumption A4 nor A4′ holds, then:

▶ the market portfolio can be inefficient; and

▶ the relationship between the asset's beta and its expected return is *not* necessarily linear.

Markowitz's observations have very serious practical implications and consequences:

1. The empirical fact that the observed expected returns are not linearly related to their betas is typically explained as reflecting the difficulty of measuring the market portfolio's return. The market portfolio return is the return of the capitalization-weighted world portfolio of risky assets, which is very hard to identify and measure exactly. Finding better approximations for the market portfolio may improve the estimation results, but if neither A4 nor A4′ holds, the expected linear relationship is likely to break down even if the measurement of the market portfolio is accurate.

2. Before the introduction of CAPM, it was common to assume that one category of investments was suitable for investors with above average willingness and ability to bear risk whereas another category of investments fitted the needs of those with below average risk tolerance. The CAPM concludes, however, that the market portfolio will efficiently serve all investors' needs. Depending on the specific investor's risk tolerance the market portfolio can be optimally combined with cash or borrowing, but the composition of the portfolio of risky assets is the same across different investors. By contrast, if neither A4 nor A4′ holds, the composition of low-risk and high-risk portfolios will be radically different: low-risk portfolios are likely to be diversified over a large number of securities, possibly overweighting low-volatility instruments relative to their market weights, whereas high-risk portfolios are likely to be concentrated in a few securities with high expected return. Thus, in the absence of unlimited borrowing and short-selling, the composition of portfolios of investors with low and high risk tolerances may become radically different from each other, consistent with traditional advice on investing.

3. The linear relationship between the expected returns and betas is the basis for risk adjustment using beta when investments or asset classes are evaluated or compared on a risk-adjusted basis. Since this linear relationship does not necessarily hold when borrowing is limited and short selling is restricted or not possible, the CAPM risk adjustment is questionable. It is important to note, however, that there are viable alternatives to the CAPM risk adjustment in practice. For example, when we are interested in the desirability of an asset class in our portfolio, a feasible solution is to generate the efficient frontier with and without the specific asset class. The comparison of the two efficient frontiers can provide us with useful information, and it is not dependent on assumptions A4 or A4′.

Because of institutional and other constraints, A4 and A4′ are seriously violated in practice. As a consequence, we should expect that:

▶ the relationship between expected return and beta is not linear and that the market portfolio may not be efficient;

▶ high risk tolerance investors hold portfolios of risky assets that differ from those held by cautious investors; and

▶ risk-adjustments using beta may be misleading.

Appendix 69A illustrates the reasoning behind Markowitz's findings.

APPENDIX 69A

Let us take the CAPM conclusion that the market portfolio is efficient, and seek to explain why this conclusion does not hold when neither A4 nor A4′ is true. Specifically, we assume that we cannot sell assets short and that borrowing at the risk-free rate is not possible. Thus, neither A4 nor A4′ is satisfied. Markowitz uses a 3-security example, where the expected returns and variances of the securities are given, and the correlations between pairs of these securities are assumed to be zero. The investments in these securities are denoted by X_1, X_2 and X_3 respectively. Let us assume that Security 3 has the highest expected return and Security 2 has the lowest expected return. When you set up a portfolio, the following constraint, known as the budget equation, must hold:

$$X_1 + X_2 + X_3 = 1.$$

If there is a constraint against short-selling (also known as non-negativity constraints), we also have the following:

$$X_1 \geq 0, \ X_2 \geq 0, \text{ and } X_3 \geq 0.$$

Let us assume all assets are risky—the case of the efficient frontier with a risk-free asset is treated separately. Portfolio allocations in this 3-security example can be nicely represented graphically: the investment in Security 1 can be plotted on the horizontal axis, and the investment in Security 2 is plotted on the vertical axis of Figure A1 below. If we know X_1 and X_2, from the budget equation we immediately

FIGURE A1   Efficient Sets with and without Non-Negativity Constraints

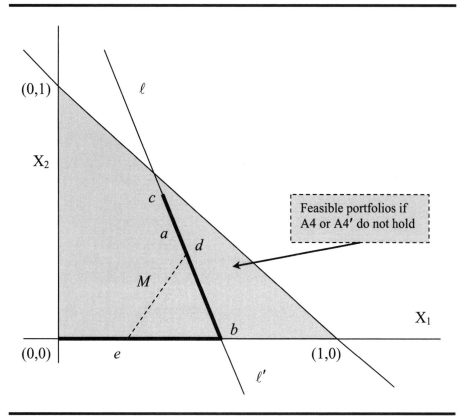

see that $X_3 = 1 - X_1 - X_2$. Furthermore, if we face non-negativity constraints, all feasible portfolio allocations are on and within the *shaded triangle* whose vertices are the points:

▶ (1,0), representing a weight of 1 on Security 1 and a weight of 0 on Security 2 and Security 3;

▶ (0,1) representing a weight of 0 on Security 1, a weight of 1 on Security 2, and a weight of 0 on Security 3; and,

▶ (0,0), representing a weight of 0 on Security 1 and Security 2, and a weight of 1 on Security 3.

Denoting the global minimum-variance portfolio by point "c", let us suppose that point "a" is another portfolio that has the lowest variance that can be achieved for a given level of expected return. (The global minimum-variance portfolio is the portfolio with absolutely smallest variance among all portfolios invested in the three securities.)

A theorem known as the two-fund separation theorem allows us to determine the security weights of other portfolios on the minimum-variance frontier using just our knowledge of the security weights of two minimum-variance portfolios (obtainable by running two optimizations). Given the single constraint that portfolio weights sum to 1 (the budget equation), the two-fund separation theorem states that the security weights of any two portfolios on the minimum-variance frontier can be combined to generate the portfolio weights of any other portfolios on the minimum-variance frontier. Using that result, drawing a line through the two points "c" and "a" generates the line $\ell\ell'$ representing the minimum-variance frontier assuming only the budget equation. The efficient frontier starts at the minimum-variance portfolio and continues through portfolios that have the lowest variance for different levels of expected returns. Thus, the efficient frontier, also known as the efficient set, is represented by the points starting at "c" in the direction of "a" and beyond on the line $\ell\ell'$. Note that as we move from "c" in the direction of "a" expected return increases (because money invested in Security 2, with lowest expected return, is reallocated to Security 1 and Security 3), but variance increases as well.

However, if we face a constraint against short selling in addition to the budget equation, we cannot move outside the triangle. As you can see in Figure A1, line $\ell\ell'$ crosses the triangle at point "b", so the line describing the weights in efficient portfolios "turns a corner" there. At point "b" the investment in Security 2 is zero ($X_2 = 0$), and we can only find efficient portfolios with higher expected returns if we move on the horizontal edge of the triangle. By searching for higher expected return portfolios, we move to the point of (0,0) representing 100% investment in Security 3, since Security 3 has the highest expected return. Ultimately, the efficient frontier in this example is located on the line segments "c"–"b" and "b"–(0,0), bolded in the figure.

With these facts in hand, we can now discuss why the market portfolio is not efficient in the case we are examining. Let us assume that there are only two types of investors: cautious investors represented by "d", located on $\ell\ell'$ between "c" and "b", and aggressive investors, represented by "e", located on the horizontal edge of the triangle between "b" and (0,0). By definition, the market portfolio reflects the average holdings of all investors, so the market portfolio M lies on the dotted line segment connecting "d" and "e". Although both "d" and "e" are located on the efficient frontier represented by the bolded line segments "c"–"b" and "b"–(0,0), the market portfolio M is *not* efficient, since it is located off this efficient frontier. In our earlier discussion, we chose words carefully in stating that when A4 and A4′ are both violated, the market portfolio *may* not be efficient (italics added). For example, if the two investors in the marketplace held portfolios on the line segment "*c*"−"*b*", the market portfolio would be efficient. The point is that the market portfolio is not *necessarily* efficient when A4 and A4′ are violated.

INTERNATIONAL ASSET PRICING
by Bruno Solnik and Dennis McLeavey

LEARNING OUTCOMES

The candidate should be able to:

a. explain international market integration and segmentation, discuss the impediments to international capital mobility, and discuss the factors that favor international market integration;

b. state the assumptions of the domestic capital asset pricing model (CAPM), explain the extension of the domestic CAPM to an international context (the extended CAPM), and describe the additional assumptions needed to justify the extended CAPM;

c. determine whether the real exchange rate has changed in a period, given the beginning-of-period (nominal) exchange rate, the inflation rates in the period, and the end-of-period (nominal) exchange rate;

d. calculate the expected 1) exchange rate and 2) domestic-currency holding period return on a foreign bond (security), given expected, predictable inflation rates, the beginning-of-period nominal exchange rate, and the constant real exchange rate;

e. calculate the end-of-period real exchange rate and the domestic-currency ex-post return on a foreign bond (security), given the end-of-period exchange rate, the beginning-of-period real exchange rate, and the inflation rates during the period;

f. calculate a foreign currency risk premium, and explain a foreign currency risk premium in terms of interest rate differentials and forward rates;

g. state the assumptions, the risk pricing relation, and the formula for the international capital asset pricing model (ICAPM);

h. calculate the expected return on a stock, given its world market beta and currency exposure as well as the appropriate risk-free rates and risk premiums;

i. explain the effect of market segmentation on the ICAPM;

j. define currency exposure and explain exposures in terms of correlations;

k. discuss the likely exchange rate exposure of a company based on a description of the company's activities, and explain the impact of both real and nominal exchange rate changes on the valuation of the company;

International Investments, Fifth Edition, by Bruno Solnik and Dennis McLeavey. Copyright © 2004 by Pearson Education. Reprinted with permission of Pearson Education, publishing as Pearson Addison Wesley.

> **l.** discuss the currency exposures of national economies, equity markets, and bond markets;
>
> **m.** contrast the traditional trade approach and the money demand approach to modeling the relationship between real exchange rate changes and domestic economic activity.

1 INTRODUCTION

In this reading, we explore the valuation and portfolio implications of international asset pricing. Several asset-pricing questions arise: What would happen if all investors diversified their portfolios internationally? What asset prices would result from such a market equilibrium? What type of risks would be priced in the marketplace? Would taking foreign currency risk be rewarded, and what would be the optimal currency-hedging policy?

Answers to these questions require some theoretical market equilibrium framework. In this reading, we review international asset pricing. All asset-pricing theories start from the assumption that markets are efficient, so the first section is devoted to this concept. The second section reviews international asset pricing models. The last section presents some discussion of the relation between exchange rates and asset prices, a central issue in international asset pricing.

Throughout this reading, we use direct currency quotes expressed as X units of domestic currency per 1 unit of foreign currency.

2 INTERNATIONAL MARKET EFFICIENCY

The notion of an efficient market is central to finance theory. In an *efficient market, any new information would be immediately and fully reflected in prices.* Because all current information is already impounded in the asset price, only news—that is, unanticipated information—could cause a change in price in the future.

Consider why a financial market *quickly*, if not instantaneously, discounts all available information. Any new information will immediately be used by some privileged investors, who will take positions to capitalize on it, thereby making the asset price adjust (almost) instantaneously to this piece of information. For example, a new balance of payments statistic would immediately be used by foreign exchange traders to buy or sell a currency until the foreign exchange rate reached a level considered consistent with the new information. Similarly, investors might use surprise information about a company, such as a new contract or changes in forecasted income, to reap a profit until the stock price reached a level consistent with the news. The adjustment in price would be so rapid that it would not pay to buy information that has already been available to other investors. Hundreds of thousands of expert financial analysts and professional investors throughout the world search for information and make the world markets *close* to fully efficient.

In an efficient market, the typical investor could consider an asset price to reflect its true *fundamental value* at all times. The notion of fundamental value is somewhat philosophical; it means that at each point in time, each asset has an **intrinsic value** that all investors try to discover. Because the true fundamental value is unknown, the only way to test for market efficiency is to detect whether some specific news is not yet impounded in the asset price and could therefore be used to make some abnormal profit in the future.

All in all, the general consensus is that individual markets across the world are quite efficient, probably due to the intense competition among professional security analysts and managers in each national market. In addition, the number of foreign investors and securities firms using their own financial analysis techniques has increased, helping to make each national market more efficient. Of course, the degree of efficiency is likely to vary among countries, depending on the maturity, liquidity, and degree of regulation of the market. However, investors must be aware that it is not easy to "beat" the market in any developed stock market. This observation also suggests that theoretical asset pricing models, based on the premise that markets are efficient, are useful guides to investment policy.

Although many national markets may be quite efficient, making it difficult to consistently outperform the local index, the question of international market efficiency still remains. Could active asset allocation among countries consistently outperform the world market index? There is less analyst competition among countries than within a single market. The fundamental issue of international market efficiency is often viewed in terms of international market *integration* or *segmentation*. An integrated world financial market would achieve international efficiency, in the sense that capital flows across markets would instantaneously take advantage of any new information throughout the world. For example, an international investor would not hesitate to move money from Germany to France if the investor forecasted an election result in France that would improve the competitiveness of French firms against German firms. Similarly, a portfolio manager would arbitrage an Italian chemical stock against a U.S. chemical stock, based on new information on their prospective earnings and market shares. In an efficient, integrated, international market, prices of all assets would be in line with their relative investment values. For example, the market consensus expectation of a prolonged period of outstanding economic growth in one country would be immediately discounted in higher current equity prices and not translate into higher future stock returns once the widely expected superior growth materializes.

The debate over integration versus segmentation involves two somewhat different concepts:

▶ The first concept has to do with impediments to capital mobility. Are there legal restrictions or other forms of constraints that segment one national market from others?

▶ The second concept has to do with international asset pricing. Are "similar" securities priced in the same manner on different national markets?

It is sometimes claimed that international markets are not integrated but segmented because of various *impediments to capital mobility*. Although each national market might be efficient, numerous factors might prevent international capital flows from taking advantage of relative mispricing among countries:

▶ *Psychological barriers.* Unfamiliarity with foreign markets, language, sources of information, and so on, might curtail foreign investment.

▶ *Legal restrictions.* Institutional investors are often constrained in their foreign investments. Also, some national markets regulate foreign investment flowing into or out of the market. Foreign ownership is sometimes constrained to avoid loss of national control.

▶ *Transaction costs.* The costs of foreign investment can be high and greater than for domestic investment. Access to sources of information throughout the world is costly, as are international transaction costs, management fees, and custodial services.

▶ *Discriminatory taxation.* Foreign investment might be more heavily taxed than domestic investment. Withholding taxes might lead to double taxation.

▶ *Political risks.* The **political risks** of foreign investment might dampen enthusiasm for international diversification. This political transfer risk might take the form of a prohibition on repatriation of profits or capital investment from a foreign country. Although the risk is extremely small in the major markets, the associated potential loss is large.

▶ *Foreign currency risks.* Foreign investments bear the risk of local market movements and unexpected changes in the foreign exchange rate. Foreign currency risk is the risk that the foreign currency *in real terms,* will depreciate or the domestic currency will appreciate during the time an investor holds an investment denominated in foreign currency.

All these factors tend to reduce international capital flows and lead to somewhat segmented national markets. This result is most apparent in emerging markets, in which foreign investment restrictions are often severe.

However, international integration requires only a sufficient flow of capital to make the world market efficient and to eliminate relative mispricing among countries. In many countries, private and institutional investors are extensively invested abroad. All major corporations have truly multinational operations; their shares are often listed on several stock exchanges. Large corporations, as well as governments, borrow internationally and quickly take advantage of relative bond mispricing between countries, thereby making the markets more efficient. The flow of foreign investment has grown rapidly over the years; thus, it does not seem that the international markets are fully segmented. What is really important for investors is whether two firms that they regard as similar are priced identically in their respective national markets. To have a meaningful discussion of market segmentation, we must first introduce asset-pricing models.

3   ASSET-PRICING THEORY

The Domestic Capital Asset-Pricing Model

The value of an asset depends on its discounted anticipated cash flows adjusted for risk. For example, the value of a risk-free bill is equal to the repayment value of the bill discounted at the risk-free interest rate. There is an inverse relation between the price of an asset and its expected return and risk. Modern portfolio theory has proposed models of asset pricing in *fully efficient markets.* All of these models attempt to determine what the expected return should be on an asset in an efficient market given the risk borne by the investor. Market equilibrium requires that the expected return be equal to the risk-free rate plus risk premiums to reward the various sources of risk borne by the investor. The major challenge is to determine the relevant measures of risk, as well as the size of the associated premiums.[1] The capital asset-pricing model (CAPM) is the first well-known model of market equilibrium. Because the reality of the international market is extremely complex, entailing a huge number of securities and sources of uncertainties, the objective of the model is to provide a simplified view of the world, capturing the major aspects of reality. This simplification is required to allow the formation of operational concepts.

The domestic (standard) CAPM is therefore built on fairly restrictive assumptions regarding investors' preferences. Many of these assumptions can be somewhat relaxed, leading to more complex (and less operational) versions. The assumptions of the standard CAPM are as follows:

▶ Investors care about risk and return. They are risk-averse and prefer less risk and more expected return.

▶ A consensus among all investors holds, and everyone agrees about the expected return and risk of all assets.

▶ Investors care about nominal returns in their domestic currency; for example, U.S. investors care about U.S. dollar returns.

▶ A risk-free interest rate exists, with unlimited borrowing or lending capacity at this rate.

▶ There are no transaction costs or taxes.

In the CAPM, all investors determine their demand for each asset by a mean–variance optimization (expected-utility maximization). They optimize a portfolio, P, made up of a set of assets, i. They do so by minimizing the variance of the portfolio, σ_p^2, for a selected level of expected return, $E(R_p)$. The selected level of expected return depends on the investor's risk aversion.

The demands from each investor are aggregated and set equal to the supply of assets, their market capitalization. The net supply of borrowing and lending (the **risk-free asset**) is assumed to be zero.

Two conclusions emerge from the domestic CAPM.

Separation Theorem   The *normative* conclusion of the domestic CAPM is that everyone should hold the same portfolio of risky assets, and the optimal combination of risky assets can be separated from the investor's preferences toward risk and return. This portfolio of risky assets must therefore be the *domestic market portfolio*, made up of all assets traded in proportion to their market capitalization. All investors should hold a combination of:

▶ the risk-free asset, and
▶ the market portfolio.

Investors adjust their risk preference by putting some of their money in the risk-free asset (more risk-oriented investors will borrow, instead of lend, at the risk-free interest rate). In other words, investors need only two portfolios to design their investment strategies: a market index fund and the risk-free asset.

Risk-Pricing Relation   The *descriptive* conclusion of the CAPM is that the equilibrium expected return of an asset should be equal to the risk-free rate plus a risk premium proportional to the covariance of the asset return with the return

---

[1] See Elton and Gruber (1995), Reilly and Brown (2003), and Sharpe, Alexander, and Bailey (1999).

on the market portfolio. The notation beta, β_i, is used to represent the ratio of the covariance between the asset and the market returns to the variance of the market return; it is the measure of the *sensitivity* of the asset return to market movements. It is sometimes called *market exposure*. The risk-pricing relation of the CAPM for asset i can be written as

$$E(R_i) = R_0 + \beta_i \times RP_m \qquad \textbf{(70-1)}$$

where

$E(R_i)$ is the expected return on asset i

$E(R_m)$ is the expected return on the market portfolio

R_0 is the risk-free interest rate

β_i is the sensitivity of asset i to market movements (i.e., market exposure)

RP_m is the **market risk premium** equal to $E(R_m) - R_0$

Equation 70-1 describes the risk-pricing relation for all assets i. So RP_m and R_0 are constant, whereas $E(R_i)$ and β_i vary, depending on the asset i considered. There is a linear relation between the expected return on all assets and their sensitivity to market movements. This straight line is usually called the *security market line*.

Intuition   The type of risk that is relevant to pricing an asset is its sensitivity to market movements, β_i, not its total risk, σ_i^2. To understand the intuitive reason for this result, let's decompose the return on asset i into two components: the market influence and a specific component.

$$R_i = \alpha_i + \beta_i \times R_m + \varepsilon_i \qquad \textbf{(70-2)}$$

where α_i and β_i are constants and R_i, R_m, and ε_i are stochastic, which means that they vary over time in a somewhat unpredictable fashion. The term ε_i is specific to asset i and independent of the market return R_m. This equation can easily be estimated as a simple regression of the asset return on the market return; β_i is the slope of the regression. Then the total risk of asset i can be decomposed into its *market* (or *systematic*) *risk* and its *specific* (or *residual*) *risk*:

$$\sigma_i^2 = \beta_i^2 \times \sigma_m^2 + \sigma_\varepsilon^2 \qquad \textbf{(70-3)}$$

A similar relation applies to any portfolio P. The beta of portfolio, β_p, is simply the weighted average of the betas of all securities included in the portfolio. As the number of securities included in the portfolio increases, its specific risk decreases. This is because the specific risks of individual securities tend to be independent of each other and tend to cancel each other out. In a well-diversified portfolio, specific risks vanish and the total risk of the portfolio reduces to its market risk σ_m^2:

$$\sigma_p^2 = \beta_p^2 \times \sigma_m^2 \qquad \textbf{(70-4)}$$

So the only risk that counts for any investor holding a **well-diversified portfolio** is market risk.

The average beta of all securities is equal to one (the beta of the market portfolio). Securities with a high beta are more sensitive to the market environment and should provide a higher expected return than securities with a low beta given a positive market risk premium. Investors should care only about the beta of a security, not about its total risk. In an international context, the domestic CAPM implies that all domestic securities would be priced in line with their risk relative to the domestic market. Even if a company has extensive foreign operations, its international risks would not be taken into account specifically.

The simplifying assumptions of any theory, including the CAPM, are never verified exactly in the real world. The empirical question is whether the results are **robust**. A major problem mentioned by Roll (1977) is that the CAPM requires an exact identification of the market portfolio, including all investable assets. Hence, a proper CAPM should include all world assets in the market portfolio, but this would require a model that accounts for a multicurrency environment.

Asset Returns and Exchange Rate Movements

As we expand the investment universe to include international assets, the currency used to measure returns becomes an issue. For example, a Swiss investor holding the Swiss company Novartis measures value and return in Swiss francs. A U.S. investor would translate Novartis' value and return into dollars. Consider an investor who uses his domestic currency (DC) to measure return on some securities of a foreign country with a foreign currency (FC). The direct exchange rate between the two currencies is S units of DC for one FC unit. For example, we could have a U.S. investor holding shares of Novartis. The value of Novartis in domestic currency (dollar), V, is equal to its foreign currency (Swiss franc) value, V^{FC}, multiplied by the spot exchange rate, S, expressed in dollars per Swiss franc:[2]

$$V = V^{FC} \times S \qquad \textbf{(70-5)}$$

Using Equation 70-5, a simple calculation of return from time 0 to time 1 shows that the DC (dollar) rate of return on an investment in Novartis, $R = (V_1 - V_0)/V_0$, is equal to the FC (Swiss franc) rate of return on Novartis, $R^{FC} = (V_1^{FC} - V_0^{FC})/V_0^{FC}$, plus the percentage exchange rate movement, $s = (S_1 - S_0)/S_0$, plus the cross-product of R^{FC} and s. This cross-product comes from the fact that the exchange rate movement applies to the original Swiss franc value of Novartis and also to the Swiss franc capital gain (loss), R^{FC}:

$$R = R^{FC} + s + (s \times R^{FC}) \qquad \textbf{(70-6)}$$

The last term is of second order and assumed to be very small for short time periods, giving the first order approximation

$$R = R^{FC} + s \qquad \textbf{(70-7)}$$

Alternatively, investors can hedge currency risk in the forward exchange market. The forward exchange rate quoted today for the period-end is F units of DC for 1 unit of FC. A 100 percent hedge would imply selling forward an amount V_1^{FC} of foreign currency. In turn, the investor knows with certainty at the start of the period what exchange rate will be used at the end of the period. So F replaces S_1, and the *hedged* return on the foreign share becomes

---

[2] We use the superscript FC when we measure return or value in the foreign currency, but no superscript when we measure return or value in the investor's domestic currency.

$$R = R^{\text{FC}} + (F - S_0)/S_0 \qquad \text{(70-8)}$$

Note that the forward discount/premium $(F - S_0)/S_0$ is fully known at the start of the period.[3]

In terms of expected returns, the DC return on an *unhedged* investment is given by

$$E(R) = E(R^{\text{FC}}) + E(s) = E(R^{\text{FC}}) + [E(S_1) - S_0]/S_0$$

and the DC expected return on a *hedged* investment is given by

$$E(R) = E(R^{\text{FC}}) + (F - S_0)/S_0$$

The Domestic CAPM Extended to the International Context

Attempts have been made to justify the use of the domestic CAPM in an international context, in which investors in different countries use different currencies and have different consumption preferences.[4] Such a domestic CAPM extension would involve the domestic rate for the risk-free rate and the market capitalization weighted portfolio of all risky assets in the world for the market portfolio. This domestic CAPM extension can be justified only with the addition of two unreasonable assumptions:

▶ Investors throughout the world have identical consumption baskets.

▶ Real prices of consumption goods are identical in every country. In other words, purchasing power parity holds exactly at any point in time.

In this type of perfect world, exchange rates would simply mirror inflation differentials between two countries. Exchange rate uncertainty would be **money illusion**; it would not matter whether investors used euros or dollars. The exchange rate would be a pure translation-accounting device, and real FC risk would not exist. The real exchange rate is defined as the actual exchange rate multiplied by the ratio of the price levels of the consumption baskets in the two countries. Recall that with direct exchange rates, the relation between the real and nominal exchange rates is

$$X = S \times (P_{\text{FC}}/P_{\text{DC}}) \qquad \text{(70-9)}$$

where

X is the real exchange rate (direct quote DC/FC)

S is the nominal exchange rate (direct quote DC/FC)

P_{FC} is the foreign country price level

P_{DC} is the domestic country price level

---

[3] Again, Equation 70-8 is a first-order approximation. We can hedge the start-of-period value V^0, but the exact end-of-period value is not known, so the unexpected capital gain (loss) cannot be hedged.

[4] See Grauer, Litzenberger, and Stehle (1976).

Real exchange rate movements are defined as movements in the exchange rates that are not explained by the inflation differential between the two countries. We can rewrite Equation 70-9 in terms of percentage changes over a time period (say a year):

$$x = s + I_{FC} - I_{DC} = s - (I_{DC} - I_{FC}) \qquad \textbf{(70-10)}$$

where

> x and s are the percentage movement in the real and nominal exchange rates I_{DC} and I_{FC} are the inflation rates in the domestic and foreign countries.

If purchasing power parity holds, the real exchange rate is constant ($x = 0\%$), and the nominal exchange rate movement (DC/FC) is equal to the inflation rate differential (domestic minus foreign inflation). For example, assume that there is a one-month inflation rate of 1 percent in the USA (DC) and 0 percent in Switzerland (FC). For the real exchange rate (dollar value of one Swiss franc) to stay constant over the month, the franc has to appreciate by 1 percent against the dollar ($x = 0\%$, $s = 1\%$). If the franc turned out to appreciate by 5 percent ($s = 5\%$) during that month, then there would be a real appreciation of 4 percent of the franc ($x = 4\%$). Any such real exchange rate movement would violate the assumptions supporting the domestic CAPM extension. To summarize, in the absence of real foreign currency risk, however, the extended CAPM would hold.

Because the real exchange rate is constant in Example 1, there is no real foreign currency risk. Note that exchange rate uncertainty due to inflation is generally very small, because inflation rates are highly predictable in the short run, especially relative to equity returns. Predictable inflation rates mean predictable exchange rates if purchasing power parity holds. Even with predictable inflation in the next example, real foreign currency risk arises.

EXAMPLE 1

Constant Real Exchange Rate

An investor in his home (domestic) country considers investing in the securities of a foreign country. The direct exchange rate between the two countries is currently two domestic currency (DC) units for one foreign currency (FC) unit. The price level of the typical consumption basket in domestic country relative to the price level of the typical consumption basket in foreign country is also 2 to 1, which means that the real exchange rate is 1 to 1. A year later the inflation rate has been 3 percent in domestic country and 1 percent in foreign country. The foreign currency has appreciated and the exchange rate is now 2.04. What is the new real exchange rate?

Solution: The new real exchange rate is equal to the new nominal exchange rate adjusted by the ratio of the new price levels: $S \times (P_{FC}/P_{DC}) = X$, or $2.04 \times (1.01/2.06) = 1$. The real exchange rate remains constant because the foreign exchange appreciation of 2 percent is equal to the inflation differential between the two countries. As the real exchange rate is fixed, the currencies have fully retained their purchasing power. The appreciation of the nominal exchange rate has no real impact.

International CAPM

Deviations from purchasing power parity can be a major source of exchange rate variation, and consumption preferences can differ among countries. In these

---

EXAMPLE 2

Foreign Currency Risk

An investor in her home (domestic) country would like to expand her portfolio to include one-year bonds in foreign countries. The expected inflation rate in domestic country is 3 percent and the expected inflation rate in one of the foreign countries is 1 percent. Inflation rates are totally predictable over the next year. The exchange rate between the two countries is currently two DC units for one FC unit. The price level of the typical consumption basket in domestic country relative to the price level of the typical consumption basket in foreign country is also 2 to 1. The real exchange rate is 1 to 1. The one-year interest rate is 5 percent in domestic country and 3 percent in foreign country. The investor expects the real exchange rate to remain constant over time.

1. What are the expected exchange rate and the expected return on the **foreign bond** in domestic currency?

A year later the inflation rates have indeed been 3 percent in DC and 1 percent in FC. The foreign exchange rate has been very volatile over the year, and the foreign currency has depreciated with an end-of-the-year exchange rate of 1.80.

2. What is the real exchange rate at the end of the year and the *ex post* return on the foreign bond?

3. How would you qualify the risk-return characteristics of this investment?

Solution to 1: The future exchange rate should be equal to 2.04 DC units per FC unit if the real exchange rate remained constant, corresponding to a 2 percent appreciation of the foreign currency. The expected return on the foreign bond should therefore be approximately 5 percent, the sum of the foreign interest rate and of the currency appreciation, or more precisely $1.03 \times (2.04/2.00) - 1 = 5.06\%$.

Solution to 2: Unfortunately, the *ex post* exchange rate is equal to 1.80 and the real exchange rate has become $S \times (P_{FC}/P_{DC}) = X$, or $1.80 \times (1.01/2.06) = 0.88$. The actual exchange rate movement is not equal to the inflation differential between the two countries, and there is a severe real depreciation of the foreign currency. The *ex post* return on the foreign bond is negative and equal to $1.03 \times (1.80/2.00) - 1 = -7.3\%$.

Solution to 3: This investment had an expected return similar to that of the domestic risk-free rate, but it carried a lot of foreign currency risk. All of the foreign currency risk is real risk, as inflation rates here were predictable. Of course, this foreign currency risk could be hedged.

---

cases, the risk that real prices of consumption goods might not be identical in every country is called *real foreign currency risk, real exchange rate risk,* or *purchasing power risk.*

In real life, daily exchange rate movements are volatile and cannot be simply explained by an adjustment to daily inflation. Because inflation rates are very stable compared with asset returns and exchange rate movements, most if not all of the short-term variability in exchange rates can be referred to as real foreign currency risk. Investors will want to hedge against real foreign currency risk. An **international CAPM** (or ICAPM) can be developed under the assumption that nationals of a country care about returns and risks measured in their *domestic currency* (e.g., the U.S. dollar for U.S. investors and the Swiss franc for Swiss investors).[5] All the assumptions of the CAPM still hold. In particular, investors can freely borrow or lend in any currency. Using interest rate parity, investors can therefore freely replicate forward currency contracts to hedge foreign currency risk. It must be stressed that a dollar short-term bill that is risk-free for U.S. investors becomes risky for foreign investors who are concerned with returns in their domestic currency because of foreign currency risk.

Interest Rate Parity   It is important here to recall the concept of interest rate parity (IRP). Interest rate parity lies behind the ability to replicate forward currency contracts. In the world of foreign currency risk and the international CAPM, we will encounter foreign currency risk premiums. These premiums will be defined in reference to the movement in the exchange rate implied by parity conditions. In review of IRP, the direct spot exchange rate times one plus the domestic risk-free rate (investing domestically the amount of DC units required to purchase 1 FC unit) equals the direct forward exchange rate times one plus the foreign risk-free rate (exchanging for 1 FC unit now, investing in the foreign country, and repatriating later). Recall that IRP with direct exchange rates is given by

$$F = S(1 + r_{DC})/(1 + r_{FC}) \qquad \textbf{(70-11)}$$

where

F is the direct forward rate

S is the direct spot rate

r_{DC} is the domestic risk-free rate

r_{FC} is the foreign risk-free rate

As a first-order linear approximation, the percentage forward premium on the exchange rate must equal the domestic risk-free rate minus the foreign risk-free rate, given as

$$(F - S)/S \cong r_{DC} - r_{FC} \qquad \textbf{(70-12)}$$

---

[5] See Solnik (1974), Sercu (1980), and Adler and Dumas (1983).

EXAMPLE 3

Interest Rate Parity

The one-year domestic country risk-free rate of return is 5 percent, and the one-year foreign country rate is 3 percent. The current exchange rate is 2 DC units for 1 FC unit. What is the current level of the forward exchange rate that is implied by these data?

Solution: The investor could invest 2 DC units at the local risk-free rate of $r_{DC} = 5$ percent and would get $2 \times (1 + r_{DC})$ or 2.1 DC units in a year. Alternately, the investor could combine three operations:

- ► Exchange those 2 DC units at the spot exchange rate S for $2/S = 1$ FC unit.
- ► Invest this FC unit at the foreign country rate of $r_{FC} = 3$ percent and get 1.03 FC units in a year.
- ► Sell forward today the proceeds of $1 + r_{FC} = 1.03$ units of FC received in a year at the forward exchange rate of F.

In a year, the investor will therefore receive, with certainty, an amount of DC units equal to

$$(2/S) \times F \times (1 + r_{FC}) \text{ or } F \times 1.03$$

This combination should yield an identical result as the first alternative, as they are both riskless in domestic currency and involve the same investment. Otherwise, an arbitrage will take place. Hence, $F \times 1.03 = 2.1$ and $F = 2.039$, giving our answer that the forward exchange rate is 2.039 DC units per 1 FC unit.

The forward premium can be approximated as the interest rate differential, or a 2 percent premium on the foreign currency. In general, with direct exchange rates, we have

$$F = S \times \frac{1 + r_{DC}}{1 + r_{FC}}$$

Foreign Currency Risk Premiums As a background for the international CAPM, it is also useful to recall the definition of a foreign currency risk premium. The risk premium on any investment is simply equal to its expected return in excess of the domestic risk-free rate:

$$RP = E(R) - R_0$$

Someone investing in a foreign currency will exchange the domestic currency (e.g., U.S. dollar) for the foreign currency (e.g., Swiss franc) and invest it at the foreign risk-free interest rate. So the expected domestic currency return on the foreign currency investment is equal to the foreign risk-free rate plus the expected percentage movement in the exchange rate. The foreign currency risk premium (SRP) is defined as the expected return on an investment minus the domestic currency risk-free rate. Thus, the foreign currency risk premium is equal to the expected movement in the exchange rate *minus* the interest rate differential (domestic risk-free rate minus foreign risk-free rate):

$$SRP = E[(S_1 - S_0)/S_0] - (r_{DC} - r_{FC}) = E(s) - (r_{DC} - r_{FC}) \quad \textbf{(70-13)}$$

Substituting for $r_{DC} - r_{FC}$ using the interest rate parity approximation, the risk premium can also be expressed as the difference between the expected exchange rate and the forward rate, in percentage of the current exchange rate: $[E(S_1) - F]/S_0$.

EXAMPLE 4

Foreign Currency Risk Premium

The one-year risk-free interest rates are 5 percent in DC and 3 percent in FC. The exchange rate between the two countries is currently 2 DC units for 1 FC unit. The expected exchange rate appreciation of FC is 3 percent. What is the foreign currency risk premium?

Solution: Because the interest differential is 2 percent (domestic minus foreign), interest rate parity implies that the forward exchange rate quotes at a premium of approximately 2 percent over the current exchange rate while the expected exchange rate appreciation of FC currency is 3 percent. Therefore, the foreign exchange risk premium is equal to +1 percent (3% − 2%). The expected DC return on the foreign investment is the 3 percent FC risk-free rate plus the 3 percent expected currency appreciation. It is also equal to the 5 percent domestic risk-free rate plus the 1 percent foreign currency risk premium. Note that the hedged investment return is the foreign risk-free rate plus the forward premium, a return of approximately 5 percent. Thus, the expected return on an unhedged foreign investment is 1 percent higher than if hedged against real foreign currency risk. However, hedging removes foreign currency risk.

In the international CAPM, as in the domestic CAPM, all investors determine their demand for each asset by a mean-variance optimization (expected-utility maximization), using their *domestic currency as base currency*. The demand from each investor is aggregated and set equal to the supply of assets, their market capitalization. The net supply of borrowing and lending (the risk-free asset) *in each currency* is assumed to be zero. Two conclusions emerge from this international CAPM.

Separation Theorem The *normative* conclusion is that the optimal investment strategy for any investor is a combination of two portfolios: a risky portfolio common to all investors, and a personalized hedge portfolio used to reduce purchasing-power risks. If there is no uncertainty about future inflation rates in any country, the personalized hedge portfolio reduces to the national risk-free asset, and a simpler separation theorem can be demonstrated.[6] All investors should hold a combination of

---

[6] It has been observed repeatedly that the variability of inflation rates is very small compared with that of exchange rates or asset returns. Therefore, using nominal returns to measure returns is quite reasonable from a practical viewpoint.

▶ the risk-free asset in their own currency, and

▶ the world market portfolio optimally hedged against foreign currency risk.

This world market portfolio is the same for each investor and is the only portfolio of risky assets that should be held, partly hedged against foreign currency risk, by any investor. However, it must be stressed that the optimal currency hedge ratio need not be unitary and will generally be different for different assets and currencies.[7] The optimal hedge ratios depend on variables such as differences among countries in relative wealth, foreign investment position, and risk aversion. Unfortunately, these variables cannot be observed or inferred from market data. The international CAPM does not provide simple, clear-cut, operational conclusions about the optimal currency-hedge ratios.

Risk-Pricing Relation   The *descriptive* conclusion of the international CAPM is an international equilibrium risk-pricing relation that is more complex than in the domestic CAPM, in which the expected return on any asset is simply a function of its covariance with the domestic market portfolio. In the presence of exchange rate risk, additional risk premiums must be added to the risk-pricing relation to reflect the covariance of the asset with the various exchange rates (the currencies' betas). If there are $k + 1$ countries, there will be k additional currency risk premiums. Hence, the expected return on an asset depends on the market risk premium plus various foreign currency risk premiums:

$$E(R_i) = R_0 + \beta_{iw} \times RP_w + \gamma_{i1} \times SRP_1 + \gamma_{i2}SRP_2 + \ldots + \gamma_{ik}SRP_k \quad \textbf{(70-14)}$$

where

R_0 is the domestic currency risk-free interest rate,

β_{iw} is the sensitivity of asset i domestic currency returns to market movements (market exposure),

RP_w is the world market risk premium equal to $E(R_w) - R_0$,

γ_{i1} to γ_{ik} are the **currency exposures**, the sensitivities of asset i domestic currency returns to the exchange rate on currencies 1 to k, and

SRP_1 to SRP_k are the foreign currency risk premiums on currencies 1 to k.

In Equation 70-14, all returns are measured in the investor's domestic currency.[8] Equation 70-14 indicates that the foreign investment return in domestic currency equals (a) the domestic risk-free rate, plus (b) a world market risk premium, times the asset's sensitivity to the world market, plus (c) foreign currency risk premiums times the investment's currency exposures.

For an asset that is uncorrelated with the various exchange rates or that is optimally hedged against currency risk, the traditional CAPM still applies with its single-market risk premium given as a function of the covariance of the asset

---

[7] The hedge ratio is the proportion of the value of the portfolio (or component of a portfolio) that is currency hedged.

[8] As stressed by Adler and Dumas (1983), Equation 70-14 applies to returns measured in any base currency. For example, one could choose arbitrarily to measure all returns in U.S. dollars; then Equation 70-14 would apply for dollar returns, and R_0 would be the U.S. risk-free rate. Or one could choose to measure all returns in euros; then Equation 70-14 would apply for euro returns, and R_0 would be the euro risk-free rate.

with the world market portfolio. So the traditional CAPM applies only to securities or portfolios perfectly hedged against currency risk.[9]

The ICAPM differs from a domestic CAPM in two respects. First, the relevant market risk is world (global) market risk, not domestic market risk. This is not surprising. Second, additional risk premiums are linked to an asset's sensitivity to currency movements. The different currency exposures of individual securities would be reflected in different expected returns.

Intuition on Foreign Currency Risk Premiums in the ICAPM   Again, the basic idea is that a risk premium should be earned for taking those risks that cannot be trivially eliminated by a naive diversification of the portfolio. Currency risks will remain in a diversified portfolio because currency movements affect all securities to some extent. One could argue that currency risks could be hedged with forward contracts and, therefore, portfolios need not bear this type of risk.[10] However, a similar argument could be developed for market risk, because futures contracts exist on stock indexes. The basic point is that the world market portfolio has to be held in aggregate, so world market risk has to be borne by investors. Similarly, because the world market portfolio is sensitive to currency risks, these currency risks have to be borne in aggregate.

A question often raised is: Why is there a non-zero currency risk premium? The theoretical answer is that investors from different countries have different net foreign investment positions and different risk aversions. In equilibrium, this will result in positive or negative currency risk premiums. Assume, for example, that Americans invest a lot abroad so that their net foreign investment position is positive while that of foreigners is negative. In other words, Americans have more wealth invested abroad than foreigners have invested in America. Also assume that Americans are more risk-averse than foreigners. Then Americans have a larger demand to hedge their foreign currency position (sell foreign currency forward) than foreigners have to hedge their dollar position (sell dollar forward). This imbalance will create, in equilibrium, a currency risk premium on

---

EXAMPLE 5

Paying/Receiving the Foreign Currency Risk Premium

Suppose Americans are big net investors in a hypothetical country, Arland, and the Arlanders invest little abroad. The Americans have a vast net foreign wealth and are worried about currency risk; hence, they have a strong demand for hedging Arlandian francs into American dollars. The Arlanders have little demand for hedging American dollars, because they do not invest much in America. The Americans are long in Arlandian stocks, and they can hedge their exposure to the Arlandian franc by

---

[9] Note, however, that optimal currency hedging does not mean 100 percent hedging. This is because the value of a foreign asset could be affected by an exchange rate movement. This is detailed in the section on currency exposures. The gammas (γ_{ik}) are sometimes called regression hedge ratios because they can be estimated from a multiple regression of the asset return on the various exchange rate movements.

[10] It is sometimes argued that on a forward or futures currency contract there is one seller for each buyer so that the expected return should be zero. This is a flawed argument. If it were true, it would apply to any forward contract. For example, there is one seller for every buyer of an S&P 500 futures contract. Still, the buyer is expected to receive the U.S. equity risk premium, while the seller is expected to lose it.

selling forward Arlandian francs (buy dollars forward). Arlandians and other speculators buy Arlandian francs forward (sell dollars forward), induced by a positive risk premium on the franc. The one-year risk-free interest rates are 5 percent in America and 3 percent in Arland. The exchange rate between the two countries is currently two dollars for one franc. The expected exchange rate appreciation of the Arlandian franc is 3 percent. The expected return on Arlandian stocks is 6 percent in francs.

1. What is the expected return on Arlandian stocks in dollars if there is no currency hedging?

2. What is the expected return on Arlandian stocks in dollars with full currency hedging?

3. What is the foreign currency risk premium on the Arlandian franc and who pays/receives it?

Solution to 1: The expected return on Arlandian stocks in dollars is equal to the expected return in francs, 6 percent, plus the expected currency appreciation of 3 percent, a total expected return of 9 percent.

Solution to 2: With currency hedging, the forward premium is equal to the interest rate differential of 2 percent. Hence, the expected return on Arlandian stocks, hedged against currency risk is 8 percent (6 percent plus 2 percent). The expected return is less than for an unhedged investment, but the risk is also less.

Solution to 3: There is a 1 percent foreign currency risk premium, that is, the difference between the expected currency appreciation of the franc and the forward premium on the franc. This risk premium is "paid" by Americans and "received" by Arlandians. In equilibrium, Americans are willing to pay this currency risk premium to remove currency risks on their net foreign position in Arlandian stocks. Arlandians (and other speculators) are willing to provide that hedge because of the expected return due to the currency risk premium.

the foreign currency. Americans will have to pay a currency risk premium on their currency hedge, while foreigners will receive a currency risk premium. This is because the selling pressure on the forward exchange rate will reduce it relative to the expected spot exchange rate. While Americans sell foreign currency forward for hedging motives, foreigners will buy forward to accommodate American needs if induced by a positive expected return, the currency risk premium. Using the dollar as the base currency, the expected exchange rate (in $ per FC units) for the foreign currency will be larger than the forward rate, and this difference as a percentage of the current exchange rate is a risk premium by definition.

Individual assets have different exposures to currencies, and these exposures affect their equilibrium pricing. Foreign currency risk premiums arise from the risk exposures of the average investor. If the average investor is sensitive to the real foreign currency risk of a particular country, he will bid up the price of those stocks that have a low or negative currency exposure (γ). Those are the stocks that are negatively correlated with real foreign currency risk. He is actually paying to hedge and thus accepts a lower expected return as a trade-off for the benefit of reducing real foreign currency risk.

EXAMPLE 6

International Asset Pricing

You are a European investor considering investing in a foreign country. The world market risk premium is estimated at 5 percent, the foreign currency offers a 1 percent risk premium, and the current risk-free rates are equal to 5 percent in euros and 3 percent in FC units. In other words, you expect the FC unit to appreciate against the euro by an amount equal to the interest rate differential (which is also equal to the expected inflation differential) plus the foreign currency risk premium, or a total of 3 percent. Your broker provides you with some statistics:

	Stock A	Stock B	Stock C	Stock D
World beta	1.0	1.0	1.2	1.4
Currency exposure (γ)	1.0	0.0	0.5	−0.5

1. According to the International CAPM, what should be the expected returns on the four stocks, in euros?
2. Stocks A and B have the same world beta, but different expected returns. Give an intuitive explanation for this difference.

Solution to 1: With one foreign currency and the euro as the base currency, the asset pricing equation of the International CAPM simplifies to

$$E(R_i) = R_0 + \beta_{iw} \times RP_w + \gamma_i \times SRP_{FC}$$

where all returns are measured in euros, RP_w is the risk premium on the world index, and SRP_{FC} is the risk premium on the foreign currency unit, assumed to be the only other currency. If the euro is used as the base currency, then all β's and γ's should be measured using euro returns. Using the exposures (or "sensitivities") given, we get the theoretical expected returns given in the following table. For example, the expected return of Stock A is equal to the euro risk-free rate of 5 percent, plus a world equity risk premium of 5 percent ($1 \times 5\%$), plus a foreign currency risk premium of 1 percent ($1 \times 1\%$).

	Stock A	Stock B	Stock C	Stock D
Theoretical expected return (€)	11.0%	10.0%	11.5%	11.5%

Solution to 2: Stock A has an expected return of 11 percent, compared with 10 percent for Stock B. The difference is explained by their different exposures to currency movements. The euro value of Stock B is insensitive to unexpected movements in the FC/euro exchange rate. As far as foreign currency risk is concerned, Stock B is less risky than Stock A (currency risk exposure of +1), so its expected return should be different from that of Stock A. Because the currency risk premium is equal to +1 percent, the difference in expected return between Stock A and Stock B should be 1 percent.

Market Imperfections and Segmentation

The international asset pricing relation described applies to all securities only in an integrated world capital market. Financial markets are segmented if securities that have the same risk characteristics, but are listed in two different markets, have different expected returns.

In many countries, various types of institutional investors face severe legal constraints on their international investments. This is often the case with public pension funds or insurance companies that have liabilities denominated in their national currencies and are required to invest in assets denominated in the same currency. The psychological aspects are also important. Investors are much more familiar with their local financial market than with foreign markets. Hence, they feel somewhat uneasy about investing their money in a remote country or an unfamiliar currency.

If currency hedging is not available, either physically or legally, the simple pricing relation breaks down. Furthermore, official restrictions, fear of expropriation, discriminatory taxes, and higher investment costs push domestic investors to underinvest in foreign assets compared with the world market portfolio. The argument for international comparative advantage in imperfect markets might be firm-specific; investors might prefer foreign companies that are not found in other parts of the world (e.g., Club Méditérranée) and avoid companies that are deemed sensitive to national interests (e.g., armament companies) or are located in countries in which foreign interests might be expropriated on short notice.

If all these impediments to international investments are of significant magnitude, buying the market is not a reasonable first-cut strategy. Although it certainly does not mean that investors should avoid foreign investments, the additional costs and risks of foreign investments may cause market segmentation and affect asset pricing.

International asset pricing under various forms of market segmentation, including differential taxes, has been studied, and more complex asset pricing relations have been found.[11] The risk premium has a more complex form than in the traditional international capital asset pricing model. It generally depends on the form of market imperfection, the relative wealth of investors, and parameters of their utility function. However, most forms of market imperfections and constraints to foreign investments cannot be easily incorporated in an equilibrium asset pricing framework. Hence, their precise influence on the resulting optimal portfolio holdings cannot be easily modeled.

4   PRACTICAL IMPLICATIONS

A Global Approach to Equilibrium Pricing

The ICAPM gives useful insights on asset pricing in an efficient world capital market and in the absence of privileged information. It tells us what should be the return on assets if we do not formulate specific forecasts for them; therefore, the ICAPM offers default values from which to start. It also proposes a simplified structure to global asset management—in other words, a benchmark or **passive investment strategy**. It basically tells us "buy the market" optimally hedged

---

[11] See Black (1974), Subrahmanyam (1975), Stapleton and Subrahmanyam (1977), Stulz (1981), Errunza and Losq (1985, 1989), Eun and Janakiramanan (1986), and Hietla (1989).

against currency risk. The conclusion to buy the market is not truly original, but the recommendations in terms of currency hedging are. We will now study the practical implications of this optimal hedging conclusion and then turn to potential usage of the international asset pricing relation.

More on Currency Hedging   The ICAPM concludes that everyone should hold the same risky portfolio, with the same amount of currency hedging. Hence, French and U.S. investors should use the same hedge ratio for their Japanese investments.[12]

Black (1989, 1990) uses this result, derived by Solnik (1974), Sercu (1980), and Adler and Dumas (1983), to suggest the existence of a "universal hedging formula" that every investor should use, independent of nationality and fairly easily estimated. Indeed, everyone hedges the world market portfolio with forward currency contracts, in the same way, because everyone holds the same risky portfolio. The aggregate hedge ratio need not be unity, and Black provides a historical estimate around 0.7. Unfortunately, this universal hedging formula gives only the aggregate dollar amount used to hedge as a proportion of the total dollar value of the world market portfolio of equity. Optimal hedge ratios vary across markets and assets. We also know that these individual currency hedge ratios are complex, because they depend on such parameters as the covariance structure of assets and currency, the risk aversion of investors from various countries, and investors' relative wealth. Because individual preferences and relative wealth are not observable, the optimal currency hedging policy cannot be deduced from market-observable data. Holding the market portfolio is a practical passive recommendation because we observe market capitalizations and can derive some proxy for the "market." This is not the case for the optimal passive currency hedging policy. To summarize, the ICAPM does not provide simple, clear-cut, operational conclusions about the optimal currency **hedge ratios**. It is not likely that any reasonable theory could ever produce simple hedging rules.

Equally important, this nice result of a unique aggregate hedge ratio breaks down if, for theoretical or practical purposes, investors do not hold the world market portfolio. For all kinds of reasons, investors tend to underweight foreign assets relative to the world market weights. If a U.S. pension fund puts its 10 percent of foreign assets in a rest-of-the-world index fund, there is no theoretical basis to suggest using the same hedge ratio that should be used if the fund were invested 70 percent in rest-of-the-world assets. Intuitively the risk diversification benefits brought to the U.S. portfolio by the foreign assets are different in the two cases. A foreign currency risk component may actually lower the total risk of a portfolio with only a small investment in foreign assets (say, 5 percent) because it provides some diversification of the U.S. monetary policy risk. For example, Jorion (1989) conducted an empirical study of optimal asset allocations for a U.S. investor. He concluded that the importance of currency hedging depends on the proportion of foreign assets held in the portfolio, and states that "this question of hedging may not matter so much if the amounts invested in the foreign assets are small, in which case overall portfolio volatility is not appreciably influenced by hedging. Hedging therefore brings no particular benefits in terms of risk reduction . . ." (p. 54). The difference between the risk diversification benefits from small versus large foreign allocations should be even more pronounced if the portfolio of foreign assets is actively managed with country weights that differ markedly from the rest-of-the-world market index.

---

[12] It appears that a Japanese investor should also hedge her domestic assets in the same proportion, but hedging yen into yen is totally neutral.

Hence, currency hedging becomes an individual empirical decision—a function of the portfolio to be hedged—and risk preferences matter. Optimal currency hedging requires the estimation of the currency risk exposure of each asset (as we discuss later).

In the absence of simple, widely accepted recommendations for a benchmark, simple hedging policy rules with a fixed hedge ratio are commonly adopted. The international benchmark typically used is either fully hedged or unhedged. But several plan sponsors, especially in Canada, have a 50 percent-hedged benchmark.

Expected Returns　Equation 70-14 describes equilibrium asset pricing in fully efficient global markets. It quantifies the risk premiums for each asset. To use this equation, one needs to estimate two types of variables:

▶ The market and currency exposures of each asset;

▶ The risk premiums on the (global) market and on currencies.

Estimating a market risk premium is a usual task in asset management. Everyone would agree that it should be positive over the long run. Historical estimates give us an order of magnitude for the future that can be refined by some conceptual forward-looking reasoning.

The task is more difficult for foreign currency risk premiums, which could be positive or negative and unstable over time. For example, a positive foreign currency risk premium on the dollar against the euro implies a negative foreign currency risk premium for the euro against the dollar. Furthermore, the demand for currency hedging is likely to change over time, affecting the risk premiums. For example, individuals and corporations of one country could progressively become large international investors, or conversely reduce their holdings in another country because of political risk or other considerations. These developments would change the magnitude and even the signs of foreign currency risk premiums. Although investors can formulate expectations about currencies over short horizons (say a year), it is harder to do so over the very long run. Hence, asset managers often assume that the risk premiums of all currencies are zero over the very long run, and use equilibrium pricing relations that only include a market risk premium. A zero long-term foreign currency risk premium assumes that the best predictor of exchange rates is the interest rate differential.[13] This leads to a linear relation between the expected return on assets and the market exposure (β), the *global market line.*

Applications of the ICAPM depend on the **investment horizon**. An assessment of the *long-term* risk premiums according to the ICAPM is usually only undertaken for asset classes or national markets, not for individual securities, because securities within the same asset class tend to be priced relative to each other and richer risk models are developed for each asset class. The ICAPM is used to anchor expected returns as default values.

An investor who believes that markets are not fully efficient could deviate from the global market line. An illustration of this is Exhibit 1 where GIM (Global Investable Market) stands for the world market portfolio of all investable assets. (In the exhibit, risk premium is the expected return in excess of the risk-free return.) Deviations can be explained by several factors:

---

[13] It is also consistent with an assumption that exchange rates revert to fundamentals in the long run and that foreign currency risk is much smaller in the long run than in the short run, thereby justifying no risk premium.

| EXHIBIT 1 | Example of Relation between Beta and Risk Premiums of Various Asset Classes |

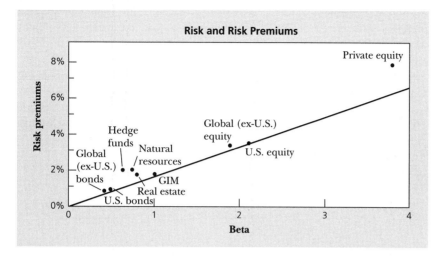

Source: B. Singer, R. Staub, and K. Terhaar, "Asset Allocation: The Alternatives Approach," *Quarterly Focus.* UBS Asset Management, June 30, 2001.

▶ The corresponding market or asset class could be felt to be undervalued.

▶ Its lack of liquidity could justify an additional risk premium.

▶ Foreign currency risk premiums could be added that translate into a deviation from the global market line.

The determination of the risk premiums will drive the strategic global asset allocation. In the shorter run, the portfolio composition could be revised to reflect changes in the risk premiums and the risk coefficients. This is often called a *tactical revision* or **tactical asset allocation**. In tactical asset allocation, a good appreciation of the risk elements becomes quite important.

Estimating Currency Exposures

The relation between asset returns and exchange rate movements is central to international asset pricing. To benefit from the insights of the ICAPM and knowledge of exchange rate determination, it now seems appropriate to investigate the link between security prices and exchange rates, in theory and in practice. We need to understand what determines the currency exposures of securities, the γ's of Equation 70-14. From a practical standpoint, any investor should be concerned about the reaction of the domestic capital market to international monetary disturbances, such as exchange rate movements. The international investor measures total return as the sum of returns on the assets, in local currencies, plus any currency movements: The investor bears both market and foreign currency risks. Setting aside considerations of portfolio diversification, the reaction of asset prices to fluctuations in currency values is a matter of prime concern for international investors. A major question is whether stocks and bonds provide a hedge against exchange rate movements. We want to get a better economic intuition for the sign and magnitude of the currency exposure γ mentioned in Equation 70-14.

Defining Currency Exposure   The currency used to measure the currency exposure of an asset is of great importance. An investor cares about the currency exposure measured in his domestic currency. The *currency exposure* of an asset can be defined as the sensitivity of the asset return, measured in the investor's domestic currency, to a movement in the exchange rate. Just like market β's, currency γ's can be estimated by a regression, namely a time-series regression of domestic currency asset returns on foreign exchange rate movements.

It is also possible to refer to the *local-currency (FC) exposure* of a non-domestic asset, γ^{FC}, which is defined as the sensitivity of the asset return, measured in the asset's local currency (the foreign currency) to a movement in the exchange rate. The relation between the two exposures follows from the relation between DC returns and FC returns given by Equation 70-7:

$$R = R^{FC} + s$$

The currency exposure of the currency itself is equal to 1. So, the currency exposure of a foreign asset is equal to its local-currency exposure plus one:

$$\gamma = \gamma_{FC} + 1 \qquad\qquad \textbf{(70-15)}$$

Perhaps an illustration will contribute to a better understanding of the concept of currency exposure. Consider a U.S. investor holding shares of the Swiss company Novartis, a leading pharmaceutical firm. We shall study various scenarios of the correlation[14] of the price of Novartis stock with the U.S. dollar/Swiss franc exchange rate. Assume a sudden depreciation of the Swiss franc (FC), giving a 1.25 percent loss on the Swiss currency for the U.S. investor (one Swiss franc loses 1.25 percent of its dollar value). The price of Novartis shares may react in different fashions to this exchange rate movement:

▶ A *zero* correlation between local-currency stock returns and exchange rate movements would mean no systematic reaction to exchange rate adjustments. The immediate rate of return on Novartis shares would tend to be zero for Swiss investors (the Swiss franc price of Novartis does not move) and −1.25 percent for U.S. investors because of the currency translation into U.S. dollars: The dollar value of one share of Novartis drops by 1.25 percent. The local-currency exposure of the Swiss franc price of Novartis is zero ($\gamma^{FC} = 0$), and the investor has a currency exposure of $\gamma = 1$: When the Swiss franc loses 1.25 percent, the investor tends to lose the same amount of 1.25 percent on Novartis in domestic (in this case U.S. dollar) currency.

▶ A *negative* correlation would mean that the local stock price benefits from a depreciation of the local currency. In other words, the loss on the Swiss currency would be partly offset by a Swiss franc capital gain on the stock price. A perfect currency hedge would be attained if the Swiss franc price of Novartis moved up 1.25 percent. Then the return to a U.S. investor would be zero, because the final dollar price of Novartis would be unchanged. In that case, the local-currency exposure of the Swiss franc price of Novartis is $\gamma^{FC} = -1$, and the investor has a currency exposure of $\gamma = 0$: When the Swiss franc loses 1.25 percent, the investor tends to have a zero return on Novartis in domestic currency.

---

[14] In this reading, we use the convention that "negative" means a correlation in which the local stock price goes up when the local currency depreciates. Also, in this illustration, we assume that the volatility of the stock's local currency return and the volatility of the exchange rate are equal.

▶ A *positive* correlation would mean that the local stock price drops in reaction to a depreciation of the local currency. With a perfect positive correlation, for example, Novartis might drop by 1.25 percent with news of the franc depreciation (or go up, following a franc appreciation). The dollar return to a U.S. investor would be −2.5 percent. In this case, foreign asset prices would compound the currency effect and might be considered a bad hedge against currency movement. Here, the currency exposure of the Swiss franc price of Novartis is $\gamma^{FC} = 1$, and the investor has a currency exposure of $\gamma = 2$; when the Swiss franc loses 1.25 percent, the investor tends to lose twice that much on Novartis in domestic currency.

The local-currency exposure simply describes the sensitivity of the stock price (measured in local currency) to a change in the value of the local currency. A statistical estimate of the currency exposure can be obtained by a regression between Swiss franc (FC) returns on Novartis and the percentage movements in the \$/SFr exchange rate. If we limit ourselves to one period, the local-currency exposure is simply equal to the return on the Swiss franc price of Novartis during this period divided by percentage movements in the \$/SFr exchange rate:

$$\gamma^{FC} = \frac{R^{FC}}{s}$$

where R^{FC} is the return on the foreign investment in local (foreign) currency and s is the percentage change in the direct exchange rate, $s = (S_1 - S_0)/S_0$.

The currency exposure is equal to

$$y = \frac{R}{s} = \frac{R^{FC} + s}{s} = \gamma^{FC} + 1$$

For example, if the Swiss franc loses 1.25 percent against the dollar (a drop in the dollar value of one Swiss franc, or a negative s) and the Swiss franc price of Novartis goes up by 1.25 percent, the local-currency exposure is $\gamma^{FC} = 1.25/(-1.25) = -1$. In this case, the currency exposure is $\gamma = 0$. If the stock price only goes up by 0.625 percent, the local-currency exposure is $\gamma^{FC} = 0.625/(-1.25) = -0.5$. Hence, the currency exposure is $\gamma = 0.5$.

We now discuss what causes the local-currency exposure to be positive or negative.

Currency Exposure of Individual Companies   To the extent that purchasing power parity holds—that is, if exchange rates exactly adjust to inflation differentials—exchange rate movements simply mirror relative inflation and do not add another dimension to the analysis. They have no specific influence on the economy or equity prices beyond that of domestic inflation. But virtually all studies indicate that purchasing power parity does not hold, especially since the advent of floating exchange rates. Short-term shocks to the exchange rate, and hence foreign exchange rate volatility, cannot be explained by an existing inflation differential. This means that real exchange rate movements (deviations from purchasing power parity) are the relevant variable to study, and the actual effect of real exchange rate movements is large compared with inflation-induced variations. As such, real currency movements may have a significant influence on domestic economies and corporations, and hence, on stock markets.

It might be useful to look at an *individual firm* to examine the influence of a *real exchange appreciation*. Consider a strong real appreciation of the U.S. dollar relative to all currencies, including the Swiss franc, as was the case from 1984 to 1985. Typically, a U.S. tourist had great incentive to spend a skiing vacation in the Swiss Alps, because the dollar purchased much more in terms of accommodations and food. Conversely, Novartis drugs manufactured in Switzerland became highly price-competitive when exported to the United States. The 50 percent *real* appreciation of the U.S. dollar in the early 1980s meant that Novartis could lower its U.S. selling price without reducing its Swiss franc profit margin. The story is only partially true, because the real dollar appreciation raises the cost of some imported goods.

The effect of this real dollar appreciation is the opposite for Merck & Co., an American pharmaceutical company; it gives them incentives for establishing plants in countries such as Switzerland, where they can benefit from lower production costs. Note, however, that the importance of the exchange rate for an individual firm depends on the currency structure of its exports, imports, and financing. For example, a French firm importing U.S. computers financed in U.S. dollars is badly hurt by the real dollar appreciation. An interesting analysis of the influence of a currency movement on the value of the firm is provided in Heckman (1985, 1986).

Another argument that would suggest that the local stock market should react favorably to a depreciation of its currency is based on the rapid internationalization of many corporations. Many corporations are now heavy foreign investors. They have operations abroad and directly own foreign companies. As such, these firms should be valued as global portfolios. For example, Novartis derives over 95 percent of its revenue outside of Switzerland. A Swiss franc depreciation should not greatly influence the "real" value of Novartis. If the Swiss franc depreciates, the Swiss franc price of Novartis should increase. Novartis can be seen as a diversified portfolio of assets in foreign currencies. As those currencies appreciate against the franc, the foreign assets should be worth more Swiss francs.

Currency exposures of individual companies could be estimated historically by regressing the company's stock returns on market returns and currency returns.[15] This estimate can be refined by a detailed analysis of the activities and financing of the company, the geographical distribution of its sales and investments, the currency origin of its profits and costs, the currency structure of its debt, and so on.

EXAMPLE 7

Individual Company Risk Exposure

Two Canadian firms are in quite different businesses:

▶ *Enga* manufactures engine parts in Canada for export, and prices are set and paid in U.S. dollars. Production costs are mostly domestic (the labor force) and considered to follow the Canadian inflation rate.

▶ *Klub* imports computers from the United States and sells them in Canada to compete with Canadian products.

The market values both at a **price–earnings ratio** of 10, so that the stock price in Canadian currency is equal to 10 times next year's expected earnings. What will happen to the earnings and valuations of the two companies if there is a sudden *real* depreciation of the Canadian dollar?

---

[15] See Diermeier and Solnik (2001).

What is likely to happen in the long-run? Would your findings be the same if the Canadian dollar depreciation only matched the Canadian–U.S. inflation differential?

Solution: Enga's earnings and stock price, measured in Canadian dollars, should increase because its revenues come from the United States and are worth more in Canadian dollars at the same time that its costs are in Canadian dollars. Enga's revenues in real terms are rising, while its costs are not. Klub faces the opposite situation. Its costs in real terms are rising, while its revenues are not. In the long run, Enga will meet competition from U.S. competitors who will be motivated to build plants in Canada. Klub will be motivated to find Canadian sources for its computers. If the Canadian dollar depreciation only matched the Canadian–U.S. interest rate differential, then the findings would be different. The effects would only be nominal and not real. Real revenues and costs would remain the same.

EXAMPLE 8

Oil and Mining Risk Exposure

In 2001, the South African rand depreciated. South African oil and mining companies sell in dollars but have costs in rand. According to these currency sensitivity factors and given that this was a real depreciation, what should have happened to South African oil and mining company revenues and valuations as a result?

Solution: According to an *Economist* (May 18, 2002, p. 71) article about the Johannesburg Stock Exchange, "for the past few months the local index has roared. The rand's slump last year helped exporters, and gave a shine to oil and mining companies, which sell in dollars but have costs in rand."

Currency Exposure of National Economies and Equity Markets   In the *macroeconomic* approach, it is widely recognized that economic activity is a major determinant of stock market returns, so the influence of exchange rate movements on domestic economic activity may explain the relation between exchange rate movements and stock returns. Various economic theories have been proposed to explain the influence of real exchange rate movements on domestic economies. The traditional approach can be sketched as follows: A decline in a currency's real exchange rate tends to improve competitiveness, whereas the concomitant deterioration in terms of trade increases the cost of imports, which creates additional domestic inflation and reduces real income and, hence, domestic demand and production. The initial reduction in real gross national product (GNP) caused by a deterioration in the terms of trade should eventually be offset by improved international competitiveness and export demand until purchasing power parity is restored.

EXHIBIT 2	The J-Curve Effect

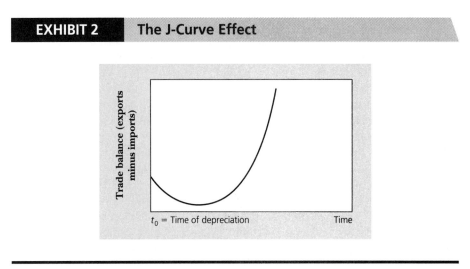

A simple example may help to illustrate this phenomenon. Let's assume a sudden 10 percent depreciation of the Swiss franc. Let's also assume that the Swiss trade balance (Swiss exports minus imports) is in deficit. The immediate effect of a 10 percent depreciation of the franc is to make current imports more expensive in terms of francs—if all imports were denominated in foreign currency, the cost of imports would immediately increase by 10 percent. This increase in cost has two major effects. First, the Swiss trade balance deficit measured in francs widens. Although the franc value of exports increases somewhat because part of the export sales are contracted in foreign currency, the percentage of exports denominated in foreign currency is usually smaller than that of imports. Second, the rise in imported goods prices leads to an increase in the domestic price index and imports inflation. Both of these effects are bad for the Swiss economy, and, in a sense, the real wealth is reduced. However, this currency depreciation makes Swiss firms more competitive; they can lower the price of their products by 10 percent in terms of foreign currency without lowering their Swiss franc income. In the long run, this should help increase foreign sales and stimulate the Swiss economy. The reaction of the deficit to the depreciation is often called the J-curve effect because of the J-shape of the trade balance curve as a function of time (Exhibit 2). However, if the economy is slow to improve, this chain of events threatens to become a vicious cycle: The immediate economic activity and trade balance worsens, leading to a further currency depreciation, which in turn may worsen domestic economic conditions, and so on.

The stock market, which immediately discounts the overall influence of an exchange rate movement on the economy, may be positively or negatively affected, depending on whether the short-term or long-term effect dominates. In late 1985, the U.S. dollar was at its highest point, well above its purchasing power parity value. The Group of Five, leading industrialized nations (United States, Japan, United Kingdom, Germany, and France), met at the Plaza Hotel in New York and made the surprising announcement that they would coordinate their intervention policies to lower the value of the dollar on the foreign exchange market. The reaction to this news was immediate; the dollar fell by 5 percent, and the U.S. stock market rose by more than 1 percent, anticipating that the dollar depreciation would have an overall positive effect on the U.S. economy. In many cases, however, a currency depreciation is not followed by this type of stock market reaction.

A money-demand model has also been proposed.[16] In this model, real growth in the domestic economy leads to increased demand for the domestic currency through a traditional money-demand equation. This increase in currency demand induces a rise in the relative value of the domestic currency. Because domestic stock prices are strongly influenced by real growth, this model justifies a positive association between real stock returns and domestic currency appreciation. Although the traditional trade approach suggests that a real exchange rate appreciation tends to reduce the competitiveness of the domestic economy and, therefore, to reduce domestic activity, the money-demand approach leads to the opposite effect: An increase in domestic economic growth leads to a real currency appreciation.

Finally, it is important to stress that the situation of emerging markets is somewhat different from that of developed countries. The economies of emerging countries are usually not very diversified. They rely heavily on foreign investment. A drop in the value of an emerging country's currency is often a signal that the country is running into severe problems. The fate of the currency and of the stock markets is closely linked to the country's economic and political situation. Their correlation is strongly positive. Hence, foreign investors are doubly affected by a drop in the value of the emerging currency: Investors lose not only in the currency translation to their domestic currency, but also in the drop in the local currency value of the emerging stock market.

Currency Exposure of Bonds   Because bond prices are directly linked to long-term interest rates, the story for bonds is told by the relation between changes in long-term interest rates and exchange rates. Bond returns are negative when bond yields rise.

There are at least two competing theories about the correlation between bond returns and currency movements:

▶ It is often stated that a rise in the national real interest rate leads to the appreciation of the home currency, because of international investment flows attracted by the higher real interest rate. This would induce a negative local-currency exposure for bonds (bond prices go down, because of the rise in yields, when the local currency goes up, and vice versa). However, it is important to be careful in differentiating between an interest rate movement caused by a rise in the real rate of interest, as mentioned, and an interest rate movement caused by changes in inflationary expectations (the Fisher effect). Increased inflationary fears in a foreign country could lead to a simultaneous rise in local interest rates (hence, a drop in bond prices) and a drop in the currency. So, investors from abroad will lose doubly.

▶ Some governments adopt monetary policies that contain foreign exchange rate targets. They attempt to stabilize their home currency's exchange rate. A fall in the domestic currency induces the monetary authorities to raise real interest rates to defend the currency, and a strong domestic currency induces the authorities to ease the interest rate policy. Branson (1984) calls this exchange rate policy reaction a "leaning-against-the-wind" policy, whereby foreign monetary authorities use interest rates to stabilize the exchange rate of their home currency. This policy would induce a positive local-currency exposure for domestic bonds.

Economic versus Accounting Currency Exposure   This reading focuses on economic exposure—the impact of a currency movement on the total return on a

---

[16] See, for example, Lucas (1982).

foreign investment. Accounting-wise investors often separate the return in local currency and the return on the currency itself. For example, most portfolio accounting systems first value an asset in its local currency and then translate it at the proper exchange rate. So, the local-currency asset return and the currency return will appear as two distinct elements. From an accounting standpoint, currency risk will only be measured by looking at the currency return. For example, consider a U.S. investor holding a foreign stock with little dollar currency exposure, so that the local-currency price tends to offset any depreciation of the foreign currency ($\gamma = 0$). From an economic standpoint, there is little foreign currency exposure: If the foreign currency depreciates by 10 percent, the local-currency stock price will rise by 10 percent, offsetting the depreciation. But from an accounting standpoint, the two returns are treated separately so that a 10 percent currency loss will be reported. If an investor only focuses on this accounting or translation measure of currency risk, then all foreign assets are fully exposed to currency risk.

Tests of the ICAPM

A brief look at investors' portfolio holdings would suggest that a major conclusion of the ICAPM is violated often. Portfolios are strongly biased toward domestic investments. U.S. investors devote almost all of their equity portfolios to U.S. securities, although the theory would have them hold the world market portfolio. French and Poterba (1991), Cooper and Kaplanis (1994), and Tesar and Werner (1995) present evidence of a home preference in portfolio investment and fail to find satisfactory explanations for such a large bias. This does not mean that financial markets are necessarily segmented and that the theory does not provide useful and robust implications regarding the pricing of securities. International capital flows, which are indeed large, could be sufficient to make the markets efficient. The international capital market would be integrated if all securities followed the same international risk-pricing relation outlined here.

Few tests of international market integration and asset pricing models have been performed so far. One problem has been the limited amount of long-term historical data available on international capital markets. Other problems are methodological and affect the testing of any CAPM, whether domestic or international. They have to do with the difficulty of exactly identifying the market portfolio and with the time-varying nature of the expected return and risk measures. The major problem is that any CAPM deals with expected returns, and those are simply not observable. Using past realized returns to proxy expected returns can be very misleading.

A test of the ICAPM investigates whether cross-sectional differences in expected returns among securities are explained by the various risk exposures, β and γ's, as described in Equation 70-14. Empirical researchers have explored several questions:

▶ Is currency risk priced?
▶ Is domestic market risk priced beyond global market risk (segmentation)?
▶ Are other firms' attributes priced beyond global market risk?

Is Currency Risk Priced? In *unconditional* tests, researchers assume that expected returns and risk measures are constant over time. This approach will not be detailed here. In *conditional* tests, expected returns and risk measures are allowed to vary in some specified way. Dumas and Solnik (1995) modeled the time variation in expected return and risk. They found that significant currency risk premiums exist, and they rejected a model that would exclude currency risk factors. De Santis and Gérard (1998) found strong support for a specification of the ICAPM that includes both market risk and currency risk. They stress the importance of a conditional approach allowing variation in market and currency risk premiums. In terms of asset management, this conclusion would encourage tactical revisions in the global asset allocation.

Segmentation   Other researchers focus on market segmentation, but exclude currency risk from their analysis. The approach is to test an alternative model, including both global risk factors and country-specific factors. If the ICAPM holds, those country-specific factors should not be priced. Bekaert and Harvey (1995) allowed conditionally expected returns in any country to be affected by their exposure to the world market portfolio (beta) *and* by the variance of the country's returns. In a perfectly integrated market, only the beta counts. In segmented markets, the country's variance is a more relevant measure of risk. Bekaert and Harvey looked at emerging markets and allowed the degree of market integration to change over time. They found evidence that many emerging markets were segmented in their early years but have become more integrated to the global market. However, several markets show signs of segmentation, which is not too surprising for most of the emerging markets. De Santis and Gérard (1997) focused on the major equity markets and introduced as country-specific factors the country's variance plus a constant to accommodate other forms of segmentation, such as differences in taxation. They concluded: "To summarize, we find that expected excess returns are positively related to their conditional covariance with a world-wide portfolio, whereas country specific risk is not priced" (p. 1901). These studies, however, suffer from the deficiency that currency factors are not introduced in the test.

Other Attributes   In a domestic or international CAPM, attributes of a firm that are not linked to the risk factors outlined here should not be priced. In a domestic framework, Fama and French (1992, 1996) find that some attributes of a firm provide a much better explanation of the differences in return among U.S. firms than their beta. For example, "value" stocks (as measured by ratios such as book-to-market value or earnings-to-price) outperform "growth" stocks. This leads to a rejection of the CAPM. Numerous criticisms have been leveled at this conclusion (see Kothari, Shanken, and Sloan, 1995). Fama and French (1998) extend their analysis to international data. They find that value stocks outperform growth stocks in 12 out of 13 major markets. Value stocks are more likely to go bankrupt than are growth stocks, and they interpret their results in terms of financial distress. They claim that financial distress is a risk that is not well captured by the standard ICAPM, and that it should be added as a factor to explain stock pricing. On the other hand, Ferson and Harvey (1998) find that the book-to-market value ratio of a firm is strongly related to its world market risk exposure. A fruitful direction of research is to refine the analysis of risk by looking at the underlying economic risk factors, rather than by summarizing all the risk information in a single beta.

Current empirical evidence is still fragmentary, and the results are likely to evolve as the world financial markets are increasingly liberalized and transaction costs are driven down. A summary of current research tends to support the conclusion that assets are priced in an integrated global financial market. The evidence is sufficiently strong to justify using the ICAPM as an anchor in structuring global portfolios. However, the evidence can be somewhat different for emerging and smaller markets, in which constraints are still serious.

SUMMARY

▶ International markets are integrated if they are efficient in the sense that securities with the same risk characteristics have the same expected return wherever in the world they are traded.

▶ International markets are segmented if they are inefficient in the sense that securities with the same risk characteristics sell at different exchange-rate-adjusted prices in different countries, thus violating the law of one price.

▶ Six impediments to international capital mobility are psychological barriers, legal restrictions, transaction costs, discriminatory taxation, political risks, and foreign exchange risks.

▶ International integration requires only a sufficient flow of capital to make the world market efficient and to eliminate relative mispricing among countries. Investment and borrowing actions of private and institutional investors, major corporations, and governments quickly take advantage of relative mispricing, thereby making the markets more efficient.

▶ The expected return on an unhedged foreign investment is

$$E(R) = E(R^{FC}) + E(s)$$

where $E(R)$ is the expected domestic-currency return on the investment, $E(R^{FC})$ is the expected foreign investment return, and $E(s)$ is the expected percentage currency movement.

▶ The expected return on a hedged foreign investment is

$$E(R) = E(R^{FC}) + (F - S)/S$$

where $E(R)$ is the expected domestic-currency return on the hedged investment, $E(R^{FC})$ is the expected foreign investment return, F is the forward rate, and S is the spot exchange rate. Both F and S are direct quotes.

▶ The extended CAPM is the domestic CAPM with the domestic rate for the risk-free rate and the market capitalization weighted portfolio of all risky assets in the world for the market portfolio.

▶ The domestic CAPM extension can be justified only with the usual domestic CAPM assumptions and the addition of two assumptions: Investors throughout the world have identical consumption baskets, and real prices of consumption goods are identical in every country (purchasing power parity holds exactly at any point in time).

▶ With direct rates, the real exchange rate is the nominal exchange rate times the ratio of the foreign price level to the domestic price level: $X = S \times (P_{FC}/P_{DC})$.

▶ The real exchange rate changes in a period if the foreign exchange appreciation during the period does not equal the inflation differential between the two countries during the period.

▶ The expected foreign currency appreciation or depreciation should be approximately equal to the interest rate differential: $E(s) = r_{DC} - r_{FC}$, where s is the percentage change in the price of foreign currency (direct exchange rate).

▶ A foreign currency risk premium (SRP) is equal to the expected movement in the exchange rate *minus* the interest rate differential (domestic risk-free rate minus foreign risk-free rate): $SRP = E[(S_1 - S_0)/S_0] - (r_{DC} - r_{FC})$.

▶ A foreign currency risk premium is equal to the difference between the expected exchange rate and the forward rate, in percentage of the current exchange rate: $SRP = [E(S_1) - F]/S_0$.

▶ The risk-pricing expression for the international CAPM (ICAPM) is that the expected return on an asset i is the sum of the market risk premium plus various currency risk premiums:

$$E(R_i) = R_0 + \beta_{iw} \times RP_w + \gamma_{i1} \times SRP_1 + \gamma_{i2} \times SRP_2 + \ldots + \gamma_{ik} \times SRP_k$$

where β is the world market exposure of the asset and the γ's are the currency exposures, sensitivities of the asset returns to the various exchange rates.

▶ With one foreign currency, for example, the asset pricing equation of the ICAPM simplifies to

$$E(R_i) = R_0 + \beta_{iw} \times RP_w + \gamma_i \times SRP_{FC}$$

▶ The international asset pricing relation applies to all securities only in an integrated world capital market with currency hedging available.

▶ Most forms of market imperfections and constraints to foreign investments cannot be easily incorporated in an equilibrium asset pricing framework.

▶ A local-currency exposure is the sensitivity of a stock price (measured in local currency) to a change in the value of the local currency. A zero correlation between stock returns and exchange rate movements would mean no systematic reaction to exchange rate adjustments. A negative correlation would mean that the local stock price would benefit from a depreciation of the local currency. A positive correlation would mean that the local stock price would drop in reaction to a depreciation of the local currency.

▶ For an investor, the currency exposure of a foreign investment is the sensitivity of the stock price (measured in the investor's domestic currency) to a change in the value of the foreign currency. It is equal to one plus the local-currency exposure of the asset.

▶ The exchange rate exposure for an individual firm depends on the currency structure of its exports, imports, and financing. Generally, for example, an importer is hurt by foreign currency appreciation and an exporter helped. If exchange rate movements only reflect inflation rate differentials, they have no specific influence on the economy or equity prices beyond that of domestic inflation. Real exchange rate movements, however, have an effect on equity prices, depending on currency exposures.

▶ In the macroeconomic approach, it is widely recognized that economic activity is a major determinant of stock market returns, so the influence of exchange rate movements on domestic economic activity may explain the relation between exchange rate movements and stock returns. On the bond side, a rise in the national real interest rate leads to an appreciation of the domestic currency, because of international investment flows attracted by the higher real interest rate. Domestic bond price declines would accompany domestic currency appreciation.

▶ The two models of how real exchange rate changes affect domestic economic activity give opposite conclusions. The traditional approach can be sketched as follows: A decline in a currency's real exchange rate tends to improve competitiveness, whereas the concomitant deterioration in terms of trade increases the cost of imports, which creates additional domestic inflation and reduces **real income** and, hence, domestic demand and production. The initial reduction in real GNP caused by a deterioration in the terms of trade should eventually be offset by improved international competitiveness and export demand until purchasing power parity is restored. In the money-demand model, on the other hand, real growth in the domestic economy leads to increased demand for the domestic currency through a traditional money-demand equation. This increase in currency demand induces a rise in the relative value of the domestic currency. Because domestic stock prices are strongly influenced by real growth, this model justifies a positive association between real stock returns and domestic currency appreciation.

PRACTICE PROBLEMS FOR READING 70

1. Consider an asset that has a beta of 1.25. If the risk-free rate is 3.25 percent and the market risk premium is 5.5 percent, calculate the expected return on the asset.

2. An asset has a beta of 0.9. The variance of returns on a market index, σ_m^2, is 90. If the variance of returns for the asset is 120, what proportion of the asset's total risk is systematic, and what proportion is residual risk?

3. A portfolio consists of three assets. Asset 1 has a beta of 0.85, Asset 2 has a beta of 1.3, and Asset 3 has a beta of 0.9. Asset 1 has an allocation of 50 percent, while Assets 2 and 3 each have an allocation of 25 percent. The variance of returns on a market index, σ_m^2, is 120. Calculate the variance of portfolio returns, assuming that the specific risk of the portfolio is negligible.

4. A Canadian investor is considering the purchase of U.K. securities. The current exchange rate is Can$1.46 per pound. Assume that the price level of a typical consumption basket in Canada is 1.46 times the price level of a typical consumption basket in the United Kingdom.

   A. Calculate the real exchange rate.

   B. One year later, price levels in Canada have risen 2 percent, while price levels in the United Kingdom have risen 4 percent. The new exchange rate is Can$1.4308 per pound. What is the new real exchange rate?

   C. Did the Canadian investor experience a change in the real exchange rate?

5. Consider a U.S. investor who wishes to purchase U.K. securities. The current exchange rate is $1.80 per pound. Assume that the price level of a typical consumption basket in the United States is three times the price level of a typical consumption basket in the United Kingdom.

   A. Calculate the real exchange rate.

   B. One year later, price levels in the United States have risen 5 percent, while price levels in the United Kingdom have risen 2 percent. The new exchange rate is $1.854 per pound. What is the new real exchange rate?

   C. Did the U.S. investor experience a change in the real exchange rate?

6. An investor based in the United States wishes to invest in Swiss bonds with a maturity of one year. Suppose that the ratio of the price levels of a typical consumption basket in the United States versus Switzerland is 1 to 1.5 and the current exchange rate is $0.62 per Swiss franc. The one-year interest rate is 2 percent in the United States and 4.5 percent in Switzerland. Assume that inflation rates are fully predictable, and expected inflation over the next year is 1.5 percent in the United States and 4 percent in Switzerland.

   A. Assuming that real exchange rates remain constant, calculate the real exchange rate, the expected exchange rate in one year, and the expected return over one year on the Swiss bond in U.S. dollar terms.

   B. Now assume that the inflation rate over the one-year period has been 1.5 percent in the United States and 4 percent in Switzerland. Further, assume that the exchange rate at the end of one year is $0.63 per Swiss franc. Calculate the real exchange rate at the end of one year. What is the return on the Swiss bond investment now? Is the return on the Swiss bond the same as in Part (a)? Explain.

7. A portfolio manager based in the United Kingdom is planning to invest in U.S. bonds with a maturity of one year. Assume that the ratio of the price levels of a typical consumption basket in the United Kingdom versus the

United States is 1.2 to 1. The current exchange rate is £0.69 per dollar. The one-year interest rate is 1.76 percent in the United States and 4.13 percent in the United Kingdom. Assume that inflation rates are fully predictable, and expected inflation over the next year is 1.5 percent in the United States and 3.75 percent in the United Kingdom.

A. Assuming that real exchange rates remain constant, calculate the real exchange rate, the expected exchange rate in one year, and the expected return over one year on the U.S. bonds in pounds.

B. Now assume that the inflation rate over the one-year period has been 1.5 percent in the United States and 3.75 percent in the United Kingdom. Further, assume that the exchange rate at the end of one year is £0.67 per dollar. Calculate the real exchange rate at the end of one year. What is the return on the U.S. bond investment now? Is the return on the U.S. bond the same as in Part A? Explain.

8. Assume that the Eurozone risk-free interest rate on bonds with one year to maturity is 4.78 percent and the U.S. risk-free interest rate on one-year bonds is 3.15 percent. The current exchange rate is $0.90 per euro. Assume that the United States is the domestic country.

A. Calculate the one-year forward exchange rate.

B. Is the euro trading at forward premium or discount?

C. Is your answer to Part (b) consistent with interest rate parity? Explain.

9. Take the case of a U.S. firm that wishes to invest some funds (U.S. dollars) for a period of one year. The choice is between investing in a U.S. bond with one year to maturity, paying an interest rate of 2.75 percent, and a U.K. bond with one year to maturity, paying an interest rate of 4.25 percent. The current exchange rate is $1.46 per pound, and the one-year forward exchange rate is $1.25 per pound. Should the U.S. firm invest in U.S. bonds or in U.K. bonds?

10. Consider a German firm that wishes to invest euro funds for a period of one year. The firm has a choice of investing in a euro bond with one year to maturity, paying an interest rate of 3.35 percent, and a U.S. dollar bond with one year to maturity, paying an interest rate of 2.25 percent. The current exchange rate is €1.12 per U.S. dollar, and the one-year forward exchange rate is €1.25 per U.S dollar. Should the German firm invest in euro bonds or in U.S. dollar bonds?

11. The interest rate on one-year risk-free bonds is 4.25 percent in the United States and 3.75 percent in Switzerland. The current exchange rate is $0.65 per Swiss franc. Suppose that you are a U.S. investor and you expect the Swiss franc to appreciate by 2.75 percent over the next year.

A. Calculate the foreign currency risk premium.

B. Calculate the domestic currency return on the foreign bond, assuming that your currency appreciation expectations are met.

12. Suppose that you are an investor based in Switzerland, and you expect the U.S. dollar to depreciate by 2.75 percent over the next year. The interest rate on one-year risk-free bonds is 5.25 percent in the United States and 2.75 percent in Switzerland. The current exchange rate is SFr1.62 per U.S. dollar.

A. Calculate the foreign currency risk premium from the Swiss investor's viewpoint.

B. Calculate the return on the U.S bond from the Swiss investor's viewpoint, assuming that the Swiss investor's expectations are met.

13. Assume you are a U.S. investor who is considering investments in the French (Stocks A and B) and Swiss (Stocks C and D) stock markets. The world market risk premium is 6 percent. The currency risk premium on the Swiss franc is 1.25 percent, and the currency risk premium on the euro is 2 percent. The interest rate on one-year risk-free bonds is 3.75 percent in the United States. In addition, you are provided with the following information:

Stock	A	B	C	D
Country	France	France	Switzerland	Switzerland
β_w	1	0.90	1	1.5
γ_ϵ	1	0.80	-0.25	-1.0
γ_{SFr}	-0.25	0.75	1.0	-0.5

    A. Calculate the expected return for each of the stocks. The U.S. dollar is the base currency.

    B. Explain the differences in the expected returns of the four stocks in terms of β_w, γ_ϵ, and γ_{SFr}.

14. A. List reasons that an international extension of the CAPM is problematic.

    B. In an international extension of the CAPM, why would the optimal portfolio differ from the world market portfolio, as suggested by the traditional CAPM, even if the markets are fully efficient?

15. You are a U.S. investor who is considering investments in the Australian stock market, but you worry about currency risk. You run a regression of the returns on the Australian stock index (in A\$) on movements in the Australian dollar exchange rate (U.S.\$ per A\$), and find a slope of -0.5.

    A. What is your currency exposure if you invest in a diversified portfolio of Australian stocks?

    B. You invest 10 million U.S. dollars in the diversified portfolio, but fear that the Australian dollar will depreciate by 10 percent relative to the U.S. dollar. How much do you expect to lose because of the currency movement?

16. Consider two French firms listed on the Paris stock market:

    ▶ *Mega* manufactures engine parts in France for export, and the prices are set and paid in dollars. Production costs are mostly domestic (the labor force) and considered to follow the French inflation rate.

    ▶ *Club* imports computers from the United States and sells them in France to compete with French products.

    A. What will happen to the earnings of the two companies in the short run if there is a sudden depreciation of the euro (say, 20 percent)?

    B. What is the difference between the short-run effect and the long-run adjustments?

    C. Would your findings be the same if the euro depreciation were only a progressive adjustment to the United States–Europe inflation differential that reflected the higher European inflation rate?

17. Consider two Australian firms listed on the Sydney stock exchange:

    ▶ *Company I.* Its stock return shows a consistent negative correlation with the euro per A\$ exchange rate. The stock price of Company I (in

Australian dollars) tends to go up when the Australian dollar depreciates relative to the euro.

▶ *Company II.* Its stock return shows a consistent positive correlation with the euro per A$ exchange rate. The stock price of Company II (in Australian dollars) tends to go down when the Australian dollar depreciates relative to the euro.

A European investor wishes to buy Australian stocks but is unsure about whether to invest in Company I or Company II. She is afraid of a depreciation of the Australian dollar. Which of the two investments would offer some protection against a weakening Australian dollar?

18. KoreaCo, a South Korean company, is a worldwide leader in widget (a hypothetical manufactured product) production. Europe is KoreaCo's single largest market.

Assumptions:

▶ KoreaCo's production capacity is located in South Korea and all of its costs are incurred in Korean won.

▶ Additions to capacity require a lead time of more than one year.

▶ KoreaCo borrows only in South Korean won.

A. Describe the effect of a short-term appreciation of the won versus the euro on the profitability of KoreaCo's sales in Europe. Address *only* the effects on KoreaCo unit sales and profit margins.

B. KoreaCo expects the appreciation of the won versus the euro to continue for the long term and is considering two business strategies:

▶ Continue to operate production plants solely in South Korea.

▶ Shift production equal to current European sales to Europe. Explain the effect of each of these strategies on the long-run profitability of KoreaCo's European sales.

19. In 2002, a strong depreciation of the U.S. dollar is expected by some observers over the next two years. Are nondollar bonds a good investment for U.S. investors? Why or why not?

20. As a money manager based in the Netherlands, you are asked to advise a domestic client about investing in foreign bonds to diversify domestic inflation risk. You fear that the strong economic recovery observed in the Netherlands and elsewhere in the Eurozone—but not yet in the Far East and North America—will feed inflationary expectations in Europe. Try to build a "marketing" case for international bond diversification.

THE THEORY OF ACTIVE PORTFOLIO MANAGEMENT

by Zvi Bodie, Alex Kane, and Alan J. Marcus

LEARNING OUTCOMES

The candidate should be able to:

a. justify the need for a theory of active portfolio management;

b. discuss the steps and the approach of the Treynor-Black model for security selection;

c. describe how an analyst's accuracy in forecasting alphas can be measured and how estimates of forecasting can be incorporated into the Treynor-Black approach.

THE LURE OF ACTIVE MANAGEMENT   1

How can a theory of active portfolio management be reconciled with the notion that markets are in equilibrium?

Market efficiency prevails when many investors are willing to depart from maximum diversification, or a passive strategy, by adding mispriced securities to their portfolios in the hope of realizing abnormal returns. The competition for such returns ensures that prices will be near their "fair" values. Most managers will not beat the passive strategy on a risk-adjusted basis. However, in the competition for rewards to investing, exceptional managers might beat the average forecasts built into market prices.

There is both economic logic and some empirical evidence to indicate that exceptional portfolio managers can beat the average forecast. Let us discuss economic logic first. We must assume that if no analyst can beat the passive strategy, investors will be smart enough to divert their funds from strategies entailing expensive analysis to less expensive passive strategies. In that case funds under active management will dry up, and prices will no longer reflect sophisticated forecasts. The consequent profit opportunities will lure back active managers who once again will become successful.[1] Of course, the critical assumption is that investors allocate management funds wisely. Direct evidence on that has yet to be produced.

> **Note:**
> Candidates are not responsible, within Reading 71, for deriving or memorizing the formulas introduced in Sections 4–6.

---

[1] This point is worked out fully in Danford J. Grossman and Joseph E. Stiglitz, "On the Impossibility of Informationally Efficient Markets," *American Economic Review* 70 (June 1980).

As for empirical evidence, consider the following: (1) Some portfolio managers have produced streaks of abnormal returns that are hard to label as lucky outcomes; (2) the "noise" in realized rates is enough to prevent us from rejecting outright the hypothesis that some money managers have beaten the passive strategy by a statistically small, yet economically significant, margin; and (3) some anomalies in realized returns have been sufficiently persistent to suggest that portfolio managers who identified them in a timely fashion could have beaten the passive strategy over prolonged periods.

These conclusions persuade us that there is a role for a theory of active portfolio management. Active management has an inevitable lure even if investors agree that security markets are nearly efficient.

Suppose that capital markets are perfectly efficient, that an easily accessible market-index portfolio is available, and that this portfolio is for all practical purposes the efficient risky portfolio. Clearly, in this case security selection would be a futile endeavor. You would be better off with a passive strategy of allocating funds to a money market fund (the safe asset) and the market-index portfolio. Under these simplifying assumptions the optimal investment strategy seems to require no effort or know-how.

Such a conclusion, however, is too hasty. Recall that the proper allocation of investment funds to the risk-free and risky portfolios requires some analysis because y, the fraction to be invested in the risky market portfolio, M, is given by

$$y = \frac{E(r_M) - r_f}{.01A\sigma_M^2}$$

(71-1)

where $E(r_M) - r_f$ is the risk premium on M, σ_M^2 its variance, and A is the investor's coefficient of risk aversion. Any rational allocation therefore requires an estimate of σ_M and $E(r_M)$. Even a passive investor needs to do some forecasting, in other words.

Forecasting $E(r_M)$ and s_M is further complicated by the existence of security classes that are affected by different environmental factors. Long-term bond returns, for example, are driven largely by changes in the term structure of interest rates, whereas equity returns depend on changes in the broader economic environment, including macroeconomic factors beyond interest rates. Once our investor determines relevant forecasts for separate sorts of investments, she might as well use an optimization program to determine the proper mix for the portfolio. It is easy to see how the investor may be lured away from a purely passive strategy, and we have not even considered temptations such as international stock and bond portfolios or sector portfolios.

In fact, even the definition of a "purely passive strategy" is problematic, because simple strategies involving only the market-index portfolio and risk-free assets now seem to call for **market analysis**. For our purposes we define purely passive strategies as those that use only index funds and weight those funds by fixed proportions that do not vary in response to perceived market conditions. For example, a portfolio strategy that always places 60% in a stock market–index fund, 30% in a bond-index fund, and 10% in a money market fund is a purely passive strategy.

More important, the lure into active management may be extremely strong because the potential profit from active strategies is enormous. At the same time, competition among the multitude of active managers creates the force driving market prices to near efficiency levels. Although enormous profits may be increasingly difficult to earn, decent profits to the better analysts should be the rule rather than the exception. For prices to remain efficient to some degree, some analysts must be able to eke out a reasonable profit. Absence of profits would decimate the active investment management industry, eventually allowing prices to stray from informationally efficient levels. The theory of managing active portfolios is the concern of this reading.

OBJECTIVES OF ACTIVE PORTFOLIOS   2

What does an investor expect from a professional portfolio manager, and how does this expectation affect the operation of the manager? If the client were risk neutral, that is, indifferent to risk, the answer would be straightforward. The investor would expect the portfolio manager to construct a portfolio with the highest possible expected rate of return. The portfolio manager follows this dictum and is judged by the realized average rate of return.

When the client is risk averse, the answer is more difficult. Without a normative theory of portfolio management, the manager would have to consult each client before making any portfolio decision in order to ascertain that reward (average return) is commensurate with risk. Massive and constant input would be needed from the client-investors, and the economic value of professional management would be questionable.

Fortunately, the theory of mean-variance efficient portfolio management allows us to separate the "product decision," which is how to construct a mean-variance efficient risky portfolio, and the "consumption decision," or the investor's allocation of funds between the efficient risky portfolio and the safe asset. We have seen that construction of the optimal risky portfolio is purely a technical problem, resulting in a single optimal risky portfolio appropriate for all investors. Investors will differ only in how they apportion investment to that risky portfolio and the safe asset.

Another feature of the mean-variance theory that affects portfolio management decisions is the criterion for choosing the optimal risky portfolio. The optimal risky portfolio for any investor is the one that maximizes the reward-to-variability ratio, or the expected excess rate of return (over the risk-free rate) divided by the standard deviation. A manager who uses this Markowitz methodology to construct the optimal risky portfolio will satisfy all clients regardless of risk aversion. Clients, for their part, can evaluate managers using statistical methods to draw inferences from realized rates of return about prospective, or ex ante, **reward-to-variability ratios**.

William Sharpe's assessment of mutual fund performance[2] is the seminal work in the area of portfolio performance evaluation. The reward-to-variability ratio has come to be known as **Sharpe's measure**:

$$S = \frac{E(r_P) - r_f}{\sigma_P}$$

It is now a common criterion for tracking performance of professionally managed portfolios.

Briefly, mean-variance portfolio theory implies that the objective of professional portfolio managers is to maximize the (ex ante) Sharpe measure, which entails maximizing the slope of the CAL (capital allocation line). A "good" manager is one whose CAL is steeper than the CAL representing the passive strategy

---

[2] William F. Sharpe, "Mutual Fund Performance," *Journal of Business, Supplement on Security Prices* 39 (January 1966).

of holding a market-index portfolio. Clients can observe rates of return and compute the realized **Sharpe measure** (the ex post CAL) to evaluate the relative performance of their manager.

Ideally, clients would like to invest their funds with the most able manager, one who consistently obtains the highest Sharpe measure and presumably has real forecasting ability. This is true for all clients regardless of their degree of risk aversion. At the same time, each client must decide what fraction of investment funds to allocate to this manager, placing the remainder in a safe fund. If the manager's Sharpe measure is constant over time (and can be estimated by clients), the investor can compute the optimal fraction to be invested with the manager from Equation 71-1, based on the portfolio long-term average return and variance. The remainder will be invested in a money market fund.

The manager's ex ante Sharpe measure from updated forecasts will be constantly varying. Clients would have liked to increase their allocation to the risky portfolio when the forecasts are optimistic, and vice versa. However, it would be impractical to constantly communicate updated forecasts to clients and for them to constantly revise their allocation between the risky portfolios and risk-free asset.

Allowing managers to shift funds between their optimal risky portfolio and a safe asset according to their forecasts alleviates the problem. Indeed, many stock funds allow the managers reasonable flexibility to do just that.

3   MARKET TIMING

Consider the results of the following two different investment strategies:

1. An investor who put $1,000 in 30-day commercial paper on January 1, 1927, and rolled over all proceeds into 30-day paper (or into 30-day T-bills after they were introduced) would have ended on December 31, 1978, fifty-two years later, with $3,600.

2. An investor who put $1,000 in the NYSE index on January 1, 1927, and reinvested all dividends in that portfolio would have ended on December 31, 1978, with $67,500.

Suppose we defined perfect **market timing** as the ability to tell (with certainty) at the beginning of each month whether the NYSE portfolio will outperform the 30-day paper portfolio. Accordingly, at the beginning of each month, the **market timer** shifts all funds into either cash equivalents (30-day paper) or equities (the NYSE portfolio), whichever is predicted to do better. Beginning with $1,000 on the same date, how would the perfect timer have ended up 52 years later?

This is how Nobel Laureate Robert Merton began a seminar with finance professors 25 years ago. As he collected responses, the boldest guess was a few million dollars. The correct answer: $5.36 *billion*.[3]

CONCEPT CHECK 1

What was the monthly and annual compounded rate of return for the three strategies over the period 1926 to 1978?

---

[3] This demonstration has been extended to recent data with similar results.

These numbers highlight the power of compounding. This effect is particularly important because more and more of the funds under management represent retirement savings. The horizons of such investments may not be as long as 52 years but are measured in decades, making compounding a significant factor.

Another result that may seem surprising at first is the huge difference between the end-of-period value of the all-safe asset strategy ($3,600) and that of the all-equity strategy ($67,500). Why would anyone invest in safe assets given this historical record? If you have internalized the lessons of previous readings, you know the reason: risk. The average rates of return and the standard deviations on the all-bills and all-equity strategies for this period are:

Arithmetic	Mean	Standard Deviation
Bills	2.55	2.10
Equities	10.70	22.14

The significantly higher standard deviation of the rate of return on the equity portfolio is commensurate with its significantly higher average return.

Can we also view the rate-of-return premium on the perfect-timing fund as a risk premium? The answer must be "no," because the perfect timer never does worse than either bills or the market. The extra return is not compensation for the possibility of poor returns but is instead attributable to superior analysis. It is the value of superior information that is reflected in the tremendous end-of-period value of the portfolio.

The monthly rate-of-return statistics for the all-equity portfolio and the timing portfolio are:

Per Month	All Equities (%)	Perfect Timer No Charge (%)	Perfect Timer Fair Charge (%)
Average rate of return	0.85	2.58	0.55
Average excess return over return on safe asset	0.64	2.37	0.34
Standard deviation	5.89	3.82	3.55
Highest return	38.55	38.55	30.14
Lowest return	−29.12	0.06	−7.06
Coefficient of skewness	0.42	4.28	2.84

Ignore for the moment the fourth column ("Perfect Timer—Fair Charge"). The results of rows 1 and 2 are self-explanatory. The third row, standard deviation, requires some discussion. The standard deviation of the monthly rate of return earned by the perfect market timer was 3.82%, far greater than the volatility of T-bill returns over the same period. Does this imply that (perfect) timing is a riskier strategy than investing in bills? No. For this analysis standard deviation is a misleading measure of risk.

To see why, consider how you might choose between two hypothetical strategies: The first offers a sure rate of return of 5%; the second strategy offers an uncertain return that is given by 5% *plus* a **random number** that is zero with probability .5 and 5% with probability .5. The characteristics of each strategy are:

	Strategy 1 (%)	Strategy 2 (%)
Expected return	5	7.5
Standard deviation	0	2.5
Highest return	5	10.0
Lowest return	5	5.0

Clearly, Strategy 2 dominates Strategy 1 because its rate of return is *at least* equal to that of Strategy 1 and sometimes greater. No matter how risk averse you are, you will always prefer Strategy 2, despite its significant standard deviation. Compared to Strategy 1, Strategy 2 provides only "good surprises," so the standard deviation in this case cannot be a measure of risk.

These two strategies are analogous to the case of the perfect timer compared with an all-equity or all-bills strategy. In every period the perfect timer obtains at least as good a return, in some cases a better one. Therefore the timer's standard deviation is a misleading measure of risk compared to an all-equity or all-bills strategy.

Returning to the empirical results, you can see that the highest rate of return is identical for the all-equity and the timing strategies, whereas the lowest rate of return is positive for the perfect timer and disastrous for all the all-equity portfolio. Another reflection of this is seen in the coefficient of skewness, which measures the asymmetry of the distribution of returns. Because the equity portfolio is almost (but not exactly) normally distributed, its coefficient of skewness is very low at .42. In contrast, the perfect timing strategy effectively eliminates the negative tail of the distribution of portfolio returns (the part below the risk-free rate). Its returns are "skewed to the right," and its coefficient of skewness is therefore quite large, 4.28.

Now for the fourth column, "Perfect Timer—Fair Charge," which is perhaps the most interesting. Most assuredly, the perfect timer will charge clients for such a valuable service. (The perfect timer may have otherworldly predictive powers, but saintly benevolence is unlikely.)

Subtracting a fair fee (discussed later) from the monthly rate of return of the timer's portfolio gives us an average rate of return lower than that of the passive, all-equity strategy. However, because the fee is *constructed* to be fair, the two portfolios (the all-equity strategy and the market-timing-with-fee strategy) must be equally attractive after risk adjustment. In this case, again, the standard deviation of the market timing strategy (with fee) is of no help in adjusting for risk because the coefficient of skewness remains high, 2.84. In other words, **mean-variance analysis** is inadequate for valuing market timing. We need an alternative approach.

Valuing Market Timing as an Option

The key to analyzing the pattern of returns to the perfect market timer is to recognize that perfect foresight is equivalent to holding a call option on the equity portfolio. The perfect timer invests 100% in either the safe asset or the equity portfolio, whichever will yield the higher return. This is shown in Figure 1. The rate of return is bounded from below by r_f.

FIGURE 1 Rate of Return of a Perfect Market Timer

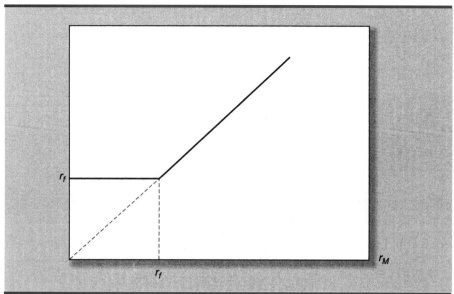

To see the value of information as an option, suppose that the market index currently is at S_0 and that a call option on the index has an exercise price of $X = S_0(1 + r_f)$. If the market outperforms bills over the coming period, S_T will exceed X, whereas it will be less than X otherwise. Now look at the payoff to a portfolio consisting of this option and S_0 dollars invested in bills:

	$S_T < X$	$S_T \geq X$
Bills	$S_0(1 + r_f)$	$S_0(1 + r_f)$
Option	0	$S_T - X$
Total	$S_0(1 + r_f)$	S_T

The portfolio pays the risk-free return when the market is bearish (i.e., the market return is less than the risk-free rate), and it pays the market return when the market is bullish and beats bills. Such a portfolio is a perfect market timer. Consequently, we can measure the value of perfect ability as the value of the call option, because a call enables the investor to earn the market return only when it exceeds r_f. This insight lets Merton[4] value timing ability using the theory of option of valuation, and calculate the fair charge for it.

The Value of Imperfect Forecasting

Unfortunately, managers are not perfect forecasters. It seems pretty obvious that if managers are right most of the time, they are doing very well. However, when we say "most of the time," we cannot mean merely the percentage of the time a manager is right. The weather forecaster in Tucson, Arizona, who *always* predicts no rain, may be right 90% of the time. But a high success rate for a "stopped-clock" strategy clearly is not evidence of forecasting ability.

Similarly, the appropriate measure of market forecasting ability is not the overall proportion of correct forecasts. If the market is up two days out of three and a

---

[4] Robert C. Merton, "On Market Timing and Investment Performance: An Equilibrium Theory of Value for Market Forecasts," *Journal of Business*, July 1981.

forecaster always predicts market advance, the two-thirds success rate is not a measure of forecasting ability. We need to examine the proportion of bull markets ($r_M > r_f$) correctly forecast *and* the proportion of bear markets ($r_M < r_f$) correctly forecast.

If we call P_1 the proportion of the correct forecasts of bull markets and P_2 the proportion for bear markets, then $P_1 + P_2 - 1$ is the correct measure of timing ability. For example, a forecaster who always guesses correctly will have $P_1 = P_2 = 1$, and will show ability of 1 (100%). An analyst who always bets on a bear market will mispredict all bull markets ($P_1 = 0$), will correctly "predict" all bear markets ($P_2 = 1$), and will end up with timing ability of $P_1 + P_2 - 1 = 0$. If C denotes the (call option) value of a perfect market timer, then $(P_1 + P_2 - 1)C$ measures the value of imperfect forecasting ability.

CONCEPT CHECK 2

What is the market timing score of someone who flips a fair coin to predict the market?

---

4 SECURITY SELECTION: THE TREYNOR-BLACK MODEL

Overview of the Treynor-Black Model

Security analysis is the other form of active portfolio management besides timing the overall market. Suppose that you are an analyst studying individual securities. It is quite likely that you will turn up several securities that appear to be mispriced. They offer positive anticipated alphas to the investor. But how do you exploit your analysis? Concentrating a portfolio on these securities entails a cost, namely, the **firm-specific risk** that you could shed by more fully diversifying. As an active manager you must strike a balance between aggressive exploitation of perceived security mispricing and diversification motives that dictate that a few stocks should not dominate the portfolio.

Treynor and Black[5] developed an optimizing model for portfolio managers who use security analysis. It represents a portfolio management theory that assumes security markets are *nearly* efficient. The essence of the model is this:

1. Security analysts in an active investment management organization can analyze in depth only a limited number of stocks out of the entire universe of securities. The securities not analyzed are assumed to be fairly priced.

2. For the purpose of **efficient diversification**, the market index portfolio is the baseline portfolio, which the model treats as the passive portfolio.

3. The macro forecasting unit of the investment management firm provides forecasts of the expected rate of return and variance of the passive (market-index) portfolio.

4. The objective of security analysis is to form an active portfolio of a necessarily limited number of securities. Perceived mispricing of the analyzed securities is what guides the composition of this active portfolio.

---

[5] Jack Treynor and Fischer Black, "How to Use Security Analysis to Improve Portfolio Selection," *Journal of Business,* January 1973.

5. Analysts follow several steps to make up the active portfolio and evaluate its expected performance:

   A. Estimate the beta of each analyzed security and its residual risk. From the beta and macro forecast, $E(r_M) - r_f$, determine the *required* rate of return of the security.

   B. Given the degree of mispricing of each security, determine its expected return and expected *abnormal* return (alpha).

   C. The cost of less-than-full diversification comes from the nonsystematic risk of the mispriced stock, the variance of the stock's residual, $\sigma^2(e)$, which offsets the benefit (alpha) of specializing in an underpriced security.

   D. Use the estimates for the values of alpha, beta, and $\sigma^2(e)$ to determine the optimal weight of each security in the active portfolio.

   E. Compute the alpha, beta, and $\sigma^2(e)$ of the active portfolio from the weights of the securities in the portfolio.

6. The macroeconomic forecasts for the passive index portfolio and the composite forecasts for the active portfolio are used to determine the optimal risky portfolio, which will be a combination of the passive and active portfolios.

Treynor and Black's model did not take the industry by storm. This is unfortunate for several reasons:

1. Just as even imperfect market timing ability has enormous value, security analysis of the sort Treynor and Black proposed has similar potential value.[6] Even with far from perfect security analysis, proper active management can add value.

2. The Treynor-Black model is conceptually easy to implement. Moreover, it is useful even when some of its simplifying assumptions are relaxed.

3. The model lends itself to use in decentralized organizations. This property is essential to efficiency in complex organizations.

Portfolio Construction

Assuming that all securities are fairly priced, and using the **index model** as a guideline for the rate of return on fairly priced securities, the rate of return on the ith security is given by

$$r_i = r_f + \beta_i(r_M - r_f) + e_i \qquad \textbf{(71-2)}$$

where e_i is the zero mean, firm-specific disturbance.

Absent security analysis, Treynor and Black (TB) took Equation 71-2 to represent the rate of return on all securities and assumed that the market portfolio, M, is the efficient portfolio. For simplicity, they also assumed that the nonsystematic components of returns, e_i, are independent across securities. As for market timing, TB assumed that the forecast for the **passive portfolio** already has been made, so that the expected return on the market index, r_M, as well as its variance, σ^2_M, has been assessed.

---

[6] Alex Kane, Alan Marcus, and Robert Trippi, "The Valuation of Security Analysis," *Journal of Portfolio Management*, Spring 1999.

Now a portfolio manager unleashes a team of security analysts to investigate a subset of the universe of available securities. The objective is to form an active portfolio of positions in the analyzed securities to be mixed with the index portfolio. For each security, k, that is researched, we write the rate of return as

$$r_k = r_f + \beta_k(r_M - r_f) + e_k + \alpha_k \qquad \textbf{(71-3)}$$

where α_k represents the extra expected return (called the *abnormal return*) attributable to any perceived mispricing of the security. Thus, for each security analyzed the research team estimates the parameters α_k, β_k, and $\sigma^2(e_k)$. If all the α_k turn out to be zero, there would be no reason to depart from the passive strategy and the index portfolio M would remain the manager's choice. However, this is a remote possibility. In general, there will be a significant number of nonzero alpha values, some positive and some negative.

One way to get an overview of the TB methodology is to examine what we should do with the active portfolio once we determine it. Suppose that the **active portfolio** (A) has been constructed somehow and has the parameters α_A, β_A, and $\sigma^2(e_A)$. Its total variance is the sum of its systematic variance, $\beta_A^2 \sigma_M^2$, plus the nonsystematic variance, $\sigma^2(e_A)$. Its covariance with the market index portfolio, M, is

$$\mathrm{Cov}(r_A, r_M) = \beta_A \sigma_M^2$$

Figure 2 shows the optimization process with the active and passive portfolios. The dashed efficient frontier represents the universe of all securities assuming that they are all fairly priced, that is, that all alphas are zero. By definition, the market index, M, is on this efficient frontier and is tangent to the (dashed) capital market line (CML). In practice, the analysts do not need to know this frontier. They need only to observe the market-index portfolio and construct a portfolio resulting in a capital allocation line that lies above the CML. Given

FIGURE 2   The Optimization Process with Active and Passive Portfolios

their perceived superior analysis, they will view the market-index portfolio as inefficient: The active portfolio, A, constructed from mispriced securities, must lie, by design, above the CML.

To locate the active portfolio A in Figure 2, we need its expected return and standard deviation. The standard deviation is

$$\sigma_A = \left[\beta_A^2 \sigma_M^2 + \sigma^2(e_A)\right]^{1/2}$$

Because of the positive alpha value that is forecast for A, it may plot above the (dashed) CML with expected return

$$E(r_A) = \alpha_A + r_f + \beta_A[E(r_M) - r_f]$$

The optimal combination of the active portfolio, A, with the passive portfolio, M, is a simple application of the construction of optimal risky portfolios from two component assets. Because the active portfolio is not perfectly correlated with the market-index portfolio, we need to account for their mutual correlation in the determination of the optimal allocation between the two portfolios. This is evident from the solid efficient frontier that passes through M and A in Figure 2. It supports the optimal capital allocation line (CAL) and identifies the optimal risky portfolio, P, which combines portfolios A and M and is the tangency point of the CAL to the efficient frontier. The active portfolio A in this example is not the ultimate efficient portfolio, because we need to mix A with the passive market portfolio to achieve optimal diversification.

Let us now outline the algebraic approach to this optimization problem. If we invest a proportion, w, in the active portfolio and $1 - w$ in the market index, the portfolio return will be

$$r_p(w) = wr_A + (1 - w)r_M$$

To find the weight, w, which provides the best (i.e., the steepest) CAL, we use Equation 71-4, which describes the optimal risky portfolio composed of two risky assets (in this case, A and M) when there is a risk-free asset:

$$w_A = \frac{\left[E(r_A) - r_f\right]\sigma_M^2 - \left[E(r_M) - r_f\right]\mathrm{Cov}(r_A, r_M)}{\left[E(r_A) - r_f\right]\sigma_M^2 + \left[E(r_M) - r_f\right]\sigma_A^2 - \left[E(r_A) - r_f + E(r_M) - r_f\right]\mathrm{Cov}(r_A, r_M)}$$

(71-4)

Now recall that

$$E(r_A) - r_f = \alpha_A + \beta_A R_M \qquad \text{where } R_M = E(r_M) - r_f$$

$$\mathrm{Cov}(R_A, R_M) = \beta_A \sigma_M^2 \qquad \text{where } R_A = E(r_A) - r_f$$

$$\sigma_A^2 = \beta_A^2 \sigma_M^2 + \sigma^2(e_A)$$

$$[E(r_A) - r_f] + [E(r_M) - r_f] = (\alpha_A + \beta R_M) + R_M = \alpha_A + R_M(1 + \beta_A)$$

Substituting these expressions into Equation 71-4, dividing both numerator and denominator by σ_M^2, and collecting terms yields the expression for the optimal weight in portfolio A, w^*,

$$w^* = \frac{\alpha_A}{\alpha_A(1 - \beta_A) + R_M \dfrac{\sigma^2(e_A)}{\sigma_M^2}}$$

(71-5)

Let's begin with the simple case where $\beta_A = 1$ and substitute into Equation 71-5. Then the optimal weight, w_0, is

$$w_0 = \frac{\dfrac{\alpha_A}{R_M}}{\dfrac{\sigma^2(e_A)}{\sigma_M^2}} = \frac{\alpha_A/\sigma^2(e_A)}{R_M/\sigma_M^2} \qquad \textbf{(71-6)}$$

Here is some intuition for this result. If the systematic risk of the active portfolio is average, that is, $\beta_A = 1$, then the optimal weight is the "relative advantage" of portfolio A as measured by the ratio: alpha/[market excess return], divided by the "disadvantage" of A, that is, the ratio: [nonsystematic risk of A]/[market risk]. Some algebra applied to Equation 71-5 reveals the relationship between w_0 and w^*:

$$w^* = \frac{w_0}{1 + (1 - \beta_A)w_0} \qquad \textbf{(71-7)}$$

w^* increases when β_A increases because the greater the systematic risk, β_A, of the active portfolio, A, the smaller is the benefit from diversifying it with the index, M, and the more beneficial it is to take advantage of the mispriced securities. However, we expect the beta of the active portfolio to be in the neighborhood of 1.0 and the optimal weight, w^*, to be close to w_0.

What is the reward-to-variability ratio of the optimal risky portfolio once we find the best mix, w^*, of the active and passive index portfolios? It turns out that if we compute the square of Sharpe's measure of the risky portfolio, we can separate the contributions of the index and active portfolios as follows:

$$S_P^2 = S_M^2 + \frac{\alpha_A^2}{\sigma^2(e_A)} = \left[\frac{R_M}{\sigma_M}\right]^2 + \left[\frac{\alpha_A}{\sigma(e_A)}\right]^2 \qquad \textbf{(71-8)}$$

This decomposition of the Sharpe measure of the optimal risky portfolio, which by the way is valid *only* for the optimal portfolio, tells us how to construct the active portfolio. Equation 71-8 shows that the highest Sharpe measure for the risky portfolio will be attained when we construct an active portfolio that maximizes the value of $\alpha_A/\sigma(e_A)$. The ratio of alpha to residual standard deviation of the active portfolio will be maximized when we choose a weight for the kth analyzed security as follows:

$$w_k = \frac{\alpha_k/\sigma^2(e_k)}{\displaystyle\sum_{i=1}^{n}\alpha_i/\sigma^2(e_i)} \qquad \textbf{(71-9)}$$

This makes sense: The weight of a security in the active portfolio depends on the ratio of the degree of mispricing, α_k, to the nonsystematic risk, $\sigma^2(e_k)$, of the security. The denominator, the sum of the ratio across securities, is a scale factor to guarantee that portfolio weights sum to one.

Note from Equation 71-8 that the square of Sharpe's measure of the optimal risky portfolio is increased over the square of the Sharpe measure of the passive (market-index) portfolio by the amount

$$\left[\frac{\alpha_A}{\sigma(e_A)}\right]^2$$

The ratio of the degree of mispricing, α_A, to the nonsystematic standard deviation, $\sigma(e_A)$, is therefore a natural performance measure of the active component of the risky portfolio. Sometimes this is called the **information ratio**.

We can calculate the contribution of a single security in the active portfolio to the portfolio's overall performance. When the active portfolio contains n analyzed securities, the total improvement in the squared Sharpe measure equals the sum of the squared information ratios of the analyzed securities,

$$\left[\frac{\alpha_A}{\sigma(e_A)}\right]^2 = \sum_{i=1}^{n}\left[\frac{\alpha_i}{\sigma(e_i)}\right]^2 \qquad \textbf{(71-10)}$$

The information ratio for each security; $\alpha_i/\sigma(e_i)$, is a measure of the contribution of that security to the performance of the active portfolio.

The best way to illustrate the Treynor-Black process is through an example that can be easily worked out in a spreadsheet. Suppose that the macroforecasting unit of Drex Portfolio Inc. (DPF) issues a forecast for a 15% market return. The forecast's standard error is 20%. The risk-free rate is 7%. The macro data can be summarized as follows:

$$R_M = E(r_M) - r_f = 8\%; \sigma_M = 20\%$$

At the same time the security analysis division submits to the portfolio manager the following forecast of annual returns for the three securities that it covers:

Stock	α	β	$\sigma(e)$	$\alpha/\sigma(e)$
1	7%	1.6	45%	.1556
2	−5	1.0	32	−.1563
3	3	0.5	26	.1154

E-INVESTMENTS: CALCULATING THE INFORMATION RATIO

Go to www.the401k.com. Click through *Reference*, then *Focus on 401(k) Newsletter*, where you can choose the Second Quarter 2001 newsletter. This choice allows you to review the calculation of the information ratio. How can the portfolio manager take extra risk to "beat" the market indexes? What does the information ratio measure?

Note that the alpha estimates appear reasonably moderate. The estimates of the residual standard deviations are correlated with the betas, just as they are in reality. The magnitudes also reflect typical values for NYSE stocks. Equations 71-10, 71-8, and the analyst input table allow a quick calculation of the DPF portfolio's Sharpe measure.

$$S_P = \left[(8/20)^2 + .1556^2 + .1563^2 + .1154^2\right]^{1/2} = \sqrt{.2220} = .4711$$

Compare the result with the Sharpe ratio for the market-index portfolio, which is only $8/20 = .40$. We now proceed to compute the composition and performance of the active portfolio.

First, let us construct the optimal active portfolio implied by the security analyst **input list**. To do so we compute the **appraisal ratios** as follows (remember to use decimal representations of returns in the formulas):

Stock	$\alpha/\sigma^2(e)$	$\dfrac{\alpha_k}{\sigma^2(e_k)} / \sum\limits_{i=1}^{3} \dfrac{\alpha_i}{\sigma^2(e_i)}$
1	$.07/.45^2 = .3457$	$.3457/.3012 = 1.1477$
2	$-.05/.32^2 = -.4883$	$-.4883/.3012 = -1.6212$
3	$.03/.26^2 = .4438$	$.4438/.3012 = 1.4735$
Total	$.3012$	1.0000

The last column presents the optimal positions of each of the three securities in the active portfolio. Obviously, Stock 2, with a negative alpha, has a negative weight. The magnitudes of the individual positions in the active portfolio (e.g., 114.77% in Stock 1) seem quite extreme. However, this should not concern us because the active portfolio will later be mixed with the well-diversified market-index portfolio, resulting in much more moderate positions, as we shall see shortly.

The forecasts for the stocks, together with the proposed composition of the active portfolio, lead to the following parameter estimates for the active portfolio:

$$\alpha_A = 1.1477 \times .07 + (-1.6212) \times (-.05) + 1.4735 \times .03$$
$$= .2056 = 20.56\%$$
$$\beta_A = 1.1477 \times 1.6 + (-1.6212) \times 1.0 + 1.4735 \times .5 = .9519$$
$$\sigma(e_A) = [1.1477^2 \times .45^2 + (-1.6212)^2 \times .32^2 + 1.4735^2 \times .26^2]^{1/2}$$
$$= .8262 = 82.62\%$$
$$\sigma^2(e_A) = .8262^2 = .6826$$

Note that the negative weight (short position) on the negative alpha stock results in a positive contribution to the alpha of the active portfolio. Note also that because of the assumption that the stock residuals are uncorrelated, the active portfolio's residual variance is simply the weighted sum of the individual stock residual variances, with the squared portfolio proportions as weights.

The parameters of the active portfolio are now used to determine its proportion in the overall risky portfolio:

$$w_0 = \frac{\alpha_A/\sigma^2(e_A)}{R_M/\sigma_M^2} = \frac{.2056/.6826}{.08/.04} = .1506$$

$$w^* = \frac{w_0}{1 + (1 - \beta_A)w_0} = \frac{.1506}{1 + (1 - .9519) \times .1506} = .1495$$

Although the active portfolio's alpha is impressive (20.56%), its proportion in the overall risky portfolio, before adjustment for beta, is only 15.06%, because of its large nonsystematic standard deviation (82.62%). Such is the importance of diversification. As it happens, the beta of the active portfolio is almost 1.0, and hence the adjustment for beta (from w_0 to w^*) is small, from 15.06% to 14.95%. The direction of the change makes sense. If the beta of the active portfolio is low (less than 1.0), there is more potential gain from diversification, hence a smaller position in the active portfolio is called for. If the beta of the active portfolio were significantly greater than 1.0, a larger correction in the opposite direction would be called for.

The proportions of the individual stocks in the active portfolio, together with the proportion of the active portfolio in the overall risky portfolio, determine the proportions of each individual stock in the overall risky portfolio.

Stock	Final Position
1	$.1495 \times 1.1477 = .1716$
2	$.1495 \times (-1.6212) = -.2424$
3	$.1495 \times 1.4735 = .2202$
Active portfolio	.1495
Market portfolio	.8505
	1.0000

The parameters of the active portfolio and market-index portfolio are now used to forecast the performance of the optimal, overall risky portfolio. When optimized, a property of the risky portfolio is that its squared Sharpe measure exceeds that of the passive portfolio by the square of the active portfolio's information ratio:

$$S_P^2 = \left[\frac{R_M}{\sigma_M}\right]^2 + \left[\frac{\alpha_A}{\sigma(e_A)}\right]^2$$
$$= .16 + .0619 = .2219$$

and hence the Sharpe measure of the DPF portfolio is $\sqrt{.2219} = .4711$, compared with .40 for the passive portfolio.

Another measure of the gain from increasing the Sharpe measure is the M^2 statistic. M^2 is calculated by comparing the expected return of a portfolio on the capital allocation line supported by portfolio P, CAL(P), with a standard deviation equal to that of the market index, to the expected return on the market index. In other words, we mix portfolio P with the risk-free asset to obtain a new portfolio P^* that has the same standard deviation as the market portfolio. Since both portfolios have equal risk, we can compare their expected returns. The M^2 statistic is the difference in expected returns. Portfolio P^* can be obtained by investing a fraction σ_M/σ_P in P and a fraction $(1 - \sigma_M/\sigma_P)$ in the risk-free asset.

The risk premium on CAL(P^*) with total risk σ_M is given by

$$R_{P^*} = E(r_{P^*}) - r_f = S_P\sigma_M = .4711 \times .20 = .0942, \text{ or } 9.42\% \qquad \textbf{(71-11)}$$

and

$$M^2 = [R_{P^*} - R_M] = 9.42 - 8 = 1.42\% \qquad \textbf{(71-12)}$$

At first blush, an incremental expected return of 1.42% seems paltry compared with the alpha values submitted by the analyst. This seemingly modest improvement is the result of diversification motives: To mitigate the large risk of individual stocks (verify that the standard deviation of stock 1 is 55%)

and maximize the portfolio Sharpe measure (which compares excess return to total volatility), we must diversify the active portfolio by mixing it with *M*. Note also that this improvement has been achieved with only three stocks, and with forecasts and portfolio rebalancing only once a year. Increasing the number of stocks and the frequency of forecasts can improve the results dramatically.

For example, suppose the analyst covers three more stocks that turn out to have alphas and risk levels identical to the first three. Use Equation 71-10 to show that the squared appraisal ratio of the active portfolio will double. By using Equation 71-8, it is easy to show that the new Sharpe measure will rise to .5327. Equation 71-12 then implies that M^2 rises to 2.65%, almost double the previous value. Increasing the frequency of forecasts and portfolio rebalancing will deploy the power of compounding to improve annual performance even more.

CONCEPT CHECK 3

A. When short positions are prohibited, the manager simply discards stocks with negative alphas. Using the preceding example, what would be the composition of the active portfolio if short sales were disallowed? Find the cost of the short-sale restriction in terms of the decline in performance (M^2) of the new overall risky portfolio.

B. What is the contribution of security selection to portfolio performance if the macro forecast is adjusted upward, for example, to $R_M = 12\%$, and short sales are again allowed?

---

5 MULTIFACTOR MODELS AND ACTIVE PORTFOLIO MANAGEMENT

Portfolio managers use various multifactor models of security returns. So far our analytical framework for active portfolio management seems to rest on the validity of the index model, that is, on a single-factor security model. Using a multifactor model will not affect the construction of the active portfolio because the entire TB analysis focuses on the residuals of the index model. If we were to replace the one-factor model with a multifactor model, we would continue to form the active portfolio by calculating each security's alpha relative to its fair return (given its betas on *all* factors), and again we would combine the active portfolio with the portfolio that would be formed in the absence of security analysis. The multifactor framework, however, does raise several new issues.

The index model simplifies the construction of the input list necessary for portfolio optimization programs. If

$$r_i - r_f = \alpha_i + \beta_i (r_M - r_f) + e_i$$

adequately describes the security market, then the variance of any asset is the sum of systematic and nonsystematic risk: $\sigma^2(r_i) = \beta_i^2 \sigma_M^2 + \sigma^2(e_i)$, and the covariance between any two assets is $\beta_i \beta_j \sigma_M^2$.

How do we generalize this rule to use in a multifactor model? To simplify, let us consider a two-factor world, and let us call the two factor portfolios M and H. Then we generalize the index model to

$$r_i - r_f = \beta_{iM}(r_M - r_f) + \beta_{iH}(r_H - r_f) + \alpha_i + e_i$$
$$= R_\beta + \alpha_i + e_i$$

(71-13)

β_{iM} and β_{iH} are the betas of the security relative to portfolios M and H. Given the rates of return on the factor portfolios, r_M and r_H, the fair excess rate of return over r_f on a security is denoted R_β and its expected abnormal return is α_i.

How can we use Equation 71-13 to form optimal portfolios? As before, investors wish to maximize the Sharpe measures of their portfolios. The factor structure of Equation 71-13 can be used to generate the inputs for the Markowitz portfolio selection algorithm. The variance and covariance estimates are now more complex, however:

$$\sigma^2(r_i) = \beta_{iM}^2 \sigma_M^2 + \beta_{iH}^2 \sigma_H^2 + 2\beta_{iM}\beta_{iH}\,\mathrm{Cov}(r_M, r_H) + \sigma^2(e_i)$$

$$\mathrm{Cov}(r_i, r_j) = \beta_{iM}\beta_{jM}\sigma_M^2 + \beta_{iH}\beta_{jH}\sigma_H^2 + (\beta_{iM}\beta_{jH} + \beta_{jM}\beta_{iH})\,\mathrm{Cov}(r_M, r_H)$$

Nevertheless, the informational economy of the factor model still is valuable, because we can estimate a covariance matrix for an n-security portfolio from

n estimates of β_{iM}
n estimates of β_{iH}
n estimates of $\sigma^2(e_i)$
1 estimate of σ_M^2
1 estimate of σ_H^2

rather than $n(n + 1)/2$ separate variance and covariance estimates. Thus the factor structure continues to simplify portfolio construction data requirements.

The factor structure also suggests an efficient method to allocate research effort. Analysts can specialize in forecasting means and variances of different factor portfolios. Having established factor betas, they can form a covariance matrix to be used together with expected security returns generated by the CAPM or APT to construct an optimal passive risky portfolio. If active analysis of individual stocks also is attempted, the procedure of constructing the optimal active portfolio and its optimal combination with the passive portfolio is identical to that followed in the single-factor case.

In the case of the multifactor market even passive investors (meaning those who accept market prices as "fair") need to do a considerable amount of work. They need forecasts of the expected return and volatility of each factor return, *and* they need to determine the appropriate weights on each factor portfolio to maximize their **expected utility**. Such a process is straightforward in principle, but it quickly becomes computationally demanding.

IMPERFECT FORECASTS OF ALPHA VALUES AND THE USE OF THE TREYNOR-BLACK MODEL IN INDUSTRY

6

Suppose an analyst is assigned to a security and provides you with a forecast of $\alpha = 20\%$. It looks like a great opportunity! Using this forecast in the Treynor-Black algorithm, we'll end up tilting our portfolio heavily toward this security.

Should we go out on a limb? Before doing so, any reasonable manager would ask: "How good is the analyst?" Unless the answer is a resounding "good," a reasonable manager would discount the forecast. We can quantify this notion.

Suppose we have a record of an analyst's past forecast of alpha, α^f. Relying on the index model and obtaining reliable estimates of the stock beta, we can estimate the true alphas (after the fact) from the average realized excess returns on the security, $\overline{R}$, and the index, $\overline{R}_M$, that is,

$$\alpha = \overline{R} - \beta \overline{R}_M$$

To measure the forecasting accuracy of the analyst, we can estimate a regression of the forecasts on the realized alpha:

$$\alpha^f = a_0 + a_1\alpha + \varepsilon$$

The coefficients a_0 and a_1 reflect potential bias in the forecasts, which we will ignore for simplicity; that is, we will suppose $a_0 = 0$ and $a_1 = 1$. Because the forecast errors are uncorrelated with the true alpha, the variance of the forecast is

$$\sigma_{\alpha^f}^2 = \sigma_\alpha^2 + \sigma_\varepsilon^2$$

The quality of the forecasts can be measured by the squared correlation coefficient between the forecasts and realization, equivalently, the ratio of explained variance to total variance

$$\rho^2 = \frac{\sigma_\alpha^2}{\sigma_\alpha^2 + \sigma_\varepsilon^2}$$

This equation shows us how to "discount" analysts' forecasts to reflect their precision. Knowing the quality of past forecasts, ρ^2, we "shrink" any new forecast, α^f, to $\rho^2\alpha^f$, to minimize forecast error. This procedure is quite intuitive: If the analyst is perfect, that is, $\rho^2 = 1$, we take the forecast at face value. If analysts' forecasts have proven to be useless, with $\rho^2 = 0$, we ignore the forecast. The quality of the forecast gives us the precise shrinkage factor to use.

Suppose the analysts' forecasts of the alpha of the three stocks in our previous example are all of equal quality, $\rho^2 = .2$. Shrinking the forecasts of alpha by a factor of .2 and repeating the optimization process, we end up with a much smaller weight on the active portfolio (.03 instead of .15), a much smaller Sharpe measure (.4031 instead of .4711), and a much smaller M^2 (.06% instead of 1.42%).

The reduction in portfolio expected performance does not reflect an inferior procedure. Rather, accepting alpha forecasts without acknowledging and adjusting for their imprecision would be naïve. We must adjust our expectations to the quality of the forecasts.

In reality, we can expect the situation to be much worse. A forecast quality of .2, that is, a correlation coefficient between alpha forecasts and realizations of $\sqrt{.2} = .45$, is most likely unrealistic in nearly efficient markets. Moreover, we don't even know this quality, and its estimation introduces yet another potential error into the optimization process. Finally, the other parameters we use in the TB model—market expected return and variance, security betas and residual variances—are also estimated with errors. Thus, under realistic circumstances, we would be fortunate to obtain even the meager results we have just uncovered.

So, should we ditch the TB model? Before we do, let's make one more calculation. The "meager" Sharpe measure of .4031 squares to .1625, larger than the market's squared Sharpe measure of .16 by .0025. Suppose we cover 300 securities instead of three, that is, 100 sets identical to the one we analyzed. From Equations 71-8 and 71-10 we know that the increment to the squared Sharpe measure will rise to $100 \times .0025 = .25$. The squared Sharpe measure of the risky portfolio will rise to $.16 + .25 = .41$, a Sharpe measure of .64, and an M^2 of 4.8%! Moreover, some of the estimation errors of the other parameters that plague us when we use three securities will offset one another and be diversified away with many more securities covered.[7]

What we see here is a demonstration of the value of security analysis we mentioned at the outset. In the final analysis, the value of the active management depends on forecast quality. The vast demand for active management suggests that this quality is not negligible. The optimal way to exploit analysts' forecasts is with the TB model.

---

[7] Empirical work along these lines can be found in: Alex Kane, Tae-Hwan Kim, and Halbert White, "The Power of Portfolio Optimization," UCSD Working Paper, July 2000.

SUMMARY

▶ A truly passive portfolio strategy entails holding the market-index portfolio and a money market fund. Determining the optimal allocation to the market portfolio requires an estimate of its expected return and variance, which in turn suggests delegating some analysis to professionals.

▶ Active portfolio managers attempt to construct a risky portfolio that maximizes the reward-to-variability (Sharpe) ratio.

▶ The value of perfect market timing ability is considerable. The rate of return to a perfect market timer will be uncertain. However, its risk characteristics are not measurable by standard measures of portfolio risk, because perfect timing dominates a passive strategy, providing "good" surprises only.

▶ Perfect timing ability is equivalent to the possession of a call option on the market portfolio, whose value can be determined using option valuation techniques such as the Black-Scholes formula.

▶ With imperfect timing, the value of a timer who attempts to forecast whether stocks will outperform bills is determined by the conditional probabilities of the true outcome given the forecasts: $P_1 + P_2 - 1$. Thus if the value of perfect timing is given by the option value, C, then imperfect timing has the value $(P_1 + P_2 - 1)C$.

▶ The Treynor-Black security selection model envisions that a macroeconomic forecast for market performance is available and that security analysts estimate abnormal expected rates of return, α, for various securities. Alpha is the expected rate of return on a security beyond that explained by its beta and the security market line.

▶ In the Treynor-Black model the weight of each analyzed security is proportional to the ratio of its alpha to its nonsystematic risk, $\sigma^2(e)$.

▶ Once the active portfolio is constructed, its alpha value, nonsystematic risk, and beta can be determined from the properties of the component securities. The optimal risky portfolio, P, is then constructed by holding a position in the active portfolio according to the ratio of α_A to $\sigma^2(e_A)$, divided by the analogous ratio for the market-index portfolio. Finally, this position is adjusted using the beta of the active portfolio.

▶ When the overall risky portfolio is constructed using the optimal proportions of the active portfolio and passive portfolio, its performance, as measured by the square of Sharpe's measure, is improved (over that of the passive, market-index, portfolio) by the amount $[\alpha_A/\sigma(e_A)]^2$.

▶ The contribution of each security to the overall improvement in the performance of the active portfolio is determined by its degree of mispricing and nonsystematic risk. The contribution of each security to portfolio performance equals $[\alpha_i/\sigma(e_i)]^2$, so that for the optimal risky portfolio,

$$S_P^2 = \left[\frac{E(r_M) - r_f}{\sigma_M}\right]^2 + \sum_{i=1}^{n}\left[\frac{\alpha_i}{\sigma(e_i)}\right]^2$$

▶ Applying the Treynor-Black model to a multifactor framework is straightforward. The forecast of the market-index mean and standard deviation must be replaced with forecasts for an optimized passive portfolio based on a multifactor model. The proportions of the factor portfolios are calculated using the familiar efficient frontier algorithm. The active portfolio is constructed on the basis of residuals from the multifactor model.

▶ Implementing the model with imperfect forecasts requires estimation of bias and precision of raw forecasts. The adjusted forecast is obtained by applying the estimated co-efficients to the raw forecasts.

WEBSITES

Learn more about the Sharpe measure at these sites:

▶ www.investorsoftware.net/InvestorPrimer/InvestmentPerformance.html
▶ www.nysscpa.org/cpajournal/2001/0600/features/f064401.htm

The sites below give valuable market timing information:

▶ www.sniper.at
▶ www.stockmarkettiming.com

Visit these sites for further information on the Treynor-Black Model:

▶ www.financewise.com/public/edit/riskm/ewrm/ewrm-port-x.htm
▶ www.financewise.com/public/edit/riskm/ewrm/ewrm-portfolio.htm
▶ www.business.com/directory/financial_services/commercial_finance/
▶ treasury/insurance_and_risk_management/sources_and_managing_risk/
portfolio_diversification

Visit these sites to gain a better understanding of the information ratio:

▶ www.russell.com/AU/Institutional_Investors/Russell_Library/Investment_
Articles_and_Updates/Information_Ratios_Explained.asp
▶ www.the401k.com/news/quarter11997/information_ratio.html

PRACTICE PROBLEMS FOR READING 71

1. A portfolio manager summarizes the input from the macro and micro forecasters in the following table:

Micro Forecasts

Asset	Expected Return (%)	Beta	Residual Standard Deviation (%)
Stock A	20	1.3	58
Stock B	18	1.8	71
Stock C	17	0.7	60
Stock D	12	1.0	55

Macro Forecasts

Asset	Expected Return (%)	Standard Deviation (%)
T-bills	8	0
Passive equity portfolio	16	23

A. Calculate expected excess returns, alpha values, and residual variances for these stocks.

B. Construct the optimal risky portfolio.

C. What is Sharpe's measure for the optimal portfolio and how much of it is contributed by the active portfolio? What is the M^2?

D. What should be the exact makeup of the complete portfolio for an investor with a coefficient of risk aversion of 2.8?

2. Recalculate problem 1 for a porfolio manager who is not allowed to short sell securities.

A. What is the cost of of the restriction in terms of Sharpe's measure and M^2?

B. What is the utility loss to the investor ($A = 2.8$) given his new complete portfolio?

3. Suppose that based on the analyst's past record, you estimate that the relationship between forecast and actual alpha is:

Actual abnormal return = .3 × Forecast of alpha

Use the alphas from problem 1. How much is expected performance affected by recognizing the imprecision of alpha forecasts?

THE PORTFOLIO MANAGEMENT PROCESS AND THE INVESTMENT POLICY STATEMENT

by John L. Maginn, Donald L. Tuttle, Dennis W. McLeavey, and Jerald E. Pinto

READING 72

LEARNING OUTCOMES

The candidate should be able to:

a. explain the importance of the portfolio perspective;

b. describe the steps of the portfolio management process and the components of those steps;

c. define investment objectives and constraints and explain and distinguish among the types of investment objectives and constraints;

d. discuss the role of the investment policy statement in the portfolio management process and explain the elements of an investment policy statement;

e. explain how capital market expectations and the investment policy statement help influence the strategic asset allocation decision and discuss how an investor's investment time horizon may influence the investor's strategic asset allocation;

f. contrast the types of investment time horizons, determine the time horizon for a particular investor, and evaluate the effects of this time horizon on portfolio choice;

g. justify ethical conduct as a requirement for managing investment portfolios.

INTRODUCTION 1

In setting out to master the concepts and tools of portfolio management, we first need a coherent description of the portfolio management process. The **portfolio management** process is an integrated set of steps undertaken in a consistent manner to create and maintain an appropriate portfolio (combination of assets) to meet clients' stated goals. The process we present in this reading is a distillation of the shared elements of current practice.

Managing Investment Portfolios: A Dynamic Process, Third Edition, John L. Maginn, Donald L. Tuttle, Dennis W. McLeavey, and Jerald E. Pinto, editors. Copyright © 2005 by CFA Institute. Reprinted with permission.

491

www.cfainstitute.org/toolkit—Your online preparation resource

Because it serves as the foundation for the process, we also introduce the investment policy statement through a discussion of its main components. An investment policy statement (IPS) is a written document that clearly sets out a client's return objectives and risk tolerance over that client's relevant time horizon, along with applicable constraints such as liquidity needs, tax considerations, regulatory requirements, and unique circumstances.

The portfolio management process moves from planning, through execution, and then to feedback. In the planning step, investment objectives and policies are formulated, capital market expectations are formed, and strategic asset allocations are established. In the execution step, the portfolio manager constructs the portfolio. In the feedback step, the manager monitors and evaluates the portfolio compared with the plan. Any changes suggested by the feedback must be examined carefully to ensure that they represent long-run considerations.

The investment policy statement provides the foundation of the portfolio management process. In creating an IPS, the manager writes down the client's special characteristics and needs. The IPS must clearly communicate the client's objectives and constraints. The IPS thereby becomes a plan that can be executed by any advisor or portfolio manager the client might subsequently hire. A properly developed IPS disciplines the portfolio management process and helps ensure against ad hoc revisions in strategy.

When combined with capital market expectations, the IPS forms the basis for a strategic asset allocation. Capital market expectations concern the risk and return characteristics of **capital market instruments** such as stocks and bonds. The **strategic asset allocation** establishes acceptable exposures to IPS-permissible asset classes to achieve the client's long-run objectives and constraints.

The portfolio perspective underlies the portfolio management process and IPS. The next sections illustrate this perspective.

2   INVESTMENT MANAGEMENT

Investment management is the service of professionally investing money. As a profession, investment management has its roots in the activities of European investment bankers in managing the fortunes created by the Industrial Revolution. By the beginning of the 21st century, investment management had become an important part of the financial services sector of all developed economies. By the end of 2003, the United States alone had approximately 15,000 money managers (registered investment advisors) responsible for investing more than $23 trillion, according to Standard & Poor's *Directory of Registered Investment Advisors* (2004). No worldwide count of investment advisors is available, but looking at another familiar professionally managed investment, the number of mutual funds stood at about 54,000 at year-end 2003; of these funds only 15 percent were U.S. based.[1]

The economics of investment management are relatively simple. An investment manager's revenue is fee driven; primarily, fees are based on a percentage of the average amount of assets under management and the type of investment program run for the client, as spelled out in detail in the investment management contract or other governing document. Consequently, an investment management firm's size is judged by the amount of assets under management, which is thus directly related to manager's revenue, another measure of size. Traditionally, the value of an investment management business (or a first estimate of value) is determined as a multiple of its annual fee income.

To understand an investment management firm or product beyond its size, we need to know not only its investment disciplines but also the type or types of investor it primarily serves. Broadly speaking, investors can be described as institutional or individual. Institutional investors are entities such as pension funds, foundations and endowments, insurance companies, and banks that ultimately serve as financial intermediaries between individuals and financial markets. The investment policy decisions of institutional investors are typically made by investment committees or trustees, with at least some members having a professional background in finance. The committee members or trustees frequently also bear a fiduciary relationship to the funds for which they have investment responsibility. Such a relationship, if it is present, imposes some legal standards regarding processes and decisions, which is reflected in the processes of the investment managers who serve that market segment.

Beginning in the second half of the 20th century, the tremendous growth of institutional investors, especially defined benefit pension plans, spurred a tremendous expansion in investment management firms or investment units of other entities (such as bank trust divisions) to service their needs.[2] As the potentially onerous financial responsibilities imposed on the sponsors by such plans became more evident, however, the 1980s and 1990s saw trends to other types of retirement schemes focused on participant responsibility for investment decisions and results. In addition, a long-lasting worldwide economic expansion created a great amount of individual wealth. As a result, investment advisors oriented to serving high-net-worth individuals as well as mutual funds (which serve the individual and, to a lesser extent, the smaller institutional market) gained in relative importance.

Such individual-investor-oriented advisors may incorporate a heavy personal financial planning emphasis in their services. Many wealthy families establish family offices to serve as trusted managers of their finances. Family offices are entities, typically organized and owned by a family, that assume responsibility for services such as financial planning, estate planning, and asset management, as well as a range of practical matters from tax return preparation to bill paying. Some family offices evolve such depth in professional staff that they open access to their services to other families (multi-family offices). In contrast to family offices, some investment management businesses service both individual and institutional markets, sometimes in separate divisions or corporate units, sometimes worldwide, and sometimes as part of a financial giant (American Express and Citigroup are examples of such financial supermarkets). In such cases, wrap-fee accounts packaging the services of outside investment managers may vie for the client's business with

---

[1] These facts are based on statistics produced by the Investment Company Institute and the International Investment Funds Association.

[2] A defined benefit pension plan specifies the plan sponsor's obligations in terms of the benefit to plan participants. The plan sponsor bears the investment risk of such plans.

in-house, separately managed accounts, as well as in-house mutual funds, external mutual funds, and other offerings marketed by a brokerage arm of the business.

Investment management companies employ portfolio managers, analysts, and traders, as well as marketing and support personnel. Portfolio managers may use both outside research produced by **sell-side analysts** (analysts employed by brokerages) and research generated by in-house analysts—so-called **buy-side analysts** (analysts employed by an investment manager or institutional investor). The staffing of in-house research departments depends on the size of the investment management firm, the variety of investment offerings, and the investment disciplines employed. An example may illustrate the variety of talent employed: The research department of one money manager with $30 billion in assets under management employs 34 equity analysts, 23 credit analysts, 3 hedge fund analysts, 12 quantitative analysts, 4 risk management professionals, 1 economist, and 1 economic analyst. That same company has a trading department with 8 equity and 8 bond traders and many support personnel. CFA charterholders can be found in all of these functions.

3   THE PORTFOLIO PERSPECTIVE

The portfolio perspective is our focus on the aggregate of all the investor's holdings: the portfolio. Because economic fundamentals influence the average returns of many assets, the risk associated with one asset's returns is generally related to the risk associated with other assets' returns. If we evaluate the prospects of each asset in isolation and ignore their interrelationships, we will likely misunderstand the risk and return prospects of the investor's total investment position—our most basic concern.

The historical roots of this portfolio perspective date to the work of Nobel laureate Harry Markowitz (1952). Markowitz and subsequent researchers, such as Jack Treynor and Nobel laureate William Sharpe, established the field of **modern portfolio theory** (MPT)—the analysis of rational portfolio choices based on the efficient use of risk. Modern portfolio theory revolutionized investment management. First, professional investment practice began to recognize the importance of the portfolio perspective in achieving investment objectives. Second, MPT helped spread the knowledge and use of quantitative methods in portfolio management. Today, quantitative and qualitative concepts complement each other in investment management practice.

In developing his theory of portfolio choice, Markowitz began with the perspective of investing for a single period. Others, including Nobel laureate Robert Merton, explored the dynamics of portfolio choice in a multiperiod setting. These subsequent contributions have greatly enriched the content of MPT.

If Markowitz, Merton, and other researchers created the supply, three developments in the investment community created demand for the portfolio perspective. First, institutional investing emerged worldwide to play an increasingly dominant role in financial markets. Measuring and controlling the risk of large pools of money became imperative. The second development was the increasing availability of ever-cheaper computer processing power and communications possibilities. As a result, a broader range of techniques for implementing MPT portfolio concepts became feasible. The third related development was the professionalization of the investment management field. This professionalization has been reflected in the worldwide growth of the professional accreditation program leading to the Chartered Financial Analyst (CFA®) designation.

PORTFOLIO MANAGEMENT AS A PROCESS

The unified presentation of portfolio management as a process represented an important advance in the investment management literature. Prior to the introduction of this concept in the first edition of this book, much of the traditional literature reflected an approach of selecting individual securities without an overall plan. Through the eyes of the professional, however, portfolio management is a *process*, an integrated set of activities that combine in a logical, orderly manner to produce a desired product. The process view is a *dynamic* and *flexible* concept that applies to all types of portfolio investments—bonds, stocks, real estate, gold, collectibles; to various organizational types—trust company, investment counsel firm, insurance company, mutual fund; to a full range of investors—individuals, pension plans, endowments, foundations, insurance companies, banks; and is independent of manager, location, investment philosophy, style, or approach. Portfolio management is a continuous and systematic process complete with feedback loops for monitoring and rebalancing. The process can be as loose or as disciplined, as quantitative or as qualitative, and as simple or as complex as its operators desire.

The portfolio management process is the same in every application: an integrated set of steps undertaken in a consistent manner to create and maintain appropriate combinations of investment assets. In the next sections, we explore the main features of this process.

THE PORTFOLIO MANAGEMENT PROCESS LOGIC

Three elements in managing any business process are planning, execution, and feedback. These same elements form the basis for the portfolio management process as depicted in Figure 1.

5.1 The Planning Step

The planning step is described in the four leftmost boxes in Figure 1. The top two boxes represent investor-related input factors, while the bottom two factors represent economic and market input.

5.1.1 Identifying and Specifying the Investor's Objectives and Constraints

The first task in investment planning is to identify and specify the investor's objectives and constraints. **Investment objectives** are desired investment outcomes. In investments, objectives chiefly pertain to return and risk. Constraints are limitations on the investor's ability to take full or partial advantage of particular investments. For example, an investor may face constraints related to the concentration of holdings as a result of government regulation, or restrictions in a governing legal document. Constraints are either internal, such as a client's specific liquidity needs, time horizon, and unique circumstances, or external, such as tax issues and legal and regulatory requirements. In Section 6, we examine the objective and constraint specification process.

FIGURE 1   The Portfolio Construction, Monitoring, and Revision Process

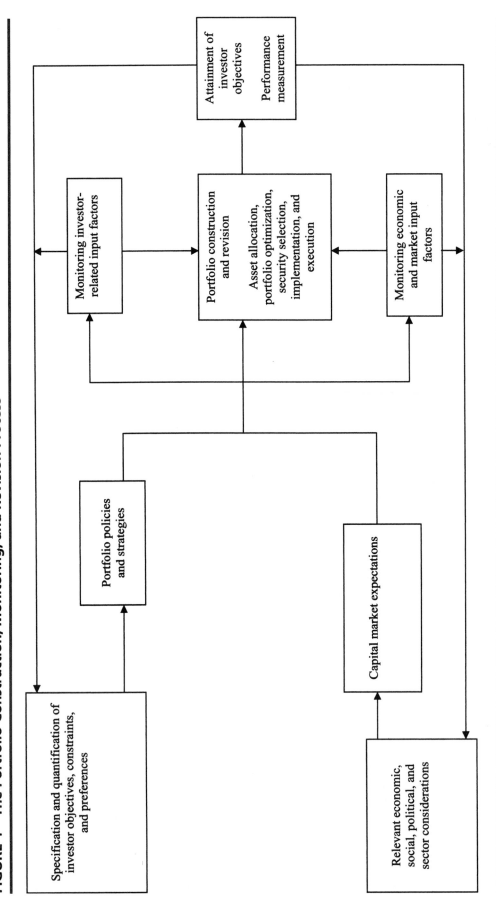

5.1.2 Creating the Investment Policy Statement

Once a client has specified a set of objectives and constraints, the manager's next task is to formulate the investment policy statement. The IPS serves as the governing document for all investment decision-making. In addition to objectives and constraints, the IPS may also cover a variety of other issues. For example, the IPS generally details reporting requirements, rebalancing guidelines, frequency and format of investment communication, manager fees, investment strategy, and the desired investment style or styles of investment managers. A typical IPS includes the following elements:

▶ a brief client description;

▶ the purpose of establishing policies and guidelines;

▶ the duties and investment responsibilities of parties involved, particularly those relating to fiduciary duties, communication, operational efficiency, and accountability. Parties involved include the client, any investment committee, the investment manager, and the bank custodian;

▶ the statement of investment goals, objectives, and constraints;

▶ the schedule for review of investment performance as well as the IPS itself;

▶ performance measures and benchmarks to be used in performance evaluation;

▶ any considerations to be taken into account in developing the strategic asset allocation;

▶ investment strategies and investment style(s); and

▶ guidelines for rebalancing the portfolio based on feedback.

The IPS forms the basis for the strategic asset allocation, which reflects the interaction of objectives and constraints with the investor's long-run capital market expectations. When experienced professionals include the policy allocation as part of the IPS, they are implicitly forming capital market expectations and also examining the interaction of objectives and constraints with long-run capital market expectations. In practice, one may see IPSs that include strategic asset allocations, but we will maintain a distinction between the two types.

The planning process involves the concrete elaboration of an **investment strategy**—that is, the manager's approach to investment analysis and security selection. A clearly formulated investment strategy organizes and clarifies the basis for investment decisions. It also guides those decisions toward achieving investment objectives. In the broadest sense, investment strategies are passive, active, or semiactive.

▶ In a passive investment approach, portfolio composition does not react to changes in capital market expectations (*passive* means *not reacting*). For example, a portfolio indexed to the MSCI-Europe Index, an index representing European equity markets, might add or drop a holding in response to a change in the index composition but not in response to changes in capital market expectations concerning the security's investment value. **Indexing**, a common passive approach to investing, refers to holding a portfolio of securities designed to replicate the returns on a specified index of securities. A second type of passive investing is a strict **buy-and-hold strategy**, such as a fixed, but non-indexed, portfolio of bonds to be held to maturity.

▶ In contrast, with an active investment approach, a portfolio manager will respond to changing capital market expectations. Active management of a portfolio means that its holdings differ from the portfolio's **benchmark** or comparison portfolio in an attempt to produce positive excess risk-adjusted returns, also known as positive **alpha**. Securities held in different-from-benchmark weights reflect expectations of the portfolio manager that differ from consensus expectations. If the portfolio manager's differential expectations are also on average correct, active portfolio management may add value.

▶ A third category, the semiactive, risk-controlled active, or enhanced index approach, seeks positive alpha while keeping tight control over risk relative to the portfolio's benchmark. As an example, an index-tilt strategy seeks to track closely the risk of a securities index while adding a targeted amount of incremental value by tilting portfolio weightings in some direction that the manager expects to be profitable.

Active investment approaches encompass a very wide range of disciplines. To organize this diversity, investment analysts appeal to the concept of investment style. Following Brown and Goetzmann (1997), we can define an investment style (such as an emphasis on growth stocks or value stocks) as a natural grouping of investment disciplines that has some predictive power in explaining the future dispersion in returns across portfolios.

5.1.3 Forming Capital Market Expectations

The manager's third task in the planning process is to form capital market expectations. Long-run forecasts of risk and return characteristics for various asset classes form the basis for choosing portfolios that maximize expected return for given levels of risk, or minimize risk for given levels of expected return.

5.1.4 Creating the Strategic Asset Allocation

The fourth and final task in the planning process is determining the strategic asset allocation. Here the manager combines the IPS and capital market expectations to determine target asset class weights; maximum and minimum permissible asset class weights are often also specified as a risk-control mechanism. The investor may seek both single-period and multiperiod perspectives in the return and risk characteristics of asset allocations under consideration. A single-period perspective has the advantage of simplicity. A multiperiod perspective can address the liquidity and tax considerations that arise from rebalancing portfolios over time, as well as serial correlation (long- and short-term dependencies) in returns, but is more costly to implement.

This reading focuses on the creation of an IPS in the planning step and thereby lays the groundwork for the discussion in other readings of tailoring the IPS to individual and institutional investors' needs. The execution and feedback steps in the portfolio management process are as important as the planning step. For now, we merely outline how these steps fit in the portfolio management process.

5.2 The Execution Step

The execution step is represented by the "portfolio construction and revision" box in Figure 1. In the execution step, the manager integrates investment strategies with capital market expectations to select the specific assets for the portfolio (the portfolio selection/composition decision). Portfolio managers initiate portfolio decisions based on analysts' inputs, and trading desks then implement these decisions (portfolio implementation decision). Subsequently, the portfolio is revised as investor circumstances or capital market expectations change; thus the execution step interacts constantly with the feedback step.

In making the portfolio selection/composition decision, portfolio managers may use the techniques of portfolio optimization. Portfolio optimization—quantitative tools for combining assets efficiently to achieve a set of return and risk objectives—plays a key role in the integration of strategies with expectations and appears in Figure 1 in the portfolio construction and revision box.

At times, a portfolio's actual asset allocation may purposefully and temporarily differ from the strategic asset allocation. For example, the asset allocation might change to reflect an investor's current circumstances that are different from normal. The temporary allocation may remain in place until circumstances return to those described in the IPS and reflected in the strategic asset allocation. If the changed circumstances become permanent, the manager must update the investor's IPS and the temporary asset allocation plan will effectively become the new strategic asset allocation. A strategy known as tactical asset allocation also results in differences from the strategic asset allocation. **Tactical asset allocation** responds to changes in short-term capital market expectations rather than to investor circumstances.

The portfolio implementation decision is as important as the portfolio selection/composition decision. Poorly managed executions result in transaction costs that reduce performance. Transaction costs include all costs of trading, including explicit transaction costs, implicit transaction costs, and missed trade opportunity costs. Explicit transaction costs include commissions paid to brokers, fees paid to exchanges, and taxes. Implicit transaction costs include bid–ask spreads and market price impacts of large trades. Missed trade opportunity costs can arise due to price changes that prevent trades from being filled.

In sum, in the execution step, plans are turned into reality—with all the attendant real-world challenges.

5.3 The Feedback Step

In any business endeavor, feedback and control are essential elements in reaching a goal. In portfolio management, this step has two components: monitoring and rebalancing, and performance evaluation.

5.3.1 Monitoring and Rebalancing

Monitoring and **rebalancing** involve the use of feedback to manage ongoing exposures to available investment opportunities so that the client's current objectives and constraints continue to be satisfied. Two types of factors are monitored: investor-related factors such as the investor's circumstances, and economic and market input factors.

One impetus for portfolio revision is a change in investment objectives or constraints because of changes in investor circumstances. Portfolio managers need a process in place to stay informed of changes in clients' circumstances. The termination of a pension plan or death of a spouse may trigger an abrupt change in a client's time horizon and tax concerns, and the IPS should list the occurrence of such changes as a basis for appropriate portfolio revision.

More predictably, changes in economic and market input factors give rise to the regular need for portfolio revision. Again, portfolio managers need to systematically review the risk attributes of assets as well as economic and capital market factors. A change in expectations may trigger portfolio revision. When asset price changes occur, however, revisions can be required even without changes in expectations. The actual timing and magnitude of rebalancing may be triggered by review periods or by specific rules governing the management of the portfolio and deviation from the tolerances or ranges specified in the strategic asset allocation, or the timing and magnitude may be at the discretion of the manager. For example, suppose the policy allocation calls for an initial portfolio with a 70 percent weighting to stocks and a 30 percent weighting to bonds. Suppose the value of the stock holdings then grows by 40 percent, while the value of the bond holdings grows by 10 percent. The new weighting is roughly 75 percent in stocks and 25 percent in bonds. To bring the portfolio back into compliance with investment policy, it must be rebalanced back to the long-term policy weights. In any event, the rebalancing decision is a crucial one that must take into account many factors, such as transaction costs and taxes (for taxable investors). Disciplined rebalancing will have a major impact on the attainment of investment objectives. Rebalancing takes us back to the issues of execution, as is appropriate in a feedback process.

5.3.2 Performance Evaluation

Investment performance must periodically be evaluated by the investor to assess progress toward the achievement of investment objectives as well as to assess portfolio management skill.

The assessment of portfolio management skill has three components. **Performance measurement** involves the calculation of the portfolio's rate of return. **Performance attribution** examines why the portfolio performed as it did and involves determining the sources of a portfolio's performance. **Performance appraisal** is the evaluation of whether or not the manager is doing a good job based on how the portfolio did relative to a benchmark (a comparison portfolio).

Often, we can examine a portfolio's performance, in terms of absolute returns, through three sources: decisions regarding the strategic asset allocation, **market timing** (returns attributable to shorter-term tactical deviations from the strategic asset allocation), and security selection (skill in selecting individual securities within an asset class). However, portfolio management is frequently conducted with reference to a benchmark, or for some entities, with reference to a stream of projected liabilities or a specified target rate of return. As a result, relative portfolio performance evaluation, in addition to absolute performance measurement, is often of key importance.

With respect to relative performance we may ask questions such as, "Relative to the investment manager's benchmark, what economic sectors were **underweighted** or **overweighted**?" or "What was the manager's rationale for these decisions and how successful were they?" Portfolio evaluation may also be conducted with respect to specific risk models, such as multifactor models, which attempt to explain asset returns in terms of exposures to a set of risk factors.

Concurrent with evaluation of the manager is the ongoing review of the benchmark to establish its continuing suitability. For some benchmarks, this review would include a thorough understanding of how economic sectors and subsectors are determined in the benchmark, the classification of securities within them, and how frequently the classifications change. For any benchmark, one would review whether the benchmark continues to be a fair measuring stick given the manager's mandate.

As with other parts of the portfolio management process, performance evaluation and performance presentation are critical. These topics play a central role in the portfolio management process.

5.4 A Definition of Portfolio Management

In sum, the process logic is incorporated in the following definition, which is the cornerstone for this book. **Portfolio management** is an ongoing process in which

▶ investment objectives and constraints are identified and specified,

▶ investment strategies are developed,

▶ portfolio composition is decided in detail,

▶ portfolio decisions are initiated by portfolio managers and implemented by traders,

▶ portfolio performance is measured and evaluated,

▶ investor and market conditions are monitored, and

▶ any necessary rebalancing is implemented.

Although we have provided general insights into the portfolio management process, we make no judgments and voice no opinions about how the process should be organized, who should make which decisions, or any other process-operating matter. How well the process works is a critical component of investment success. In a survey of pension fund chief operating officers, Ambachtsheer, Capelle, and Scheibelhut (1998) found that 98 percent of the respondents cited a poor portfolio management process as a barrier to achieving excellence in organizational performance. The organization of the portfolio management process of any investment management company should be the result of careful planning.

INVESTMENT OBJECTIVES AND CONSTRAINTS
6

As previously discussed, the IPS is the cornerstone of the portfolio management process. Because of the IPS's fundamental importance, we introduce its main components in this reading. In this section, we return to the tasks of identifying and specifying the investor's objectives and constraints that initiate the planning step.

Although we discuss objectives first and then constraints, the actual process of delineating these for any investor may appropriately start with an examination of investor constraints. For example, a short time horizon affects the investor's ability to take risk.

6.1 Objectives

The two objectives in this framework, risk and return, are interdependent—one cannot be discussed without reference to the other. The risk objective limits how high the investor can set the return objective.

6.1.1 Risk Objective

The first element of the risk–return framework is the risk objective because it will largely determine the return objective. A 10 percent standard deviation risk objective, for example, implies a different asset allocation than a 15 percent standard deviation risk objective, because expected asset risk is generally positively correlated with expected asset return. In formulating a risk objective, the investor must address the following questions:

1. *How do I measure risk?* Risk measurement is a key issue in investments, and several approaches exist for measuring risk. In practice, risk may be measured in absolute terms or in relative terms with reference to various risk concepts. Examples of absolute risk objectives are a specified level of standard deviation or variance of total return. The **variance** of a random variable is the expected value of squared deviations from the random variable's mean. Variance is often referred to as volatility. **Standard deviation** is the positive square root of variance. An example of a relative risk objective is a specified level of tracking risk. **Tracking risk** is the standard deviation of the differences between a portfolio's and the benchmark's total returns.

Downside risk concepts, such as value at risk (VAR), may also be important to an investor. **Value at risk** is a probability-based measure of the loss that one anticipates will be exceeded only a specified small fraction of the time over a given horizon—for example, in 5 percent of all monthly holding periods. Besides statistical measures of risk, other risk exposures, such as exposures to specific economic sectors, or risk with respect to a factor model of returns, may be relevant as well.

2. *What is the investor's willingness to take risk?* The investor's stated willingness to take risk is often very different for institutional versus individual investors. Managers should try to understand the behavioral and, for individuals, the personality factors behind an investor's willingness to take risk. In the reading on individual investors, we explore behavioral issues in reference to the investor's willingness to take risk.

3. *What is the investor's ability to take risk?* Even if an investor is eager to bear risk, practical or financial limitations often limit the amount of risk that can be prudently assumed. For the sake of illustration, in the following discussion we talk about risk in terms of the volatility of asset values.

▶ In terms of spending needs, how much volatility would inconvenience an investor who depends on investments (such as a university in relationship to its endowment fund)? Or, how much volatility would inconvenience an investor who otherwise cannot afford to incur substantial short-term losses? Investors with high levels of wealth relative to probable worst-case short-term loss scenarios can take more risk.

▶ In terms of long-term wealth targets or obligations, how much volatility might prevent the investor from reaching these goals? Investors with high levels of wealth relative to long-term wealth targets or obligations can take more risk.

▶ What are the investor's liabilities or pseudo liabilities? An institution may face legally promised future payments to beneficiaries (liabilities) and an individual may face future retirement spending needs (pseudo liabilities).

▶ What is the investor's financial strength—that is, the ability to increase the savings/contribution level if the portfolio cannot support the planned spending? More financial strength means more risk can be taken.

4. *How much risk is the investor both willing and able to bear?* The answer to this question defines the investor's risk tolerance. Risk tolerance, the capacity to accept risk, is a function of both an investor's willingness and ability to do so. Risk tolerance can also be described in terms of **risk aversion**, the degree of an investor's inability and unwillingness to take risk. The investor's specific risk objectives are formulated with that investor's level of risk tolerance in mind. Importantly, any assessment of risk tolerance must consider both an investor's willingness and that investor's ability to take risk. When a mismatch exists between the two, determining risk tolerance requires educating the client on the dangers of excess risk taking or of ignoring inflation risk, depending on the case. In our presentation in this book, we assume that such education has taken place and that we are providing an appropriate risk objective in the IPS proposed to the client. When an investor's willingness to accept risk exceeds ability to do so, ability prudently places a limit on the amount of risk the investor should assume. When ability exceeds willingness, the investor may fall short of the return objective because willingness would be the limiting factor. These interactions are shown in Table 1.

An investor with an above-average ability to assume risk may have legitimate reasons for choosing a lower risk strategy. As well, an investor may face the pleasant situation of having an excess of wealth to meet financial needs for a long period of time. In these cases, the investor needs to have a clear understanding of the eventual consequences of the decision to effectively spend down excess wealth over time. As with any strategy, such a decision must be reevaluated periodically. In the case of a high-net-worth investor who has earned substantial wealth from entrepreneurial risk taking, such an investor may now simply not want to lose wealth and may desire only liquidity to spend in order to maintain her current lifestyle.

5. *What are the specific risk objective(s)?* Just as risk may be measured either absolutely or relatively, we may specify both absolute risk and relative risk objectives. In practice, investors often find that quantitative risk objectives are easier to specify in relative than in absolute terms. Possibly as a consequence, absolute risk objectives in particular are frequently specified in qualitative rather than quantitative terms.

What distinguishes the risk objective from risk tolerance is the level of specificity. For example, the statement that a person has a "lower than average risk tolerance" might be converted operationally into "the loss in any one year is not to exceed x percent of portfolio value" or "annual volatility of the portfolio is not to exceed y percent." Often, clients—particularly individual investors—do not understand or appreciate this level of specificity, and more-general risk-tolerance statements substitute for a quantitative risk objective.

6. *How should the investor allocate risk?* This is how some investors frame **capital allocation decisions** today, particularly when active strategies will play a role in the portfolio. The question may concern the portfolio as a whole or some part of it. **Risk budgeting** disciplines address the above question most directly. After the investor has determined the *measure* of risk of concern to him (e.g., VAR or tracking risk) and the *desired total quantity of risk* (the

TABLE 1   Risk Tolerance

Willingness to Take Risk	Ability to Take Risk	
	Below Average	**Above Average**
Below Average	Below-average risk tolerance	Resolution needed
Above Average	Resolution needed	Above-average risk tolerance

overall risk budget), an investor using **risk budgeting** would allocate the overall risk budget to specific investments so as to maximize expected overall risk-adjusted return. The resulting optimal risk budgets for the investments would translate to specific allocations of capital to them.

6.1.2 *Return Objective*

The second element of the investment policy framework is the return objective, which must be consistent with the risk objective. Just as tension may exist between willingness and ability in setting the risk objective, so the return objective requires a resolution of return desires versus the risk objective. In formulating a return objective, the investor must address the following four questions:

1. *How is return measured?* The usual measure is **total return**, the sum of the return from price appreciation and the return from investment income. Return may be stated as an absolute amount, such as 10 percent a year, or as a return relative to the benchmark's return, such as benchmark return plus 2 percent a year. Nominal returns must be distinguished from real returns. Nominal returns are unadjusted for inflation. Real returns are adjusted for inflation and sometimes simply called **inflation-adjusted returns**. Also, pretax returns must be distinguished from post-tax returns. Pretax returns are returns before taxes, and post-tax returns are returns after taxes are paid on investment income and realized capital gains.

2. *How much return does the investor say she wants?* This amount is the stated return desire. These wants or desires may be realistic or unrealistic. For example, an investor may have higher than average return desires to meet high consumption desires or a high ending wealth target: for instance, "I want a 20 percent annual return." The advisor or portfolio manager must continually evaluate the desire for high returns in light of the investor's ability to assume risk and the reasonableness of the stated return desire, especially relative to capital market expectations.

3. *How much return does the investor need to achieve, on average?* This amount is the required return or return requirement. Requirements are more stringent than desires because investors with requirements typically must achieve those returns, at least on average. An example of a return requirement is the average return a pension fund projects it must earn to fund liabilities to current and future pensioners, based on actuarial calculations. The compound rate of return that an individual investor must earn to attain the asset base needed for retirement is another example of a return requirement. A third example would be the return that a retired investor must earn on his investment portfolio to cover his annual living expenses. We illustrate these last two cases.

   Suppose that a married couple needs £2 million in 18 years to fund retirement. Their current investable assets total £1,200,000. The projected future need (£2 million) incorporates expected inflation. The couple would need to earn $(£2,000,000/£1,200,000)^{1/18} - 1.0 = 2.88$ percent per year after-tax to achieve their goal. Every cash flow needs to be accounted for in such calculations. If the couple needed to liquidate £25,000 from the portfolio at the end of each year (keeping all other facts unchanged), they would need to earn 4.55 percent per year on an after-tax basis to have £2 million in 18 years (a financial calculator is needed to confirm this result). If all investment returns were taxed at 35 percent, 4.55 percent after tax would correspond to a 7 percent pretax required return $[4.55/(1 - 0.35) = 7\%]$.

A retiree may depend on his investment portfolio for some or all of his living expenses. That need defines a return requirement. Suppose that a retiree must achieve a 4 percent after-tax return on his current investment portfolio to meet his current annual living expenses. Thus, his return requirement on a real, after-tax basis is 4 percent per year. If he expects inflation to be 2 percent per year and a 40 percent tax rate applies to investment returns from any source, we could estimate his pretax nominal return requirement as (After-tax real return requirement + Expected inflation rate)/(1 − Tax rate) = (4% + 2%)/(1 − 0.40) = 10 percent.

In contrast to desired returns, which can be reduced if incongruent with risk objectives, large required returns are an important source of potential conflict between return and risk objectives. Other required return issues that are relevant to specific situations include the following:

► What are the needs and desires for current spending versus ending wealth?

► How do nominal total return requirements relate to expected rates of price inflation? If assets fund obligations subject to inflation, the return requirements should reflect expected rates of inflation.

4. *What are the specific return objectives?* The return objective incorporates the required return, the stated return desire, and the risk objective into a measurable annual total return specification. For example, an investor with a 5 percent after-tax, required, inflation-adjusted annual rate of return but above-average risk tolerance might reasonably set a higher than 5 percent after-tax, inflation-adjusted annual rate of return objective to maximize expected wealth.

An investor's return objective should be consistent with that investor's risk objective. A high return objective may suggest an asset allocation with an expected level of risk that is too great in relation to the risk objective, for example. In addition, the anticipated return from the portfolio should be sufficient to meet wealth objectives or liabilities that the portfolio must fund.

For investors with current investment income needs, the return objective should be sufficient to meet spending needs from capital appreciation and investment income: When a well-considered return objective is not consistent with risk tolerance, other adjustments may need to take place, such as increasing savings or modifying wealth objectives.

An investor delegating portfolio management to an investment manager will communicate a mandate—a set of instructions detailing the investment manager's task and how his performance will be evaluated—that includes a specification of the manager's benchmark. Because the manager's performance will be evaluated against the benchmark, the benchmark's total return is an effective return objective for the investment manager. These instructions may be part of the investment policy statement or, in the case of a portfolio with multiple managers, outlined in separate instructions for each mandate to each manager.

Although an absolute return objective is sometimes set (e.g., 8 percent), the reality of the markets suggests that a relative return objective may be more plausible. A relative return objective is stated as a return relative to the portfolio benchmark's total return (e.g., 1 percent higher than the benchmark).

Table 2 illustrates the variation in return requirement and risk tolerance among various categories of investors.

TABLE 2	Return Requirements and Risk Tolerances of Various Investors	
Type of Investor	**Return Requirement**	**Risk Tolerance**
Individual	Depends on stage of life, circumstances, and obligations	Varies
Pension Plans (Defined Benefit)	The return that will adequately fund liabilities on an inflation-adjusted basis	Depends on plan and sponsor characteristics, plan features, funding status, and workforce characteristics
Pension Plans (Defined Contribution)	Depends on stage of life of individual participants	Varies with the risk tolerance of individual participants
Foundations and Endowments	The return that will cover annual spending, investment expenses, and expected inflation	Determined by amount of assets relative to needs, but generally above-average or average
Life Insurance Companies	Determined by rates used to determine policyholder reserves	Below average due to factors such as regulatory constraints
Non-Life-Insurance Companies	Determined by the need to price policies competitively and by financial needs	Below average due to factors such as regulatory constraints
Banks	Determined by cost of funds	Varies

6.2 Constraints

The investor's risk and return objectives are set within the context of several constraints: liquidity, time horizon, tax concerns, legal and regulatory factors, and unique circumstances. Although all of these factors influence portfolio choice, the first two constraints bear directly on the investor's ability to take risk and thus constrain both risk and return objectives.

6.2.1 Liquidity

A liquidity requirement is a need for cash *in excess of new contributions* (for pension plans and endowments, for example) or *savings* (for individuals) at a specified point in time. Such needs may be anticipated or unanticipated, but either way they stem from liquidity events. An example of a liquidity event is planned construction of a building in one year.

The liquidity requirement may reflect nonrecurring needs or the desire to hold cash against unanticipated needs (a safety or reserve fund). This requirement may be met by holding cash or cash equivalents in the portfolio or by converting other assets into cash equivalents. Any risk of economic loss because of the need to sell relatively less liquid assets to meet liquidity requirements is **liquidity risk**. (An asset that can be converted into cash only at relatively high total cost is said to be relatively less liquid.) Liquidity risk, therefore, arises for two reasons: an asset-side reason (asset liquidity) and a liability-side reason (liquidity requirements). Portfolio managers control asset selection but not liquidity requirements; as a result, in practice, managers use asset selection to manage liquidity risk. If the portfolio's asset and income base are large relative to its potential liquidity requirements, relatively less liquid assets can be held. A distinct consideration is liquidity requirements in relation to **price risk** of the asset—the risk of fluctuations in market price.

Assets with high price risk are frequently less liquid, especially during market downturns. If the timing of an investor's liquidity requirements is significantly correlated with market downturns, these requirements can influence asset selection in favor of less risky assets. In many cases, therefore, consideration of both liquidity risk and price risk means that an investor will choose to hold some part of the portfolio in highly liquid and low-price-risk assets in anticipation of future liquidity requirements. Investors may also modify the payoff structure of a risky portfolio to address liquidity requirements using derivative strategies, although such modifications often incur costs. (**Derivatives** are contracts whose payoffs depend on the value of another asset, often called the underlying asset.)

6.2.2 Time Horizon

Time horizon most often refers to the time period associated with an investment objective. Investment objectives and associated time horizons may be short term, long term, or a combination of the two. (A time horizon of 10 years or more is often considered to be long term. Investment performance over the long term should average results over several market and business cycles.) A multistage horizon is a combination of shorter term and longer term horizons. An example of a multistage horizon is the case of funding children's education shorter term and the investor's retirement longer term.

Other constraints, such as a unique circumstance or a specific liquidity requirement, can also affect an investor's time horizon. For example, an individual investor's temporary family living arrangement can dictate that his time horizon constraint be stated in multistage terms. Similarly, an institutional investor's need to make an imminent substantial disbursement of funds for a capital project can necessitate a multistage approach to the time horizon constraint.

In general, relevant time horizon questions include the following:

▶ *How does the length of the time horizon modify the investor's ability to take risk?* The longer the time horizon the more risk the investor can take. The longer the time horizon, the greater the investor's ability to replenish investment resources by increasing savings. A long-term investor's labor income may also be an asset sufficiently stable to support a higher level of portfolio risk.[3] Cash may be safe for a short-term investor but risky for a long-term investor who will be faced with continuously reinvesting.

▶ *How does the length of the time horizon modify the investor's asset allocation?* Many investors allocate a greater proportion of funds to risky assets when they address long-term as opposed to short-term investment objectives. Decreased risk-taking ability with shorter horizons can thus constrain portfolio choice.

▶ *How does the investor's willingness and ability to bear fluctuations in portfolio value modify the asset allocation?* With a focus on risk, even an investor with a long-term objective may limit risk taking because of sensitivity to the possibility of substantial interim losses. The chance of unanticipated liquidity needs may increase during market downturns, for instance, because a market downturn may be linked to a decline in economic activity affecting income or other sources of wealth. An investor that often faces unanticipated short-term liquidity needs will usually favor investments with a shorter time horizon so as to limit the risk of loss of value.

[3] See Campbell and Viceira (2002) for a discussion of this and the following point.

► *How does a multistage time horizon constrain the investor's asset allocation?* The investment policy must be designed to accommodate all time horizons in a multistage horizon case. Such design will probably entail some compromise in the setting of objectives to attain short-, medium-, and long-term goals.

6.2.3 Tax Concerns

A country's tax policy can affect important aspects of investment decision-making for investors who reside there. Tax concerns arise for taxable investors because tax payments reduce the amount of the total return that can be used for current needs or reinvested for future growth. Differences between the tax rates applying to investment income and capital gains will influence taxable investors' choice of investments and their timing of sales. Estate taxes on wealth triggered by the investor's death can also affect investment decisions. Finally, tax policy changes that affect security prices affect both taxable and tax-exempt investors.

6.2.4 Legal and Regulatory Factors

Legal and regulatory factors are external factors imposed by governmental, regulatory, or oversight authorities to constrain investment decision-making. In the United Kingdom, for example, regulations issued by the Financial Services Authority (FSA) limit the concentration of holdings in debt and equity securities for U.K. mutual funds. Another example is the United States' Employee Retirement Income Security Act (ERISA) of 1974, as interpreted by regulatory agencies and the courts. ERISA limits the acquisition and holding of employer securities by certain pension plans. Some countries limit the use of certain asset classes in retirement accounts.

6.2.5 Unique Circumstances

Unique circumstances are internal factors (other than a liquidity requirement, time horizon, or tax concern) that may constrain portfolio choices. For example, a university endowment may be constrained to avoid certain investments against which there may be ethical objections or social responsibility considerations. Similarly, an individual investor's portfolio choices may be constrained by circumstances focusing on health needs, support of dependents, and other circumstances unique to the particular individual. Investors may specify avoidance of nondomestic shares or derivatives. Portfolio choices may also be constrained by investor capability in terms of both human resources and financial resources such as time, interest, background, and technical expertise.

7   THE DYNAMICS OF THE PROCESS

One of the truly satisfying aspects of portfolio management as a professional activity is the underlying logic and the dynamism of the portfolio process concept. In a broad sense, the work of analysts, economists, and market strategists is all a matter of "getting ready." The work of portfolio management is the action: taking the inputs and moving step by step through the orderly process of converting this raw material into a portfolio that maximizes expected return relative to the investor's ability to bear risk, that meets the investor's constraints and preferences, and that integrates portfolio policies with expectational factors and market uncertainties.

Portfolio management is where the payoff is, because this is where it all comes together. Of course, it is the end result of this process that is judged: the performance of the portfolio relative to expectations and comparison standards.

Professionalism is enhanced and practice improved by managing portfolios as a process that

► consists of the steps outlined in this book,

► flows logically and systematically through an orderly sequence of decision-making, and

► is continuous once put into motion with respect to a given investor.

This view approaches portfolio management not as a set of separate elements operating by fits and starts as intuition or inspiration dictates but rather as an integrated whole in which every decision moves the portfolio down the process path and in which no decision can be skipped without sacrificing functional integrity.

THE FUTURE OF PORTFOLIO MANAGEMENT

In the last few decades, portfolio management has become a more science-based discipline somewhat analogous to engineering and medicine. As in these other fields, advances in basic theory, technology, and market structure constantly translate into improvements in products and professional practices.

Among the most significant recent theoretical advances in investments is the recognition that the risk characteristics of the nontradable assets owned by an individual client, such as future earnings from a job, a business, or an expected inheritance, should be included in the definition of that client's portfolio. In the institutional area also, there is an increasing awareness and use of multifactor risk models and methods of managing risk.

Among the most significant market developments is the emergence of a broad range of new standardized derivative contracts—swaps, futures, and options. As active trading in these standardized products continues to develop, they make possible the creation of an infinite variety of customized investment products tailored to the needs of specific clients. As analysts continue to develop a more comprehensive view of risk, they also command a wider set of tools with which to manage it.[4]

THE ETHICAL RESPONSIBILITIES OF PORTFOLIO MANAGERS

In this reading, we have initiated a course of study that we hope will further the reader in his or her career as an investment professional. We select the term investment *professional* advisedly. The dictionary defines professional as "conforming to the standards of a profession." Every thoughtful person who has explored the subject has concluded that professional standards are of two types: standards of competence and standards of conduct. Merely drawing a livelihood from managing or advising on the investment of client monies is insufficient in itself to make an investment professional.

---

[4] This section on the future of portfolio management was contributed by Dr. Zvi Bodie.

But verbal distinctions are not the most important point. The conduct of a portfolio manager affects the well-being of clients and many other people. The connection to individuals and their welfare is always present; it is no less important in those institutional contexts in which the portfolio manager may never meet the client. In the first years of the 21st century press attention focused on abuses in the U.S. mutual fund industry such as late trading, abusive market timing, selective disclosure of information on portfolio holdings, and undisclosed payments for "shelf space" to gain placement on brokers' preferred lists.[5] Certain fund executives facilitated or participated in these activities for personal enrichment, at the expense of the well-being of their clients, mutual fund shareholders. In truth, the docket of cases of professional misconduct is never empty, but the profession can and must work towards minimizing it. The portfolio manager must keep foremost in mind that he or she is in a position of trust, requiring ethical conduct towards the public, client, prospects, employers, employees, and fellow workers. For CFA Institute members, this position of trust is reflected in the Code of Ethics and Standards of Professional Conduct to which members subscribe, as well as in the Professional Conduct Statement they submit annually. Ethical conduct is the foundation requirement for managing investment portfolios.

---

[5] The listing follows the enumeration of William H. Donaldson, CFA, chair of the U.S. Securities and Exchange Commission, in a speech to the Mutual Fund Directors Forum on 7 January 2004.

SUMMARY

In this reading, we have presented the portfolio management process and the elements of the investment policy statement.

▶ According to the portfolio perspective, individual investments should be judged in the context of how much risk they add to a portfolio rather than on how risky they are on a stand-alone basis.

▶ The three steps in the portfolio management process are the planning step (objectives and constraint determination, investment policy statement creation, capital market expectation formation, and strategic asset allocation creation); the execution step (portfolio selection/composition and portfolio implementation); and the feedback step (performance evaluation and portfolio monitoring and rebalancing).

▶ Investment objectives are specific and measurable desired performance outcomes, and constraints are limitations on the ability to make use of particular investments. The two types of objectives are risk and return. The two types of constraints are internal (posed by the characteristics of the investor) and external (imposed by outside agencies).

▶ An investment policy statement is a written planning document that governs all investment decisions for the client. This document integrates a client's needs, preferences, and circumstances into a statement of that client's objectives and constraints.

▶ A policy or strategic asset allocation establishes exposures to IPS-permissible asset classes in a manner designed to satisfy the client's long-run objectives and constraints. The plan reflects the interaction of objectives and constraints with long-run capital market expectations.

▶ In a passive investment strategy approach, portfolio composition does not react to changes in expectations; an example is indexing, which involves a fixed portfolio designed to replicate the returns on an index. An active approach involves holding a portfolio different from a benchmark or comparison portfolio for the purpose of producing positive excess risk-adjusted returns. A semiactive approach refers to an indexing approach with controlled use of weights different from the benchmark.

▶ The portfolio selection/composition decision concerns portfolio construction and often uses portfolio optimization to combine assets efficiently to achieve return and risk objectives. The portfolio implementation decision concerns the trading desk function of implementing portfolio decisions and involves explicit and implicit transaction costs.

▶ The elements of performance evaluation are performance measurement, attribution, and appraisal. Performance measurement is the calculation of portfolio rates of return. Performance attribution is the analysis of those rates of return to determine the factors that explain how the return was achieved. Performance appraisal assesses how well the portfolio manager performed on a risk-adjusted basis, whether absolute or relative to a benchmark.

▶ Portfolio monitoring and rebalancing use feedback to manage ongoing exposures to available investment opportunities in order to continually satisfy the client's current objectives and constraints.

▶ Portfolio management is an ongoing process in which the investment objectives and constraints are identified and specified, investment policies and strategies are developed, the portfolio composition is decided in detail, portfolio decisions are initiated by portfolio managers and implemented by traders, portfolio performance is evaluated, investor and market conditions are monitored, and any necessary rebalancing is implemented.

▶ To determine a risk objective, there are several steps: specify a risk measure (or measures) such as standard deviation, determine the investor's willingness to take risk, determine the investor's ability to take risk, synthesize the investor's willingness and ability into the investor's risk tolerance, and specify an objective using the measure(s) in the first step above.

▶ To determine a return objective, there are several steps: specify a return measure such as total nominal return, determine the investor's stated return desire, determine the investor's required rate of return, and specify an objective in terms of the return measure in the first step above.

▶ A liquidity requirement is a need for cash in excess of the contribution rate or the savings rate at a specified point in time. This need may be either anticipated or unanticipated.

▶ A time horizon is the time period associated with an investment objective. Investment objectives and associated time horizons may be short term, long term, or a combination of these two. A multistage horizon is a combination of shorter term and longer term horizons. A time horizon can be considered a constraint because shorter time horizons generally indicate lower risk tolerance and hence constrain portfolio choice, making it more conservative.

▶ A tax concern is any issue arising from a tax structure that reduces the amount of the total return that can be used for current needs or reinvested for future growth. Tax concerns constrain portfolio choice. If differences exist between the tax rates applying to investment income and capital gains, tax considerations will influence the choice of investment.

▶ Legal and regulatory factors are external considerations that may constrain investment decision making. For example, a government agency may limit the use of certain asset classes in retirement portfolios.

▶ Unique circumstances are internal factors (other than a liquidity requirement, time horizon, or tax concerns) that may constrain portfolio choices. For example, an investor seeking to avoid investments in tobacco companies will place an internal constraint on portfolio choice.

1. A. An individual expects to save €50,000 during the coming year from income from non-portfolio sources, such as salary. She will need €95,000 within the year to make a down payment for a house purchase. What is her liquidity requirement for the coming year?

B. Endowments are funds that are typically owned by non-profit institutions involved in educational, medical, cultural, and other charitable activities. Classified as institutional investors, endowments are almost always established with the intent of lasting into perpetuity.

    The Wilson-Fowler Endowment was established in the United States to provide financial support to Wilson-Fowler College. An endowment's spending rate defines the fraction of endowment assets distributed to the supported institution. The Wilson-Fowler Endowment has established a spending rate of 4 percent a year; the endowment follows the simple rule of spending, in a given year, an amount equal to 4% × (Market value of the endowment at the end of the prior year). This amount is committed to the budgetary support of the college for the coming year. At the end of the prior year, the market value of the Wilson-Fowler Endowment's assets stood at $75,000,000. In addition, the Wilson-Fowler Endowment has committed to contribute $1,000,000 in the coming year to the construction of a new student dormitory. Planners at the endowment expect the endowment to receive contributions or gifts (from alumni and other sources) of $400,000 over the coming year. What is the anticipated liquidity requirement of the Wilson-Fowler Endowment for the coming year?

2. The Executive Director of the Judd University Endowment estimates that the capital markets will provide a 9 percent expected return for an endowment portfolio taking above-average risk, and a 7 percent expected return for an endowment portfolio taking average risk. The Judd Endowment provides tuition scholarships for Judd University students. The spending rate has been 4 percent, and the expected tuition inflation rate is 3 percent. Recently university officials have pressured the endowment to increase the spending rate to 6 percent. The endowment has an average to below-average ability to accept risk and only an average willingness to take risk, but a university official claims that the risk tolerance should be raised because higher returns are needed. Discuss an appropriate return objective and risk tolerance for the Judd Endowment.

3. Stux (1994) describes a country allocation strategy across five major equity markets: the United States, the United Kingdom, Germany, France, and Japan. In this strategy, a measure of relative attractiveness among the five equity markets is used as a factor in determining the weights of the five equity markets in the overall portfolio. The investment in each country, however, whatever the country's weight, is an indexed investment in the equity market of that country. The weights of the five equity markets in the overall portfolio generally are expected to differ from benchmark weights (the weights of the countries in an appropriate benchmark for the international equity market), within limits.

A. Characterize the two components (portfolio weights and within-country investments) of the country allocation strategy using the text's framework for classifying investment strategies.

B. Characterize the country allocation strategy overall.

4. Characterize each of the investment objectives given below as one of the following: an absolute risk objective, a relative risk objective, an absolute return objective, or a relative return objective.

A. Achieve a rate of return of 8 percent a year.

B. Limit the standard deviation of portfolio returns to 20 percent a year or less.

C. Achieve returns in the top quartile of the portfolio's peer universe (the set of portfolios with similar investment objectives and characteristics).

D. Maintain a 10 percent or smaller probability that the portfolio's return falls below the threshold level of 5 percent per annum over a one-year time horizon.

E. Achieve a tracking risk of no more than 4 percent per annum with respect to the portfolio's benchmark.

Questions 5–10 relate to James Stephenson

Select and justify the best answer.

James Stephenson, age 55 and single, is a surgeon who has accumulated a substantial investment portfolio without a clear long-term strategy in mind. Two of his patients who work in financial markets comment as follows:

▶ James Hrdina: "My investment firm, based on its experience with investors, has standard investment policy statements in five categories. You would be better served to adopt one of these standard policy statements instead of spending time developing a policy based on your individual circumstances."

▶ Charles Gionta: "Developing a long-term policy can be unwise given the fluctuations of the market. You want your investment advisor to react continuously to changing conditions and not be limited by a set policy."

Stephenson hires a financial advisor, Caroline Coppa. At their initial meeting, Coppa compiles the following notes:

Stephenson currently has a $2.0 million portfolio that has a large concentration in small-capitalization U.S. equities. Over the past five years, the portfolio has averaged 20 percent annual total return on investment. Stephenson hopes that, over the long term, his portfolio will continue to earn 20 percent annually. When asked about his risk tolerance, he described it as "average." He was surprised when informed that U.S. small-cap portfolios have experienced extremely high volatility.

He does not expect to retire before age 70. His current income is more than sufficient to meet his expenses. Upon retirement, he plans to sell his surgical practice and use the proceeds to purchase an annuity to cover his post-retirement cash flow needs.

Both his income and realized capital gains are taxed at a 30 percent rate. No pertinent legal or regulatory issues apply. He has no pension or retirement plan but does have sufficient health insurance for post-retirement needs.

---

5. The comments about investment policy statements made by Stephenson's patients are *best* characterized as

	Hrdina	Gionta
A.	correct	correct
B.	correct	incorrect
C.	incorrect	correct
D.	incorrect	incorrect

6. In formulating the return objective for Stephenson's investment policy statement, the *most* appropriate determining factor for Coppa to focus on is

A. return desires.

B. ability to take risk.

C. return requirement.

D. Stephenson's returns over last five years.

7. Stephenson's willingness and ability to accept risk can be *best* characterized as

	Willingness to accept risk	Ability to accept risk
A.	below average	below average
B.	below average	above average
C.	above average	below average
D.	above average	above average

8. Stephenson's tax and liquidity constraints can be *best* characterized as

	Tax constraint	Liquidity constraint
A.	significant	significant
B.	significant	insignificant
C.	insignificant	significant
D.	insignificant	insignificant

9. Stephenson's time horizon is best characterized as

   A. short-term and single-stage.

   B. short-term and multistage.

   C. long-term and single-stage.

   D. long-term and multistage.

10. Stephenson's return objective and risk tolerance are most appropriately described as

	Return Objective	Risk Tolerance
A.	below average	below average
B.	below average	above average
C.	above average	below average
D.	above average	above average

11. *James Stephenson Investment Profile*

Case Facts

Type of investor	Individual; surgeon, 55 years of age, in good health
Asset base	$2 million
Stated return desire *or* investment goal	10 percentage points above the average annual return on U.S. small-capitalization stocks
Annual spending needs	$150,000
Annual income from non-portfolio sources (before tax)	$350,000 from surgical practice
Other return factors	Inflation is 3%
Risk considerations	Owns large concentration in U.S. small-capitalization stocks
Specific liquidity requirements	$70,000 charitable donation in 10 months
Time specifications	Retirement at age 70
Tax concerns	Income and capital gains taxed at 30 percent

Questions

11-1. Underline the word at right that best describes the client's:

A. *Willingness to accept risk*	Below average	Above average
B. *Ability to accept risk*	Below average	Above average
C. *Risk tolerance*	Below average	Above average
D. *Liquidity requirement*	Significant	Not significant
E. *Time horizon*	Single stage	Multistage
F. *Overall time horizon*	Short to intermediate term	Long term
G. *Tax concerns*	Significant	Not significant

11-2. Discuss appropriate client objectives:

A. *Risk*

B. *Return*

12. *Foothill College Endowment Fund*

Case Facts

Type of investor	Institutional; endowment
Purpose	Provide annual scholarships currently totaling $39.5 million
Asset base	$1 billion ˉ
Stated return desire	6 percent, calculated as spending rate of 4 percent plus previously expected college tuition inflation of 2 percent
Other return factors	Revised expectation of college tuition inflation is 3 percent
Tax concerns	Tax-exempt

Questions

12-1. Underline the word at right that best describes the client's:

A. *Risk tolerance*	Below average	Above average
B. *Liquidity requirement*	Significant	Not significant
C. *Time horizon*	Single stage	Multistage
D. *Overall time horizon*	Short to intermediate term	Long term
E. *Tax concerns*	Significant	Not significant

12-2. Discuss appropriate client objectives:

A. *Risk*

B. *Return*

---

13. [**Adapted from the 1998 CFA Level III Examination**] *Vincenzo Donadoni Investment Profile*

Case Facts

Type of investor	Individual; 56 year old male in good health
Asset base	13.0 million Swiss francs (CHF)
Stated return desire *or* investment goal	Leave a trust fund of CHF 15.0 million for three children
Annual spending needs	CHF 250,000 rising with inflation
Annual income from other sources (after tax)	CHF 125,000 consulting income for next two years only
Ability to generate additional income	No
Willingness to accept risk	Impulsive, opinionated, successful with large bets as a businessman, believes success depends on taking initiative
Specific liquidity requirements	CHF 1.5 million immediately to renovate house CHF 2.0 million in taxes due in nine months
Time specifications	Long term except for liquidity concerns
Legal and regulatory factors	None
Unique circumstances	None

Questions

13-1. Underline the word at right that best describes the client's:

A. *Willingness to accept risk*	Below average	Above average
B. *Ability to accept risk*	Below average	Above average
C. *Risk tolerance*	Below average	Above average
D. *Liquidity requirement*	Significant	Not significant
E. *Time horizon*	Single stage	Multistage
F. *Overall time horizon*	Short to intermediate term	Long term

13-2. Discuss appropriate client objectives:

A. *Risk*

B. *Return*

Questions 14–19 relate to Gina Benedetti

Gina Benedetti, a trust officer at an Italian bank, interviewed Alessandro Santalucia, a new client. A summary of her interview appears in Exhibit 1.

EXHIBIT 1	Interview Summary for Client Alessandro Santalucia
Age	45
Family	Married but divorce is pending; three children ages 16, 17, and 18
Hobbies	Speed boat racing, mountain climbing
Business	Real estate speculation, buying firms with turn-around potential
Assets	€1 million in his private business and real estate and €500,000 in a nondiversified investment portfolio
Retirement plans	None; wishes to continue working until physically unable to do so
Current income	Spending modestly exceeds income
Spending plans/ Requirements	Children's college education (estimated at €30,000/year per child); divorce settlement may be up to one-half of his assets

Benedetti develops an investment policy statement and recommended asset allocation for Santalucia and puts the following notes in Santalucia's file:

1. I met with our staff economist to review his thinking on short-term trends in the economy and financial markets. I relied greatly on his forecast to draft an investment policy statement for Santalucia.

2. Santalucia's situation is very similar to that of another client from several years ago. I used that client's asset allocation as a basis for my portfolio recommendations for Santalucia.

Benedetti next meets with her firm's research analyst, Kurt Westerlund, to discuss changes to the firm's recommended list. One company of interest is an upcoming initial public offering (IPO) for Palladio Corp. To analyze this IPO, Westerlund used data from 20 publicly traded peer companies with business lines similar to Palladio's. He combined them into an equally weighted portfolio to approximate the anticipated behavior of Palladio's stock once it becomes publicly traded. Some of this information is presented in Exhibit 2.

During their conversation, Westerlund makes several statements about Palladio and the capital markets:

1. "I estimated the Palladio proxy portfolio's beta over several different time periods, and this portfolio beta has always been stable, with the high and low estimates within 5 percent of each other. However, Palladio's estimated beta will be more volatile over time than that of the proxy portfolio."

2. "The estimation of beta is affected by several factors, including regression to the mean, volume of trading, and the market proxy used."

3. "The capital market line (CML) uses a measure of total risk, and the SML uses a standardized measure of systematic risk."

4. "The SML is the equation that specifies the required/expected return for a security that is implied by the CML when the market is in equilibrium."

EXHIBIT 2	Data for Palladio Peer Firms Monthly Data, May 2000–May 2006	
	Palladio Proxy Portfolio	**Market**
Average monthly return	0.0051	0.0025
Variance of returns	0.0033	0.0021
Covariance with market return	0.0015	0.0021
Correlation with market return	0.567	1.000

Note: Returns measured as decimal; 1% = 0.01.

Benedetti notes that the current short-term government bill rate offers 2.5 percent annually and her firm's economist anticipates a market risk premium of 7.0 percent on stock market investments.

In addition to her consideration of Palladio, Benedetti wants to review Borgonovo, Inc., and decide whether it should remain on the bank's recommended list or be removed. Borgonovo has a beta of 1.2, and a forecasted return of 9.0 percent.

CFA
2006 exam

14. Which of the following *best* describes Santalucia's current risk tolerance and liquidity constraint? Santalucia's risk tolerance is

A. below average, and his liquidity constraint is significant.

B. below average, and his liquidity constraint is insignificant.

C. above average, and his liquidity constraint is significant.

D. above average, and his liquidity constraint is insignificant.

CFA
2006 exam

15. Do Benedetti's two notes for Santalucia's file describe the correct process for constructing an investment policy statement and for developing portfolio recommendations?

	Note #1 on Investment Policy Statement Process	Note #2 on Developing Portfolio Recommendations
A.	No	No
B.	No	Yes
C.	Yes	No
D.	Yes	Yes

16. Are Westerlund's statements #1 and #2 correct regarding the:

	Palladio systematic risk?	factors affecting beta estimation?
A.	No	No
B.	No	Yes
C.	Yes	No
D.	Yes	Yes

17. Are Westerlund's statements #3 and #4 correct regarding:

	types of risk measures?	equilibrium?
A.	No	No
B.	No	Yes
C.	Yes	No
D.	Yes	Yes

18. Based on Exhibit 2, the estimated beta for Palladio is *closest* to

   A. 0.40.

   B. 0.45.

   C. 0.57.

   D. 0.71.

19. Based on the relationship of Borgonovo's stock to the SML, what is the *most* appropriate decision Benedetti should make regarding the Borgonovo stock?

   A. Keep Borgonovo on the recommended list because it plots below the SML.

   B. Keep Borgonovo on the recommended list because it plots above the SML.

   C. Remove Borgonovo from the recommended list because it plots below the SML.

   D. Remove Borgonovo from the recommended list because it plots above the SML.

APPENDIX

Appendix A Solutions to End-of-Reading Problems, Practice Questions, and Concept Checks

SOLUTIONS FOR READING 62

1. A. $S_0 = \$1{,}000$

$F(0,T) = \$1{,}100$

$T = 1$

$V_0(0,T) = \$1{,}000 - \$1{,}100/(1.0675) = -\$30.44$

B. Because the value is negative, the payment is made by the short to the long.

2. A. $S_0 = \$500$

$T = 2/12 = 0.1667$

$r = 0.035$

$F(0,T) = \$500 \times (1.035)^{0.1667} = \$502.88$

B. Sell the security for $500 and invest at 3.5 percent for two months. At the end of two months, you will have $502.88. Enter into a forward contract now to buy the security at $498 in two months.

Arbitrage profit = $\$502.88 - \$498 = \$4.88$

C. $S_t = \$490$

$t = 1/12 = 0.0833$

$T = 2/12 = 0.1667$

$T - t = 0.0834$

$r = 0.035$

$V_t(0,T) = \$490.00 - \$502.88/(1.035)^{0.0834} = -\$11.44$. This represents a gain to the short position.

3. A. $S_0 = \$100$

$T = 1$

$r = 0.05$

$F(0,T) = \$100(1.05) = \$105$

B. $S_t = \$90$

$t = 3/12 = 0.25$

$T = 1$

$T - t = 0.75$

$r = 0.05$

$V_t(0,T) = \$90 - \$105/(1.05)^{0.75} = -\$11.23$

The investor is short so this represents a gain.

C. $S_t = \$107$

$t = 5/12 = 0.4167$

$T = 1$

$T - t = 0.5834$

$r = 0.05$

$V_t(0,T) = \$107 - \$105/(1.05)^{0.5834} = \$4.95$

The investor is short, so this represents a loss to the short position.

D. $S_t = \$98$

   $F(0,T) = \$105$

   $V_T(0,T) = \$98 - \$105 = -\$7$

   Gain to short position $= \$7$

   Loss on asset $\qquad = -\$2$ (based on $\$100 - \$98$)

   Net gain $\qquad\qquad = \$5$

   This represents a return of 5 percent on an asset worth $100, the same as the risk-free rate.

E. $S_t = \$110$

   $F(0,T) = \$105$

   $V_T(0,T) = 110 - 105 = \$5$

   Loss to short position $= -\$5$

   Gain on asset $\qquad = \$10$ (based on $\$110 - \$100$)

   Net gain $\qquad\qquad = \$5$

   This represents a return of 5 percent on an asset worth $100, the same as the risk-free rate. The overall gain on the transaction is the same as in Part D because the forward contract was executed at the no-arbitrage price of $105.

4. A. $S_0 = \$225$

   $T = 1$

   $r = 0.0475$

   $F(0,T) = \$225(1.0475) = \$235.69$

B. $S_t = \$250$

   $t = 4/12 = 0.3333$

   $T = 1$

   $T - t = 0.6667$

   $r = 0.0475$

   $V_t(0,T) = \$250.00 - \$235.69/(1.0475)^{0.6667} = \$21.49$

   The investor is long, so a positive value represents a gain.

C. $S_t = \$200$

   $t = 8/12 = 0.6667$

   $T = 1$

   $T - t = 0.3333$

   $r = 0.0475$

   $V_t(0,T) = \$200.00 - \$235.69/(1.0475)^{0.3333} = -\$32.07$

   The investor is long, so this represents a loss to the long position.

D. $S_t = \$190$

   $F(0,T) = \$235.69$

   $V_T(0,T) = \$190.00 - \$235.69 = -\$45.69$

   Loss to long position $= -\$45.69$

   Gain on asset $\qquad = \$35.00$ (based on $\$225 - \$190$)

   Net loss $\qquad\qquad = -\$10.69$

E. $S_t = \$240$

$F(0,T) = \$235.69$

$V_T(0,T) = \$240.00 - \$235.69 = \$4.31$

Gain to long position = $4.31

Loss on asset   = −$15.00 (based on $240 − $225)

Net loss   = −$10.69

This loss is the same as the loss in Part D. In fact, the loss would be the same for any other price as well, because the forward contract was executed at the no-arbitrage price of $235.69. The loss of $10.69 is the risk-free rate of 4.75 percent applied to the initial asset price of $225.

5. A. The no-arbitrage forward price is $F(0,T) = \$200(1.05)3/12 = \$202.45$.

Because the forward contract offered by the dealer is overpriced, sell the forward contract and buy the security now. Doing so will yield an arbitrage profit of $2.55.

Borrow $200 and buy security. At the end of three months, repay $202.45

At the end of three months, deliver the security for $205.00

Arbitrage profit $2.55

B. At a price of $198.00, the contract offered by the dealer is underpriced relative to the no-arbitrage forward price of $202.45. Enter into a forward contract to buy in three months at $198.00. Short the stock now, and invest the proceeds. Doing so will yield an arbitrage profit of $4.45.

Short security for $200 and invest proceeds for three months $202.45

At the end of three months, buy the security for $198.00

Arbitrage profit $4.45

6. A. $S_0 = \$150$

$T = 250/365$

$r = 0.0525$

$PV(D,0,T) = \$1.25/(1.0525)^{30/365} + \$1.25/(1.0525)^{120/365} +$
                $\$1.25/(1.0525)^{210/365}$

        $= \$3.69$

$F(0,T) = (\$150.00 - \$3.69)(1.0525)^{250/365} = \$151.53$

B. $S_t = \$115$

$F(0,T) = \$151.53$

$t = 100/365$

$T = 250/365$

$T - t = 150/365$

$r = 0.0525$

After 100 days, two dividends remain: the first one in 20 days, and the second one in 110 days.

$PV(D,t,T) = \$1.25/(1.0525)^{20/365} + \$1.25/(1.0525)^{110/365} = \$2.48$

$V_t(0,T) = \$115.00 - \$2.48 - \$151.53/(1.0525)^{150/365} = -\$35.86$

A negative value is a gain to the short.

C. $S_T = \$130$

$F(0,T) = \$151.53$

$V_T(0,T) = \$130.00 - \$151.53 = -\$21.53$

The contract expires with a value of negative $21.53, a gain to the short.

7. A. $S_0 = \$1,145$

$T = 90/365 = 0.2466$

$r = 0.0425$

$r^c = \ln(1 + 0.0425) = 0.0416$

$\delta^c = 0.0175$

$F(0,T) = (\$1,145 \times e^{-0.0175(0.2466)})(e^{0.0416(0.2466)}) = \$1,151.83$

B. $S_t = \$1,225$

$T = 90/365 = 0.2466$

$t = 28/365 = 0.0767$

$T - t = 0.1699$

$r = 0.0425$

$r^c = \ln(1 + 0.0425) = 0.0416$

$\delta^c = 0.0175$

$V_t(0,T) = (\$1,225 \times e^{-0.0175(0.1699)}) - (1151.83e^{-0.0416(0.1699)}) = \$77.65$

This is a gain to the long position.

C. $S_T = \$1,235$

$F(0,T) = \$1,151.83$

$V_T(0,T) = \$1,235.00 - \$1,151.83 = \$83.17$

The contract expires with a value of $83.17, a gain to the long.

8. A. The investor should enter into a short forward contract, locking in the price at which he can sell the bond in 365 days.

$B_0{}^c(T + Y) = \$1,146.92$
$T = 365/365 = 1$
$r = 0.06$

Between now (i.e., 200 days since the original purchase) and the next 365 days, the investor will receive two coupons, the first 165 days from now and the second 347 days from now.

$PV(CI,0,T) = \$40/(1.06)^{165/365} + \$40/(1.06)^{347/365} = \$76.80$

$F(0,T) = (\$1,146.92 - \$76.81)(1.06)^{365/365} = \$1,134.32$

B. $B_t^c(T + Y) = \$1,302.26$

$F(0,T) = \$1,134.32$

$t = 180/365$

$T = 365/365$

$T - t = 185/365$

$r = 0.04$

We are now on the 380th day of the bond's life. One more coupon payment remains until the expiration of the forward contract. The coupon payment is in $547 - 380 = 167$ days.

$PV(CI,0,T) = \$40/(1.04)^{167/365} = \$39.29$

$V_t(0,T) = \$1,302.26 - \$39.29 - \$1,134.32/(1.04)^{185/365} = \$150.98$

A positive value is a loss to the short position.

9. A. A 6×12 FRA expires in 180 days and is based on 180-day LIBOR.

    B. $h = 180$

        $m = 180$

        $h + m = 360$

        $L_0(h + m) = 0.0595$

        $L_0(h) = 0.057$

$$FRA(0,h,m) = \left[\frac{1 + 0.0595\left(\frac{360}{360}\right)}{1 + 0.0570\left(\frac{180}{360}\right)} - 1 \right]\left(\frac{360}{180}\right) = 0.0603$$

    C. $h = 180$

        $m = 180$

        $g = 45$

        $h - g = 135$

        $h + m - g = 315$

        $L_{45}(h - g) = 0.0590$

        $L_{45}(h + m - g) = 0.0615$

$$V_t(0,h,m) = \frac{1}{1 + 0.0590\left(\frac{135}{360}\right)} - \frac{1 + 0.0603\left(\frac{180}{360}\right)}{1 + 0.0615\left(\frac{315}{360}\right)} = 0.00081$$

    For \$10,000,000 notional principal, the value of the FRA would be $= 0.00081 \times 10,000,000 = \$8,100$.

    D. $h = 180$

        $m = 180$

        $L_{180}(h + m) = 0.0625$

$$\text{At expiration, the payoff is } \frac{(0.0625 - 0.0603)\left(\frac{180}{360}\right)}{1 + 0.0625\left(\frac{180}{360}\right)} = 0.001067$$

    Based on a notional principal of \$10,000,000, the corporation, which is long, will receive $\$10,000,000 \times 0.001067 = \$10,670$ from the dealer.

10. A. A 3×6 FRA expires in 90 days and is based on 90-day LIBOR.

    B. $h = 90$

        $m = 90$

        $h + m = 180$

        $L_0(h) = 0.06$

        $L_0(h + m) = 0.0614$

$$FRA(0,h,m) = \left[\frac{1 + 0.0614\left(\frac{180}{360}\right)}{1 + 0.06\left(\frac{90}{360}\right)} - 1 \right]\left(\frac{360}{90}\right) = 0.0619$$

C. $h = 90$

$m = 90$

$g = 30$

$h - g = 60$

$h + m - g = 150$

$L_{30}(h - g) = 0.055$

$L_{30}(h + m - g) = 0.0562$

$$V_t(0,h,m) = \frac{1}{1 + 0.055\left(\dfrac{60}{360}\right)} - \frac{1 + 0.0619\left(\dfrac{90}{360}\right)}{1 + 0.0562\left(\dfrac{150}{360}\right)}$$

$$= -0.001323$$

For \$15,000,000 notional principal, the value of the FRA would be $= -0.001323 \times 15,000,000 = -\$19,845$. Because the manager is short, this represents a gain to his company.

11. A. The risk to the U.S. company is that the value of the Swiss franc will decline and it will receive fewer U.S. dollars on conversion. To hedge this risk, the company should enter into a contract to sell Swiss francs forward.

B. $S_0 = \$0.5974$

$T = 90/365$

$r = 0.02$

$r^f = 0.05$

$$F(0,T) = \left[\frac{0.5974}{(1.05)^{90/365}}\right](1.02)^{90/365} = \$0.5931$$

C. $S_t = \$0.55$

$T = 90/365$

$t = 30/365$

$T - t = 60/365$

$r = 0.02$

$r^f = 0.05$

$$V_t(0,T) = \frac{\$0.55}{(1.05)^{60/365}} - \frac{\$0.5931}{(1.02)^{60/365}} = -\$0.0456$$

This represents a gain to the short position of \$0.0456 per Swiss franc. In this problem, the U.S. company holds the short forward position.

12. First calculate the fair value or arbitrage-free price of the forward contract:

$S_0 = \$1.0231$

$T = 180/365$

$r = 0.04$

$r^f = 0.05$

$$F(0,T) = \left[\frac{1.0231}{(1.05)^{180/365}}\right](1.04)^{180/365} = \$1.0183$$

The dealer quote for the forward contract is $1.0225; thus, the forward contract is overpriced. To earn a risk-free profit, you should enter into a forward contract to sell euros forward in six months at $1.0225. At the same time, buy euros now.

  i. Take $\dfrac{\$1.0231}{(1.05)^{180/365}} = \$0.9988$. Use it to buy $\dfrac{1}{(1.05)^{180/365}} = 0.9762$ euros.

  ii. Enter a forward contract to deliver €1.00 at $1.0225 in six months.

  iii. Invest €0.9762 for six months at 5 percent per year and receive €0.9762 × $1.05^{180/365}$ = €1.00 at the end of six months.

  iv. At expiration, deliver the euro and receive $1.0225. Return over six months is $\dfrac{\$1.0225}{\$0.9988} - 1 = 0.0237$, or 4.74 percent a year.

This risk-free annual return of 4.74 percent exceeds the U.S. risk-free rate of 4 percent.

13. A. The risk to you is that the value of the British pound will rise over the next 30 days and it will require more U.S. dollars to buy the necessary pounds to make payment. To hedge this risk you should enter a forward contract to buy British pounds.

  B. $S_0 = \$1.50$

     $T = 30/365$

     $r = 0.055$

     $r^f = 0.045$

     $F(0,T) = \left[\dfrac{\$1.50}{(1.045)^{30/365}}\right](1.055)^{30/365} = \$1.5018$

  C. $S_t = \$1.53$

     $T = 30/365$

     $t = 10/365$

     $T - t = 20/365$

     $r = 0.055$

     $r^f = 0.045$

     $V_t(0,T) = \dfrac{\$1.53}{1.045^{20/365}} - \dfrac{\$1.5012}{1.055^{20/365}} = \$0.0295$

     Because you are long, this is a gain of $0.0295 per British pound.

14. A. $r^{fc} = \ln(1.04) = 0.0392$

     $r^c = \ln(1.06) = 0.0583$

  B. $S_0 = \$0.6667$

     $T = 90/365$

     $r^{fc} = 0.0392$

     $r^c = 0.0583$

     $F(0,T) = (\$0.6667 \times e^{-0.0392(90/365)})(e^{0.0583(90/365)}) = \$0.6698$

C. $S_t = \$0.65$

$T = 90/365$

$t = 25/365$

$T - t = 65/365$

$r^{fc} = 0.0392$

$r^c = 0.0583$

$V_t(0,T) = (\$0.65 \times e^{-0.0392(65/365)}) - (\$0.6698 \times e^{-0.0583(65/365)}) = -\$0.0174$

The value of the contract is $-\$0.0174$ per Swiss franc.

15. First, calculate the fair value or arbitrage free price of the forward contract:

$S_0 = \$0.00812$ per yen

$T = 90/365$

$r = 0.045$

$r^f = 0.02$

$$F(0,T) = \left[\frac{\$0.00812}{(1.02)^{90/365}} \right](1.045)^{90/365} = \$0.00817$$

The dealer quote for the forward contract is $\$0.00813$. Therefore, the forward contract is underpriced. To earn a risk-free profit, you should enter into a forward contract to buy yen in three months at $\$0.00813$. At the same time, sell yen now.

   i. The spot rate of $\$0.00812$ per yen is equivalent to ¥123.15 per U.S. dollar. Take $\dfrac{¥123.15}{(1.045)^{90/365}} = ¥121.82$. Use it to buy $\dfrac{1}{(1.045)^{90/365}} = 0.9892$ U.S. dollars.

   ii. Enter a forward contract to buy yen at $\$0.00813$ in three months. One U.S. dollar will buy $\dfrac{1}{\$0.00813} = ¥123.00$

   iii. Invest $\$0.9892$ for three months at 4.5 percent a year and receive $\$0.9892 \times 1.045^{90/365} = \$1.00$ at the end of three months.

   iv. At expiration, deliver the dollar and receive ¥123. The return over three months is $\dfrac{¥123.00}{¥121.82} - 1 = 0.00969$, or 3.88 percent a year.

Because we began our transactions in yen, the relevant comparison for the return from our transactions is the Japanese risk-free rate. The 3.88 percent return above exceeds the Japanese risk-free rate of 2 percent. Therefore, we could borrow yen at 2 percent and engage in the above transactions to earn a risk-free return of 3.88 percent that exceeds the rate of borrowing.

SOLUTIONS FOR READING 63

1. Her gain caused by the increase in the price of Dow Jones Industrial Average futures is $10(9,086 - 9,020) = 660. Because Craft had a short position in S&P Midcap 400 futures, her loss caused by the increase in the price of S&P Midcap 400 futures is $500(370.20 - 369.40) = 400. Craft's net gain is $660 - $400 = 260.

2. **A.** $T = 90/365 = 0.2466$. The futures price is

$$f_0(T) = S_0(1 + r)^T$$
$$f_0(0.2466) = 300(1.06)^{0.2466} = \$304.34 \text{ per ounce}$$

   B. Do the following:

   ▶ Enter a short futures position—that is, sell the futures at $306.

   ▶ Buy gold at $300.

   ▶ At expiration, deliver an ounce of gold and receive $306.

   This amount is $1.66 more than $304.34, which is the sum of the cost of the asset ($300) and the loss of interest on this amount at the rate of 6 percent a year ($4.34). Thus, the overall strategy results in a riskless arbitrage profit of $1.66 per futures contract. You can also look at this scenario in terms of returns: Investing $300 and receiving $306 90 days later is an annual return of 8.36 percent, because $300(1.0836)^{(90/365)} = 306$. This return is clearly greater than the risk-free return of 6 percent.

   C. The steps in this case would be the reverse of the steps in Part B above. So, do the following:

   ▶ Enter a long futures position; that is, buy the futures at $303.

   ▶ Sell short the gold at $300.

   ▶ At expiration, take the delivery of an ounce of gold and pay $303.

   This amount paid is $1.34 less than $304.34, which is the sum of the funds received from the short sale of the asset ($300) and the interest earned on this at the rate of 6 percent per year ($4.34). Thus, the overall strategy results in a riskless arbitrage profit of $1.34 per futures contract. In terms of rates, receiving $300 up front and paying $303 90 days later represents an annual rate of 4.12 percent, because $300(1.0412)^{(90/365)} = 303$. This rate is clearly less than the risk-free rate of 6 percent. Thus, the overall transaction is equivalent to borrowing at a rate less than the risk-free rate.

3. **A.** $T = 75/365 = 0.2055$. The futures price is $f_0(0.2055) = 90(1.07)^{0.2055} = 91.26$.

   B. Storage costs must be covered in the futures price, so we add them:

$$f_0(0.2055) = 91.26 + 3 = 94.26$$

   C. A positive cash flow, such as interest or dividends on the underlying, reduces the futures price:

$$f_0(0.2055) = 91.26 - 0.50 = 90.76$$

Solutions to 1–8 taken from *Analysis of Derivatives for the CFA® Program*, by Don M. Chance. Copyright © 2003 by AIMR. Reprinted with permission. All other solutions copyright © 2006 by CFA Institute.

D. We add the storage costs and subtract the positive cash flow:

$$f_0(0.2055) = 91.26 + 3 - 0.50 = 93.76$$

E. We would do the following:

- ▶ Sell the futures at $95.
- ▶ Buy the asset at $90.
- ▶ Because the asset price compounded at the interest rate is $91.26, the interest forgone is 1.26. So the asset price is effectively $91.26 by the time of the futures expiration.
- ▶ We have incurred storage costs of $3 on the asset. We have received $0.50 from the asset. At expiration, we deliver the asset and receive $95. The net investment in the asset is $91.26 + $3.00 − $0.50 = $93.76. If we sell it for $95, we make a net gain of $1.24. Thus, the overall strategy results in a riskless arbitrage profit of $1.24 per futures contract. One can also look at this profit in terms of returns. Investing $90 and receiving a net of $95.00 − $3.00 + $0.50 = $92.50 75 days later is an annual return of 14.26 percent, because $90(1.14264)^{(75/365)} = 92.50. This return is clearly greater than the risk-free return of 7 percent.

F. The last settlement price was $89.50, and the price in our answer in Part A is $91.26. The value of a long futures contract is the difference between these prices, or $1.76.

G. When the futures contact is marked to market, the holder of the futures contract receives a gain of $1.76, and the value of the futures contract goes back to a value of zero.

4. A. Because the futures contract expires in 18 months, T = 1.5. The risk-free rate, $r_0(T)$, is 0.05. When computing the accumulated value of the coupons on the bond and the interest on them until the futures contract expires, note that the first coupon is paid in exactly six months and reinvested for the one year remaining until expiration. Also, the second coupon is paid in exactly one year and reinvested for the six months remaining until expiration, and the third coupon is paid in exactly one and a half years and not reinvested. So, the accumulated value of the coupons on the bond and the interest on them is

$$0.04(1.05)^1 + 0.04(1.05)^{0.5} + 0.04 = 0.1230$$

Because the underlying bond is the only deliverable bond in this simplistic problem, the conversion factor is 1.0, so no adjustment is required. Now the futures price is easily obtained as

$$f_0(T) = B_0^c(T + Y)[1 + r_0(T)]^T - FV(CI,0,T)$$
$$f_0(1.5) = 1.1488(1.05)^{1.5} - 0.1230$$
$$= 1.1130$$

B. Buy the five-year bond for $1.1488 and sell the futures for $1.1130. Hold the position for one and a half years until the futures expiration. Collect and reinvest the coupons in the meantime. When the futures contract expires, deliver the bond and receive the futures price of $1.1130. In addition, you will have the coupons and interest on them of $0.1230 for a total of $1.1130 + $0.1230 = $1.2360. You invested $1.1488 and end up with $1.2360 a year and a half later, so the return per dollar invested is $1.2360/$1.1488 = 1.0759$. Because this amount is paid in 1.5 years, the annual equivalent of this is

$$1.0759^{1/1.5} = 1.05$$

This return is equivalent to the 5 percent risk-free rate.

5. A. Because the futures contract expires in 15 months, T = 1.25. The risk-free rate, $r_0(T)$, is 0.05. To compute the accumulated value of the coupons on the bond and the interest on them until the futures contract expires, we note that the first coupon is paid in exactly six months and reinvested for the nine months (0.75 years) remaining until expiration. Also, the second coupon is paid in exactly one year and reinvested for the three months (0.25 years) remaining until expiration. So, the accumulated value of the coupons on the bond and the interest on them is

$$0.03(1.05)^{0.75} + 0.03(1.05)^{0.25} = 0.0615$$

B. Because the underlying bond is the only deliverable bond in this part of the problem, the conversion factor is 1, and no adjustment is required. So, the futures price is

$$f_0(T) = B_0^c(T + Y)[1 + r_0(T)]^T - FV(CI,0,T)$$
$$f_0(1.25) = 1(1.05)^{1.25} - 0.0615$$
$$= 1.0014$$

C. The futures price now is the price computed in Part B above divided by the conversion factor. Because the conversion factor is 1.0567, the futures price is

$$\frac{1.0014}{1.0567} = 0.9477$$

6. A. T = 73/365 = 0.20. The futures price should be

$$f_0(T) = S_0(1 + r)^T - FV(D,0,T)$$
$$f_0(0.20) = 1,521.75(1.0610)^{0.20} - 5.36$$
$$= 1,534.52$$

Alternatively, we can find the present value of the dividends:

$$PV(D,0,T) = \frac{FV(D,0,T)}{(1 + r)^T}$$

$$PV(D,0,0.20) = \frac{5.36}{(1.0610)^{0.20}} = 5.30$$

Then the futures price would be

$$f_0(T) = [S_0 - PV(D,0,T)](1 + r)^T$$
$$f_0(0.20) = (1,521.75 - 5.30)(1.061)^{0.20}$$
$$= 1,534.52$$

B. One specification based on the yield δ is

$$\frac{1}{(1 + \delta)^T} = 1 - \frac{FV(D,0,T)}{S_0(1 + r)^T}$$

$$= 1 - \frac{5.36}{1,521.75(1.061)^{0.20}} = 0.9965$$

So, $(1 + \delta)^T$ is $1/0.9965 = 1.0035$. Then the futures price is

$$f_0(T) = \left(\frac{S_0}{(1 + \delta)^T}\right)(1 + r)^T$$

$$f_0(0.20) = \left(\frac{1,521.75}{1.0035}\right)(1.061)^{0.20}$$

$$= 1,534.51$$

The difference comes from rounding.

Under the other specification, the yield would be found as

$$\delta^* = \frac{PV(D,0,T)}{S_0}$$

$$= \frac{5.30}{1,521.75} = 0.0035$$

Then the futures price would be

$$f_0(T) = S_0(1 - \delta^*)(1 + r)^T$$
$$f_0(0.20) = 1,521.75(1 - 0.0035)(1.061)^{0.20}$$
$$= 1,534.49$$

The difference comes from rounding.

C. The continuously compounded risk-free rate is $r^c = \ln(1 + r) = \ln(1.061) = 0.0592$. The continuously compounded dividend yield is $\delta^c = \ln(1 + \delta) = (1/T)\ln[(1 + \delta)^T] = (1/0.20)\ln(1.0035) = 0.0175$. The futures price is

$$f_0(T) = S_0 e^{(r^c - \delta^c)T}$$
$$f_0(0.20) = 1,521.75 e^{(0.0592 - 0.0175)0.20}$$
$$= 1,534.49$$

The difference comes from rounding.

7. A. $T = 201/365 = 0.5507$. The futures price should be

$$f_0(T) = S_0(1 + r)^T - FV(D,0,T)$$
$$f_0(0.5507) = 443.35(1.0650)^{0.5507} - 5.0 = 454.0$$

Alternatively, we can find the present value of the dividends:

$$PV(D,0,T) = \frac{FV(D,0,T)}{(1 + r)^T}$$

$$PV(D,0,0.5507) = \frac{5.0}{(1.0650)^{0.5507}} = 4.83$$

Then the futures price would be

$$f_0(T) = [S_0 - PV(D,0,T)](1 + r)^T$$
$$f_0(0.5507) = (443.35 - 4.83)(1.065)^{0.5507}$$
$$= 454.0$$

Because the futures contract is selling at 458.50, which is higher than the price computed above, the futures contract is overpriced.

B. The arbitrageur will buy the stocks underlying the index at their current price of \$443.35. Also, the arbitrageur will sell the futures contract at the settlement price of \$458.50. The arbitrageur will collect and reinvest the dividends, which would be worth \$5 at the time of the futures expiration. At the time of expiration, the arbitrageur will get the settlement price of \$458.50. So, the arbitrageur invests \$443.35 at the beginning and receives \$5.00 + \$458.50 = \$463.50 at the expiration 201 days later. The return per dollar invested over the 201-day period is

$$\frac{463.50}{443.35} = 1.0454$$

The annual risk-free rate is 6.5 percent, equivalent to a return per dollar invested of $(1.065)^{0.5507} = 1.0353$ over the 201-day period. Thus, the return to the arbitrageur from the transactions described above exceeds the risk-free return. Alternatively, one could see that to the arbitrageur, the return per dollar invested, over a year, is $1.0454^{365/201} = 1.0832$. This annualized return of 8.32 percent is clearly greater than the annual risk-free rate of 6.5 percent.

8. $T = 100/365 = 0.274$

A. The futures price is

$$f_0(T) = \left(\frac{S_0}{(1 + r^f)^T}\right)(1 + r)^T$$

$$f_0(0.274) = \left(\frac{1.4390}{1.058^{0.274}}\right)(1.063)^{0.274}$$

$$= 1.4409$$

B. The continuously compounded equivalent rates are

$$r^{fc} = \ln(1.058) = 0.0564$$
$$r^c = \ln(1.063) = 0.0611$$

The futures price is

$$f_0(T) = (S_0 e^{-r^{fc}T}) e^{r^c T}$$
$$f_0(T) = (1.4390 e^{-0.0564(0.274)}) e^{0.0611(0.274)}$$
$$= 1.4409$$

C. The actual futures price of \$1.4650 is higher than the price computed above—the futures contract is overpriced. To take advantage, the arbitrageur needs to buy the foreign currency and sell the futures contract. First, however, we must determine how many units of the currency to buy. Because we need to have 1 unit of currency, including the interest, the number of units to buy is

$$\frac{1}{(1.058)^{0.274}} = 0.9847$$

So we buy 0.9847 units, which costs 0.9847(\$1.4390) = \$1.417. We sell the futures at \$1.4650 and hold until expiration. During that time, the accumulation of interest will make the 0.9847 units of the currency grow to one unit. Using the futures contract, at expiration we convert this unit at the futures rate of \$1.4650. The return per dollar invested is

$$\frac{1.4650}{1.417} = 1.0339$$

or a return of 3.39 percent over 100 days. The U.S. annual risk-free rate is 6.3 percent, which is equivalent to a return per dollar invested of $(1.063)^{0.274} = 1.0169$, over the 100-day period. Thus, the return to the arbitrageur from the transactions described above exceeds the risk-free return. Alternatively, one could see that to the arbitrageur, the return per dollar invested, over a year, is $(1.0339)^{365/100} = 1.1294$. This annualized return of 12.94 percent is more than double the annual risk-free rate of 6.3 percent.

9. B is correct. The implied forward rate in this question can be found using:

$$FRA(0,h,m) = \left[\frac{1 + L_0(h+m)\left(\frac{h+m}{360}\right)}{1 + L_0(h)\left(\frac{h}{360}\right)} - 1 \right]\left(\frac{360}{m}\right)$$

For this problem, $FRA = \left[\dfrac{1 + 0.412\left(\frac{270}{360}\right)}{1 + 0.0371\left(\frac{90}{360}\right)} - 1 \right]\left(\dfrac{360}{180}\right) = 0.04285.$

10. A is correct. The payoff at expiration of an FRA is found by solving:

$$V(0,h,m) = \frac{[L_h(m) - FRA(0,h,m)] \times (^m/_{360})}{1 + L_h(m)(^m/_{360})}$$

Then multiply the notional principal by the above calculated value. For this problem, $[(0.0448 - 0.0468) \times (180/360)]/[1 + 0.0448 \times (180/360)] = -0.00097809$. Multiply this value by the notional principal of $300,000,000 to get the answer of $-\$293,427$.

11. B is correct. Due to the design features of the Eurodollar futures contract, the rate implied by the futures contract will differ from the implied forward rate of the FRA. Thus, a "perfect" hedge cannot be accomplished. "The difference between the FRA rate and the Eurodollar rate is called convexity bias."

12. B is correct. Use $F(0,T) = [S_0/(1 + r^f)^T] \times (1 + r)^T$ where $F(0,T)$ is the futures price for the contract that expires at time T, T is the time to expiration, S_0 is current spot rate, r^f is the foreign interest rate, and r is the domestic interest rate. In this problem, solve $[0.6892/(1.0328)^{(244/365)}] \times (1.0417)^{(244/365)} = 0.6932$.

13. D is correct. By definition, to exploit an arbitrage, buy the (relatively) undervalued and sell the (relatively) overvalued. Malquist states that the futures contract on the euro is trading above its fair value. Thus, the correct answer is to buy euros and sell euro futures contract.

14. D is correct. As stated in the problem, Malquist "finds that the 244-day arbitrage-free futures price (GBP/EUR) is below the 244-day expected spot exchange rate." Normal backwardation is defined as "futures prices are lower than expected spot prices."

SOLUTIONS FOR READING 64

1. Call price, $c_0 = \$4.50$

Put price, $p_0 = \$6.80$

Exercise price, $X = \$70$

Risk-free rate, $r = 5$ percent

Time to expiration $= 139/365 = 0.3808$

Current stock price, $S_0 = \$67.32$

Bond price $= X/(1 + r)^T = 70/(1 + 0.05)^{0.3808} = \$68.71$

A. Synthetic call $= p_0 + S_0 - X/(1 + r)^T = 6.8 + 67.32 - 68.71 = \$5.41$

Synthetic put $= c_0 + X/(1 + r)^T - S_0 = 4.5 + 68.71 - 67.32 = \$5.89$

Synthetic bond $= p_0 + S_0 - c_0 = 6.8 + 67.32 - 4.5 = \$69.62$

Synthetic underlying $= c_0 + X/(1 + r)^T - p_0 = 4.5 + 68.71 - 6.8 = \$66.41$

B.

Instrument	Actual Price	Synthetic Price	Mispricing/Profit
Call	4.50	5.41	0.91
Put	6.80	5.89	0.91
Bond	68.71	69.62	0.91
Stock	67.32	66.41	0.91

Thus, the mispricing is the same regardless of the instrument used to look at it.

C. The actual call is cheaper than the synthetic call. Therefore, an arbitrage transaction where you buy the call (underpriced) and sell the synthetic call (overpriced) will yield a risk-free profit of $\$5.41 - \$4.50 = \$0.91$.

As shown below, at expiration no cash will be received or paid out.

	Value at Expiration	
Transaction	$S_T < 70$	$S_T > 70$
Buy call	0	$S_T - 70$
Sell synthetic call		
Short put	$-(70 - S_T)$	0
Short stock	$-S_T$	$-S_T$
Long bond	70	70
Total	0	0

D. The actual put is more expensive than the synthetic put. Therefore, an arbitrage transaction in which you buy the synthetic put (underpriced) and sell the put (overpriced) will yield a risk-free profit of $\$6.80 - \$5.89 = \$0.91$. As shown below, at expiration no cash will be received or paid out.

	Value at Expiration	
Transaction	$S_T < 70$	$S_T > 70$
Sell put	$-(70 - S_T)$	
Buy synthetic put		
Long call	0	$S_T - 70$
Long bond	70	70
Short stock	$-S_T$	$-S_T$
Total	0	0

2. Current stock price, S = \$100

  Up move, u = 1.1

  Down move, d = 0.85

  Exercise price, X = \$90

  Risk-free rate, r = 6.5 percent

  A. Stock prices one period from now are

$$S^+ = Su = 100(1.1) = \$110$$
$$S^- = Sd = 100(0.85) = \$85$$

Call option values at expiration one period from now are

$$c^+ = Max(0,110 - 90) = \$20$$
$$c^- = Max(0,85 - 90) = \$0$$

The risk-neutral probability is

$$\pi = \frac{1.065 - 0.85}{1.1 - 0.85} = 0.86 \text{ and } 1 - \pi = 0.14$$

The call price today is

$$c = \frac{0.86(20) + 0.14(0)}{1.065} = 16.15$$

  B. If the current call price is \$17.50, it is overpriced. Therefore, we should sell the call and buy the underlying stock. The hedge ratio is

$$n = \frac{20 - 0}{110 - 85} = 0.8$$

For every option sold we should purchase 0.8 shares of stock. If we sell 100 calls we should buy 80 shares of stock.

Sell 100 calls at 17.50 =	1,750
Buy 80 shares at 100 =	−8,000
Net cash flow =	−6,250

At expiration the value of this combination will be

$$80(110) - 100(20) = \$6{,}800 \text{ if } S_T = 110$$
$$80(85) - 100(0) = \$6{,}800 \text{ if } S_T = 85$$

We invested \$6,250 for a payoff of \$6,800. The rate of return is $(6{,}800/6{,}250) - 1 = 0.088$. This rate is higher than the risk-free rate of 0.065.

C. If the current call price is \$14, it is underpriced. Therefore, we should buy the call and sell the underlying stock. The hedge ratio is

$$n = \frac{20 - 0}{110 - 85} = 0.8$$

For every option purchased we should sell 0.8 shares of stock. If we buy 100 calls we should sell 80 shares of stock.

Buy 100 calls at 14   = −1,400
Sell 80 shares at 100   = 8,000
Net cash flow   = 6,600

Thus, we generate \$6,600 up front.

At expiration the value of this combination will be

$$100(20) - 80(110) = -\$6{,}800 \text{ if } S_T = 110$$
$$100(0) - 80(85) = -\$6{,}800 \text{ if } S_T = 85$$

We generated \$6,600 up front and pay back \$6,800. The rate of return is $(6{,}800/6{,}600) - 1 = 0.0303$. This borrowing rate is lower than the risk-free rate of 0.065.

3. Current stock price, S = \$150

Up move, u = 1.33

Down move, d = 0.85

Exercise price, X = \$150

Risk-free rate, r = 4.5 percent

A. Stock prices one period from now are

$$S^+ = Su = 150(1.33) = \$199.5$$
$$S^- = Sd = 150(0.85) = 127.5$$

Put option values at expiration one period from now are

$$p^+ = \text{Max}(0, 150 - 199.5) = \$0$$
$$p^- = \text{Max}(0, 150 - 127.5) = \$22.5$$

The risk-neutral probability is

$$\pi = \frac{1.045 - 0.85}{1.33 - 0.85} = 0.4063, \text{ and } 1 - \pi = 0.5937$$

The put price today is

$$\pi = \frac{0.4063(0) + 0.5937(22.50)}{1.045} = 12.78$$

B. If the current put price is $14, it is overpriced. In order to create a hedge portfolio, we should sell the put and short the underlying stock. The hedge ratio is

$$n = \frac{p^+ - p^-}{S^+ - S^-} = \frac{0 - 22.5}{199.5 - 127.5} = -0.3125$$

For every option sold, we should sell 0.3125 shares of stock. If we sell 10,000 puts, we should sell 3,125 shares of stock.

    Sell 10,000 puts at 14   = 140,000
    Sell 3,125 shares at 150 = 468,750
    Net cash flow   = 608,750

Thus, we generate $608,750 up front.

At expiration, the value of this combination will be

$$-3,125(199.5) - 10,000(0) = -\$623,437 \text{ if } S_T = \$199.5$$
$$-3,125(127.5) - 10,000(22.5) = -\$623,437 \text{ if } S_T = \$127.5$$

We generated $608,750 up front and pay back $623,437. The rate of return is

$$\frac{623,437}{608,750} - 1 = 0.0241$$

This borrowing rate is lower than the risk-free rate of 0.045.

C. If the current put price is $11, it is underpriced. In order to create a hedge portfolio, we should buy the put and buy the underlying stock. The hedge ratio is

$$n = \frac{p^+ - p^-}{S^+ - S^-} = \frac{0 - 22.5}{199.5 - 127.5} = -0.3125$$

For every option purchased we should buy 0.3125 shares of stock. If we buy 10,000 puts we should buy 3,125 shares of stock.

    Buy 10,000 puts at 11   = -110,000
    Buy 3,125 shares at 150 = -468,750
    Net cash flow   = -578,750

That is, we invest $578,750.

At expiration, the value of this combination will be

$$3,125(199.5) + 10,000(0) = \$623,437 \text{ if } S_T = \$199.5$$
$$3,125(127.5) + 10,000(22.5) = \$623,437 \text{ if } S_T = \$127.5$$

We invested $578,750 for a payoff of $623,437. The rate of return is
$\frac{623,437}{578,750} - 1 = 0.0772$. This rate is higher than the risk-free rate of 0.045.

4. Current stock price, S = $65

Up move, u = 1.20

Down move, d = 0.83

Risk-free rate, r = 5 percent

A. Exercise price, X = $60

Stock prices in the binomial tree one and two periods from now are

$$S^+ = Su = 65(1.20) = \$78$$
$$S^- = Sd = 65(0.83) = \$53.95$$
$$S^{++} = Su^2 = 65(1.20)(1.20) = \$93.60$$
$$S^{+-} = Sud = 65(1.20)(0.83) = \$64.74$$
$$S^{--} = Sd^2 = 65(0.83)(0.83) = \$44.78$$

Call option values at expiration two periods from now are

$$c^{++} = Max(0, 93.60 - 60) = \$33.6$$
$$c^{+-} = Max(0, 64.74 - 60) = \$4.74$$
$$c^{--} = Max(0, 44.78 - 60) = \$0$$

The risk-neutral probability is

$$\pi = \frac{1.05 - 0.83}{1.20 - 0.83} - 0.5946, \text{ and } 1 - \pi = 0.4054$$

Now find the option prices at time 1:

$$c^+ = \frac{0.5946(33.6) + 0.4054(4.74)}{1.05} = \$20.86$$

$$c^- = \frac{0.5946(4.74) + 0.4054(0)}{1.05} = \$2.68$$

The call price today is

$$c = \frac{0.5946(20.86) + 0.4054(2.68)}{1.05} = \$12.85$$

B. The hedge ratios at each point in the binomial tree are calculated as follows:

At the current stock price of $65,

$$n = \frac{c^+ - c^-}{S^+ - S^-} = \frac{20.86 - 2.68}{78 - 53.95} = 0.7559$$

Therefore, today at time 0, the risk-free hedge would consist of a short position in 10,000 calls and a long position in 7,559 shares of the underlying stock.

At a stock price of $78,

$$n^+ = \frac{c^{++} - c^{+-}}{S^{++} - S^{+-}} = \frac{33.6 - 4.74}{93.6 - 64.74} = 1$$

Now the risk-free hedge would consist of a short position in 10,000 calls and a long position in 10,000 shares of the underlying stock.

At a stock price of $53.95,

$$\frac{n^- = c^{+-} - c^{--}}{S^{+-} - S^{--}} = \frac{4.74 - 0}{64.74 - 44.78} = 0.2375$$

Now the risk-free hedge would consist of a short position in 10,000 calls and a long position in 2,375 shares of the underlying stock.

C. Exercise price, $X = \$70$

Stock prices in the binomial tree one and two periods from now are

$$S^+ = Su = 65(1.20) = \$78$$
$$S^- = Sd = 65(0.83) = \$53.95$$
$$S^{++} = Su^2 = 65(1.20)(1.20) = \$93.6$$
$$S^{+-} = Sud = 65(1.20)(0.83) = \$64.74$$
$$S^{--} = Sd^2 = 65(0.83)(0.83) = \$44.78$$

Call option values at expiration two periods from now are

$$c^{++} = Max(0,93.6 - 70) = \$23.6$$
$$c^{+-} = Max(0,64.74 - 70) = \$0$$
$$c^{--} = Max(0,44.78 - 70) = \$0$$

The risk-neutral probability is

$$\pi = \frac{1.05 - 0.83}{1.20 - 0.83} = 0.5946, \text{ and } 1 - \pi = 0.4054$$

Now find the option prices at time 1:

$$c^+ = \frac{0.5946(23.6) + 0.4054(0)}{1.05} = \$13.36$$
$$c^- = \frac{0.5946(0) + 0.4054(0)}{1.05} = \$0$$

The call price today is

$$c = \frac{0.5946(13.36) + 0.4054(0)}{1.05} = \$7.57$$

D. The hedge ratios at each point in the binomial tree are calculated as follows.

At the current stock price of $65,

$$n = \frac{c^+ - c^-}{S^+ - S^-} = \frac{13.36 - 0}{78 - 53.95} = 0.5555$$

Therefore, today at time 0, the risk-free hedge would consist of a short position in 10,000 calls and a long position in 5,555 shares of the underlying stock.

At a stock price of $78,

$$n^+ = \frac{c^{++} - c^{+-}}{S^{++} - S^{+-}} = \frac{23.6 - 0}{93.6 - 64.74} = 0.8177$$

Now, the risk-free hedge would consist of a short position in 10,000 calls and a long position in 8,177 shares of the underlying stock.

At a stock price of $53.95,

$$n^- = \frac{c^{+-} - c^{--}}{S^{+-} - S^{--}} = \frac{0 - 0}{64.74 - 44.78} = 0$$

Zero shares of the underlying stock are needed for the short position in calls.

5. Current stock price, $S_0 = \$65$

Up move, $u = 1.20$

Down move, $d = 0.83$

Risk-free rate, $r = 5$ percent

A. Exercise price, $X = \$60$

Stock prices in the binomial tree one and two periods from now are

$$S^+ = Su = 65(1.20) = \$78$$
$$S^- = Sd = 65(0.83) = \$53.95$$
$$S^{++} = Su^2 = 65(1.20)(1.20) = \$93.6$$
$$S^{+-} = Sud = 65(1.20)(0.83) = \$64.74$$
$$S^{--} = Sd^2 = 65(0.83)(0.83) = \$44.78$$

Put option values at expiration two periods from now are

$$p^{++} = \text{Max}(0, 60 - 93.6) = \$0$$
$$p^{+-} = \text{Max}(0, 60 - 64.74) = \$0$$
$$p^{--} = \text{Max}(0, 60 - 44.78) = \$15.22$$

The risk-neutral probability is

$$\pi = \frac{1.05 - 0.83}{1.20 - 0.83} = 0.5946 \text{ and } 1 - \pi = 0.4054$$

Now find the option prices at time 1:

$$p^+ = \frac{0.5946(0) + 0.4054(0)}{1.05} = \$0$$

$$p^- = \frac{0.5946(0) + 0.4054(15.22)}{1.05} = \$5.88$$

The put price today is

$$p = \frac{0.5946(0) + 0.4054(5.88)}{1.05} = \$2.27$$

B. Unlike the hedge portfolio for calls, which has the opposite positions in the two instruments (calls and underlying stock), the hedge portfolio for puts has the same positions in the two instruments. Therefore, the current value of the hedge portfolio for puts is

$$H = nS + p$$

The possible values of the hedge portfolio one period later are

$$H^+ = nS^+ + p^+$$
$$H^- = nS^- + p^-$$

Setting H^+ equal to H^- and solving for n,

$$n = \frac{p^- - p^+}{S^+ - S^-}$$

Note that the above formula is the same as that for the hedge portfolio for calls, except that the p^+ and p^- have switched positions in the numerator. Similarly, the hedge ratios for the next time point are

$$n^+ = \frac{p^{+-} - p^{++}}{S^{++} - S^{+-}}$$
$$n^- = \frac{p^{--} - p^{+-}}{S^{+-} - S^{--}}$$

At the current stock price of $65,

$$n = \frac{p^- - p^+}{S^+ - S^-} = \frac{5.88 - 0}{78 - 53.95} = 0.2445$$

Therefore, today at time 0, the risk-free hedge would consist of a long position in 10,000 puts and a long position in 2,445 shares of the underlying stock.

At a stock price of $78,

$$n^+ = \frac{p^{+-} - p^{++}}{S^{++} - S^{+-}} = \frac{0 - 0}{93.6 - 64.74} = 0$$

Zero shares of the underlying stock are needed for the long position in puts.

At a stock price of $53.95,

$$n^- = \frac{p^{--} - p^{+-}}{S^{+-} - S^{--}} = \frac{15.22 - 0}{64.74 - 44.78} = 0.7625$$

Now the risk-free hedge would consist of a long position in 10,000 puts and a long position in 7,625 shares of the underlying stock.

C. Exercise price, X = $70

Stock prices in the binomial tree, one and two periods from now are

$$S^+ = Su = 65(1.20) = \$78$$
$$S^- = Sd = 65(0.83) = \$53.95$$
$$S^{++} = Su^2 = 65(1.20)(1.20) = \$93.6$$

$$S^{+-} = Sud = 65(1.20)(0.83) = \$64.74$$
$$S^{--} = Sd^2 = 65(0.83)(0.83) = \$44.78$$

Put option values at expiration two periods from now are

$$p^{++} = Max(0, 70 - 93.6) = \$0$$
$$p^{+-} = Max(0, 70 - 64.74) = \$5.26$$
$$p^{--} = Max(0, 70 - 44.78) = \$25.22$$

The risk-neutral probability is

$$\pi = \frac{1.05 - 0.83}{1.20 - 0.83} = 0.5946, \text{ and } 1 - \pi = 0.4054$$

Now find the option prices at time 1:

$$p^+ = \frac{0.5946(0) + 0.4054(5.26)}{1.05} = \$2.03$$

$$p^- = \frac{0.5946(5.26) + 0.4054(25.22)}{1.05} = \$12.72$$

The put price today is

$$p = \frac{0.5946(2.03) + 0.4054(12.72)}{1.05} = \$6.06$$

D. The hedge ratios at each point in the binomial tree are calculated as follows:

At the current stock price of $65,

$$n = \frac{p^- - p^+}{S^+ - S^-} = \frac{12.72 - 2.03}{78 - 53.95} = 0.4445$$

Therefore, today at time 0, the risk-free hedge would consist of a long position in 10,000 puts and a long position in 4,445 shares of the underlying stock.

At stock price $78,

$$n^+ = \frac{p^{+-} - p^{++}}{S^{++} - S^{+-}} = \frac{5.26 - 0}{93.6 - 64.74} = 0.1823$$

Therefore, at time 1, the risk-free hedge would consist of a long position in 10,000 puts and a long position in 1,823 shares of the underlying stock.

At stock price $53.95,

$$n^- = \frac{p^{--} - p^{+-}}{S^{+-} - S^{--}} = \frac{25.22 - 5.26}{64.74 - 44.78} = 1$$

Now, the risk-free hedge would consist of a long position in 10,000 puts and a long position in 10,000 shares of the underlying stock.

SOLUTIONS FOR READING 65

1. A. The present value factors for 180, 360, 540, and 720 days are as follows:

$$B_0(180) = \frac{1}{1 + 0.0585(180/360)} = 0.9716$$

$$B_0(360) = \frac{1}{1 + 0.0605(360/360)} = 0.9430$$

$$B_0(540) = \frac{1}{1 + 0.0624(540/360)} = 0.9144$$

$$B_0(720) = \frac{1}{1 + 0.0665(720/360)} = 0.8826$$

The semiannual fixed rate (or payment per \$1 of notional principal) is calculated as

$$FS(0, n, m) = FS(0,4,180) = \frac{1 - 0.8826}{0.9716 + 0.9430 + 0.9144 + 0.8826}$$
$$= 0.0316$$

The annualized fixed rate (or payment per \$1 of notional principal) is $0.0316(360/180) = 0.0632$. Because the notional principal is \$25,000,000, the semiannual fixed payment is $25,000,000(0.0316) = \$790,000$.

B. The new present value factors for 60, 240, 420, and 600 days are as follows:

$$B_{120}(180) = \frac{1}{1 + 0.0613(60/360)} = 0.9899$$

$$B_{120}(360) = \frac{1}{1 + 0.0629(240/360)} = 0.9598$$

$$B_{120}(540) = \frac{1}{1 + 0.0653(420/360)} = 0.9292$$

$$B_{120}(720) = \frac{1}{1 + 0.0697(600/360)} = 0.8959$$

The present value of the remaining fixed payments plus the \$1 hypothetical notional principal is $0.0316(0.9899 + 0.9598 + 0.9292 + 0.8959) + 1(0.8959) = 1.0152$.

The present value of the floating payments plus the hypothetical \$1 notional principal is $1.0293(0.9899) = 1.0189$, where

▶ 1.0293 is the first floating payment, $0.0585(180/360) + 1$, which is the market value of the remaining payments plus the \$1 notional principal, and

▶ 0.9899 is the discount factor.

Based on a notional principal of \$25,000,000, the market value of the swap to the pay-floating, receive-fixed party is $(1.0152 - 1.0189)$ $25,000,000 = -\$92,500$. Thus, the market value of the swap to opposite party that pays fixed and receives floating is \$92,500.

2. A. The present value factors for 90, 180, 270, and 360 days are as follows:

$$B_0(90) = \frac{1}{1 + 0.0656(90/360)} = 0.9839$$

$$B_0(180) = \frac{1}{1 + 0.0640(180/360)} = 0.9690$$

$$B_0(270) = \frac{1}{1 + 0.0621(270/360)} = 0.9555$$

$$B_0(360) = \frac{1}{1 + 0.0599(360/360)} = 0.9435$$

The quarterly fixed rate (or payment per \$1 of notional principal) is calculated as

$$FS(0, n, m) = FS(0,4,90) = \frac{1 - 0.9435}{0.9839 + 0.9690 + 0.9555 + 0.9435}$$

$$= 0.0147$$

The annualized fixed rate (or payment per \$1 of notional principal) is $0.0147(360/90) = 0.0588$. Because the notional principal is \$15,000,000, the quarterly fixed payment is $15,000,000(0.0147) =$ \$220,500.

B. The new present value factors for 60, 150, 240, and 330 days are as follows:

$$B_{30}(90) = \frac{1}{1 + 0.0384(60/360)} = 0.9936$$

$$B_{30}(180) = \frac{1}{1 + 0.0379(150/360)} = 0.9845$$

$$B_{30}(270) = \frac{1}{1 + 0.0382(240/360)} = 0.9752$$

$$B_{30}(360) = \frac{1}{1 + 0.0406(330/360)} = 0.9641$$

The present value of the remaining fixed payments plus the \$1 notional principal is $0.0147(0.9936 + 0.9845 + 0.9752 + 0.9641) + 1(0.9641) =$ 1.0217.

The present value of the floating payments plus hypothetical \$1 notional principal is $1.0164(0.9936) = 1.0099$, where

▶ 1.0164 is the first floating payment, $0.0656(90/360) + 1$, which is the market value of the remaining payments plus the \$1 notional principal, and

▶ 0.9936 is the discount factor.

Based on a notional principal of \$15,000,000, the market value of the swap to the pay-floating, receive-fixed party is $(1.0217 - 1.0099)15,000,000 = \$177,000$. Thus, the market value of the swap to the pay-fixed, receive-floating party is $-\$177,000$.

3. A. First calculate the fixed payment in dollars. The dollar present value factors for 180, 360, 540, and 720 days are as follows:

$$B_0(180) = \frac{1}{1 + 0.0585(180/360)} = 0.9716$$

$$B_0(360) = \frac{1}{1 + 0.0605(360/360)} = 0.9430$$

$$B_0(540) = \frac{1}{1 + 0.0624(540/360)} = 0.9144$$

$$B_0(720) = \frac{1}{1 + 0.0665(720/360)} = 0.8826$$

The semiannual fixed payment per \$1 of notional principal is calculated as

$$FS(0, n, m) = FS(0,4,180) = \frac{1 - 0.8826}{0.9716 + 0.9430 + 0.9144 + 0.8826}$$

$$= 0.0316$$

The annualized fixed payment per \$1 of notional principal is calculated as $0.0316(360/180) = 0.0632$.

Now calculate the fixed payment in pounds. The pound present value factors for 180, 360, 540, and 720 days are as follows:

$$B_0^\pounds(180) = \frac{1}{1 + 0.0493(180/360)} = 0.9759$$

$$B_0^\pounds(360) = \frac{1}{1 + 0.0505(360/360)} = 0.9519$$

$$B_0^\pounds(540) = \frac{1}{1 + 0.0519(540/360)} = 0.9278$$

$$B_0^\pounds(720) = \frac{1}{1 + 0.0551(720/360)} = 0.9007$$

The semiannual fixed payment per £1 of notional principal is calculated as

$$FS(0, n, m) = FS(0,4,180) = \frac{1 - 0.9007}{0.9759 + 0.9519 + 0.9278 + 0.9007}$$

$$= 0.0264$$

The annualized fixed payment per £1 of notional principal is calculated as $0.0264(360/180) = 0.0528$.

B. The new dollar discount factors for 60, 240, 420, and 600 days are as follows:

$$B_{120}(180) = \frac{1}{1 + 0.0613(60/360)} = 0.9899$$

$$B_{120}(360) = \frac{1}{1 + 0.0629(240/360)} = 0.9598$$

$$B_{120}(540) = \frac{1}{1 + 0.0653(420/360)} = 0.9292$$

$$B_{120}(720) = \frac{1}{1 + 0.0697(600/360)} = 0.8959$$

The present value of the remaining fixed payments plus the \$1 notional principal is $0.0316(0.9899 + 0.9598 + 0.9292 + 0.8959) + 1(0.8959) = 1.0152$.

The present value of the floating payments plus hypothetical \$1 notional principal discounted back 120 days is $1.0293(0.9899) = 1.0189$, where

▶ 1.0293 is the first floating payment, $0.0585(180/360) + 1$, which is the market value of the remaining payments plus the \$1 notional principal, and

▶ 0.9899 is the discount factor.

The new pound discount factors for 60, 240, 420, and 600 days are as follows:

$$B_{120}{}^{£}(180) = \frac{1}{1 + 0.0517(60/360)} = 0.9915$$

$$B_{120}{}^{£}(360) = \frac{1}{1 + 0.0532(240/360)} = 0.9657$$

$$B_{120}{}^{£}(540) = \frac{1}{1 + 0.0568(420/360)} = 0.9379$$

$$B_{120}{}^{£}(720) = \frac{1}{1 + 0.0583(600/360)} = 0.9114$$

The present value of the remaining fixed payments plus the £1 notional principal is $0.0264(0.9915 + 0.9657 + 0.9379 + 0.9114) + 1(0.9114) = 1.0119$. Convert this amount to the equivalent of \$1 notional principal; that is, $1/\$1.41$: $1.0119(1/1.41) = £0.7177$. Now convert to dollars at the current exchange rate $\$1.35/£$: $0.7177(1.35) = \$0.9688$.

The present value of the floating payments plus hypothetical £1 notional principal is $1.0247(0.9915) = 1.016$, where

▶ 1.0247 is the first floating payment, $0.0493(180/360) + 1$, which is the market value of the remaining payments plus the £1 notional principal, and

▶ 0.9915 is the discount factor.

Convert this amount to the equivalent of \$1 notional principal; that is, $1/\$1.41$: $1.016(1/1.41) = £0.7206$. Now convert to dollars at the current exchange rate $\$1.35/£$: $0.7206(1.35) = \$0.9728$.

The market values based on notional principal of \$1 are as follows:

i. Pay £ fixed and receive \$ fixed = \$0.0464 = 1.0152 − 0.9688
ii. Pay £ floating and receive \$ fixed = \$0.0424 = 1.0152 − 0.9728
iii. Pay £ floating and receive \$ floating = \$0.0461 = 1.0189 − 0.9728
iv. Pay £ fixed and receive \$ floating = \$0.0501 = 1.0189 − 0.9688

4. A. First calculate the fixed payment in dollars. The dollar present value factors for 90, 180, 270, and 360 days are as follows:

$$B_0(90) = \frac{1}{1 + 0.0656(90/360)} = 0.9839$$

$$B_0(180) = \frac{1}{1 + 0.0640(180/360)} = 0.9690$$

$$B_0(270) = \frac{1}{1 + 0.0621(270/360)} = 0.9555$$

$$B_0(360) = \frac{1}{1 + 0.0599(360/360)} = 0.9435$$

The quarterly fixed payment per \$1 of notional principal is calculated as

$$FS(0, n, m) = FS(0,4,90) = \frac{1 - 0.9435}{0.9839 + 0.9690 + 0.9555 + 0.9435}$$
$$= 0.0147$$

The annualized fixed payment per \$1 of notional principal is $0.0147(360/90) = 0.0588$.

Now calculate the fixed payment in euros. The euro present value factors for 90, 180, 270, and 360 days are as follows:

$$B_0^{€}(90) = \frac{1}{1 + 0.0682(90/360)} = 0.9832$$

$$B_0^{€}(180) = \frac{1}{1 + 0.0673(180/360)} = 0.9674$$

$$B_0^{€}(270) = \frac{1}{1 + 0.0661(270/360)} = 0.9528$$

$$B_0^{€}(360) = \frac{1}{1 + 0.0668(360/360)} = 0.9374$$

The quarterly fixed payment per €1 of notional principal is calculated as

$$FS(0, n, m) = FS(0,4,90) = \frac{1 - 0.9374}{0.9832 + 0.9674 + 0.9528 + 0.9374}$$
$$= 0.0163$$

The annualized fixed payment per €1 of notional principal is $0.0163(360/90) = 0.0652$.

B. The new dollar discount factors for 60, 150, 240, and 330 days are as follows:

$$B_{30}(90) = \frac{1}{1 + 0.0384(60/360)} = 0.9936$$

$$B_{30}(180) = \frac{1}{1 + 0.0379(150/360)} = 0.9845$$

$$B_{30}(270) = \frac{1}{1 + 0.0382(240/360)} = 0.9752$$

$$B_{30}(360) = \frac{1}{1 + 0.0406(330/360)} = 0.9641$$

The present value of the remaining fixed payments plus the \$1 notional principal is $0.0147(0.9936 + 0.9845 + 0.9752 + 0.9641) + 1(0.9641) = 1.0217$.

The present value of the floating payments plus hypothetical \$1 notional principal is $1.0164(0.9936) = 1.0099$, where

▶ 1.0164 is the first floating payment, $0.0656(90/360) + 1$, which is the market value of the remaining payments plus the \$1 notional principal, and

▶ 0.9936 is the discount factor.

The new euro discount factors for 60, 150, 240, and 330 days are as follows:

$$B_{30}^{€}(90) = \frac{1}{1 + 0.0583(60/360)} = 0.9904$$

$$B_{30}^{€}(180) = \frac{1}{1 + 0.0605(150/360)} = 0.9754$$

$$B_{30}^{€}(270) = \frac{1}{1 + 0.0613(240/360)} = 0.9604$$

$$B_{30}^{€}(360) = \frac{1}{1 + 0.0651(330/360)} = 0.9437$$

The present value of the remaining fixed payments plus the €1 notional principal is $0.0163(0.9904 + 0.9754 + 0.9604 + 0.9437) + 1(0.9437) = 1.0068$. Convert this amount to the equivalent of $1 notional principal; that is, 1/$0.86: $1.0068(1/0.86) = €1.1707$. Now convert to dollars at the current exchange rate of $0.82 per euro: $1.1707(0.82) = \$0.96$.

The present value of the floating payments plus hypothetical €1 notional principal is $1.0171(0.9904) = 1.0073$, where

▶ 1.0171 is the first floating payment, $0.0682(90/360) + 1$, which is the market value of the remaining payments plus the €1 notional principal, and

▶ 0.9904 is the discount factor.

Convert this amount to the equivalent of $1 notional principal; that is, 1/$0.86: $1.0073(1/0.86) = €1.1713$. Now convert to dollars at the current exchange rate of $0.82 per euro: $1.1713(0.82) = \$0.9605$. The market values based on notional principal of $1 are

  i. Pay € fixed and receive $ fixed = $0.0617 = 1.0217 − 0.96$

  ii. Pay € floating and receive $ fixed = $0.0612 = 1.0217 − 0.9605$

  iii. Pay € floating and receive $ floating = $0.0494 = 1.0099 − 0.9605$

  iv. Pay € fixed and receive $ floating = $0.0499 = 1.0099 − 0.96$

5. A. First calculate the fixed payment in pounds. The pound present value factors for 180 and 360 days are as follows:

$$B_0^{£}(180) = \frac{1}{1 + 0.0623(180/360)} = 0.9698$$

$$B_0^{£}(360) = \frac{1}{1 + 0.0665(360/360)} = 0.9376$$

The semiannual fixed payment per £1 of notional principal is calculated as

$$FS(0, n, m) = FS(0,2,180) = \frac{1 - 0.9376}{0.9698 + 0.9376} = 0.0327$$

The annualized fixed payment per £1 of notional principal is calculated as $0.0327(360/180) = 0.0654$.

Now calculate the fixed payment in euros. The euro present value factors for 180 and 360 days are as follows:

$$B_0^{\text{€}}(180) = \frac{1}{1 + 0.0563(180/360)} = 0.9726$$

$$B_0^{\text{€}}(360) = \frac{1}{1 + 0.0580(360/360)} = 0.9452$$

The quarterly fixed payment per €1 of notional principal is calculated as

$$FS(0, n, m) = FS(0,2,180) = \frac{1 - 0.9452}{0.9726 + 0.9452} = 0.0286$$

The annualized fixed payment per €1 of notional principal is $0.0286(360/180) = 0.0572$.

B. The new pound present value factors for 120 and 300 days are as follows:

$$B_{60}^{\text{£}}(180) = \frac{1}{1 + 0.0585(120/360)} = 0.9809$$

$$B_{60}^{\text{£}}(360) = \frac{1}{1 + 0.0605(300/360)} = 0.9520$$

The present value of the remaining fixed payments plus the £1 notional principal is $0.0327(0.9809 + 0.9520) + 1(0.9520) = 1.0152$.

The present value of the floating payments plus hypothetical £1 notional principal is $1.0312(0.9809) = 1.0115$, where

▶ 1.0312 is the first floating payment, $0.0623(180/360) + 1$, which is the market value of the remaining payments plus the £1 notional principal, and

▶ 0.9809 is the discount factor.

The new euro discount factors for 120 and 300 days are as follows:

$$B_{60}^{\text{€}}(180) = \frac{1}{1 + 0.0493(120/360)} = 0.9838$$

$$B_{60}^{\text{€}}(360) = \frac{1}{1 + 0.0505(300/360)} = 0.9596$$

The present value of the remaining fixed payments plus the €1 notional principal is $0.0286(0.9838 + 0.9596) + 1(0.9596) = 1.0152$. Convert this to the equivalent of £1 notional principal; that is, $1/\text{£}0.61$: $1.0152(1/0.61) = \text{€}1.6643$.

Now convert to pounds at the current exchange rate of £0.57 per euro: $1.6643(0.57) = \text{£}0.9487$. The present value of the floating payments plus hypothetical €1 notional principal is $1.0282(0.9838) = 1.0115$, where

▶ 1.0282 is the first floating payment, $0.0563(180/360) + 1$, which is the market value of the remaining payments plus the €1 notional principal, and

▶ 0.9838 is the discount factor.

Convert this amount to the equivalent of £1 notional principal; that is, 1/£0.61: 1.0115(1/0.61) = €1.6582. Now convert to pounds at the current exchange rate of £0.57 per euro: 1.6582(0.57) = £0.9452. The market values based on notional principal of £1 are:

i. Pay £ fixed and receive € fixed = −£0.0665 = 0.9487 − 1.0152
ii. Pay £ floating and receive € fixed = −£0.0628 = 0.9487 − 1.0115
iii. Pay £ floating and receive € floating = −£0.0663 = 0.9452 − 1.0115
iv. Pay £ fixed and receive € floating = −£0.07 = 0.9452 − 1.0152

6. A. The present value factors for 180, 360, 540, and 720 days are as follows:

$$B_0(180) = \frac{1}{1 + 0.0458(180/360)} = 0.9776$$

$$B_0(360) = \frac{1}{1 + 0.0528(360/360)} = 0.9499$$

$$B_0(540) = \frac{1}{1 + 0.0624(540/360)} = 0.9144$$

$$B_0(720) = \frac{1}{1 + 0.0665(720/360)} = 0.8826$$

The semiannual fixed payment per $1 of notional principal is calculated as

$$FS(0, n, m) = FS(0,4,180) = \frac{1 - 0.8826}{0.9776 + 0.9499 + 0.9144 + 0.8826}$$
$$= 0.0315$$

The annualized fixed payment per $1 of notional principal is 0.0315(360/180) = 0.0630.

B. The new present value factors for 20, 200, 380, and 560 days are as follows:

$$B_{160}(180) = \frac{1}{1 + 0.0544(20/360)} = 0.9970$$

$$B_{160}(360) = \frac{1}{1 + 0.0629(200/360)} = 0.9662$$

$$B_{160}(540) = \frac{1}{1 + 0.0679(380/360)} = 0.9331$$

$$B_{160}(720) = \frac{1}{1 + 0.0697(560/360)} = 0.9022$$

The present value of the remaining fixed payments plus the $1 notional principal is 0.0315(0.9970 + 0.9662 + 0.9331 + 0.9022) + 1(0.9022) = 1.0219. The value of the equity payment is

$$\left(\frac{1204.10}{1150.89}\right) = 1.0462$$

Based on a notional principal of $100,000,000, the market value of a swap to pay the fixed and receive the equity return is (1.0462 − 1.0219)100,000,000 = $2,430,000.

7. The asset manager enters into the swap at time t = 0. After moving forward 100 days the next floating payment is due on day 180—that is, 80 days from now. Based on the rate in effect on day 100, the present value factor is

$$B_{100}(180) = \frac{1}{1 + 0.0427(80/360)} = 0.9906$$

The next floating payment, based on the rate in effect on day 90, will be $0.0432(90/360) = 0.0108$. The present value of the next floating payment plus the $1 market value of the remaining floating payments is $0.9906(1.0108) = 1.0013$. The value of the equity payment is

$$\left(\frac{1595.72}{1561.27}\right) = 1.0221$$

Based on a notional principal of $50 million, the market value of the swap to the party that pays floating and receives the equity return is $(1.0221 - 1.0013)50,000,000 = \$1,040,000$.

8. The value of the equity payment received on the Russell 2000 is

$$\left(\frac{524.29}{478.19}\right) = 1.0964$$

The value of the equity payment made on the DJIA is

$$\left(\frac{10016}{9867.33}\right) = 1.0151$$

Based on a notional principal of $15 million, the market value of the swap to the pay the return on the DJIA and receive the return on the Russell 2000 is $(1.0964 - 1.0151)15,000,000 = \$1,219,500$.

9. A. The present value factors for 180, 360, 540, and 720 days are as follows:

$$B_0(180) = \frac{1}{1 + 0.042(180/360)} = 0.9794$$

$$B_0(360) = \frac{1}{1 + 0.0474(360/360)} = 0.9547$$

$$B_0(540) = \frac{1}{1 + 0.0554(540/360)} = 0.9246$$

$$B_0(720) = \frac{1}{1 + 0.0661(720/360)} = 0.8832$$

The semiannual fixed payment per $1 of notional principal is calculated as

$$FS(0, n, m) = FS(0,4,180) = \frac{1 - 0.8832}{0.9794 + 0.9547 + 0.9246 + 0.8832}$$
$$= 0.0312$$

The annualized fixed payment per $1 of notional principal is $0.0312(360/180) = 0.0624$. Based on a notional principal of $50,000,000, the four possible ways to exercise this swaption are

i. Exercise the swaption, entering into a receive-fixed, pay-floating swap. The fixed receipt is (based on the exercise rate of 7 percent) $50,000,000(0.07 \times 180/360)$ $1,750,000.

The first floating payment is (based on the 180-day rate of 4.20 percent in effect at the time the swap is initiated) $50,000,000(0.0420 \times 180/360) = $1,050,000.

ii. Exercise the swaption, entering into a receive-fixed, pay-floating swap *and* entering into a pay-fixed, receive-floating swap at the market rate.

The fixed receipt is (based on the exercise rate of 7 percent) $1,750,000.

The fixed payment is (based on the rate of 6.24 percent) $50,000,000 (0.0624 \times 180/360) = $1,560,000.

The first floating payment and receipt of $1,050,000 offset each other.

iii. Exercise the swaption with offsetting swap netted.

The holder would receive a net payment stream of $1,750,000 − $1,560,000 = $190,000.

iv. The holder can choose to receive an up-front cash payment now of $190,000 (0.9794 + 0.9547 + 0.9246 + 0.8832) = $710,961.

B. At expiration, the market value of a bond with face (exercise price) of $1 and annual coupon 7 percent $= (0.07 \times 180/360)(0.9794 + 0.9547 + 0.9246 + 0.8832) + 1(0.8832) = 1.0142$. The payoff on a call option on this bond with exercise price $1 is Max $[0,(1.0142 − 1)] = 0.0142$. Based on notional principal of $50,000,000, the payoff is $50,000,000(0.0142) = $710,000. This amount is the same as the payoff on the swaption computed in Part A (iv) above (the difference comes from rounding).

10. A. The present value factors for 180, 360, 540, and 720 days are as follows:

$$B_0(180) = \frac{1}{1 + 0.0583(180/360)} = 0.9717$$

$$B_0(360) = \frac{1}{1 + 0.0605(360/360)} = 0.9430$$

$$B_0(540) = \frac{1}{1 + 0.0614(540/360)} = 0.9157$$

$$B_0(720) = \frac{1}{1 + 0.0651(720/360)} = 0.8848$$

The semiannual fixed payment per $1 of notional principal is calculated as

$$FS(0, n, m) = FS(0,4,180) = \frac{1 - 0.8848}{0.9717 + 0.9430 + 0.9157 + 0.8848}$$
$$= 0.031$$

The annualized fixed payment per $1 of notional principal is $0.031 (360/180) = 0.062$.

Based on a notional principal of $10,000,000, the four possible ways to exercise this payer swaption are

i. Exercise the swaption, entering into pay-fixed and receive-floating swap.

The fixed payment is (based on the exercise rate of 5 percent) $10,000,000 (0.05 × 180/360) = $250,000.

The first floating receipt is (based on the 180-day rate in effect at the time the swap is initiated of 5.83 percent) $10,000,000(0.0583 × 180/360) = $291,500.

ii. Exercise the swaption, entering into pay-fixed and receive-floating swap, and entering into receive-fixed pay-floating swap at the market rate.

The fixed payment is (based on the exercise rate of 5 percent) $250,000.

The fixed receipt is (based on the rate of 6.2 percent) $10,000,000(0.062 × 180/360) = $310,000.

The first floating payment and receipt of $291,500 offset each other.

iii. Exercise the swaption with offsetting swap netted.

The holder would receive a net payment stream of $310,000 − $250,000 = $60,000.

iv. The holder can choose to receive an up-front cash payment now of 60,000 (0.9717 + 0.9430 + 0.9157 + 0.8848) = $222,912.

B. At expiration, the market value of a bond with face (exercise price) of $1 and annual coupon 5 percent = (0.05 × 180/360) (0.9717 + 0.9430 + 0.9157 + 0.8848) + 1(0.8848) = 0.9777. The payoff on a put option on this bond with exercise price $1 is Max [0,(1 − 0.9777)] = 0.0223. The payoff based on a notional principal of $10,000,000 is 0.0223(10,000,000) = $223,000. This amount is the same as the payoff on the swaption as computed in Part A (iv) above (the difference comes from rounding).

11. A. The present value factors for 90, 180, 270, and 360 days are as follows:

$$B_0(180) = \frac{1}{1 + 0.0373(90/360)} = 0.9908$$

$$B_0(360) = \frac{1}{1 + 0.0429(180/360)} = 0.9790$$

$$B_0(540) = \frac{1}{1 + 0.0477(270/360)} = 0.9655$$

$$B_0(720) = \frac{1}{1 + 0.0538(360/360)} = 0.9489$$

The quarterly fixed payment per $1 of notional principal is calculated as

$$FS(0, n, m) = FS(0,4,180) = \frac{1 - 0.9489}{0.9908 + 0.9790 + 0.9655 + 0.9489}$$
$$= 0.0132$$

The annualized fixed payment per $1 of notional principal is 0.0132(360/90) = 0.0528. The market value at expiration of the receiver swaption is Max {0,[0.065 × (90/360) − 0.0132](0.9908 + 0.9790 + 0.9655 + 0.9489)} = 0.012. Based on notional principal of $100,000,000, the market value is 100,000,000(0.012) = $1,200,000.

B. At expiration, the market value of a bond with face (exercise price) of $1 and annual coupon of 6.5 percent is $(0.065 \times 90/360)(0.9908 + 0.9790 + 0.9655 + 0.9489) + 1(0.9489) = 1.012$. The payoff on a call option on this bond with exercise price $1 is Max $[0,(1.012 - 1)] = 0.012$. This is the same as the payoff on the swaption.

12. A. The present value factors for 180, 360, 540, and 720 days are as follows:

$$B_0(180) = \frac{1}{1 + 0.0583(180/360)} = 0.9717$$

$$B_0(360) = \frac{1}{1 + 0.0616(360/360)} = 0.9420$$

$$B_0(540) = \frac{1}{1 + 0.0680(540/360)} = 0.9074$$

$$B_0(720) = \frac{1}{1 + 0.0705(720/360)} = 0.8764$$

The semiannual fixed payment per $1 of notional principal is calculated as

$$FS(0, n, m) = FS(0,4,180) = \frac{1 - 0.8764}{0.9717 + 0.9420 + 0.9074 + 0.8764}$$

$$= 0.0334$$

The annualized fixed payment per $1 of notional principal is calculated as $0.0334(360/180) = 0.0668$.

The new present value factors for 180, 360, and 540 days are as follows:

$$B_{180}(180) = \frac{1}{1 + 0.0429(180/360)} = 0.9790$$

$$B_{180}(360) = \frac{1}{1 + 0.0583(360/360)} = 0.9489$$

$$B_{180}(540) = \frac{1}{1 + 0.0618(540/360)} = 0.9152$$

The present value of the remaining fixed payments plus the $1 notional principal is $0.0334(0.9790 + 0.9489 + 0.9152) + 1(0.9152) = 1.0102$.

Because we are on the payment date, the present value of the remaining floating payments plus hypothetical $1 notional principal is automatically 1.0.

The market value of the swap to the pay-floating, receive-fixed party is $(1.0102 - 1) = \$0.0102$. So the market value of the swap to the pay-fixed, receive-floating party is $-\$0.0102$. Because the swap is marked to market, the party that pays floating will now receive $0.0102 per $1 of notional principal from the party that pays fixed. The two parties would then reprice the swap.

B. The new fixed-rate payment per $1 of notional principal is

$$FS(r0, n, m) = FS(0,3,180) = \frac{1 - 0.9152}{0.9790 + 0.9489 + 0.9152}$$

$$= 0.0298$$

13. A. The present value factors for 90, 180, 270, and 360 days are as follows:

$$B_0(90) = \frac{1}{1 + 0.0252(90/360)} = 0.9937$$

$$B_0(180) = \frac{1}{1 + 0.0305(180/360)} = 0.9850$$

$$B_0(270) = \frac{1}{1 + 0.0373(270/360)} = 0.9728$$

$$B_0(360) = \frac{1}{1 + 0.0406(360/360)} = 0.9610$$

The quarterly fixed payment per $1 of notional principal is calculated as

$$FS(0, n, m) = FS(0,4,90) = \frac{1 - 0.9610}{0.9937 + 0.9850 + 0.9728 + 0.9610}$$

$$= 0.01$$

The annualized fixed payment per $1 of notional principal is calculated as $0.01(360/90) = 0.04$.

The new present value factors for 90, 180, and 270 days are as follows:

$$B_{90}(90) = \frac{1}{1 + 0.0539(90/360)} = 0.9867$$

$$B_{90}(180) = \frac{1}{1 + 0.0608(180/360)} = 0.9705$$

$$B_{90}(270) = \frac{1}{1 + 0.0653(270/360)} = 0.9533$$

The present value of the remaining fixed payments plus the $1 notional principal is $0.01(0.9867 + 0.9705 + 0.9533) + 1(0.9533) = 0.9824$.

Because we are on the payment date, the present value of the remaining floating payments plus hypothetical $1 notional principal is automatically 1.0.

The market value of the swap to the pay-floating, receive-fixed party is $(0.9824 - 1) = -\$0.0176$. So, the market value of the swap to the pay-fixed, receive-floating party is $0.0176. Because the swap is marked to market, the party that pays floating will now pay $0.0176 per $1 of notional principal to the party that pays fixed. The two parties would then reprice the swap.

B. The new fixed-rate payment per $1 of notional principal is

$$FS(0, n, m) = FS(0,3,90) = \frac{1 - 0.9533}{0.9867 + 0.9705 + 0.9533} = 0.0160$$

14. A is correct. Burke's statement #1 has the price of the protective put above that of the fiduciary call. Put–call parity establishes that the two should be equal. To exploit an arbitrage condition, one buys the (relatively) undervalued and sells the (relatively) overvalued. Thus, in this problem, one would sell the overvalued protective put (sell the put and sell the asset) and buy the undervalued fiduciary call (buy the call and buy the appropriate risk-free bond). Only answer A is a correct statement in exploiting this arbitrage.

15. B is correct. In statement #2, Burke mischaracterizes put–call parity. Put–call parity is

$$p_0 = c_0 - S_0 + X/(1 + r)^T$$

Solving for the underlying asset, $S_0 = c_0 + [X/(1 + r)^T] - p_0$.

Therefore, the synthetic long asset is a combination of long the call, long the risk-free bond, and short the put option.

16. B is correct. When dealing with forward contracts, as in Burke's statement #3, put-call parity must be modified. The current stock price, S_0, drops out of the formula. Then, adjust the last term to be the difference between the strike price and the forward price. That is:

$$p_0 = c_0 + [X - F(0,T)]/(1 + r)^T$$

Substituting the values from Exhibit 1:

$$p_0 = 7.5 + (55 - 46)/(1.04)^{(175/365)} = \$16.33$$

17. A is correct. Burke has valued the call at $7.44. Exhibit P-2 reports the market price of the call is $7.75. The call is overvalued from Burke's perspective. To arbitrage this difference, Burke should sell calls and buy the underlying shares. Thus, the answer is either A or B. Next, consider the question of how many calls per share to form the arbitrage. Note these facts: the delta of a call is the change in value of the call for a unit ($1.00) change in the value of the stock. Deltas range from +1.00 (very deep in the money) to 0.00 (very far out of the money). Ignoring very deep in the money options, in order to form a delta-neutral hedge, one needs more calls (on a per unit basis) than underlying assets.

Confirmation comes from solving the binomial model for the given values. The expiration date values for the stock are $56 (up 12%) or $42.5 (down 15%). Assume one borrows the present value of $42.50 at time zero. The payoffs at expiration from a portfolio of long the stock and short the bond are zero in the down state and $13.50 in the up state (i.e., $56 - 42.50$). The terminal values of the call with a strike of $45 are $11.00 in the up-state and $0.00 in the down-state. To make the expiration payoffs match, multiply the call payoffs by 13.50/11. As the payoffs now match at expiration, it must also be true, to avoid arbitrage, that the time zero values are equal. That is, one share of stock minus the present value of $42.50 equals 13.50/11 calls. For 1,000 calls, the replicating portfolio would need 815 shares of stock (i.e., $(11/13.5) \times 1,000$).

18. B is correct. The value of the swaption is the sum of the present values of the related cash flows. The net cash flows reflect the fixed rate of 6.20%, adjusted for semi-annual payments, minus the exercise rate of 5.10%, adjusted for semi-annual payments, times the notional principal of $15 million. Thus, the semi-annual payments are $(0.062/2) - (0.051/2) \times \$15,000,000 = \$82,500$. Find the PV of these cash flows at the given interest rates: $\$82,500 \times (0.9717 + 0.9430 + 0.9157 + 0.8848) = \$306,504$.

19. D is correct. Under the terms of the swap Client 2 entered into last year, Client 2 is currently committed to paying fixed and receiving floating. By entering into a receiver swaption to receive fixed and pay floating, the client can offset the current swap commitment if future conditions make it attractive to do so.

SOLUTIONS FOR READING 66

1. There is no payoff to the cap if the cap rate exceeds 3-month LIBOR. For Periods 2 and 3, there is no payoff because 3-month LIBOR is below the cap rate. For Periods 1 and 4, there is a payoff and the payoff is determined by:

$10 million $\times$ (3-month LIBOR $-$ cap rate)/4

The payoffs are summarized below:

Period	3-month LIBOR (%)	Payoff ($)
1	8.7%	17,500
2	8.0	0
3	7.8	0
4	8.2	5,000

2. There is a payoff to the floor if 3-month LIBOR is less than the floor rate. For Periods 1 and 2, there is no payoff because 3-month LIBOR is greater than the floor rate. For Periods 3 and 4, there is a payoff and the payoff is determined by:

$20 million $\times$ (floor rate $-$ 3-month LIBOR)/4

The payoffs are summarized below:

Period	3-month LIBOR (%)	Payoff ($)
1	4.7%	0
2	4.4	0
3	3.8	10,000
4	3.4	30,000

3. Once the fee for the interest rate floor is paid, the seller of an interest rate floor is not exposed to counterparty risk. Only the seller, not the buyer, must perform.

4. A. An interest rate cap or floor is equivalent to a package of interest rate options.

  B. Since a cap is equivalent to a package of interest rate options, each option in the package is called a caplet.

Fixed Income Analysis for the Chartered Financial Analyst® Program, Second Edition, by Frank J. Fabozzi.
Copyright © 2005 by CFA Institute. Reprinted with permission.

SOLUTIONS FOR READING 66

Solutions for Practice Questions found in Reading

1. The invoice price is equal to

contract size × futures settlement price × conversion factor
    + accrued interest

The futures settlement price is 97-24 or 97.75 (= 97 + 24/32). The futures settlement price per $1 of par value is therefore 0.9775. The invoice price is then:

$$\$100{,}000 \times 0.9775 \times 1.17 + \$3{,}800 = \$118{,}167.50$$

2. The proceeds received are:

converted price = futures price × conversion factor
    = \$97 × 0.9710 = \$94.1870

The term repo rate is 4.7%, so the interest from reinvesting the interim coupon payment is

interest from reinvesting the interim coupon payment

$$= \$3.5 \times 0.047 \times \left(\frac{37}{360}\right) = \$0.0169$$

Summary:

converted price	= $94.1870
accrued interest received	= 0.7096
interim coupon payment	= 3.5000
interest from reinvesting the interim coupon payment	= 0.0169
proceeds received	= $98.4135

The cost of the investment is the purchase price for the issue plus the accrued interest paid, as shown below:

cost of the investment = \$95 + \$3.0110 = \$98.0110

The implied repo rate is then:

$$\text{implied repo rate} = \frac{\$98.4135 - \$98.0110}{\$98.0110} \times \frac{360}{62} = 0.0238 = 2.38\%$$

3. A. The investor will exercise the call option because the price of the futures contract exceeds the strike price. By exercising the investor receives a long position in the Treasury bond futures contract and the call option writer receives the corresponding short position. The futures price for both parties is the strike price of $98. The positions are then marked-to-market using the futures price of $103 and the option writer must pay the option buyer $5 (the difference between the futures price of $103 and the strike price of $98).

After this, the positions look as follows:

► the investor (the buyer of the call option) has a long position in the Treasury bond futures contract at $103 and cash of $5

► the writer of the call option has a short position in the Treasury bond futures contract at $103 and has paid cash of $5

B. The investor will exercise the put option because the price of the futures contract is less than the strike price. By exercising the investor receives a short position in the Treasury bond futures contract and the put option writer receives the corresponding long position. The futures price for both parties is the strike price of $105. The positions are then marked-to-market using the futures price of $105 and the option writer must pay the option buyer $9 (the difference between the strike price of $105 and the futures price of $96).

After this, the positions look as follows:

► the investor (the buyer of the put option) has a short position in the Treasury bond futures contract at $105 and cash of $9

► the writer of the call option has a long position in the Treasury bond futures contract at $105 and has paid cash of $9

4. Although the payments are quarterly rather than semiannual as illustrated in the text illustration, the concept is the same.

A. Since the swap rate is 4.4%, the fixed-rate payment each quarter will be:

$100 million $\times$ (0.044/4) = $1.1 million

(In the next reading, this number will be fine tuned to allow for the fact that not every quarter has the same number of days.)

B. Since 3-month LIBOR is 7.2%, the first quarterly payment will be:

$100 million $\times$ (0.072/4) = $1.8 million

5. There is a payoff to the cap if the cap rate exceeds 3-month LIBOR. For Periods 1 and 2, there is no payoff because the 3-month LIBOR is below the cap rate. For Periods 3 and 4, there is a payoff and the payoff is determined by:

$100 million $\times$ (3-month LIBOR − cap rate)/4

The payoffs are summarized below:

Period	3-month LIBOR (%)	Payoff ($)
1	6.7%	$ 0
2	7.0	0
3	7.4	100,000
4	7.6	150,000

SOLUTIONS FOR READING 68

1. The expected return is $0.75E$(return on stocks) $+ 0.25E$(return on bonds)

$$= 0.75(15) + 0.25(5)$$
$$= 12.5 \text{ percent}$$

The standard deviation is

$$\sigma = [w_{\text{stocks}}^2 \sigma_{\text{stocks}}^2 + w_{\text{bonds}}^2 \sigma_{\text{bonds}}^2 + 2w_{\text{stocks}}w_{\text{bonds}}$$
$$\text{Corr}(R_{\text{stocks}}, R_{\text{bonds}})\sigma_{\text{stocks}}\sigma_{\text{bonds}}]^{1/2}$$
$$= [0.75^2(225) + 0.25^2(100) + 2(0.75)(0.25)(0.5)(15)(10)]^{1/2}$$
$$= (126.5625 + 6.25 + 28.125)^{1/2}$$
$$= (160.9375)^{1/2}$$
$$= 12.69\%$$

2. Use the expression

$$\sigma_p^2 = \sigma^2 \left(\frac{1 - \rho}{n} + \rho \right)$$

The square root of this expression is standard deviation. With variance equal to 625 and correlation equal to 0.3,

$$\sigma_p = \sqrt{625 \left(\frac{1 - 0.3}{100} + 0.3 \right)}$$
$$= 13.85\%$$

3. Find portfolio variance using the following expression

$$\sigma_p^2 = \sigma^2 \left(\frac{1 - \rho}{n} + \rho \right)$$
$$\sigma_p^2 = 625 \left[(1 - 0.3)/24 + 0.3 \right] = 205.73$$

With 24 stocks, variance of return is 205.73 (equivalent to a standard deviation of 14.34 percent). With an unlimited number of securities, the first term in square brackets is 0 and the smallest variance is achieved:

$$\sigma_{\text{min}}^2 = \sigma^2 \rho = 625(0.30) = 187.5$$

This result is equivalent to a standard deviation of 13.69 percent. The ratio of the variance of the 24-stock portfolio to the portfolio with an unlimited number of securities is

$$\frac{\sigma_p^2}{\sigma_{\text{min}}^2} = \frac{205.73}{187.5} = 1.097$$

The variance of the 24-stock portfolio is approximately 110 percent of the variance of the portfolio with an unlimited number of securities.

4. Define

R_p = return on the portfolio
R_1 = return on the risk-free asset
R_2 = return on the risky asset
w_1 = fraction of the portfolio invested in the risk-free asset
w_2 = fraction of the portfolio invested in the risky asset

Then the expected return on the portfolio is

$$E(R_p) = w_1 E(R_1) + w_2 E(R_2)$$
$$= 0.10(5\%) + 0.9(13\%) = 0.5 + 11.7 = 12.2\%$$

To calculate standard deviation of return, we calculate variance of return and take the square root of variance:

$$\sigma^2(R_p) = w_1^2\sigma^2(R_1) + w_2^2\sigma^2(R_2) + 2w_1 w_2 \text{Cov}(R_1, R_2)$$
$$= 0.1^2(0^2) + 0.9^2(23^2) + 2(0.1)(0.9)(0)$$
$$= 0.9^2(23^2)$$
$$= 428.49$$

Thus the portfolio standard deviation of return is $\sigma(R_p) = (428.49)^{1/2} = 20.7$ percent.

5. According to the market model, $\text{Var}(R_p) = \beta_p^2\sigma_M^2 + \sigma_{\varepsilon_p}^2$. The S&P 500 index fund should have a beta of 1 with respect to the S&P 500. By moving 10 percent of invested funds from the index fund to a security with a beta of 2, we necessarily will increase $\beta_p^2\sigma_M^2$ (systematic risk) for the portfolio. An individual assset will also have higher nonsystematic risk (residual risk) than the highly diversified index fund, so $\sigma_{\varepsilon_p}^2$ will increase as well. Thus the new portfolio cannot have a lower standard deviation of return than the old portfolio.

6. A. With R_T the return on the tangency portfolio and R_F the risk-free rate,

$$\text{Expected risk premium per unit of risk} = \frac{E(R_T) - R_F}{\sigma(R_T)} = \frac{14 - 6}{24} = 0.33$$

B. First, we find the weight w of the tangency portfolio in the investor's portfolio using the expression $\sigma(R_p) = w\sigma(R_T)$, so

$$w = (20/24) = 0.8333$$

Then

$$E(R_p) = wE(R_T) + (1 - w)R_F = 0.833333(14\%) + 0.166667(6\%)$$
$$= 12.67\%$$

7. A. According to the Markowitz decision rule, Martínez should prefer Portfolio B to Portfolio C because B has the same expected return as C with lower standard deviation of return than C. Thus he can eliminate C from consideration as a stand-alone portfolio. The Markowitz decision rule is inconclusive concerning the choice between A and B, however, because although A has higher mean return, it also has higher standard deviation of return.

B. With a risk-free asset, we can evaluate portfolios using the Sharpe ratio (the ratio of mean return in excess of the risk-free rate divided by standard deviation of return). The Sharpe ratios are

Portfolio A: $(12 - 2)/15 = 0.67$
Portfolio B: $(10 - 2)/8 = 1.00$
Portfolio C: $(10 - 2)/9 = 0.89$

With risk-free borrowing and lending possible, Martínez will choose Portfolio B because it has the highest Sharpe ratio.

8. The quantity (Sharpe ratio of existing portfolio) $\times$ (Correlation of U.S. bonds with existing portfolio) $= 0.15(0.20) = 0.03$. Because U.S. bonds' predicted Sharpe ratio of 0.10 exceeds 0.03, it is optimal to add them to the existing portfolio.

9. With R_M the return on the market portfolio, and all the other terms as defined in previous answers, we have

$$\begin{aligned} E(R_p) &= wE(R_M) + (1 - w)R_F \\ 17 &= 13w + 5(1 - w) = 8w + 5 \\ 12 &= 8w \\ w &= 1.5 \end{aligned}$$

Thus $1 - 1.5 = -0.5$ of initial wealth goes into the risk-free asset. The negative sign indicates borrowing: $-0.5(\$1 \text{ million}) = -\$500,000$, so the investor borrows \$500,000.

10. We start from the definition of correlation (first line below). In the numerator, we substitute for covariance using Equation 68-14; in the denominator we use Equation 68-13 to substitute for the standard deviations of return.

$$\begin{aligned} \text{Corr } (R_1, R_2) &= \frac{\text{Cov}(R_1, R_2)}{\sigma_1 \sigma_2} \\ &= \frac{\beta_1 \beta_2 \sigma_M^2}{\sqrt{\beta_1^2 \sigma_M^2 + \sigma_{\epsilon_1}^2} \sqrt{\beta_2^2 \sigma_M^2 + \sigma_{\epsilon_2}^2}} \\ &= \frac{1.5(1.2)(8)^2}{\sqrt{1.5^2(8^2) + 2^2} \sqrt{1.2^2(8^2) + 4^2}} \\ &= 0.91 \end{aligned}$$

11. $\begin{aligned} \beta_{adj} &= 0.33 + (0.67)(1.2) \\ &= 0.33 + 0.80 \\ &= 1.13 \end{aligned}$

$$\begin{aligned} E(R_p) = E(R_i) &= R_F + \beta_i[E(R_M) - R_F] \\ &= 5\% + 1.13(8.5\%) \\ &= 14.6\% \end{aligned}$$

12. The surprise in a factor equals actual value minus expected value. For the interest rate factor, the surprise was 2 percent; for the GDP factor, the surprise was -3 percent.

$$\begin{aligned} R = {}& \text{Expected return} - 1.5(\text{Interest rate surprise}) + 2(\text{GDP surprise}) \\ & + \text{Company-specific surprise} \\ = {}& 11\% - 1.5(2\%) + 2(-3\%) + 3\% \\ = {}& 5\% \end{aligned}$$

13. Portfolio inflation sensitivity is the weight on Manumatic stock multiplied by its inflation sensitivity, plus the weight on Nextech stock multiplied by its inflation sensitivity: $0.5(-1) + 0.5(2) = 0.5$. So a 1 percent interest rate surprise increase in inflation is expected to produce a 50 basis point increase in the portfolio's return.

14. The arbitrage portfolio must have zero sensitivity to the factor. We first need to find the proportions of A and B in short position that combine to produce a factor sensitivity equal to 0.45, the factor sensitivity of C, which we will hold long. Using w as the weight on A in the short position,

$$2w + 0.4(1 - w) = 0.45$$
$$2w + 0.4 - 0.4w) = 0.45$$
$$1.6w = 0.05$$
$$w = 0.05/1.6 = 0.03125$$

Hence, the weights on A and B are -0.03125 and -0.96875, respectively. These sum to -1. The arbitrage portfolio has zero net investment. The weight on C in the arbitrage portfolio must be 1, so that combined with the short position, the net investment is 0. The expected return on the arbitrage portfolio is $1(0.08) - 0.03125(0.15) - 0.96875(0.07) = 0.08 - 0.0725 = 0.0075$ or 0.75 percent. For \$10,000 invested in C, this represents a \$10,000 × $0.0075 = \$75$ arbitrage profit.

15. We need to combine Portfolios K and L in such a way that sensitivity to the inflation factor is zero. The inflation sensitivities of Portfolios K and L are 0.5 and 1.5, respectively. With w the weight on Portfolio L, we have

$$0 = 0.5(1 - w) + 1.5w$$
$$0 = 0.5 - 0.5w + 1.5w$$
$$0 = 0.5 + w$$
$$w = -0.5$$

The weight on Portfolio L in the new portfolio is -0.5, and the weight on Portfolio K is 1.5 $(-0.5 + 1.5 = 1)$. For every \$1.50 invested on Portfolio K, the institution shorts \$0.50 of Portfolio L. The new portfolio's return is

$$R = 0.125 + 0.25F_{GDP}$$

The intercept is computed as $(1.50 \times 0.12) + (-0.5 \times 0.11) = 0.125$, and the sensitivity to the GDP factor is computed as $(1.50 \times 1.0) + (-0.5 \times 2.5) = 0.25$.

16. $E(R_A) = 6 + 0.5\lambda = 10.25$
$E(R_B) = 6 + 1.2\lambda = 16.2$
Using either equation, we can calculate the price of factor risk as

$$\lambda = \frac{10.25 - 6}{0.5} = \frac{16.2 - 6}{1.2} = 8.5$$

The risk premium for each unit of factor risk, or price of risk, is 8.5 percent.

17. With w the weight on Portfolio A, $(1 - w)$ the weight on Portfolio B, and 1.71 the sensitivity of the S&P 500 to the business cycle factor, we have

$$2.25w + 1.00(1 - w) = 1.71$$
$$2.25w + 1 - w = 1.71$$
$$1.25w = 0.71$$

Thus

$w = 0.568$, weight on Portfolio A
$1 - w = 0.432$, weight on Portfolio B

With a weight of 0.568 on A and 0.432 on B, the resulting inflation factor sensitivity is $0.568(-0.12) + 0.432(-0.45) = -0.263$.

18. If the average investor has income from employment, then this income makes this investor recession sensitive. Hence, the average investor requires a risk premium to hold recession-sensitive securities. The average investor's need for a risk premium for these stocks influences their prices. Cyclical stocks and high-yield bonds are both very sensitive to economic conditions. For example, the debt-paying ability of high-yield bond issuers is strongly affected by recessions. The wealthy investor with no labor income can take the recession risk for which she would receive a premium (pay a lower price than would be the case if the average investor were not recession sensitive). The high-wealth investor can afford to take the risk because she does not face recession risk from labor income.

SOLUTIONS FOR READING 70

1. According to the CAPM, expected return = 3.25 + 1.25(5.5) = 10.125%.

2. The total risk of the asset is 120 percent. The systematic risk = $0.9^2(90)$ = 72.9. Thus, the portion of total risk that can be attributed to market risk is 72.9/120 = 60.75%. The balance, 39.25 percent, can be attributed to asset-specific risk.

3. The portfolio beta, β_p = 0.5(0.85) + 0.25(1.3) + 0.25(0.90) = 0.975.

Total portfolio risk, $\sigma_p^2 = 0.975^2(120)$ = 114.1. So, σ_p = 10.7%.

4. A. Current real exchange rate = Can$1.46(1/1.46) = Can$1 per pound.

B. Real exchange rate one year later = Can$1.4308(1.04/1.4892) = Can$1 per pound.

C. The Canadian investor did not experience a change in the real exchange rate. While inflation in the United Kingdom is greater than inflation in Canada by two percentage points, the pound has depreciated relative to the Canadian dollar by 2 percent. Thus, the real exchange rate is unchanged.

5. A. Current real exchange rate = $1.80(1/3) = $0.60 per pound.

B. Real exchange rate one year later = $1.854(1.02/3.15) = $0.60 per pound.

C. The U.S. investor did not experience a change in the real exchange rate. This is because while inflation in the United Kingdom is less than inflation in the United States by three percentage points, the pound has appreciated relative to the dollar by 3 percent. Thus, the real exchange rate is unchanged.

6. A. The current real exchange rate = $0.62(1.5/1) = $0.93 per Swiss franc.

The inflation differential between the United States and Switzerland is 2.5%. That is, U.S. inflation minus Swiss inflation is −2.5%. Thus, for real exchange rates to remain the same, the Swiss franc would have to depreciate by 2.5 percent.

The expected exchange rate = 0.62(1 − 0.025) = $0.6045 per Swiss franc.

The real exchange rate would then be = $0.6045(1.56/1.015) = $0.93 per Swiss franc.

The expected return on the Swiss bond = (1 + 0.045)(1 − 0.025) − 1 = 0.0189, or 1.9 percent.

B. If the exchange rate at the end of one year is $0.63 per Swiss franc, the Swiss franc has appreciated by 1.61 percent.

The real exchange rate is = $0.63(1.56/1.015) = $0.9683 per Swiss franc.

The return on the Swiss bond = (1 + 0.045)(1 + 0.0161) − 1 = 0.0618, or 6.18 percent.

The return on the Swiss bond is higher than in Part A because the Swiss franc has appreciated by 1.61%, whereas in Part A, the Swiss Franc depreciated by 2.5 percent.

7. A. The current real exchange rate = 0.69(1/1.2) = £0.575 per U.S. dollar.

The inflation differential between the United Kingdom and the United States is 2.25 percent. That is, U.K. inflation minus U.S. inflation is 2.25

percent. Thus, for real exchange rates to remain the same, the U.S. dollar would have to appreciate by 2.25 percent.

The expected exchange rate = 0.69(1 + 0.0225) = £0.7055 per U.S. dollar.

The real exchange rate would then be = 0.7055(1.015/1.245) = £0.575 per U.S. dollar.

The expected return on the U.S. bond = (1 + 0.0176)(1 + 0.0225) − 1 = 0.0405, or 4.05 percent. This is close to the U.K. one-year interest rate of 4.13 percent.

B. If the exchange rate at the end of one year is £0.67 per U.S. dollar, the U.S. dollar has depreciated by approximately 2.9 percent.

The real exchange rate is = 0.67(1.015/1.245) = £0.5462 per dollar.

The return on the U.S. bond is = (1 + 0.0176)(1 − 0.029) − 1 = −0.0119, or −1.19 percent.

The return on the U.S. bond is lower than in Part A because the U.S. dollar has depreciated by 2.9 percent, whereas in Part (a), the U.S. dollar appreciated by 2.25 percent.

8. A. The forward rate = 0.90(1.0315/1.0478) = $0.886 per euro.

B. The euro is trading at a forward discount = (0.886 − 0.90)/0.90 = −0.0156, or −1.56 percent.

C. The interest rate differential between the domestic interest rate and the foreign interest rate (U.S. minus Eurozone) is 3.15 − 4.78 = −1.63%. This is in line with the forward discount on the foreign currency (euro) of 1.56 percent. This result is consistent with interest rate parity.

9. If the U.S. firm invests funds (say, $1) in one-year U.S. bonds, at the end of one year it will have 1(1 + 0.0275) = $1.0275.

Alternatively the U.S. firm could convert $1 into £(1/1.46) = £0.6849. This amount would be invested in one-year U.K. bonds, and at the end of one year it will have 0.6849(1 + 0.0425) = £0.714.

This can be converted back to U.S. dollars at the forward exchange rate = 0.714(1.25) = $0.8925.

The firm is better off investing domestically in U.S. bonds.

10. If the German firm invests funds (say, €1) in one-year euro bonds, at the end of one year it will have 1(1 + 0.0335) = €1.0335.

Alternatively the German firm could convert €1 into $(1/1.12) = $0.8929. This amount would be invested in one-year U.S. bonds, and at the end of one year it will have 0.8929(1 + 0.0225) = $0.913.

This can be converted back to euros = 0.913(1.25) = €1.1412.

The firm is better off investing in U.S. bonds.

11. A. The interest rate differential (U.S. minus Swiss) = 0.0425 − 0.0375 = 0.005, or 0.50 percent. This implies that the Swiss Franc trades at a forward premium of 0.50 percent. That is, the forward exchange rate is quoted at a premium of 0.50 percent over the spot exchange rate of $0.65 per Swiss franc.

The foreign currency risk premium = 0.0275 − 0.005 = 0.0225, or 2.25 percent.

B. The domestic currency (U.S.$) return on the foreign bond is 6.5%. This can be calculated in one of two ways:

▶ Domestic risk-free rate + Foreign currency risk premium = 4.25% + 2.25% = 6.5%.

▶ Foreign risk-free rate + Expected exchange rate movement = 3.75% + 2.75% = 6.5%.

12. A. The interest rate differential (Swiss minus U.S.) = $0.0275 - 0.0525 =$ -0.025, or -2.50 percent. This implies that the U.S. dollar trades at a forward discount of 2.50 percent. That is, the forward exchange rate is quoted at a discount of 2.50 percent over the spot exchange rate, SFr 1.62 per dollar.

The foreign currency risk premium = $-0.0275 - (-0.025) = -0.0025$ $= -0.25\%$.

B. The domestic currency (Swiss franc) return on the foreign (U.S.) bond is 2.5 percent. This can be calculated in one of two ways:

▶ Domestic risk-free rate + Foreign currency risk premium = 2.75% + (-0.25%) = 2.5%.

▶ Foreign risk-free rate + Expected exchange rate movement = 5.25% + (-2.75%) = 2.5%.

13. A. The expected return for each of the stocks is calculated using the following version of the ICAPM:

$$E(R_i) = R_0 + \beta_{iw}(RP_w) + \gamma_{i\text{€}}(SRP_\text{€}) + \gamma_{iSF}(SRP_{SF})$$

Thus, the expected returns for Stocks A, B, C, and D are

$E(R_A) = 0.0375 + 1(0.06) + 1(0.02) - 0.25(0.0125) = 0.1144$, or 11.44%
$E(R_B) = 0.0375 + 0.90(0.06) + 0.80(0.02) + 0.75(0.0125) =$
0.1169, or 11.69%
$E(R_C) = 0.0375 + 1(0.06) - 0.25(0.02) + 1(0.0125) = 0.1050$, or 10.50%
$E(R_D) = 0.0375 + 1.5(0.06) - 1(0.02) - 0.50(0.0125) = 0.1013$, or 10.13%

B. Stock B has the lowest world beta but the highest expected return, whereas Stock D has the highest world beta and the lowest expected return. The reason lies with differences in currency exposures of the stocks. The negative currency exposures of Stock D result in a lower expected return. Stock B, on the other hand, has positive currency exposures, which increase expected returns in this example.

14. A. The derivation of the traditional CAPM relies on assumptions about investors' expectations and market perfection.

In the international context, tax differentials, high transaction costs, regulations, capital, and exchange controls are obvious market imperfections. Their magnitude is greater than in a domestic context and is more likely to create problems in the model.

Because of deviations from purchasing power parity (real exchange rate movements), investors from different countries have a different measure of the real return of a given asset. For example, if the euro depreciates by 20 percent, a U.S. investor may obtain a negative (real dollar) return on his Club Med investment, while a French investor could obtain a positive (real euro) return on Club Med.

B. Even if markets were fully efficient and integrated, deviations from purchasing power parity alone could explain why, in theory, optimal portfolios differ from the world market portfolio.

15. A. From a U.S. dollar viewpoint, the currency exposure of a diversified Australian portfolio (similar to the index) is equal to +0.5. The regression coefficient $\gamma^{A\$}$ measures the sensitivity of the Australian dollar value of the portfolio to changes in the value of the Australian dollar— this coefficient is -0.50. Thus, the currency exposure of the Australian portfolio is $= \gamma = 1 + \gamma^{A\$} = 1 - 0.5 = 0.5$.

B. Because the currency exposure is 0.5, if the Australian dollar declined by 10 percent against the U.S. dollar, you can expect to lose approximately 5 percent of U.S.$10 million, i.e.; $500,000.

16. A. For *Mega:* Assume a sudden and unanticipated depreciation of the euro. Production costs are unaffected in the short run; they stay constant in euros. Product prices stay constant in dollars and therefore increase by 20 percent in euros. The earnings are vastly increased in the short run.

For *Club:* The short-run effect is opposite to that of *Mega.* The import costs rise while the product prices must stay constant to match French competition.

B. For *Mega:* In the longer run, this unanticipated depreciation of the euro could have several effects. *Mega* could use it to lower the dollar price of its products and increase its sales (and earnings) as it becomes more competitive. On the other hand, this euro depreciation could "import" inflation into Europe. The price of imported goods and inflation rise. Wages consequently adjust. In the long run, *Mega*'s production costs in euros will rise.

For *Club:* In the long run, the importer will still be in a difficult position. However, French and European competitors may seize this opportunity to raise the price of their products.

C. For *Mega:* Assume now that the euro depreciation is simply an adjustment to the existing inflation differential (high inflation rate in Europe). This purchasing power parity movement has no real effect on *Mega.* It will simply make the euro price of its products rise at the same rate as the inflated production costs.

For *Club:* Again, the effect should be neutral as on *Mega.*

17. Because you want an asset whose price will go up if the Australian dollar depreciates, you would choose Company I. However, this is only one factor of the investment choice. For example, it may be more interesting to buy the most attractive assets (even if they exhibit a positive correlation with the euro per A$ exchange rate) and hedge the currency risk using currency futures.

18. A. In general, the short-term appreciation of the won versus the euro would make South Korean goods more expensive to European buyers and would make European goods cheaper for South Korean citizens.

The likely effect of a short-term appreciation of the won versus the euro on KoreaCo's unit sales in Europe would be a decline in KoreaCo's sales resulting from the increased cost of the imported KoreaCo widgets relative to domestic alternatives (or other imports). European widgets or other imports would become more attractive, and purchases would shift to them.

A decline in unit sales as a result of the appreciation, and an assumption that variable costs are not subjected to change, implies a higher cost per unit *because of* the lower number of units over which the fixed costs can be spread. Profit margins would contract.

In the short run, KoreaCo could absorb the currency impact by lowering the won price in an effort to maintain the euro price of widgets and unit sales/market share in Europe. The lower price would cause a decline in profit margins on European sales unless KoreaCo could stabilize margins through manipulation of such variable costs as labor and materials.

B. The traditional trade approach suggests that real exchange rate appreciation tends to reduce the competitiveness of a domestic economy and, therefore, reduce domestic activity over time. Worsening economic conditions resulting from reduced competitiveness would be expected to lead to a depreciation of the currency at some point, restoring competitiveness and foreign sales.

In the long run, industries from countries with overvalued currencies will make direct investments in countries with undervalued currencies. In time, such activity will contribute to restoration of purchasing power parity.

▶ If KoreaCo elects to maintain all production facilities in South Korea based on its expectation of a long-term currency appreciation, such a strategy would be expected to have a *negative effect* on its competitive position in the European market, and thus on the long-run profitability of its European sales. Such a decision would result in downward pressure on unit European sales. Because all costs are variable in the long run, KoreaCo may be able to adjust capacity utilization and other factors of production to maintain margins in the face of declining sales.

▶ KoreaCo's shift of production facilities to Europe would be expected to have a beneficial or positive effect on its long-run competitive position in Europe. The proposed strategy would lower average total costs on KoreaCo's European sales as it establishes production facilities in the cheaper currency. KoreaCo's lower cost-structure and improved competitiveness would be expected to have a positive effect on the profitability of KoreaCo's European sales.

19. The dollar value of the foreign bonds would rise because the foreign currency appreciates relative to the dollar. Furthermore, many countries practice a "leaning against the wind" exchange rate policy. Foreign bond yields are likely to drop to stabilize the exchange rate against the dollar. The local currency price of foreign bonds tends to go up when the dollar depreciates relative to the local currency. Hence, the dollar value of the foreign bonds would rise both because the foreign currency appreciates relative to the dollar and because the foreign bond prices rise.

20. The following are some arguments in favor of international bond diversification:

▶ A rise in European inflationary anticipations is bad for European bond prices (increasing nominal yields), but should not affect foreign bond prices. Because foreign economies are lagging the European economy, inflationary pressures are not yet felt abroad.

▶ Increased European inflation would lead to a depreciation of the euro, which would be good for the euro return of assets denominated in foreign currencies.

▶ An inflation-induced depreciation of the euro (appreciation of the foreign currency) is good for investing in foreign bond markets, if foreign governments lower their interest rates to avoid too strong an appreciation of their domestic currency ("leaning against the wind").

SOLUTIONS FOR READING 71

1. A.

	Alpha (α) $\alpha_i = r_i - [r_f + \beta_i(r_M - r_f)]$	Expected excess return $E(r_i) - r_f$
$\alpha_A = 20\% - [8\% + 1.3(16\% - 8\%)] = 1.6\%$		$20\% - 8\% = 12\%$
$\alpha_B = 18\% - [8\% + 1.8(16\% - 8\%)] = -4.4\%$		$18\% - 8\% = 10\%$
$\alpha_C = 17\% - [8\% + 0.7(16\% - 8\%)] = 3.4\%$		$17\% - 8\% = 9\%$
$\alpha_D = 12\% - [8\% + 1.0(16\% - 8\%)] = -4.0\%$		$12\% - 8\% = 4\%$

Stocks A and C have positive alphas, whereas stocks B and D have negative alphas.

The residual variances are:

$$\sigma^2(e_A) = 58^2 = 3,364$$
$$\sigma^2(e_B) = 71^2 = 5,041$$
$$\sigma^2(e_C) = 60^2 = 3,600$$
$$\sigma^2(e_D) = 55^2 = 3,025$$

B. To construct the optimal risky portfolio, we first determine the optimal active portfolio. Using the Treynor-Black technique, we construct the active portfolio:

	$\dfrac{\alpha}{\sigma^2(e)}$	$\dfrac{\alpha/\sigma^2(e)}{\Sigma\alpha/\sigma^2(e)}$
A	0.000476	−0.6142
B	−0.000873	1.1265
C	0.000944	−1.2181
D	−0.001322	1.7058
Total	−0.000775	1.0000

Do not be concerned that the positive alpha stocks have negative weights and vice versa. We will see that the entire position in the active portfolio will be negative, returning everything to good order.

With these weights, the forecast for the active portfolio is:

$$\alpha = [-0.6142 \times 1.6] + [1.1265 \times (-4.4)] - [1.2181 \times 3.4] +$$
$$[1.7058 \times (-4.0)]$$
$$= -16.90\%$$
$$\beta = [-0.6142 \times 1.3] + [1.1265 \times 1.8] - [1.2181 \times 0.70] +$$
$$[1.7058 \times 1] = 2.08$$

The high beta (higher than any individual beta) results from the short positions in the relatively low beta stocks and the long positions in the relatively high beta stocks.

$$\sigma^2(e) = [(-0.6142)^2 \times 3364] + [1.1265^2 \times 5041] + [(-1.2181)^2 \times 3600]$$
$$+ [1.7058^2 \times 3025]$$
$$= 21,809.6$$
$$\sigma(e) = 147.68\%$$

Here, again, the levered position in stock B [with high $\sigma^2(e)$] overcomes the diversification effect, and results in a high residual standard deviation. The optimal risky portfolio has a proportion w* in the active portfolio, computed as follows:

$$w_0 = \frac{\alpha/\sigma^2(e)}{[E(r_m) - r_f]/\sigma_M^2} = \frac{-16.90/21,809.6}{8/23^2} = -0.05124$$

The negative position is justified for the reason stated earlier. The adjustment for beta is:

$$w* = \frac{w_0}{1 + (1 - \beta)w_0} = \frac{-0.05124}{1 + (1 - 2.08)(-0.05124)} = -0.0486$$

Since w* is negative, the result is a positive position in stocks with positive alphas and a negative position in stocks with negative alphas. The position in the index portfolio is:

$$1 - (-0.0486) = 1.0486$$

C. To calculate Sharpe's measure for the optimal risky portfolio, we compute the information ratio for the active portfolio and Sharpe's measure for the market portfolio. The information ratio for the active portfolio is computed as follows:

$$A = \alpha/\sigma(e) = -16.90/147.68 = -0.1144$$
$$A^2 = 0.0131$$

Hence, the square of Sharpe's measure (S) of the optimized risky portfolio is:

$$S^2 = S_M^2 + A^2 = \left(\frac{8}{23}\right)^2 + 0.0131 = 0.1341$$
$$S = 0.3662$$

Compare this to the market's Sharpe measure:

$$S_M = 8/23 = 0.3478$$

The difference is: 0.0184

Note that the only-moderate improvement in performance results from the fact that only a small position is taken in the active portfolio A because of its large residual variance.

We calculate the "Modigliani-squared" (M^2) measure, as follows:

$$E(r_{P*}) = r_f + S_P\sigma_M = 8\% + (0.3662 \times 23\%) = 16.423\%$$
$$M^2 = E(r_{P*}) - E(r_M) = 16.423\% - 16\% = 0.423\%$$

D. To calculate the exact makeup of the complete portfolio, we first compute the mean excess return of the optimal risky portfolio and its variance. The risky portfolio beta is given by:

$$\beta_P = w_M + (w_A \times \beta_A) = 1.0486 + [(-0.0486) \times 2.08] = 0.95$$
$$E(R_P) = \alpha_P + \beta_P E(R_M) = [(-0.0486) \times (-16.90\%)] +$$
$$(0.95 \times 8\%) = 8.42\%$$
$$\sigma_P^2 = \beta_P^2 \sigma_M^2 + \sigma^2(e_P) = (0.95 \times 23)^2 + ((-0.0486^2) \times 21,809.6)$$
$$= 528.94$$
$$\sigma_P = 23.00\%$$

Since A = 2.8, the optimal position in this portfolio is:

$$y = \frac{8.42}{0.01 \times 2.8 \times 528.94} = 0.5685$$

In contrast, with a passive strategy:

$$y = \frac{8}{0.01 \times 2.8 \times 23^2} = 0.5401$$

This is a difference of: 0.0284

The final positions of the complete portfolio are:

Bills	$1 - 0.5685 =$	43.15%
M	$0.5685 \times 1.0486 =$	59.61%
A	$0.5685 \times (-0.0486) \times (-0.6142) =$	1.70%
B	$0.5685 \times (-0.0486) \times 1.1265 =$	−3.11%
C	$0.5685 \times (-0.0486) \times (-1.2181) =$	3.37%
D	$0.5685 \times (-0.0486) \times 1.7058 =$	−4.71%
		100.00%

[sum is subject to rounding error]

Note that M may include positive proportions of stocks A through D.

2. A. If a manager is not allowed to sell short he will not include stocks with negative alphas in his portfolio, so he will consider only A and C:

	α	$\sigma^2(e)$	$\dfrac{\alpha}{\sigma^2(e)}$	$\dfrac{\alpha/\sigma^2(e)}{\Sigma\alpha/\sigma^2(e)}$
A	1.6	3,364	0.000476	0.3352
C	3.4	3,600	0.000944	0.6648
			0.001420	1.0000

The forecast for the active portfolio is:

$$\alpha = (0.3352 \times 1.6) + (0.6648 \times 3.4) = 2.80\%$$
$$\beta = (0.3352 \times 1.3) + (0.6648 \times 0.7) = 0.90$$
$$\sigma^2(e) = (0.3352^2 \times 3,364) + (0.6648^2 \times 3,600) = 1,969.03$$
$$\sigma(e) = 44.37\%$$

The weight in the active portfolio is:

$$w_0 = \frac{\alpha/\sigma^2(e)}{E(R_M)/\sigma_M^2} = \frac{2.80/1,969.03}{8/23^2} = 0.0940$$

Adjusting for beta:

$$w* = \frac{w_0}{1 + (1 - \beta)w_0} = \frac{0.094}{1 + [(1 - 0.90) \times 0.094]} = 0.0931$$

The information ratio of the active portfolio is:

$$A = \alpha/\sigma(e) = 2.80/44.37 = 0.0631$$

Hence, the square of Sharpe's measure is:

$$S^2 = (8/23)^2 + 0.0631^2 = 0.1250$$

Therefore: S = 0.3535

The market's Sharpe measure is: $S_M = 0.3478$

When short sales are allowed (Problem 1), the manager's Sharpe measure is higher (0.3662). The reduction in the Sharpe measure is the cost of the short sale restriction.

We calculate the "Modigliani-squared" or M^2 measure as follows:

$$E(r_{P*}) = r_f + S_P\sigma_M = 8\% + (0.3535 \times 23\%) = 16.1305\%$$
$$M^2 = E(r_{P*}) - E(r_M) = 16.1305\% - 16\% = 0.1305\%$$

When short sales are allowed: $M^2 = 0.423\%$

The characteristics of the optimal risky portfolio are:

$$\beta_P = w_M + w_A \times \beta_A = (1 - 0.0931) + (0.0931 \times 0.9) = 0.99$$
$$E(R_P) = \alpha_P + \beta_P E(R_M) = (0.0931 \times 2.8\%) + (0.99 \times 8\%) = 8.18\%$$
$$\sigma_P^2 = \beta_P^2\sigma_M^2 + \sigma^2(e_P) = (0.99 \times 23)^2 + (0.0931^2 \times 1,969.03) = 535.54$$
$$\sigma_P = 23.14\%$$

With A = 2.8, the optimal position in this portfolio is:

$$y = \frac{8.18}{0.01 \times 2.8 \times 535.54} = 0.5455$$

The final positions in each asset are:

Bills	$1 - 0.5685 =$	45.45%
M	$0.5455 \times (1 - 0.0931) =$	49.47%
A	$0.5455 \times 0.0931 \times 0.3352 =$	1.70%
C	$0.5455 \times 0.0931 \times 0.6648 =$	3.38%
		100.00%

B. The mean and variance of the optimized complete portfolios in the unconstrained and short-sales constrained cases, and for the passive strategy are:

	$E(R_C)$	σ_c^2
Unconstrained	$0.5685 \times 8.42 = 4.79$	$0.5685^2 \times 528.94 = 170.95$
Constrained	$0.5455 \times 8.18 = 4.46$	$0.5455^2 \times 535.54 = 159.36$
Passive	$0.5401 \times 8.00 = 4.32$	$0.5401^2 \times 529.00 = 154.31$

The utility levels below are computed using the formula:
$E(r_C) - 0.005A\sigma_C^2$

Unconstrained	$8 + 4.79 - (0.005 \times 2.8 \times 170.95) = 10.40$
Constrained	$8 + 4.46 - (0.005 \times 2.8 \times 159.36) = 10.23$
Passive	$8 + 4.32 - (0.005 \times 2.8 \times 154.31) = 10.16$

3. All alphas are reduced to 0.3 times their values in the original case. Therefore, the relative weights of each security in the active portfolio are unchanged, but the alpha of the active portfolio is only 0.3 times its previous value: $0.3 \times -16.90\% = -5.07\%$. The investor will take a smaller position in the active portfolio. The optimal risky portfolio has a proportion w* in the active portfolio as follows:

$$w_0 = \frac{\alpha/\sigma^2(e)}{E(r_M - r_f)/\sigma_M^2} = \frac{-5.70/21,809.6}{8/23^2} = -0.01537$$

The negative position is justified for the reason given earlier.

The adjustment for beta is:

$$w^* = \frac{w_0}{1 + (1 - \beta)w_0} = \frac{-0.01537}{1 + [(1 - 2.08) \times (-0.01537)]} = -0.0151$$

Since w* is negative, the result is a positive position in stocks with positive alphas and a negative position in stocks with negative alphas. The position in the index portfolio is:

$$1 - (-0.0151) = 1.0151$$

To calculate Sharpe's measure for the optimal risky portfolio we compute the information ratio for the active portfolio and Sharpe's measure for the market portfolio. The information ratio of the *active portfolio* is 0.3 times its previous value:

$$A = \alpha/\sigma(e) = -5.07/147.68 = -0.0343 \text{ and } A^2 = 0.00118$$

Hence, the square of Sharpe's measure of the *optimized risky portfolio* is:

$$S^2 = S^2_M + A^2 = (8/23)^2 + 0.00118 = 0.1222$$
$$S = 0.3495$$

Compare this to the market's Sharpe measure: $S_M = 8/23 = 0.3478$

The difference is: 0.0017

Note that the reduction of the forecast alphas by a factor of 0.3 reduced the squared information ratio and the improvement in the squared Sharpe ratio by a factor of:

$0.3^2 = 0.09$

SOLUTIONS FOR READING 71

Solutions for Concept Checks found in Reading

1. We show the answer for the annual compounded rate of return for each strategy and leave the monthly rate for you to compute. Beginning-of-period fund:

$$F_0 = \$1,000$$

End-of-period fund for each strategy:

$$F_1 = \begin{cases} \$3,600 & \text{Strategy} = \text{Bill only} \\ \$67,500 & \text{Strategy} = \text{Market only} \\ \$5,360,000,000 & \text{Strategy} = \text{Perfect timing} \end{cases}$$

Number of periods: $N = 52$ years
Annual compounded rate:

$$[1 + r_Z]^N = \frac{F_1}{F_0}$$

$$r_A = \left(\frac{F_1}{F_0}\right)^{1/N} - 1$$

$$r_A = \begin{cases} 2.49\% & \text{Strategy} = \text{Bills only} \\ 8.44\% & \text{Strategy} = \text{Market only} \\ 34.71\% & \text{Strategy} = \text{Perfect timing} \end{cases}$$

2. The timer will guess bear or bull markets completely randomly. One-half of all bull markets will be preceded by a correct forecast, and similarly for bear markets. Hence $P_1 + P_2 - 1 = \frac{1}{2} + \frac{1}{2} - 1 = 0$.

3. **A.** When short positions are prohibited, the analysis is identical except that negative-alpha stocks are dropped. In that case the sum of the ratios of alpha to residual variance for the remaining two stocks is .7895. This leads to the new composition of the active portfolio. If x denotes new portfolio weights, then

$$x_1 = .3457/.7895 = .4379$$
$$x_2 = .4438/.7895 = .5621$$

The alpha, beta, and residual standard deviation of the active portfolio are now

$$\alpha_A = .4379 \times .07 + .5621 \times .03 = .0475$$
$$\beta_A = .4379 \times 1.6 + .5621 \times .5 = .9817$$
$$\sigma(e_A) = [.4379^2 \times .45^2 + .5621^2 \times .26^2]^{\frac{1}{2}} = .2453$$

The cost of the short sale restriction is already apparent. The alpha has shrunk from 20.56% to 4.75%, while the reduction in the residual standard deviation is more moderate, from 82.62% to 24.53%. In fact, a negative-alpha stock is potentially more attractive than a positive-alpha one: Since most stocks are positively correlated, the negative position that is required for the negative-alpha stock creates a better diversified active portfolio.

The optimal allocation of the new active portfolio is

$$w_0 = \frac{.0475/.6019}{.08/.04} = .3946$$

$$w^* = \frac{.3946}{1 + (1 - .9817) \times .3946} = .3918$$

Here, too, the beta correction is essentially irrelevant because the portfolio beta is so close to 1.0.

Finally, the performance of the overall risky portfolio is estimated at

$$S_P^2 = .16 + \left[\frac{.0475}{.2453}\right]^2 = .1975; \ S_P = .44$$

It is clear that in this case we have lost about half of the original improvement in the Sharpe measure. Note, however, that this is an artifact of the limited coverage of the security analysis division. When more stocks are covered, then a good number of positive-alpha stocks will keep the residual risk of the active portfolio low. This is the key to extracting large gains from the active strategy.

We calculate the "Modigliani-square," or M^2 measure, as follows:

$$E(r_{P*}) = r_f + S_p\sigma_M = .07 + .44 \times .20 = .158, \text{ or } 15.8\%$$
$$M^2 = E(r_{P*}) - E(r_M) = 15.8\% - 15\% = 0.8\%$$

which is a bit less than half the M^2 value of the unconstrained portfolio.

B. When the forecast for the market-index portfolio is more optimistic, the position in the active portfolio will be smaller and the contribution of the active portfolio to the Sharpe measure of the risky portfolio also will be smaller. In the original example the allocation to the active portfolio would be

$$w_0 = \frac{.2056/.6826}{.12/.04} = .1004$$

$$w^* = \frac{.1004}{1 + (1 - .9519) \times .1004} = .0999$$

Although the Sharpe measure of the market is now better, the improvement derived from security analysis is smaller:

$$S_P^2 = \left(\frac{.12}{.20}\right)^2 + \left(\frac{.2056}{.8262}\right)^2 = .4219$$
$$S_P = .65; \qquad S_M = .60$$

SOLUTIONS FOR READING 72

1. **A.** The liquidity requirement for this individual is her need for cash in excess of her savings during the coming year. Therefore, her liquidity requirement is €95,000 − €50,000 = €45,000.

   B. The Wilson-Fowler Endowment's anticipated liquidity requirement is $600,000, calculated as $1,000,000 (the planned contribution to the construction of the new dormitory) minus $400,000 (the anticipated amount of new contributions to the endowment). Note that the amount of 4% × $75,000,000 = $3,000,000, as provided for in the spending rule, is fully committed to budgetary support; thus this amount is not available to help meet the endowment's planned contribution to the building project.

2. The Judd Endowment's risk tolerance is limited by its ability and willingness to accept risk. Risk tolerance is *not* a function of a need for higher returns. The return objective should be consistent with risk tolerance, so an appropriate return objective for the Judd Endowment is 7 percent. A spending rate of 6 percent is too high for this endowment; raising the return objective to 9 percent would only compound the problem created by a 6 percent spending rate, which is inappropriately high for this endowment.

3. **A.** The country allocation strategy as described mixes elements of active and passive investment approaches. The portfolio weights are actively determined and differ from benchmark weights, within limits. However, the investments in individual countries are passive, indexed investments.

   B. Overall, we can classify the country allocation strategy as a semiactive or controlled-active investment approach.

4. **A.** This is an absolute return objective because it does not reference a comparison to the performance of another portfolio but rather is stated in terms of a fixed number (an 8 percent annual return).

   B. This is an absolute risk objective because it does not reference a comparison to the performance of another portfolio but rather is stated in terms of a fixed number (a standard deviation of return of 20 percent a year).

   C. This is a relative return objective because it references a comparison to the performance of other portfolios.

   D. This is an absolute risk objective because it addresses the risk that a portfolio's return will fall below a minimum acceptable level over a stated time horizon.

   E. This is a relative risk objective because it references a comparison to the performance of another portfolio, the benchmark.

5. D is correct. The IPS identifies pertinent investment objectives and constraints for a *particular* investor. Clearly identified objectives and constraints ensure that the policy statement is accurate and relevant to the investor's specific situation and desires. The result should be an optimal balance between return and risk for that investor. The IPS provides a long-term plan for an investor and a basis for making disciplined investment decisions over time. The absence of an investment policy statement reduces decision making to an individual-event basis and often leads to pursuing short-term opportunities that may not contribute to, or may even detract from, reaching long-term goals.

Solutions to 1–13 taken from *Managing Investment Portfolios: A Dynamic Process*, Third Edition, John L. Maginn, Donald L. Tuttle, Jerald E. Pinto, and Dennis W. McLeavey, editors. Copyright © 2007 by CFA Institute. Reprinted with permission. All other solutions copyright © 2006 by CFA Institute.

6. B is correct. An investor's ability to take risk puts an upper limit on a reasonable return objective.

7. D is correct. Even though Stephenson describes his risk tolerance as "average," his present investment portfolio and his desire for large returns indicate an above-average willingness to take risk. His financial situation (large asset base, ample income to cover expenses, lack of need for liquidity, and long time horizon) indicates an above-average ability to accept risk.

8. B is correct. Stephenson has adequate income to cover his living expenses and has no major outlays for which he needs cash, so his liquidity needs are minimal. He is not a tax-exempt investor (both income and capital gains are taxed at 30%), so taxes should play a considerable role in his investment decisions.

9. D is correct. Stephenson's time horizon is long—he is currently only 55 years old. The time horizon consists of two stages: the first stage extends to his retirement in 15 years; the second stage may last for 20 years or more and extends from retirement until his death.

10. D is correct.

    Risk: Stephenson has an above-average risk tolerance based on both his ability and willingness to assume above-average risk. His large asset base, long time horizon, ample income to cover expenses, and lack of need for liquidity or cash flow indicate an above-average ability to assume risk. His concentration in U.S. small-capitalization stocks and his desire for high returns indicate substantial willingness to assume risk.

    Return: Stephenson's financial circumstances (long time horizon, sizable asset base, ample income, and low liquidity needs) and his risk tolerance warrant an above-average total return objective. His expressed desire for a continued return of 20 percent, however, is unrealistic. Coppa should counsel Stephenson on what level of returns to reasonably expect from the financial markets over long periods of time and to define an achievable return objective.

11–1. *James Stephenson*

   Underline the word at right that best describes the client's:

A.	*Willingness to accept risk*	Below average	<u>Above average</u> Explanation in 2A below
B.	*Ability to accept risk*	Below average	<u>Above average</u> Explanation in 2A below
C.	*Risk tolerance*	Below average	<u>Above average</u> Explanation in 2A below
D.	*Liquidity requirement*	Significant	<u>Not significant</u> $70,000 can be met by expected annual saving of $350,000 × (1 − 0.3) − $150,000 = $95,000
E.	*Time horizon*	Single stage	<u>Multistage</u> Stage 1: Pre-retirement Stage 2: Retirement
F.	*Overall time horizon*	Short to intermediate term	<u>Long term</u> Overall time horizon could be 20 to 30 years or more
G.	*Tax concerns*	<u>Significant</u> Taxed at 30% rate	Not significant

11–2.

    A. *Risk:* Stephenson has an above-average risk tolerance based on both his ability and willingness to assume above-average risk. His large asset base, long time horizon, ample income to cover expenses, and lack of need for liquidity or cash flow indicate an above-average ability to assume risk. His concentration in U.S. small-capitalization stocks and his desire for high returns indicate substantial willingness to assume risk.

    B. *Return:* Stephenson's financial circumstances (long time horizon, sizable asset base, ample income, and low liquidity needs) and his risk tolerance warrant an above-average total return objective. His expressed desire for a return 10 percentage points above the average return on U.S. small capitalization stocks, however, is unrealistic. The portfolio manager should counsel Stephenson on what level of returns to reasonably expect from the financial markets over long periods of time and to define an achievable return objective.

12–1. *Foothill College Endowment Fund*

    Underline the word at right that best describes the client's:

A. *Risk tolerance*	Below average	<u>Above average</u> Explanation in 2A below
B. *Liquidity requirement*	Significant	<u>Not significant</u> Budgeted support at 4% × $1 billion exceeds scholarship needs of $39.5 million
C. *Time horizon*	<u>Single stage</u>	Multistage
D. *Overall time horizon*	Short to intermediate term	<u>Long term</u> Provide support in perpetuity
E. *Tax concerns*	Significant	<u>Not significant</u> Tax-exempt

    Discuss appropriate client objectives:

    A. *Risk:* The endowment fund, with a large asset base and very long time horizon, has an above-average risk tolerance.

    B. *Return:* An estimate for the endowment's required annual return is the sum of the spending rate (4 percent) plus the expected annual college tuition inflation rate (3 percent) for a total of 7 percent.

       The endowment's objective is to maintain the long-term purchasing power of its assets while providing a stable flow of funds for scholarships.

13–1. *Vincenzo Donadoni*

    Underline the word at right that best describes the client's:

A. *Willingness to accept risk*	Below average	<u>Above average</u> Explanation in 2A below
B. *Ability to accept risk*	Below average	<u>Above average</u> Explanation in 2A below
C. *Risk tolerance*	Below average	<u>Above average</u> Explanation in 2A below
D. *Liquidity requirement*	<u>Significant</u> CHF 1.5 million needed now CHF 2 million due in nine months	Not significant

E. *Time horizon*   Single stage   <u>Multistage</u>
                                                                 Three stages:
                                                                 First nine months
                                                                 Next 20 to 30 years
                                                                 Life of trust

F. *Overall time horizon*   Short to intermediate term   <u>Long term</u>
                                                                 Overall time horizon
                                                                 is approximately 20 to
                                                                 30 years

13–2.

   A. *Risk:* Donadoni has an above-average risk tolerance based on both his willingness and ability to accept above-average risk. He is a risk taker with a long time horizon, a relatively low need for income, and a large asset base.

   B. *Return:* To meet his long-term goal of a leaving a CHF 15.0 million trust fund for his three children, Donadoni must also achieve growth of his current assets. In accordance with his above-average risk tolerance and his goal of leaving the trust, Donadoni should adopt an above-average total real return objective.

   Donadoni has a minimal need for additional cash flow given his current expenses, income, and asset base: $(250{,}000 - 125{,}000)/(13 \text{ million} - 1.5 \text{ million}) = 1.1\%$. In nine months, his need will grow due to inflation of his expenses, his reduction in income, and his reduced asset base: $(250{,}000 - 0)/(13 \text{ million} - 1.5 \text{ million} - 2 \text{ million in taxes}) = 2.6\%$ return. As a long-run average, a 2.6 percent real return should be achievable.

14. A is correct. Santalucia's lifestyle and business career (speedboats, mountain climbing, real estate speculation, turnarounds) show a *willingness* to take risks. His current *ability* to take risks is diminished, given his total assets and his current income/spending situation, by his expected divorce settlement and upcoming college bills. When an investor's willingness to accept risk exceeds the ability to do so, ability prudently places a limit on the amount of risk the investor should assume. Santalucia's pending divorce and college education bills create a significant liquidity constraint.

15. A is correct. Neither note describes the correct process. The IPS process requires that members first identify and specify the investor's objectives and constraints and then create the investment policy statement. Incorporating short-term economic trends into the policy statement is inappropriate. Only after the IPS has been created should members form capital market expectations and then create the strategic asset allocation. Using another client's asset allocation from several years earlier is inappropriate because it does not include current capital market expectations.

16. D is correct. Westerlund's first statement is correct: Beta is more stable for portfolios than for individual stocks. The second statement is also correct: Beta estimation is affected by all the listed items.

17. D is correct. The first statement is correct: Variance, or total risk, is the relevant risk measure for the CML; the SML uses beta, the asset's risk standardized by the market's risk. The second statement is also correct: The SML is based on the CML and both are equilibrium relationships.

18. D is correct. The estimated beta is the covariance of Palladio's returns with the market's returns divided by the variance of the market's returns, or 0.0015/0.0021 = 0.714.

19. C is correct. The SML required return for Borgonovo is 2.5% + 1.2(7%) = 10.9%. With a forecasted return of 9.0%, Borgonovo lies below the SML (indicating it is overvalued) and should be removed from the bank's recommended list.

Abandonment option   The ability to terminate a project at some future time if the financial results are disappointing.

Abnormal earnings   See *Residual income.*

Abnormal rate of return   The amount by which a security's actual return differs from its expected rate of return which is based on the market's rate of return and the security's relationship with the market.

Abnormal return   Return on a stock beyond what would be predicted by market movements alone. Cumulative abnormal return (CAR) is the total abnormal return for the period surrounding an announcement or the release of information.

Absolute dispersion   The amount of variability present without comparison to any reference point or benchmark.

Absolute frequency   The number of observations in a given interval (for grouped data).

Absolute priority rule   The hierarchy whereby claims are satisfied in corporate liquidation.

Absolute valuation model   A model that specifies an asset's intrinsic value.

Accounting   A detailed report to the trust beneficiaries by a trustee of his stewardship, also used to discharge the trustee.

Accounting earnings   Earnings of a firm as reported on its income statement.

Accounting estimates   Estimates of items such as the useful lives of assets, warranty costs, and the amount of uncollectible receivables.

Accounting profit   Total revenues minus total explicit costs.

Accounting risk   The risk associated with accounting standards that vary from country to country or with any uncertainty about how certain transactions should be recorded.

Accounting Standards Board (ASB)   The Accounting Standards Board issues Financial Reporting Standards (FRSs) for the United Kingdom. It took over the task of setting accounting standards from the Accounting Standards Committee in 1990.

Accounts payable   A liability that results from the purchase of goods or services on open account, that is, without a signed note payable.

Accounts receivable   Amounts owed to a company by customers as a result of delivering goods or services and extending credit in the ordinary course of business. Also referred to as *trade receivables.*

Accrual accounting   The system of recording financial transactions as they come into existence as a legally enforceable claim, rather than when they settle.

Accrued interest   Interest earned but not yet paid.

Accumulate   Wall Street expression for buying on a large scale over time, typically by an institution. "Accumulation" of a stock is said to occur if a number of institutions are gradually adding to their holdings.

Accumulated other comprehensive income   Cumulative gains or losses reported in shareholders' equity that arise from changes in the fair value of available-for-sale securities, from the effects of changes in foreign-currency exchange rates on consolidated foreign-currency financial statements, from certain gains and losses on financial derivatives and from adjustments for underfunded pension plans.

Acquiring company or acquirer   The company in a merger or acquisition that is acquiring the target.

Acquisition   The purchase of some portion of one company by another; the purchase may be for assets, a definable segment of another entity, or the purchase of an entire company.

Active factor risk   The contribution to active risk squared resulting from the portfolio's different-than-benchmark exposures relative to factors specified in the risk model.

Active investment managers   Managers who hold portfolios that differ from their benchmark portfolio in an attempt to produce positive risk-adjusted returns.

Active management   Attempts to achieve portfolio returns more than commensurate with risk, either by forecasting broad market trends or by identifying particular mispriced sectors of a market or securities in a market.

Active portfolio   In the context of the Treynor-Black model, the portfolio formed by mixing analyzed stocks of perceived nonzero alpha values. This portfolio is ultimately mixed with the passive market index portfolio.

Active return   The return on a portfolio minus the return on the portfolio's benchmark.

Active risk   The standard deviation of active returns.

Active risk squared   The variance of active returns; active risk raised to the second power.

Active specific risk or asset selection risk   The contribution to active risk squared resulting from the portfolio's active weights on individual assets as those weights interact with assets' residual risk.

Addition rule for probabilities A principle stating that the probability that *A* or *B* occurs (both occur) equals the probability that *A* occurs, plus the probability that *B* occurs, minus the probability that both *A* and *B* occur.

Additional information Information that is required or recommended under the GIPS standards and is not considered as "supplemental information" for the purposes of compliance.

Additions Assets transferred to a trust after the initial funding.

Add-on interest A procedure for determining the interest on a bond or loan in which the interest is added onto the face value of a contract.

Adjustable-rate mortgage A mortgage whose interest rate varies according to some specified measure of the current market interest rate.

Adjusted beta Historical beta adjusted to reflect the tendency of beta to be mean reverting.

Adjusted present value (APV) As an approach to valuing a company, the sum of the value of the company, assuming no use of debt, and the net present value of any effects of debt on company value.

Adjusted R^2 A measure of goodness-of-fit of a regression that is adjusted for degrees of freedom and hence does not automatically increase when another independent variable is added to a regression.

Administrative fees All fees other than the trading expenses and the investment management fee. Administrative fees include custody fees, accounting fees, consulting fees, legal fees, performance measurement fees, or other related fees. These administrative fees are typically outside the control of the investment management firm and are not included in either the gross-of-fees return or the net-of-fees return. However, there are some markets and investment vehicles where administrative fees are controlled by the firm.

After-tax cash flow (ATCF) Net operating income less debt service and less taxes payable on income from operations.

Agency costs Agency costs are the incremental costs arising from conflicts of interest when an agent makes decisions for a principal. In the context of a corporation, agency costs arise from conflicts of interest between managers, shareholders, and bondholders.

Agency problem or principal-agent problem or agency conflict A conflict of interest that arises when the agent in an agency relationship has goals and incentives that differ from those of the principal.

Agency relationships An arrangement whereby someone, an agent, acts on behalf of another person, the principal.

Agency trade A trade in which a broker acts as an agent only, not taking a position on the opposite side of the trade.

Aggregate demand (1) The relationship between the quantity of real GDP demanded and the price level. (2) The total of all planned expenditures for the entire economy.

Aggregate production function The relationship between the quantity of real GDP supplied and the quantities of labor and capital and the state of technology.

Aggressive With respect to equity valuation, the term implies a concentrated portfolio holding smaller capitalization stocks than the general market, often with higher price/earnings and lower yields, together with low reserves. Often implies unusual volatility.

AICPA The American Institute of Certified Public Accountants. The AICPA is the national association of CPAs in the United States.

AIMR Performance presentation standards (AIMR-PPS®) A comprehensive set of reporting guidelines created by the Association for Investment Management and Research (AIMR) (now CFA Institute) in 1993 that converged to the Global Investment Performance Standards on 1 January 2006.

Allocative efficiency A situation in which we cannot produce more of any good without giving up some of another good that we value more highly.

Alpha (or abnormal return) The return on an asset in excess of the asset's required rate of return; the risk-adjusted excess return.

Alternative hypothesis The hypothesis accepted when the null hypothesis is rejected.

Alternative investments Hedge funds, venture capital pools, options and other derivatives, real estate, and other non-stock or -bond market assets.

American Depositary Receipt (ADR) A certificate of ownership issued by a U.S. bank to promote local trading in a foreign stock. The U.S. bank holds the foreign shares and issues ADRs against them.

American option An option contract that can be exercised at any time until its expiration date.

American terms With reference to U.S. dollar exchange rate quotations, the U.S. dollar price of a unit of another currency.

Amortizing or accreting swaps A swap in which the notional principal changes according to a formula related to changes in the underlying.

Analysis of variance (ANOVA) The analysis of the total variability of a dataset (such as observations on the dependent variable in a regression) into components representing different sources of variation; with reference to regression, ANOVA provides the inputs for an *F*-test of the significance of the regression as a whole.

Annual percentage rate The cost of borrowing expressed as a yearly rate.

Annuity A finite set of level sequential cash flows.

Annuity due An annuity having a first cash flow that is paid immediately.

Anomalies (1) Security price relationships that appear to contradict a well-regarded hypothesis; in this case, the efficient market hypothesis. (2) Patterns of returns that seem to contradict the efficient market hypothesis.

Antitrust legislation or antitrust laws Laws that restrict the formation of monopolies and regulate certain anticompetitive business practices.

A priori probability A probability based on logical analysis rather than on observation or personal judgment.

Appraisal ratio The ratio of alpha to residual standard deviation.

Appreciation An increase in the exchange value of one nation's currency in terms of the currency of another nation.

Arbitrage The simultaneous purchase of an undervalued asset or portfolio and sale of an overvalued but equivalent asset or portfolio, in order to obtain a riskless profit on the price differential.

Arbitrage opportunity An opportunity to conduct an arbitrage; an opportunity to earn an expected positive net profit without risk and with no net investment of money.

Arbitrage portfolio The portfolio that exploits an arbitrage opportunity.

Arbitrage pricing theory (APT) An asset pricing theory that is derived from a factor model, using diversification and arbitrage arguments. The theory describes the relationship between expected returns on securities, given that there are no opportunities to create wealth through risk-free arbitrage investments.

Arithmetic mean The sum of the observations divided by the number of observations.

Arrears swap A type of interest rate swap in which the floating payment is set at the end of the period and the interest is paid at that same time.

Asian call option A European-style option with a value at maturity equal to the difference between the stock price at maturity and the average stock price during the life of the option, or $0, whichever is greater.

Ask price The price at which a market maker is willing to sell a security (also called *offer price*).

Asset allocation Dividing of investment funds among several asset classes to achieve diversification.

Asset allocation decision Choosing among broad asset classes such as stocks versus bonds.

Asset beta The unlevered beta; reflects the business risk of the assets; the asset's systematic risk.

Asset class Securities that have similar characteristics, attributes, and risk/return relationships.

Asset purchase An acquisition in which the acquirer purchases the target company's assets and payment is made directly to the target company.

Asset turnover (ATO) The annual sales generated by each dollar of assets (sales/assets).

Asset-based valuation An approach to valuing natural resource companies that estimates company value on the basis of the market value of the natural resources the company controls.

Assets under management (AUM) The total market value of the assets managed by an investment firm.

Assets Amounts owned; all items to which a business or household holds legal claim.

Asymmetric information Possession of information by one party in a financial transaction but not by the other party.

At the money option An option for which the underlying's market price equals the option's exercise price.

Auction market A market in which the orders of multiple buyers compete for execution.

Autocorrelation The correlation of a time series with its own past values.

Autoregressive (AR) model A time series regressed on its own past values, in which the independent variable is a lagged value of the dependent variable.

Available-for-sale security A default classification for an investment in a debt or equity security that is not classified as either a held-to-maturity security or a trading security.

Average tax rate The total tax payment divided by total income. It is the proportion of total income paid in taxes.

Backward integration A merger involving the purchase of a target ahead of the acquirer in the value or production chain; for example, to acquire a supplier.

Backwardation Condition in which spot price of commodity exceeds the futures price (cf. *contango*).

Balance of payments A system of accounts that measures transactions of goods, services, income, and financial assets between domestic households, businesses, and governments and residents of the rest of the world during a specific time period.

Balance of payments accounts   A country's record of international trading, borrowing, and lending.

Balance sheet   A financial statement that shows what assets the firm controls at a fixed point in time and how it has financed these assets.

Balanced budget   A government budget in which tax revenues and expenditures are equal.

Balanced fund   A mutual fund with, generally, a three-part investment objective: (1) to conserve the investor's principal, (2) to pay current income, and (3) to increase both principal and income. The fund aims to achieve this by owning a mixture of bonds, preferred stocks, and common stocks.

Balloon payment   Large final payment (e.g., when a loan is repaid in installments).

Band-of-investment method   A widely used approach to estimate an overall capitalization rate. It is based on the premise that debt and equity financing is typically involved in a real estate transaction.

Bank discount basis   A quoting convention that annualizes, on a 360-day year, the discount as a percentage of face value.

Barriers to entry   Legal or natural constraints that protect a firm from potential competitors.

Barter   The direct exchange of goods and services for other goods and services without the use of money.

Base year   The year that is chosen as the point of reference for comparison of prices in other years.

Basic earnings per share   Total earnings divided by the weighted average number of shares actually outstanding during the period.

Basis point   A hundredth of a percent; thus 75 basis points equals three-quarters of 1 percentage point.

Basis point value (BPV)   Also called *present value of a basis point* or *price value of a basis point* (PVBP), the change in the bond price for a 1 basis point change in yield.

Basis swap   A swap in which both parties pay a floating rate.

Bayes' formula   A method for updating probabilities based on new information.

Bear hug   A tactic used by acquirers to circumvent target management's objections to a proposed merger by submitting the proposal directly to the target company's board of directors.

Bear market   Widespread decline in security prices (cf. *bull market*).

Bear spread   An option strategy that involves selling a put with a lower exercise price and buying a put with a higher exercise price. It can also be executed with calls.

Before-tax cash flow   A measure of the expected annual cash flow from the operation of a real estate investment after all expenses but before taxes.

Behavioral finance   (1) The analysis of various psychological traits of individuals and how these traits affect how they act as investors, analysts, and portfolio managers. (2) Branch of finance that stresses aspects of investor irrationality.

Benchmark   A comparison portfolio used to evaluate performance; a point of reference or comparison.

Benchmark bond   A bond representative of current market conditions and used for performance comparison.

Benchmark value of the multiple   In using the method of comparables, the value of a price multiple for the comparison asset; when we have comparison assets (a group), the mean or median value of the multiple for the group of assets.

Bernoulli random variable   A random variable having the outcomes 0 and 1.

Bernoulli trial   An experiment that can produce one of two outcomes.

Beta   A measure of an asset's systematic risk based upon an asset's covariance with the market portfolio.

Bid price   The price at which a dealer is willing to purchase a security.

Bid-ask spread (or bid-asked spread)   The difference between the quoted ask and the bid prices.

Bidder   The acquiring firm.

Bilateral arbitrage   With reference to currencies, an arbitrage involving two currencies only.

Bill-and-hold basis   Sales on a bill-and-hold basis involve selling products but not delivering those products until a later date.

Binomial model   A model for pricing options in which the underlying price can move to only one of two possible new prices in each specified time interval.

Binomial random variable   The number of successes in n Bernoulli trials for which the probability of success is constant for all trials and the trials are independent.

Binomial tree   The graphical representation of a model of asset price dynamics in which, at each period, the asset moves up with probability p or down with probability $(1 - p)$.

Black-Scholes or Black-Scholes-Merton option pricing model (formula)   An equation to value a call option based on five variables: the price of the underlying, the exercise price, the risk-free interest rate, the time to maturity, and the standard deviation of the underlying's return.

Block Orders to buy or sell that are too large for the liquidity ordinarily available in dealer networks or stock exchanges.

Blue chip A large, stable, well-known, widely held, seasoned company with a strong financial position, usually paying a reasonable dividend.

Boilerplate Standard terms and conditions, e.g., in a debt contract.

Bond A security issued by a borrower that obligates the issuer to make specified payments to the holder over a specific period. A *coupon bond* obligates the issuer to make interest payments called coupon payments over the life of the bond, then to repay the *face value* at maturity.

Bond-equivalent yield The yield to maturity on a basis that ignores compounding.

Bond indenture A legal contract specifying the terms of a bond issue.

Bond option An option in which the underlying is a bond; primarily traded in over-the-counter markets.

Bond rating Rating of the likelihood of bond's default.

Bond yield plus risk premium method A method of determining the required rate of return on equity (cost of equity) for a company as the sum of the yield to maturity on the company's long-term debt plus a risk premium.

Bonding costs Costs borne by management to assure owners that they are working in the owners' best interest (e.g., implicit cost of non-compete agreements).

Book entry Registered ownership of stock without issue of stock certificate.

Book value of equity (or book value) Shareholders' equity (total assets minus total liabilities) minus the value of preferred stock; common shareholders' equity; book value per share is book value of equity divided by the number of common shares outstanding.

Books In accounting, a shorthand reference to shareholder as opposed to income tax financial information.

Bootstrapping earnings An increase in a company's earnings that results as a consequence of the idiosyncrasies of a merger transaction itself rather than because of resulting economic benefits of the combination.

Bottom-up forecasting approach A forecasting approach that involves aggregating the individual company forecasts of analysts into industry forecasts, and finally into macroeconomic forecasts.

Bottom-up or bottom-up investing An approach to investing that focuses on the individual characteristics of securities rather than on macroeconomic or overall market forecasts.

Bourse A French term often used to refer to a stock market.

Box spread An option strategy that combines a bull spread and a bear spread having two different exercise prices, which produces a risk-free payoff of the difference in the exercise prices.

Breakeven point The number of units produced and sold at which the company's net income is zero (revenues = total costs).

Breakup value (or private market value) The value that can be achieved if a company's assets are divided and sold separately.

Breusch–Pagan test A test for conditional heteroskedasticity in the error term of a regression.

Broker An agent who executes orders to buy or sell securities on behalf of a client in exchange for a commission.

Brokerage The business of acting as agents for buyers or sellers, usually in return for commissions.

Brokered market A market where an intermediary (a broker) offers search services to buyers and sellers.

Budget constraint All of the possible combinations of goods that can be purchased (at fixed prices) with a specific budget.

Budget deficit The amount by which government spending exceeds government revenues.

Build-up method A method for determining the required rate of return on equity as the sum of risk premiums, in which one or more of the risk premiums is typically subjective rather than grounded in a formal equilibrium model.

Bull market Widespread rise in security prices (cf. *bear market*).

Bull spread An option strategy that involves buying a call with a lower exercise price and selling a call with a higher exercise price. It can also be executed with puts.

Bullet payment Single final payment, e.g., of a loan (in contrast to payment in installments).

Bund Long-term German government *bond*.

Business cycle The periodic but irregular up-and-down movement in production.

Business risk The risk associated with operating earnings; risk that is related to the uncertainty of revenues.

Butterfly spread An option strategy that combines two bull or bear spreads and has three exercise prices.

Buy-and-hold strategy A passive portfolio management strategy in which securities (bonds or stocks) are bought and held to maturity.

Buyback   Repurchase agreement.

Buy-side analysts   Analysts who work for investment management firms, trusts, and bank trust departments, and similar institutions.

Call   An option that gives the holder the right to buy an underlying asset from another party at a fixed price over a specific period of time.

Callable bond   A bond that the issuer may repurchase at a given price in some specified period.

Call auction   See *fixing*.

Call option   A contract that gives its holder the right to buy an asset, typically a financial instrument, at a specified price through a specified date.

Call provision   Provision that allows an issuer to buy back the *bond* issue at a stated price.

Cannibalization   Cannibalization occurs when an investment takes customers and sales away from another part of the company.

Cap agreement (or cap)   A contract that on each settlement date pays the holder the greater of the difference between the reference rate and the cap rate or zero; it is equivalent to a series of call options at the reference rate.

Capital   The tools, equipment, buildings, and other constructions that businesses now use to produce goods and services.

Capital account   Foreign investment in a country minus its investment abroad.

Capital accumulation   The growth of capital resources.

Capital allocation decision   Allocation of invested funds between risk-free assets versus the risky portfolio.

Capital allocation line (CAL)   A graph line that describes the combinations of expected return and standard deviation of return available to an investor from combining the optimal portfolio of risky assets with the risk-free asset.

Capital appreciation   A return objective in which the investor seeks to increase the portfolio value, primarily through capital gains, over time to meet a future need rather than dividend yield.

Capital asset pricing model (CAPM)   An equation describing the expected return on any asset (or portfolio) as a linear function of its beta.

Capital budget   List of planned investment projects, usually prepared annually.

Capital budgeting   The allocation of funds to relatively long-range projects or investments.

Capital charge   The company's total cost of capital in money terms.

Capital consumption   The decrease in the capital stock that results from wear and tear and obsolescence.

Capital Employed (Real Estate)   The denominator of the return expressions, defined as the "weighted-average equity" (weighted-average capital) during the measurement period. Capital employed should not include any income or capital return accrued *during* the measurement period. Beginning capital is adjusted by weighting the cash flows (contributions and distributions) that occurred during the period. Cash flows are typically weighted based on the actual days the flows are in or out of the portfolio. Other weighting methods are acceptable; however, once a methodology is chosen, it should be consistently applied.

Capital expenditures   Expenditures made in the purchase of long-term productive assets, such as property, plant, and equipment, whose cost is amortized against income in future periods.

Capital gain   The amount by which the sale price of an asset exceeds the purchase price. If a share of stock is bought for $5 and then sold for $15, the capital gain is $10.

Capital goods   Producer durables; nonconsumable goods that firms use to make other goods.

Capital lease   A lease that transfers, in an economic sense, the risks and rewards of ownership to the lessee without transferring title. Lease payments made are comprised of interest and principal. Property held under a capital-lease agreement is accounted for as an asset. This cost is amortized over the relevant useful life.

Capital loss   The amount by which the sale price of an asset is less than the purchase price. If a share of stock is bought for $15 and then sold for $5, the capital loss is $10.

Capital market   Financial market (particularly the market for long-term securities).

Capital market instruments   Fixed-income or equity investments that trade in the secondary market.

Capital market line (CML)   The line with an intercept point equal to the risk-free rate that is tangent to the efficient frontier of risky assets; represents the efficient frontier when a risk-free asset is available for investment.

Capital rationing   Shortage of funds that forces a company to choose between worthwhile projects.

Capital stock   The total quantity of plant, equipment, buildings, and inventories.

Capital structure   The mix of debt and equity that a company uses to finance its business.

Capitalization   Long-term debt plus preferred stock plus net worth.

Capitalization rate   The divisor in the expression for the value of a perpetuity.

Capitalized interest   Interest incurred during the construction period on monies invested in assets under construction that is added to the cost of the assets.

Caplet   Each component call option in a cap.

CAPM   Capital asset pricing model.

Capped swap   A swap in which the floating payments have an upper limit.

Capture hypothesis   A theory of regulatory behavior that predicts that the regulators will eventually be captured by the special interests of the industry being regulated.

Capture theory   A theory of regulation that states that the regulations are supplied to satisfy the demand of producers to maximize producer surplus.

Cash   Currency, coin, and funds on deposit that are available for immediate withdrawal without restriction. Money orders, certified checks, cashier's checks, personal checks, and bank drafts are also considered cash.

Cash and carry   Purchase of a security and simultaneous sale of a *future,* with the balance being financed with a loan or *repo.*

Cash earnings   Cash revenue minus cash expenses.

Cash equivalents   Short-term and highly liquid investments readily convertible into known amounts of cash and close enough to maturity that there is insignificant risk of changes in value from interest rate movements.

Cash flow   A flow based on cash receipts and cash disbursements; may refer to either total cash flow or, more commonly, operating cash flow.

Cash flow additivity principle   The principle that dollar amounts indexed at the same point in time are additive.

Cash flow analysis   The search for the fundamental drivers that underlie a company's cash flow stream and affect its sustainability.

Cash flow at risk (CFAR)   A variation of VAR that reflects the risk of a company's cash flow instead of its market value.

Cash flow from operations   A term used on the cash flow analysis statement that consists of cash flow available for debt service less total interest paid. The term also is used to refer to cash provided or used by operating activities and operating cash flow as those terms are defined by generally accepted accounting principles.

Cash offering   A merger or acquisition that is to be paid for with cash; the cash for the merger might come from the acquiring company's existing assets or from a debt issue.

Cash operating expense   A Uniform Credit Analysis®–defined cash flow amount that consists of cash paid for sales and marketing, general and administrative, and research and development expenditures. The term is defined the same way on the cash flow analysis statement.

Cash price or spot price   The price for immediate purchase of the underlying asset.

Cash settlement   A procedure used in certain derivative transactions that specifies that the long and short parties engage in the equivalent cash value of a delivery transaction.

Catalyst   An event or piece of information that causes the marketplace to re-evaluate the prospects of a company.

Caution   One of the three components of the standard of prudence governing trustees; avoidance of undue risk and attentiveness to the protection of trust property.

Central bank   A bank's bank and a public authority that regulates a nation's depository institutions and controls the quantity of money.

Central limit theorem   A result in statistics that states that the sample mean computed from large samples of size n from a population with finite variance will follow an approximate normal distribution with a mean equal to the population mean and a variance equal to the population variance divided by n.

Centralized risk management or companywide risk management   When a company has a single risk management group that monitors and controls all of the risk-taking activities of the organization. Centralization permits economies of scale and allows a company to use some of its risks to offset other risks. See also *enterprise risk management.*

CEO   Chief executive officer.

Certificate of deposit (CD)   An unsecured evidence of indebtedness of a bank, which may be sold to others. Usually with a face value of $100,000 or more and bearing interest below the prime rate.

Ceteris paribus   Other things being equal—all other relevant things remaining the same.

CFO   Chief financial officer.

CFTC   Commodity Futures Trading Commission.

Chaebol   A Korean conglomerate.

Chain rule of forecasting   A forecasting process in which the next period's value as predicted by the forecasting equation is substituted into the right-hand side of the equation to give a predicted value two periods ahead.

Chapter 11   A U.S.bankruptcy procedure designed to reorganize and rehabilitate defaulting firm.

Chapter 7   A U.S. bankruptcy procedure whereby a debtor's assets are sold and the proceeds are used to repay creditors.

Cheapest to deliver   A bond in which the amount received for delivering the bond is largest compared with the amount paid in the market for the bond.

Cherry-picking When a bankrupt company is allowed to enforce contracts that are favorable to it while walking away from contracts that are unfavorable to it.

CHIPS Clearinghouse Interbank Payments System.

Classical growth theory A theory of economic growth based on the view that real GDP growth is temporary and that when real GDP per person increases above subsistence level, a population explosion brings real GDP back to subsistence level.

Clayton Act A federal antitrust law passed in 1914. Section 7, which is most relevant to mergers and acquisitions, prohibits the acquisition of stock and assets of a company when the effect is to lessen competition.

Clean surplus accounting Accounting that satisfies the condition that all changes in the book value of equity other than transactions with owners are reflected in income.

Clean surplus relation The relationship between earnings, dividends, and book value in which ending book value is equal to the beginning book value plus earnings less dividends, apart from ownership transactions.

Clearinghouse An entity associated with a futures market that acts as middleman between the contracting parties and guarantees to each party the performance of the other.

Clientele effect The preference some investors have for shares that exhibit certain characteristics.

Closed-end fund An investment company with a fixed number of shares. New shares cannot be issued and the old shares cannot be redeemed. Shares are traded in the marketplace, and their value may differ from the underlying net asset value of the fund.

Closeout netting Netting the market values of *all* derivative contracts between two parties to determine one overall value owed by one party to another in the event of bankruptcy.

CMOs Collateralized mortgage obligations.

Coefficient of variation (CV) The ratio of a set of observations' standard deviation to the observations' mean value.

Cointegrated Describes two time series that have a long-term financial or economic relationship such that they do not diverge from each other without bound in the long run.

Collar An option strategy involving the purchase of a put and sale of a call in which the holder of an asset gains protection below a certain level, the exercise price of the put, and pays for it by giving up gains above a certain level, the exercise price of the call. Collars also can be used to provide protection against rising interest rates on a floating-rate loan by giving up gains from lower interest rates.

Collateral A specific asset pledged against possible default on a bond. Mortgage bonds are backed by claims on property. Collateral trust bonds are backed by claims on other securities. Equipment obligation bonds are backed by claims on equipment.

Collateralized mortgage obligation (CMO) A mortgage pass-through security that partitions cash flows from underlying mortgages into classes called tranches that receive principal payments according to stipulated rules.

Combination A listing in which the order of the listed items does not matter.

Commercial bank A firm that is licensed by the Comptroller of the Currency in the U.S. Treasury or by a state agency to receive deposits and make loans.

Commercial paper Unsecured short-term corporate debt that is characterized by a single payment at maturity.

Commingled fund Typically, an investment pool run by a bank, in which participation is represented by accounting units rather than shares.

Commission recapture Credit for brokerage generated is then applied to such services as custody and appraisal.

Commodity forward A contract in which the underlying asset is oil, a precious metal, or some other commodity.

Commodity futures Futures contracts in which the underlying is a traditional agricultural, metal, or petroleum product.

Commodity option An option in which the asset underlying the futures is a commodity, such as oil, gold, wheat, or soybeans.

Commodity swap A swap in which the underlying is a commodity such as oil, gold, or an agricultural product.

Common size statements Financial statements in which all elements (accounts) are stated as a percentage of a key figure such as revenue for an income statement or total assets for a balance sheet.

Common stock Equities, or equity securities, issued as ownership shares in a publicly held corporation. Shareholders have voting rights and may receive dividends based on their proportionate ownership.

Company fundamental factors Factors related to the company's internal performance, such as factors relating to earnings growth, earnings variability, earnings momentum, and financial leverage.

Company share-related factors Valuation measures and other factors related to share price or the trading characteristics of the shares, such as earnings yield, dividend yield, and book-to-market value.

Comparative advantage A person or country has a comparative advantage in an activity if that person or country can perform the activity at a lower opportunity cost than anyone else or any other country.

Competitive environment The level of intensity of competition among firms in an industry, determined by an examination of five competitive forces.

Competitive market A market that has many buyers and many sellers, so no single buyer or seller can influence the price.

Competitive strategy The search by a firm for a favorable competitive position within an industry within the known competitive environment.

Complement With reference to an event S, the event that S does not occur.

Complete portfolio The entire portfolio, including risky and risk-free assets.

Composite A universe of portfolios with similar investment objectives.

Composition Voluntary agreement to reduce payments on a firm's debt.

Compound interest Reinvestment of each interest payment on money invested to earn more interest (cf. *simple interest*).

Compounding The process of accumulating interest on interest.

Comprehensive income All changes in equity other than contributions by, and distributions to, owners; income under clean surplus accounting.

Concentration ratio The percentage of all sales contributed by the leading four or leading eight firms in an industry; sometimes called the *industry concentration ratio*.

Conditional expected value The expected value of a stated event given that another event has occurred.

Conditional heteroskedasticity Heteroskedasticity in the error variance that is correlated with the values of the independent variable(s) in the regression.

Conditional probability The probability of an event given (conditioned on) another event.

Conditional variances The variance of one variable, given the outcome of another.

Confidence interval A range that has a given probability that it will contain the population parameter it is intended to estimate.

Conglomerate A combination of unrelated firms.

Conglomerate merger A merger involving companies that are in unrelated businesses.

Consistency A desirable property of estimators; a consistent estimator is one for which the probability of estimates close to the value of the population parameter increases as sample size increases.

Consistent With reference to estimators, describes an estimator for which the probability of estimates close to the value of the population parameter increases as sample size increases.

Consolidation A merger in which both companies terminate their previous legal existence and become part of a newly formed company.

Constant growth model A form of the dividend discount model that assumes dividends will grow at a constant rate.

Constant maturity swap or CMT swap A swap in which the floating rate is the rate on a security known as a constant maturity treasury or CMT security.

Constant maturity treasury or CMT A hypothetical U.S. Treasury note with a constant maturity. A CMT exists for various years in the range of 2 to 10.

Consumer Price Index (CPI) An index that measures the average of the prices paid by urban consumers for a fixed "basket" of the consumer goods and services.

Consumption The use of goods and services for personal satisfaction. Can also be viewed as spending on new goods and services out of a household's current income. Whatever is not consumed is saved. Consumption includes such things as buying food and going to a concert.

Consumption expenditure The total payment for consumer goods and services.

Consumption goods Goods bought by households to use up, such as food and movies.

Contango A situation in a futures market where the current futures price is greater than the current spot price for the underlying asset.

Contestable market A market in which firms can enter and leave so easily that firms in the market face competition from potential entrants.

Contingent claims Derivatives in which the payoffs occur if a specific event occurs; generally referred to as options.

Continuing residual income Residual income after the forecast horizon.

Continuous compounding Interest compounded continuously rather than at fixed intervals.

Continuous random variable A random variable for which the range of possible outcomes is the real line (all real numbers between $-\infty$ and $+\infty$) or some subset of the real line.

Continuous time Time thought of as advancing in extremely small increments.

Continuously compounded return The natural logarithm of 1 plus the holding period return, or equivalently, the natural logarithm of the ending price over the beginning price.

Contract price The transaction price specified in a forward or futures contract.

Contraction A business fluctuation during which the pace of national economic activity is slowing down.

Contribution margin The amount available for fixed costs and profit after paying variable costs; revenue minus variable costs.

Control premium An increment or premium to value associated with a controlling ownership interest in a company.

Controller Officer responsible for budgeting, accounting, and auditing in a firm (cf. *treasurer*).

Convenience yield The nonmonetary return offered by an asset when the asset is in short supply, often associated with assets with seasonal production processes.

Conventional cash flow A conventional cash flow pattern is one with an initial outflow followed by a series of inflows.

Conversion factor An adjustment used to facilitate delivery on bond futures contracts in which any of a number of bonds with different characteristics are eligible for delivery.

Conversion parity price The price at which common stock can be obtained by surrendering the convertible instrument at par value.

Conversion premium The excess of the market value of the convertible security over its equity value if immediately converted into common stock. Typically expressed as a percentage of the equity value.

Conversion ratio The number of shares of common stock for which a convertible security may be exchanged.

Conversion value The value of the convertible security if converted into common stock at the stock's current market price.

Convertible A bond or preferred stock that offers the investor the right to convert his holding into common stock under set terms.

Convertible bond A bond with an option allowing the bondholder to exchange the bond for a specified number of shares of common stock in the firm. A *conversion ratio* specifies the number of shares. The *market conversion price* is the current value of the shares for which the bond may be exchanged. The *conversion premium* is the excess of the bond's value over the conversion price.

Convexity A measure of the degree to which a bond's price-yield curve departs from a straight line. This characteristic affects estimates of a bond's price volatility for a given change in yields.

Corporate bonds Long-term debt issued by private corporations typically paying semiannual coupons and returning the face value of the bond at maturity.

Corporate governance The system of principles, policies, procedures, and clearly defined responsibilities and accountabilities used by stakeholders to overcome the conflicts of interest inherent in the corporate form.

Corporate raider A person or organization seeking to profit by acquiring a company and reselling it, or seeking to profit from the takeover attempt itself (e.g. greenmail).

Corporate trustee A bank or trust company having federal or state authority to serve as a trustee.

Corporation A legal entity that may conduct business in its own name just as an individual does; the owners of a corporation, called shareholders, own shares of the firm's profits and enjoy the protection of limited liability.

Correlation analysis The analysis of the strength of the linear relationship between two data series.

Correlation or correlation coefficient A number between -1 and $+1$ that measures the co-movement (linear association) between two random variables.

Cost averaging The periodic investment of a fixed amount of money.

Cost leadership The competitive strategy of being the lowest cost producer while offering products comparable to those of other firms, so that products can be priced at or near the industry average.

Cost of capital Opportunity cost of capital.

Cost of carry The cost associated with holding some asset, including financing, storage, and insurance costs. Any yield received on the asset is treated as a negative carrying cost.

Cost of carry model A model for pricing futures contracts in which the futures price is determined by adding the cost of carry to the spot price.

Cost of equity The required rate of return on common stock.

Cost-of-service regulation Regulation based on allowing prices to reflect only the actual cost of production and no monopoly profits.

Cost structure The mix of a company's variable costs and fixed costs.

Counterparty Party on the other side of a *derivative* contract.

Coupon The interest rate on a bond, expressed as a percentage of its face (not market) value. At one time bonds (and indeed stocks) contained coupons resembling postage stamps, which one "clipped" or cut periodically and presented for payment of interest (or dividends).

Coupon rate A bond's interest payments per dollar of par value.

Covariance A measure of the co-movement (linear association) between two random variables.

Covariance matrix A matrix or square array whose entries are covariances; also known as a variance-covariance matrix.

Covariance stationary Describes a time series when its expected value and variance are constant and finite in all periods and when its covariance with itself for a fixed number of periods in the past or future is constant and finite in all periods.

Covenant Clause in a loan agreement.

Covered call An option strategy involving the holding of an asset and sale of a call on the asset.

Covered interest arbitrage A transaction executed in the foreign exchange market in which a currency is purchased (sold) and a forward contract is sold (purchased) to lock in the exchange rate for future delivery of the currency. This transaction should earn the risk-free rate of the investor's home country.

Covered option *Option* position with an offsetting position in the underlying asset.

Creative response Behavior on the part of a firm that allows it to comply with the letter of the law but violates the spirit, significantly lessening the law's effects.

Credit analysis An active bond portfolio management strategy designed to identify bonds that are expected to experience changes in rating. This strategy is critical when investing in high-yield bonds.

Credit derivatives A contract in which one party has the right to claim a payment from another party in the event that a specific credit event occurs over the life of the contract.

Credit enhancement Contract for *hedging* against loan default or changes in credit risk (see *default swap*).

Credit-linked notes Fixed-income securities in which the holder of the security has the right to withhold payment of the full amount due at maturity if a credit event occurs.

Credit risk or default risk The risk of loss due to nonpayment by a counterparty.

Credit scoring A procedure for assigning scores to borrowers on the basis of the risk of default.

Credit spread option An option on the yield spread on a bond.

Credit swap A type of swap transaction used as a credit derivative in which one party makes periodic payments to the other and receives the promise of a payoff if a third party defaults.

Credit VAR, Default VAR, or Credit at Risk A variation of VAR that reflects credit risk.

Creditor nation A country that during its entire history has invested more in the rest of the world than other countries have invested in it.

Cross-product netting Netting the market values of all contracts, not just derivatives, between parties.

Cross-rate The exchange rate between two currencies, derived from their exchange rates with a third currency.

Cross-sectional data Observations over individual units at a point in time, as opposed to time-series data.

Cum dividend With dividend.

Cumulative distribution function A function giving the probability that a random variable is less than or equal to a specified value.

Cumulative relative frequency For data grouped into intervals, the fraction of total observations that are less than the value of the upper limit of a stated interval.

Currency The bills and coins that we use today.

Currency appreciation The rise in the value of one currency in terms of another currency.

Currency depreciation The fall in the value of one currency in terms of another currency.

Currency exposure The sensitivity of the asset return, measured in the investor's domestic currency, to a movement in the exchange rate.

Currency forward A forward contract in which the underlying is a foreign currency.

Currency option An option that allows the holder to buy (if a call) or sell (if a put) an underlying currency at a fixed exercise rate, expressed as an exchange rate.

Currency swap A contract to exchange streams of fixed cash flows denominated in two different currencies.

Current account A record of the payments for imports of goods and services, receipts from exports of goods and services, the interest income, and net transfers.

Current asset Asset that will normally be turned into cash within a year.

Current credit risk The risk associated with the possibility that a payment currently due will not be made.

Current income A return objective in which the investor seeks to generate income rather than capital gains; generally a goal of an investor who wants to supplement earnings with income to meet living expenses.

Current liability Liability that will normally be repaid within a year.

Current ratio A ratio representing the ability of the firm to pay off its current liabilities by liquidating current assets (current assets/current liabilities).

Current yield A bond's annual coupon payment divided by its price. Differs from yield to maturity.

Custodians Agents who hold property in safekeeping for others, usually without inherent investment management responsibility.

Customer acquisition costs Initial direct costs incurred in adding to a company's customer base, including direct-response advertising, commissions, and related administrative costs. When capitalized, prospective customer-related revenues must be expected to exceed amounts capitalized. Depending on the industry, such costs may have other names, including subscriber acquisition costs and policy acquisition costs.

Cyclical businesses or cyclical companies Businesses with high sensitivity to business- or industry-cycle influences.

Cyclical industries Industries with above-average sensitivity to the state of the economy.

Cyclical stock A stock with a high beta; its gains typically exceed those of a rising market and its losses typically exceed those of a falling market.

Cyclicals Some industries are perennially subject to the vagaries of the business cycle: mining, steel, construction, automobiles, chemicals, machine tools, and the like. It is impossible to get away from the cyclical effect in business, just as there is always alternation between good and bad weather, so a cyclical company will have an irregular earnings pattern, and usually an irregular stock price pattern too.

Daily settlement See *marking to market.*

Data mining The practice of determining a model by extensive searching through a dataset for statistically significant patterns.

Day trader A trader holding a position open somewhat longer than a scalper but closing all positions at the end of the day.

DCF Discounted cash flow.

DDM Dividend discount model.

Dead-hand provision A poison pill provision that allows for the redemption or cancellation of a poison pill provision only by a vote of continuing directors (generally directors who were on the target company's board prior to the takeover attempt).

Dealer An agent that buys and sells securities as a principal (for its own account) rather than as a broker for clients. A dealer may function, at different times, as a broker or as a dealer. Sometimes called a *market maker.*

Debenture Unsecured bond.

Debt ratings An objective measure of the quality and safety of a company's debt based upon an analysis of the company's ability to pay the promised cash flows, as well as an analysis of any indentures.

Debtor nation A country that during its entire history has borrowed more from the rest of the world than it has lent to it.

Decentralized risk management A system that allows individual units within an organization to manage risk. Decentralization results in duplication of effort but has the advantage of having people closer to the risk be more directly involved in its management.

Deciles Quantiles that divide a distribution into 10 equal parts.

Decision rule With respect to hypothesis testing, the rule according to which the null hypothesis will be rejected or not rejected; involves the comparison of the test statistic to rejection point(s).

Decision tree Method of representing alternative sequential decisions and the possible outcomes from these decisions.

Declaration date The day that the corporation issues a statement declaring a specific dividend.

Deep in the money Said of call options for which the market price of the underlying is far above the exercise price or of put options for which the market price of the underlying is far below the exercise price.

Deep out of the money Said of call options for which the market price of the underlying is far below the exercise price or of put options for which the market price of the underlying is far above the exercise price.

Default risk The risk that an issuer will be unable to make interest and principal payments on time.

Default risk premium A differential in promised return relative to default-free debt that compensates investors for the possibility that the borrower will fail to make a promised payment at the contracted time and in the contracted amount.

Default swap *Credit derivative* in which one party makes fixed payments while the payments by the other party depend on the occurrence of a loan default.

Defeasance Practice whereby the borrower sets aside cash or *bonds* sufficient to service the borrower's debt. Both the borrower's debt and the offsetting cash or bonds are removed from the balance sheet.

Defensive industries Industries with little sensitivity to the state of the economy.

Deferred tax assets Future tax benefits that result from (1) the origination of a deductible temporary difference, that is, a tax deduction that can be used in a future period, or (2) a loss or tax-credit carryover. These future tax benefits are realized upon the reversal of deductible temporary differences. In addition, realization can occur by the offsetting of a loss carryforward against taxable income or a tax credit carryforward against taxes currently payable.

Deferred tax liabilities Future tax obligations that result from the origination of taxable temporary differences. Upon origination, these temporary difference cause pretax financial income to exceed taxable income. These future tax obligations are paid later when temporary differences reverse, now causing taxable income to exceed pretax book income.

Defined benefit pension plan or defined benefit plan A pension plan to which the company contributes a certain amount each year and promises to pay employees a specified income after they retire. The benefit size is based on factors such as workers' salary and time of employment.

Defined contribution pension plan or defined contribution plan A pension plan in which worker benefits are determined by the size of employees' contributions to the plan and the returns earned on the fund's investments.

Definitive merger agreement A contract signed by both parties to a merger that clarifies the details of the transaction, including the terms, warranties, conditions, termination details, and the rights of all parties.

Deflation The situation in which the average of all prices of goods and services in an economy is falling.

Degree of confidence The probability that a confidence interval includes the unknown population parameter.

Degree of financial leverage (DFL) The ratio of the percentage change in net income to the percentage change in operating income; the sensitivity of the cash flows available to owners when operating income changes.

Degree of operating leverage (DOL) The ratio of the percentage change in operating income to the percentage change in units sold; the sensitivity of operating income to changes in units sold.

Degree of total leverage The ratio of the percentage change in net income to the percentage change in units sold; the sensitivity of the cash flows to owners to changes in the number of units produced and sold.

Degrees of freedom (df) The number of independent observations used.

Delivery A process used in a deliverable forward contract in which the long pays the agreed-upon price to the short, which in turn delivers the underlying asset to the long.

Delivery option The feature of a futures contract giving the short the right to make decisions about what, when, and where to deliver.

Delta The relationship between the option price and the underlying price, which reflects the sensitivity of the price of the option to changes in the price of the underlying.

Delta hedge An option strategy in which a position in an asset is converted to a risk-free position with a position in a specific number of options. The number of options per unit of the underlying changes through time, and the position must be revised to maintain the hedge.

Delta-normal method A measure of VAR equivalent to the analytical method but that refers to the use of delta to estimate the option's price sensitivity.

Demand The relationship between the quantity of a good that consumers plan to buy and the price of the good when all other influences on buyers' plans remain the same. It is described by a demand schedule and illustrated by a demand curve.

Demand curve A curve that shows the relationship between the quantity demanded of a good and its price when all other influences on consumers' planned purchases remain the same.

Demand for labor The relationship between the quantity of labor demanded and the real wage rate when all other influences on a firm's hiring plans remain the same.

Dependent With reference to events, the property that the probability of one event occurring depends on (is related to) the occurrence of another event.

Dependent variable The variable whose variation about its mean is to be explained by the regression; the left-hand-side variable in a regression equation.

Depreciation Reduction in the value of capital goods over a one-year period due to physical wear and tear and also to obsolescence; also called *capital consumption allowance*. Can also be viewed as a decrease in the exchange value of one nation's currency in terms of the currency of another nation.

Depression An extremely severe recession.

Deregulation   The elimination or phasing out of regulations on economic activity.

Derivative   A financial instrument that offers a return based on the return of an underlying asset.

Derivatives dealers   The commercial and investment banks that make markets in derivatives. Also referred to as market makers.

Descriptive statistics   The study of how data can be summarized effectively.

Devaluation   Deliberate downward adjustment of a currency against its fixed parity.

Differential expectations   Expectations that differ from consensus expectations.

Differential swap or diff swap or diff   A swap in which the payments are based on the difference between interest rates in two countries but payments are made in only a single currency.

Differentiation   The competitive strategy of offering unique products or services along some dimensions that are widely valued by buyers so that the firm can command premium prices.

Diffuse prior   The assumption of equal prior probabilities.

Diluted earnings per share   Total earnings divided by the number of shares that would be outstanding if holders of securities such as executive stock options and convertible bonds exercised their options to obtain common stock.

Dilution   Reduction in shareholders' equity per share or earnings per share that arises from some changes among shareholders' proportionate interests.

Diminishing marginal returns   The tendency for the marginal product of an additional unit of a factor of production to be less than the marginal product of the previous unit of the factor.

Direct exchange rate   The amount of local or domestic currency required to purchase one unit of foreign currency.

Direct income capitalization approach   Division of net operating income by an overall capitalization rate to arrive at market value.

Direct Investments (Private Equity)   An investment made directly in venture capital or private equity assets (i.e., not via a partnership or fund).

Direct quote   For foreign exchange, the number of U.S. dollars needed to buy one unit of a foreign currency (cf. *indirect quote*).

Directed brokerage   A manager is asked to direct business to a specified broker, usually to pay for services.

Dirty surplus items   Items that affect comprehensive income but which bypass the income statement.

Discontinued operations   Net income and the gain or loss on disposal of a discontinued business segment or separately measured business unit.

Discount   To reduce the value of a future payment in allowance for how far away it is in time; to calculate the present value of some future amount. Also, the amount by which an instrument is priced below its face value.

Discount factor   *Present value* of $1 received at a stated future date.

Discount interest   A procedure for determining the interest on a loan or bond in which the interest is deducted from the face value in advance.

Discount rate   (1) Rate used to calculate the present value of future cash flows. (2) The interest rate at which the U.S. Federal Reserve System stands ready to lend reserves to depository institutions.

Discounted cash flow (DCF)   Future cash flows multiplied by discount factors to obtain present value.

Discounted cash flow analysis   Analysis of value in terms of the present value of expected future cash flows.

Discounting   The conversion of a future amount of money to its present value.

Discrete random variable   A random variable that can take on at most a countable number of possible values.

Discrete time   Time thought of as advancing in distinct finite increments.

Discretionary account   An account of a customer who gives a broker the authority to make buy and sell decisions on the customer's behalf.

Discriminant analysis   A multivariate classification technique used to discriminate between groups, such as companies that either will or will not become bankrupt during some time frame.

Dispersion   The variability around the central tendency.

Diversifiable risk   Risk attributable to firm-specific risk, or nonmarket risk. *Nondiversifiable* risk refers to systematic or market risk.

Diversification   (1) Spreading a portfolio over many investments to avoid excessive exposure to any one source of risk. (2) In mergers and acquisitions, a term that refers to buying companies or assets outside the companies' current lines of business.

Divestiture   The sale, liquidation, or spin-off of some major component of a business.

Dividend   Payment by a company to its stockholders.

Dividend discount model (DDM)   A present value model of stock value that views the intrinsic value of a stock as present value of the stock's expected future dividends.

Dividend displacement of earnings The concept that dividends paid now displace earnings in all future periods.

Dividend payout policy The strategy a company follows with regard to the amount and timing of dividend payments.

Dividend payout ratio Percentage of earnings paid out as dividends.

Dividend rate The most recent quarterly dividend multiplied by four.

Dividend reinvestment plan (DRIP) Plan that allows shareholders to reinvest dividends automatically.

Dividend yield Annual dividend divided by share price.

Dividends paid A term used on the cash flow analysis statement that refers to cash disbursements for dividends on common and preferred stock.

Double taxation With reference to certain tax jurisdictions, the practice of taxing corporate earnings twice. First, corporate earnings are taxed regardless of whether they will be distributed as dividends or retained at the corporate level, and second, dividends are taxed again at the individual shareholder level.

Dow Jones Industrial Average (DJI or DJIA) A price-weighted average of thirty industrial companies.

Down transition probability The probability that an asset's value moves down in a model of asset price dynamics.

Due diligence Investigation and analysis in support of a recommendation; the failure to exercise due diligence may sometimes result in liability according to various securities laws.

Dummy variable A type of qualitative variable that takes on a value of 1 if a particular condition is true and 0 if that condition is false.

Dumping The sale by a foreign firm of exports at a lower price that the cost of production.

Duration A measure of an option-free bond's average maturity. Specifically, the weighted average maturity of all future cash flows paid by a security, in which the weights are the present value of these cash flows as a fraction of the bond's price. A measure of a bond's price sensitivity to interest rate movements.

Dutch Book Theorem A result in probability theory stating that inconsistent probabilities create profit opportunities.

Dynamic hedging Hedging that involves making frequent adjustments to the quantity of the instrument used for hedging in relation to the instrument being hedged.

Early stage With reference to venture capital financing, the stage associated with moving into operation and before commercial manufacturing and sales have occurred. Includes the start-up and first stages.

Earnings at risk (EAR) A variation of VAR that reflects the risk of a company's earnings instead of its market value.

Earnings before interest and taxes (EBIT) Net income measured before interest expense and before income tax expense. EBIT has a long history of being used as a basis for measuring fixed-charge coverage.

Earnings before interest, taxes, depreciation, and amortization (EBITDA) An earnings-based measure that often serves as a surrogate for cash flow. The measure actually represents working capital provided by operations before interest and taxes.

Earnings management The practice of using flexibility in accounting rules to improve the apparent profitability of the firm.

Earnings momentum A strategy in which portfolios are constructed of stocks of firms with rising earnings.

Earnings retention ratio Plowback ratio.

Earnings surprise A company announcement of earnings that differs from analysts' prevailing expectations.

Earnings yield Earnings per share divided by price; the reciprocal of the P/E ratio.

EBIT Earnings before interest and taxes.

EBITDA Earnings before interest, taxes, depreciation, and amortization.

Economic depreciation The change in the market value of capital over a given period.

Economic efficiency A situation that occurs when the firm produces a given output at the least cost.

Economic exposure Risk that arises from changes in real exchange rates (cf. *transaction exposure, translation exposure*).

Economic growth (1) Increases in per capita real GDP measured by its rate of change per year. (2) The expansion of production possibilities that results from capital accumulation and technological change.

Economic growth rate The percentage change in the quantity of goods and services produced from one year to the next.

Economic income Cash flow plus change in *present value*.

Economic model A description of some aspect of the economic world that includes only those features of the world that are needed for the purpose at hand.

Economic profit Total revenue minus total opportunity costs of all inputs used, or the total of all implicit and explicit costs; a firm's after-tax net operating profit minus its opportunity cost of capital.

Economic rent A payment for the use of any resource over and above its opportunity cost.

Economic risk As used in currency risk management, the risk that arises when the foreign currency value of a foreign investment reacts systematically to an exchange rate movement.

Economic sectors Large industry groupings.

Economic theory A generalization that summarizes what we think we understand about the economic choices that people make and the performance of industries and entire economies.

Economic value added (EVA®) The spread between ROA and cost of capital multiplied by the capital invested in the firm. It measures the dollar value of the firm's return in excess of its opportunity cost.

Economic welfare A comprehensive measure of the general state of economic well-being.

Economics The social science that studies the choices that individuals, businesses, governments, and entire societies make and how they cope with scarcity and the incentives that influence and reconcile those choices.

Economies of scale The reduction of a company's average costs due to increasing output and spreading out fixed costs over higher output levels; the savings achieved through the consolidation of operations and elimination of duplicate resources.

Economies of scope The ability of a firm to utilize one set of inputs to provide a broader range of outputs or services.

Effective annual rate The amount by which a unit of currency will grow in a year with interest on interest included.

Effective annual yield (EAY) An annualized return that accounts for the effect of interest on interest; EAY is computed by compounding 1 plus the holding period yield forward to one year, then subtracting 1.

Effective tax rate The income tax provision divided by income before the income tax provision.

Efficiency In statistics, a desirable property of estimators; an efficient estimator is the unbiased estimator with the smallest variance among unbiased estimators of the same parameter.

Efficient capital market A market in which security prices rapidly reflect all information about securities.

Efficient diversification The organizing principle of modern portfolio theory, which maintains that any risk-averse investor will search for the highest expected return for any level of portfolio risk.

Efficient frontier The portion of the minimum-variance frontier beginning with the global minimum-variance portfolio and continuing above it; the graph of the set of portfolios offering the maximum expected return for their level of variance of return.

Efficient market A market in which any relevant information is immediately impounded in asset prices.

Efficient portfolio A portfolio offering the highest expected return for a given level of risk as measured by variance or standard deviation of return.

Elasticity A measure of sensitivity; the incremental change in one variable with respect to an incremental change in another variable.

Electronic crossing networks Order-driven trading systems in which market orders are anonymously matched at prespecified times at prices determined in the primary market for the system.

Emerging Issues Task Force (EITF) The EITF assists the Financial Accounting Standards Board through the timely identification, discussion, and resolution of financial accounting issues based on existing authoritative literature.

Emerging markets Often, countries so defined by the International Finance Corporation (IFC), based on their per capita income.

Empirical Relying on real-world data in evaluating the usefulness of a model.

Empirical duration Measures directly the interest rate sensitivity of an asset by examining the percentage price change for an asset in response to a change in yield during a specified period of time.

Employee Retirement Income Security Act (ERISA) Governs most private pension and benefit plans.

Endogenous growth theory A theory of economic growth that does not assume that the marginal productivity of capital declines as capital is added.

Endowment funds Organizations chartered to invest money for specific purposes.

Endowments The various resources in an economy, including both physical resources and such human resources as ingenuity and management skills.

Enhanced derivatives products companies (EDPC) or special purpose vehicles (SPVs) A type of subsidiary engaged in derivatives transactions that is separated from the parent company in order to have a higher credit rating than the parent company.

Enterprise risk management A form of *centralized risk management* that typically encompasses the management of a broad variety of risks, including insurance risk.

Enterprise value (EV) Total company value (the market value of debt, common equity, and preferred equity) minus the value of cash and investments.

EPS Earnings per share.

Equilibrium The condition in which supply equals demand.

Equilibrium price The price at which the quantity demanded equals the quantity supplied.

Equities Another name for shares. The capitalization of a company consists of "equity"—or owner-ship—represented by common or preferred shares (stock), and debt, represented by bonds, notes, and the like. (In England, "corporation stock" means municipal bonds, incidentally.)

Equitizing cash A strategy used to replicate an index. It is also used to take a given amount of cash and turn it into an equity position while maintaining the liquidity provided by the cash.

Equity (1) *Common stock* and *preferred stock*. Often used to refer to common stock only. (2) *Net worth*.

Equity carve-out A form of restructuring that involves the creation of a new legal entity and the sale of equity in it to outsiders.

Equity charge The estimated cost of equity capital in money terms.

Equity dividend rate Income rate that reflects the relationship between equity income and equity capital.

Equity forward A contract calling for the purchase of an individual stock, a stock portfolio, or a stock index at a later date at an agreed-upon price.

Equity options Options on individual stocks; also known as stock options.

Equity risk premium The expected return on equities minus the risk-free rate.

Equity security An ownership interest in an enterprise, including preferred and common stock.

Equity swap A swap transaction in which at least one cash flow is tied to the return to an equity portfolio position, often an index.

Error autocorrelation The autocorrelation of the error term.

Error term The portion of the dependent variable that is not explained by the independent variable(s) in the regression.

Estimate The particular value calculated from sample observations using an estimator.

Estimated (or fitted) parameters With reference to regression analysis, the estimated values of the population intercept and population slope coefficient(s) in a regression.

Estimated rate of return The rate of return an investor anticipates earning from a specific investment over a particular future holding period.

Estimation With reference to statistical inference, the subdivision dealing with estimating the value of a population parameter.

Estimator An estimation formula; the formula used to compute the sample mean and other sample statistics are examples of estimators.

Euribor Interbank offer rate for short-term deposits in euros. Euribor is determined by an association of European banks.

Eurobond A bond underwritten by a multinational syndicate of banks and placed mainly in countries other than the country of the issuer; sometimes called an *international bond*.

Eurodollar A dollar deposited outside the United States.

Eurodollar deposit Dollar deposit with a bank outside the United States.

Eurodollar market The U.S. dollar segment of the Eurocurrency market.

European option An option that can be exercised only at expiration.

European terms With reference to U.S. dollar exchange rate quotations, the price of a U.S. dollar in terms of another currency.

European Union (EU) A formal association of European countries founded by the Treaty of Rome in 1957. Formerly known as the EEC.

EVA Economic value added.

Event Any outcome or specified set of outcomes of a random variable.

Excess kurtosis Degree of peakedness (fatness of tails) in excess of the peakedness of the normal distribution.

Excess return Rate of return in excess of the risk-free rate.

Exchange for physicals (EFP) A permissible delivery procedure used by futures market participants, in which the long and short arrange a delivery procedure other than the normal procedures stipulated by the futures exchange.

Exchange of assets Acquisition of another company by purchase of its assets in exchange for cash or shares.

Exchange rate Price of a unit of one country's currency in terms of another country's currency.

Exchange rate risk Uncertainty due to the denomination of an investment in a currency other than that of the investor's own country.

Exchange ratio The number of shares that target stockholders are to receive in exchange for each of their shares in the target company.

Exchanges National or regional auction markets providing a facility for members to trade securities. A seat is a membership on an exchange.

Exchange-traded funds (ETFs)   A type of mutual fund traded like other shares on a stock market, having special characteristics particularly related to redemption, and generally designed to closely track the performance of a specified stock market index.

Ex-dividend date   The first date that a share trades without (i.e. "ex") the right to a declared dividend.

Executor   The legal representative of a person who dies with a will.

Exercise or exercising the option   The process of using an option to buy or sell the underlying.

Exercise price (striking price)   Price at which a call option or put option may be exercised.

Exercise rate or strike rate   The fixed rate at which the holder of an interest rate option can buy or sell the underlying.

Exhaustive   Covering or containing all possible outcomes.

Expansion   A business cycle phase between a trough and a peak—phase in which real GDP increases.

Expectational arbitrage   Investing on the basis of differential expectations.

Expectations theory   Theory that forward interest rate (forward exchange rate) equals expected spot rate.

Expected holding-period return   The expected total return on an asset over a stated holding period; for stocks, the sum of the expected dividend yield and the expected price appreciation over the holding period.

Expected return or expected rate of return   Average of possible returns weighted by their probabilities.

Expected return–beta relationship   Implication of the CAPM that security risk premiums (expected excess returns) will be proportional to beta.

Expected utility   The average utility arising from all possible outcomes.

Expected value   The probability-weighted average of the possible outcomes of a random variable.

Expiration date   The date on which a derivative contract expires.

Exports   The goods and services that we sell to people in other countries.

Ex-Post   After the fact.

External financing   A term used on the cash flow analysis statement that consists of net debt and equity capital raised from external sources.

External growth   Company growth in output or sales that is achieved by buying the necessary resources externally (i.e., achieved through mergers and acquisitions).

Externality   A consequence of an economic activity that spills over to affect third parties; a situation in which the costs (or benefits) of an action are not fully borne (or gained) by the two parties engaged in exchange or by an individual engaging in a scarce-resource-using activity.

Extra dividend   *Dividend* that may or may not be repeated (cf. *regular dividend*).

Extraordinary item   Gain or loss that is unusual and infrequent in occurrence.

Face value   The promised payment at maturity separate from any coupon payment. Sometimes referred to as *par value*.

Factor   A common or underlying element with which several variables are correlated.

Factor beta   Sensitivity of security returns to changes in a systematic factor. Alternatively, factor loading; factor sensitivity.

Factor loading   See *factor beta*.

Factor model   A way of decomposing the factors that influence a security's rate of return into common and firm-specific influences.

Factor portfolio   A well-diversified portfolio constructed to have a beta of 1.0 on one factor and a beta of zero on any other factor.

Factor risk premium (or factor price)   The expected return in excess of the risk-free rate for a portfolio with a sensitivity of 1 to one factor and a sensitivity of 0 to all other factors.

Factor sensitivity (also factor betas or factor loadings)   An asset's sensitivity to a particular factor (holding all other factors constant).

Factors of production   The productive resources that businesses use to produce goods and services.

Fair value   (1) The amount at which an asset could be acquired or sold in a current transaction between willing parties in which the parties each acted knowledgeably, prudently, and without compulsion. (2) The theoretical value of a security based on current market conditions. The fair value is the value such that no arbitrage opportunities exist.

FASB   Financial Accounting Standards Board.

Federal Deposit Insurance Corporation (FDIC)   A government agency that insures the deposits held in banks and most other depository institutions; all U.S. banks are insured this way.

Federal funds   Non-interest-bearing deposits by banks at the Federal Reserve. Excess reserves are lent by banks to each other.

Federal funds rate   The interest rate that depository institutions pay to borrow reserves in the interbank federal funds market.

Fictitious revenue   Revenue recognized on a nonexistent sale or service transaction.

Fiduciary   A person who supervises or oversees the investment portfolio of a third party, such as in a trust account, and makes investment decisions in accordance with the owner's wishes.

Fiduciary call A combination of a European call and a risk-free bond that matures on the option expiration day and has a face value equal to the exercise price of the call.

Fiduciary relationship An arrangement under which a person (the fiduciary) has a duty to act for another's benefit (the beneficiary).

FIFO The first-in first-out accounting method of inventory valuation.

Financial account A component of the balance of payments covering investments by residents abroad and investments by nonresidents in the home country. Examples include direct investment made by companies, portfolio investments in equity and bonds, and other investments and liabilities.

Financial Accounting Standards Board (FASB) The principal standard-setting body in the United States. Its primary standards are Statements of Financial Accounting Standards (SFASs).

Financial assets Financial assets such as stocks and bonds are claims to the income generated by real assets or claims on income from the government.

Financial capital Funds used to purchase physical capital goods such as buildings and equipment.

Financial distress Heightened uncertainty regarding a company's ability to meet its various obligations because of lower or negative earnings.

Financial engineering Combining or dividing existing instruments to create new financial products.

Financial futures Futures contracts in which the underlying is a stock, bond, or currency.

Financial innovation The development of new financial products—new ways of borrowing and lending.

Financial intermediaries Institutions that transfer funds between ultimate lenders (savers) and ultimate borrowers.

Financial lease (capital lease, full-payout lease) Long-term, noncancelable lease (cf. *operating lease*).

Financial risk The variability of future income arising from the firm's fixed financing costs, for example, interest payments. The effect of fixed financial costs is to magnify the effect of changes in operating profit on net income or earnings per share.

Firm (1) An economic unit that hires factors of production and organizes those factors to produce and sell goods and services. (2) For purposes of the GIPS standards, the term "firm" refers to the entity defined for compliance with the GIPS standards.

Firm-specific risk See *diversifiable risk.*

First-differencing A transformation that subtracts the value of the time series in period $t-1$ from its value in period t.

First-order serial correlation Correlation between adjacent observations in a time series.

Fiscal policy The government's attempt to achieve macroeconomic objectives such as full employment, sustained economic growth, and price level stability by setting and changing taxes, making transfer payments, and purchasing goods and services.

Fixed costs Costs that remain at the same level regardless of a company's level of production and sales.

Fixed investment Purchases by businesses of newly produced producer durables, or capital goods, such as production machinery and office equipment.

Fixed-income forward A forward contract in which the underlying is a bond.

Fixed-income security A security such as a bond that pays a specified cash flow over a specific period.

Fixed-rate perpetual preferred stock Stock with a specified dividend rate that has a claim on earnings senior to the claim of common stock, and no maturity date.

Fixing A method for determining the market price of a security by finding the price that balances buyers and sellers. A fixing takes place periodically each day at defined times. Sometimes called a *call auction.*

Flexible exchange rates Exchange rates that are allowed to fluctuate in the open market in response to changes in supply and demand. Sometimes called *floating exchange rates.*

Flexible exchange rate system A system in which exchange rates are determined by supply and demand.

Flip-in pill A poison pill takeover defense that dilutes an acquirer's ownership in a target by giving other existing target company shareholders the right to buy additional target company shares at a discount.

Flip-over pill A poison pill takeover defense that gives target company shareholders the right to purchase shares of the acquirer at a significant discount to the market price, which has the effect of causing dilution to all existing acquiring company shareholders.

Floating-rate bond A bond whose interest rate is reset periodically according to a specified market rate.

Floating-rate loan A loan in which the interest rate is reset at least once after the starting date.

Floating-rate note (FRN) Short- to intermediate-term bonds with regularly scheduled coupon payments linked to a variable interest rate, most often LIBOR.

Floor A combination of interest rate put options designed to hedge a lender against lower rates on a floating-rate loan.

Floor agreement A contract that on each settlement date pays the holder the greater of the difference between the floor rate and the reference rate or zero; it is equivalent to a series of put options on the reference rate.

Floor traders or locals Market makers that buy and sell by quoting a bid and an ask price. They are the primary providers of liquidity to the market.

Floored swap A swap in which the floating payments have a lower limit.

Floorlet Each component put option in a floor.

Flotation cost Fees charged to companies by investment bankers and other costs associated with raising new capital.

Flow A quantity measured per unit of time; something that occurs over time, such as the income you make per week or per year or the number of individuals who are fired every month.

Focus The competitive strategy of seeking a competitive advantage within a target segment or segments of the industry, either on the basis of cost leadership (cost focus) or differentiation (differentiation focus).

Foreign bond A bond issued on the domestic capital market of another country.

Foreign currency risk premium The expected movement in the (direct) exchange rate minus the interest rate differential (domestic risk-free rate minus foreign risk-free rate).

Foreign direct investment The acquisition of more than 10 percent of the shares of ownership in a company in another nation.

Foreign exchange The purchase (sale) of a currency against the sale (purchase) of another.

Foreign exchange expectation A relation that states that the forward exchange rate, quoted at time 0 for delivery at time 1, is equal to the expected value of the spot exchange rate at time 1. When stated relative to the current spot exchange rate, the relation states that the forward discount (premium) is equal to the expected exchange rate movement.

Foreign exchange market The market in which the currency of one country is exchanged for the currency of another.

Foreign exchange rate The price at which one currency exchanges for another.

Forex Foreign exchange.

Forward contract An agreement between two parties in which one party, the buyer, agrees to buy from the other party, the seller, an underlying asset at a later date for a price established at the start of the contract.

Forward discount or premium Refers to the percentage difference between the forward exchange rate and the spot exchange rate (premium if positive, discount if negative).

Forward exchange rate Exchange rate fixed today for exchanging currency at some future date (cf. *spot exchange rate*).

Forward integration A merger involving the purchase of a target that is farther along the value or production chain; for example, to acquire a distributor.

Forward interest rate (1) Interest rate fixed today on a loan to be made at some future date (cf. *spot interest rate*). (2) Rate of interest for a future period that would equate the total return of a long-term bond with that of a strategy of rolling over shorter-term bonds. The forward rate is inferred from the term structure.

Forward premium A situation where, from the perspective of the domestic country, the spot exchange rate is larger than the forward exchange rate with a foreign country.

Forward price or forward rate The fixed price or rate at which the transaction scheduled to occur at the expiration of a forward contract will take place. This price is agreed on at the initiation date of the contract. With respect to the yield curve, a short-term yield for a future holding period implied by the spot rates of two securities with different maturities.

Forward rate agreement (FRA) A forward contract calling for one party to make a fixed interest payment and the other to make an interest payment at a rate to be determined at the contract expiration.

Forward swap A forward contract to enter into a swap.

Franchise factor A firm's unique competitive advantage that makes it possible for a firm to earn excess returns (rates of return above a firm's cost of capital) on its capital projects. In turn, these excess returns and the franchise factor cause the firm's stock price to have a *P/E* ratio above its base *P/E* ratio that is equal to $1/k$.

Franchise value In P/E ratio analysis, the present value of growth opportunities divided by next year's expected earnings.

Free cash flow The actual cash that would be available to the company's investors after making all investments necessary to maintain the company as an ongoing enterprise (also referred to as free cash flow to the firm); the internally generated funds that can be distributed to the company's investors (e.g., shareholders and bondholders) without impairing the value of the company.

Free cash flow hypothesis The hypothesis that higher debt levels discipline managers by forcing them to make fixed debt service payments and by reducing the company's free cash flow.

Free cash flow to equity The cash flow available to a company's common shareholders after all operating expenses, interest, and principal payments have been made, and necessary investments in working and fixed capital have been made.

Free cash flow to equity model A model of stock valuation that views a stock's intrinsic value as the present value of expected future free cash flows to equity.

Free cash flow to the firm The cash flow available to the company's suppliers of capital after all operating expenses (including taxes) have been paid and necessary investments in working and fixed capital have been made.

Free cash flow to the firm model A model of stock valuation that views the value of a firm as the present value of expected future free cash flows to the firm.

Frequency distribution A tabular display of data summarized into a relatively small number of intervals.

Frequency polygon A graph of a frequency distribution obtained by drawing straight lines joining successive points representing the class frequencies.

Friendly transaction A potential business combination that is endorsed by the managers of both companies.

Full price (or dirty price) The total price of a bond, including accrued interest.

Fundamental beta A beta that is based at least in part on fundamental data for a company.

Fundamental factor models A multifactor model in which the factors are attributes of stocks or companies that are important in explaining cross-sectional differences in stock prices.

Fundamentals Economic characteristics of a business such as profitability, financial strength, and risk.

Funded debt Debt maturing after more than one year (cf. *unfunded debt*).

Funds Traditionally defined as working capital, that is, the excess of current assets over current liabilities.

Funds from operations (FFO) A term used by real estate investment trusts (REITs) and defined as net income or loss excluding gains or losses from debt restructuring and sales of property, plus depreciation and amortization of real estate assets.

Future value (FV) The amount to which a payment or series of payments will grow by a stated future date.

Futures commission merchants (FCMs) Individuals or companies that execute futures transactions for other parties off the exchange.

Futures contract A standardized contract to buy (sell) an asset at a specified date and a specified price (futures price). The contract is traded on an organized exchange, and the potential gain/loss is realized each day (marking to market).

Futures exchange An exchange on which futures contracts are traded.

Futures option The right to enter a specified futures contract at a futures price equal to the stipulated exercise price.

Futures price The price at which a futures trader commits to make or take delivery of the underlying asset.

GAAP See generally accepted accounting principles.

Game theory A tool that economists use to analyze strategic behavior—behavior that takes into account the expected behavior of others and the mutual recognition of independence.

Gamma A numerical measure of how sensitive an option's delta is to a change in the underlying.

GDP deflator One measure of the price level, which is the average of current-year prices as a percentage of base-year prices.

Gearing Financial leverage.

General Agreement on Tariffs and Trade An international agreement signed in 1947 to reduce tariffs on international trade.

General Partner (Private Equity) (GP) A class of partner in a partnership. The GP retains liability for the actions of the partnership. In the PRIVATE EQUITY world, the GP is the fund manager and the LIMITED PARTNERS (LPs) are the institutional and high-net-worth investors in the partnership. The GP earns a management fee and a percentage of profits.

Generalized least squares A regression estimation technique that addresses heteroskedasticity of the error term.

Generally accepted accounting principles (GAAP) A common set of standards and procedures for the preparation of general-purpose financial statements that either have been established by an authoritative accounting rule-making body, such as the Financial Accounting Standards Board (FASB), or have over time become common accepted practice.

Generic   See *plain-vanilla.*

Geometric mean   A measure of central tendency computed by taking the *n*th root of the product of *n* non-negative values.

Global   Of a fund or portfolio, invested both in the United States and abroad.

Global Investment Performance Standards™ (GIPS®)   A global industry standard for the ethical presentation of investment performance results promulgated by CFA Institute.

Globalization   Tendency toward a worldwide investment environment, and the integration of national capital markets.

Going-concern assumption   The assumption that the business will maintain its business activities into the foreseeable future.

Going-concern value   A business's value under a going-concern assumption.

Gold standard   An international monetary system in which the parity of a currency is fixed in terms of its gold content.

Golden parachute   Employment contract of upper management that provides a larger payout upon the occurrence of certain control transactions, such as a certain percentage share purchase by an outside entity or when there is a tender offer for a certain percentage of the company's shares.

Goods   All things from which individuals derive satisfaction or happiness.

Goods and services   The objects that people value and produce to satisfy their wants.

Goodwill   An intangible asset that represents the excess of the purchase price of an acquisition over the value of the net assets acquired.

Governance   The oversight of a firm's management.

Government debt   The total amount of borrowing that the government has borrowed. It equals the sum of past budget deficits minus budget surpluses.

Government sector surplus or deficit   An amount equal to net taxes minus government purchases of goods and services.

Great Depression   A decade (1929-1939) of high unemployment and stagnant production throughout the world economy.

Greenmail   The purchase of the accumulated shares of a hostile investor by a company that is targeted for takeover by that investor, usually at a substantial premium over market price.

Gross domestic product   A money measure of the goods and services produced within a country's borders over a stated time period.

Gross investment   The total amount spent on purchases of new capital and on replacing depreciated capital.

Gross margin   Revenue minus cost of goods sold. Also referred to as *gross profit.*

Gross national product (GNP)   Total value of a country's output produced by residents both within the country's physical borders and abroad.

Growth accounting   A method of calculating how much real GDP growth results from growth of labor and capital and how much is attributable to technological change.

Growth company   A company that consistently has the opportunities and ability to invest in projects that provide rates of return that exceed the firm's cost of capital. Because of these investment opportunities, it retains a high proportion of earnings, and its earnings grow faster than those of average firms.

Growth investing   Emphasizes the future over apparent immediate undervaluation. Thus, usually implies buying companies with higher than average price-earnings ratios and lower dividend yields.

Growth option or expansion option   The ability to make additional investments in a project at some future time if the financial results are strong.

Growth phase   A stage of growth in which a company typically enjoys rapidly expanding markets, high profit margins, and an abnormally high growth rate in earnings per share.

Growth stock   A stock issue that generates a higher rate of return than other stocks in the market with similar risk characteristics.

Harmonic mean   A type of weighted mean computed by averaging the reciprocals of the observations, then taking the reciprocal of that average.

Hedge fund   An investment vehicle designed to manage a private, unregistered portfolio of assets according to any of several strategies. The investment strategy often employs arbitrage trading and significant financial leverage (e.g., short selling, borrowing, derivatives) while the compensation arrangement for the manager typically specifies considerable profit participation.

Hedge ratio   The relationship of the quantity of an asset being hedged to the quantity of the derivative used for hedging.

Hedging   A general strategy usually thought of as reducing, if not eliminating, risk.

Herfindahl Index or Herfindahl–Hirschman Index   A measure of market concentration that is calculated by summing the squared market shares for competing companies in an industry; high HHI readings or mergers that would result in large HHI increases are more likely to result in regulatory challenges.

Heteroskedastic With reference to the error term of a regression, having a variance that differs across observations.

Heteroskedasticity The property of having a nonconstant variance; refers to an error term with the property that its variance differs across observations.

Heteroskedasticity-consistent standard errors Standard errors of the estimated parameters of a regression that correct for the presence of heteroskedasticity in the regression's error term.

High-yield bond A bond rated below investment grade. Also referred to as *speculative-grade bonds* or *junk bonds.*

Histogram A bar chart of data that have been grouped into a frequency distribution.

Historical method A method of estimating VAR that uses data from the returns of the portfolio over a recent past period and compiles this data in the form of a histogram.

Historical simulation (or back simulation) method Another term for the historical method of estimating VAR. This method involves not a simulation of the past but rather what actually happened in the past, sometimes adjusted to reflect the fact that a different portfolio may have existed in the past than is planned for the future.

Holder-of-record date The date that a shareholder listed on the corporation's books will be deemed to have ownership of the shares for purposes of receiving an upcoming dividend; two business days after the ex-dividend date.

Holding company A company that owns the stock of other corporations. A holding company may not engage in actual operations of its own but merely manages various operating units that it owns an interest in.

Holding period return The return that an investor earns during a specified holding period; a synonym for total return.

Homogenization Creating a contract with standard and generally accepted terms, which makes it more acceptable to a broader group of participants.

Homoskedasticity The property of having a constant variance; refers to an error term that is constant across observations.

Horizontal merger A merger involving companies in the same line of business, usually as competitors.

Hostile transaction An attempt to acquire a company against the wishes of the target's managers.

Hot issue A newly issued stock that is in strong demand; often it will go to a premium over its original issue price.

Human capital The value of skills and knowledge possessed by the workforce.

Hurdle rate The rate of return that must be offered for a project to be accepted.

Hypothesis With reference to statistical inference, a statement about one or more populations.

Hypothesis testing With reference to statistical inference, the subdivision dealing with the testing of hypotheses about one or more populations.

Impairment As used in accounting, a downward adjustment.

Impairment of capital rule A legal restriction that dividends cannot exceed retained earnings.

Implicit costs Expenses that managers do not have to pay out of pocket and hence do not normally explicitly calculate, such as the opportunity cost of factors of production that are owned; examples are owner-provided capital and owner-provided labor.

Implied repo rate The rate of return from a cash-and-carry transaction implied by the futures price relative to the spot price.

Implied volatility The volatility of an asset that is implicit in the current market price of an option on that asset and a particular option-pricing model (e.g., the Black-Scholes-Merton formula).

Imports The goods and services that we buy from people in other countries.

Imputation In reference to corporate taxes, a system that imputes, or attributes, taxes at only one level of taxation. For countries using an imputation tax system, taxes on dividends are effectively levied only at the shareholder rate. Taxes are paid at the corporate level but they are attributed to the shareholder. Shareholders deduct from their tax bill their portion of taxes paid by the company.

Imputation tax system Arrangement by which investors who receive a *dividend* also receive a tax credit for corporate taxes that the firm has paid.

In the money An option that has positive intrinsic value.

Incentive A reward that encourages or a penalty that discourages an action.

Incentive system A method of organizing production that uses a market-like mechanism inside the firm.

Income approach Measuring national income by adding up all components of national income, including wages, interest, rent, and profits.

Income beneficiary A person entitled to all or a share of the income of a trust.

Income effect The effect of a change in income on consumption, other things remaining the same.

Income from continuing operations After-tax net income before discontinued operations, extraordinary items, and the cumulative effect of changes in accounting principle.

Income fund　A mutual fund providing for liberal current income from investments.

Income statement　A financial statement showing a firm's revenues and expenses during a specified period.

Income stock　*Common stock* with high *dividend yield* and few profitable investment opportunities (cf. *growth stock*).

Incremental cash flow　The changes or increments to cash flow resulting from a decision or action; the cash flow with a decision minus the cash flow without that decision.

Indenture　The legal agreement that lists the obligations of the issuer of a bond to the bondholder, including payment schedules, call provisions, and sinking funds.

Independent　With reference to events, the property that the occurrence of one event does not affect the probability of another event occurring.

Independent and identically distributed (IID)　With respect to random variables, the property of random variables that are independent of each other but follow the identical probability distribution.

Independent projects　Independent projects are projects whose cash flows are independent of each other.

Independent variable　A variable used to explain the dependent variable in a regression; a right-hand-side variable in a regression equation.

Index amortizing swap　An interest rate swap in which the notional principal is indexed to the level of interest rates and declines with the level of interest rates according to a predefined scheduled. This type of swap is frequently used to hedge securities that are prepaid as interest rates decline, such as mortgage-backed securities.

Index fund　A portfolio designed to replicate the performance of an index.

Index model　A model of stock returns using a market index such as the SP 500 to represent common or systematic risk factors.

Index option　An option in which the underlying is a stock index.

Indexing　An investment strategy in which an investor constructs a portfolio to mirror the performance of a specified index.

Indirect exchange rate　The amount of foreign currency required to purchase one unit of domestic currency.

Indirect quote　For foreign exchange, the number of units of a foreign currency needed to buy one U.S. dollar (cf. *direct quote*).

Industry life cycle　Stages through which firms typically pass as they mature.

Industry structure　An industry's underlying economic and technical characteristics.

Infant-industry argument　The argument that it is necessary to protect a new industry to enable it to grow into a mature industry that can compete in world markets.

Inflation　The rate at which the general level of prices for goods and services is rising.

Inflation-adjusted return　A rate of return that is measured in terms of real goods and services; that is, after the effects of inflation have been factored out.

Inflation premium　An extra return that compensates investors for expected inflation.

Inflation rate　The percentage change in the price level from one year to the next.

Information　An attribute of a good market that includes providing buyers and sellers with timely, accurate information on the volume and prices of past transactions and on all currently outstanding bids and offers.

Information ratio (IR)　Mean active return divided by active risk.

Initial margin　The amount that an investor must deposit to open a position in futures and some other derivatives; also used to refer to the initial equity required when a stock is purchased using borrowed money.

Initial margin requirement　The margin requirement on the first day of a transaction as well as on any day in which additional margin funds must be deposited.

Initial public offering (IPO)　The initial issuance of common stock registered for public trading by a formerly private corporation.

Innovation　Transforming an invention into something that is useful to humans.

Input list　List of parameters such as expected returns, variances, and covariances necessary to determine the optimal risky portfolio.

In-sample forecast errors　The residuals from a fitted time-series model within the sample period used to fit the model.

Inside information　Nonpublic knowledge about a corporation possessed by corporate officers, major owners, or other individuals with privileged access to information about a firm.

Insider trading　Trading by officers, directors, major stockholders, or others who hold private inside information allowing them to benefit from buying or selling stock.

Instability in the minimum-variance frontier　The characteristic of minimum-variance frontiers that they are sensitive to small changes in inputs.

Institution A retirement fund, bank, investment company, investment advisor, insurance company, or other large pool of investment buying power.

Intangible asset Nonmaterial asset, such as technical expertise, a trademark, or a patent (cf. *tangible asset*).

Interest The payment for current rather than future command over resources; the cost of obtaining credit. Also, the return paid to owners of capital.

Interest rate A rate of return that reflects the relationship between differently dated cash flows; a discount rate.

Interest rate call An option in which the holder has the right to make a known interest payment and receive an unknown interest payment.

Interest rate cap, or cap A series of call options on an interest rate, with each option expiring at the date on which the floating loan rate will be reset, and with each option having the same exercise rate. A cap in general can have an underlying other than an interest rate.

Interest rate collar A combination of a long cap and a short floor, or a short cap and a long floor.

Interest rate floor, or floor A series of put options on an interest rate, with each option expiring at the date on which the floating loan rate will be reset, and with each option having the same exercise rate. A floor in general can have an underlying other than the interest rate.

Interest rate forward (See *forward rate agreement*).

Interest rate option An option in which the underlying is an interest rate.

Interest rate parity A formula that expresses the equivalence or parity of spot and forward rates, after adjusting for differences in the interest rates.

Interest rate put An option in which the holder has the right to make an unknown interest payment and receive a known interest payment.

Interest rate risk The uncertainty of returns on an investment due to possible changes in interest rates over time.

Interest rate swap An agreement calling for the periodic exchange of cash flows, one based on an interest rate that remains fixed for the life of the contract and the other that is linked to a variable-rate index.

Intergenerational data mining A form of data mining that applies information developed by previous researchers using a dataset to guide current research using the same or a related dataset.

Intermediate Of bonds, usually five to seven years' maturity.

Intermediate goods Goods used up entirely in the production of final goods.

Internal rate of return (IRR) The discount rate that makes net present value equal 0; the discount rate that makes the present value of an investment's costs (outflows) equal to the present value of the investment's benefits (inflows).

International Accounting Standard (IAS) An accounting standard issued by the International Accounting Standards Committee. This committee has been replaced by the International Accounting Standards Board (IASB). IAS standards have been adopted by the IASB.

International Accounting Standards Board (IASB) An international standard setting body. Its principal standard-setting products are International Financial Reporting Standards (IFRSs). The IASB assumed its duties from the International Accounting Standards Committee (IASC). Existing International Accounting Standards issued by the IASC were adopted by the IASB.

International CAPM An equilibrium theory that relates the expected return of an asset to its world market and foreign exchange risks.

International Financial Reporting Standard (IFRS) A financial reporting standard issued by the International Accounting Standards Board.

International Fisher relation The assertion that the interest rate differential between two countries should equal the expected inflation rate differential over the term of the interest rates.

International monetary market (IMM) The financial futures market within the Chicago Mercantile Exchange.

International Swaps and Derivatives Association (ISDA) An association of swap dealers formed in 1985 to promote uniform practices in the writing, trading, and settlement procedures of swaps and other derivatives.

Interquartile range The difference between the third and first quartiles of a dataset.

Interval With reference to grouped data, a set of values within which an observation falls.

Interval scale A measurement scale that not only ranks data but also gives assurance that the differences between scale values are equal.

In-the-money Options that, if exercised, would result in the value received being worth more than the payment required to exercise.

Intrinsic value The value of the asset given a hypothetically complete understanding of the asset's investment characteristics; for options, the greater of zero and the amount of money realized if the option were to be exercised.

Inventory investment Changes in the stocks of finished goods and goods in process, as well as changes in the raw materials that businesses keep on hand. Whenever inventories are decreasing, inventory investment is negative; whenever they are increasing, inventory investment is positive.

Inverse floater A floating-rate note or bond in which the coupon is adjusted to move opposite to a benchmark interest rate.

Inverse relationship A relationship between variables that move in opposite directions.

Invested Capital (Private Equity) The amount of paid-in capital that has been invested in portfolio companies.

Investing Buying an asset, such as a bond, corporate stock, rental property, or farm, with reasonably determinable underlying earnings.

Investment (1) Any use of today's resources to expand tomorrow's production or consumption. Can also be viewed as spending by businesses on things such as machines and buildings, which can be used to produce goods and services in the future. The investment part of total output is the portion that will be used in the process of producing goods in the future. (2) The current commitment of dollars for a period of time in order to derive future payments that will compensate the investor for the time the funds are committed, the expected rate of inflation, and the uncertainty of future payments.

Investment Advisor (Private Equity) Any individual or institution that supplies investment advice to clients on a per fee basis. The investment advisor inherently has no role in the management of the underlying portfolio companies of a partnership/fund.

Investment bankers Firms specializing in the sale of new securities to the public, typically by underwriting the issue.

Investment company A firm that issues (sells) shares, and uses the proceeds to invest in various financial instruments or other assets.

Investment Company Act of 1940 One of several pieces of federal legislation passed after the October 1929 stock market crash and the Great Depression. This law regulated the activities and reporting requirements of investment companies, which are firms whose principal business is the trading and management of securities.

Investment constraints Internal or external limitations on investments.

Investment decision process Estimation of intrinsic value for comparison with market price to determine whether or not to invest.

Investment grade Bonds rated AAA to BBB.

Investment horizon The time period used for planning and forecasting purposes or the future time at which the investor requires the invested funds.

Investment management company A company separate from the investment company that manages the portfolio and performs administrative functions.

Investment Management Fee The fee payable to the investment management firm for the ongoing management of a portfolio. Investment management fees are typically asset based (percentage of assets), performance based (based on performance relative to a benchmark), or a combination of the two but may take different forms as well.

Investment objectives Desired investment outcomes; includes risk objectives and return objectives.

Investment portfolio Set of securities chosen by an investor.

Investment strategy An approach to investment analysis and security selection.

IPO Initial public offering.

IRR Internal rate of return.

Joint probability The probability of the joint occurrence of stated events.

Joint probability function A function giving the probability of joint occurrences of values of stated random variables.

Joint venture When companies jointly pursue a certain business activity.

Junior debt Subordinated debt.

Justified (fundamental) P/E The price-to-earnings ratio that is fair, warranted, or justified on the basis of forecasted fundamentals.

Justified price multiple (or warranted price multiple or intrinsic price multiple) The estimated fair value of the price multiple, usually based on forecasted fundamentals or comparables.

Just-in-time System of inventory management that requires minimum inventories of materials and very frequent deliveries by suppliers.

Keiretsu A network of Japanese companies organized around a major bank.

Keynesian An economist who believes that left alone, the economy would rarely operate at full employment and that to achieve full employment, active help from fiscal policy and monetary policy is required.

kth Order autocorrelation The correlation between observations in a time series separated by k periods.

Kurtosis The statistical measure that indicates the peakedness of a distribution.

Labor The work time and work effort that people devote to producing goods and services.

Labor force Individuals aged 16 years or older who either have jobs or are looking and available for jobs; the number of employed plus the number of unemployed.

Labor productivity Total real domestic output (real GDP) divided by the number of workers (output per worker).

Labor unions Worker organizations that seek to secure economic improvements for their members; they also seek to improve the safety, health, and other benefits (such as job security) of their members.

Land The natural resources that are available from nature. Land as a resource includes location, original fertility and mineral deposits, topography, climate, water, and vegetation.

Law of demand The observation that there is a negative, or inverse, relationship between the price of any good or service and the quantity demanded, holding other factors constant.

Law of diminishing returns As a firm uses more of a variable input, with a given quantity of other inputs (fixed inputs), the marginal product of the variable input eventually diminishes.

Law of one price The rule stipulating that equivalent securities or bundles of securities must sell at equal prices to preclude arbitrage opportunities.

Leading dividend yield Forecasted dividends per share over the next year divided by current stock price.

Leading P/E (or forward P/E or prospective P/E) A stock's current price divided by next year's expected earnings.

Lease Long-term rental agreement.

Lease receivables Amounts due from customers on long-term sales-type lease agreements.

Legal risk The risk that the legal system will not enforce a contract in case of dispute or fraud; the risk that failures by company managers to effectively manage a company's risk exposures will lead to lawsuits and other judicial remedies, resulting in potentially catastrophic losses for the company.

Legislative and regulatory risk The risk that governmental laws and regulations directly or indirectly affecting a company's operations will change with potentially severe adverse effects on the company's continued profitability and even its long-term sustainability.

Leptokurtic Describes a distribution that is more peaked than a normal distribution.

Lessee User of a leased asset (cf. *lessor*).

Lessor Owner of a leased asset (cf. *lessee*).

Letter of credit Letter from a bank stating that it has established a credit in the company's favor.

Level of significance The probability of a Type I error in testing a hypothesis.

Leverage In the context of corporate finance, leverage refers to the use of fixed costs within a company's cost structure. Fixed costs that are operating costs (such as depreciation or rent) create operating leverage. Fixed costs that are financial costs (such as interest expense) create financial leverage.

Leverage ratio Ratio of debt to total capitalization of a firm.

Leveraged buyout (LBO) A transaction whereby the target company management team converts the target to a privately held company by using heavy borrowing to finance the purchase of the target company's outstanding shares.

Leveraged floating-rate note or leveraged floater A floating-rate note or bond in which the coupon is adjusted at a multiple of a benchmark interest rate.

Leveraged recapitalization A post-offer takeover defense mechanism that involves the assumption of a large amount of debt that is then used to finance share repurchases; the effect is to dramatically change the company's capital structure while attempting to deliver a value to target shareholders in excess of a hostile bid.

Liabilities Amounts owed; the legal claims against a business or household by nonowners.

LIFO The last-in first-out accounting method of valuing inventories.

LIFO liquidation A reduction in the physical quantity of an inventory that is accounted for using the LIFO method. A LIFO liquidation usually produces a nonrecurring increase in earnings because the older costs associated with the liquidated units are lower than current inventory costs.

Likelihood The probability of an observation, given a particular set of conditions.

Limit down A limit move in the futures market in which the price at which a transaction would be made is at or below the lower limit.

Limit move A condition in the futures markets in which the price at which a transaction would be made is at or beyond the price limits.

Limit order An order to buy or sell a security at a specific price or better (lower for a buy order and higher for a sell order).

Limit up A limit move in the futures market in which the price at which a transaction would be made is at or above the upper limit.

Limited liability A legal concept whereby the responsibility, or liability, of the owners of a corporation is limited to the value of the shares in the firm that they own.

Limited partnership *Partnership* in which some partners have *limited liability* and general partners have unlimited liability.

Linear association A straight-line relationship, as opposed to a relationship that cannot be graphed as a straight line.

Linear interpolation   The estimation of an unknown value on the basis of two known values that bracket it, using a straight line between the two known values.

Linear regression   Regression that models the straight-line relationship between the dependent and independent variable(s).

Linear trend   A trend in which the dependent variable changes at a constant rate with time.

Liquid   Term used to describe an asset that can be quickly converted to cash at a price close to fair market value.

Liquid asset   Asset that is easily and cheaply turned into cash—notably cash itself and short-term securities.

Liquidating dividend   *Dividend* that represents a return of capital.

Liquidation   To sell the assets of a company, division, or subsidiary piecemeal, typically because of bankruptcy; the form of bankruptcy that allows for the orderly satisfaction of creditors' claims after which the company ceases to exist.

Liquidation value   The value of a company if the company were dissolved and its assets sold individually.

Liquidity   With reference to an entity, the ability to satisfy short-term obligations using assets that are most readily converted into cash; with reference to an asset, the degree to which the asset can be acquired or disposed of quickly without loss relative to its fair value.

Liquidity discount   A reduction or discount to value that reflects the lack of depth of trading or liquidity in that asset's market.

Liquidity preference theory   Theory that the forward rate exceeds expected future interest rates.

Liquidity premium   An extra return that compensates investors for the risk of loss relative to an investment's fair value if the investment needs to be converted to cash quickly.

Liquidity risk   The risk that a financial instrument cannot be purchased or sold without a significant concession in price due to the size of the market.

Locked limit   A condition in the futures markets in which a transaction cannot take place because the price would be beyond the limits.

Logit model   A qualitative-dependent-variable multiple regression model based on the logistic probability distribution.

Log-linear model   With reference to time-series models, a model in which the growth rate of the time series as a function of time is constant.

Log-log regression model   A regression that expresses the dependent and independent variables as natural logarithms.

London Interbank Offer Rate (LIBOR)   The Eurodollar rate at which London banks lend dollars to other London banks; considered to be the best representative rate on a dollar borrowed by a private, high-quality borrower.

Long   The buyer of an asset or derivative contract. Also refers to the position of owning an asset or derivative contract.

Longitudinal data   Observations on characteristic(s) of the same observational unit through time.

Long position   The buyer of a commodity or security or, for a forward contract, the counterparty who will be the eventual buyer of the underlying asset.

Long run   (1) The time period during which all factors of production can be varied. (2) A period of time in which the quantities of all resources can be varied.

Long-run average cost curve   The locus of points representing the minimum unit cost of producing any given rate of output, given current technology and resource prices.

Long-term equity anticipatory securities (LEAPS)   Options originally created with expirations of several years.

Look-ahead bias   Bias that may result from the use of information that was not available on the test date.

Lower bound   The lowest possible value.

LP   Linear programming.

Macaulay duration   The duration without dividing by 1 plus the bond's yield to maturity. The term, named for one of the economists who first derived it, is used to distinguish the calculation from modified duration. See also *modified duration.*

Macroeconomic factor   A factor related to the economy, such as the inflation rate, industrial production, or economic sector membership.

Macroeconomic factor model   A multifactor model in which the factors are surprises in macroeconomic variables that significantly explain equity returns.

Macroeconomics   The study of the behavior of the economy as a whole, including such economywide phenomena as changes in unemployment, the general price level, and national income.

MACRS   Modified accelerated cost recovery system.

Maintenance margin   The minimum margin that an investor must keep on deposit in a margin account at all times.

Maintenance margin requirement   The margin requirement on any day other than the first day of a transaction.

Management buyout (MBO)   A corporate transaction in which management repurchases all outstanding common stock, usually using the proceeds of debt issuance; a leveraged buyout (LBO) led by management.

Management fee The compensation an investment company pays to the investment management company for its services. The average annual fee is about 0.5 percent of fund assets.

Managerialism theories Theories that posit that corporate executives are motivated to engage in mergers to maximize the size of their company rather than shareholder value.

Margin or margin deposit The amount of money that a trader deposits in a margin account. The term is derived from the stock market practice in which an investor borrows a portion of the money required to purchase a certain amount of stock. In futures markets, there is no borrowing so the margin is more of a down payment or performance bond.

Margin account The collateral posted with the futures exchange clearinghouse by an outside counterparty to insure its eventual performance; the *initial* margin is the deposit required at contract origination while the *maintenance* margin is the minimum collateral necessary at all times.

Margin call A request by an investor's broker for additional capital for a security bought on margin if the investor's equity value declines below the required maintenance margin.

Marginal benefit The benefit that a person receives from consuming one more unit of a good or service. It is measured as the maximum amount that a person is willing to pay for one more unit of the good or service.

Marginal cost The opportunity cost of producing one more unit of a good or service; the change in total cost due to a one-unit increase in production.

Marginal cost pricing A system of pricing in which the price charged is equal to the opportunity cost to society of producing one more unit of the good or service in question. The opportunity cost is the marginal cost to society.

Marginal product The increase in total product that results from a one-unit increase in the variable input, with all other inputs remaining the same. It is calculated as the increase in total product divided by the increase in the variable input employed, when the quantities of all other inputs are constant.

Marginal revenue The change in total revenue that results from a one-unit increase in the quantity sold. It is calculated as the change in total revenue divided by the change in quantity sold.

Marginal tax rate The part of each additional dollar in income that is paid as tax.

Market All of the arrangements that individuals have for exchanging with one another. Thus, for example, we can speak of the labor market, the automobile market, and the credit market.

Market analysis With respect to investing, the analysis of a the current conditions of a financial market.

Market capitalization (market cap) The number of shares a company has outstanding times the price per share.

Market demand The demand of all consumers in the marketplace for a particular good or service. The summation at each price of the quantity demanded by each individual.

Market efficiency The subject dealing with the relationship of price to intrinsic value. The traditional efficient markets formulation asserts that an asset's price is the best available estimate of its intrinsic value. The rational efficient markets formulation asserts that investors should expect to be rewarded for the costs of information gathering and analysis by higher gross returns.

Market failure A state in which the market does not allocate resources efficiently.

Market impact With reference to execution costs, the difference between the actual execution price and the market price that would have prevailed had the manager not sought to trade the security.

Market maker An institution or individual quoting firm bid and ask prices for a security and standing ready to buy or sell the security at those quoted prices. Also called a *dealer*.

Market model (1) Model suggesting a linear relationship between actual returns on a stock and on the market portfolio. (2) A method that is used in event studies. Regression analysis is used to compute the return that is attributable to market forces. It is used to compute "excess returns" that may be attributable to the occurrence of an event.

Market order An order to buy or sell a security immediately at the best price available.

Market portfolio The portfolio that includes all risky assets with relative weights equal to their proportional market values.

Market power The ability to influence the market, and in particular the market price, by influencing the total quantity offered for sale.

Market price of risk The slope of the capital market line, indicating the market risk premium for each unit of market risk.

Market return The standard (typically the SP 500) against which stock portfolio performance can be measured.

Market risk (systematic risk) Risk that cannot be diversified away. In risk management, *market risk* refers to the risk associated with interest rates, exchange rates, and equity prices.

Market risk premium The expected excess return on the market over the risk-free rate.

Market share test The percentage of a market that a particular firm supplies, used as the primary measure of monopoly power.

Market timer An investor who speculates on broad market moves rather than on specific securities.

Market timing Trying to catch short-term market movements. Extremely difficult.

Market Value The current listed price at which investors buy or sell securities at a given time.

Market value added (MVA) External management performance measure to compare the market value of the company's debt and equity with the total capital invested in the firm.

Marketability discount A reduction or discount to value for shares that are not publicly traded.

Marking to market or mark to market The settlement process used to adjust the margin account of a futures contract for (traditionally) daily gains or losses. Also known as the *daily settlement* although some futures contracts are now marked to market more frequently than daily.

Markowitz decision rule A decision rule for choosing between two investments based on their means and variances.

Mature growth rate The earnings growth rate in a company's mature phase; an earnings growth rate that can be sustained long term.

Mature phase A stage of growth in which the company reaches an equilibrium in which investment opportunities on average just earn their opportunity cost of capital.

Maturity premium An extra return that compensates investors for the increased sensitivity of the market value of debt to a change in market interest rates as maturity is extended.

Maturity strategy A portfolio management strategy employed to reduce the interest rate risk of a bond portfolio by matching the maturity of the portfolio with its investment horizon. For example, if the investment horizon is 10 years, the portfolio manager would construct a portfolio that will mature in 10 years.

MBO Management buyout.

MDA Multiple-discriminant analysis.

Mean The sum of all values in a distribution or dataset, divided by the number of values summed; a synonym of arithmetic mean.

Mean absolute deviation With reference to a sample, the mean of the absolute values of deviations from the sample mean.

Mean excess return The average rate of return in excess of the risk-free rate.

Mean reversion The tendency of a time series to fall when its level is above its mean and rise when its level is below its mean; a mean-reverting time series tends to return to its long-term mean.

Mean–variance analysis An approach to portfolio analysis using expected means, variances, and covariances of asset returns.

Means of payment A method of settling a debt.

Measure of central tendency A quantitative measure that specifies where data are centered.

Measure of location A quantitative measure that describes the location or distribution of data; includes not only measures of central tendency but also other measures such as percentiles.

Measurement error Errors in measuring an explanatory variable in a regression that leads to biases in estimated parameters.

Measurement scales A scheme of measuring differences. The four types of measurement scales are nominal, ordinal, interval, and ratio.

Median The value of the middle item of a set of items that has been sorted into ascending or descending order; the 50th percentile.

Merger The absorption of one company by another; that is, two companies become one entity and one or both of the pre-merger companies ceases to exist as a separate entity.

Mesokurtic Describes a distribution with kurtosis identical to that of the normal distribution.

Method based on forecasted fundamentals An approach to using price multiples that relates a price multiple to forecasts of fundamentals through a discounted cash flow model.

Method of comparables An approach to valuation that involves using a price multiple to evaluate whether an asset is relatively fairly valued, relatively undervalued, or relatively overvalued when compared to a benchmark value of the multiple.

Microcap Refers to companies with a market capitalization in the $100 million to $300 million range.

Microeconomics The study of the choices that individuals and businesses make, the way those choices interact, and the influence governments exert on them.

Midcap Companies with a market capitalization in the $3 billion to $4 billion range.

Minimum-variance frontier The graph of the set of portfolios that have minimum variance for their level of expected return.

Minimum-variance portfolio The portfolio with the minimum variance for each given level of expected return.

Mispricing Any departure of the market price of an asset from the asset's estimated intrinsic value.

Mixed factor models Factor models that combine features of more than one type of factor model.

Mixed offering A merger or acquisition that is to be paid for with cash, securities, or some combination of the two.

Modal interval With reference to grouped data, the most frequently occurring interval.

Mode The most frequently occurring value in a set of observations.

Model risk The use of an inaccurate pricing model for a particular investment, or the improper use of the right model.

Model specification With reference to regression, the set of variables included in the regression and the regression equation's functional form.

Modern portfolio theory (MPT) Principles underlying analysis and evaluation of rational portfolio choices based on risk-return trade-offs and efficient diversification.

Modified accelerated cost recovery system (MACRS) Schedule of *depreciation* deductions allowed for tax purposes.

Modified duration Measure of a bond's price sensitivity to interest rate movements. Equal to the duration of a bond divided by one plus its yield to maturity.

Molodovsky effect The observation that P/Es tend to be high on depressed EPS at the bottom of a business cycle, and tend to be low on unusually high EPS at the top of a business cycle.

Momentum indicators Valuation indicators that relate either price or a fundamental (such as earnings) to the time series of their own past values (or in some cases to their expected value).

Monetarists Macroeconomists who believe that inflation in the long run is always caused by excessive monetary growth and that changes in the money supply affect aggregate demand both directly and indirectly.

Monetary policy The Fed conducts the nation's monetary policy by changing interest rates and adjusting the quantity of money.

Money Any medium that is universally accepted in an economy both by sellers of goods and services as payment for those goods and services and by creditors as payment for debts.

Money illusion Reacting to changes in money prices rather than relative prices. If a worker whose wages double when the price level also doubles thinks he or she is better off, that worker is suffering from money illusion.

Money market The market for short-term debt instruments (one-year maturity or less).

Money market yield (or CD equivalent yield) A yield on a basis comparable to the quoted yield on an interest-bearing money market instrument that pays interest on a 360-day basis; the annualized holding period yield, assuming a 360-day year.

Money supply The amount of money in circulation.

Moneyness The relationship between the price of the underlying and an option's exercise price.

Money-weighted rate of return The internal rate of return on a portfolio, taking account of all cash flows.

Monitoring costs Costs borne by owners to monitor the management of the company (e.g., board of director expenses).

Monopolist The single supplier of a good or service for which there is no close substitute. The monopolist therefore constitutes its entire industry.

Monopolization The possession of monopoly power in the relevant market and the willful acquisition or maintenance of that power, as distinguished from growth or development as a consequence of a superior product, business acumen, or historical accident.

Monopoly A market structure in which there is one firm, which produces a good or service that has no close substitute and in which the firm is protected from competition by a barrier preventing the entry of new firms.

Monte Carlo simulation method A methodology using a computer to generate random outcomes according to specified probability models to find approximate solutions to complex problems.

Mortgage-backed security Ownership claim in a pool of mortgages or an obligation that is secured by such a pool. Also called a *pass-through*, because payments are passed along from the mortgage originator to the purchaser of the mortgage-backed security.

Moving average The continually recalculating average of security prices for a period, often 200 days, to serve as an indication of the general trend of prices and also as a benchmark price.

Multicollinearity A regression assumption violation that occurs when two or more independent variables (or combinations of independent variables) are highly but not perfectly correlated with each other.

Multifactor model Model of security returns positing that returns respond to multiple systematic factors.

Multiple Short for price-earnings multiple.

Multiple linear regression Linear regression involving two or more independent variables.

Multiple linear regression model A linear regression model with two or more independent variables.

Multiple R The correlation between the actual and forecasted values of the dependent variable in a regression.

Multiplication rule for probabilities The rule that the joint probability of events A and B equals the probability of A given B times the probability of B.

Multiplier The amount by which a change in autonomous expenditure is magnified or multiplied to determine the change in equilibrium expenditure and real GDP.

Multivariate distribution A probability distribution that specifies the probabilities for a group of related random variables.

Multivariate normal distribution A probability distribution for a group of random variables that is completely defined by the means and variances of the variables plus all the correlations between pairs of the variables.

Municipal bonds Tax-exempt bonds issued by state and local governments, generally to finance capital improvement projects. General obligation bonds are backed by the general taxing power of the issuer. Revenue bonds are backed by the proceeds from the project or agency they are issued to finance.

Mutual fund An investment company that pools money from shareholders and invests in a variety of securities, including stocks, bonds, and money market securities. A mutual fund ordinarily stands ready to buy back (redeem) its shares at their current net asset value, which depends on the market value of the fund's portfolio of securities at the time. Mutual funds generally continuously offer new shares to investors.

Mutually exclusive events Events such that only one can occur at a time.

Mutually exclusive projects Mutually exclusive projects compete directly with each other. For example, if Projects A and B are mutually exclusive, you can choose A or B, but you cannot choose both.

n Factorial For a positive integer n, the product of the first n positive integers; 0 factorial equals 1 by definition. n factorial is written as $n!$.

NASDAQ National Association of Securities Dealers Automated Quotations. It is the trading system for the over-the-counter market.

Nash equilibrium The outcome of a game that occurs when player A takes the best possible action given the action of player B and player B takes the best possible action given the action of player A.

National income (NI) The total of all factor payments to resource owners.

Natural monopoly A monopoly that arises from the peculiar production characteristics in an industry. It usually arises when there are large economies of scale relative to the industry's demand such that one firm can produce at a lower average cost than can be achieved by multiple firms.

Negative relationship A relationship between variables that move in opposite directions.

Negative serial correlation Serial correlation in which a positive error for one observation increases the chance of a negative error for another observation, and vice versa.

Neoclassical growth theory A theory of economic growth that proposes that real GDP grows because technological change induces a level of saving and investment that makes capital per hour of labor grow.

Net asset value (NAV) (1) The market value of the assets owned by a fund. (2) The value of each share expressed as assets minus liabilities on a per-share basis.

Net borrower A country that is borrowing more from the rest of the world than it is lending to it.

Net capital expenditures Gross capital expenditures minus proceeds from the disposal of productive assets.

Net debt Total debt minus cash on hand.

Net exports The value of exports minus the value of imports.

Net income plus depreciation Often referred to as traditional cash flow, its calculation removes an important noncash expense from net income.

Net investment Net increase in the capital stock-gross investment minus depreciation.

Net lender A country that is lending more to the rest of the world than it is borrowing from it.

Net operating profit less adjusted taxes (NOPLAT) A company's operating profit with adjustments to normalize the effects of capital structure.

Net present value (NPV) The present value of an investment's cash inflows (benefits) minus the present value of its cash outflows (costs).

Net public debt Gross public debt minus all government interagency borrowing.

Netting When parties agree to exchange only the net amount owed from one party to the other.

Network effect A situation in which a consumer's willingness to purchase a good or service is influenced by how many others also buy the item.

Net working capital Current assets minus current liabilities.

Net worth   (1) The difference between assets and liabilities. (2) Book value of a company's *common stock,* surplus, and *retained earnings.*

New growth theory   A theory of economic growth based on the idea that real GDP per person grows because of the choices that people make in the pursuit of ever greater profit and that growth can persist indefinitely.

New issue   Common stocks or bonds offered by companies for public sale.

Node   Each value on a binomial tree from which successive moves or outcomes branch.

No-growth company   A company without positive expected net present value projects.

No-growth value per share   The value per share of a no-growth company, equal to the expected level amount of earnings divided by the stock's required rate of return.

Nominal GDP   The value of the final goods and services produced in a given year valued at the prices that prevailed in that same year. It is a more precise name for GDP.

Nominal interest rate   The interest rate in terms of nominal (not adjusted for purchasing power) dollars.

Nominal risk-free interest rate   The sum of the real risk-free interest rate and the inflation premium.

Nominal scale   A measurement scale that categorizes data but does not rank them.

Nominal values   The values of variables such as GDP and investment expressed in current dollars, also called money values; measurement in terms of the actual market prices at which goods and services are sold.

Nominal yield   A bond's yield as measured by its coupon rate.

Noncontrolling interest   Generally, minority interest. However, the term is used to reflect a minority shareholder interest when the definition of control is extended beyond a simple majority share ownership interest. Any interest in an entity besides that of a controlling shareholder.

Nonconventional cash flow   In a nonconventional cash flow pattern, the initial outflow is not followed by inflows only, but the cash flows can flip from positive (inflows) to negative (outflows) again (or even change signs several times).

Nondeliverable forwards (NDFs)   Cash-settled forward contracts, used predominately with respect to foreign exchange forwards.

Nondiversifiable risk   See *systematic risk.*

Nonlinear relation   An association or relationship between variables that cannot be graphed as a straight line.

Nonparametric test   A test that is not concerned with a parameter, or that makes minimal assumptions about the population from which a sample comes.

Nonrecurring cash flow   Operating cash flow that appears infrequently or that may appear with some regularity but is very irregular in amount. In addition, even though included in operating cash flow, nonrecurring cash flow often is not closely tied to the core operating activities of the firm.

Nonstationarity   With reference to a random variable, the property of having characteristics such as mean and variance that are not constant through time.

Nonsystematic risk   Nonmarket or firm-specific risk factors that can be eliminated by diversification. Also called *unique risk* or *diversifiable risk.* Systematic risk refers to risk factors common to the entire economy.

Nontariff barrier   Any action other than a tariff that restricts international trade.

Normal backwardation   The condition in futures markets in which futures prices are lower than expected spot prices.

Normal contango   The condition in futures markets in which futures prices are higher than expected spot prices.

Normal distribution   A continuous, symmetric probability distribution that is completely described by its mean and its variance.

Normal rate of return   The amount that must be paid to an investor to induce investment in a business; also known as the *opportunity cost of capital.*

Normalized (or normal) earnings per share   The earnings per share that a business could achieve currently under mid-cyclical conditions.

North American Free Trade Agreement   An agreement, which became effective on January 1, 1994, to eliminate all barriers to international trade between the United States, Canada, and Mexico after a 15-year phasing in period.

Note   Unsecured debt with a maturity of up to 10 years.

Notes payable   Promissory notes that are evidence of a debt and state the terms of interest and principal payment.

Notional principal   (1) Principal amount used to calculate swap payments. (2) The principal value of a swap transaction, which is not exchanged but is used as a scale factor to translate interest rate differentials into cash settlement payments.

***n*-Period moving average**   The average of the current and immediately prior $n-1$ values of a time series.

NPV   Net present value.

NPV rule   An investment decision rule that states that an investment should be undertaken if its NPV is positive but not undertaken if its NPV is negative.

Null hypothesis   The hypothesis to be tested.

NYSE   New York Stock Exchange.

Objective probabilities   Probabilities that generally do not vary from person to person; includes a priori and objective probabilities.

Objectives   In investments, the investor's goals expressed in terms of risk and return and included in the policy statement.

Off-balance-sheet financing   Financing that is not shown as a liability in a company's balance sheet.

Offer price   The price at which a market maker is willing to sell a security (also called *ask price*).

Official reserves   The amount of reserves owned by the central bank of a government in the form of gold, Special Drawing Rights, and foreign cash or marketable securities.

Official settlements account   A record of the change in a country's official reserves.

Off-market forward rate agreement (off-market FRA)   A contract in which the initial value is intentionally set at a value other than zero and therefore requires a cash payment at the start from one party to the other.

Offsetting   A transaction in exchange-listed derivative markets in which a party re-enters the market to close out a position.

One third rule   The rule that, with no change in technology, a 1 percent increase in capital per hour of labor brings, on the average, a one third of 1 percent increase in real GDP per hour of labor.

One-sided hypothesis test (or one-tailed hypothesis test)   A test in which the null hypothesis is rejected only if the evidence indicates that the population parameter is greater than (smaller than) θ_0. The alternative hypothesis also has one side.

Open-end fund   An investment company that continuously offers to sell new shares, or redeem them, at prices based on the market value of the assets owned by the fund (net asset value).

Operating breakeven   The number of units produced and sold at which the company's operating profit is zero (revenues = operating costs).

Operating cash flow   Cash flow from operating activities computed in accordance with generally accepted accounting principles.

Operating earnings   An earnings measure that excludes selected items of nonrecurring gain, revenue, loss, and expense. This is not a GAAP measure, and its determination may vary widely among different companies.

Operating income   See *operating profit.*

Operating lease   A lease that does not transfer the risks and rewards of ownership to the lessee. Operating lease payments are expensed as incurred.

Operating profit   Core pretax profit from central operations calculated as revenue minus cost of goods sold, selling, general and administrative expense, and research and development expense.

Operating risk   The risk attributed to the operating cost structure, in particular the use of fixed costs in operations; the risk arising from the mix of fixed and variable costs; the risk that a company's operations may be severely affected by environmental, social, and governance risk factors.

Operating working capital   Current assets, including operating receivables, inventory, and prepaid expenses, that are used in operations minus current liabilities, including operating payables and accrued expenses payable that are incurred in operations.

Operations risk or operational risk   The risk of loss from failures in a company's systems and procedures (for example, due to computer failures or human failures) or events completely outside of the control of organizations (which would include "acts of God" and terrorist actions).

Opportunity cost   The alternative return that investors forgo by choosing a particular course of action; the value of something in its best alternative use.

Opportunity cost of capital   The normal rate of return, or the available return on the next-best alternative investment. Economists consider this a cost of production, and it is included in our cost examples.

Opportunity set   The set of assets available for investment.

Optimal capital structure   The capital structure at which the value of the company is maximized.

Optimal portfolio   The portfolio on the efficient frontier that has the highest utility for a given investor. It lies at the point of tangency between the efficient frontier and the curve with the investor's highest possible utility.

Optimal risky portfolio   An investor's best combination of risky assets to be mixed with safe assets to form the complete portfolio.

Optimizer   A specialized computer program or a spreadsheet that solves for the portfolio weights that will result in the lowest risk for a specified level of expected return.

Option   A financial instrument that gives one party the right, but not the obligation, to buy (for a call option) or sell (for a put option) an underlying asset from or to another party at a fixed price over a specific period of time.

Option-adjusted spread A type of yield spread that considers changes in the term structure and alternative estimates of the volatility of interest rates. It is spread after adjusting for embedded options.

Option contract An agreement that grants the owner the right, but not the obligation, to make a future transaction in an underlying commodity or security at a fixed price and within a predetermined time in the future.

Option delta Hedge ratio.

Option price, option premium, or premium The amount of money a buyer pays and seller receives to engage in an option transaction.

Options Clearing Corporation (OCC) A company designed to guarantee, monitor margin accounts, and settle exchange-traded option transactions.

Order-driven market A market without active market makers in which buy-and-sell orders directly confront each other; an auction market.

Ordinal scale A measurement scale that sorts data into categories that are ordered (ranked) with respect to some characteristic.

Ordinary annuity An annuity with a first cash flow that is paid one period from the present.

Ordinary least squares (OLS) An estimation method based on the criterion of minimizing the sum of the squared residuals of a regression.

Organic growth Company growth in output or sales that is achieved by making investments internally (i.e., excludes growth achieved through mergers and acquisitions).

Origin The intersection of the *y* axis and the *x* axis in a graph.

Orthogonal Uncorrelated; at a right angle.

OTC Over-the-counter.

Other comprehensive income Changes to equity that bypass (are not reported in) the income statement; the difference between comprehensive income and net income.

Outcome A possible value of a random variable.

Outliers Small numbers of observations at either extreme (small or large) of a sample.

Out-of-sample forecast errors The differences between actual and predicted value of time series outside the sample period used to fit the model.

Out-of-sample test A test of a strategy or model using a sample outside the time period on which the strategy or model was developed.

Out-of-the-money Said of options that, if exercised, would require the payment of more money than the value received and therefore would not be currently exercised.

Overnight A deal from today to the next business day.

Overnight index swap (OIS) A swap in which the floating rate is the cumulative value of a single unit of currency invested at an overnight rate during the settlement period.

Over-the-counter (OTC) Informal market that does not involve a securities exchange. Specifically used to refer to the Nasdaq dealer market for *common stocks*.

Overweighted A condition in which a portfolio, for whatever reason, includes more of a class of securities than the relative market value alone would justify.

P/E ratio Share price divided by earnings per share.

Paid-In Capital (Private Equity) The amount of committed capital a limited partner has actually transferred to a venture fund. Also known as the *cumulative drawdown amount.*

Paired comparisons test A statistical test for differences based on paired observations drawn from samples that are dependent on each other.

Paired observations Observations that are dependent on each other.

Pairs arbitrage trade A trade in two closely related stocks that involves buying the relatively undervalued stock and selling short the relatively overvalued stock.

Panel data Observations through time on a single characteristic of multiple observational units.

Par value (1) The principal amount repaid at maturity of a bond. Also called *face value.* (2) The officially determined value of a currency.

Par yield curve The yield curve drawn for government coupon bonds of different maturities that trade at, or around, par.

Parameter A descriptive measure computed from or used to describe a population of data, conventionally represented by Greek letters.

Parameter instability The problem or issue of population regression parameters that have changed over time.

Parametric test Any test (or procedure) concerned with parameters or whose validity depends on assumptions concerning the population generating the sample.

Partial regression coefficients or partial slope coefficients The slope coefficients in a multiple regression.

Partnership A business owned by two or more joint owners, or partners, who share the responsibilities and the profits of the firm and are individually liable for all the debts of the partnership.

Passive investment strategy See *passive management.*

Passive management Buying a well-diversified portfolio to represent a broad-based market index without attempting to search out mis-priced securities.

Passive portfolio   A market index portfolio.

Passive strategy   See *passive management*.

Pass-through securities   *Notes* or *bonds* backed by a package of assets such as home mortgage loans.

Patent   A government-sanctioned exclusive right granted to the inventor of a good, service, or productive process to produce, use, and sell the invention for a given number of years.

Payables   Accounts payable.

Payback   The time required for the added income from the convertible security relative to the stock to offset the conversion premium.

Payer swaption   A swaption that allows the holder to enter into a swap as the fixed-rate payer and floating-rate receiver.

Payment date   The day that the company actually mails out (or electronically transfers) a dividend payment.

Payment netting   A means of settling payments in which the amount owed by the first party to the second is netted with the amount owed by the second party to the first; only the net difference is paid.

Payoff   The value of an option at expiration.

Payout ratio   The percentage of total earnings paid out in dividends in any given year (in per-share terms, DPS/EPS).

Peak   The point at which a business cycle turns from expansion into recession.

Pecking order theory   The theory that managers take into account how their actions might be interpreted by outsiders and thus order their preferences for various forms of corporate financing. Forms of financing that are least visible to outsiders (e.g., internally generated funds) are most preferable to managers and those that are most visible (e.g., equity) are least preferable.

Peer group comparison   A method of measuring portfolio performance by collecting the returns produced by a representative universe of investors over a specific period of time.

PEG   The P/E-to-growth ratio, calculated as the stock's P/E divided by the expected earnings growth rate.

Per capita   Latin, meaning "by the head." Distributing to "issue per capita" means to distribute trust property to persons who take, in their own right, an equal portion of the property.

Per unit contribution margin   The amount that each unit sold contributes to covering fixed costs—that is, the difference between the price per unit and the variable cost per unit.

Percentiles   Quantiles that divide a distribution into 100 equal parts.

Perfect collinearity   The existence of an exact linear relation between two or more independent variables or combinations of independent variables.

Perfect competition   An industry structure characterized by certain conditions, including many buyers and sellers, homogeneous products, perfect information, easy entry and exit, and no barriers to entry. The existence of these conditions implies that each seller is a price taker.

Performance appraisal   The evaluation of risk-adjusted performance; the evaluation of investment skill.

Performance attribution   The attribution of investment performance to specific investment decisions (such as asset allocation and country weighting).

Performance guarantee   A guarantee from the clearinghouse that if one party makes money on a transaction, the clearinghouse ensures it will be paid.

Performance measurement   The calculation of returns in a logical and consistent manner.

Periodic rate   The quoted interest rate per period; the stated annual interest rate divided by the number of compounding periods per year.

Permutation   An ordered listing.

Perpetuity   A perpetual annuity, or a set of never-ending level sequential cash flows, with the first cash flow occurring one period from now; a stream of level payments extending to infinity.

Personal income (PI)   The amount of income that households actually receive before they pay personal income taxes.

Personal trust   An amount of money set aside by a grantor and often managed by a third party, the trustee. Often constructed so one party receives income from the trust's investments and another party receives the residual value of the trust after the income beneficiaries' death.

Pet projects   Projects in which influential managers want the corporation to invest. Often, unfortunately, pet projects are selected without undergoing normal capital budgeting analysis.

Physical capital   All manufactured resources, including buildings, equipment, machines, and improvements to land that is used for production.

PIK   Pay-in-kind bond.

Plain-vanilla   Refers to a security, especially a bond or a swap, issued with standard features. Sometimes called *generic*.

Plain vanilla swap   An interest rate swap in which one party pays a fixed rate and the other pays a floating rate, with both sets of payments in the same currency.

Platykurtic Describes a distribution that is less peaked than the normal distribution.

Point One percent (1%).

Point estimate A single numerical estimate of an unknown quantity, such as a population parameter.

Poison pill A pre-offer takeover defense mechanism that makes it prohibitively costly for an acquirer to take control of a target without the prior approval of the target's board of directors.

Poison puts A pre-offer takeover defense mechanism that gives target company bondholders the right to sell their bonds back to the target at a prespecified redemption price, typically at or above par value; this defense increases the need for cash and raises the cost of the acquisition.

Policy statement A statement in which the investor specifies investment goals, constraints, and risk preferences.

Political risk Possibility of the expropriation of assets, changes in tax policy, restrictions on the exchange of foreign currency for domestic currency, or other changes in the business climate of a country.

Pooling of interest Method of accounting for *mergers* (no longer available in the US). The consolidated balance sheet of the merged firm is obtained by combining the balance sheets of the separate firms (cf. *purchase accounting*).

Population All members of a specified group.

Population mean The arithmetic mean value of a population; the arithmetic mean of all the observations or values in the population.

Population standard deviation A measure of dispersion relating to a population in the same unit of measurement as the observations, calculated as the positive square root of the population variance.

Population variance A measure of dispersion relating to a population, calculated as the mean of the squared deviations around the population mean.

Portfolio A group of investments. Ideally, the investments should have different patterns of returns over time.

Portfolio implementation problem The part of the execution step of the portfolio management process that involves the implementation of portfolio decisions by trading desks.

Portfolio investment The purchase of less than 10 percent of the shares of ownership in a company in another nation.

Portfolio management Process of combining securities in a portfolio tailored to the investor's prefer-

ences and needs, monitoring that portfolio, and evaluating its performance.

Portfolio performance attribution The analysis of portfolio performance in terms of the contributions from various sources of risk.

Portfolio possibilities curve A graphical representation of the expected return and risk of all portfolios that can be formed using two assets.

Portfolio selection/composition problem The part of the execution step of the portfolio management process in which investment strategies are integrated with expectations to select a portfolio of assets.

Position trader A trader who typically holds positions open overnight.

Positive market feedback A tendency for a good or service to come into favor with additional consumers because other consumers have chosen to buy the item.

Positive relationship A relationship between two variables that move in the same direction.

Positive serial correlation Serial correlation in which a positive error for one observation increases the chance of a positive error for another observation, and a negative error for one observation increases the chance of a negative error for another observation.

Posterior probability An updated probability that reflects or comes after new information.

Potential credit risk The risk associated with the possibility that a payment due at a later date will not be made.

Power of a test The probability of correctly rejecting the null—that is, rejecting the null hypothesis when it is false.

Preferences A description of a person's likes and dislikes.

Preferred habitat theory Holds that investors prefer specific maturity ranges but can be induced to switch if risk premiums are sufficient.

Preferred stock A class of stock with priority rights, both as to dividends and in liquidation, over the common stock of the same company. Corporations pay a much lower income tax on dividends from their investments in other corporations (where it has already been taxed) than on direct business earnings. Preferred stock is usually priced at the level that makes it attractive to a corporation, taking account of this tax exemption, and as a result is rarely tax-efficient for individuals.

Pre-investing The strategy of using futures contracts to enter the market without an immediate outlay of cash.

Premium (1) A bond selling at a price above par value due to capital market conditions. (2) The purchase price of an option.

Present value (PV) The current (discounted) value of a future cash flow or flows.

Present (price) value of a basis point (PVBP) The change in the bond price for a 1 basis point change in yield. Also called *basis point value* (BPV).

Present value model or discounted cash flow model A model of intrinsic value that views the value of an asset as the present value of the asset's expected future cash flows.

Present value of growth opportunities (or value of growth) The difference between the actual value per share and the no-growth value per share.

Price controls Government-mandated minimum or maximum prices that may be charged for goods and services.

Price discovery A feature of futures markets in which futures prices provide valuable information about the price of the underlying asset.

Price discrimination Selling a given product at more than one price, with the price difference being unrelated to differences in cost.

Price-driven market A market in which dealers (market makers) adjust their quotes continuously to reflect supply and demand; also known as a *dealer market*.

Price–earnings multiple See *price–earnings ratio*.

Price–earnings ratio The ratio of a stock's price to its earnings per share. Also referred to as the *P/E multiple*.

Price effect The effect of a change in the price on the quantity of a good consumed, other things remaining the same.

Price level The average level of prices as measured by a price index.

Price limits Limits imposed by a futures exchange on the price change that can occur from one day to the next.

Price momentum A valuation indicator based on past price movement.

Price multiple The ratio of a stock's market price to some measure of value per share.

Price relative A ratio of an ending price over a beginning price; it is equal to 1 plus the holding period return on the asset.

Price risk The component of interest rate risk due to the uncertainty of the market price of a bond caused by changes in market interest rates.

Price-setting option The operational flexibility to adjust prices when demand varies from forecast. For example, when demand exceeds capacity, the company could benefit from the excess demand by increasing prices.

Price war A pricing campaign designed to capture additional market share by repeatedly cutting prices.

Priced risk Risk that investors require an additional return for bearing.

Primary market The market in which newly issued securities are sold by their issuers, who receive the proceeds.

Prime rate Benchmark lending rate set by U.S. banks.

Principal The amount of funds originally invested in a project or instrument; the face value to be paid at maturity.

Principal-agent problem The problem of devising compensation rules that induce an agent to act in the best interest of a principal.

Principal trade A trade through a broker who guarantees full execution at specified discount/premium to the prevailing price.

Prior probabilities Probabilities reflecting beliefs prior to the arrival of new information.

Private equity *Equity* that is not publicly traded and that is used to finance business start-ups, *leveraged buy-outs,* etc.

Private placement A new issue sold directly to a small group of investors, usually institutions.

Private sector surplus or deficit An amount equal to saving minus investment.

Private trusts A term used to identify trusts created by individuals for individuals, either during life or under will.

Pro forma Projected.

Probability A number between 0 and 1 describing the chance that a stated event will occur.

Probability density function A function with non-negative values such that probability can be described by areas under the curve graphing the function.

Probability distribution A distribution that specifies the probabilities of a random variable's possible outcomes.

Probability function A function that specifies the probability that the random variable takes on a specific value.

Probit model A qualitative-dependent-variable multiple regression model based on the normal distribution.

Producer Price Index (PPI) A statistical measure of a weighted average of prices of goods and services that firms produce and sell.

Product differentiation The distinguishing of products by brand name, color, and other minor attributes. Product differentiation occurs in other than perfectly competitive markets in which products are, in theory, homogeneous, such as wheat or corn.

Production Any activity that results in the conversion of resources into products that can be used in consumption.

Production-flexibility The operational flexibility to alter production when demand varies from forecast. For example, if demand is strong, a company may profit from employees working overtime or from adding additional shifts.

Productivity curve A relationship that shows how real GDP per hour of labor changes as the amount of capital per hour of labor changes with a given state of technology.

Productivity growth slowdown A slowdown in the growth rate of output per person.

Profit The income earned by business.

Profit margin or Net profit margin Net income divided by sales.

Profitability index Ratio of a project's *NPV* to the initial investment.

Pro-forma earnings A measure of earnings performance that selectively excludes nonrecurring as well as some noncash items.

Program trading Coordinated buy orders and sell orders of entire portfolios, usually with the aid of computers, often to achieve index arbitrage objectives.

Project sequencing To defer the decision to invest in a future project until the outcome of some or all of a current project is known. Projects are sequenced through time, so that investing in a project creates the option to invest in future projects.

Property rights Social arrangements that govern the ownership, use, and disposal of resources or factors of production, goods, and services that are enforceable in the courts.

Proprietorship A business owned by one individual who makes the business decisions, receives all the profits, and is legally responsible for the debts of the firm.

Prospectus Summary of the *registration* statement providing information on an issue of securities.

Protective put An option strategy in which a long position in an asset is combined with a long position in a put.

Proxy An instrument empowering an agent to vote in the name of the shareholder.

Proxy fight or proxy contest An attempt to take control of a company through a shareholder vote.

Proxy statement A public document that provides the material facts concerning matters on which shareholders will vote.

Proxy vote Vote cast by one person on behalf of another.

Prudent investor rule An investment manager must act in accord with the actions of a hypothetical prudent investor.

Pseudo-random numbers Numbers produced by random number generators.

Public good A good or service that is both nonrival and nonexcludable—it can be consumed simultaneously by everyone and from which no one can be excluded.

Purchase accounting Method of accounting for *mergers*. The assets of the acquired firm are shown at market value on the balance sheet of the acquirer (cf. *pooling of interest*).

Purchased in-process research and development costs Costs of research and development in progress at an acquired company; often, part of the purchase price of an acquired company is allocated to such costs.

Purchasing power The value of money for buying goods and services. If your money income stays the same but the price of one good that you are buying goes up, your effective purchasing power falls, and vice versa.

Purchasing power parity (PPP) A theory stating that the exchange rate between two currencies will exactly reflect the purchasing power of the two currencies.

Pure discount instruments Instruments that pay interest as the difference between the amount borrowed and the amount paid back.

Pure factor portfolio A portfolio with sensitivity of 1 to the factor in question and a sensitivity of 0 to all other factors.

Put An option that gives the holder the right to sell an underlying asset to another party at a fixed price over a specific period of time.

Put–call parity An equation expressing the equivalence (parity) of a portfolio of a call and a bond with a portfolio of a put and the underlying, which leads to the relationship between put and call prices.

Put–call–forward parity The relationship among puts, calls, and forward contracts.

Put option A contract that gives its holder the right to sell an asset, typically a financial instrument, at a specified price through a specified date.

_p_-Value The smallest level of significance at which the null hypothesis can be rejected; also called the marginal significance level.

Pyramiding Controlling additional property through reinvestment, refinancing, and exchanging.

_q_ Ratio of the market value of an asset to its replacement cost.

Qualified Institutional buyers (QIBs) Institutions that are allowed to trade unregistered stock among themselves.

Qualitative dependent variables Dummy variables used as dependent variables rather than as independent variables.

Quality of earnings The realism and conservatism of the earnings number and the extent to which we might expect the reported level of earnings to be sustained.

Quality of earnings analysis The investigation of issues relating to the accuracy of reported accounting results as reflections of economic performance; quality of earnings analysis is broadly understood to include not only earnings management, but also balance sheet management.

Quantile (or fractile) A value at or below which a stated fraction of the data lies.

Quartiles Quantiles that divide a distribution into four equal parts.

Quick ratio A measure of liquidity similar to the current ratio except for exclusion of inventories (cash plus receivables divided by current liabilities).

Quintiles Quantiles that divide a distribution into five equal parts.

Quota A quantitative restriction on the import of a particular good, which specifies the maximum amount that can be imported in a given time period.

Random number An observation drawn from a uniform distribution.

Random number generator An algorithm that produces uniformly distributed random numbers between 0 and 1.

Random variable A quantity whose future outcomes are uncertain.

Random walk A time series in which the value of the series in one period is the value of the series in the previous period plus an unpredictable random error.

Range The difference between the maximum and minimum values in a dataset.

Rate of return The future financial benefit to making a current investment.

Ratio scales A measurement scale that has all the characteristics of interval measurement scales as well as a true zero point as the origin.

Ratio spread An option strategy in which a long position in a certain number of options is offset by a short position in a certain number of other options on the same underlying, resulting in a risk-free position.

Rational efficient markets formulation See "Market efficiency."

Rational expectation The most accurate forecast possible, a forecast that uses all the available information, including knowledge of the relevant eco-nomic forces that influence the variable being forecasted.

Real assets Tangible assets and intangible assets used to carry on business (cf. financial assets).

Real Estate Traditionally, land and any structures permanently attached to the land.

Real exchange rate The exchange rate adjusted by the inflation differential between the two countries.

Real foreign currency risk The risk that real prices of consumption goods might not be identical in different countries. Also known as *real exchange rate risk*, or *purchasing power risk*.

Real gross domestic product (real GDP) The value of final goods and services produced in a given year when valued at constant prices.

Real income A household's income expressed as a quantity of goods that the household can afford to buy.

Real interest rate The nominal interest rate adjusted for inflation; the nominal interest rate minus the inflation rate.

Real options Options embedded in a firm's real assets that give managers valuable decision-making flexibility, such as the right to undertake, abandon, modify or postpone an investment project.

Real rate of interest The nominal rate of interest minus the anticipated rate of inflation.

Real risk-free interest rate The single-period interest rate for a completely risk-free security if no infla-tion were expected.

Real values Measurement of economic values after adjustments have been made for changes in the average of prices between years.

Real wage rate The quantity of goods and services that an hour's work can buy. It is equal to the money wage rate divided by the price level.

Realized capital gains Capital gains that result when an appreciated asset is sold; realized capital gains are taxable.

Rebalancing Realigning the proportions of assets in a portfolio as needed.

Recapture premium Provision for a return of invest-ment, net of value appreciation.

Receivables Accounts receivable.

Receiver A bankruptcy practitioner appointed by secured creditors in the United Kingdom to over-see the repayment of debts.

Receiver swaption A swaption that allows the holder to enter into a swap as the fixed-rate receiver and floating-rate payer.

Recession There are two common definitions of recession. They are: (1) A business cycle phase in which real GDP decreases for at least two successive quarters. (2) A significant decline in activity spread across the economy, lasting for more than a few months, visible in industrial production, employment, real income, and wholesale-retail trade.

Reclassification adjustment An adjustment to reported operating cash flow that moves a cash flow item from one classification to another, such as from operating cash flow to investing cash flow or from financing cash flow to operating cash flow. An example would be the reclassification of a tax benefit from stock options from operating cash flow to financing cash flow. The goal of these reclassifications is to produce a more sustainable measure of operating cash flow.

Record date Date set by directors when making dividend payment. *Dividends* are sent to stockholders who are registered on the record date.

Recycling The reuse of raw materials derived from manufactured products.

Regime With reference to a time series, the underlying model generating the times series.

Registration Process of obtaining *SEC* approval for a public issue of securities.

Registration statement Required to be filed with the SEC to describe the issue of a new security.

Regression analysis In statistics, a technique for finding the line of best fit.

Regression coefficients The intercept and slope coefficient(s) of a regression.

Regression equation An equation that describes the average relatinship between a dependent variable and a set of explanatory variables.

Regular dividend *Dividend* that the company expects to maintain in the future.

Regulation Rules administrated by a government agency to influence economic activity by determining prices, product standards and types, and conditions under which new firms may enter an industry.

Regulatory risk The risk associated with the uncertainty of how derivative transactions will be regulated or with changes in regulations.

Reinvestment Profits (or depreciation reserves) used to purchase new capital equipment.

Rejection point (or critical value) A value against which a computed test statistic is compared to decide whether to reject or not reject the null hypothesis.

Relative dispersion The amount of dispersion relative to a reference value or benchmark.

Relative frequency With reference to an interval of grouped data, the number of observations in the interval divided by the total number of observations in the sample.

Relative price The ratio of the price of one good or service to the price of another good or service. A relative price is an opportunity cost.

Relative return A portfolio's return compared with its benchmark.

Relative strength (RSTR) indicators Valuation indicators that compare a stock's performance during a period either to its own past performance or to the performance of some group of stocks.

Relative valuation models A model that specifies an asset's value relative to the value of another asset.

Remainder The trust corpus existing at the termination of the life beneficiary's interest.

Rent seeking Any attempt to capture a consumer surplus, a producer surplus, or an economic profit.

Reorganization Agreements made by a company in bankruptcy under which a company's capital structure is altered and/or alternative arrangements are made for debt repayment; U.S. Chapter 11 bankruptcy. The company emerges from bankruptcy as a going concern.

Replacement cost Cost to replace a firm's assets. "Reproduction" cost.

Replacement value With reference to swaps, the market value of a swap.

Repo See *repurchase agreement.*

Reported operating cash flow Cash flow from operating activities computed in accordance with generally accepted accounting principles. Also see *operating cash flow.*

Repurchase agreement (RP, repo, buy-back) Purchase of Treasury securities from a securities dealer with an agreement that the dealer will repurchase them at a specified price.

Reputational risk The risk that a company will suffer an extended diminution in market value relative to other companies in the same industry due to a demonstrated lack of concern for environmental, social, and governance risk factors.

Required rate of return The minimum rate of return required by an investor to invest in an asset, given the asset's riskiness.

Reserves (1) Cash in a bank's vault plus the bank's deposits at Federal Reserve banks. (2) The fixed-income component of a portfolio, notably shorter-term highly liquid instruments.

Residual autocorrelations The sample autocorrelations of the residuals.

Residual claim Refers to the fact that shareholders are at the bottom of the list of claimants to assets of a corporation in the event of failure or bankruptcy.

Residual dividend approach   A dividend payout policy under earnings in excess of the funds necessary to finance the equity portion of company's capital budget are paid out in dividends.

Residual income (or abnormal earnings)   Earnings for a given time period, minus a deduction for common shareholders' opportunity cost in generating the earnings.

Residual income model (RIM)   A model of stock valuation that views intrinsic value of stock as the sum of book value per share plus the present value of the stock's expected future residual income per share.

Residual loss   Agency costs that are incurred despite adequate monitoring and bonding of management.

Residual risk   The specific risk contained in a security, as distinct from the general market risk.

Residual Value (Private Equity)   The remaining equity that a limited partner has in the fund. (The value of the investments within the fund.) Also can be referred to as *ending market value* or *net asset value.*

Residuals   Parts of stock returns not explained by the explanatory variable (the market-index return). They measure the impact of firm-specific events during a particular period.

Resources   Things used to produce other things to satisfy people's wants.

Restatement of the Law Third, Trusts   A book of rules and principles promulgated by the American Law Institute, concerning the conduct of a trustee in the management of a trust. It serves as a guide for lawyers, trustees, and investment advisors.

Restructuring charge(s)   Costs associated with restructuring activities, including the consolidation and/or relocation of operations or the disposition or abandonment of operations or productive assets. Such charges may be incurred in connection with a business combination, a change in an enterprise's strategic plan, or a managerial response to declines in demand, increasing costs, or other environmental factors.

Retained earnings   Earnings that a corporation saves, or retains, for investment in other productive activities; earnings that are not distributed to stockholders.

Return on assets (ROA)   A profitability ratio; earnings before interest and taxes dividend by total assets.

Return on equity (ROE)   (1) An accounting ratio of net profits divided by equity. (2) An excellent definition is profit margin $\times$ turnover $\times$ leverage, where profit margin is sales $\div$ profits, turnover is sales $\div$ assets, and leverage is assets $\div$ equity. It is extremely high in industries with high RD that is expensed rather than capitalized and added to equity, such as pharmaceuticals.

Return on invested capital (ROIC)   The after-tax net operating profits as a percent of total assets or capital.

Return on investment (ROI)   Generally, book income as a proportion of net book value.

Return on sales (ROS)   See *profit margin.*

Revenue bond   A bond that is serviced by the income generated from specific revenue-producing projects of the municipality such as toll roads or athletic stadiums.

Reverse stock split   A reduction in the number of shares outstanding with a corresponding increase in share price, but no change to the company's underlying fundamentals.

Revolving credit   Legally assured *line of credit* with a bank.

Reward-to-variability ratio   Ratio of a portfolio's risk premium to its standard deviation.

Rho   The sensitivity of the option price to the risk-free rate.

Risk   A situation in which more than one outcome might occur and the probability of each possible outcome can be estimated.

Risk aversion   Describes the fact that investors want to minimize risk for the same level of expected return. To take more risk, they require compensation by a risk premium.

Risk budgeting   The establishment of risk objectives for individuals, groups, or divisions of an organization that takes into account the allocation of an acceptable level of risk.

Risk-free asset   An asset with a certain rate of return; often taken to be short-term T-bills.

Risk-free rate   The interest rate that can be earned with certainty.

Risk governance   The setting of overall policies and standards in risk management

Risk management   The process of identifying the level of risk an entity wants, measuring the level of risk the entity currently has, taking actions that bring the actual level of risk to the desired level of risk, and monitoring the new actual level of risk so that it continues to be aligned with the desired level of risk.

Risk premium   The expected return on an investment minus the risk-free rate.

Risk-neutral   See *risk-averse.*

Risk-neutral probabilities   Weights that are used to compute a binomial option price. They are the probabilities that would apply if a risk-neutral investor valued an option.

Risk-neutral valuation The process by which options and other derivatives are priced by treating investors as though they were risk neutral.

Risky asset An asset with uncertain future returns.

Rival A good or service or a resource is rival if its use by one person decreases the quantity available for someone else.

Robust The quality of being relatively unaffected by a violation of assumptions.

Robust standard errors Standard errors of the estimated parameters of a regression that correct for the presence of heteroskedasticity in the regression's error term.

Root mean squared error (RMSE) The square root of the average squared forecast error; used to compare the out-of-sample forecasting performance of forecasting models.

Roy's safety first criterion A criterion asserting that the optimal portfolio is the one that minimizes the probability that portfolio return falls below a threshold level.

Rule 144a *SEC* rule allowing *qualified institutional buyers* to buy and trade unregistered securities.

Rule of 72 The principle that the approximate number of years necessary for an investment to double is 72 divided by the stated interest rate.

Russell 1000 Index The 1000 largest companies in the Russell 3000 index.

Russell 2000 Index The 2000 smallest companies in the Russell 3000 index.

Russell 3000 Index The 3000 largest U.S. companies, capital-weighted, which represent about 98 percent of the investible equity market.

Safe harbor Practices that satisfy such requirements as the Prudent Investor Rule.

Safety-first rules Rules for portfolio selection that focus on the risk that portfolio value will fall below some minimum acceptable level over some time horizon.

Sales risk Uncertainty with respect to the quantity of goods and services that a company is able to sell and the price it is able to achieve.

Salvage value Scrap value of plant and equipment.

Sample A subset of a population.

Sample excess kurtosis A sample measure of the degree of a distribution's peakedness in excess of the normal distribution's peakedness.

Sample kurtosis A sample measure of the degree of a distribution's peakedness.

Sample mean The sum of the sample observations, divided by the sample size.

Sample selection bias Bias introduced by systematically excluding some members of the population according to a particular attribute—for example, the bias introduced when data availability leads to certain observations being excluded from the analysis.

Sample skewness A sample measure of degree of asymmetry of a distribution.

Sample standard deviation The positive square root of the sample variance.

Sample statistic or statistic A quantity computed from or used to describe a sample.

Sample variance A sample measure of the degree of dispersion of a distribution, calculated by dividing the sum of the squared deviations from the sample mean by the sample size (n) minus 1.

Sampling The process of obtaining a sample.

Sampling distribution The distribution of all distinct possible values that a statistic can assume when computed from samples of the same size randomly drawn from the same population.

Sampling error The difference between the observed value of a statistic and the quantity it is intended to estimate.

Sandwich spread An option strategy that is equivalent to a short butterfly spread.

Sarbanes-Oxley Act An act of the U.S. Congress signed into law on 30 July 2002 that tightened the oversight of firms that audit public companies, added criminal penalties for earnings management activities, and took steps generally to improve company internal controls and corporate governance.

Saving The act of not consuming all of one's current income. Whatever is not consumed out of spendable income is, by definition, saved. Saving is an action measured over time (a flow), whereas savings are a stock, an accumulation resulting from the act of saving in the past.

Scaled earnings surprise Unexpected earnings divided by the standard deviation of analysts' earnings forecasts.

Scalper A trader who offers to buy or sell futures contracts, holding the position for only a brief period of time. Scalpers attempt to profit by buying at the bid price and selling at the higher ask price.

Scatter plot or scatter diagram A two-dimensional plot of pairs of observations on two data series.

Scenario analysis A risk management technique involving the examination of the performance of a portfolio under specified situations. Closely related to *stress testing*.

Screening The application of a set of criteria to reduce an investment universe to a smaller set of investments.

Seasoned issue Issue of a security for which there is an existing market (cf. *unseasoned issue*).

Seats Memberships in a derivatives exchange.

SEC   Securities and Exchange Commission.

Secondary issue   (1) Procedure for selling blocks of *seasoned issues* of stock; (2) more generally, sale of already issued stock.

Secondary market   The market in which outstanding securities are bought and sold by owners other than the issuers. Purpose is to provide liquidity for investors.

Sector neutral   Said of a portfolio for which economic sectors are represented in the same proportions as in the benchmark, using market-value weights.

Sector rotation   An investment strategy which entails shifting the portfolio into industry sectors that are forecast to outperform others based on macroeconomic forecasts.

Sector rotation strategy   A type of top-down investing approach that involves emphasizing different economic sectors based on considerations such as macroeconomic forecasts.

Securities Exchange Act of 1934   The federal law that established the Securities and Exchange Commission. It also added further regulations for securities markets. The law has been amended several times since its initial passage. One of the amendments that is relevant to mergers is the Williams Act of 1968.

Securities   Stocks and bonds.

Securities offering   A merger or acquisition in which target shareholders are to receive shares of the acquirer's common stock as compensation.

Securitization   Substitution of tradable securities for privately negotiated instruments.

Security analysis   Determining correct value of a security in the marketplace.

Security market line (SML)   The graph of the capital asset pricing model.

Self-interest   The choices that you think are the best for you.

Sell-side analysts   Analysts who work at brokerages.

Semideviation   The positive square root of semivariance (sometimes called semistandard deviation).

Semilogarithmic   Describes a scale constructed so that equal intervals on the vertical scale represent equal rates of change, and equal intervals on the horizontal scale represent equal amounts of change.

Semivariance   The average squared deviation below the mean.

Senior debt   Debt that, in the event of bankruptcy, must be repaid before *subordinated debt* receives any payment.

Sensitivity analysis   Analysis of the effect on project profitability of possible changes in sales, costs, and so on.

Serially correlated   With reference to regression errors, errors that are correlated across observations.

Services   Mental or physical labor or help purchased by consumers. Examples are the assistance of physicians, lawyers, dentists, repair personnel, housecleaners, educators, retailers, and wholesalers; things purchased or used by consumers that do not have physical characteristics.

Settlement date or payment date   With reference to swaps, the date on which the parties to a swap make payments.

Settlement period   The time between settlement dates.

Settlement price   The official price, designated by the clearinghouse, from which daily gains and losses will be determined and marked to market.

Settlement risk   When settling a contract, the risk that one party could be in the process of paying the counterparty while the counterparty is declaring bankruptcy.

Settlor   The creator of an inter vivos trust; also same as *grantor, trustor,* or *creator.*

Share of stock   A legal claim to a share of a corporation's future profits; if it is common stock, it incorporates certain voting rights regarding major policy decisions of the corporation; if it is preferred stock, its owners are accorded preferential treatment in the payment of dividends.

Share repurchase   A transaction in which a company buys back its own shares. Unlike stock dividends and stock splits, share repurchases use corporate cash.

Shareholders' equity   Total assets minus total liabilities.

Share-the-gains, share-the-pains theory   A theory of regulatory behavior in which the regulators must take account of the demands of three groups: legislators, who established and who oversee the regulatory agency; members of the regulated industry; and consumers of the regulated industry's products or services.

Shark repellents   A pre-offer takeover defense mechanism involving the corporate charter (e.g., staggered boards of directors and supermajority provisions).

Sharpe ratio or Sharpe measure   The average return in excess of the risk-free rate divided by the standard deviation of return; a measure of the average excess return earned per unit of standard deviation of return.

Short   The seller of a derivative contract. Also refers to the position of being short a derivative.

Short interest rate   A one-period interest rate.

Short position   The seller of a commodity or security or, for a forward contract, the counterparty who will be the eventual seller of the underlying asset.

Short run   The short run in microeconomics has two meanings. (1) For the firm, it is the period of time in which the quantity of at least one input is fixed and the quantities of the other inputs can be varied. The fixed input is usually capital—that is, the firm has a given plant size. (2) For the industry, the short run is the period of time in which each firm has a given plant size and the number of firms in the industry is fixed.

Short sale   The sale of shares not owned by the investor but borrowed through a broker and later repurchased to replace the loan. Profit is earned if the initial sale is at a higher price than the repurchase price.

Shortage   A situation in which quantity demanded is greater than quantity supplied at a price below the market clearing price.

Shortfall risk   The risk that portfolio value will fall below some minimum acceptable level over some time horizon.

Should   Encouraged (recommended) to follow the recommendation of the GIPS standards but not required.

Signal   (1) Action that demonstrates an individual's unobservable characteristics (because it would be unduly costly for someone without those characteristics to take the action). (2) An action taken by an informed person (or firm) to send a message to uninformed people or an action taken outside a market that conveys information that can be used by that market.

Simple interest   The interest earned each period on the original investment; interest calculated on the principal only.

Simple random sample   A subset of a larger population created in such a way that each element of the population has an equal probability of being selected to the subset.

Simulation   Monte Carlo simulation.

Simulation trial   A complete pass through the steps of a simulation.

Single-factor model   A model of security returns that acknowledges only one common factor. See *factor model*.

Single-payment loan   A loan in which the borrower receives a sum of money at the start and pays back the entire amount with interest in a single payment at maturity.

Sinking fund   Bond provision that requires the issuer to redeem some or all of the bond systematically over the term of the bond rather than in full at maturity.

Sinking fund factor   Amount that must be set aside each period to have $1 at some future point in time.

Skewed   Not symmetrical.

Skewness   A quantitative measure of skew (lack of symmetry); a synonym of skew.

Skill   One of the three components of the standard of prudence governing trustees; familiarity with business matters.

Slope   The change in the value of the variable measured on the y-axis divided by the change in the value of the variable measured on the x-axis.

Soft dollars   The value of research services that brokerage houses supply to investment managers "free of charge" in exchange for the investment managers' business.

Sole proprietorship   A business owned and operated by a single person.

Sovereign risk   The risk that a government may default on its debt.

Spearman rank correlation coefficient   A measure of correlation applied to ranked data.

Special purpose entity (SPE)   A non-operating entity created to carry out a specified purpose, such as leasing assets or securitizing receivables. Also known as a special purpose vehicle (SPV).

Specialist   A trader who makes a market in the shares of one or more firms and who maintains a "fair and orderly market" by dealing personally in the stock.

Specialization   The division of productive activities among persons and regions so that no one individual or one area is totally self-sufficient. An individual may specialize, for example, in law or medicine. A nation may specialize in the production of coffee, computers, or cameras.

Speculation   Undertaking a risky investment with the objective of earning a greater profit than an investment in a risk-free alternative (a risk premium).

Speculative stock   A stock that appears to be highly overpriced compared to its intrinsic valuation.

Spin-off   A form of restructuring in which a corporation separates off and separately capitalizes a component business, which is then transferred to the corporation's common stockholders; shareholders end up owning stock in two different companies where there used to be one.

Split   When a stock reaches a high price, the management of the company will split it two for one, three for two, or whatever, to create a lower price per share and thus facilitate trading. The dividend may be raised at the same time.

In a "reverse split," a low-priced stock, often of a failing company, is consolidated to bring the price per share up to a reasonable level. On the Canadian exchanges such stocks are thereafter called "Consolidated Gold Bug" (or whatever).

Split-off   A form of restructuring in which shareholders of the parent company are given shares in a newly created entity in exchange for their shares of the parent company.

Split-rate   In reference to corporate taxes, a split-rate system taxes earnings to be distributed as dividends at a different rate than earnings to be retained. Corporate profits distributed as dividends are taxed at a lower rate than those retained in the business.

Spot exchange rate   Exchange rate on currency for immediate delivery (cf. *forward exchange rate*).

Spot price   Price of asset for immediate delivery (in contrast to forward or futures price).

Spot rate   The required yield for a cash flow to be received at some specific date in the future-for example, the spot rate for a flow to be received in one year, for a cash flow in two years, and so on.

Spread   With reference to options strategies, a strategy involving the purchase of one option and sale of another option that is identical to the first in all respects except either exercise price or expiration.

Spreadsheet modeling   As used in this book, the use of a spreadsheet in executing a dividend discount model valuation, or other present value model valuation.

Spurious correlation   A correlation that misleadingly points towards associations between variables.

Squeeze   The possibility that enough long positions hold their contracts to maturity that supplies of the commodity are not adequate to cover all contracts. A *short squeeze* describes the reverse: short positions threaten to deliver an expensive-to-store commodity.

Staggered board   Also called a *classified board*. This is an antitakeover measure in which the election of directors is split in separate periods so that only a percentage of the total number of directors come up for election in a given year. It is designed to make taking control of the board of directors more difficult.

Stakeholder   Any entity that is affected by the actions of a company, which may include shareholders, management, workers, communities, consumers, and so on.

Standard deviation   The positive square root of the variance; a measure of dispersion in the same units as the original data.

Standard error   In statistics, a measure of the possible error in an estimate.

Standard normal distribution (or unit normal distribution)   The normal density with mean (μ) equal to 0 and standard deviation (σ) equal to 1.

Standardized beta   With reference to fundamental factor models, the value of the attribute for an asset minus the average value of the attribute across all stocks, divided by the standard deviation of the attribute across all stocks.

Standardized unexpected earnings (SUE)   Unexpected earnings per share divided by the standard deviation of unexpected earnings per share over a specified prior time period.

Standardizing   A transformation that involves subtracting the mean and dividing the result by the standard deviation.

Standstill agreement   An agreement that a potential hostile bidder enters into with the target corporation whereby the bidder agrees, in exchange for some consideration, not to purchase more than an agreed-upon number of shares.

Start-up stage   The opening period in a company's life cycle during which operating losses often are reported and operating cash flow is consumed.

Stated annual interest rate or quoted interest rate   A quoted interest rate that does not account for compounding within the year.

Statement of cash flows   A financial statement showing a firm's cash receipts and cash payments during a specified period.

Static trade-off theory of capital structure   A theory pertaining to a company's optimal capital structure; the optimal level of debt is found at the point where additional debt would cause the costs of financial distress to increase by a greater amount than the benefit of the additional tax shield.

Statistic   A quantity computed from or used to describe a sample of data.

Statistical factor models   A multifactor model in which statistical methods are applied to a set of historical returns to determine portfolios that best explain either historical return covariances or variances.

Statistical inference   Making forecasts, estimates, or judgments about a larger group from a smaller group actually observed; using a sample statistic to infer the value of an unknown population parameter.

Statistically significant   A result indicating that the null hypothesis can be rejected; with reference to an estimated regression coefficient, frequently understood to mean a result indicating that the corresponding population regression coefficient is different from 0.

Statistics   The science of describing, analyzing, and drawing conclusions from data; also, a collection of numerical data.

Statutory merger   A merger in which one company ceases to exist as an identifiable entity and all its assets and liabilities become part of a purchasing company.

Stock   The quantity of something, measured at a given point in time—for example, an inventory of goods or a bank account. Stocks are defined independently of time, although they are assessed at a point in time.

Stock dividend   *Dividend* in the form of stock rather than cash.

Stock exchanges   Secondary markets where already-issued securities are bought and sold by members.

Stock option   A contract that gives its holder the right to buy (call option) or sell (put option) an interest in stock at a specified price through a specified date.

Stock purchase   An acquisition in which the acquirer gives the target company's shareholders some combination of cash and securities in exchange for shares of the target company's stock.

Stock selection   An active portfolio management technique that focuses on advantageous selection of particular stocks rather than on broad asset allocation choices.

Stock split   Issue by a corporation of a given number of shares in exchange for the current number of shares held by stockholders. Splits may go in either direction, either increasing or decreasing the number of shares outstanding. A *reverse split* decreases the number outstanding.

Storage costs or carrying costs   The costs of holding an asset, generally a function of the physical characteristics of the underlying asset.

Straddle   An option strategy involving the purchase of a put and a call with the same exercise price. A straddle is based on the expectation of high volatility of the underlying.

Straight-line depreciation   An equal dollar amount of *depreciation* in each period.

Strangle   A variation of a straddle in which the put and call have different exercise prices.

Strap   An option strategy involving the purchase of two calls and one put.

Strategic alliance   A more flexible alternative to a joint venture whereby certain companies agree to pursue certain common activities and interests.

Strategic asset allocation   The allocation to the major investment asset classes that is determined to be appropriate, given the investor's long-run investment objectives and constraints.

Strategy   Any rule that is used to make a choice, such as "Always pick heads."

Stratified random sampling   A procedure by which a population is divided into subpopulations (strata) based on one or more classification criteria. Simple random samples are then drawn from each stratum in sizes proportional to the relative size of each stratum in the population. These samples are then pooled.

Stress testing   A risk management technique in which the risk manager examines the performance of the portfolio under market conditions involving high risk and usually high correlations across markets. Closely related to *scenario analysis*.

Strike price   Price at which an option can be exercised (same as *exercise price*).

Strip   An option strategy involving the purchase of two puts and one call.

Structural change   Economic trend occurring when the economy is undergoing a major change in organization or in how it functions.

Structured note   A debt security with an embedded derivative designed to create a payoff distribution that satisfies the needs of a specific investor clientele.

Style analysis   An attempt to explain the variability in the observed returns to a security portfolio in terms of the movements in the returns to a series of benchmark portfolios designed to capture the essence of a particular security characteristic such as size, value, and growth.

Subjective probability   A probability drawing on personal or subjective judgment.

Subordinated debt (junior debt)   Debt over which *senior debt* takes priority. In the event of bankruptcy, subordinated debtholders receive payment only after senior debt is paid off in full.

Subsidiary merger   A merger in which the company being purchased becomes a subsidiary of the purchaser.

Subsidy   A payment that the government makes to a producer.

Subsistence real wage rate   The minimum real wage rate needed to maintain life.

Substitute   A good that can be used in place of another good.

Sunk cost   A cost that has already been incurred and cannot be reversed.

Supermajority   Provision in a company's charter requiring a majority of, say, 80 percent of shareholders to approve certain changes, such as a *merger*.

Supernormal growth   Above average or abnormally high growth rate in earnings per share.

Supplemental Information   Any performance-related information included as part of a compliant performance presentation that supplements or enhances the required and/or recommended disclosure and presentation provisions of the GIPS standards.

Supply   A schedule showing the relationship between price and quantity supplied for a specified period of time, other things being equal.

Supply curve   The graphical representation of the supply schedule; a line (curve) showing the supply schedule, which generally slopes upward (has a positive slope), other things being equal.

Supply shock   An event that influences production capacity and costs in the economy.

Supply-side economics   The notion that creating incentives for individuals and firms to increase productivity will cause the aggregate supply curve to shift outward.

Surplus   A situation in which quantity supplied is greater than quantity demanded at a price above the market clearing price.

Surprise   The actual value of a variable minus its predicted (or expected) value.

Survivorship bias   The bias resulting from a test design that fails to account for companies that have gone bankrupt, merged, or are otherwise no longer reported in a database.

Sustainable growth rate   The rate of dividend (and earnings) growth that can be sustained for a given level of return on equity, keeping the capital structure constant over time and without issuing additional common stock.

Swap   A contract whereby two parties agree to a periodic exchange of cash flows. In certain types of swaps, only the net difference between the amounts owed is exchanged on each payment date.

Swap spread   The difference between the fixed rate on an interest rate swap and the rate on a Treasury note with equivalent maturity; it reflects the general level of credit risk in the market.

Swaption   An option to enter into a swap.

Synergy   2 1 2 5 5; a combination of businesses in which the combined entity is more valuable than the sum of the parts.

Synthetic call   The combination of puts, the underlying, and risk-free bonds that replicates a call option.

Synthetic forward contract   The combination of the underlying, puts, calls, and risk-free bonds that replicates a forward contract.

Synthetic index fund   An index fund position created by combining risk-free bonds and futures on the desired index.

Synthetic put   The combination of calls, the underlying, and risk-free bonds that replicates a put option.

Systematic factors   Factors that affect the average returns of a large number of different assets.

Systematic risk   (1) The variability of returns that is due to macroeconomic factors that affect all risky assets. Because it affects all risky assets, it cannot be eliminated by diversification. (2) Market risk.

Systematic sampling   A procedure of selecting every kth member until reaching a sample of the desired size. The sample that results from this procedure should be approximately random.

Tactical asset allocation   Short-term adjustments to the long-term asset allocation to reflect views on the current relative attractiveness of asset classes.

Takeover   A merger; the term may be applied to any transaction, but is often used in reference to hostile transactions.

Takeover premium   The amount by which the takeover price for each share of stock must exceed the current stock price in order to entice shareholders to relinquish control of the company to an acquirer.

Tangible asset   Physical asset, such as plant, machinery, and offices (cf. *intangible assets*).

Tangible book value per share   Common shareholders' equity minus intangible assets from the balance sheet, divided by the number of shares outstanding.

Target capital structure   A company's chosen proportions of debt and equity.

Target company, or target   The company in a merger or acquisition that is being acquired.

Target payout ratio   A strategic corporate goal representing the long-term proportion of earnings that the company intends to distribute to shareholders as dividends.

Target semideviation   The positive square root of target semivariance.

Target semivariance   The average squared deviation below a target value.

Tariffs   Taxes on imported goods.

Tax adjustments   Restatements of nonrecurring items of operating cash flow to place them on an after-tax basis. For example, an outsized tax-deductible pension contribution of $50 million would be reduced to an after-tax amount of $30 million if a combined federal and state marginal tax rate of 40 percent is assumed: $50 million $\times$ (1 − 40 percent) = $30 million.

Tax bracket   A specified interval of income to which a specific and unique marginal tax rate is applied.

Tax credits A direct dollar-for-dollar reduction in taxes payable.

Tax risk The uncertainty associated with tax laws.

T-bill Treasury bill.

t-Distribution A symmetrical distribution defined by a single parameter, degrees of freedom, that is largely used to make inferences concerning the mean of a normal distribution whose variance is unknown.

Technical indicators Momentum indicators based on price.

Technological change The development of new goods and better ways of producing goods and services.

Technology (1) Any method of producing a good or service. (2) Society's pool of applied knowledge concerning how goods and services can be produced.

TED spread Difference between *LIBOR* and U.S. *Treasury bill* rate.

Temporary difference A difference between the book and tax basis of both assets and liabilities. Alternatively, a temporary difference is a difference between book and tax return earnings that will reverse at some future point in time. Temporary differences give rise to deferred tax assets and liabilities.

Tender offer A public offer whereby the acquirer invites target shareholders to submit ("tender") their shares in return for the proposed payment.

Tenor The original time to maturity on a swap or loan.

Term bond A bond that has a single maturity date.

Term structure See *yield curve.*

Term structure of interest rates The relationship between term to maturity and yield to maturity for a sample of comparable bonds at a given time. Popularly known as the *yield curve.*

Term to maturity Specifies the date or the number of years before a bond matures or expires.

Terminal price multiple The price multiple for a stock assumed to hold at a stated future time.

Terminal share price The share price at a particular point in the future.

Terminal value of the stock (or continuing value of the stock) The analyst's estimate of a stock's value at a particular point in the future.

Termination date The date of the final payment on a swap; also, the swap's expiration date.

Terms of trade The quantity of goods and services that a country exports to pay for its imports of goods and services.

Test statistic A quantity, calculated based on a sample, whose value is the basis for deciding whether or not to reject the null hypothesis.

Testamentary trust A trust created by will.

The Fed The Federal Reserve System; the central bank of the United States.

Theory of contestable markets A hypothesis concerning pricing behavior that holds that even though there are only a few firms in an industry, they are forced to price their products more or less competitively because of the ease of entry by outsiders. The key aspect of a contestable market is relatively costless entry into and exit from the industry.

Theta The rate at which an option's time value decays.

Third parties Parties who are not directly involved in a given activity or transaction.

Thrift institutions Financial institutions that receive most of their funds from the savings of the public; they include mutual savings banks, savings and loan associations, and credit unions.

Tick Minimum amount the price of a security may change.

Time deposit A deposit in a financial institution that requires notice of intent to withdraw or must be left for an agreed period. Withdrawal of funds prior to the end of the agreed period may result in a penalty.

Time-period bias The possibility that when we use a time-series sample, our statistical conclusion may be sensitive to the starting and ending dates of the sample.

Time series A set of observations on a variable's outcomes in different time periods.

Time-series data Observations of a variable over time.

Time to expiration The time remaining in the life of a derivative, typically expressed in years.

Time value (of an option) The part of the value of an option that is due to its positive time to expiration. Not to be confused with present value or the time value of money.

Time value decay The loss in the value of an option resulting from movement of the option price toward its payoff value as the expiration day approaches.

Time value of money The principles governing equivalence relationships between cash flows with different dates.

Time value or speculative value The difference between the market price of the option and its intrinsic value, determined by the uncertainty of the underlying over the remaining life of the option.

Time-weighted rate of return The compound rate of growth of one unit of currency invested in a portfolio during a stated measurement period; a measure of investment performance that is not sensitive to the timing and amount of withdrawals or additions to the portfolio.

Tobin's q The ratio of the market value of debt and equity to the replacement cost of total assets.

Top-down With respect to investment approaches, the allocation of money first to categories such as asset classes, countries, or industry followed by the selection of individual securities within category.

Top-down forecasting approach A forecasting approach that involves moving from international and national macroeconomic forecasts to industry forecasts and then to individual company and asset forecasts.

Top-down investing An approach to investing that typically begins with macroeconomic forecasts.

Total cash flow The change in reported cash and cash equivalents during a reporting period.

Total cost The cost of all the productive resources that a firm uses; the sum of total fixed cost and total variable cost.

Total fixed cost The cost of the firm's fixed inputs.

Total income The yearly amount earned by the nation's resources (factors of production). Total income therefore includes wages, rent, interest payments, and profits that are received, respectively, by workers, landowners, capital owners, and entrepreneurs.

Total interest paid A term used on the cash flow analysis statement that consists of cash payments for interest on debt and capital leases, including capitalized interest.

Total probability rule A rule explaining the unconditional probability of an event in terms of probabilities of the event conditional on mutually exclusive and exhaustive scenarios.

Total return A return objective in which the investor wants to increase the portfolio value to meet a future need by both capital gains and current income reinvestment.

Total return swap A swap in which one party agrees to pay the total return on a security. Often used as a credit derivative, in which the underlying is a bond.

Total revenue The value of a firm's sales.

Total Value (Private Equity) Residual value of the portfolio plus distributed capital.

Tracking error A synonym for tracking risk; also, the condition in which the performance of a portfolio does not match the performance of an index that serves as the portfolio's benchmark.

Tracking portfolio A portfolio having factor sensitivities that are matched to those of a benchmark or other portfolio.

Tracking risk or tracking error or tracking error volatility or active risk The standard deviation of the differences between a portfolio's returns and its benchmark's returns; a synonym of active risk.

Trade balance The balance of a country's exports and imports; part of the current account.

Trade credit Accounts receivable.

Tradeoff An exchange—giving up one thing to get something else.

Trading turnover The percentage of outstanding shares traded during a period of time.

Traditional efficient markets formulation See *Market efficiency.*

Trailing dividend yield Current market price divided by the most recent quarterly per-share dividend multiplied by four.

Trailing P/E (or current P/E) A stock's current market price divided by the most recent four quarters of earnings per share.

Tranche Refers to a portion of an issue that is designed for a specific category of investors. French for "slice."

Transaction cost (1) The cost of executing a trade. Low costs characterize an operationally efficient market. (2) All of the costs associated with exchanging, including the informational costs of finding out price and quality, service record, and durability of a product, plus the cost of contracting and enforcing that contract. Can also be viewed as all costs associated with making, reaching, and enforcing agreements.

Transaction exposure The risk associated with a foreign exchange rate on a specific business transaction such as a purchase or sale.

Transfer payments Money payments made by governments to individuals for which in return no services or goods are concurrently rendered. Examples are welfare, Social Security, and unemployment insurance benefits.

Transition phase The stage of growth between the growth phase and the mature phase of a company in which earnings growth typically slows.

Translation exposure The risk associated with the conversion of foreign financial statements into domestic currency.

Treasurer Principal financial manager (cf. *controller*).

Treasury bill Short-term, highly liquid government securities issued at a discount from the face value and returning the face amount at maturity.

Treasury bond A U.S. government security with a maturity of more than 10 years that pays interest periodically.

Treasury note A U.S. government security with maturities of 1 to 10 years that pays interest periodically.

Treasury shares Shares that were issued and subsequently repurchased by the company.

Treasury stock A corporation's issued stock that has subsequently been repurchased by the company and not retired.

Tree diagram A diagram with branches emanating from nodes representing either mutually exclusive chance events or mutually exclusive decisions.

Trend A long-term pattern of movement in a particular direction.

Triangular arbitrage With respect to currencies, an arbitrage involving three currencies only.

Trimmed mean A mean computed after excluding a stated small percentage of the lowest and highest observations.

Trough The transition point between recession and recovery.

Trust agreement or trust indenture or trust instrument The document that creates an inter vivos trust, between a grantor and a trustee, for the benefit of the beneficiaries.

*t***-Test** A hypothesis test using a statistic (*t*-statistic) that follows a *t*-distribution.

Turnover The ratio of the trading activity of a portfolio to the assets of the portfolio.

Two-sided hypothesis test (or two-tailed hypothesis test) A test in which the null hypothesis is rejected in favor of the alternative hypothesis if the evidence indicates that the population parameter is either smaller or larger than a hypothesized value.

Type I error The error of rejecting a true null hypothesis.

Type II error The error of not rejecting a false null hypothesis.

U.S. interest rate differential A gap equal to the U.S. interest rate minus the foreign interest rate.

U.S. Official reserves The government's holdings of foreign currency.

Unanticipated inflation Inflation at a rate that comes as a surprise, either higher or lower than the rate anticipated.

Unbiasedness Lack of bias. A desirable property of estimators, an unbiased estimator is one whose expected value (the mean of its sampling distribution) equals the parameter it is intended to estimate.

Uncertainty A situation in which more than one event might occur but it is not known which one.

Unconditional heteroskedasticity Heteroskedasticity of the error term that is not correlated with the values of the independent variable(s) in the regression.

Unconditional probability (or marginal probability) The probability of an event *not* conditioned on another event.

Uncovered interest rate parity The assertion that expected currency depreciation should offset the interest differential between two countries over the term of the interest rate.

Underlying With reference to derivatives, the asset on which a derivative contract is written.

Underlying earnings (or persistent, continuing, or core earnings) Earnings excluding nonrecurring components.

Underweighted A condition in which a portfolio, for whatever reason, includes less of a class of securities than the relative market value alone would justify.

Underwriter Firm that buys an issue of securities from a company and resells it to investors.

Unemployment The total number of adults (aged 16 years or older) who are willing and able to work and who are actively looking for work but have not found a job.

Unemployment rate The percentage of the people in the labor force who are unemployed.

Unexpected earnings (also earnings surprise) The difference between reported earnings per share and expected earnings per share.

Unit root A time series that is not covariance stationary is said to have a unit root.

Univariate distribution A distribution that specifies the probabilities for a single random variable.

Unlimited funds An unlimited funds environment assumes that the company can raise the funds it wants for all profitable projects simply by paying the required rate of return.

Unlimited liability A legal concept whereby the personal assets of the owner of a firm can be seized to pay off the firm's debts.

Unsystematic risk Risk that is unique to an asset, derived from its particular characteristics. It can be eliminated in a diversified portfolio.

Unwind The negotiated termination of a forward or futures position before contract maturity.

Valuation The process of determining the value of an asset or service on the basis of variables perceived to be related to future investment returns, or on the basis of comparisons with closely similar assets.

Valuation analysis An active bond portfolio management strategy designed to capitalize on expected price increases in temporarily undervalued issues.

Valuation process Part of the investment decision process in which you estimate the value of a security.

Value The amount for which one can sell something, or the amount one must pay to acquire something.

Value at risk (VAR) A money measure of the minimum value of losses expected during a specified time period at a given level of probability.

Value chain The set of transformations to move from raw material to product or service delivery.

Value stocks Stocks that appear to be undervalued for reasons besides earnings growth potential. These stocks are usually identified based on high dividend yields, low *P/E* ratios, or low price-to-book ratios.

Value-weighted index An index calculated as the total market value of the securities in the sample. Market value is equal to the number of shares or bonds outstanding times the market price of the security.

Variable costs Costs that fluctuate with the level of production and sales.

Variance The expected value (the probability-weighted average) of squared deviations from a random variable's expected value.

Variation margin Additional margin that must be deposited in an amount sufficient to bring the balance up to the initial margin requirement.

Vega The relationship between option price and volatility.

Vendor financing Amounts owed vendors for purchased goods or services, reported as accounts payable.

Venture capital Capital to finance a new firm.

Vertical merger A merger involving companies at different positions of the same production chain; for example, a supplier or a distributor.

Visibility The extent to which a company's operations are predictable with substantial confidence.

Volatility As used in option pricing, the standard deviation of the continuously compounded returns on the underlying asset.

Volatility risk The risk in the value of options portfolios due to unpredictable changes in the volatility of the underlying asset.

Voluntary export restraint An agreement between two governments in which the government of the exporting country agrees to restrain the volume of its own exports.

Wages The income that labor earns.

Warrant An instrument that allows the holder to purchase a specified number of shares of the firm's common stock from the firm at a specified price for a given period of time.

Wealth The stock of assets owned by a person, household, firm, or nation. For a household, wealth can consist of a house, cars, personal belongings, stocks, bonds, bank accounts, and cash.

Weighted-average cost of capital (WACC) A weighted average of the after-tax required rates of return on a company's common stock, preferred stock, and long-term debt, where the weights are the fraction of each source of financing in the company's target capital structure.

Weighted mean An average in which each observation is weighted by an index of its relative importance.

Well-diversified portfolio A portfolio spread out over many securities in such a way that the weight in any security is close to zero.

White-corrected standard errors A synonym for robust standard errors.

White knight A third party that is sought out by the target company's board to purchase the target in lieu of a hostile bidder.

White squire A third party that is sought out by the target company's board to purchase a substantial minority stake in the target-enough to block a hostile takeover without selling the entire company.

Wholesale Price Index (WPI) A price index defined on a basket of goods produced.

Window dressing Toward the end of a reporting period, particularly at year end, mutual funds and banks will sometimes round up their holdings to even thousands, or sell positions that have gone down and thus constitute an eyesore.

Winner's curse The tendency for the winner in certain competitive bidding situations to overpay, whether because of overestimation of intrinsic value, emotion, or information asymmetries.

Winsorized mean A mean computed after assigning a stated percent of the lowest values equal to one specified low value, and a stated percent of the highest values equal to one specified high value.

Withholding tax A tax levied by the country of source on income paid.

Working capital Current assets minus current liabilities.

Working capital management The management of a company's short-term assets (such as inventory) and short-term liabilities (such as money owed to suppliers).

Workout period Realignment period of a temporary misaligned yield relationship.

World Bank A supranational organization of several institutions designed to assist developing countries. The International Bank for Reconstruction and Development (IBRD) and the International Finance Corporation (IFC) are the more important members of the World Bank group.

World Trade Organization An international organization that places greater obligations on its member countries to observe the GATT rules.

Write-down A reduction in the value of an asset as stated in the balance sheet.

Writer of an option A term used for the person or institution selling an option and therefore granting the right to exercise it to the buyer of the option.

x axis The horizontal axis in a graph.

y axis The vertical axis in a graph.

Yield The promised rate of return on an investment under certain assumptions.

Yield beta A measure of the sensitivity of a bond's yield to a general measure of bond yields in the market that is used to refine the hedge ratio.

Yield curve A curve showing the relationship between yield (interest rate) and maturity for a set of similar securities. For example, the yield curve can be drawn for U.S. Treasuries or for LIBOR. Typically, different yield curves are drawn for zero-coupon bonds (zero-coupon yield curve) and for coupon bonds quoted at par (par yield curve).

Yield spread The difference between the yield on a bond and the yield on a default-free security, usually a government note, of the same maturity. The yield spread is primarily determined by the market's perception of the credit risk on the bond.

Yield to maturity The total yield on a bond obtained by equating the bond's current market value to the discounted cash flows promised by the bond. Also called *actuarial yield.*

Zero-beta portfolio The minimum-variance portfolio uncorrelated with a chosen efficient portfolio.

Zero-cost collar A transaction in which a position in the underlying is protected by buying a put and selling a call with the premium from the sale of the call offsetting the premium from the purchase of the put. It can also be used to protect a floating-rate borrower against interest rate increases with the premium on a long cap offsetting the premium on a short floor.

Zero-coupon bond A bond that pays its par value at maturity but no periodic interest payments. Its yield is determined by the difference between its par value and its discounted purchase price. Also called *original issue discount (OID).*

Z-score Measure of the likelihood of bankruptcy.

Page numbers followed by n refer to footnotes.